CHRISTOPHER PLANTIN AND ENGRAVED BOOK ILLUSTRATIONS
IN SIXTEENTH-CENTURY EUROPE

This is an interdisciplinary study of Christopher Plantin's pioneering role in the production
and distribution of books with engraved and etched illustrations in sixteenth-century Europe.
Using the rich archival sources at the Plantin-Moretus Museum in Belgium, Karen Bowen and
Dirk Imhof examine the artists who worked on these illustrations, the types of illustrations that
appealed to specific markets, and the technological, cultural, and economic constraints under
which Christopher Plantin operated as he ventured into this new area of publishing. They
demonstrate how Plantin's innovations led to a revolutionary change in taste for book
illustrations, and place his work within the broader context of the European book trade of the
late sixteenth century and Antwerp's political, economic, cultural, and religious history. This
is a major contribution to the history of the book, art history, and the economic and social
history of early modern Europe.

KAREN L. BOWEN is an independent scholar and lecturer on book illustration.

DIRK IMHOF is the curator of rare books and archives at the Plantin-Moretus Museum
of Antwerp.

CHRISTOPHER PLANTIN AND ENGRAVED BOOK ILLUSTRATIONS IN SIXTEENTH-CENTURY EUROPE

KAREN L. BOWEN AND DIRK IMHOF

CAMBRIDGE UNIVERSITY PRESS

CAMBRIDGE UNIVERSITY PRESS
Cambridge, New York, Melbourne, Madrid, Cape Town, Singapore, São Paulo, Delhi

Cambridge University Press
The Edinburgh Building, Cambridge CB2 8RU, UK

Published in the United States of America by Cambridge University Press, New York

www.cambridge.org
Information on this title: www.cambridge.org/9780521852760

First published 2008

Printed in the United Kingdom at the University Press, Cambridge

A catalogue record for this publication is available from the British Library

ISBN 978-0-521-85276-0 hardback

CONTENTS

ILLUSTRATIONS

FIGURES

TABLES

Sources

All of the images reproduced here are taken from works in the collection of the Plantin-Moretus Museum, and reproduced by courtesy of the director of that museum unless noted specifically among the remaining credits. The following illustrations are reproduced with the kind permission of: the director of the Stadsbibliotheek, Antwerp (figs. 3.3, 3.8, 5.10, 5.11, 6.4, 6.13, and 6.20); the director of the Staats- und Stadtbibliothek, Augsburg (figs. 4.2 and 4.3); the director of the Royal Library, Brussels (figs. 1.1, 1.2, 5.7, 5.19, 6.26, and 6.29a); the Master and Fellows of Trinity College, Cambridge (figs. 4.6, 4.7, 4.8, 4.9, and 4.10); the head librarian of the Universiteitsbibliotheek, Ghent (figs. 3.4, 4.1, and 6.21); the director of the Maurits Sabbebibliotheek, Katholieke Universiteit Leuven (figs. 3.18, 3.19, 3.20, 3.21, 3.25, and 4.17); the Biblioteca Nacional de España, Madrid (photograph courtesy of the Laboratorio Fotográfico, Biblioteca Nacional de España, Madrid) (fig. 4.12); and a private collector in Antwerp (figs. 6.1 and 6.2).

ACKNOWLEDGMENTS

We gladly extend this prefatory word of thanks to the many friends and colleagues who have generously supported our work on this book during the past years. Unmissable in this regard are: the staff at the Plantin-Moretus Museum – who brought up more books and documents to the museum's reading room than any of us would care to count – friends who found the time to read and comment on the drafts of our text, and librarians throughout Europe and the United States, who patiently sent us ever informative responses to each of our queries. We would also like to mention Dr. David McKitterick in particular, for his great support of this project from beginning to end. Finally, we are also indebted to both the Historians of Netherlandish Art and the College Art Association for their generous financial support of this book. Our warm thanks to you all.

MEASUREMENTS

All measurements are given in millimeters, with height preceding width.

SPELLING

The spelling of words in transcriptions has often been "normalized" as follows:

the use of u and v and of i and j has been altered according to contemporary norms; standard abbreviations, such as ū (for "um"), have been written out in full.

CURRENCY

Unless noted otherwise, all of the sums of money in the cited records from Christopher Plantin's business were noted in florins (= fl.), which is another name for Carolus or Brabant guilders. The following equivalencies are relevant here:

1 florin (fl.) — 20 stuivers (or patards) (st.); where 1 stuiver — 4 oorden
6 florins = 1 Flemish pound ("groten Vlaams") (£) = 20 schellingen (sh.) = 240 deniers (d.)
2 florins = 1 Spanish "escus," or "escudos"

Owing to ever fluctuating rates of currency, it is difficult to give a current (modern) value for this currency. Rather, often the most effective means of putting these values in some sort of perspective is by comparing them with contemporary wages or the purchasing power of certain groups of people. For examples of such comparative figures, see Scholliers 1976. For a more detailed list of monetary values, as well as weights and measures, in different regions in Flanders, see Vandewalle 1984.

BOOK FORMATS AND PAPER

The format of a book is an indication of its size with regard to the size of the original sheet of paper used to print it. It is determined by the number of times the original sheet has been folded (and possibly cut) in order to form the individual leaves of the book. For a more detailed discussion of the identification of book formats, with accompanying diagrams of the possible lay-out of the pages, see, e.g., Gaskell 1972, pp. 80–107. The following standard book formats are cited here:

folio (f° or 2°) = two leaves or four pages per sheet of paper;
quarto (4°) = four leaves or eight pages per sheet of paper;
octavo (8°) = eight leaves or sixteen pages per sheet of paper;
duodecimo (12°) = twelve leaves or twenty-four pages per sheet of paper;
sedecimo (16°) = sixteen leaves or thirty-two pages per sheet of paper;
vigesimoquarto (24°) = twenty-four leaves or forty-eight pages per sheet of paper;
trigesimosecundo (32°) = thirty-two leaves or sixty-four pages per sheet of paper.

In the sixteenth century, paper was typically sold by reams or quires (usually "rames" and "mains," respectively, in the Plantin archives), where one ream of paper usually (among Plantin's purchases at least) comprised 500 sheets or 20 quires of 25 sheets each.

CITATION OF RARE BOOKS AND MANUSCRIPTS

Whenever possible, we have attempted to give not only the full title of each work cited, but also at least one general reference to it and/or reference to at least one known copy of it. No attempt is made to give an exhaustive list of either the known copies of particular books or the reference works in which specific editions are discussed.

The following abbreviations are used for the frequently cited collections housing the works discussed here. All other collections are cited in full in the notes. The collection number of the given book is cited within parentheses immediately following the reference to the collection.

BL	London, The British Library
BN Madrid	Madrid, Biblioteca Nacional de España
BN Paris	Paris, Bibliothèque Nationale de France
BS Munich	Munich, Bayerische Staatsbibliothek
KB Den Haag	The Hague, Koninklijke Bibliotheek
KBR	Brussels, The Royal Library, Rare Books Department
KBR PK	Brussels, The Royal Library, Print Department
KULG	Leuven, Katholieke Universiteit Leuven, Maurits Sabbebibliotheek
MPM	Antwerp, Museum Plantin-Moretus
MPM PK	Antwerp, Museum Plantin-Moretus, Prentenkabinet
ONB	Vienna, Österreichische Nationalbibliothek
RG	Antwerp, Universiteit Antwerpen, Bibliotheek van het Ruusbroecgenootschap

RUG	Ghent, Universiteitsbibliotheek, Kostbare werken
SAA	Antwerp, Stadsarchief
SBA	Antwerp, Stadsbibliotheek
UL Utrecht	Utrecht, Universiteit Utrecht, Centrale Bibliotheek

REFERENCES TO PRIMARY SOURCES IN THE PLANTIN-MORETUS MUSEUM OF ANTWERP (MPM)

The vast majority of the archival documents and other primary materials cited here are preserved in the Plantin-Moretus Museum of Antwerp. References to these items typically consist of the following: the abbreviations MPM (for the Plantin-Moretus Museum) and then Arch. (for archive), or M (for manuscript), or KP (for copper plate), or Tek (for drawing), and then a number. The full title of each archival document or manuscript is given in the bibliography.

Usually one of three basic systems was used to identify the pages in the archival documents in the Plantin-Moretus Museum:

1 conventional (modern) page numbers (reflected in the notes here by the abbreviations p. or pp.);

2 a standard folio system, whereby a number (e.g., 20) was noted only in the upper right corner of the right-hand page and that page is then identified as "fol. 20 recto" (or abbreviated as fol. 20r) and the subsequent page (the back of the first) as "fol. 20 verso" (or abbreviated as fol. 20v); or

3 an accounting system, whereby one number (e.g., 100) was written in the upper corners of both pages in a single opening of a "debit–credit" balance, i.e., the recto of the right-hand leaf and the verso of the preceding leaf. In this case, we refer to the right and left sides of the single opening, with the following abbreviations: e.g., fol. 100 rht (for the right side) and fol. 100 lft (for the left side).

FREQUENTLY USED ABBREVIATIONS FROM SECONDARY LITERATURE

Corr.. M. Rooses and J. Denucé, eds., Correspondance de Christophe Plantin, 9 vols. (Antwerp: De Groote Boekhandel-'s Granvenhage, Martinus Nijhoff, 1883–1918); and M. Van Durme, ed., Supplément à la correspondance de Christophe Plantin (Antwerp: De Nederlandsche Boekhandel, 1955; reprint Kraus, Nendeln, Liechenstein, 1968).

Holl. Dutch & Flemish: refers to one of the numerous volumes (listed in full in the bibliography) of the series: F. W. Hollstein, Dutch & Flemish Etchings, Engravings and Woodcuts, c.1450–1700 (Amsterdam: Menno Hertzberger, 1949–c.1964; Amsterdam: Van Gendt & Co., 1974–1987; Roosendaal: Koninklijke van Poll, 1988–1994; Rotterdam, Sound & Vision, 1995–2004; Ouderkerk aan den Ijssel: Sound & Vision, 2005–).

M-H (followed by a number): catalogue entries from Marie Mauquoy-Hendrickx's, Les estampes des Wierix, 3 vols. in 4 parts (Brussels: The Royal Library, 1978–1982).

M-H Wierix: refers to one of the preceding volumes.

New Holl. (followed by artist's name): refers to one of the numerous volumes (listed in full in the bibliography) of the series: *The New Hollstein Dutch & Flemish Etchings, Engravings, and Woodcuts, 1450–1700* (Roosendaal: Koninklijke van Poll, 1993–1994; Rotterdam: Sound & Vision, 1995–2004; Ouderkerk aan den Ijssel: Sound & Vision, 2005–).

PP (followed by a number): catalogue entries from Voet, PP (see below).

Voet, GC: Leon Voet, *The Golden Compasses: The History of the House of Plantin-Moretus,* 2 vols. (Amsterdam: Vangendt & Co.; London; Routledge & Kegan Paul; New York: Abner Schram, 1969 and 1972).

Voet, PP: Leon Voet, *The Plantin Press (1555–1589): A Bibliography of the Works Printed and Published by Christopher Plantin at Antwerp and Leiden,* 6 vols. (Amsterdam: Van Hoeve, 1980–1983).

INTRODUCTION: PRECEDENTS FOR PLANTIN'S WORK

LABORE ET CONSTANTIA (WORK AND PERSEVERANCE)

This motto, combined with its visual counterpart of a pair of compasses, became the standard, readily recognizable symbol of the *Officina Plantiniana* of Antwerp, the printing-publishing business begun by the Frenchman Christopher Plantin in 1555.[1] It was renowned throughout sixteenth- and seventeenth-century Europe for both the exceptional scale and the quality of its numerous publications. Plantin's editions were often highly influential, as others sought to emulate or compete against them. As we will document in the following pages, this was also the case in the realm of book illustration, where Plantin's persistent effort – his "Labore et constantia" – to sustain a novel, systematic production of books with engraved or etched illustrations irrevocably altered the market for these publications. Drawing from the uncommonly rich archival sources documenting the work at the *Officina Plantiniana*, we will delve into essential, but often ignored topics on the production and distribution of books with such illustrations in sixteenth-century Europe. We will demonstrate how one publisher – Christopher Plantin – could make such production viable economically and practically, and we will reveal the means by which a revolution in book design came about.

That such trends would come to dominate book illustration was far from clear when printers first started to produce illustrated editions in the later fifteenth century. Then, there were three primary means available for illustrating typographically printed texts: manually added illuminations, woodcuts, or engravings. Hand-painted illustrations were clearly the most labor-intensive, time-consuming approach to illustrating numerous copies of a printed edition. Books with such illustrations are usually associated with wealthier buyers who liked the appearance of illuminated manuscripts but were ready to compromise and accept a faster, cheaper, standardized printing of the text. Antoine Vérard, a scribe in Paris turned book printer-publisher, is perhaps

---

[1] Here, the stationary point of the compass represents *constantia* and the moving point *labore*. The third printer's mark Plantin used (starting in 1557), this would continue to be favored by Plantin and his successors for the next three centuries (cf. Voet, GC, I, p. 31).

the best-known producer of texts with this combination of techniques, but he was far from the only one. Gilles and Germain Hardouyn (also active in Paris) are, for example, known for carrying the tradition on into the early sixteenth century.[2]

Woodcuts are a "relief" print technique, like that of the movable type with which the texts themselves were printed, whereby the image to be printed is left raised on the top of the woodblock. Woodcuts were the most economical means of illustrating texts, both because they were usually cheaper to make than engravings and because one could pull thousands of impressions from a single, well-cared for block. Woodcuts were also technically the most logical medium to combine with printed texts because they could be set, inked, and printed together with the movable type in a single operation under the supervision of the printer of the text.

Engravings, like etchings, are an "intaglio" print technique, namely, one in which ink is left in lines made in a metal plate and the paper used to pull the impression has to be pressed down into the lines in order to catch the ink. Engravings offered several advantages over the preceding two techniques. Often producing a finer, more detailed image than a woodcut, engravings also provided a more efficient means of producing multiple copies of a subject than employing someone to paint each image by hand. Nevertheless, there were also limitations and disadvantages to using this technique to illustrate typographically printed texts. Financially, intaglio prints were generally more costly to make than woodcuts and, particularly in this early stage in the development of the technique, could produce significantly fewer impressions than woodcuts.[3] Furthermore, because intaglios had to be printed on a different press than that used for type, their combination with a typographically printed text brought extra technical challenges and resulted in a longer "time to completion" of the illustrated copies than if the text had simply been illustrated with woodcuts from the start.

Which technique was a printer to use if seeking to make his name in the new world of printing? It was not simply a matter of determining which technique one's potential customers preferred – it had to be practical technically to combine with printed texts and economically viable to produce and sell. Which considerations carried the greatest weight: ease of printing and fewer costs, or a finer, but more costly illustration that would be a credit to one's publications and have a better chance of appealing to a more affluent and potentially influential buying public? The choice could be critical because, as was the case with any business, the bottom line for most printer-publishers was to devise a product that would sell and not constitute a financial loss.

The books (printed and manuscript) that have come down to us from this period of experimentation in the production of texts attest to the fact that there was no single, clear-cut answer.[4] While woodcuts quickly became the most common medium for

---

[2] For several examples of hand-colored illustrations added to printed books, as well as references to additional literature on the topic, see McKitterick 2003, pp. 67–68, 75, 79–80, and 87.

[3] See ch. 1 for more information on intaglio print techniques, how they were combined with letterpress, and their relative cost in comparison with woodcuts. See Bowen and Imhof 2005 and ch. 5 for the varying number of impressions that can be pulled from a single copper plate.

[4] For examples of manuscripts illustrated with either woodcuts or engravings, see, e.g., McKitterick 2003, pp. 53–64; for a recent case study, see Schmidt 2003. For examples of illuminated illustrations in printed books, see n. 2 above. Examples of printed books with woodcut and intaglio illustrations are given below.

illustrating printed texts, experiments with the other media – particularly engravings – continued.[5] Nearly a century passed before one printer, Christopher Plantin, was able to coordinate everything he needed to make the systematic production of books with intaglio illustrations a practical, desirable component of his total output.

The significance of Plantin's success was recognized at the time, as his novel editions with intaglio illustrations were quickly imitated and emulated throughout Europe.[6] Plantin is also regularly cited in modern literature as a pivotal figure in the history of book illustration because his publications furthered the widespread switch to engravings as the favored means of embellishing books in the seventeenth century.[7] Engravings continued to enjoy this privileged position for two hundred years until they were supplanted by new printmaking techniques – wood-engraving and lithography – in the nineteenth century.[8] Nevertheless, the following is much more than a simple success story of one well-known printer. Rather, this examination of Plantin's production of these influential texts has significant ramifications that are, for example, of fundamental importance for the ostensibly distinct fields of bibliography and the cataloguing of a graphic artist's œuvre.[9] Such far-reaching results are possible thanks to the juxtaposition of a thorough knowledge of copies of Plantin's publications with uncommonly extensive archival sources documenting his production and the distribution of his works with intaglio illustrations. This combination has enabled us to describe in unprecedented detail not only how these books were made and what the actual, as yet not fully understood, implications were of this process, but also what the usually indeterminable "market demand" for books with intaglio illustrations genuinely comprised: who, specifically, throughout Europe, purchased which texts and in what quantities? These results will, in turn, improve historians' ability to assess accurately both the illustrated books that have survived and the place of their intaglio illustrations in the œuvre of the artists concerned.[10] But, in order properly to evaluate Plantin's contribution to this manifest alteration in book illustration, we need to go back in time and consider the antecedents to Plantin's own richly illustrated editions. First we will examine the publications of the early entrepreneurs in this field and determine what they reveal concerning the initial technical expertise in printing such books, the development of the market for them, and the common, modern perspective on these publications. With this essential background information, we will then turn to Plantin

---

5 For numerous examples of incunabula with woodcut illustrations, see, e.g., the extensive BMC series. The earliest known printed book to be illustrated with printed illustrations (in this case woodcuts) is a 1461 edition of Ulrich Boner's *Der Edelstein*, printed by Albrecht Pfister in Bamberg (cf. GW, IV (1930), no. 4839). The early use of engraved illustrations is discussed in greater detail below.

6 See ch. 4 and the Conclusion for such examples.

7 For a sampling of such appraisals, see, e.g., Harthan 1981, p. 98; Bland 1969, p. 161; Pastoureau 1982, p. 508; and Landau and Parshall 1994, p. 222.

8 For a brief account of wood-engraving and lithography, see, e.g., Griffiths 1996, pp. 22–25 and 100–108, respectively.

9 For a standard guide to historical bibliography, see Gaskell 1972. Examples of the implications for discussions of artists' work are given below.

10 See Gaskell 2004 for a call for further work to clarify the implications of this combination of printing techniques. Although highly valuable sources of information, the Hollstein series on graphic artists often provides misleading information on prints used to illustrate books owing to its rigid adherence to certain faulty assumptions concerning book illustrations. These publications are discussed in greater detail below.

and discuss what this study of his illustrated editions will contribute to our understanding of how editions with intaglio illustrations were produced and what the expectations and markets for such books were.

Regrettably, our knowledge of how early printed books were illustrated is usually limited to the often unrepresentative selection of books that have come down to us. This problem is all too often overlooked, although evidence of it is widespread. In the case of books, it is frequently the cheaper and/or smaller editions for everyday reading or prayer that have disappeared from view. Thousands of prints were also "used up" and are known only through archival records.[11] Consequently, all of the trends described below must remain tentative generalizations based upon incomplete sources. Similarly, attempts to document "the first ever" appearance of a particular print technique in a printed text are, to some extent, a lost cause from the start, as we will never know precisely all that was printed centuries ago.

Despite these pitfalls inherent in studies of early printed books, we can nevertheless derive useful information from the often unique examples of illustrated editions that have been documented thus far. For example, a succinct list of the twenty-eight known fifteenth-century editions with engraved or etched illustrations supports the following observations.[12] The use of intaglios as book illustrations began in earnest around 1476, some fifteen years after the earliest known use of woodcuts as such. At first glance, this initial group of publications is noteworthy for the frequency with which a new edition with intaglio illustrations appeared – a little more than one per year, on average – and the number of cities throughout western Europe in which printers attempted to combine an intaglio printmaking technique with letterpress. This variety, however, is simultaneously symptomatic of both the early widespread interest in illustrating texts with intaglios and the difficulty in doing so successfully. Specifically, the strikingly diverse selection of cities represented here – Bruges (Low Countries), Lyon (France), Cologne, Nuremberg, Würzburg, and Eichstätt (Germany), and Bologna, Florence, Rome, and Milan (Italy) – attests to a pervasive, contemporaneous interest throughout western Europe in illustrating books in this fashion.[13] Nevertheless, the fact that many of these works appear to constitute one printer's solitary attempt to combine these two dissimilar printing techniques suggests that other concerns – technical, as well as financial, perhaps – ultimately frustrated an initial inclination (possibly based on aesthetic preferences) to try working with the intaglio technique. Technical difficulties in printing the illustrations properly on to the sheets of text – the accurate "registration" of the plate on the sheet – are evident from the numerous books in which the illustrations were printed askew, did not fit properly into the space left open for them, or were

---

[11] For the case of books, consider, e.g., the number of Plantin's small books of hours that are known only via archival records (see Bowen 1997a, pp. 223–258, *passim*). For the case of prints, see, e.g., Van der Stock 1998, pp. 173–181.

[12] See Von Arnim 1984, pp. 119–121, for this list, which contains references to more detailed discussions of the cited books. Hofer 1934, pp. 203–227, provides a more descriptive (but often less detailed), chronologically arranged account of many of the books cited by Von Arnim.

[13] We will be using the term "Low Countries" to refer to territories now part of present-day Belgium and the Netherlands. These may also be referred to as the Southern and Northern Netherlands, respectively. Other countries cited here are referred to according to their current names and national boundaries.

simply printed separately and then pasted in.[14] Such difficulties may reflect the often overlooked consideration that a true intaglio (roller) printing press, with fixed rollers and a movable bed on which the paper and plates could be systematically and accurately registered, may not yet have been invented. Although some system of printing images with the use of weighted drums appears to have been in use in Italy, at least, by the late fifteenth century, it may still have been difficult to align the plates properly and print the larger runs desired for the illustration of an entire edition.[15] The switch to woodcut variants of a set of engraved illustrations for the embellishment of subsequent editions of a given text is also often cited by Philip Hofer as yet another indication of technical or financial concerns. For, even if a printer was able to arrange for the technically successful combination of intaglio images and letterpress, a switch to woodcuts for the illustration of subsequent editions of the text might reflect the fact that he could not find a market to support his continued production of the work with intaglio illustrations.[16] As is discussed in greater detail below in connection with the Würzburg liturgical editions, it is also possible that the illustration of some publications was split, such that some copies were illustrated with woodcuts and others (that happen to be unknown to us) were illustrated with intaglios.

Indeed, of the thirteen printers/publishers known to have produced books with intaglio illustrations in the fifteenth century, only three appear to have found it worth repeating the experiment. These are the Florentine Nicolò di Laurenzo (or Nicolaus Laurentii) and the German printers Georg and Michael Reyser, active in Würzburg and Eichstätt respectively. While di Laurenzo printed at least three texts with engraved illustrations between 1477 and 1482, the Reysers are credited with printing at least fifteen liturgical editions with an intaglio coat of arms (and, depending upon the publication, an engraving of the Crucifixion), between 1479 and 1499.[17]

Di Laurenzo's first publication with engraved illustrations, a 1477 edition of Antonio Bettini's *Monte sancto di Dio*, is often cited as the first printed book with true engraved text illustrations – although occasionally poorly printed.[18] Di Laurenzo never succeeded in finding printers who could combine these two techniques successfully on one sheet of paper, however. His second known edition with engraved illustrations – a 1481 edition

---

[14] For two well-known examples of the initial technical difficulties of adding intaglio illustrations, consider *De la ruyne des nobles hommes et femmes*, a French translation of Giovanni Boccacio's *De casibus virorum illustrium*, printed by Colard Mansion in Bruges in 1476 (see Von Arnim 1984, no. 63), and a 1481 edition of Dante's *Divina commedia*, printed in Florence by Nicolò di Laurenzo (see Von Arnim 1984, no. 115).

[15] For discussions of the development of the roller press, see, e.g., Landau and Parshall 1994, pp. 29–30, and Meier 1941. The earliest known reference to a press for printing engravings dates from 1540. Although Landau and Parshall erroneously refer to the pertinent document as an inventory, it is actually (as discussed in Van der Stock 1998, p. 155 and appendix III, docs. 22 and 26) an agreement for the loan of the press, copper plates, and other materials needed to print engravings.

[16] Hofer 1934, p. 214.

[17] For an overview of di Laurenzo's work as a printer and descriptions of many of his publications, see BMC, VI (1930), pp. 624–631. The most complete, succinct list of the Reysers' publications with intaglio illustrations is provided in Von Arnim 1984, I, pp. 119–121. Several of Georg Reyser's publications are also discussed in BMC, II (1912), pp. 569–572 (which also has a brief introductory note on Reyser); and in Von Rath 1927, pp. 64–65.

[18] For a sampling of accounts of this book, see, e.g., McKitterick 2003, p. 81; Von Arnim 1984, no. 14; Hofer 1934, pp. 209–214; BMC, VI (1930), pp. 626–627; and GW, II (1926), no. 2204.

of Dante's *Divina commedia* – similarly suffers from technical difficulties in adding the engraved illustrations to the printed sheets of text, while in his third such publication – a 1480–1482 edition of Francesco Berlinghieri's *Geographia* – he avoided this difficulty altogether by having the accompanying engraved maps printed separately and inserted into copies of the book.[19] Thus, despite having earned the honor of being one of the first printers to persist in producing books with engraved text illustrations, his efforts appear to have been foiled by technical difficulties and, potentially, an insufficient market for them.

While admittedly less ambitious than the illustrated works conceived of by di Laurenzo, the numerous editions including an intaglio coat of arms that were published by the German printers Georg and Michael Reyser attest to a more lasting, basic achievement in the combination of these two media. For here, various factors point to an active production of books with intaglio illustrations that was not simply successful technically, but clearly was sustained by a demand for them – albeit, perhaps, one dictated by the idiosyncratic wishes of the local bishops.[20] Of particular importance are the adeptness with which the plates were usually (although not always) printed directly on to the sheets with letterpress, the frequency with which editions bearing the bishops' and chapters' coats of arms were produced, as well as the evidence of several different plates being used in the course of time for the printing of them. As of 1495, however, woodcut variants of these coats of arms began to appear.[21] One might argue that the essentially simultaneous use of woodcut and etched (or engraved) coats of arms for these publications represented a savvy broadening of the market for these editions for buyers with distinct budgets, interested either in copies with more costly intaglios or in copies with cheaper woodcuts. It was a practice that Plantin and his successors successfully exploited for decades.[22] The apparent disappearance of editions with intaglio illustrations soon thereafter, however, suggests that something in the earlier success formula had changed. The passing away of the bishops who had instigated this practice, for example, may have meant the end of a guaranteed market for such books and, hence, the loss of the incentive to produce them.[23]

The initial success enjoyed by the Eichstätt and Würzburg editions would not be achieved again until the mid-sixteenth century. Philip Hofer attributes this lack primarily to inadequate public interest in buying these richly illustrated editions, arguing

---

[19] For a few of the numerous discussions of di Laurenzo's Dante edition, see McKitterick 2003, pp. 81–82; Caron 1998, cat. 13; Von Arnim 1984, no. 115; and Hofer 1934, pp. 218 220. For extensive bibliographic descriptions of this book, see, e.g., GW, VII (1938), no. 7966, and BMC, VI (1930), pp. 628–629. For di Laurenzo's edition of the *Geographia*, see, e.g., von Arnim 1984, no. 40; Levarie 1995, p. 126; Hofer 1934, p. 216; and BMC, VI (1930), pp. 629–630.

[20] On the importance of Bishop Rudolf von Scherenberg for the Würzburg editions, see Von Rath 1927, p. 64. On the involvement of Bishop Wilhelm von Reichenau of Eichstätt, see Von Arnim 1984, no. 321, in which Von Arnim observes that the coat of arms used to illustrate this edition (in addition to three similar ones) was etched and not engraved – as is suggested in Hofer 1934, pp. 223–224, and BMC, III (1913), p. 665. Our examination of a copy of this work in the British Library (BL) (I B 12803) supports Von Arnim's attribution. See also Hofer 1934, p. 222, on the relative success of these editions.

[21] Hofer 1934, p. 225, and Von Rath 1927, p. 65.

[22] See pp. 29 and 172 for a more detailed discussion of Plantin's application of this system and ch. 1, n. 45, and ch. 4, n. 136 for examples of editions with both series of woodcut and intaglio illustrations.

[23] Bishop Rudolf von Scherenberg of Würzburg passed away in 1495, just as the woodcuts came into use, while Bishop Wilhelm von Reichenau of Eichstätt died a year later in 1496.

that if there had been sufficient willingness to pay for such books, resourceful printers would have resolved any remaining technical problems.[24] Evidence from the various editions produced in the intervening years (from 1500 to 1545) supports this hypothesis.

Far fewer editions with engraved or etched illustrations are commonly known from the first half of the sixteenth century than the preceding twenty-five years.[25] The implied significant reduction in the production of such books may, in fact, be exaggerated owing to simple scholarly neglect. For, these decades constitute neither the intriguing period of "firsts" among incunabula nor the triumphant phase of the second half of the sixteenth century when numerous printers throughout western Europe began to produce richly illustrated editions with engravings.[26] Despite the uncertain numbers, editions with intaglio illustrations are known to have been produced in at least seven different western European cities between 1500 and 1545.[27] Attesting to a comparably diverse, widespread production of such books as was observed for the incunabula period, these editions similarly document a continued, pervasive interest in attempting to illustrate printed texts with engravings and etchings. The essential difference in the works produced in these two periods is the new proficiency evident in the early sixteenth-century editions in combining these two distinct printing techniques.[28] Perhaps not unrelated to this phenomenon was the development of a true roller printing press in these decades – the earliest known reference to one is included in a legal document from 1540, which was composed in Antwerp, then a burgeoning center for the production of prints.[29] These observations, combined with the lack of evidence that any one of these editions was popular enough to be reprinted and imitated like the Würzburg and Eichstätt editions, support one of Hofer's recurring arguments: that at this stage, the lack of a sufficient market to support the continued production of books with intaglio illustrations was the primary factor impeding a more active production of such works, rather than practical, technical concerns.

Had publishers simply not hit upon a type of illustrated text that would appeal to a broader public, or were too many potential buyers still reluctant to pay extra

---

[24] Hofer 1934, p. 227.   [25] For a brief overview of most of these works, see Hofer 1934, pp. 295–303.

[26] Discussions of books with intaglio illustrations from the first half of the sixteenth century are often limited to what happens to be cited in a general survey of illustrated books (cf., e.g., Levarie 1995, Harthan 1981, Bland 1969), catalogues of particular collections (although older publications, Mortimer 1964 and Mortimer 1974 are good examples for this given the extra attention to illustration in the entries and despite the periodic confusion between etchings and engravings), or sales catalogues of rare books.

[27] Consider, for example, the following publications: Domenicus Lupi, *Figurae ad devotionem excitantes de passione Christi cum alia figura rosarii virginis* (Bruges: Hendrick de Valle, 1503) (NK 3448); editions of the *Heiltumbuch*, printed in Wittenberg in 1509 (cf. Hofer 1934, pp. 298–299) and Halle in 1520 (cf. Hofer 1934, pp. 301–303) (see, e.g., the Deutsche Historische Museum of Berlin for copies of both); Thomas Aquinas, *Della purita della consciencia & del modo da confessarsi* (Florence, 1512) (cf. Bland 1969, pp. 121 and 142; and Hofer 1934, pp. 299–301); Ambrosius Leo, *De Nola* (Venice: Giovanni Rosso, 1514) (cf. Mortimer 1974, no. 255); Amadeus Berrutus, *Dialogus . . . de amicitia vera* (Rome, 1517) (Hofer 1934, p. 301; and STC Italian, p. 89); and Augustin Hirschvogel, *Ein aigentliche und grundtliche Anweysung in die Geometria* (Nuremberg: Johann vom Berg and Ulrich Neuber, 1543) (Hofer 1934, pp. 303–304; copy in, e.g., BS Munich).

[28] The primary example of difficulties in this regard is Ambrosius Leo's *De Nola* (Venice: Giovanni Rosso, 1514). In this case, while pages were left blank for the addition of the illustrations, they were ultimately printed separately and inserted, resulting in an ad hoc placement of the illustrations and an unintended waste of valuable paper (see Mortimer 1974, no. 255).

[29] See n. 15 above for sources on this legal document and ch. 2 on the print world in sixteenth-century Antwerp.

for this more costly, but nevertheless mechanically produced form of illustration? The two books that initiated the dramatic shift in the market for works with intaglio illustrations suggest that the content of the book was significant. For, the "success" of these books – Thomas Geminus's pirated edition of Andreas Vesalius's anatomical work, the *Compendiosa totius anatomiae delineatio* (London: John Herford, 1545), and a history of the kings of France, *Epitome des rois* (Lyon: Balthasar Arnoullet, 1546) – is usually measured on the following two counts. First, by the reuse of their plates for the illustration of other comparable texts and, second, by the emulation of both of these types of illustrated editions by other publishers working with their own distinct sets of intaglios. Geminus's plates, for example, were used to illustrate several other editions of this text, including two subsequent editions printed in London in 1553 and 1559, as well as Jacques Grévin's revision of it, printed by André Wechel in Paris in 1564–1565 and 1569.[30] In addition, other publishers had comparable sets of engravings made to illustrate their own anatomical editions, including: (1) Paulus Fabricius in Nuremberg for his 1551 publication of Jacob Bauman's *Anatomia Deudsch*; (2) Antonio Salamanca and Antonio Lafreri in Rome for their 1556 Spanish edition of Juan de Valverde's anatomical edition; and (3) Christopher Plantin, who had a set of plates made after the Italian engravings first used by Salamanca and Lafreri.[31] The French portrait edition of the kings of France had similar repercussions, as several related editions were printed in Lyon with many of the same plates, while other texts with engraved series of portraits were made.[32]

In the decades following the publication of these "breakthrough" editions, a wide sample of texts boasting engraved and etched illustrations appeared throughout western Europe. Accounts of these books now tend to arise in discussions concerning a specific artist's or publisher's achievements, or else in more general surveys that either highlight the evolution of particular trends in book illustration (title-pages, for example) or are devoted to specific types of texts (emblem books, for example) or collections in which editions with engraved or etched illustrations appear.[33]

It is true that during the third quarter of the sixteenth century – in contrast with the preceding decades – certain cities and even specific individuals began to dominate

[30] For a full discussion of Geminus's and related editions, see Cushing 1962, pp. 119–130. For discussions of the influence of the original Geminus plates, see, e.g., Hind 1952, pp. 39–52. On the reuse of the plates for the Parisian editions, see also Mortimer 1964, no. 541.

[31] For a brief account of the first two editions, see, e.g., Cushing 1962, pp. 132 and 146–147. For a more detailed discussion of the Italian plates, see Mortimer 1974, no. 513. See ch. 3 for an extensive discussion Plantin's anatomical editions.

[32] For the original and some subsequent French editions using this series of portraits, see, e.g., Mortimer 1964, nos. 208–209 (for the original issues), and nos. 456 and 51 for later uses of many of the same plates. For examples of other successful texts with engraved series of portraits, see, e.g., Mortimer 1964, no. 518, and Mortimer 1974, nos. 40, 100, 117, 173, and 460.

[33] For examples of studies focused on specific artists and publishers who were important figures in this stage of the evolution of engraved book illustration, see, e.g., Iwai 1986 or Seelig et al. 2001–2003, or the discussion of the work of Antonio Lafreri in Bury 2001 (which includes references to several other works devoted to Lafreri). Studies of engraved title-pages range from Alfred Johnson's original work (e.g., Johnson 1936) to Remmert 2005. For catalogues of emblem books, one of the most prominent genres that, as of the mid-sixteenth century, would boast numerous editions with intaglio illustrations, see, e.g., Adams et al. 2002 and Landwehr 1976, although these authors cannot be relied upon to distinguish between engraved and etched illustrations. For examples of other more general publications on illustrated books from the sixteenth century, see n. 26 above.

the production of texts with intaglio illustrations. Notably, while publications from Germany figured prominently in the incunabula period, this was no longer the case by the second half of the sixteenth century, when works with intaglio illustrations, such as Melchior Jamnitzer's *Perspectiva corporum regularium* (published in Nuremberg in 1568 with illustrations etched by Joost Amman), were seldom published.[34] This relative lack of editions with intaglio illustrations may be a result of a generally poor national market for such works. As we will discuss in greater detail in the chapters that follow, Plantin's editions with engravings and etchings sold well in most of western Europe except Germany, where buyers exhibited a persistent preference for books with woodcut illustrations.[35] The Low Countries – at least prior to the 1570s, when Plantin began to produce books with engraved illustrations on an unprecedented scale – similarly declined in its relative importance in this market. For while publishers from Bruges, like their counterparts in the fifteenth and early sixteenth centuries, occasionally contributed a solitary edition with etched illustrations in the mid-sixteenth century, this rate of production did not increase, as it did in cities in France and Italy. Consequently, while the then Bruges-based artist Marcus Gheeraerts I and the Bruges antiquarian Hubertus Goltzius were engaged in the production of a few editions with etched illustrations in 1557 and periodically during the 1560s, these remained the exception, rather than the rule.[36]

It was, rather, in France and Italy that the initial burst in the production of works with intaglio illustrations took place from c.1548 to the early 1570s. The sudden rise in importance of France in this area is particularly striking given the previous paucity of such illustrated editions. Indeed, prior to the appearance of the 1546 edition of the *Epitome des rois* in Lyon, only one other French publication with intaglio illustrations is known, namely, the 1488 French edition of Bernhard von Breidenbach's *Peregrinatio in terram sanctam*, which was similarly published in Lyon.[37] Thereafter, however, numerous such editions were printed in both Paris and Lyon in the 1550s and 1560s.[38] Although the intaglios were often successfully printed on the sheets with letterpress in the Lyon publications, in these initial Parisian editions text and illustrations were typically printed separately. Either the plates were inserted among the pages of text or else the publication consisted primarily of a large series of plates whereby the letterpress text was subordinated to a brief introduction. Thus, while the Lyon editions attest to

34 On this and related publications, see, e.g., May 1985, pp. 161–165 and cat. nos. 756–757.
35 See also appendix 3.
36 For a more extensive discussion of Goltzius's editions and Gheeraerts's illustrations to Edward de Dene's *De warachtighe fabulen der dieren* (Bruges: Pieter de Clerck for Marcus Gheeraerts I, 1567), see ch. 5.
37 See, for example, GW, IV (1930), no. 5080, and Von Arnim 1984, no. 85, for this publication.
38 Consider, for example, Leonard Thiry, ed. by J. de Mauregard, *Livre de la conqueste de la toison d'or* (Paris: 1563) (Mortimer 1964, nos. 519–520); Jacques Androuet du Cerceau, *Livre d'architecture* (Paris: B. Prévost, 1559) (Mortimer 1964, no. 22); and A. Wechel's anatomical editions discussed in ch. 3, as well as Pierre Woeiriot, *Pinax iconicus antiquorum ac variorum in sepulturis rituum ex Lilio Gregorio excerpta* (Lyon: printed for C. Baudin, 1556) (Mortimer 1964, no. 555); Georgette de Montenay, *Emblemes ou devises chrestiennes* (Lyon: J. Marcorelle, 1567 and 1571) (see Adams 2000 for the 1567 edition and Mortimer 1964, no. 380, for the better-known 1571 edition); and Nicolas de Nicolay, *Les quatre premiers livres des navigations et peregrinations orientales* (Lyon: G. Rouillé, 1568) (Mortimer 1964, no. 386). Jacques Besson's *Instrumentorum et machinarum liber primus* is also dated to this period (c.1569) and is believed to be a rare example of the production of a work with intaglio illustrations in Orléans (see Mortimer 1964, no. 56).

the ability of both text printers and print workshops to work together to create a real integration of the two media, the Parisian editions suggest a continued de facto separation of the two realms of printing that must have impeded, at least temporarily, a more varied production of books with intaglio illustrations.[39]

Italy's flourishing production of books illustrated with engravings or etchings comes as less of a surprise, although there were some significant shifts in the centers of production of such works. For example, while Florence had been home to a couple of fifteenth-century printers – in particular, Nicolò di Laurenzo – who are known for their early endeavors to produce works with intaglio illustrations, it was not until the 1580s that other Florentine printers – in particular, members of the Giunti family – took up the production of such works again.[40] Similarly, while one Bolognese edition with engraved illustrations is known from 1477, very few have been documented from the mid-sixteenth century either.[41] It was, rather, Venice and Rome – famous, respectively, for the printing of books and the printing of engravings – that would dominate this production from the 1550s to the early 1570s.[42]

Venice's unheralded emergence as an important center for the printing of books with engraved illustrations is noticeably reminiscent of Lyon's. While neither can be credited with any significant contributions to the development of this aspect of book illustration in the preceding decades, in both cities the combination of an established, significant body of book printers and a growing group of engravers or etchers evidently gave rise to the ready publication of numerous richly illustrated editions for the new emerging market for books with intaglio illustrations. The number of distinct printers and artists engaged in the production of the Venetian editions attests to the great potential of the city in this area of book production in mid-sixteenth-century Europe. However, some have seen a potential decline in the prosperity of printing and the graphic arts in Venice around 1575–1577 when the plague rampaged the city.[43]

In contrast to Venice, Rome both gave rise to some of the original fifteenth-century editions with engraved illustrations and was subsequently home to entrepreneurs who were influential in the development of professional print publishers.[44] Consequently,

[39] See Martin 1954, p. 257, for similar conclusions regarding the Parisian editions, although he credits the lack of true engraved text illustrations to a simple preference for woodcuts in Paris at that time.

[40] For examples of some of the editions with intaglio illustrations published by Filippo and Jacopo Giunti in Florence as of 1579, see, e.g., Mortimer 1974, nos. 83 and 223.

[41] Consider, a 1477 edition of Ptolemaeus's *Cosmographia* printed by Dominicus de Lapis (see von Arnim 1984, no. 280), and a 1555 edition of Achille Bocchi's *Symbolicarum quaestionum libri quinque* (see Mortimer 1974, no. 76).

[42] On Rome's leading position in the area of engraved prints and Venice's own growing importance in the same in mid-sixteenth-century Italy, see Bury 2001, pp. 121–131 and 171–174. On Venetian book production, see, e.g., Grendler 1977 and di Filippo Bareggi 1994 for a more recent re-evaluation of the subject.

[43] A few of the better-known Venetian publications include: Enea Vico, *Le imagini delle donne auguste. Libro primo* (Venice: Enea Vico and Vincenzo Valgrisi, 1557); Girolamo Ruscelli, *Le imprese illustri* (Venice: Francesco Rampazetto [for Damiano Zenaro], 1566); and Giovanni Battista Mutiano, *Il primo libro di fogliami antiqui* (Venice: Giovanni Francesco Camocio, 1571). These and several other editions with intaglio illustrations published between 1548 and 1570 (the year in which Plantin's production of editions with intaglio illustrations began in earnest) are described in Mortimer 1974, nos. 15, 104, 108, 197, 316 (Mutiano's study), 318, 404, 449 (Ruscelli's work), 460, 467, 475, 532–533 (Vico's *Imagini*), and 556. On Venice's ascribed decline, cf. Bury 2001, pp. 174–175.

[44] The earliest known Roman edition with intaglio illustrations is a 1478 edition of Ptolemaeus's *Cosmographia*, printed by A. Buckinck (see, e.g., Hofer 1934, pp. 214–215, and Von Arnim 1984,

Rome's burgeoning production of books with intaglio illustrations in the mid-sixteenth century is not surprising. What is of interest, however, is how this production differs from that in Venice, particularly in terms of who appears to have been the moving force behind it. As observed above, Venetian publications document a diverse range of printers, artists, and authors contributing to the production of a variety of these richly illustrated editions. When one examines a sample of similar works published in Rome, however, one figure alone clearly dominates the field, namely, the print dealer Antonio Lafreri.[45] Lafreri is best known for his leading role in invigorating the print publishing business, most likely serving, along with his one-time partner, Antonio Salamanca, as the model for Hieronymus Cock's prosperous print publishing business in Antwerp in the second half of the sixteenth century. Notably, the majority of the books with engraved illustrations in which he was involved post-date his partnership with Salamanca, which ended in 1562 upon the latter's death. These works include several remarkable and well-known editions.[46] Although some are essentially print series with an introductory text – as was common among Parisian editions with engraved illustrations from this period – others exhibit a true integration of text and image, with both media appearing on the same leaf.[47] Some of Lafreri's publications are also of interest because he had the text printed by a Venetian printer. While cooperative ventures between Venice and Rome were not uncommon in the worlds of prints and books in this period, it does raise the question as to what extent letterpress printers active in mid-sixteenth-century Rome were capable or willing to take on the challenge of producing works in which these two media were combined.[48]

Around 1573, Lafreri published a list of the publications he had for sale.[49] Famous as one of his innovative approaches to the print publishing business, this list provides a valuable overview of all the works he wanted to sell at that time, including his "Libri et Stampe di Rame" (books with engraved prints). While this last group is predictably far outweighed by the numerous independent prints he was simultaneously offering for sale – that is, prints sold separately and independently from a printed book – it includes, nevertheless, some twenty items. Regrettably, it is not always clear when a work from

no. 282). See Bury 2001, pp. 9–10, for a brief summary of the emergence of "print publishers" in Rome in the sixteenth century and arguments as to why one must be careful in the use of the term "print publisher" (a point that has been emphasized by other authors writing on print production elsewhere, see, for example, Orenstein 1996, pp. 12–14).

45 Lafreri is discussed at length and in various contexts in Bury 2001, see especially pp. 9–10 and 121–123.

46 For descriptions of many of these, see Mortimer 1974, nos. 170, 173, 245, 329, 356, 454, and 513. Lafreri is also associated with Ippolito Salviani's *Aquatilium animalium historiae, liber primus* (Rome: Ippolito Salviani, 1557–1558), as he published the plates separately (see Mortimer 1974, no. 454).

47 For an example of the former see, e.g., [Aquiles Estaço, ed.], *Inlustrium virorum ut exstant in urbe expressi vultus* (Rome: Antonio Lafreri, 1569); for the latter, see, e.g., Onufrio Panvinio, *XXVII pontificum maximorum elogia et imagines* (Rome: Antonio Lafreri, 1568) (Mortimer 1974, nos. 173 and 356, respectively).

48 On cooperative ventures involving individuals based in Venice and Rome at this time, see Bury 2001, pp. 171–172. For examples of such works among Lafreri's publications, see, e.g., his 1560 Italian edition of Juan de Valverde's anatomical study, printed in Venice by Niccolò Bevilacqua for Lafreri and Antonio Salamanca (see Mortimer 1974, no. 513); and Lafreri's 1570 edition of Fulvio Orsini's *Imagines et elogia virorum illustrium*, printed for him in Venice by Pietro Dehuchino (see Mortimer 1974, no. 329).

49 See Bury 2001, p. 121 and n. 11, for a discussion of the significance of this document and its dating. For a transcription of this stock list, see Ehrle 1908, pp. 53–59 (p. 59 in particular for the "Libri et Stampe di Rame").

this list comprised a body of printed text (rather than consisting primarily of just an extensive print series and a title-page). Nevertheless, this list of approximately twenty editions boasting numerous engraved illustrations from diverse sets of plates produced under the direction of just one publisher was a significant, new accomplishment in the history of book illustration. This fact clarifies why Lafreri (and, by implication, Rome and Italy in general, if one complements his work with the numerous editions produced contemporaneously in Venice) was so well known for the production of editions with engravings in the mid-sixteenth century.

Nonetheless, as observed above, in various studies of the ultimate triumph of engravings over woodcuts as the preferred medium for illustrating books in the seventeenth and eighteenth centuries, it is not Lafreri, but Plantin who is routinely cited. These assertions of Plantin's significance are rarely justified in any detail, perhaps because some of the reasons seem self-evident. For example, Plantin's total production far outstripped that of any contemporary European printer: Plantin had some ten to fifteen presses for letterpress work in operation during his peak production years (1570–1575) and six to seven at other times, whereas most sixteenth-century printers operated only two to four presses at most.[50] Consequently, although Plantin's hundreds of illustrated editions represented a relatively small percentage of his total production (around 18 percent), this group nevertheless comprised almost two hundred editions with some form of engraved or etched embellishment.[51] Even if one discounts those publications with just one or two text illustrations or some image on the title-page, in addition to the works Plantin actually printed for someone else who owned the plates used for the illustrations, one is still left with some 115 editions with three or more engraved or etched text illustrations. This is an astounding leap from the approximately twenty publications with engraved illustrations cited in Lafreri's stock list. Representing thousands of books that were distributed throughout Europe, Plantin's unprecedented production indicates that he had overseen fundamental changes in both the mechanics of producing these illustrated editions and finding a large enough market to support (and justify) such a production. These observations, combined with the evidence of both explicit imitations and a more general emulation of his editions in sundry European cities, fully justify the prominent recognition his editions with intaglio illustrations have received.[52]

---

[50] For an overview of Plantin's total production, see Voet 1984, which is based upon the detailed descriptions of Plantin's editions in Voet, PP. For a succinct list of the number of presses Plantin (and his successors) had in operation in any given year, see Voet, GC, I, pp. 437–439. For evidence of the number of presses operated by other important sixteenth-century printers, see, e.g., Veyrin-Forrer 1982, p. 279, and Martin 1984, I, pp. 312–313.

[51] For Voet's calculations concerning Plantin's production of illustrated editions (he arrives at 91 meagerly illustrated works and 238 richly illustrated ones), see Voet 1985, pp. 38–41. Voet's subsequent (pp. 42–43) assessment of the costs of including intaglio illustrations and the relative importance of Plantin's 1566 publication of Juan de Valverde's *Vivae imagines partium corporis humani* (PP 2413) must be read with caution. See ch. 1 and ch. 3, respectively, for our assessment of the relative costs of producing a book with intaglio illustrations and Plantin's de Valverde editions. The number of editions Plantin printed with intaglios is derived from the descriptions of his editions in Voet, PP and in Bowen 1997a, ch. 8.

[52] See n. 6 for references to the imitations of Plantin's books with intaglio illustrations.

There are, however, numerous other reasons why a detailed examination of Plantin's production of works with intaglio illustrations – and not just another overview of the highlights – should be undertaken. Foremost among these is the valuable archive of the Plantin-Moretus Press. The foregoing survey of the preliminary production of books with engraved and etched illustrations is based almost entirely upon those books that have happened to survive and receive the attention of some researcher or librarian. Our study, by contrast, will benefit from a more extensive (archival-based) knowledge of what Plantin printed and sold, regardless of whether copies of the texts concerned are currently known. Whenever possible, we set surviving copies beside the record of their production and sale.

Indeed, not only can we learn more about Plantin's original production, but we often also know exactly how many copies of a given text were actually illustrated with engravings or etchings and at what cost. Such knowledge would be immensely valuable, for example, in determining the true significance of the production of the Würzburg and Eichstätt liturgical editions printed at the end of the fifteenth century. Do the known copies of these books represent just a limited production of special, presentation copies, or are they the remains of a more extensive production? How significant was the extra cost of embellishing some copies with a single etched or engraved coat of arms? A relatively low added cost would help clarify the surprising frequency with which these copies appear to have been printed.

Similarly, while earlier studies of the initial production of books with intaglio illustrations often focus on the technical issues of combining letterpress and intaglio printing techniques, once enough books appeared in which these distinct media were competently combined, the implied assumption is that such technical matters were no longer a concern. The records of the production of Plantin's seemingly highly successful editions, however, indicate that this was not always the case. Rather, they reveal numerous difficulties, ranging from finding artists who were willing to work at an affordable price, to delays in production due to either an overload of commissions for new texts or the slow delivery of the desired plates. This evidence not only corrects inaccurate assumptions, but also heightens our appreciation of what was ultimately accomplished.

The question of "market demand" is another case in point. Once the great breakthrough in the production of editions with intaglio illustrations came in the mid-sixteenth century, the common assumption appears to be that the issue of finding enough buyers to support the production of these editions was resolved. The records of Plantin's sales of his editions with intaglio illustrations, however, reflect a significantly different state of affairs, in which he was constantly having to modify his total production to accommodate the ever-changing selection of potential buyers available to him. Perhaps a more attuned search for comparable circumstances – either in terms of unimagined complications in the technical execution of these illustrated editions, or shifting markets for the texts concerned – might help explain why earlier printers did not succeed in producing more editions with intaglio illustrations than they did.

As the above sample of new questions suggests, an in-depth look at how Plantin succeeded in making the systematic production of books with intaglio illustrations a desirable component of his total output can generate far-reaching results that go beyond a study of his publications alone. Thus, in the course of this book, we will also address the following broader issues.

On one level, we will amass fundamental, practical information on what such a production required: for example, finding artists who were capable and willing to make the necessary plates at a reasonable price; resolving how the illustrations could best be combined with the letterpress text; finding a competent printer of copper plates who could perform the desired work at an acceptable fee; and determining which types of texts would be popular enough among potential clients to make the investment in the copper plates worthwhile financially. As this account will make clear, it was not simply a question of artists knowing how to make the necessary plates and printers of texts and plates working out how to combine the two on one sheet of paper. Rather, we will recount the various ways in which one could produce books with intaglio illustrations, and explore the implications of the potential, often ignored, pitfalls to sustaining such a production. Consequently, the "Mysterious Collaboration," or working relationship between a press and a print shop, highlighted by Roger Gaskell in his recent article on this topic, need no longer be so mysterious.[53]

When we combine this fundamental information, derived primarily from archival sources, with the examination of multiple copies of the books concerned, we are then able to move beyond the "ideal," generalized account of how books were made and assumptions of a single, "ideal" copy. Instead, we can gather evidence for yet another order of observations. Namely, what did the actual, day-in, day-out, year-in, year-out realities of the illustration of books with intaglios imply in terms of the resulting, potentially variable appearance of the entire edition? In particular, we will elucidate the following topics: (1) why was a publisher's choice of which artist would make which plates not necessarily free, nor necessarily motivated by a connoisseur's desire to have a complete series of top-quality prints executed by a single artist? (2) Why did a publisher not necessarily commission plates for the illustration of just one edition, but, rather, seek to supplement a general stock of plates such that they could then be used for the illustration of several editions simultaneously or over extended periods of time? (3) Why weren't all copies of a given edition illustrated with a single set of plates immediately following the initial printing of the text, but occasionally left to be illustrated later on and then perhaps with a different set of plates? And (4) what were the relative advantages and disadvantages of using etchings instead of engravings as book illustrations? All of these issues attest to the fact that the commissioning, printing, and maintenance of intaglio plates for book illustrations were most likely (and logically) determined by other factors than what would have directed a publisher of independent prints when ordering and publishing comparable images. Consequently, accounts of engravings (or etchings) used to illustrate books that are composed with the same conventions and underlying assumptions that are typically applied to a series of independent prints will often end up misconstruing the image and its context. This is regrettably the case in even the most recent volumes of the respected Hollstein series of print catalogues,

---

[53] See Gaskell 2004.

where, for example, a rigid adherence to the underlying assumption that engravings were ordered in book-specific groups – like an independent series of numbered prints – occasionally results in a confusing, misleading presentation of the prints concerned.[54] A better understanding of the issues presented in the following chapters will hopefully, on the one hand, clarify why such an approach can be inherently faulty and, on the other hand, further a historically more accurate appraisal of such illustrated books and what they do (and do not necessarily) represent. This knowledge would also further the project called for by Roger Gaskell of developing a better bibliographic description of illustrated editions that would reflect the potential and inevitable variation in the appearance of books that are strictly regarded as a single edition.[55]

Just as important as the production side of this equation is the demand, for one could not exist without the other. While we are used to vague references to an amorphous "market" or "demand" for books with intaglio illustrations, in this study of Plantin's production we will periodically step back and examine who, specifically, purchased selected works under consideration and in which quantities. In this way, we will discover how certain markets for new types of books with intaglio illustration arose (and collapsed). That for liturgical editions with engraved illustrations resulted, for example, from the unforeseeable combination of reforms instigated by the Council of Trent and the personal preferences of members of the Spanish court and clerical elite. Thus, we will also derive a heightened appreciation of what the usually indeterminable sixteenth-century market for books with intaglio illustrations actually comprised and how variable it could be. For it was influenced by numerous factors beyond a printer's control, such as the changeable financial means of potential buyers and the state of war in sixteenth-century Europe. Consequently, our examination of these issues – often not considered to such an extent owing to a paucity of information – will provide new insights into which were the relatively reliable and which the variable markets for such books in sixteenth-century Europe. This will further, in turn, our appreciation of the potential distribution of other contemporary works with intaglio illustrations.

Thus, this study will not only justify Plantin's place in the history of book illustration. It will also reveal the intriguing elements that inform how this process worked, when it did not work as well, and how Plantin endeavored to resolve a variety of impediments in his attempt to maintain his production of books with intaglio illustrations. All of these aspects will emerge in the course of the following chapters. A brief introductory account of how, generally, printed texts were illustrated with intaglio prints will set the stage by detailing some of the basic technical and financial concerns inherent to producing books with engraved or etched illustrations. We will then describe the context in which Plantin worked, sixteenth-century Antwerp, which was, when Plantin arrived, a burgeoning city of trade and a leading European center for the production of

---

54 Numerous examples of this basic fallacy can be found in *Holl. Dutch & Flemish, Wierix*, LXX, and the *New Holl., Van der Borcht, Book Illustrations*. See also *New Holl., Van Groeningen*, II, nos. 365–396, where the contrived cataloguing of thirty-two plates as all being made for just one edition that was ultimately printed late in 1583 results in the citation of "(Later) use of the plates" in books that were printed prior to the cited work – either by just a year (as is the case with the 1583 bible cited) or by some eight years (as is the case with the 1575 *Officium B. Mariae Virginis* [BMV] cited).

55 Cf. Gaskell 2004, pp. 233–234.

both texts and printed images. By examining the opportunities this city offered Plantin throughout his career, we will be better able to determine to what degree his ultimate success in this area of book illustration was fortuitous and to what degree it was a sought and fought-for achievement. In the next three chronologically arranged chapters we will trace Plantin's production of these luxuriously illustrated books. These will reveal Plantin's surprising evolution from one initially reluctant to take on such projects, to one who revolutionized the production of editions with intaglio illustrations, but also had to struggle to maintain his position in this realm of book production in the face of unpredictable complications arising from working in a war-ravaged region. In the final chapter, we will examine Plantin's unexpectedly extensive work for others, as the simple "hired hand" who just printed the letterpress for another publisher's or author's illustrated edition. This evidence of Plantin's willingness to perform these tasks at various points in his career provides a telling complement to what otherwise might be seen as just a hero's tale. It underscores the reality of the times in which he worked, when even the trend-setting Plantin, on occasion, deemed it best to facilitate the production of another's – ultimately, a potential competitor's – illustrated editions. Thus, far from a simple success story, this account will reveal the unpredictable combination of factors, happenstance, and perseverance – Plantin's "Labore et constantia" – that enabled one person to alter irrevocably publishers' perspectives and buyers' tastes for illustrated books.

CHAPTER ONE

PRINTING WITH INTAGLIO ILLUSTRATIONS

"It is to you I turn . . . since you offer to do me the favor of telling about this marvelous art of printing." E.: "I do not wish to stop to speak of its excellence, knowing your appreciation of that is as good as I could make it. But as for the procedure which we follow, I will take it up gladly."[1]

Thus begins the rather obscure account of how texts were printed in Christopher Plantin's 1567 publication of dialogues to help Dutch-speaking children learn French. While several individuals are associated with the writing and translation of these various pieces, Plantin is usually credited with writing that on printing himself.[2] Consisting of brief technical explanations that often leave the reader uncertain, this dialogue remains important as it contains the earliest known description of the printing press and its use, appearing some 120 years prior to the first edition of Joseph Moxon's more substantive and routinely cited work, *Mechanick Exercises*.[3] However, as is soon indicated in this dialogue, the speaker (and hence the author) is concerned primarily with the printing of texts ("the types, the forme or assemblage of them, and the press") per se, and not how texts were illustrated. Rather, the decorative materials used to embellish the printed text are noted merely in passing, at the end of the discussion of making type, when the question is posed "is everything printed at the press done from foundry material?" and the following answer is given: "No. Sometimes they cut on wood lettres grises and flowered letters, fleurons, chapter headings and vignettes. And most of the portraits and figures which are put in a book [are cut in wood], save those engraved on copper."[4]

---

[1] Nash 1964, p. 37. See pp. 10, 18, and 36 for the identification of the speakers in this dialogue.
[2] The original title is: *La premiere et la seconde partie des dialogues françois, pour les ieunes enfans. Het eerste ende tweede deel van de Françoische t'samensprekinghen* (Antwerp: Christopher Plantin, 1567). See the notes to PP 1081 for a summary of who may have been involved in composing this publication.
[3] Moxon's text was first published in parts in London in 1683–1684 and was frequently cited (or plagiarized) thereafter. See Moxon 1958 for a critical edition of this text.
[4] Nash 1964, pp. 37 and 59.

1.1 Anonymous artist after Joannes Stradanus, *Impressio librorum (The Printing of Books)*, engraving, 201 × 265 (Brussels, The Royal Library, Print Department, s i 1445 f°).

In this chapter, we will focus on exactly what was of notably negligible import in Plantin's 1567 publication, namely, how the printed text was illustrated. In particular, we will discuss how images engraved or etched on copper were combined with printed text, and consider what this combination of two distinct printing techniques implied technically, practically, and financially for anyone wishing to produce a book with intaglio illustrations. The resulting understanding of these essential issues will further our appreciation of what all fifteenth- and sixteenth-century publishers of books with intaglio illustrations had to negotiate once they decided to produce such a work. It will also underscore the significance of Plantin's own great resourcefulness, opportunism, and perseverance. For, it was these traits that enabled him to alter the exceptional production of such distinctively illustrated books into a systematic practice.

In order to apprehend fully the added complications of illustrating printed texts with engravings and etchings, it is necessary to review briefly the essential, basic steps to printing a text with movable type (see fig. 1.1).[5] The production of a book always started

5 For a detailed account of the printing of books in the "hand-press period," see Gaskell 1972, which includes a diagram of all the parts of a printing press (p. 119). For examples of the various costs inherent in printing books in early sixteenth-century France, see Veyrin-Forrer 1982, pp. 279–280. For examples of what Plantin and his successors paid for such items, see Voet, GC, II, chs. 2–7 and 13. For a brief account of the relative weight of each of these costs per book, see Voet, GC, II, ch. 15.

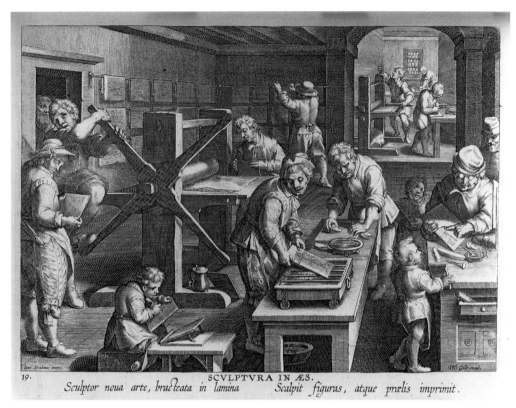

19.   SCVLPTVRA IN ÆS.

Sculptor noua arte, bracteata in lamina   *Scalpit figuras, atque prælis imprimit.*

1.2 Anonymous artist after Joannes Stradanus, *Sculptura in aes (Cutting in Copper)*, engraving, 202 × 273 (Brussels, The Royal Library, Print Department, s i 1532 f°).

from a model, otherwise called the "copy," which could be either an earlier edition of the printed text or else a handwritten document, for example from the author of a new text. The copy was set above the cases with the desired type, such that the compositor – the workman who arranged the type for the text – could set the type, line by line, and group the lines in pages. Once the text was set, decorative material, such as cast fleurons or lines, large or decorative initials, tail pieces, printer's devices, and text illustrations cut in wood, could be added. All of these elements, as well as the letter type, had the image or the letter to be printed sticking out in "relief" at the top of the piece of metal or wood. Consequently, as long as the height of all the metal and wood pieces was the same, they could all be printed simultaneously on an ordinary printing press for type. All of the type, as well as the cast and woodcut decorative materials needed to print the full front or back of a sheet of paper, was set and locked into place in a metal frame (all together, this was called the "forme"). The forme was then placed on the press and inked. Dampened paper was fixed on the press and brought down on top of the type. Paper and type were then rolled under the platen, a flat rectangular block that was large enough to cover roughly half the length of a sheet of paper. One movement of the bar or handle of the press brought down the platen, the pressure of which forced the transfer of the ink on to the dampened paper. The paper and type were then rolled further in for the printing of the other half of the sheet. Trial proofs of the initially set forme were always made and then corrected before the full, definitive run of the text was printed, though in practice further corrections were also made during the press run.

Because of the limited size of the platen, four pulls of the press handle were required before both the front and back of a full sheet of paper were printed. If a text was to be printed in red and black ink – which was common for many liturgical and devotional works – then as many as eight pulls of the handle may have been needed. Consequently, although the basic procedure for printing a text seems straightforward and possible to complete in a single, small workshop, there were, nonetheless, time-consuming aspects of it and many opportunities between the four to eight pulls of the press handle to make a mistake and ruin a costly sheet of paper. It remains, thus, truly astounding that as many successfully printed books resulted as they did. Following the printing of the sheets of paper, each was hung up to dry and then they were stacked in individual piles according to the forme used to print the given sheets. As copies of the completed text were needed, one sheet from each group was taken, folded, and possibly cut according to the distribution of the pages, and then gathered together to form a book that was often sold – in the sixteenth and seventeenth centuries, at least – without a binding.

Such was the production of the vast majority of the texts – illustrated or not – in the fifteenth and sixteenth centuries. Everything could be done in one location, under the control of the master printer or publisher. If engraved or etched illustrations were to be added, however, various aspects of this process had to be modified. What, then, enticed publishers consciously to complicate matters by deciding to illustrate their works in this fashion? In contrast with most woodcuts, intaglio prints could provide highly detailed images, a greater range of tone (as against just alternating areas of black and white), and a finer resulting effect. It is, consequently, not surprising that many of the early publications boasting such prints were cartographic, architectural, and scientific works, where the precise detailing of the image was of great importance.[6] Of these two fundamental intaglio techniques, engraving emerged as a viable and reliable print technique first, alongside the development of printing texts with movable type in the mid-fifteenth century.[7] Engravings also give sharper, finer images and appear to have been preferred generally in the sixteenth century. The qualitative differences between etchings and engravings are the result of the distinct means by which each is made. In an etching, the lines forming the composition are bitten down and out of the plate by an acid, leaving an often irregular line behind of (particularly early in the sixteenth century) frequently unpredictable depth. In an engraving, the lines of the composition are cut out of the plate with a sharp, v-shaped tool called a burin, which, when in well-trained hands, can be manipulated to make lines of subtly varying depths and widths that, in turn, create the clear, finely defined forms and range of tones that characterize these prints. Both of these techniques were often combined, although one

---

[6] See the Introduction for various examples of early editions with intaglio prints and ch. 3 for examples of scientific works with intaglio illustrations.

[7] There are numerous accounts of these and related print techniques (e.g., dry point). Two succinct sources with clear, informative descriptions and illustrations of the technical aspects are Griffiths 1996 and Ivins 1987.

usually dominates. For example, while the outlines of a composition might be quickly etched in, the body of the composition would be engraved, for a detailed, finished look. Or, while a composition might be almost fully etched, extra shading lines would be engraved in afterwards with a burin to enhance the tonal quality of the print.

Whether these print techniques were combined or kept separate, the manner in which the resulting plates had to be printed was the same and – the essential point here – significantly different from and more time-consuming than the relief printing technique of type and woodblocks. In order to pull an impression from an intaglio plate, like an engraving, first the plate has to be warmed, then a slightly less viscous form of a text-printer's ink (one with a higher ratio of oil to the ground lamp black base, for example) has to be rubbed into the lines cut into the plate. The excess ink is then wiped away from the surface of the plate with cloths and the plate is laid face up on the bed of a roller (intaglio) press, after which the dampened paper and a series of blankets for cushioning the paper and the plate are put on. A roller press (see fig. 1.2), in contrast with a press for printing type (see fig. 1.1), requires immense strength to push the press bed, complete with the plate, paper, and blankets, between two rollers. The rollers have to exert a much greater force upon the paper than the platen of a type press, because they must push the paper into the inked lines in the copper plate so that it can pull out the ink, and not merely stamp the paper down (as a platen does) on to the raised surface of a woodcut or type. It is for this reason that intaglio plates cannot be printed together with woodcuts or type and often were printed separately, beyond the text printer's premises, in a workshop specializing in their printing.

The decision to illustrate a book with engravings or etchings had, consequently, practical, technical implications, as well as financial. The practical complications began with the acquisition of the necessary copper plates, if the publisher did not have them in stock already. This could be accomplished in a variety of ways. Occasionally, a publisher bought up a group of plates for an edition that he wished to republish in one form or another. For example, the plates used to illustrate Nicolas de Nicolay's *Les quatre premiers livres des Navigations et peregrinations orientales* (first published in Lyon by G. Rouillé in 1568) subsequently came into the hands of the Parisian publishers Abel L'Angelier and Mathieu Guillemot. Their widows then used them, along with other plates, to illustrate their 1612 publication of Laonicos Chalcondylas's *L'Histoire de la décadence de l'Empire Grec*.[8] Plantin's successors, the Moretuses, also periodically purchased used plates, with the intent of bringing out new editions of such works as Hubertus Goltzius's antiquarian studies, Abraham Ortelius's atlas, and Jerome Nadal's *Evangelicae historiae imagines*, a project with which Plantin had been associated for several years, but never published himself.[9] Occasionally people were not willing to sell their copper plates, but were willing to print extra impressions from them (for a price) for others to include

---

[8] On de Nicolay's original publication, see, e.g., Mortimer 1964, no. 386. For the subsequent owners and use of these plates, see Balsamo and Simonin 2002, pp. 126 and 132, and cat. no. 522 (pp. 393–395).

[9] For their purchase of Goltzius's plates in 1632 from Peter Paul Rubens, see Imhof 2004, p. 25. For their purchase of the plates for Ortelius's atlas from the widow of J. B. Vrints I in 1612, see Imhof 1998c, cat. 52. For examples of other sets of copper plates that the Moretuses purchased from the widow of Jan Baptist Vrints I, see appendix 5. n. 27. Finally, for the purchase of the Nadal plates from the Antwerp Jesuits in 1605, see MPM Arch. 101, fols. 7 (lft and rht) and 8 (lft and rht), and MPM Arch. 1075, fol. 72v.

in their own publications. For example, several publishers appear to have "borrowed" the plates that were originally used to illustrate John Herford's 1545 publication of T. Geminus's edition of Andreas Vesalius's anatomic work. Similarly, on a few occasions when Plantin (and later the Moretuses) wanted to use plates that were in the possession of the print publishers Philips (or Theodoor) Galle, they paid for both the printing of the illustrations and for the loan of the plates.[10] Or else, as is discussed in greater detail in chapter 6, text printers could work together on an edition with someone else – an author or another publisher – who obtained the desired plates, but also retained the ownership of them.

More often than not, however, it appears that publishers interested in producing books with engraved illustrations had the necessary plates that they did not already own made specially for themselves.[11] As was the case with ordering woodcuts, the compositions were either designed specifically for the new illustrations or else drawn on the basis of existing visual sources, such as earlier editions of comparable texts or independent prints or maps.[12] Plantin also often paid separately for the basic material on which the illustration was made – wood for woodcuts or copper for engravings or etchings.[13] Plantin usually purchased individual copper plates ("planches") by the pound. In one such record, the copper was identified as red copper ("cuivre rouge"), which appears to have been the preferred type of copper for making engravings.[14] Plantin then paid a separate fee (often to the same supplier of the copper) for having the plates cleaned and polished such that they could be engraved. In the period c.1569– 1571, when Plantin began to commission large numbers of engravings from a variety of artists, he obtained the copper plates from various sources. These included independent dealers in copper, such as a certain Cornelis Snyders "vendeur de cuivre"; Hans van Luyck (alias Jan Godle), a local goldsmith, engraver, and dealer in prints;[15] and some of the artists Plantin had engaged to help make these book illustrations. For example, the engraver Pieter van der Heyden was paid for supplying and cleaning the copper he needed for some of the engravings he made for the Polyglot Bible. In the 1580s, at least, Peeter vander Borcht, Plantin's most faithful designer and etcher, regularly supplied, cleaned, and polished plates for Plantin.[16]

---

[10] See ch. 3 for examples of the reuse of Geminus's plates. For Plantin's "borrowing" of some of Philips Galle's engravings, see the discussion of his 1584 edition of A. Barlandus's *Hollandiae comitum historia et icones* (PP 625) in ch. 6. Woodcuts were also occasionally lent between publishers, see, e.g., Imhof 2001.

[11] In the following section, all of the examples will be taken from the Plantin archives owing to the exceptional records of this process preserved there. Other publishers probably worked in a similar fashion.

[12] Many of these options are evident, for example, among the suite of engraved illustrations used to embellish Plantin's Polyglot Bible (PP 644) (see ch. 3).

[13] For examples of Plantin's purchases of wood (occasionally specified as "bois de buis" or boxwood), see Voet, GC, II, n. 3, pp. 225–226.

[14] See MPM Arch. 29, fol. 12 rht (between February 28 and March 1, 1571) for this purchase. See, e.g., Landau and Parshall 1994, p. 24, for a discussion of the desirability of red copper.

[15] For Plantin's purchase of copper from Cornelis Snyders, see MPM Arch. 29, fol. 48 rht, between August 10 and 13, 1571. For examples of his purchases from Hans van Luyck, see, e.g., MPM Arch. 28, fol. 4 rht, between February 1 and 10, 1570, and MPM Arch. 29, fol. 68 rht, between December 15 and 22, 1571. For the identification of van Luyck, see Van der Stock 1998, p. 210, n. 55, and p. 237, n. 17.

[16] See ch. 2 and appendix 1 for more information on van der Heyden and vander Borcht and their work for Plantin. For this specific reference to van der Heyden supplying and cleaning some of the plates he

Obviously, in addition to the compositional designs and copper plates required for the illustrations, one also needed to find an artist who was willing to make the desired plates for a reasonable price and within an acceptable time frame. As is discussed in greater detail in the following chapters, not every artist was willing to devote his time to making engravings for someone else's publications.[17] This fact often went hand in hand with some artists' ability to demand exceptionally high fees for their work, thereby pricing themselves beyond the budget of the book publisher.[18]

The potential problem of how long it took to complete a set of engravings is also commonly associated with books illustrated with this medium. For example, we know that it took Pieter Huys nearly two years to complete forty full-page engravings for Plantin's *quarto* edition of Juan de Valverde's *Vivae imagines partium corporis humani*, implying that Huys often finished just two or three engravings per month for this project.[19] Some authors and publishers even laid the blame for the delayed publication of a given work on the slow progress made by the artists executing the plates.[20] It is, consequently, not surprising that when Plantin was negotiating a potential agreement for the production of a large set of book illustrations with Hieronymus and Anton Wierix – two engravers whom he repeatedly described as being highly unreliable – the timing of the completion of the plates was also an issue.[21] However, Plantin apparently had similar concerns regarding the "time to completion" of some of his woodcuts, as he also made up contracts with one woodcutter, Arnold Nicolai, in which it was stated that if Nicolai did not keep to the agreed-upon schedule for the delivery of the woodcuts, he would be paid less. Nicolai was, indeed, late on at least one occasion and received less for his work as a result.[22] Thus, the delayed delivery of illustrative material was not necessarily strictly a matter of the medium concerned, but also, perhaps, a reflection of the artist involved, be he a woodcutter or engraver. Moreover, even if it generally took longer to have a suite of engravings completed than woodcuts or etchings, Plantin discovered how to work around that problem early on by simply employing several different engravers simultaneously to complete all of the illustrations required for any one project.[23]

Nevertheless, if one examines what is known about when certain artists completed specific plates for some of Plantin's projects, there are a striking number of significant

engraved, see MPM Arch. 757, fol. 370 rht, which is transcribed in Voet, GC, II, p. 226, n. 2. For examples of such payments to vander Borcht, see, e.g., MPM Arch. 14, bundle 2, fol. 11 rht (under September 6, 1580); MPM Arch. 60, fol. 185r (under November 10, 1582); and MPM Arch. 14, bundle 6, fol. 1 rht (under January 8, 1587).

[17] See ch. 2 and ch. 6.
[18] On differing artists fees, see Bowen and Imhof 2003.
[19] See ch. 3.
[20] For one such example, see the discussion of Principio Fabricii's *Delle allusioni, imprese, et emblemi sopra la vita, opere, et attioni di Gregorio. XIII. pontefice massimo libri vi* (Rome: Bartolomeo Grassi and Giacomo Ruffinelli, 1588) in Mortimer 1974, no. 177.
[21] For an example of such negotiations, see *Corr.*, VIII, no. 1193, a letter from January 13, 1587 that Plantin wrote to Emmanuel Ximenes regarding his negotiations for the production of the illustrations to Jerome Nadal's *Evangelicae historiae imagines*. Part of this letter is discussed and transcribed below (pp. 50–51).
[22] For these contracts see MPM Arch. 31, fol. 50 rht, under September 2, 1564 and January 12, 1565. The timing of and payments for Nicolai's work under this contract are recorded in MPM Arch. 31, fol. 50 lft, and are discussed in greater detail in Bowen 1997a, pp. 85–86.
[23] For an account of one such project see Bowen 1997b. See also table A1.2 for a visual record of the large number of distinct engravers Plantin employed simultaneously for work on various projects.

discrepancies between the completion of some of the desired plates for a publication and the ultimate publication date on the book itself. These range from two or three years' difference to as many as nine years'. Was Plantin simply waiting for the remaining engravings to be cut, or was the printing of the text delayed for some other reason? There does not seem to be a single, consistent answer to this question. The illustration of Plantin's large *octavo* book of hours from 1573, for example, appears to have suffered from delays in the completion of new engravings. For here, there is an unusual combination of twelve larger plates (c.168/170 × 113/115 mm, including three dated either 1570 or 1571), with six smaller plates (c.114/117 × 73/75 mm), which had already been used to illustrate other texts and had to be printed here with an extra border around the image in order to fill the page.[24] This hypothesis is supported by the fact that when Plantin reprinted this text in this same format in 1575 (see PP 1776), all eighteen of the illustrations were now generally the same, larger size. In the case of his 1583 *quarto* edition of Benito Arias Montano's *Humanae salutis monumenta*, however, nearly all of the seventy or so engravings needed to illustrate the book were ready by January 1, 1576. It seems unlikely that it took seven years to complete the few missing plates. Rather, Plantin probably delayed the publication of this book for other reasons.[25] Thus, while the switch to illustrating books with engravings may well have complicated a printer's production schedule, it was not the only potential source of delays.

Once the basic plate was engraved, it was, in theory, ready for use. There were two primary exceptions to this general practice, however. First, for special projects, funded, for example, by a particular client, proof impressions of the engravings might be made first and sent to the client for approval prior to the definitive printing of the illustrations for the book.[26] The second potential extra step toward the final completion of an engraving was the addition of engraved texts. This was often done by someone specializing in such work and not necessarily by the engraver of the rest of the plate. Some proof impressions of plates, as well as subsequent payments to other artists for the addition of the engraved letters, indicate that this was the case. For examples of the former, consider the numerous proof impressions of plates engraved and already signed with the IHW monogram of Jan Wierix, but still lacking the finely engraved, cursive rendition of "Crispine" for the designer, Crispin van den Broeck.[27] Although there are no concrete examples of separate payments to individuals for engraving letters on to plates Plantin used exclusively for his book illustrations, it is clear that he did ask the engraver and print publisher Adriaen Huberti to perform this work for a few independent projects. Soon after Plantin's death, the engraver Ferdinandus Arsenius

---

[24] See Bowen 1997a, pp. 236–237, for a list of the illustrations included in this edition (PP 1769).

[25] See ch. 5 for more information regarding when most of the plates for this publication were completed (probably between 1574 and 1576). See Plantin's publication of M. Victorius's edition of St. Jerome's *Opera divi Hieronymi Stridoniensis* (PP 1333, in particular the list of illustrations, fig. 20, and n. 2) for another example of the printing of a book being delayed although the engraved illustrations were ready on time.

[26] See, e.g., cat. 11a in Imhof 1996a, a discussion of Jan Moretus I's production of an exceptional book of hours for the archduke and duchess of the Low Countries, Albert and Isabella, for such a case.

[27] For these proof impressions, see MPM Arch. 1228, fols. 244–248 *passim*. The distinct states of some of these plates are described under M-H 2239 and M-H 2250–2252.

appears to have become the Moretuses' regular contact for the engraving of letters on plates.[28]

When the desired plates were fully and satisfactorily engraved, the printer then had to resolve the last significant complication intrinsic to illustrating books with intaglio prints instead of woodcuts, namely, how the illustrations were to be combined with the printed sheets of text. As noted above, neither engravings nor etchings could be printed on an ordinary press and had to be added separately, often by an independent "copper-plate printer" who did not work exclusively for any one book printer.[29] One solution was to have the text and the illustrations printed separately and just append one to the other. This was commonly done when a suite of illustrations was simply accompanied by a brief introductory text, as was the case, for example, with Antonio Labacco's *Libro appartenente a l'architettura* (Rome: for the author, 1559). Independently printed illustrations were also commonly inserted between the printed pages of texts, as was often done with cartographic works, for example.[30] Some of Plantin's editions were also printed with inserted intaglio illustrations; consider, for example, his 1568 Dutch and 1579 Latin edition of Juan de Valverde's anatomical work (PP 2416 and PP 2415) and his 1588 edition of Justus Lipsius's *Saturnalium sermonum libri duo* (PP 1558).

However, in most of Plantin's publications with intaglio illustrations, as well as in many other sixteenth-century editions, the engraved illustrations were printed directly on to pages as true text illustrations, with typographically printed text on one or both sides of the leaf. This implied that when the original formes of text were set, blank filler had to be placed in the areas where the engravings were to be printed, so as to keep those areas free for the subsequent, independent addition of the illustrations. While the full intended run of the letterpress was printed at once, the illustrations were usually added to discrete numbers of copies, as the demand for the complete, illustrated work required. This was a logical means of saving the plates from unnecessary wear, as well as saving money, by avoiding payments for too many impressions that might never be sold. Jan Moretus I, at least, also clearly saw advantages to having a text illustrated in smaller quantities, so he would not have to wait longer for an entire, larger run to be illustrated before some copies could be sold.[31] The illustration of copies in smaller batches may also have been desirable from the point of view of the pictorial printers who were usually employed to do this work. As they also worked independently on

---

[28] See ch. 2 for Huberti's work for Plantin. See MPM Arch. 1079, p. 9, for a note from Jan Moretus II that Ferdinandus Arsenius received $1/2$ st. per word for the engraving of letters.

[29] For the various individuals Plantin employed for the printing of his intaglio images, see ch. 2.

[30] For Labacco's architectural work, see Mortimer 1974, no. 245. Examples of cartographic publications with inserted maps are numerous and constitute some of the earliest examples of books with intaglio illustrations, including, e.g., Francesco Berlinghieri's *Geographia* (Florence: Niccolò di Lorenzo, 1480–1482), discussed in Von Arnim 1984, no. 40. Many other types of publications also had inserted intaglio illustrations, like Nicolas de Nicolay's *Les quatre premiers livres des Navigations et peregrinations orientales*, cited above (n. 8).

[31] For this view, see a letter written by Jan Moretus to the Spanish bookseller Juan Boyer on March 14, 1589 (*Corr.*, IX, no. 1446), in which he states: "les figures ne se impriment audit Theatre sinon par 25 exemplaires a la fois et ce pour eviter la longue attente qu'il fauldroit avoir pour la perfection de 200 ou 150 exemplaires avec lesdites figures" (the illustrations are only printed in 25 copies of the *Theatrum* at one time in order to avoid having to wait a long time before the completion of 200 or 150 copies with these illustrations).

other projects, they may not have wanted to devote their presses and staff exclusively to printing someone else's book illustrations. Indeed, it is possible that book publishers may even have been forced to wait for some copies of their illustrated publications as a consequence of other more urgent projects (at least in the view of the pictorial printer) beyond their control. The results of this staggered printing of the illustrations in one and the same edition of text are evident not only in the payments made to Plantin's printers of intaglio illustrations, but also in the surviving books themselves, where different states or even different plates are found among distinct copies of the same text.[32]

As has already been observed, the basic printing of a text required at least four pulls of the press handle to print each sheet for texts in just black ink and eight pulls per sheet for texts in red and black. If woodcut illustrations were included, these numbers did not change. The addition of intaglio illustrations, however, implied that the initial series of steps of dampening the paper, printing it, drying and stacking it, was followed by another comparable series of steps of re-dampening the sheets with the text printed on it, running them through a roller press to make the necessary impressions of the copper plates, and re-drying and stacking the now illustrated sheets. Because the entire length of a sheet of paper could be passed through a roller press in one go, the number of extra times the sheet would have to be printed was primarily a function of whether the illustrations were concentrated on just one side of the sheet (for one run through), or appeared on both (requiring two runs through). Having to print a larger number of text illustrations on any given side does not appear to have affected the number of times the sheet would have to be printed, just the cost of printing it.[33] The best indication that several plates were printed simultaneously on one sheet is the number of instances when two plates that should have appeared on the same side of the original sheet of paper were switched.[34] Instances in which an image was originally printed upside down may support other indications that engraved plates were occasionally printed with their inked side down on the sheet with letterpress, which would then lie directly on the press bed itself.[35]

[32] For a detailed account of the implications of the staggered illustration of one of Plantin's editions, see Bowen 2003. For references to several copies of one of Plantin's publications, each of which is illustrated by a distinct selection of engravings, see the list of plates used to illustrate a book of hours Plantin published in 1575 (PP 1775) in Bowen 1997b, pp. 145–150. For evidence that other printers had their publications with engraved illustrations printed in a similar fashion, such that variations in the illustrations appear while the printed text remains the same, see, e.g., Mortimer 1974, nos. 449, 454, 467, and 532.
[33] See pp. 54–56 for a sample of the rates Plantin paid to have his copper plates printed.
[34] For copies of books in which a pair of illustrations from the same side of the original sheet were switched, see, e.g., KBR (VH 15.384 A LP), a copy of Plantin's 1577 edition of L. Hillessemius, *Sacrarum antiquitatum monumenta* (PP 1335), and the illustrations on pp. 36 and 40 = fols. C2v and C4v, and on pp. 44 and 48 = fols. C6v and C8v. See also copies of Plantin's 1583 edition of Benito Arias Montano's *Humanae salutis monumenta* (PP 590) in the Bibliothèque de la Sorbonne, Paris (R BA 37; the illustrations on fols. M2r and M4r) and in the Bibliothèque de l'Arsenal, Paris (4° T 583; the illustrations on fols. B2r and B4r).
[35] For an example of an image that was originally printed upside down, see, e.g., a copy of Plantin's 1583 edition of Benito Arias Montano's *Humanae salutis monumenta* (PP 590) in the ONB Vienna, Bildarchiv und Porträtsammlung (261.755-B.Fid; the illustration on fol. O4r). For other indications that engravings were occasionally printed face down, see, e.g., Gaskell 2004, pp. 230–231, and the markings on the back of a couple of round engravings that Plantin commissioned (see, e.g., MPM KP 826 B). Our thanks to Erik Breuls for sharing his observations on these plates.

Only in the case of some of Plantin's *octavo* books of hours (which were also printed in red and black ink) and *octavo* editions of Arias Montano's *Humanae salutis monumenta*, when engraved borders were printed around engraved text illustrations, did the sheets of paper have to be run through a roller press twice per side – once for the text illustrations and once for the borders (see, for example, figs. 3.23, 3.25, 4.17, 4.18, and 4.19).[36] This was an exceptional, labor-intensive (and costly) undertaking, requiring careful, astute craftsmanship by all involved to ensure that no mistake was made (in the case of Plantin's books of hours) during any one of the twelve runs through a press made by each sheet in these richly illustrated books. For, while the proper alignment of movable type and woodcut or cast decorative materials was essentially guaranteed when they were all set together in a forme, this was not the case when works were illustrated with engravings and etchings. Rather, when intaglio illustrations were added, the intaglio printer not only had to determine which plate was to be printed on which page, but also which side was up (for both the image and the printed sheet of text) and how to fit the plate into the blank space within the text that was reserved for it. Despite the fact that the printer occasionally only had a few millimeters to spare in the alignment of the illustration within the printed text, the images are generally remarkably well aligned, without any overlapping between the print and the text. Only rarely, as in fig. 3.23, are overlapping prints – visible here in the upper right corner – evident. Among the surviving copies of Plantin's editions, at least, examples of images printed upside down or the switching of two plates are more common. In both of these cases, the solution was to print an extra impression of the incorrectly printed illustration and paste it on over the erroneously printed image.[37] Plantin, himself, apparently tried to simplify matters later on in his career by having a group of four borders etched together into one plate, so that it would be possible, if the setting of the text was aligned according to the distribution of the four borders on the plate, to embellish simultaneously four pages of text with borders with the printing of a single plate. Regrettably, no impression of these borders is known. Comprising images of everyday occupations, they may have been used to decorate such secular works as the almanacs Plantin had printed with intaglio illustrations.[38]

One final, unavoidable feature of working with engravings and etchings instead of woodcuts was the limited "life" of the plate. Intaglio plates are, by definition, ones in which fine lines are cut into a plate and great pressure must be used in order to push the paper on which the image is to be printed into these grooves to pull out whatever ink has been placed in them. Predictably, in addition to pushing the paper into the grooves, the great pressure of the roller press also incrementally, but relentlessly flattens the metal of the plate, such that the lines cut or etched into it are gradually flattened and made steadily shallower. Consequently, the finely detailed, rich visual effects of an engraving

---

[36] For more information on this combination of engraved borders and illustrations, see Bowen 2003, pp. 19–20, and the discussion of these editions in ch. 3.

[37] For examples of such misprinted and corrected illustrations, see notes 34 and 35 above. Woodcuts were also, on occasion, printed upside down. See, e.g., the examples given in McKitterick 2003, pp. 87–88.

[38] Plantin had four such plates made (cf. MPM KP 5–8 D). See, e.g., MPM Arch. 18, fol. 158 rht, under 1575; and MPM Arch. 20, fol. 194 rht, under September 17, 1584, for payments to Mynken Liefrinck for illustrating almanacs with intaglios.

are inevitably worn away (or down) by the basic process of pulling impressions from that plate. This was not an issue with woodcuts, where the fundamental difference in technique – a raised surface that could be printed with much less pressure – ensured that a well cared-for block would not suffer as noticeably from wear. Precisely how many "acceptable" impressions could be pulled from a sixteenth-century engraving or etching is a perpetual subject of debate and speculation.[39] Regardless of the true answer to this question, the essential fact that only a limited number of impressions could be pulled from the original plate was well known and a concern to printers like Plantin. It implied that if an edition illustrated with engravings was successful, the publisher would need to have the original set of engravings repeatedly reworked – that is, individual lines re-engraved and thereby strengthened – and potentially replaced with entirely new plates in order to print as many impressions as might have been made from a single set of woodcuts.[40]

The financial implications of illustrating texts with intaglio plates are, at first glance, hard to quantify owing to the difficulties in finding truly comparable accounts of the relative costs of, for example, purchasing wood for woodblocks versus copper for engravings, or employing a respected woodcutter versus an often relatively young engraver, as Plantin regularly did.[41] There are, nevertheless, other irrefutable pieces of evidence indicating that books with intaglio illustrations were significantly more expensive to produce than comparable ones illustrated with woodcuts.

First, as may be surmised from the above account of the extra concerns inherent in the use of engravings or etchings as book illustrations, many of these aspects also comprised an added cost that would not have been accrued if the book had been illustrated with woodcuts. Unavoidable here were the extra costs of having the illustrations made and printed, regardless of how they were ultimately incorporated into the text. For more successful editions, a printer would also have to make additional outlays to have the original copper plates reworked and, potentially, replaced. This fundamental distinction between the added costs intrinsic to the use of intaglios and the lack thereof for woodcuts is tellingly confirmed in a document that Plantin compiled in the early 1570s when he began to produce large quantities of illustrated liturgical editions for the Spanish court. In this document, Plantin tried to quantify these additional expenses by calculating how much a buyer would have to pay for the addition of certain quantities of engravings in specific formats – as both the size of individual plates and the number that were included determined how expensive it would be to print and replace them. Essential here is the fact that Plantin simultaneously indicated that he did not reckon on any extra costs for the inclusion of woodcut illustrations.[42]

---

[39] See Bowen and Imhof 2005 for a discussion of this matter and evidence that, by the early seventeenth century, at least, thousands of impressions could be (and were) pulled from engravings (new and reworked). See ch. 5 for evidence that far fewer (a maximum of approximately 1,500) impressions could be pulled from the etchings made for Plantin and Jan Moretus I in the 1580s–1590s.

[40] See Bowen 2003 and ch. 4 for a more extensive discussion of this topic.

[41] Comparisons of the standard wages paid to woodcutters and engravers are difficult to make because the wages paid were a function not only of the work done, but also of the reputation and skill of the artist. For more on this issue, as well as a few isolated examples of how the amounts Plantin paid for woodcuts c.1570 could even exceed what he paid for comparably scaled engravings, see Bowen and Imhof 2003. See ch. 5 for evidence that etchings were less expensive (and faster) to make than engravings.

[42] This document is discussed extensively in ch. 4 and is transcribed and translated in full in appendix 2.

Even more definitive than these indications of an accumulating extra cost for the inclusion of engraved or etched illustrations – be it from the initial production of the plates, their printing, or their potential reworking and replacement – is the price for which the books containing them were sold, the bottom line for Plantin and his customers. In this case, Plantin's production practices and account books provide numerous undeniable, justifiable comparisons between two issues of the same text, namely, one with woodcut illustrations and one with engraved or etched illustrations.[43] Consisting primarily of breviaries, missals, books of hours, and Petrus Canisius's popular Catholic handbook, these books provide ideal opportunities for comparing the price of illustrating a text with woodcuts versus engravings because the other essential components of the printed text are identical: the paper needed to print each copy and the basic setting of the text.[44] For all of these publications for which the price of the two issues is known – that with woodcuts and that with engravings or etchings – the price of that with the intaglio illustrations is consistently greater, occasionally even twice as much as that for copies with woodcuts.[45]

Given the numerous practical, technical complications intrinsic to the use of engravings and etchings as book illustrations instead of woodcuts, not to mention the various inherent extra costs, it is not surprising that the production of such books was often initially limited to special editions or types of texts. It is, thus, all the more understandable that even entrepreneurial publishers, like Plantin, would have been hesitant about taking on such projects, particularly given the uncertain market for these costly, exceptional editions. And also that, once that decision was made, the ownership of – and, hence, the control over the plates used to illustrate these special projects was of immense importance. For while a competitive publisher might easily order copies of a set of woodcut illustrations, this was not the case with intaglio illustrations. Thus, not only would the ownership of a set of intaglio illustrations determine what one publisher could print (and reprint), but the competition would have thought more than twice about imitating it.

In the chapters that follow, we will see how and why Plantin's understandable initial unwillingness to enter into the world of printing books with intaglio illustrations changed. We will begin by introducing Plantin and the city of Antwerp, where he chose to settle, probably attracted by its fame in mid-sixteenth-century Europe as a thriving,

---

43 We are using the term "issue" here to refer to, using Gaskell's terminology, "a consciously planned printed unit distinct from the basic form of the ideal copy" (see Gaskell 1972, p. 315). Although one cannot determine which would have been the "ideal copy," those copies with woodcuts or those with engravings, it is clear that these subgroups of the original edition were envisioned as two distinct variants intended for two distinct groups of buyers, characterized by both their taste in prints and how much they could afford to pay for a copy of the text. Production records preserved for the period 1590–c.1650 also confirm the routine subdivision of the total number of copies printed of certain editions into predetermined subgroups according to the medium of the illustration (see, e.g., MPM M 39). While others may prefer to speak of different "states" of the same edition when discussing differences in illustration technique, we prefer to reserve that term for the variations in the precise selection of plates used to illustrate the various copies of the intaglio issue of the edition.

44 A few select copies may also have been printed on notably better paper, but this was usually noted in conjunction with yet another distinct price for the book.

45 For examples of these price differences, see the notes to: PP 823–834 (various breviaries); PP 890–895 (for sundry editions of Canisius's *Manuale catholicorum*); PP 1688, PP 1699, and PP 1701–1702 (for some missal editions); and PP 1769–1773, PP 1777–1778, and PP 1785 (editions of books of hours).

leading center for international trade and, among other professions, the production and sale of printed matter. Although being in Antwerp was not always advantageous for Plantin's sundry business ventures, it seems unlikely that he could have undertaken his daring, revolutionizing approach to illustrating books with engravings and etchings without the numerous, essential resources it offered.

CHAPTER TWO

"L'EXCELLENTE, & FAMEUSE CITÉ D'ANVERS"*: ANTWERP AND ITS ARTISTS

Although I would have been able to secure better conditions for myself in other regions and cities, I still preferred the Low Countries above all the rest and in particular this city of Antwerp, where I settled, primarily because I believed that there was no city in the world that offered better opportunities for the trade that I had undertaken. Besides the ready supply of daily provisions at that time, the abundant stock of sundry materials essential for the practicing of our trades that are imported from various regions and, in addition, the workers who, in this area, can be selected and trained in all occupations in a short period of time, what appealed to me the most was how this whole region and society, more so than all neighboring lands, seemed to excel so superbly in honoring the Catholic faith.[1]

In this letter written to Pope Gregory XIII on October 9, 1574, Christopher Plantin is primarily concerned with persuading the pope of his love of the Catholic faith and his commitment to being of service to (that is, printing the texts required by) the Catholic church. The timing of the composition of this letter is critical to understanding it. Writing nearly twenty-five years after his arrival in Antwerp, Plantin had recently been awarded privileges for the lucrative printing of several newly reformed texts essential to the practice of the Catholic faith. Plantin was clearly grateful for the pope's favor and wished to maintain it.[2] But who was Plantin and can we believe his reasons for settling in Antwerp were indeed those given above? Plantin's profession of such a strong, common, pervasive love of the Catholic faith and his own personal stake in it is highly suspect, for

---

* Thus begins Plantin's 1582, revised French translation of Ludovico Guicciardini's often-cited contemporary account of sixteenth-century Antwerp. See Guicciardini 1920 for a reprint of this text and ch. 5 for a more extensive discussion of Plantin's editions of it.

[1] *Corr.*, IV, no. 566, pp. 158–159: "Atque ad eam rem etsi aliis in locis et urbibus commodiores mihi oblatas conditiones consequi poteram, tamen una haec prae ceteris placuit Belgica regio, atque adeo haec urbs Antverpia in qua sedem figerem, eo potissimum nomine, quod nullam in orbe terrarum ad eam quam instituebam artem maiores habere commoditates existimarem. Nam praeter facilem eo tempore commeatum et affluentem copiam variae materiae nostris officinis necessariae quae ex variis provinciis comportabatur, ac etiam operarum, quae ad omnes artes in hac provincia brevi tempore instrui et deligi possunt, illa cum primis mihi probabantur, quod haec una provincia et respub. omnis in catholica religione colenda tum egregie praeter finitimas omnes, florere videretur."

[2] See ch. 4 for a more detailed discussion of Plantin's printing of the reformed Catholic texts.

2.1 One of the Wierixes?, *Christopher Plantin, Portrayed within his Printer's Device*, engraving, 62 × 40 (Antwerp, Museum Plantin-Moretus, Prentenkabinet, I/W 622).

example. Antwerp was a pivotal city in the revolts in the Low Countries at the time – partly due to its economic importance and inhabitants' desire for more independent self-rule, and partly due to matters of faith.[3] Plantin's important personal and business contacts reflected the ambiguous character of the city, for while some were staunch supporters of Spain and the Catholic faith, many others neither loved nor actively adhered to either. For example, Plantin's regular contact with Cardinal Antoine Perrenot de Granvelle, the archbishop of Mechelen and later representative of Philip II in Rome, Gabriel de Çayas, Philip II's secretary for international affairs, and Benito Arias Montano, a theological scholar and chaplain to Philip II – each of whom is discussed in greater detail later on – attests to Plantin's strong associations with adherents to Spain and the Catholic faith. On the other hand, Plantin often received important financial backing from non-Catholics and is himself frequently associated with a distinct spiritual group called the "Family of Love."[4] Thus, the importance Plantin places on his and others' love of the Catholic faith above all else must be read with pockets-full of salt and an eye to the person to whom this letter was written, Pope Gregory XIII, to whom Plantin must have been immensely grateful from a purely business point of view. What of the other reasons Plantin gave for settling in Antwerp that were certainly of no import to the

---

[3] For a brief, general overview of the major issues at stake during the rebellion of the Low Countries and the evolution of that fight, see Graham Darby's introductory "Narrative of events," in Darby 2001, pp. 8–28. On the importance of Antwerp's printers for religious refugees, see, e.g., Imhof et al. 1994.

[4] For examples of Plantin's non-Catholic backers see Voet, GC, I, pp. 41–49, and Kingdon 1963. For Plantin's personal association with the "Huis der liefde" or the "Family of Love," see ch. 6, n. 106.

pope? To what extent might they have been true and what role may they have played in Plantin's subsequent successful production of illustrated books?

After discussing Antwerp's position in sixteenth-century Europe and what is actually known of Plantin when he first came to Antwerp in around 1550, we will, in this chapter, focus on the following two basic issues, which will provide essential background information for the chapters to come. First, to what degree was Plantin initially interested in the production of illustrated books generally and familiar with the trade in independent (intaglio) prints and maps in particular? Second, who were the artists and printers of intaglio plates who ultimately agreed to work for Plantin and thereby made his production of books with engraved and etched illustrations possible? By examining these questions we will learn more about the general context in which Plantin worked and the various contacts he had to make in order to print these special illustrated editions. This information, combined with what we know about the basic technical and economic considerations behind the production of such books, will in turn furnish us with a better, truer understanding of all the elements that had to be combined – fortuitously or by design – to generate what would ultimately become a body of internationally influential works.

PLANTIN AND ANTWERP IN THE MID-SIXTEENTH CENTURY

In 1550 Christopher Plantin (c.1520–July 1, 1589) (fig. 2.1) was registered as a citizen of Antwerp in the city records and as a printer at the guild of St. Luke. Prior to these first official references to Plantin's establishment in Antwerp, however, little is known of his life.[5] On the basis of these records and a few other documents, it is presumed that Plantin was born in or near Tours, France, and that he traveled in the later 1530s to Caen, where he may have trained with the printer-bookbinder Robert Macé II. Plantin is also supposed to have met and married Jeanne Rivière in Caen and remained there until the later 1540s, at which point some authors speculate that they went to Paris briefly before emigrating to Antwerp.[6] Once in Antwerp, Plantin worked as a bookbinder first, not obtaining the necessary patents to work as a printer until 1555.[7] Given that Plantin was a Frenchman and would certainly have been knowledgeable of the potential of working as a bookbinder or printer in France, where both Paris and Lyon were thriving, important centers of the business, it is all the more striking that he did, indeed, decide to pass by these cities and emigrate to Antwerp instead. This begs the question of what Antwerp was like in the mid-sixteenth century and why it might have attracted someone seeking to establish himself in the world of printing and binding books.

By around 1550, Antwerp's population had grown from approximately 30,000 at the beginning of the sixteenth century to nearly 100,000, thereby making it (albeit briefly) a true urban center in Europe, at least in terms of its sheer size, on a par with

[5] See *Corr. supplément*, no. 226, for a full transcription and citation of the record in the city archives. For evidence of Plantin's membership in the St. Luke's guild, see Rombouts and van Lerius, I, p. 170.

[6] For a detailed account of what is known and hypothesized about Plantin's life up until his arrival in Antwerp, see Voet, GC, I, pp. 3–12.

[7] Cf. Voet, GC, I, p. 17.

such cities as Paris, Venice, Naples, and Istanbul.[8] This stunning population growth was brought about not by simple patterns of increasing local birth rates, but rather by immigration. For the period 1533–1584, an average of 300 people registered themselves annually in Antwerp. The majority (approximately two-thirds) of these immigrants came from the southern Low Countries, followed by a sizable number from the northern Low Countries. Far behind were groups of immigrants from Germany, France, and a sprinkling of cities in other countries.[9] While these figures attest to the great (mostly national) attraction Antwerp had for those from rural areas in search of work, they say nothing about Antwerp's potential as an influential international center within Europe. As Peter Burke justifiably asserts, a city with far fewer inhabitants – just 50,000–60,000, like Rome or Florence in the early sixteenth century – could, nevertheless, exert a major cultural, artistic influence in Europe, while larger cities (like Paris) might not to the same degree. In his study of the extent to which Antwerp might be termed a "cultural metropolis," Burke defines such a city as one "which functioned as the central place of a large region (western Europe, if not Europe as a whole), and did so – if not for the whole range of culture – at least for some major cultural activities," whereby, Burke continues, "its artists (writers, actors, printers, etc.) influence the world outside, whether by travelling abroad themselves, by exporting their products, or by attracting outsiders to the city . . ."[10]

There is no doubt that for much of the sixteenth century Antwerp was known as the center of trade not only for the Low Countries, but for Europe as a whole. It maintained this status readily until the general disruptions that arose throughout the Low Countries at the start of revolts against Spanish domination in the later 1560s. But the city did not lose its privileged place definitively until Alessandro Farnese's decisive siege, which led to Antwerp's capitulation as a result of starvation in August 1585. Significant numbers of people fled the city – in particular those involved in international trade or other specialty crafts – as a consequence both of matters of faith and of the subsequent costly blockage of Antwerp's main artery for trade, the River Schelde.[11] Regardless of the subsequent turn of events, when Plantin was deciding where he should establish himself in the mid-sixteenth century Antwerp was thriving. Not only did it serve as the European warehouse and distribution center for English textiles, spices from Asia, and various luxury items produced in northern France and the Low Countries, but these activities were supported by the presence of a foreign exchange, in which numerous bankers, money traders, and foreign investors were involved.[12] Consequently, by the mid-sixteenth century, Antwerp was home to both a large body of local merchants (perhaps 400–500) and numerous foreign merchants: approximately 300 from Spain,

---

[8] For telling statistics, recording Antwerp's spectacular growth to become by far the largest city in the Low Countries by the mid-sixteenth century, and its subsequent return (by 1600) to being one of several larger cities, see table 5.1 in Darby 2001.

[9] For this overview of Antwerp's demographics in the sixteenth and seventeenth centuries, see Van der Wee and Materné 1993, pp. 19–21.

[10] Burke 1993, pp. 49 and 53.

[11] For Antwerp's initial boom as a center of trade and its subsequent decline, see Van der Wee and Materné 1993, pp. 21–25. For a brief account of the implications of the fall of Antwerp in 1585, see Marnef 2001, pp. 101–103.

[12] Van der Wee and Materné 1993, pp. 23–24.

another 300 from Upper Germany and Hanseatic ports, around 200 from Italy, 150 from Portugal, and 100 from France (the 300–400 British salesmen active in Antwerp in this period were only occasionally present).[13] Thus, in addition to a large, ready body of people experienced in the financial backing of ventures (which must have been appealing given the sizable "start-up" costs of a printing business), there was an even larger body of merchants experienced in the distribution of goods throughout Europe and beyond.

The presence of so many dealers in goods and money was certainly advantageous to anyone with ambitions to start up an internationally oriented business. Indeed, Antwerp's clear dominance of the production of books in the sixteenth-century Low Countries is often attributed, at least in part, to these factors, which were present to some degree in Antwerp as of the early sixteenth century.[14] However, sixteenth-century Antwerp was not only a leading national center in the book trade, it was also important internationally. Where, precisely, Antwerp falls in relation to other sixteenth-century centers of printing varies depending upon what is estimated – the number of printers active vs. the number of distinct editions printed vs. the visual and qualitative influence of the works produced. Nevertheless, authors agree that it was among the most important players in the international arena of book production and trade behind, primarily, Venice and Paris.[15] Numerous factors contributed to Antwerp's international import. The various communities of émigrés in the city from sundry nations meant that there was a ready market for a variety of texts in numerous vernacular languages – French, English, Spanish, Italian, German, as well as Dutch – in addition to the broader-based international market for books in Latin. Moreover, the presence of so many local traders from throughout Europe greatly facilitated the subsequent distribution of these same books, thereby making Antwerp a logical location for the production and sale of books intended for an international market.

Antwerp's renown as an influential center of printing was also buoyed by the products of the intimately related world of printed images, which were published in Antwerp for an international market. Indeed, while in the realm of printing books Antwerp had to compete with influential Italian centers of book production, like Venice, as well as important centers close by in Paris and Lyon, in the market for paintings and prints Antwerp's position was stronger. As Burke observed in terms of the production of paintings, Antwerp was the only city in sixteenth-century Europe that could be compared with the then famous artistic centers of Florence, Rome, and Venice, while David Landau and Peter Parshall describe Antwerp as "the most artistically vibrant city in northern Europe."[16] This was due to several factors. Antwerp was an active center of production that attracted foreign artists, as a place both to visit and to work. It also served as an important bridge between northern and southern Europe, as artists from northern climes often passed through the city on their way to and from their artistic pilgrimage to Italy, exchanging impressions of styles and new artistic trends, often via the medium of prints. Finally, Antwerp also had active art markets that supported

[13] Ibid., p. 24.   [14] Cf. Voet 1975, esp. p. 234; and De Nave 1993, p. 87 in particular.
[15] Cf., e.g., McKitterick 2005, pp. 11 and 14; De Nave 1993, p. 88; and Burke 1993, p. 55.
[16] Burke 1993, pp. 50–53; and Landau and Parshall 1994, p. 223.

the sale of all forms of artistic productions, from paintings and sculptures, to books and prints, that could then be readily distributed via the numerous established trading networks already present there.[17] This was in significant contrast to Paris, which had, quantitatively, a larger population and was perhaps even more active in the production of books than Antwerp, but lacked an artistic appeal and structures of patrons and markets to support a comparably active and stimulating production of works of art.[18]

The same arguments could certainly be made for the production and trade in prints as well, particularly in the mid-sixteenth century, when Plantin was determining where he would establish himself. The print publisher Hieronymus Cock is often cited as the epitome of the great international aspect of Antwerp's print production at this time. Not only did he produce a variety of prints, many intended for an international market, but he also employed draughtsmen, etchers, and engravers from in and beyond Antwerp: Giorgio Ghisi from Mantua, Maarten van Heemskerck and Philips Galle from Haarlem, Lambert Lombard and Pierre Dufour from Liège, the van Doetecum brothers from the northern Low Countries (perhaps Deventer), Hans Bol from Mechelen, Hans Collaert I from Brussels, and such local artists as Pieter Bruegel I, Frans Floris, Pieter van der Heyden, and Frans Huys.[19] However, neither Cock nor Gerard de Jode, another famous Antwerp print publisher, was active in this business in Antwerp until around 1550, just when Plantin arrived, and thus could not have contributed to the aura of activity and potential that evidently attracted Plantin. Rather, if Plantin had known of any leading figure from the Antwerp print world, it would most likely have been Hans Liefrinck. While Italian artists and dealers in prints are commonly credited with the conceptualization of and first profitable engagement in the occupation of a print publisher in the early sixteenth century, Liefrinck played a critical role in developing print publishing into a commercially viable, internationally oriented business in Antwerp, which figures like Cock, de Jode, and (later on) Philips Galle continued.[20]

But, as already observed and as will be underscored periodically in the coming pages, the worlds of printing independent prints (the work of "pictorial printers," in Jan Van der Stock's terminology) and printing texts were intimately linked, by craft, guild, marriage, and often simply by the physical proximity of the pertinent shops and businesses. True generally, this was certainly the case in sixteenth-century Antwerp. For example, on a professional level, as of 1558 everyone related to the production of books was required to join the St. Luke's guild for artists, where people involved in making and distributing independent prints were already commonly registered. On a personal level, many of the 300–450 or so people professionally involved in the production of

---

[17] On Antwerp's art markets see, for example, Van der Stock 1998, pp. 60 and 69 (for prints) and Vermeylen 2003 (for paintings). For a recent study that underscores the important northern flow of Antwerp prints, see Verheggen 2006.

[18] Cf. Burke 1993, p. 53.

[19] On Cock, see Riggs 1977. For references to his international renown, see, e.g., Landau and Parshal 1994, pp. 365–366; and Diels 2005, pp. 13–14.

[20] On the origins of print publishing in Italy, see Landau and Parshall 1994, pp. 6, 299, 302–309, and 365; and Bury 2001, pp. 9–10. For Liefrinck's importance, see Landau and Parshall 1994, pp. 222–223. While not disputing Liefrinck's importance as a print publisher, Van der Stock (1998, p. 107) suggests that Antwerp's great production of prints may have had more diverse origins than indicated by Landau and Parshall.

books and prints in Antwerp in the 1560s and 1570s all lived within one square mile of one another in an area of the city that comprised the original main art market. The numbers are such that Van der Stock ventures to assert that this "concentration of graphic industry . . . was without a doubt the largest in sixteenth-century Europe."[21] Plantin lived and worked in the middle of it all.

Antwerp's importance as a center for the production of art, books, and prints began to decline in the later 1560s with the growing religious upheavals, many of which, under the banner of "iconoclasm," deliberately sought to destroy certain works of art. As occurred with its self-supporting networks of trade and finance, the 1585 fall of the city similarly brought a more definitive end to its glory days as the center in northern Europe for the production of prints. Once again, the diaspora of talented figures from Antwerp and the general demise of the markets and transportation routes there that had facilitated the sale and distribution of these products resulted in the establishment of new influential centers of print production elsewhere, in particular in Haarlem and Amsterdam in the last decades of the sixteenth century, and Paris by the seventeenth century.[22] Plantin, however, together with several other established families of text printers and the renowned print publishers Philips Galle and Gerard de Jode, was among the leading figures in the field of printing texts and images who did not flee following Antwerp's 1585 surrender to Farnese. In fact, Plantin returned to the city in the fall of that year following a brief sojourn in Leiden during the worst years of the siege. He evidently hoped to maintain his business in Antwerp despite the difficult years of rebuilding that were to come. How Plantin managed this, at least in terms of his production of luxurious books illustrated with engraved and etched illustrations, is one of the topics for the chapters that follow (see chapter 5). For now, we would like to conclude this general consideration of Antwerp's place in the sixteenth-century world of books and prints with a more detailed examination of Plantin's own initial contacts with those engaged in the city's famed production of prints and the artists he subsequently employed for his own production of books with intaglio illustrations.

PLANTIN AND ANTWERP'S WORLD OF GRAPHIC ARTS

From the very first year in which he printed and published his own books (1555), Plantin produced editions with some woodcut illustrations or other decorative elements.[23] As is discussed in greater detail in the following chapters, it would take another fifteen years (until around 1570) before Plantin began to print books with engraved or etched illustrations on an annual basis. Despite the delayed appearance of intaglio prints in

---

[21] For estimates of the numbers of people affiliated with the production of books in fifteenth- and sixteenth-century Antwerp, see Van den Branden 1985, pp. 169–178. For Van der Stock's discussion of those living in this area, see Van der Stock 1998, pp. 60–68, fig. 26 on p. 61, and p. 68 in particular for the concluding citation. He uses the term "pictorial printer" throughout this book.

[22] On the rising importance of cities in the northern Low Countries for the production of prints, see Leeflang 1993. For the growing importance of Paris for prints, see, e.g., Grivel 1986.

[23] See his and Jan Steelsius's co-publication of Petrus Bellonius's *Les observations de plusieurs singularitez et choses memorables, trouvées en Grece, Asie, Iudée, Egypte, Arabie, et autres pays estranges* (PP 637), which contains some forty-five woodcuts, executed by a local woodcutter, Arnold Nicolai.

his books, Plantin was involved in the trade of independent prints and maps much earlier. In fact, Plantin's first known agreement concerning the sale of intaglio prints dates to March 1553, just a few years following his arrival in Antwerp and two years prior to the appearance of his own first publications. In this case, Plantin arranged to have the exclusive rights to sell a series of Apostles, engraved by the Liège artist Lambert Suavius.[24] At this point (c.1553–1556) one could reasonably argue that Plantin was simply endeavoring to earn his living by any of a variety of means: as a leather craftsman, as a dealer in prints and lace, and as a printer and publisher of books.[25] As of 1557–1558, however, Plantin's dealings in prints, maps, and other cartographic items had grown into a thriving business with national contacts and numerous international sales. For example, by this time, Plantin was buying large quantities of independent prints and maps from such leading Antwerp print publishers as Hieronymus Cock and Hans Liefrinck and was selling them in turn to dealers in Paris and at the Frankfurt book fair, among others.[26] Similarly, while the earliest records of Plantin's trade in maps date to 1556–1557, by 1558 he was actively engaged in this market as well, dealing with various people in and beyond Antwerp.[27] His activities in this field were such in this period that Jan Denucé observed that one might think that Plantin sought to specialize in this trade.[28]

There can be no doubt, then, that as early as the later 1550s Plantin was familiar with how business was transacted in the Antwerp print world and with those involved in it, from the local, delegating print publishers to the artists (local and international) who were asked to produce the desired images. Although most scholars focus on Plantin's subsequent production of books and not his involvement in the print trade, his dealings with Philips Galle alone in the 1570s–1580s make clear the continued importance for him of this complementary occupation.[29] When Plantin finally decided to attempt the production of books with fully integrated intaglio illustrations – as against, for example, simply an appended series of prints, as was the case with his and Cock's co-publication of La pompe funèbre (see chapter 3) – it is evident that he made use of the pool of artists attracted to Antwerp's burgeoning print world. And yet, as we will see below, this same competitive world of independent artists and print publishers, all endeavoring to distinguish themselves, also came to frustrate Plantin's attempts to maintain his production of these richly illustrated editions.

There are three primary sources of information on the artists Plantin employed: (1) the pure visual records of the prints they made, as they have survived in Plantin's publications and fragments thereof; (2) an incomplete and not necessarily representative selection of payments made by Plantin for the work various artists completed;

---

[24] See Delen 1932, pp. 22–23, for this reference and a transcription of their agreement.

[25] For the initial evidence of each of these occupations, see Voet, GC, I, pp. 14–17.

[26] For examples of Plantin's earliest transactions with Cock and Liefrinck in this regard, see Delen 1932, pp. 2–4 and 13–14, respectively. For examples of Plantin's early shipments of prints to Paris and Frankfurt, see ibid., pp. 8–12 and 12–13, respectively.

[27] For examples of Plantin's early flurry of activity in this area, see, e.g., Denucé 1912–1913, I, pp. 4, 8, 20–22, 33, 42–45, 52, 67, 81–82, 101–102, 135–136, and 210.

[28] See ibid., I, p. 17.

[29] For Plantin's and Galle's varied business contacts, see ch. 6. Other isolated examples of Plantin's subsequent involvement in commissioning independent prints for others are given below.

and (3) Plantin's correspondence. Although each of these sources exists, in essence, in isolation from the others, it is only when one considers them in conjunction with one another that a more accurate picture emerges of which work was completed when and Plantin's actual relationship with individual figures. Of these three basic sources, the most complete single overview of all the illustrations Plantin ever commissioned comes from the existing books and surviving parts thereof. That said, Plantin's fragmentary payment records for work completed for his book illustrations often provide useful correctives of, for example, the relative completion dates of specific prints that might be misconstrued from the dates of the publications in which they were used, potentially several years after they had been made. In addition, these records often help clarify which artists were involved in making otherwise anonymous prints and identify the publication(s) for which the given prints were originally intended. Payment records for engravings made by the Liège artist Pierre Dufour are good examples of this, as they help identify which (unsigned) engravings he provided for which books.[30] Records of payments for the designing, engraving or etching, and printing of Plantin's intaglio book illustrations must also, however, be interpreted carefully, as some, for example, were recorded after the fact and consequently post-date the actual completion of the noted activity.[31] Finally, while Plantin's correspondence contains only sporadic references to a selection of the artists he employed, the very subjectivity of these remarks and a consideration of who, precisely, is discussed in which context, itself enriches our view of Plantin's contact with these figures and who was willing to work for him under which circumstances.

Together, these sources provide a much clearer view of two essential matters, namely: (1) the inevitably variable time lapse between the completion of the illustrations and the printing of the text in which they were used; and (2) determining when, precisely, an artist was employed by Plantin. For example, as was discussed above, one usually imagines the printer of a book delaying his publication of the text until the engravings for it were ready. This was the case with Plantin's first edition of Juan de Valverde's *Vivae imagines partium corporis humani* (PP 2413) from 1566, for which Pieter Huys took nearly two years to finish all of the necessary engravings, immediately after which the text was printed.[32] However, there are also numerous examples where either the date of a payment record, the date on the print itself, or else a print's appearance amid fragments of Plantin's editions significantly pre-dates the first "official" appearance of that print in one of Plantin's publications.[33] Consider as well printers' common habit of reusing their decorative materials – be they woodblocks, cast metal, or intaglio plates – any number of years after they were first made. If one only works on the basis of which plates appear in which books, one can occasionally derive a false sense of when, precisely, any given artist worked for a particular publisher. In the case of Plantin's publications, this problem is most prevalent among his frequently reprinted

---

[30] See appendix 1, under Dufour, for a full discussion of these records.

[31] See Bowen 2003, p. 14, n. 30, for an example of a late payment for the engraving of a plate. Plantin's payment records for Mynken Liefrinck's work printing his illustrations can also be imprecise, as they are occasionally noted in a long list just under the date of the year concerned (see appendix 1, under Liefrinck, for references to these records).

[32] See the discussion of this book in ch. 3.   [33] See pp. 23–24 and appendix 1 for examples of this.

and similarly illustrated devotional and liturgical editions – his missals, breviaries, and books of hours. It arises because our lack of knowledge of several of the earliest editions of these books makes it impossible to document when, exactly, a specific plate by a particular artist was first used. For example, impressions of an engraving of the *Visitation* by Jan Sadeler I after a design by Gerard van Groeningen are known only in Plantin's late folio missals from 1587 and 1589. But the impressions of this print in these books are clearly worn, indicating that they were made from an older plate that had an earlier, as yet unknown use.[34] As all other evidence of van Groeningen's and Jan Sadeler's work for Plantin indicates that neither of them worked for Plantin after 1576, it would be most logical to date the original execution of this print to that period as well, despite what is known (or not) from copies of Plantin's publications.[35] Consequently, the overview given below of the periods in which certain artists are known to have worked for Plantin – which is documented in appendix 1 and illustrated in tables A1.1 and A1.2 – will differ, in such cases, from the impression one might otherwise derive from references to the appearance of particular artists' signatures on the engravings illustrating Plantin's numerous publications.

THE DRAUGHTSMEN PLANTIN EMPLOYED

The artist Plantin engaged the most regularly throughout the years that he produced books with engraved or etched illustrations was, without doubt, the draughtsman, etcher, and painter, Peeter vander Borcht.[36] Vander Borcht was not the first designer Plantin employed – that honor goes to the Antwerp painter, draughtsman, and engraver, Pieter Huys (discussed in greater detail below) and the Parisian designer and illuminator, Geoffroy Ballain, both of whom were supplying Plantin with designs for woodcut figures as of 1563–1564.[37] Nevertheless, Plantin employed vander Borcht the longest and most intensely, asking him to supply not only compositions for woodcuts and engravings, but also etchings after his own designs. Vander Borcht first worked for Plantin as a designer of woodcut illustrations for botanical texts and emblem books around 1565–1566.[38] Soon thereafter, however (by 1569), he began to provide Plantin with designs for engravings. The majority of these compositions (supplied primarily in the period 1569–1575) were engraved by Jan and Hieronymus Wierix, as well

---

[34] See PP 1700 and PP 1702 for these two late missals. See *New Holl., Van Groeningen*, 11, no. 247, for this print.

[35] For example, this plate may have been used to illustrate any of the following missal editions (all in *quarto* or folio and published in 1574 or 1575) for which there are currently no known copies with engraved illustrations: PP 1686 A, PP 1688 B, PP 1689 B, PP 1690 A, and PP 1691. Although there are no records indicating that Plantin bought up other printers' stocks of religious engravings for the illustration of his books, it is always possible that such plates were previously used by someone else.

[36] For an overview of his work on Plantin's intaglio illustrations, see appendix 1 and table A1.1.

[37] For an overview of Huys's career and work on Plantin's engraved illustrations in particular, see appendix 1 and table A1.2. For sources on Ballain's work for Plantin, see Voet, GC, 11, p. 233, n. 3. Voet notes here that Ballain began to work for Plantin in 1563, but all of the sources we have seen indicate that he started to supply Plantin with designs in 1564. We are grateful to the late Myra Dickman Orth for our conversations concerning Ballain's work as an illuminator.

[38] For examples of vander Borcht's initial projects, see PP 1095, Plantin's 1566 edition of Rembert Dodoens's *Frumentorum, leguminum, palustrium et aquatilium herbarum . . .*; and PP 2169, Joannes Sambucus's *Emblemata et aliquot nummi antiqui operis*, also from 1566.

as Abraham de Bruyn (see, for example, figs. 4.1 and 4.17).[39] Although Jan Sadeler I also worked for Plantin at this time, he made strikingly few engravings after vander Borcht's designs.[40] Finally, by 1581, vander Borcht appears to have stopped designing new illustrations for Plantin and begun to make hundreds of etchings for him instead (see figs. 5.12 and 5.17). Consequently, vander Borcht supplied Plantin with etchings and designs for engravings for nearly twenty years straight. The only brief lacunas were the years 1576–1578, when many in Antwerp were recovering from the ransacking of the city by Spanish troops in November 1576, the so-called "Spanish Fury," and Plantin commissioned notably few new intaglio illustrations, and perhaps the years 1584 and 1587 – depending on when, precisely, vander Borcht completed the etchings Plantin commissioned in the 1580s. Following Plantin's death in 1589, vander Borcht continued to work for Plantin's successor, Jan Moretus I, supplying him with etchings or compositional drawings for a little more than a decade.[41]

Vander Borcht was much more, however, than a favored artist; he was also clearly close to Plantin and his family, even helping them with more mundane chores, such as the acquisition of butter for family members in Leiden.[42] Vander Borcht was also on good terms with Plantin's close friend, the Spanish theological scholar Benito Arias Montano, whom Philip II had sent to Antwerp in 1568 to supervise Plantin's printing of his famed Polyglot Bible.[43] Arias Montano apparently valued vander Borcht as a painter, as he commissioned 120 small paintings from him around 1571 for Sebastián de Santoyo, a royal official.[44] But vander Borcht was also evidently part of a small group of close friends. The first indication of their mutual friendship is a letter Plantin wrote to Arias Montano on November 1, 1572, in which he recounted how "our Peeter," together with his family, arrived sick and naked in Antwerp, seeking (and finding) refuge with Plantin after fleeing the sacking of Mechelen by Spanish troops between October 2 and 4, 1572. In subsequent letters (dated to 1585, 1587, and 1588) Plantin systematically

---

[39] For examples of this, see the entries for these artists in appendix 1.

[40] For examples of this, see the entry for Jan Sadeler I in appendix 1.

[41] For examples of vander Borcht's work for Jan Moretus, see the forthcoming *New Holl., Van der Borcht*, Book illustration vols.

[42] See MPM Arch. 64, fol. 159v (under December 14, 1587), for a payment to vander Borcht for butter that he purchased at the request of Margareta Plantin, the wife of Franciscus Raphelengius I, who was then in Leiden.

[43] Arias Montano and the production of the Polyglot Bible are discussed at greater length in ch. 3.

[44] Arias Montano's basic commission of these paintings from vander Borcht is recorded in MPM Arch. 98, fol. 223r, a document headed "Quae C. P. me absente curanda sunt hoc indice annotavi" (What C[hristopher] P[lantin] should do when I am not here), item 20 of which reads: "Petrus Mechliniensis pictor habet a me commissionem curand. ut depingantur telae centum et viginti, quas depingi iussi pro Dno. Sebast° Santoyo singulis binis florenis, quarum rationibus ille accepit certam summam florenorum et ego vicissem certum numerum telarum consolidanda est ratio ubi ille tradiderit telas pictas, habet iam hoc nomine centum triginta octo florenos." (I have asked Petrus, the painter from Mechelen, to make 120 small paintings on canvas for me, that I had made for Sebastian Santoyo for 2 fl. per piece, for which vander Borcht will receive certain amounts in florins and I, a certain number of canvases in return. The accounts must be consolidated as soon as he has delivered the painted canvases. He has already received 138 florins for this account.) Although this document is not signed, periodic payments in 1570 and 1571 to vander Borcht for the delivery of paintings, some of which are expressly cited as being for Arias Montano, document his work on this project (see MPM Arch. 28, fols. 52r, 56r, and 73r; and MPM Arch. 29, fols. 1r, 5r, 9r, 22r, and 31r). On the basis of Arias Montano's correspondence, it appears that he left Antwerp between January 4, and May 13, 1572 (Dávila Pérez 2002, I, letters 10 and 11). For the identification of de Santoyo, see Bécares Botas 1999, p. 277; and *Corr.*, VIII, no. 1109.

sends Arias Montano not only his and his family's greetings, but also those of a few additional individuals, often including vander Borcht, the print publisher Philips Galle, the cartographer Abraham Ortelius, and the artist Crispin van den Broeck.[45] Perhaps this was why vander Borcht, along with Galle and Ortelius, was charged with compiling an inventory of Plantin's stock of copper plates in 1590, as part of the settlement of Plantin's estate (see appendix 4).

It is noteworthy that Plantin's two other favored designers for his engraved illustrations – Crispin van den Broeck and Gerard van Groeningen – also had particular ties with Arias Montano, who was involved in the production of several editions with engraved illustrations in the period around 1569–1575.[46] Van den Broeck, who was also active as a painter, began to supply Plantin with compositions for engravings by 1570, essentially contemporaneous with vander Borcht. However, as is indicated in table A1.1, far fewer compositions can be positively attributed to van den Broeck in this period, than to vander Borcht. Van den Broeck's and vander Borcht's work for Plantin also differed in terms of the general scale of the compositions they tended to execute, as well as in the selection of engravers who ultimately executed the prints after their designs. Specifically, while Plantin commissioned numerous larger compositions from van den Broeck – in *quarto* or folio – the majority of vander Borcht's designs for Plantin's engravings tended to be for books in *octavo* or smaller.[47] Similarly, while the majority of van den Broeck's book illustration designs appear to have been engraved by either Jan Sadeler I (see, for example, fig. 5.2) or his reputed father-in-law, Abraham de Bruyn (see, for example, fig. 4.4), these engravers do not dominate the execution of vander Borcht's designs to the same degree; rather, Jan Wierix does.

It is striking that what distinguishes van den Broeck's work for Plantin (in contrast with vander Borcht's) – fewer compositions, but more in a larger scale – may also typify the difference in Arias Montano's orders of paintings from the two men. For, in the same document in which Arias Montano asked Plantin to oversee (and pay for) vander Borcht's execution of paintings for Sebastián de Santoyo, he made a similar request for

---

[45] For these letters, see *Corr.*, III, no. 421 (from November 1, 1572), *Corr.*, VII, no. 1045 (dated to early November 1585 on the basis of the contents), *Corr.*, VIII–IX, no. 1263 (from June 3–7, 1587), and *Corr.*, VIII–IX, no. 1399 (from August 27, 1588). Plantin's 1572 account of vander Borcht's arrival in Antwerp reads: "Petrus noster cum uxore ambo morbo correpti et prolibus nudi ad nos venerunt. Cum et necessarius ad huc essem in Galliis ab uxore mea hic fuerunt suis induti et adjuti . . . Habitat cum fratre in cubiculo, domum nostram illi obtuli jubeoque illum boni esse animi, pecunia neque rebus aliis necessariis non plus per Dei gratiam carere permittam quam ipse velim in tali casu. Deus misereatur nostri et benedicat nobis." (Our Peeter and his wife, both sick, have come here with their children without anything; and because I had to be in France up until this time, my wife clothed and helped them here . . . He lives in a room in our house with his brother. I offered him our house and I ask him to keep himself in good spirits. With God's grace, I will not allow him to be lacking either the money or essential items that I would want myself in such a situation.)

[46] See chs. 3 and 6 for more on Arias Montano's association with projects involving engravings. For an overview of the lives of van den Broeck and van Groeningen and their work for Plantin, see appendix 1 and table A1.1. As alluded to above, van den Broeck was also regularly included among the group of special friends whose greetings Plantin conveyed in his letters to Arias Montano. For examples of such letters, see *Corr.*, IV, no. 643 (from August 13–14, 1575) and *Corr.*, VIII–IX, nos. 1303 (from September 16, 1587). See below for van Groeningen's contacts with Arias Montano.

[47] Van den Broeck's varied selection of larger compositions for Plantin's editions is compensated by the one suite of nearly forty *octavo* compositional drawings that he made for Plantin's 1577 edition of L. Hillessemius's *Sacrarum antiquitatum monumenta* (PP 1335).

paintings to be made by van den Broeck for the same man. But, while vander Borcht was to make some 120 paintings at just 2 fl. per painting (for a total of 240 fl.), van den Broeck was to paint only 48 scenes, but at an average of 6 fl. per piece, for a larger total of 288 fl.[48] Regrettably we do not know what either vander Borcht's or van den Broeck's paintings looked like, or how big they were. Thus, it is impossible to determine whether the difference in their wages reflected simply a difference in the scale of the works concerned, or a differing appreciation of the capabilities of both artists. In another, potentially related list of watercolors on canvas that vander Borcht made for Arias Montano by 1573, however, the paintings are identified and differentiated in their cost by their relative scale, which suggests that the relative physical scale of the work did influence how much was paid for it.[49] Given what is known of their work for Plantin, it is all the more tempting to associate at least some of the difference in wage with a commensurate difference in the scale of the paintings concerned. Regardless of the precise mix of factors, it remains clear that Arias Montano was willing to pay van den Broeck more per painting – be it larger or "better" – than for the ones executed by vander Borcht.

Our knowledge of the work and general activities of van Groeningen are, regrettably, much more limited. In contrast with the two other designers Plantin regularly employed, van Groeningen is not known for any body of independent paintings – only some work as a glass painter. Rather, van Groeningen is known primarily for his work as a graphic artist, either as a designer of engravings or as an etcher, active in a relatively limited period of time, from around 1561 to 1575. Like all of the other designers who worked for Plantin, van Groeningen was active making or designing prints for more than a decade (often for recognized Antwerp print publishers like Philips Galle and Gerard de Jode) before Plantin employed him. Although the lack of references to van Groeningen in Plantin's correspondence makes it impossible to determine whether he, too, was part of Plantin's and Arias Montano's circle of artist friends, he may at least have known Arias Montano, as they both worked on several projects organized by Philips Galle in the early 1570s, just prior to Plantin's employment of van Groeningen.[50] Van Groeningen's work for Plantin is concentrated in just two years, 1574 and 1575, when he produced nearly forty designs for Plantin's own publications, as well as an additional twenty-five designs for an edition that Plantin and Galle published

---

48 For Arias Montano's original charge for van den Broeck, see MPM Arch. 98, fol. 223r, item 21, which reads: "Crispinus pictor depingit etiam quadraginta octo tabulas pro eodem D. S. Oyo quas ubi depinxerit et tradiderit accipiet ducentos octoginta et octo florenos detracta summa quam antea acceperit quae usque in hodiernum diem est florenorum quinquaginta." (The painter Crispin must also paint forty-eight scenes for the same S. Oyo, for which he will receive 288 fl. once he has painted and delivered them, minus the amount that he has already received, which at this moment amounts to 50 fl.) Plantin discusses van den Broeck's work on these paintings (referred to as "tabula") in his correspondence with Arias Montano in the summer of 1572 (see *Corr.*, III, nos. 191, 396, and 409), where the main topic is that while van den Broeck was finishing all of the requested paintings, Plantin did not have enough ready cash to pay him. According to Plantin's last letter on the topic (no. 409), he ultimately asked his and Arias Montano's good friend and occasional financier, the Spanish merchant Louis Perez, to pay van den Broeck. Perez is discussed in greater detail in ch. 3.

49 See MPM Arch. 204, p. 12, for this list of "Waterverf doeken a° 73 Peeter vander Borcht p^r Montano" (Watercolor canvases 1573 Peeter vander Borcht for [B. Arias] Montano).

50 For van Groeningen's work on these projects, see *New Holl., Van Groeningen*, nos. 265–364 and 406–417. For a discussion of Arias Montano's involvement in them, see Hänsel 1991, pp. 90–129.

jointly (see, for example, figs. 4.7 and 6.11).[51] The abrupt end of his work for Plantin might simply be part of the striking, general decline in Plantin's commissions for new engravings as of 1576 (see table A1.1). However, the lack of knowledge of any other artistic production following his work for Plantin suggests that he may also have simply died in these troubled times.[52]

The last artist who is known to have supplied Plantin (as well as his successor, Jan Moretus I) with a number of designs for book illustrations is Maarten de Vos. De Vos was an established painter in Antwerp by the 1560s, but it was not until the 1580s that he began an active career as a designer of prints.[53] Plantin's first known contact with de Vos stems from the later period of his career when, in 1582, Plantin engaged him to design a large image of the *Last Judgment*, which was ultimately engraved by Jan Wierix.[54] This was not a commission for a book illustration, as is suggested in some discussions of de Vos's drawing, but should rather be associated with Plantin's ongoing activities as a dealer in independent prints. For, the finished engraving, along with a plate of the *Crucifixion*, supposedly designed by Hans Bol and engraved by Jan Sadeler I, were sent to Jan Poelman, who dealt with the sale of Plantin's editions in Salamanca.[55]

Plantin asked de Vos to design another engraving – an image of St. Bruno – for a third party in 1588.[56] Plantin's accounts reveal that the main image was engraved by Crispijn van de Passe, who had only recently attained the status of master in the Antwerp St. Luke's guild, while Adriaen Huberti, who is perhaps better known for his activities as a print publisher than as an engraver, was paid for engraving the text into the plate.[57] In this case, it is less clear for whom the print was ultimately intended. According to Plantin's correspondence, in June 1588 he sent a proof impression to Don Bernardino de Mendoza, Philip II's ambassador to France, asking him whether any alterations should be made in the plate.[58] In November 1588, the plate itself was included in a shipment of various items to the Parisian bookseller Michel Sonnius I, with the note that it was intended for Isuardo Capello, an Italian merchant and banker, residing in Paris, who had previously helped with the shipment of Plantin's liturgical editions and

---

[51] For details of each of these projects, see the entry for van Groeningen in appendix 1.

[52] The real possibility that van Groeningen passed away in the later 1570s would also account for the lack of references to him in Plantin's subsequent correspondence with Arias Montano.

[53] See appendix 1 for more on de Vos and his work for Plantin.

[54] De Vos's drawing is still preserved in MPM Tek. 354 and measures 260 × 202 mm. For a payment to de Vos for this drawing, see MPM Arch. 60, fol. 160r (under September 23, 1582). For Wierix's engraving of it (>246 × 192 mm), see *Holl. Dutch & Flemish*, LX, no. 395, and *New Holl., de Vos*, no. 612. For a payment to Jan Wierix for engraving it, see MPM Arch. 61, fol. 28v (under March 12, 1583). This is transcribed in M-H Wierix, III.2, p. 542 (last item of document 36), but with the name of the recipient of the engraving incorrectly read as J. Rutenas instead of J. Poelman.

[55] For a discussion of earlier misattributions of this drawing, see Bowen and Imhof 2001, p. 261, n. 6. For the shipment of various items to Jan Poelman on March 15, 1583, including this engraving and that of the *Crucifixion*, attributed in this record to [Hans?] Bol and [Jan?] Sadeler, see MPM Arch. 61, fol. 30v. On Poelman and his special business arrangements with Plantin, see Robben 1993.

[56] For de Vos's original drawing (161 × 124 mm), see MPM Tek. 272. No impression of this image is known. For a discussion of this project, see Veldman 2001, p. 31.

[57] See MPM Arch. 65, fol. 73r (under May 28, 1588), for payments made to van de Passe and Huberti for their work on this plate. This payment is transcribed in Veldman 2001, n. 50, pp. 381–382.

[58] See *Corr.*, VIII–IX, no. 1378, pp. 401–402, for this letter, a relevant section of which is also transcribed in Veldman 2001, n. 51, p. 382.

subsequently served as an intermediary for the shipment of other items to Fulvio Orsini in Rome.[59] Was Capello going to convey the plate to the Spanish ambassador, or were both middlemen for someone else? Regrettably, we will never know. Regardless, the main point remains the same: de Vos continued to provide Plantin with drawings for independent engravings that Plantin had made specially at the request of third parties.

By this time, however, de Vos also served Plantin in another capacity, namely, as the middleman for the delivery of both woodcuts and engravings that he designed and had executed by other artists, presumably for the illustration of Plantin's publications. The best-documented example of this practice concerns the production of a group of forty-six small plates (all c.90 × 70 mm) engraved by van de Passe (who was then most likely in Germany), which comprised thirty-five subjects from Christ's Passion, as well as eleven additional plates with images that were common to Plantin's liturgical editions.[60] Although one could argue that the Passion images may have been intended for an independent print series on the Passion of Christ – and, consequently, were more in line with Plantin's other commissions of independent prints from de Vos – the existence of the comparably scaled extra liturgical images speaks against this. Not only can one not make up a logical subset of prints for an independent print series with these images, but it is only by combining subsets of these plates with some of the subjects that fit in with the Passion series that one can arrive at a full, standard series of subjects for Plantin's missals or breviaries. Given the potential practical use of these plates for Plantin's editions, it remains odd that no contemporary impressions or use of these plates to illustrate any of Plantin's or his successors' publications are known. In the next few years, however, de Vos did go on to provide designs for book illustrations that were used and reused by Plantin's successors, thereby underscoring his new role (albeit somewhat late for Plantin's own editions) as a designer of illustrations for the publications of the *Officina Plantiniana* (see fig. 5.19).[61]

Of the six remaining artists who are known to have supplied Plantin with designs or etchings for his publications with intaglio illustrations, each appears to have worked on just one of Plantin's projects. The painter-designer Lambert van Noort, for example, was the first person Plantin hired to design an engraving for one of his own publications – the title-frame for Juan de Valverde's *Vivae imagines partium corporis humani* from 1566 (see fig. 3.2). Whether or not he and Plantin were satisfied with this type of arrangement, van Noort's death a few years later prevented him from working for Plantin again.[62] Each of the other artists whom Plantin seems to have employed just once – Jan and Lucas van Doetecum, Maarten van Heemskerck, Hans Vredeman de Vries, and Otto van Veen – may well have agreed to do so only at the exceptional request of a third party.[63] For example, the van Doetecum brothers, who were responsible for the suite of plates

---

[59] For the record of this shipment, see MPM Arch. 65, fol. 151v (under November 4, 1588). For Capello, see Bécares Botas 1999, pp. 153 and 306; *Corr.*, VII, no. 956, and *Corr. Supplément*, nos. 95, 170, and 172.

[60] See appendix 1 under de Vos and van de Passe for more on them and these plates. For an example of Plantin paying de Vos for the delivery of unspecified woodcuts, see MPM Arch. 65, fol. 44v (under March 29, 1588).

[61] On de Vos's work as a designer of illustrations for Plantin's successors, see Bowen and Imhof 2001.

[62] For more on van Noort, see appendix 1.

[63] For extra information on each of these artists and their work for Plantin, see appendix 1.

appended to Plantin and Hieronymus Cock's joint publication, *Le pompe funèbre*, from 1559 (see fig. 3.1), regularly worked for Cock at the time. Thus, it is most likely that Cock arranged for them to make the plates for this publication.[64] The Haarlem-based artist van Heemskerck, who drew a composition of the *Crucifixion* for Plantin's folio missals, which was then engraved by Philips Galle (see fig. 4.2), may have been asked to design the image by Galle himself. Galle had only recently moved from Haarlem, where he had regularly made prints after van Heemskerck's designs.[65] Otto van Veen, who is only known to have designed (if not etched) the illustrations to Plantin's first illustrated edition of Justus Lipsius's *Saturnalium sermonum libri duo, qui de gladiatoribus* from 1585 (see fig. 5.14), may well have been asked to make these images by or on behalf of Lipsius himself. Van Veen was clearly on good terms with Lipsius – Lipsius signed van Veen's *Liber amicorum* when they were together in Leiden in 1584, just when Plantin would have been working on this edition – and Lipsius expressed both his admiration for van Veen's designs and his resulting regret that van Veen decided to leave Leiden in 1584.[66] Finally, Vredeman de Vries was paid, if not contracted, by the city of Antwerp for the designing of the illustrations for the commemorative album of the state entry of the duke of Anjou into Antwerp in 1582 (see figs. 5.10 and 5.11). Nevertheless, Plantin retained possession of the plates and acted as the sole publisher of the resulting printed accounts. Thus, in addition to having the plates printed, he may also have paid to have Vredeman de Vries's compositions etched and engraved.[67]

Consequently, Plantin had the illustrations for the vast majority of his publications executed by just a few artists, some of whom were evidently also on good personal terms with Plantin. Nearly all of the designers who worked for Plantin (regularly or not) were also, notably, often in the middle or towards the end of their productive years when they did so.[68] None was a novice endeavoring to establish himself in this fashion. As will become evident in the following discussion of the engravers Plantin hired, these basic characteristics of the group of designers he employed are in telling contrast with the numerous young, ambitious engravers he engaged.

THE ENGRAVERS PLANTIN EMPLOYED

Plantin's first independent publication to be illustrated with engravings was a 1566 edition of Juan de Valverde's anatomical work, *Vivae imagines partium corporis humani*

---

[64] See ch. 3 for more on this publication (PP 939).

[65] For examples of Galle's work after van Heemskerck, see, e.g., *New Holl., Van Heemskerck*, II, p. 269, under Galle.

[66] See ch. 5 for more on Lipsius and van Veen.

[67] See ch. 5 for more on this project. For evidence that these plates stayed in Plantin's possession, see the list of copper plates in Leiden in appendix 4. The work of Marcus Gheeraerts for the illustrations of Gerard de Jode's 1584 publication the *Apologi creaturarum* (PP 1706) and the van Doetecums' work for Lucas Waghenaer's sea atlases (PP 2480–2489) from 1584–1585 are not included here because in these and similar cases discussed in ch. 6 Plantin only served as the hired printer and was not the person behind the publication who contacted the artists and retained possession of the plates.

[68] The main exceptions here are van Veen (who was approximately twenty-eight years old when he made the designs for Lipsius's publication) and vander Borcht (who was approximately thirty years old when he first began to design woodcuts for Plantin and thirty-four when he began to design engravings). All of the other artists (except for van Groeningen, for whom no birth date is known) were in their forties, fifties, or even seventy-four (van Heemskerck) when they supplied Plantin with designs.

(see figs. 3.2, 3.6, 3.7, and 3.9).[69] In his dedicatory letter to the Antwerp magistrates, Plantin emphasized how he had searched assiduously for a skilled engraver to make the engravings for this book.[70] Plantin ultimately hired Frans Huys, an established local artist who was known for his successful engravings after designs by Pieter Bruegel I for Hieronymus Cock.[71] Unfortunately, Frans Huys died in 1562, soon after he began work on the project, having completed only three of the forty-three plates needed. Work on these engravings was further delayed by the subsequent sale of all of Plantin's belongings (including Huys's three engravings) during Plantin's self-imposed exile in Paris (to avoid being implicated in the printing of heretical texts by his pressmen).[72] When Plantin was able to return to it in 1564, he hired Frans Huys's brother Pieter, a painter, draughtsman, and engraver, who had been designing woodcut illustrations for Plantin as of 1563.[73] Plantin continued to employ Pieter Huys for more than a decade following the completion of the illustrations for de Valverde's anatomical treatise. In this period, Huys is known to have made approximately sixty engravings for Plantin. He was, consequently (as we will discuss below), one of the more productive engravers working for Plantin at this time, at least in terms of the sheer number of plates completed. These engravings varied significantly from full-page folio engravings (often essentially diagrams) for the Polyglot Bible (see fig. 3.17), to small text illustrations for a book of hours and several borders used to decorate Plantin's *octavo* editions of Arias Montano's *Humanae salutis monumenta* and books of hours. His single most spectacular project, however, is an engraved title-plate, first made in 1578 for Georges de la Hèle's *Octo missae quinque, sex et septem vocum* and subsequently reused for the title-page of all of Plantin's and Jan Moretus's large folio music editions.[74] This collection of images is noteworthy for the relative predominance of either more decorative images (like the borders or the title-plate for Plantin's musical editions) or diagrams (for the Polyglot Bible). The simultaneous relative paucity of conventional, narrative text illustrations for books in *octavo* or *quarto*, which Plantin was ordering from other artists in large quantities at this time, suggests that a sort of specialization existed among the engravers Plantin hired in the early 1570s.

When Plantin first asked Frans and Pieter Huys to make engraved book illustrations for him, both were in their early forties and had been active in the Antwerp art world for more than fifteen years. Thus, they do not represent the young aspiring engravers alluded to above, but were exceptions to the general pattern that will become evident below. Perhaps this was owing to Plantin himself being something of a novice in the production of books with engraved illustrations when he hired them. Or was he truly guided in his decision by his desire, expressed in his dedicatory letter to de Valverde's text, to find a "craftsman [in Antwerp] who could measure up to the Italians" (that is, the engravers responsible for the plates in an earlier edition of de Valverde's text

---

[69] See ch. 3 for more on this publication (PP 2413).   [70] See p. 67 for this text.
[71] See appendix 1 for more on Huys.   [72] See p. 77 for a more extensive discussion of these events.
[73] See appendix 1 for more on Pieter Huys and his work for Plantin. For examples of Huys's subsequent designs for woodcuts for Plantin, completed while Huys was also making engravings for him, see PP 2168, n. 5 (a 1564 edition of J. Sambucus's *Emblemata*), PP 1476, n. 8 (a 1565 edition of H. Junius's *Emblemata*), and PP 1238, n. 4 (a 1571 edition of E. de Garibay y Zamalloa's history of Spain).
[74] See Voet, PP, III, fig. 15, for a reproduction of this plate.

that served as a model for Plantin's).[75] If so, then a respected engraver employed by Cock, whose own business was inspired by that of famed Italian publishers, was a logical choice. Regardless of the precise reasons behind Plantin's initial selection of engravers, the majority of the artists he subsequently employed differed significantly in the types of engravings they executed, as well as in their age and status in the Antwerp print world when they worked for Plantin.

As is evident from table A1.2, the years 1569–1575 represented an intensely active period in the production of engraved illustrations for a variety of Plantin's editions.[76] While three designers were responsible for making the vast majority of the compositions needed, Plantin employed at least seven different engravers to execute all of the plates required. As many as three, four, or even six (in 1570) engravers were employed simultaneously in some years, presumably to ensure that the number of plates desired could be completed within a "reasonable" amount of time. Aside from Pieter Huys (then around fifty years old), these engravers included three other older, established artists – Pieter van der Heyden (aged around forty), Abraham de Bruyn (aged around thirty), and Philips Galle (about thirty-three) – and three young engravers, who were not yet even registered as masters in the St. Luke's guild, namely, Jan Sadeler I and Jan Wierix (both twenty years old when they completed their first work for Plantin) and Hieronymus Wierix, who was only seventeen when he made his first engravings for Plantin.[77] Once again, Plantin may well have known of at least two of the established artists – van der Heyden and Galle (who had most likely just moved to Antwerp from Haarlem when he made his first engraving for Plantin – see fig. 4.2) – through their work for Antwerp print publishers, in particular Hieronymus Cock. It is not clear how Plantin learned of de Bruyn, who, despite having been born in Antwerp, was, according to Plantin's own records, living near Breda when he supplied Plantin with engravings in 1570 and 1571.[78] It is similarly not known how Plantin came into contact with the young engravers. Hieronymus and Jan Wierix, in any case, had been producing engravings for some five years, including impressive copies after Dürer when they were just twelve or fourteen years old, and had, presumably, some local notoriety as a result. With the exception of de Bruyn, all of these engravers were based in Antwerp by the time they actively began to work for Plantin.

Of these artists, Jan Wierix worked the most consistently and extensively for Plantin, producing a minimum of 120 engravings for him between 1569 and January 1, 1576 alone.[79] In contrast with the sixty or so engravings executed by Pieter Huys (who follows Jan Wierix in terms of the total number of engravings he is known to have completed for Plantin), Jan Wierix's work consists primarily of figural (mostly biblical) text illustrations for books in *octavo* and *quarto* (see, for example, figs. 3.24 and 5.4).

[75] See p. 67 for this excerpt.
[76] The primary projects on which each of these artists worked is given in appendix 1, under the respective artists' names.
[77] See appendix 1 for more biographical information on these figures.
[78] See, e.g., MPM Arch. 28, fol. 35 rht, under June 2, 1570, which reads: "Paye a Abraham de Bruyn tailleur en cuivre pres Breda fl. 20" (Paid to Abraham de Bruyn, engraver in copper, near Breda, 20 fl.).
[79] This figure remains notably less than the hundreds of etchings vander Borcht made single handedly in 1574 and in the 1580s (cf. the work of each artist listed in appendix 1).

After Jan Wierix and Pieter Huys, Jan Sadeler I and de Bruyn completed the most work for Plantin in the period 1569–1576, with some fifty-two and thirty-five plates, respectively. While both Jan Wierix and Pieter Huys were systematically employed by Plantin for work on a variety of projects during his initial "start-up" period for the production of books with engravings (1569–1574/5), both Sadeler and de Bruyn worked more intermittently on select projects. The bulk of the plates made by both men were figural or narrative subjects for books in *octavo*, supplemented by comparable images in a slightly larger *quarto* format (see, for example, figs. 4.17, 5.2, and 5.5). However, Sadeler's earliest known work for Plantin consisted of engraving several decorative borders for Plantin's *octavo* books of hours, which were comparable to ones executed simultaneously by Pieter Huys. Sadeler also made a few larger borders for Plantin around 1574–1575. Of all the other engravers Plantin employed in the early 1570s only Jan Wierix is also known to have engraved a border for Plantin, but this time a large, detailed narrative composition (see fig. 4.3).

The fact that Plantin employed Jan Wierix far more frequently than of all these figures was not simply a matter of his being, for example, the cheapest engraver of the lot. While his fees appear to have been significantly less than the rates charged by van der Heyden, who was a well-known and respected engraver by this time thanks to his work for Cock, Jan Wierix's fees were equivalent to those charged by Pieter Huys, who was then also an established artist, but is known to have made only half as many engravings for Plantin in the same period. Indeed, Jan Wierix's fees were consistently higher than the amounts charged by either his younger brother Hieronymus Wierix or the older artist Abraham de Bruyn, both of whom appear to have worked on far fewer projects for Plantin.[80] Rather, what clearly played a role here was not simply whom Plantin could afford to pay to make engraved book illustrations, but who was willing and able to make them for Plantin.

For van der Heyden, Huys, and de Bruyn, for example, it may simply have been impractical to supply Plantin with more engravings. Van der Heyden's engravings for the Polyglot Bible (see, for example, fig. 3.11) appear to be the last he made before his reputed death in 1576 during the Spanish Fury.[81] Huys, at least by the later 1570s when he would have been nearly sixty, may similarly have become too old to keep working extensively for Plantin. Finally, de Bruyn, whose whereabouts in the period 1572–1575 are unknown, may simply have been engaged elsewhere or too far away to make working for Plantin convenient.

Galle, Jan Sadeler I, and Hieronymus Wierix appear to have limited their work for Plantin for other reasons, namely, the desire to establish themselves as independent engravers and print publishers. That this was the case for Galle and Sadeler is clear from numerous allusions to them in Plantin's correspondence from the later 1580s when he was seeking competent engravers who could make the plates for Jerome Nadal's *Evangelicae historiae imagines*.[82] The relatively few engravings that Galle or members of

---

[80] For an overview of what Plantin's engravers charged for their work in the period 1569–1571, see Bowen and Imhof 2003, pp. 161–172, and table 1, p. 190.

[81] See appendix 1 under van der Heyden for the sources of these speculations.

[82] See p. 248 for such remarks.

his workshop made for Plantin is all the more striking given his and Plantin's close personal ties.[83] Sadeler's evident reluctance to make book illustrations for Plantin in the period 1582–1586 is also noteworthy because he was in Antwerp periodically in those years and did agree to make a single, independent engraving of the *Crucifixion* in 1583 for Plantin for a third party.[84]

The reasons behind Hieronymus Wierix's unwillingness to make book illustrations for Plantin are less certain. All indications are, however, that he actively sought to work as an independent print publisher and soon became a sought-after engraver who could set his own conditions and exceptionally high fees for whichever work he took on – none of which would have appealed to a profit-minded book publisher with his own production schedule. Such was the case, for example, with his and his younger brother's (Anton II, whom Plantin never appears to have hired to make illustrations for his own publications) response to Plantin's inquiries concerning engraving the plates for Nadal's *Evangelicae historiae imagines*. Both were willing, in principle, to work on the project, but only if granted extra time to complete the work – three years instead of the previously agreed upon two – and exorbitant sums per engraving – 60 fl. per plate for Hieronymus and 40 fl. for Anton, instead of the previously agreed upon rate of 30 fl. per plate – among other demands.[85] It was not an offer that Plantin was inclined to take up. For, as he remarked in a letter to Emmanuel Ximenes from January 13, 1587 in which he related the Wierixes' latest set of conditions, the brothers were, in his view, stubborn, unreliable men who unabashedly demanded unreasonably high prices for their work, did not stick to their agreements, and were too wont to waste their time indulging in alcohol and other disrespectful activities.[86] Although the three Wierix brothers did, ultimately, engrave the majority of the illustrations for this project, Plantin did not arrange it. Rather, the series of images were first published in 1593 by the Antwerp Jesuits, while Martinus Nutius II printed the first edition of the accompanying text, the *Adnotationes et meditationes in evangelia* in 1594.[87] Nevertheless, in 1587, Plantin did, with much exasperation and effort, arrange for Hieronymus Wierix to make an exceptionally large, independent engraving of the *Seven Sorrows of the Virgin*, at the request of Jean Moflin, the abbot of St. Winoc in Bergues (formerly in the Low Countries, now part of France).[88] Thus, as was the case with Jan Sadeler I, while neither artist,

---

[83] See ch. 6 for more on Galle's and Plantin's personal and professional relationships.

[84] See also ch. 6 for Plantin's interest in independent prints.

[85] See Plantin's letter to Emmanuel Ximenes from January 13, 1587 (*Corr.*, VIII–IX, no. 1193) for these demands.

[86] Plantin alludes to this view of the Wierixes in several of his letters. See, e.g., *Corr.*, VIII–IX, nos. 1160, 1182, 1188, and 1193, the last of which comprises the highlighted excerpt, which reads: "Vides morositatem horum juvenum e quorum praeterea manibus vix puto vel illis preciis ultra modum impudenter et praeter rationem postulatis nos vel sexennio extorqueri posse quamvis aliter polliciti essent et stricte obligati. Tantus siquidem est in illis ardor potandi et loca inhonesta frequentandi ut quovis discrimine malint tempus in illis perdere quam ullis pollicitis satisfacere."

[87] For a summary of the history of the publication of these images and the accompanying text, see, e.g., M-H Wierix, III.1, Annex I (especially pp. 491–493).

[88] See M-H 775 for this engraving (> 446 × 306 mm), which Moflin never saw, as he died in 1587 before it was completed. For additional information on Moflin, see, e.g., Imhof 1998a, p. 133. While the plate was listed in the inventories of Plantin's copper plates made up after his death (see appendix 4, p. 384), it subsequently came into the hands of Theodoor Galle, who published it in 1601. This project is discussed in Rooses 1882, pp. 233–235; and in *Corr.*, VIII–IX, nos. 1170 (Plantin to Jean Moflin,

once an established, recognized engraver, was willing to make book illustrations for Plantin, Plantin was still able to negotiate with them for the production of independent engravings for third parties. This underscores an essential aspect of which engravers were willing to work for Plantin when and in which capacity.

Given Plantin's clear exasperation with the Wierixes, it would not be surprising if he, himself, preferred to work with other artists for his own projects, unless a third party, like those seeking to arrange for the publication of Nadal's work, expressly asked about employing them. Such may also have been the case with Jan Wierix. Notably absent from Plantin's correspondence concerning the work on Nadal's publication, Jan Wierix was back in Antwerp as of 1580 (following a brief period in Delft from c.1577–1579), and was enjoying great success with his own print production. While he continued to provide Plantin with some engravings in the years 1580–1583, the quantity and type of commissions had changed significantly in comparison with his earlier work for Plantin. Now his one major project for Plantin's publications consisted of a series of illustrations for a lengthy poem on courting by Jan-Baptist Houwaert, in addition to an author's portrait (see fig. 5.6), which were paid for, at least in part, by the author himself.[89] Thus, this may represent yet another example, typical of Plantin's contacts with the Wierixes in the 1580s, of how engravings ordered by Plantin were actually commissioned at the request of a third party. Beyond these plates, Jan Wierix executed just two author's portraits and perhaps one additional illustration for Plantin's extensively illustrated folio bible from 1583. Perhaps Jan Wierix, like his brother Hieronymus, Jan Sadeler I, and Philips Galle, also wanted to focus his energies on his own print production and publications and consequently began to price himself beyond Plantin's reach or simply refused to take on additional projects for him. Indeed, beyond Hieronymus and Anton Wierix II's work on Nadal's *Evangelicae historiae imagines*, none of these figures is known to have made any significant number of book illustrations for other publishers either.[90]

In the mid-1570s, when the original group of local engravers were, mostly, no longer able or willing to work for him, Plantin sought alternative solutions for the continued production of his intaglio book illustrations. One option open to him was to try working with the less certain technique of etching as a means of producing such illustrations. Finding a willing etcher was simple, as his established friend Peeter vander Borcht had been making etchings for many years prior to doing so for Plantin's publications as of 1574.[91] The other solution was, obviously, to find new engravers. At least three of the four engravers Plantin is known to have engaged for the first time between 1574 and 1577 were most likely living beyond Antwerp at the time. They were Pierre Dufour in Liège (see fig. 4.12), Paul Uten Waele from Utrecht (see fig. 6.2), and Julius Goltzius in

November 4, 1586), 1191 (Plantin to Jean Moflin, January 7, 1587), and 1229 (Plantin to Garcia de Loasia, chaplain to Philip II and instructor of Philip III, March 23, 1587). The compositional drawing for this print is attributed, at least in part, to Crispin van den Broeck (cf. MPM Tek. 355).

[89] See the discussion of this book in ch. 5.

[90] See the lists of book illustrations in the relevant Hollstein volumes for each of these artists, as cited in appendix 1.

[91] See ch. 5 for Plantin's use of etchings as book illustrations. See appendix 1 for references to many of the etchings vander Borcht made for Plantin.

Bruges.[92] Each of these figures appears to have worked only intermittently for Plantin, however. All of Dufour's known contacts with Plantin are, for example, concentrated in the year 1574, when he executed some twenty-two engravings and delivered numerous independent prints to Plantin. Prior to this, Dufour had made several engravings that were published by Cock in 1570 and 1573, which may well have been how Plantin came to know of him. Despite evidence indicating that Dufour did not die young, but continued to live in Liège until around 1610, it is not clear why he stopped working for Plantin (and Cock) so abruptly following the completion of these initial commissions. Given the relatively few prints known by him, it seems unlikely that he shunned such commissions in favor of his own print production. He evidently decided to devote himself to other activities – perhaps painting – instead.

Paul Uten Waele and Julius Goltzius are different cases, once again. Snippets of Plantin's correspondence indicate that he would have liked to have employed Goltzius more, but hoped to encourage him to move to Antwerp in order to do so.[93] However, when Goltzius finally did move to Antwerp in around 1586, there was no immediate, evident increase in Plantin's orders of plates from him, although Plantin did have Goltzius make a series of engravings for the German bookseller Hans Gundlach in 1586.[94] Thus, once again, perhaps, while Plantin continued to negotiate the engraving of plates for third parties with some of his past engravers, this did not always go hand in hand with his own employment of them for the execution of his book illustrations. It was only in the months following Plantin's death that Goltzius once again executed some small engravings for Plantin's successor, Jan Moretus I.[95] Uten Waele appears to be a similar case of an artist Plantin employed on occasion, but was hindered in doing so regularly, at least in part, by his place of residence. For while it is clear – both from various records in the Plantin archives and from the evidence of what independent print publishers like Cock published – that the shipment of copper plates between distant engravers and paying publishers was a common transaction, it must also have represented an additional cost and complication in terms of monitoring the work on the illustrations for a particular publication.[96] Among Plantin's

[92] For brief biographical sketches and lists of their work for Plantin, see appendix 1. We do not know where the as yet unidentified "Gil Hor" was residing.

[93] See *Corr.*, VII, no. 1044, a letter from November 5, 1585 that Plantin wrote to the Jesuit Ludovico Tovardus, concerning "an experienced engraver who is living in Bruges" ("de quodam perito artifice qui Brugis vivit") who, given Plantin's known contacts at the time, was most likely Julius Goltzius. This is distinct from Plantin's subsequent (unsuccessful) attempt in 1586 to convince Hendrick Goltzius to come to Antwerp to engrave the plates for Jerome Nadal's *Evangelicae historiae imagines* (for more information on both of these cases, see Delen 1924–1935, II.1, pp. 151–152).

[94] For Plantin's arrangements for one of Gundlach's projects, just identified as the "Monumentum," see *Corr.*, VII, no. 1107, a letter from Plantin to Gundlach dated May 31, 1586. A confirmation of the charges Plantin outlined in this letter (105 fl. for engraving the plates and an additional 4 fl. 10 st. for having 200 impressions printed of them) is noted in Plantin's accounts with Gundlach in MPM Arch. 20, fol. 96 lft. Plantin performed similar services for other printer-publishers. For evidence of this, see MPM Arch. 86, fol. 127r, for a letter written on October 19, 1594 by the Parisian printer-publisher Abel L'Angelier to Jan Moretus I, in which he asks Moretus to have some engravings made for him as Plantin had done. This letter is also cited in Balsamo and Simonin 2002, p. 127.

[95] For examples of such work, see MPM Arch. 30, fol. 1 verso (under July 24, 1589), for a payment to Goltzius for making six illustrations for a small book of hours; and Bowen and Imhof 2001, pp. 276–277, for engravings he made for a small book on St. Francis for the Capuchins.

[96] De Bruyn clearly shipped his plates to Plantin on several occasions (e.g., those completed around 1570–1571 when he was in Breda) and Plantin sent Dufour copper plates, which Dufour then sent back

Leiden editions, one work, G. Stewechius's *Commentarius ad flavi vegeti renati libros* from 1585, was embellished with an engraving of the author that was executed by the famed Haarlem engraver Hendrick Goltzius. However, as the engraving is dated 1583, it is possible that Goltzius had originally made it as an independent project and not specifically for Plantin's publication. For, as Plantin's subsequent fruitless correspondence with Goltzius concerning the execution of engravings for Jerome Nadal's *Evangelicae historiae imagines* indicates, Goltzius was not inclined to provide Plantin with book illustrations.[97]

Plantin may have been driven to try to employ engravers located beyond Antwerp, despite these necessary complications, as a result of a lack of competent, willing artists in Antwerp itself, particularly following the fall of Antwerp to Spanish troops in 1585. Plantin certainly repeats this sentiment regularly in his correspondence from the mid- to late 1580s and there was, without doubt, a great exodus of skilled craftsman from the city because of the siege and the resulting definitive return of the city to Catholic rule. Crispijn van de Passe, for example, may have initially been a likely, willing candidate to provide Plantin with book illustrations, having supplied him with nearly fifty plates in just four years immediately following his registration as a master in the St. Luke's guild in Antwerp at the age of twenty. However, his settlement in Germany owing to religious reasons, following the fall of Antwerp, must have impeded Plantin's continued employment of him. And he, too, clearly wished to establish himself as an independent engraver and print publisher. The Sadelers and Abraham de Bruyn similarly appear to have left Antwerp for such reasons. Indeed, it appears from both the books Plantin published and his payment records that he never succeeded in finding an engraver who was willing or able to work regularly for him during the last four years of his life, following the fall of Antwerp.[98] Adriaen Huberti, who is perhaps best known as a print publisher, was, for example, only occasionally paid for completing small tasks, like the engraving of letters on to copper plates. Only Hans Collaert II, who is known to have delivered just two unspecified plates to Plantin shortly after his registry as a master in the St. Luke's guild in 1586, continued to work periodically for Plantin's successor, Jan Moretus I. This may help clarify why Plantin switched to working primarily with etchers in the 1580s, in particular his friend Peeter vander Borcht, who produced hundreds of etchings for him in the years 1582–1583 and 1588–1589 alone. But, as is discussed in chapter 5, etchings were not always the best solution for book illustrations. A lasting solution to this problem did not come for another decade, until 1600, when the Galle workshop – under the new direction of Philips Galle's son Theodoor, who had recently become Jan Moretus's son-in-law – began to work regularly for the Moretuses. Only then did the *Officina Plantiniana* return to a period of relative stability in terms of the production of their desired copper plates and freedom from an incessant search for competent engravers who were willing to work.

engraved (see, for example, the transcriptions of these accounts with Dufour in Delen 1924–1935, II.1, p. 164, n. 3).

[97] See the discussion of Goltzius's work and his correspondence with Plantin in appendix 1. It is possible that this solitary engraving was produced at the author's request.

[98] See table A1.2 for an overview of this trend and appendix 1 for more on the last engravers discussed here.

PLANTIN'S INTAGLIO PRINTERS

As is discussed in greater detail in chapter 1, using etchings or engravings as book illustrations also implied finding someone who could print the images on the distinct intaglio (roller) press, following the printing of the text on a conventional typographical (relief) press. As is indicated in table A1.2, Plantin employed three people for this task in the course of his career: the painter and engraver Pieter Huys, a seller and colorer of prints, Mynken Liefrinck, and a certain Jacques vander Hoeven.[99]

Huys was the first of the three Plantin hired for this work and also the one employed for the shortest amount of time. This situation is readily clarified by the circumstances. For Huys was asked to print the very plates he had just finished engraving for Plantin's first fully independent projects with engraved illustrations, namely his 1566 edition (and 1568 Dutch reissue) of Juan de Valverde's *Vivae imagines partium corporis humani* (PP 2413 and PP 2416). Most likely, this was simply the easiest solution to a problem that had presented itself for the first time. It was, evidently, not the best solution, for just when Plantin paid Huys for printing groups of these plates a third time (c.1568) he also paid Huys's sister-in-law Mynken Liefrinck to print the title-plate for the same project for the first time. These payments represent the last Plantin made to Huys for printing images and the first of a long series of such payments that were made to Liefrinck throughout the remainder of Plantin's life. Although Huys himself may have indicated that he no longer wished to serve Plantin in this capacity, the more probable explanation is that Liefrinck was cheaper to employ and perhaps more willing, as the printing of plates may have been closer to her primary occupation. Specifically, while Huys charged 20 st. for every hundred sheets printed with the de Valverde plates, Liefrinck charged just 12 st. for every hundred impressions made of the title-plate (the "commencement") for this work.[100] Although it is true that the printing of some number of (most often one, two, or three) text illustrations on one sheet of paper was more complicated work than just printing the title-plate, Huys's rate of 20 st. per hundred sheets remained on the high end for printing images. The rates that Liefrinck charged for printing copper plates ranged from 8 st. per hundred sheets printed (her initial fee for printing the text illustrations in *octavo* missals) to 80 st. (or 4 fl.) per hundred sheets, for adding both text illustrations and engraved borders to Plantin's *octavo* editions of books of hours and Arias Montano's *Humanae salutis monumenta*.[101] Usually, however, she asked just 10, 12, or 13 st. per hundred sheets for printing any number of text illustrations in varying sizes.[102] Higher rates of, for example, 15 or 18 st. per hundred sheets were reserved for illustrating Plantin's 1583 folio bible or small books of hours, where, in both cases,

---

[99] More information on each of these figures and their work for Plantin is given in appendix 1.

[100] For references to these records, see the discussion of each individual's work on this project in appendix 1.

[101] For an example of Liefrinck's low rate of 8 st. per hundred sheets, see MPM Arch. 18, fol. 235 rht. For an example of her high rate of 4 fl. (80 st.) per hundred sheets, see MPM Arch. 16, fol. 146 rht.

[102] For various examples of Liefrinck charging 10 st. per hundred sheets printed, see MPM Arch. 16, fol. 240 rht and MPM Arch. 18, fol. 158 rht. See also the latter for other work completed at a rate of 12 st. per hundred sheets. See MPM Arch. 18, fol. 430 rht, and MPM Arch. 20, fol. 119 rht, for examples of printing charged at 13 st. per hundred sheets.

more than one illustration often had to be printed per sheet of paper.[103] Even Philips Galle charged just 14 st. per hundred sheets printed for the illustrations Plantin needed for his 1584 edition of Adrianus Barlandus's *Hollandiae comitum historia et icones*. This comparison is particularly telling because the plates were comparable in scale to those used to illustrate de Valverde's work and the inclusion of them represented a comparable "difficulty" level in terms of the number of plates that had to be printed per sheet of paper.[104] Indeed, as the accounts with Plantin's third intaglio printer, Jacques vander Hoeven, make clear, the printing of illustrations was a job that could be performed by people working at the low rates of unskilled day laborers and not just specialized artists.

As is indicated in table A1.2, once he began to employ Liefrinck and vander Hoeven, Plantin continued to do so virtually continually, until his own death in 1589. Mynken Liefrinck's occupation as a seller and colorer of prints is readily accounted for as an off-shoot of a family business, for both her father and brother, Willem and Hans Liefrinck, were prominent printmakers and publishers in Antwerp. Jacques vander Hoeven, on the other hand, remains largely unknown, except for the few references to him in the Plantin archives. Apparently not registered in the St. Luke's guild, vander Hoeven was, rather, more likely one of the many, often anonymous copper-plate printers, employed by sundry owners of intaglio plates, from renowned print publishers like Hieronymus Cock to individuals with a more specialized business, like the cartographer Abraham Ortelius, who maintained his own stock of plates for the atlases he published.[105] In Van den Branden's survey of archival documents pertaining to the printing of books and images in Antwerp in the fifteenth and sixteenth centuries, he found 90 people out of his sample of 1,200 names who were active as either "kunstdrukkers," "coperdruckers," "printers van beelden," etc. (namely, the printers of images), or "verlichters" and "constafsetters" (illuminators or colorers of prints), like Mynken Liefrinck and even Abraham Ortelius, before he conceived of the production of his atlas.[106] This was the third largest subdivision out of the eleven that he formed, behind only the large, general category of printers, booksellers, and publishers, and that of book binders. The number of "pictorial printers" and illuminators cited is even significantly greater than the number of paper merchants or letter cutters or correctors of texts, etc., listed.[107] The earliest known records of vander Hoeven's work for Plantin, noted on and off in

[103] For Liefrinck's charges for printing the illustrations for the 1583 folio bible, see MPM Arch. 18, fol. 430 rht, under July 14, August 5, and August 25, 1581. See MPM Arch. 20, fol. 237 rht, under October 25, 1585 and April 26, 1586, for examples of Liefrinck illustrating small books of hours at a rate of 18 st. per hundred sheets printed.

[104] See the discussion of the printing of Barlandus's work in ch. 6. While the de Valverde plates are c.235 × 145 mm, those used to illustrate Barlandus's work are c.205 × 120 mm. Galle is not included in the list of Plantin's intaglio printers because when he was involved in the printing of plates for Plantin, it was always part of some special cooperative venture (discussed in greater detail in ch. 6) and not – as was the case with Liefrinck and vander Hoeven – part of Plantin's independent production.

[105] See Van der Stock 1998, p. 145, for Cock's personal printer of his copper plates, a certain Sander Jansens. For the identification of Ortelius's copper-plate printer, Hans Rogghe (or Hans de Roge), see Imhof 1998b, pp. 202–203.

[106] For references to Ortelius as a "verlichter" or "afsetter" of printed images, see Van der Stock 1998, p. 273, and Imhof 1999b, pp. 79–80. There are numerous references to Liefrinck supplying Plantin with colored images in the records cited under her name in appendix 1.

[107] For these figures, see Van den Branden 1985, pp. 175–178.

the period March 5, 1571 to June 21, 1572, were for unspecified days of work, paid at a standard rate of 7 st. per day (as against the variable "piece rate" Liefrinck, Huys, and Galle always charged).[108] This wage was, notably, the equivalent of the high, daily summer wage paid to unskilled masons working in Antwerp in the period 1567–1572, which suggests that the routine, physically demanding task of working a roller press was something for unskilled laborers and not the likes of successful, aspiring artists.[109]

Regrettably, owing to the scant and rarely detailed records of vander Hoeven's work for Plantin, it is impossible fully to describe or quantify what he did for him. A comparison of the more detailed records of payments to Mynken Liefrinck with lists of Plantin's illustrated editions does indicate that Liefrinck printed the illustrations for the majority of the editions Plantin had embellished with intaglio plates. Nevertheless, it does not appear, for example, that vander Hoeven only printed certain types of images. The few records that specify precisely which projects he worked on indicate that he and Liefrinck occasionally split the work illustrating some editions – for Plantin's folio bible from 1583 and a small book of hours from 1584, for example – and that he illustrated other texts on his own. Similarly, no clear subdivision can be made in the texts that might be attributed to vander Hoeven and Liefrinck in terms of the general scale of the book – vander Hoeven (as Liefrinck) worked on both large folio editions and small books of hours.

It is also difficult to define their work in terms of the relative "difficulty level" of the task. As indicated above, both completed relatively simple printing jobs – like printing impressions of one large plate – as well as more complex ones – like printing several smaller plates on one sheet of text.[110] The main lingering question, then, is why Plantin employed both Liefrinck and vander Hoeven simultaneously for so many years. Was it simply impossible (or just not desirable) for Liefrinck (or vander Hoeven) to illustrate all of Plantin's editions with intaglio plates? Did vander Hoeven provide Plantin with a certain guarantee of always being able to have at least a selection of his plates printed as needed at a moment's notice? By the end of his career, Plantin also owned a press for printing copper plates, which would have facilitated such "spur-of-the-moment" printing.[111] Or did vander Hoeven, as is suggested in one record from 1579, also serve a more practical function, such as caring for Plantin's stock of plates, in addition to at least occasionally pulling impressions from them?[112]

Despite these limitations to our knowledge of how, precisely, vander Hoeven and Liefrinck may have complemented or supplemented each other's contributions to

---

[108] For these records, see MPM Arch. 31, fol. 181 lft, and MPM Arch. 32, fol. 27 rht.

[109] For the daily summer wages paid to skilled and unskilled masons in Antwerp in this period, see Scholliers 1976, table 1, p. 165.

[110] For examples of the simpler printing of images that were subsequently just inserted into the relevant books, consider the illustrations to Justus Lipsius's *Saturnalium sermonum libri duo* from 1588 (PP 1558) (printed by vander Hoeven; see MPM Arch. 98, p. 499) and the illustrations to A. de Pasino's *Discours sur plusieurs poincts de l'architecture de guerre concernants les fortifications . . .* (PP 1955) (printed by Liefrinck; see MPM Arch. 18, fol. 278 rht, under February 14, 1580). For vander Hoeven's and Liefrinck's work on the 1583 bible and a more complex, small book of hours, see the discussion of vander Hoeven's work in appendix 1.

[111] See MPM Arch. 99, p. 19, for a reference to "une presse pour imprimer en cuivre" in an inventory of Plantin's possessions in Antwerp.

[112] See the discussion of vander Hoeven in appendix 1 for evidence of this function.

Plantin's production of editions with intaglio illustrations, the simple, astounding fact that Plantin employed both of them for so many years remains. It attests to Plantin's own commitment, once he began, to the production of these specially illustrated editions despite the more obvious vicissitudes in employment of various artists for the completion of the compositions, engravings, and etchings they required.

CONCLUSION

Looking back on this brief overview of Antwerp's potential attraction to one like Plantin, an entrepreneur in the world of printing who was seeking to establish himself somewhere, it is clear that mid-sixteenth-century Antwerp was an appealing city in which to settle. In particular (and in notable contrast with Paris, for example), Antwerp was home to innovative, influential artists and businessmen, while the numerous foreigners present there supported the climate of an international exchange of objects and ideas.[113] Thus, as Plantin may have truly recalled when reflecting upon the reasons why he came to Antwerp, the availability of everything and anyone that he could possibly need to perform any of the numerous, superficially diverse occupations that he assumed in his first years in Antwerp must have been an enticing advantage indeed. In particular, Antwerp's then burgeoning and renowned worlds of prints and books were fluid and interactive in both the materials required and the people one needed to engage in order to complete specific projects.

And yet, despite the wealth of opportunities that Antwerp offered Plantin when he first arrived in the city, his subsequent influential production of books with intaglio illustrations remains a remarkable accomplishment that should not be taken for granted. There were numerous factors beyond Plantin's control that also influenced what he could do. The general state of war, for example, affected transport routes essential for the acquisition of necessary supplies and the subsequent distribution of his books. And, when endeavoring to produce illustrated editions, Plantin had to contend with an artist's own ambitions, current status, and resulting willingness (or not) to help make book illustrations for someone else. With all of these independent forces limiting his options, it appears that – at least in terms of the illustration of his books – Plantin was often left in an oddly dichotomous situation. For the designs for his plates, he relied primarily on just three artists, two of whom – Peeter vander Borcht and Crispin van den Broeck – were clearly on good personal terms with both Plantin and his friend the Spanish theologian Arias Montano. The third artist, Gerard van Groeningen, was most likely at least known to Arias Montano (if not on friendly terms) through their mutual work on several print projects organized by Philips Galle, who was also part of Plantin's and Arias Montano's intimate circle of artist friends. Noteworthy here, particularly in contrast with the engravers Plantin hired, is the fact that all of the draughtsmen Plantin employed were established figures, active designing prints for prominent Antwerp print publishers for several years before they worked for Plantin. Some, like Maarten van Heemskerck, Hans Vredeman de Vries, and Otto

[113] Cf. Burke 1993, pp. 53 and 56.

van Veen, were only engaged to work on an exceptional project for Plantin. For others, however, like vander Borcht, van den Broeck, van Groeningen, and even de Vos, this was clearly an acceptable form of employment throughout or at least toward the end of their careers.

Plantin could not, by contrast, rely upon similar good contacts with a comparable circle of respected figures to make the engravings he needed. Of all the engravers Plantin worked with, he was on friendly terms with just one, Philips Galle, who rarely provided him with engravings. Matters were significantly different for etched plates, as Plantin's close friend Peeter vander Borcht appears to have made most of those. And while a few of the engravers he initially hired were established artists who had previously (or simultaneously) furnished the famed Antwerp print publisher Hieronymus Cock with engravings, they rarely worked for Plantin for long. Either they happened to die soon thereafter (as was the case with Frans Huys and Pieter van der Heyden) or else they simply declined to work further for Plantin (as was the case with Philips Galle). Plantin presumably also had his own, independent contacts in the Antwerp print world through his early and continued dealings in maps and independent prints. Perhaps this is how he learned of young local artists who were willing to work for him in the years just prior to or following their registration as masters in the St. Luke's guild – as occurred with the Wierix brothers, Jan Sadeler I, Crispijn van de Passe, and Hans Collaert II. But these younger artists were all less inclined to continue to work for Plantin as they endeavored to establish themselves as independent engravers. Either they sought more money for their work than Plantin wished to pay (as was the case with the Wierixes) or else they did not wish to devote their time and energy to producing engravings that they, aspiring top engravers and print publishers, would not control (as was the case with Jan Sadeler, for example).

Thus, while Plantin presumably learned of the artists who could help produce his intaglio illustrations via the Antwerp print world generally, it was precisely the fame and draw of this world for aspiring young artists that made Plantin's efforts to secure the engravings he needed for his publications all the more difficult. The prevailing disinclination of established engravers to make someone else's book illustrations, and the growing scarcity of artists as a result of the siege and subsequent fall of Antwerp in 1585, were probably the primary factors that forced Plantin into his ever more frustrating, perpetual search for new engravers in the 1580s and resulting increasing reliance on etchers in this decade. These concerns, however, do not seem to have affected Plantin's primary copper-plate printers, for Mynken Liefrinck and Jacques vander Hoeven were evidently content to work – even, periodically, at low, day-laborer's wages – printing other people's copper plates. Thus, they became the people upon whom Plantin relied most regularly for the production of his luxury editions with intaglio illustrations.

Personal contacts, personal prestige, and matters of money. With such a combination of issues to juggle and resolve in order to find the best affordable and willing mix of artists to make and print intaglio book illustrations, is it surprising that, at certain points in his career, Plantin was not eager to undertake such projects? This was the case, for example, in August 1567, just one year after Plantin's publication of Juan de

Valverde's *Vivae imagines partium corporis humani*, with forty-two engraved illustrations.[114] Regardless of the precise mix of concerns that influenced Plantin in the summer of 1567, he changed his perspective dramatically within just two years. In the following chapters we will examine his extraordinary shift from this unwilling stance. For, not only was Plantin to become the leader in the production of books with intaglio illustrations by the mid-1570s, he even fought to maintain his position in the market for such books in the 1580s, when Antwerp had ceased to function as the northern European center of prints and trade.

[114] See ch. 3 for a fuller discussion of this issue and Plantin's first editions with intaglio illustrations.

CHAPTER THREE

PLANTIN'S FIRST PROJECTS WITH ENGRAVINGS (1559–1571)

But as for illustrations engraved in copper, I do not think that this is something I can have anything to do with, nor be involved in; yet if it is a matter of some figures for books that might be woodcuts, then I will gladly do this job.[1]

This was Christopher Plantin's response (sent on August 8, 1567) to a request from the Italian theologian and scholar, Onufrio Panvinio, to print a book of his on Roman antiquity with engraved illustrations.[2] Plantin's reluctance to take on the project is all the more poignant, as the request had been made via an influential patron, Cardinal Granvelle, whom Plantin would normally seek to accommodate. The crux of the problem is clarified in Plantin's and Granvelle's subsequent correspondence on the matter in the fall of 1567. Although Panvinio already had some of the twenty-four desired illustrations engraved and had designs ready for the rest, someone had to be found to engrave the remaining images (and presumably print the lot). Panvinio suggested that Plantin ask the well-known (and also local) print publisher Hieronymus Cock to assist in the matter and offered to split the costs and the profits for the entire project. But, according to Plantin, Cock refused to become involved, citing numerous existing commitments and a reluctance to work with someone living as far away as Rome.[3] This brought a definite end to the discussion, and Panvinio's own death several months later, in April 1568, meant that he would never see the realization of this publication.

---

[1] See Corr., III, no. 342, Plantin to Cardinal Granvelle, on August 8, 1567, for the following excerpt: "Mais quant est des figures taillées en cuivre, je ne voys pas que ce soit chose là où je m'entende ne de quoy je me doibve mesler aucunement: bien s'il est besoing de quelques figures aux livres, les quelles se puissent tailler en bois, en feray-je volontiers le devoir."

[2] It is not clear which of Panvinio's texts was involved here. On this matter, see Ferrary 1996, pp. 23–28.

[3] For Plantin's and Granvelle's correspondence on this matter see Corr., III, no. 342, and Corr. supplément, nos. 33, 36, and 41. Plantin's report of Cock's refusal to take on this project is recorded in Corr. supplément, no. 41, and reads as follows: "J'ay communiqué avec nostre compere et amy Hierosme Cocq l'intention dudict Padre Onoffrio touchant les figures des antiquites et remonstré le bon espoir de la distribution dudict œuvre. Mais il m'a respondu absolument que, outre ce qu'il est par trop occupé a dautres ouvrages commencés, il ne fut onques d'advis de se mectre en compagnie daucun, ne d'accueillir aucun en la sienne, et moins le vouldroit il faire avec aucun tant eslongne du lieu de sa demeure comme est Romme."

Such circumstances were not unique at this point in Plantin's career. Another Italian scholar, Fulvio Orsini, whose work Granvelle had also recommended to Plantin for publication around 1567, similarly found engraved illustrations more attractive than woodcuts. But once again, Plantin had to disappoint his Italian author by persisting with using woodcuts instead.[4] Plantin may have consequently lost potential commissions for books to other publishers, like Antonio Lafreri in Rome, who would satisfy Panvinio's and Orsini's wishes to have their publications illustrated with engravings as early as 1568 and 1570, respectively.[5]

Why was Plantin so hesitant to take on these requests for books with engraved illustrations? He had been actively engaged in the sale of independent engravings since 1558 and had already worked on the publication of two works with such illustrations by 1567.[6] Thus, he was capable of surmounting the essential difficulties inherent in such a production, namely, amassing the financial means necessary to cover the extra production costs and finding an artist or print publisher who could produce and print the engraved illustrations. Nevertheless, these initial ventures apparently did not assure Plantin of his ability to take on new commissions of this sort. Within a few years, however, Plantin's earlier concerns were vanquished, as he then produced three stunning independent publications with engraved illustrations between 1570 and 1572. These were a landmark, scholarly polyglot bible in eight large folio volumes; a sumptuous, old-fashioned book of hours; and a novel theological emblem book.[7]

These three editions do not simply represent a great, one-time effort on Plantin's part. Rather, they mark a dramatic and significant shift in Plantin's work, as he proceeded to establish himself as the leading publisher of books with engraved illustrations in all of Europe. In order to understand this important alteration in Plantin's production better, we will devote this chapter to a detailed examination of Plantin's production of books with engraved illustrations during the first sixteen years of his career as a printer-publisher (c.1555–c.1571). Given Plantin's later reputation, it may come as a surprise that in this period Plantin published just seven distinct texts with engraved illustrations.[8] Although clearly representing a very small percentage of Plantin's total

---

[4] Consider Plantin's 1568 edition of Orsini's *Carmina novem illustrium feminarum* (PP 917), which comprises a woodcut image of Sappho, that instigated the following remark from Orsini (as related to Plantin by Granvelle), namely: "L'effigie de Sapho luy plaict bien, mais il vouldroit qu'elle fut taillée en cuyvre, et a la verité elle seroit plus belle, oyres que celluy qu'a taillé le bois . . ." (He likes the image of Sappho, but he would like to have it engraved in copper; in truth, it would be even more attractive than if it is cut in wood . . .) (Van Durme 1962, p. 282).

[5] For examples of Lafreri's (and others') publications of both Orsini's and Panvinio's texts with engraved illustrations (albeit posthumously in the case of the latter), see, e.g., Mortimer 1974, nos. 329 and 330 (for Orsini) and nos. 356 and 357 (for Panvinio).

[6] On Plantin's sale of independent prints, see Delen 1932 and ch. 2. For his first two publications with engraved illustrations, see the discussion below of *La pompe funèbre* (PP 939) from 1559, and Juan de Valverde's *Vivae imagines partium corporis humani* (PP 2413), first published by Plantin in 1566.

[7] The respective titles of these works are: *Biblia sacra* (PP 644), *Horae beatissimae Virginis Mariae* (PP 1565–1568), and Benito Arias Montano's *Humanae salutis monumenta* (PP 588). Each of these works is discussed in greater detail below.

[8] In addition to the five works cited in nn. 6 and 7, Plantin also produced a Dutch edition of his anatomical work in 1568 (PP 2416) and Clemens Perret's engraved examples of calligraphy, his *Exercitatio alphabetica nova et utilissima*, in 1569 (PP 1961). We have not included Plantin's 1568 publication of Petrus Bacherius's *Panicus tumultus, rebus in Belgio pacatis, ac mire tranquillis, quorundam improbitate iniectus* (PP 620) in this

production at this time,[9] these works are worth examining in full for the information they provide on Plantin's evolving position in this still uncommon, yet burgeoning realm of publishing. Specifically, after serving as a "guest co-publisher" of a regal commemorative print series in 1559, Plantin then experimented with the production of an anatomical text with engraved illustrations in the early 1560s, as several printers had done before him. It was not until 1569–1571, however, when Plantin was nearly fifty years old, that he began his own trend-setting ventures in the field of intaglio book illustration with his stunning and technically unprecedented book of hours and emblem book. In the course of this chapter we will endeavor to determine what motivated Plantin to attempt each of these projects, how he resolved the difficulties inherent in producing such books, and what he ultimately achieved. The answers to these questions may not be so simple, for as Plantin's dealings with his potential Italian clients around 1567 reveal, he, alone, was not always able to determine the outcome of his projects. Rather, their successful completion depended upon the participation of several other individuals, from the author of the text to the craftsmen needed to make and print the plates. In addition, the resulting publication had to be an appealing product that Plantin could both finance and sell. As we investigate Plantin's first attempts to produce books with engraved illustrations, we will examine the interplay of these various interdependent aspects. The result will be a thorough appreciation of what Plantin achieved (or did not) with each edition, enhanced by a heightened understanding of what led to his breakthrough. Could Plantin have anticipated the forthcoming transformation of his production? Probably not. But this is what makes an examination of the process all the more worthwhile.

SELF-CONSCIOUS VENERATION AND PROPAGANDA IN SUPPORT OF THE SPANISH CROWN: *LA POMPE FUNÈBRE* IN HONOR OF CHARLES V

Several years before he died, the Holy Roman Emperor Charles V (1500–1558) began the process of transferring the rule of the Low Countries, along with other parts of his vast empire, to his son Philip II (1527–1598). This process included arranging state entries for Philip in all of the important cities in the Low Countries in 1549 and Charles's official abdication of the throne in 1555.[10] Nevertheless, the definitive transfer of his title of king of Spain to Philip could not take place until his death. When Charles died in September 1558 at a hieronymite monastery in the Spanish city of Yuste, a simple service was performed by the monks residing there. It was all part of Charles V's desire to pass his final years in a devout religious retreat.[11] Philip II,

---

group because there is no evidence that the engraved portrait of the author inserted in some copies was originally part of the publication, as produced by Plantin.

[9] According to Voet's estimates (Voet 1984, pp. 363–365), Plantin produced approximately 650 distinct publications in the period 1555–1571.

[10] For more on these state entries, see, e.g., Schrader 1998, p. 70 and n. 11. For references to contemporary accounts of them, see n. 13 below.

[11] For a detailed account of both Charles V's death and Philip's subsequent use of the occasion for his own political needs, see Schrader 1998. While highly informative, two important corrections must be made.

3.1 Jan or Lucas van Doetecum after Hieronymus Cock, *Procession with Musicians*, from *La magnifique et sumptueuse pompe funèbre faite aus obseques et funerailles du . . . empereur Charles Cinquième . . . en la ville de Bruxelles* (Antwerp: Christopher Plantin, 1559; oblong f°), plates 2–3, etching and engraving, *c.*240 × 32.5 each (Antwerp, Museum Plantin-Moretus, R 44.8).

however, decided to stage an unusually large and extravagant commemoration of Charles V's death in Brussels on December 28–29, 1558. Philip's goal appears to have been "to create a spectacle of royal strength" within the tradition of Burgundian funerary rites at a moment when the Spanish crown might otherwise have been perceived as weak. Through the various classes of people assembled, the symbolic floats created, and the concluding religious service, Charles V's achievements as a great military and Christian ruler were highlighted, while Philip's role as the successor to Charles's accomplishments and kingdom was emphasized.[12]

Although this elaborately devised commemoration-coronation was a one-time event, a more lasting record of it was published in 1559 in a textual and visual form. This was not unusual in the Low Countries. A printed account of the mass held in Brussels for Charles V's grandfather Ferdinand of Aragon appeared in 1515, while works commemorating Charles V's numerous state entries in the former German empire and the Low Countries, including those made with his son Philip in 1549, were also regularly published.[13] Within this familiar context, however, the commemorative publication for Charles V's death stands out dramatically because of the exceptional use of engraved and etched illustrations instead of the traditional woodcuts.

First, when Plantin printed the text for *La pompe funèbre* in 1559, he was not the royal printer in the Low Countries, as Schrader suggests (p. 89). Rather, one of Plantin's competitors, Willem Silvius, was granted this title in 1560 (Rouzet 1975, p. 201); Plantin did not receive comparable titles for another decade (Voet, GC, I, pp. 70–72). Second, the artists who executed the prints for *La pompe funèbre*, the van Doetecum brothers, were most likely employed by the print publisher Hieronymus Cock (see Riggs 1977, pp. 60 and 292). There is no evidence that they were ever employed by Plantin directly, as Schrader suggests (p. 89).

[12] Schrader 1998, pp. 70, 79–81, and 86.

[13] For a summary description of these publications and later editions thereof, cf., e.g., Landwehr 1971, nos. 1–26, and Simon and Watanabe-O'Kelly 2000, nos. 1, 2, and 6–9. For a more general discussion of these types of publications, see, e.g., Mulryne et al. 2004.

Degrees of responsibility for La pompe funèbre

Commonly referred to as La pompe funèbre (an abbreviated form of the French title), this work comprised two parts.[14] The visual record of the funeral procession consisted of a series of thirty-four prints designed by Hieronymus Cock and executed by Joannes and Lucas van Doetecum in a combination of etching and engraving. The prints themselves bear inscriptions identifying some of the individuals represented, in addition to an occasional explanatory text in Latin (fig. 3.1). An accompanying textual account of the funeral procession was printed separately by Plantin in each of the then common vernacular languages: Dutch, French, German, Italian, and Spanish. It is evident from both archival records and preserved copies that this series of prints was sold either as a roll, such that the entire procession could be viewed as a single frieze, approximately twenty meters long, or else as a book, with each of the plates bound in individually, together with the accompanying text.[15]

The division of labor among the aforementioned figures is documented by the publication itself. The van Doetecums, whom Cock regularly employed as of 1554,[16] signed plate 2 "Ioannes a duetecum Lucas duetecum. Fecit," while plate 32 is signed "Hieronymus Cock. Inve[nit] 1559." Cock does appear to have sold some copies of this publication. For example, among the few sales records still preserved for this period, Cock is noted to have purchased three copies of La pompe funèbre with the Italian text on April 28, 1561, while he supplied Plantin with two copies of the German version of the publication in roll form on December 9, 1566.[17] However, the same archival documents make it equally clear that Plantin played a greater role in organizing the production and distribution of this publication.[18]

The largest single quantity of copies known to have passed through Plantin's hands is a selection of 143 copies of La pompe funèbre that he had received from Philip's herald of arms, Pierre de Vernois.[19] De Vernois invested at least 2,000 fl. himself in the production of La pompe funèbre, and also requested a subsidy from the Spanish regent of the Low Countries, Margaret of Parma.[20] Aside from 12 copies that were to be sent to Paris, the remainder of this large consignment was sent to the Frankfurt book fair. It included copies in all five languages, some in book form, some in rolls, some already bound in parchment, and two that were hand-painted. In addition, however, at least 197 rolls

---

[14] A more complete version of the French title is La magnifique et sumptueuse pompe funèbre faite aus obseques et funerailles du . . . empereur Charles Cinquième . . . en la vile de Bruxelles. The full title of this work, as it appears in each of the cited languages, is given in PP 939 and in New Holl., Van Doetecum, 1, pp. 67–68. Both of these works have a detailed discussion of this publication with bibliographic references. Predictably, the former is better for commentary on the typographical aspects and sales of the series, while the latter provides a useful overview of the states in which the various prints are found. See also Riggs 1977, pp. 288–294. While S. Schrader's 1998 article is by far the most substantive of the publications that have appeared since Voet, PP and New Holl., Van Doetecum, the entry (no. 63) by Javier Docampo Capilla in Seville 2000 and the catalogue's extensive concluding list of references are also highly useful.

[15] See below for examples of the sale of this publication in both book and roll form.

[16] Riggs 1977, p. 292.　　[17] See MPM Arch. 35, fol. 183v, and MPM Arch. 37, fol. 50 rht, respectively.

[18] Voet notes (PP 939c) that Cock is also cited as the seller in the imprint found on a copy of the Dutch version of the text (KB Den Haag: 1043 B). However, the reference to Cock comes from a separately printed piece of paper that was affixed to one of the prints. Thus, it is not certain that Cock was named as a seller of this series on all copies of the Dutch version. Plantin's name was included in the imprint of each language variant.

[19] See MPM Arch. 35, fol. 177 rht.　　[20] PP 939, n. 2.

of the prints, as well as an unspecified number of extra copies, were also sold at the auction of Plantin's possessions held on April 28, 1562.[21] These two large collections of copies, together with another 40 copies sold individually at various points in time, imply that more than 400 copies of this publication had been in Plantin's hands between 1560 and 1562.[22] As will become evident in the course of this book, 400 impressions or more of one set of intaglios was a significant number at this time. Thus, these copies may well have represented the bulk of those printed.

Just as important, however, in determining "degrees of responsibility" in the production of this work is another entry from the April 1562 auction of Plantin's property, which documents the sale of the copper plates used to print the illustrations.[23] This is particularly significant when one recalls how Cock and the van Doetecums made their involvement in the production of the plates for this project undeniably clear through the inclusion of their names on the thirty-second and second plates, respectively. Plantin's possession of the plates is all the more noteworthy given that the form of the publication, a series of prints with a brief, separately printed and appended text, was closer to what a print publisher would produce than would a printer of books.

Consequently, despite the various indications of some sort of cooperative venture – the external funding of the project by de Vernois and Margaret of Parma and Cock's part in the production of the prints and the sale of some copies – Plantin appears to have been the one who was ultimately in charge of the publication. Not only did he control the sale of a sizable number of copies of the work, but he had also retained the plates (at least initially) and with them the control over any subsequent publication and sale of the images. This would have impeded even a partner in the production of the original edition, like Cock, from independently producing a comparable (and hence competitive) publication. Whether Plantin had simply purchased the plates, during or following the initial production of this work, or gained control of them through other means, remains unclear. Regardless of how it was arranged, Plantin was hereby initiated into the world of publishing texts with engraved illustrations.

Fitting La pompe funèbre in Plantin's œuvre

Why Plantin would have been favored with this spectacular commission instead of any of the other established publishers in Antwerp remains a mystery. For example, as noted above, Willem Silvius had enough stature and connections to be named the "royal printer" in 1560.[24] The publication was also highly exceptional for Plantin's œuvre at the time, while other established printers – the Nutius family and Gilles Coppens van Diest I, for example – had already produced comparable works.[25] Although some

---

[21] This auction is discussed in greater detail below.   [22] For these sales, see PP 939, nn. 5–7.

[23] See MPM Arch. 27, fol. 38r, for the following reference to the sale of the original copper plates: "de plaeten ende figuren vande vuytvaert vande keyser xxi £ × s" (the plates and the figures of the funeral of the king, for 21 Flemish pounds and 10 schellingen [= 129 fl.]). In 1601, a number of these plates were cited in an inventory of the possessions of Cock's widow, Volcxken Diericx (see New Holl., Van Doetecum, I, p. 67).

[24] Compare n. 11 above.

[25] See Riggs 1977, p. 292, and Voet, GC, I, p. 33, for similar observations. For related editions printed by other known Antwerp printers, see, e.g., Landwehr 1971, nos. 23–25.

of Plantin's other publications to date were illustrated, none contained engravings or etchings. Similarly, in terms of the content of his publications, Plantin had thus far favored texts that would sell readily and appeal to a broader audience instead of the more limited elite class who would have been interested in and could pay for *La pompe funèbre*. Even in terms of Plantin's subsequent production, which would feature a variety of texts with engraved illustrations, this remains an anomaly owing to the predominance of the suite of engravings and the brief, occasionally appended text. As observed above, the structure of this work is much more akin to what a print publisher would produce than a printer-publisher of books, like Plantin. The best single comparison among Plantin's publications from this period is an album of thirty-three examples of calligraphy designed by Clemens Perret and engraved by other artists, which Plantin published in 1569. And yet, despite having obtained a privilege to publish this series of plates and paid for the printing of the plate bearing this text, along with his name, Plantin does not appear to have played an important role in its publication or distribution. He had to buy copies of the work from Etienne Perret – who is assumed to be the father of Clemens – and he does not appear to have owned or arranged for the printing of the main plates used to produce it.[26]

If *La pompe funèbre* was exceptional in terms of Plantin's work to date as a printer, persuasive personal connections may offer the best explanation yet for his being asked to work on this grand project. In 1556 Plantin published two poems in honor of Philip II. One was by an Antwerp orator, Cornelius Ghistelius, while the other was written by Plantin himself supposedly with the encouragement of a few loyal members of Philip's retinue. Two copies of Plantin's poem are mentioned in a catalogue of Philip II's library.[27] Although the "few loyal members" of Philip's retinue are not named in Plantin's text, he does allude to Philip's "tresprudent secretaire," which could refer to either Gabriel de Çayas or Gonzalo Perez.[28] Although both men had dealings with Plantin in this period, de Çayas is the better candidate as a persuasive advocate for Plantin. Said to have met when the latter was still working as a bookbinder and tooler of leather around 1554–1555, de Çayas supported Plantin throughout his career.[29] In particular, in the later 1560s de Çayas played an important role in garnering Philip II's financial support for Plantin's famed Polyglot Bible, which was also illustrated with engravings.[30]

Regardless of the origin of this commission, however, Plantin's introduction to the realm of producing texts with engraved illustrations had occurred via an overtly

[26] See ch. 5 for more on Etienne Perret and PP 1961, n. 2, for Plantin's privilege for Clemens Perret's publication. In *New Holl., Van Doetecum*, II, nos. 483–517, the borders to these plates for the latter project are identified as the work of the van Doetecum brothers, after designs by Hans Vredeman de Vries, the engraved letters are attributed to Cornelis de Hooghe, and the edition is said to have also been printed and published by Ameet Tavernier in Antwerp in 1569.

[27] For Ghistelius's work, see Landwehr 1971, no. 26; for Plantin's, see PP 2058. Both are discussed in Imhof 1992, nos. 76–77.

[28] Imhof 1992, p. 193.

[29] For the account of Plantin's first contact with de Çayas – involving an attack on Plantin in 1554 or 1555, when he was bringing de Çayas a leather box he had made – and his subsequent importance to Plantin, see Voet, GC, I, pp. 18–20 and 56.

[30] Plantin's Polyglot (or "Royal") Bible is discussed at length below.

propagandistic account of the lavish funeral procession Philip II had organized in the name of Charles V and in his own name as Charles V's successor. Apparently it appealed to Plantin, for within a year of the completion of *La pompe funèbre*, Plantin began on another publication with engraved illustrations, namely, an edition of Juan de Valverde's anatomical treatise. This time, however, the resulting book would be an independently conceived project that Plantin sought to present to the magistrates of the city of Antwerp as a token of his gratitude to them, an example of the skill of Antwerp's artists, and, let us not forget, an exemplary publication by one of its typographers as well.

ANATOMICAL ILLUSTRATIONS FOR JUAN DE VALVERDE'S *VIVAE IMAGINES PARTIUM CORPORIS HUMANI*

In the foreword to his 1566 edition of Juan de Valverde's *Vivae imagines partium corporis humani* (Images of the Human Body taken from Life), an anatomical work illustrated with forty-two engravings and dedicated to the Antwerp city magistrates, Plantin suggests why he decided to attempt to produce this book:[31]

Having long sought an opportunity to produce a token of my thankfulness for your lofty station,[32] renowned sirs, I finally learned that an anatomical book by a certain ingenious de Valverde had been published in Italy with engraved illustrations. It was done with such skill that it easily surpassed the efforts of all those who had previously taken on the same task. As soon as I had obtained a copy of the publication, I immediately began an assiduous search to see if there was no craftsman in your city who could measure up to the Italians. Once I found such a person (and after having put his expertise and skill to the test first), I immediately immersed myself in the project, hoping that speed would also bring some esteem with it.[33]

Clearly seeking to appeal to feelings of local pride, Plantin even had the city arms (along with those of Philip II) included in the engraved architectural frame used for the title-page (fig. 3.2). It is equally evident from this same foreword, however, that Plantin simultaneously sought to promote himself as the local printer who could

---

[31] Plantin's dedicatory text was included on fols. A2r–A3v of both the original 1566 Latin edition (PP 2413) and the 1572/1579 reprint thereof (PP 2414–2415). The excerpt cited here reads: "Cum autem, ut meae erga vestram celsitudinem, clatissimi [sic] domini, gratitudinis indicium exhiberem, diu oportunitatem captassem; tandem intellexi ingeniosissimi cuiusdam Valverdae Anatomen illustratam imaginibus aeri insculptis, in Italia excusam esse: idque tanto artificio, ut omnes qui prius huic labori operam navassent, facile superaret. Hanc ut primum nancisci potui, continuo diligenter inquisivi, an nullus in hac vestra civitate artifex esset, qui cum Italis paria facere posset: talem cum invenissem, facto imprimis illius solertiae atque dexteritatis periculo, statim operi adhibui, sperans celeritatem aliquid etiam commendationis allaturam." This text was replaced in the 1568 Dutch edition (PP 2416) with a dedication (in French) to Gérard Grammay, the treasurer of the city of Antwerp.

[32] Further on in this same foreword, Plantin clarifies his feelings of gratitude towards the city magistrates, by recalling how they eased his return to Antwerp following the "trouble" at his Press concerning the printing of a heretical text and his resulting self-imposed exile in Paris. This topic is discussed in greater detail below.

[33] For the Italian edition of de Valverde's text, *Anatomia del corpo humano* (Venice: Niccolò Bevilacqua, for Antonio Salamanca and Antoine Lafreri at Rome, 1559 and 1560), see, e.g., Cushing 1962, p. 148, and Mortimer 1974, no. 513. Although a copy of the 1560 issue is preserved in the Plantin-Moretus Museum (B 850), this was purchased in 1872 (see the note on the front flyleaf) and thus cannot have served as the copy that Plantin used as his model.

3.2 Pieter Huys after Lambert van Noort, title-plate to Juan de Valverde, *Vivae imagines partium corporis humani* (Antwerp: Christopher Plantin, 1566; 4°), engraving, 251 × 165 (Antwerp, Museum Plantin-Moretus, A 1358).

produce quality publications such as this, which were prepared together with learned individuals. Not only does Plantin lament the poor quality of his contemporaries' publications, but he is so bold as to assert the superiority of his own. When discussing the present publication in particular, Plantin is also careful to defend its scholarly value, noting what it has to offer in contrast with recent editions of comparable texts.[34]

[34] See p. [5] of Plantin's foreword for these remarks.

Thus, it appears that Plantin hoped to achieve two distinct, but related goals with this publication, namely, to produce a work that would, on the one hand, comprise remarkable illustrations and, on the other, represent a valuable scholarly asset. Through both of these aspects, as well as his flattering dedication, he clearly hoped to garner positive acclaim for himself as the printer responsible for producing it. Representing Plantin's first fully independent attempt to produce a book with engraved illustrations, this work is obviously of great significance for this study. But was Plantin's rendition of this anatomical work also a successful, satisfactory means of winning the recognition he clearly hoped to gain at that point in time? In order to answer this question, we first need to examine the most important precedents for Plantin's edition.

Precedents for Plantin's anatomical publications

Although Plantin cites the Italian edition of de Valverde's work as the primary source of inspiration for his own, much of de Valverde's text and, more to the point, the vast majority of the illustrations were based upon Andreas Vesalius's groundbreaking text, *De humani corporis fabrica* (first edition: Basel: Johannes Oporinus, 1543).[35] Vesalius's text was revolutionary owing to its break from the old theories of Galenic anatomy, whereby human anatomy was explained on the basis of animals and not, as was the case with Vesalius's and de Valverde's work, on the basis of human dissections. The illustrations – eye-catching woodcuts attributed to Jan (or Hans) Stephan van Calcar (or Kalcar) – ranged from emotive, full-length skeletons and details of individual groups of bones, to diagrams of the muscles, internal organs, and the arteries (see, for example, figs. 3.3 and 3.8).

Not surprisingly, Vesalius's publication was imitated by others. The first such work was Thomas Geminus's *Compendiosa totius anatomie delineatio* (London: John Herford, 1545).[36] Textually, this publication was noteworthy for Geminus's reworking of Vesalius's own summary of his *Fabrica*, the so-called *Epitome* (first edition: Basel: Johannes Oporinus, 1543), which would, in turn, be used by other authors. It is also famous for the forty-seven engravings used to illustrate it. Renowned as an exceptionally early example of engravings used as book illustrations in England (if not the first), most of these plates were relatively faithful copies of the original Vesalian woodcuts that would, themselves, be reused and imitated (see figs. 3.3 and 3.4). Consequently, as is discussed in the Introduction, Geminus's *Compendiosa totius anatomie delineatio* is often regarded as a landmark in the history of producing books with engraved illustrations because it was one of the first books with such illustrations to achieve what appears to have been

---

[35] For more on Vesalius, de Valverde, their publications, and numerous imitations and variants thereof, see, e.g., BB, V, pp. 688–722, under "Vesale"; Cockx-Indestege 1994; and Cushing 1962. For a detailed examination of the original Vesalian illustrations, see, for example, Saunders and O'Malley 1950. For a detailed comparison of the "Vesalius" and "de Valverde" illustrations, see Meyer and Wirt 1943. The specific number of imitated and truly "original" images among de Valverde's illustrations varies according to the author.

[36] For accounts of Geminus's influential publication and related editions, see, for example, Cushing 1962, pp. 119–130.

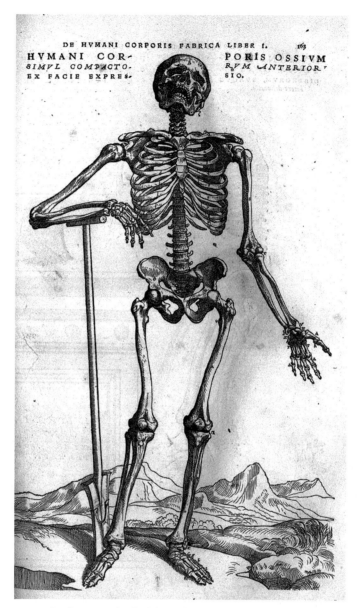

3.3 Jan Stephan van Calcar?, *Skeleton*, from Andreas Vesalius, *De humani corporis fabrica* (Basel: Johannes Oporinus, 1543; f°), p. 163, woodcut, 248 × 145 (Antwerp, Stadsbibliotheek, J 5833). See figs. 3.4–3.6 for copies of this image.

real commercial success, as a result of the then exceptional reuse of its illustrations for subsequent publications. And yet, it was not this publication (or any of the editions derived from it), but de Valverde's, the third significant plagiarism of Vesalius's work and illustrations, that attracted Plantin's attention. The forty-two engravings used in the 1559/1560 Italian edition cited by Plantin were originally engraved for Lafreri's and Salamanca's Spanish edition of de Valverde's text, which was printed in Rome in

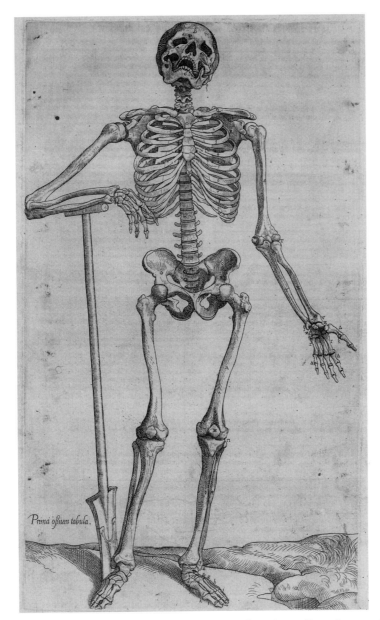

3.4 Anonymous artist, *Skeleton*, from Thomas Geminus, *Compendiosa totius anatomie delineatio* (London: John Herford, 1545; f°), "Prima ossium tabula," inserted following fol. ʙiii, engraving, 336 × 195 (Ghent, Universiteitsbibliotheek, Kostbare werken, Acc. 9952). This was based on fig. 3.3.

1556. Most were relatively free and (in de Valverde's own words) occasionally corrected copies of the Vesalian woodcuts (compare figs. 3.3 and 3.5).[37] Ultimately, however, it

37 For de Valverde's original Spanish edition, *Historia de la composicion del cuerpo humano* (Rome: Antonio Blado for Antonio Salamanca and Antoine Lafreri, 1556), see, for example, Cushing 1962, pp. 146–147, and Mortimer 1974, no. 513. Mortimer notes that the design of these plates and the title-page are

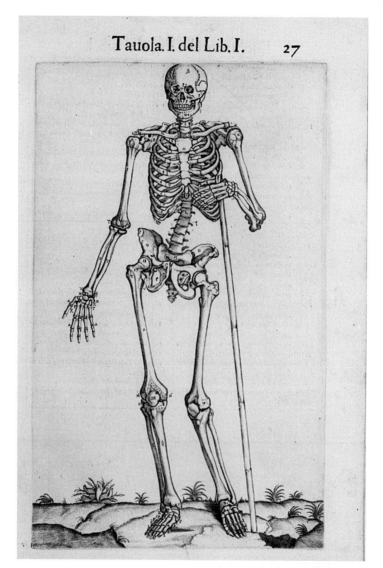

3.5 Nicolas Beatrizet after Gaspar Becerra, *Skeleton*, from Juan de Valverde, *Anatomia del corpo humano* (Venice: Niccolò Bevilacqua for Antonio Salamanca and Antonio Lafreri at Rome, 1560; f°), fol. 27r, engraving, *c.*235 × 140 (Antwerp, Museum Plantin-Moretus, B 850).

was only this set of engravings (and their accompanying explanatory notes) that Plantin had copied from de Valverde's publications (see figs. 3.5 and 3.6) and not his more extensive commentary. Rather, Plantin combined his set of illustrations with Jacques Grévin's revision of Geminus's rendition of Vesalius's own *Epitome*. Cited explicitly in Plantin's foreword to his own 1566 edition, Grévin's work was published in 1564

attributed to Gaspar Becerra, while Nicolas Beatrizet engraved them. The plates subsequently came into the hands of the Giunta Press, which used them for its own editions of de Valverde's text (see Cushing 1962, pp. 148–150). For references to de Valverde's remarks on the relationship between his plates and Vesalius's, see, e.g., the notes on the first de Valverde edition in Cushing 1962, p. 146.

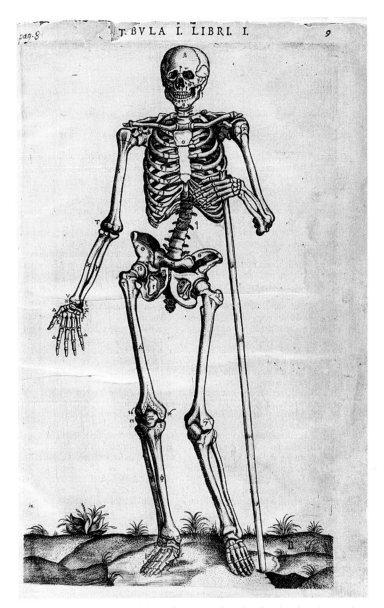

3.6 Frans or Pieter Huys, *Skeleton*, from Juan de Valverde, *Vivae imagines partium corporis humani* (Antwerp: Christopher Plantin, 1566; 4°), p. 9, engraving, 238 × 142 (Antwerp, Museum Plantin-Moretus, A 1358). This was based on fig. 3.5.

by the Parisian printer André Wechel and illustrated with impressions of Geminus's plates.[38]

As the preceding sample of illustrations (figs. 3.3–3.6) indicates, the original Vesalian woodcuts were copied with varying degrees of faithfulness, artistic license,

---

[38] See J. de Valverde, *Vivae imagines . . .* (Antwerp: Christopher Plantin, 1566), fols. A2v–A3r, for these remarks. On the Grévin edition, see, e.g., Cushing 1962, pp. 128–130, and Mortimer 1964, no. 541.

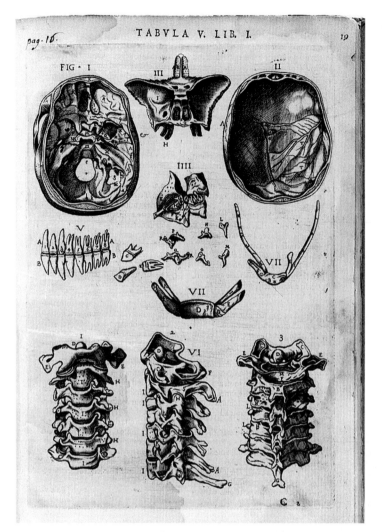

3.7 Frans or Pieter Huys, *Bones*, from Juan de Valverde, *Vivae imagines partium corporis humani* (Antwerp: Christopher Plantin, 1566; 4°), p. 19, engraving, 238 × 142 (Antwerp, Museum Plantin-Moretus, A 1358). Compare details VII here with fig. 3.8.

and, in the case of the illustrations de Valverde commissioned and Plantin had copied, occasional deliberate deviations from the 1543 originals.[39] Generally, while the Geminus plates appear to have been the most faithful to the originals, de Valverde's illustrations document how some artists took greater liberties with the Vesalian models, altering the facial expressions, the accompanying scenery, and reversing some figures. Although the engravers Frans and Pieter Huys, who copied de Valverde's illustrations for Plantin, attempted to do so faithfully, they did reverse some plates, with the more serious result of producing factually inaccurate diagrams in two cases. The fact that

[39] See n. 35 above for references to detailed comparative studies of the Vesalian and Valverdian illustrations.

3.8 Jan Stephan van Calcar?, *Bones*, from Andreas Vesalius, *De humani corporis fabrica* (Basel: Johannes Oporinus, 1543; f°), p. 55, woodcuts, 47 × 49 and 19 × 42 (Antwerp, Stadsbibliotheek, J 5833).

these errors were allowed into print – and were noted by some readers (see fig. 3.9) – is particularly significant given Plantin's assertions in his foreword concerning the superior quality of his own scholarly publications in general and the advantages of this edition in particular.[40]

These formal issues aside, all of these sets of engravings do share some important traits in comparison with the Vesalian woodcuts, simply because of the inherent differences between engraved and woodcut illustrations. One of the most obvious issues is that of clarity in rendering the desired detail and lettered keys. This concern surely contributed to the early success of engravings in the fifteenth and sixteenth centuries for the illustration of minutely described, information-carrying images, such as maps, architectural designs, and other scholarly aids.[41] An additional, less obvious matter, however, also had significant consequences for how these books were illustrated. For, as is demonstrated by a comparison of figs. 3.7 and 3.8, images that were originally true (woodcut) text illustrations, set within the columns of text wherever appropriate, became, with the switch to engravings, part of a larger plate containing a collection of detailed drawings, independent of a textual content. Although one may argue that the new combination of smaller images would have eased the comparison of related figures that had previously been separated by pages of text, that does not appear to have been the primary goal of the new arrangement. Rather, a decision to illustrate these texts with engravings instead of woodcuts, which was made on visual grounds, necessitated, owing to practical concerns of cost and technique, a change in layout that resulted in the loss of the immediate connection between text and image. It would have been much more costly and extremely complicated technically to produce several smaller individual plates for true text illustrations instead of one larger plate. Consider fig. 3.7. If de Valverde (and Plantin) had tried to imitate the placement of Vesalius's illustrations faithfully, they would have had to commission at least six separate plates instead of the single more compact "group plate" seen here, which would have represented a much more significant total investment in copper and labor for the preparation of the plates.[42] In addition, even if someone had decided to invest in the numerous extra plates, there was then the even greater technical challenge of fitting (or "registering") each of the smaller plates correctly within the space left open in the printed text. Such precise work had rarely been attempted before the mid-sixteenth century and was evidently a challenge that the initial printers of these anatomical editions wished to avoid. Indeed, even the more rudimentary technical feat of having the engraved illustrations printed together with (on the recto or verso) a full page of typographically printed text was rarely achieved in these early anatomical editions – the 1560 Italian edition of

---

[40] Plantin's use of the incorrect plates and readers' comments on them are discussed at greater length below.

[41] For examples of such engraved illustrations, see, e.g., Von Arnim 1984, nos. 40, 280, and 282 (for early editions with engraved maps), and Mortimer 1974, nos. 22, 245, and 475 (for architectural studies) and no. 454 for Ippolito Salviani's study of fish, *Aquatilium animalium historiae, liber primus* (Rome: Ippolito Salviani, 1558). See also the Introduction for references to sixteenth-century German mathematical studies with etched illustrations.

[42] Specifically, the various bones shown in the Plantin illustration are found on pp. 24, 25, 33, 45, 55, and 60 of Vesalius's 1543 edition of the *Fabrica*.

de Valverde's text and Plantin's 1566 adaptation thereof are two exceptional examples of this accomplishment. More often than not, the illustrations were simply inserted among the pages of text, as Plantin did himself in his 1568 Dutch edition and a Latin edition completed in 1579 (PP 2415–2416).

Must one then conclude that the early printers of the engraving-illustrated anatomical editions were not concerned with how the illustrations were integrated into the text? Not necessarily. Rather, the final appearance of these anatomical studies was most likely simply dominated by technical and financial concerns. Indeed, the potential influence of the factors inherent in using engravings (or etchings) as book illustrations is much greater and more pervasive than is usually suspected. Affecting not only the appearance of the illustrations, the cost to produce them, and their placement in conjunction with the text, the decision to illustrate with engravings (or etchings) also meant that the printer himself was no longer capable of fully governing the rate at which his publications would be finished, down to the printing of the illustrations. In order to gain a better perspective of the full impact of the use of intaglios as illustrations we will return to Plantin's production of these texts in the 1560s and examine how he negotiated these inescapable issues in his first independent attempt to illustrate books with engravings. Then we will be able to resolve the initial question of whether Plantin's production of the *Vivae imagines* might have earned him the fame and success he evidently hoped to garner with this work.

The production of Plantin's Vivae imagines partium corporis humani

As noted above, in his foreword to the 1566 edition Plantin asserted that he began work on his edition of the *Vivae imagines* as soon as he had obtained a copy of the 1559/1560 Italian edition of de Valverde's *Anatomia del corpo humano* that had inspired him. The first stage in this process consisted of finding a suitable engraver and arranging for him to produce the necessary plates. But, as Plantin observed himself, shortly after the engraver had started to make the plates, all work on this and other projects was brought to a halt because "disaster struck my family" ("ea familiae meae accidit calamitas").[43] The cause of the disaster (which Plantin does not specify) was the production of a heretical text at his Press in February 1562 during one of his business trips to Paris. Although the three employees who were directly responsible for the work were sentenced to be hanged (sentences that they all seem to have ultimately escaped), Plantin himself was cleared of involvement in the affair, largely because of his prolonged sojourn in Paris at the time. But, while he remained in Paris, all of his property, including three plates for the *Vivae imagines*, as well as the plates and copies of *La pompe funèbre* discussed above, was confiscated and sold at public auction on April 28, 1562 to satisfy the demands of his creditors.[44]

---

[43] See J. de Valverde, *Vivae imagines* . . . (Antwerp: Christopher Plantin, 1566), fol. A2v.

[44] For a detailed account of the circumstances around the production of the questionable text and the subsequent sale of Plantin's goods, see Voet, GC, I, pp. 34–44. See MPM Arch. 27, fols. 15r and 15v for the following entry in the record of this sale: "Dryen coperen platen van anathomia ij £ ii s. vi d." (Three copper plates of "Anathomia" 2 Flemish pounds 2 schellingen 6 deniers [=12 fl. 15 st.].)

By September 14, 1564, approximately one year after his return to Antwerp from his self-imposed Parisian exile and at least three years after his initial decision to undertake this project, Plantin returned to it. As he stated in his foreword:

When in some way or another peace was finally restored and I had begun to repair the resulting damage as best I could, I came upon the anatomical illustrations again, among various other incomplete projects. Although they were not yet finished, they had already cost me a significant sum of money. First I saw to it that the remaining images were engraved with the same diligence as the first and then I had their indices translated from Italian into Latin, so that they could be of use to all scholars.[45]

While this is related in a matter-of-fact manner, all was not so simple in practice. Frans Huys, a prominent local engraver whom Plantin had first asked to make the plates, had since died, while the three plates that he had completed prior to Plantin's sojourn in Paris were no longer in Plantin's possession, having been sold at auction the year before. Thus, Plantin not only had to buy back the first three plates – which had been purchased at the auction by an important local competitor, Willem Silvius – but he also had to engage another engraver, ultimately Frans Huys's brother Pieter Huys, to execute the remaining forty plates. It would take more than one and a half years (from September 1564 to January or February 1566) before all of the necessary plates were engraved. Both of the Huys brothers were paid 11 fl. per engraving, or 462 fl. total, while Silvius received an equivalent sum of 33 (or 36) fl. for the return of the first three plates. In addition, the painter Lambert van Noort was paid 3 fl. 10 st. for designing the frame for the title-page.[46] The text itself was printed between February 2 and March 9, 1566, at a tenth of the cost of having the engravings made – only 45 fl. 8 st. – and ten days later (on March 19, 1566) Pieter Huys was paid an additional 44 fl. for printing the illustrations in 200 of the 600 copies printed of this text (the illustrations for the remaining copies were paid for nearly eighteen months later, on August 22, 1567). All told, the production and printing of the illustrations cost nearly 600 fl. out of the approximately 788 fl. paid for the production of the book as a whole.[47] A summary comparison of these costs with those for a sample of other works Plantin printed at this time reveals that the 188 fl. paid for everything but the production of the illustrations

---

[45] See J. de Valverde, *Vivae imagines* . . . (Antwerp: Christopher Plantin, 1566), fol. A2v, for the following excerpt: "Itaque cum tandem rebus utcunque pacatis, ad acceptum damnum, quo ad possem, sarciendum me convertissem, occurrerunt inter plurima alia imperfecta opera, tabulae illae anatomicae, quae, licet nondum absolutae essent, plurimum tamen iam tum sumptibus constiterant. Primum igitur tabulas quae restarent, pari ut priores industria desculpendas, deinde harum indices ex Italicis Latinos fieri curavi, ut omnibus eruditis hoc pacto subvenirem."

[46] See PP 2413, nn. 6–7, for all of the basic sums Plantin paid for these engravings, including his ambiguous note regarding his repurchase of three plates from Silvius. We believe that Plantin used the original three plates executed prior to the April 1562 sale of his property and that they were included in the first, large summary entry in MPM Arch. 4, fol. 81 lft, for work on this publication and that no extra plates were engraved, as Voet suggests. For more on the artists involved, see ch. 2 and appendix 1, which includes the timetable for Pieter Huys's delivery of these plates.

[47] For this summary of the costs, see Voet, GC, 11, p. 384. As noted by Voet, this includes the cost of good quality paper, wages, illustrating all 600 copies, translation costs (for the translation of the Italian indices from de Valverde's text into Latin), and the purchase of three copies of de Valverde's text. This excludes the extra 33 (or 36) fl. paid to Silvius for the first three plates engraved by Frans Huys.

would have been in the normal range for an unillustrated text using that quantity of good quality paper. The immense extra costs incurred for the illustrations were clearly not.[48] In his foreword to this publication, Plantin himself states that he found the cost of having just the first three plates engraved (33 fl.) "a significant sum of money."[49] Regardless of whether this was his true opinion, the total cost for the production and printing of the illustrations for all 600 copies of this book – approximately 600 fl. – was clearly much more. It was the equivalent of approximately 1,500 days of work for an unskilled mason, or 800 days of work for a skilled one.[50] This clarifies, for example, why Plantin did not simply have all the illustrations printed at once – why sink extra money into completing books that might not sell? Similarly, returning to an earlier question, it is no longer surprising that Plantin, like the other printers of anatomical texts before him, would have attempted to minimize these extraordinary costs by using engraved plates as fully and efficiently as possible, even if that meant altering the more immediate text–image relationship of Vesalius's woodcut-illustrated editions.

While these costs were huge in terms of Plantin's standard production at the time, did he at least recoup them through the sale of this edition? According to Leon Voet, the first known sale of this publication dates to March 27, 1566. By the end of 1568, 352 of the 600 copies printed had been sold at an average price of 2 fl. 10 st. per book. More than 100 copies each went to dealers in present-day Belgium and Paris, while another 30 copies went to London, 25 to dealers in Heidelberg, and around 20 to individuals in Lyon, as well as at the Frankfurt book fair.[51] At this point, Plantin would not only have covered all of the production costs, but he would have been left with a profit of nearly 100 fl. These sales apparently encouraged him enough to prepare a new edition (now in Dutch) in 1568. In 1576, he had a Spanish version of the text prepared and obtained a privilege to publish it. And in 1579, another Latin edition finally appeared (after having been begun in 1572), thirteen years after the first.[52] In addition to the routine investments in producing new editions of a text, Plantin also paid Pieter Huys an extra 22 fl. for the engraving of two new plates between the fall of 1571 and the spring of 1572, presumably in preparation for the printing of the new Latin edition. These plates were needed to ensure the scholarly value and rigor that Plantin claimed as one of his goals in his foreword to the first edition. As already mentioned, two of the original engravings made for Plantin were reversed during the initial copying of

---

[48] For Voet's sampling of Plantin's printing costs in 1566–1567, see Voet, GC, II, pp. 380–384. The most effective comparisons are made when the quantity of paper required to print the edition is equated, for aside from illustrations, this was generally the most costly single component of a book.

[49] See p. 78.

[50] The wages paid to skilled and unskilled laborers are the standard means of price comparisons for this period. This comparison is based upon the average daily summer wages paid c.1566. Masons were among the better-paid day laborers in Antwerp at the time and their summer wages would have been relatively high, for the working day was longer. For these figures, see Scholliers 1976, p. 165.

[51] Voet, GC, II, pp. 523–525.

[52] On the preparations for the Spanish edition (which was ultimately never printed), see Voet, PP, V, p. 2328; and De Nave and De Schepper 1990, cat. no. 31. For the 1568 Dutch and 1579 Latin edition, see PP 2416 and PP 2415, respectively. There is no evidence that the printing of a second Latin edition begun by Plantin in 1572 (PP 2414) was ever completed at that time. All known copies with the 1572 date on the title-page have a colophon dated 1579 (see, for example, MPM (A 2003) and SBA (J 11395)).

the designs from the 1559/1560 Italian edition and consequently provided factually inaccurate information, as noted by readers of both Plantin's 1566 Latin and 1568 Dutch editions.[53] For example, one reader of the 1566 Latin edition noted by the fourth illustration to book VI: "In this and the next print, the engraver incorrectly placed what should be on the right, on the left, and vice versa. This occurs frequently, elsewhere, but if the reader has been warned once about this, it should not confuse him." In another note, this reader went on to clarify for himself the real problem with this image, namely that the aorta, the main artery that distributes blood from the heart to all the other arteries in the body, actually starts in the left ventricle and not the right, as suggested in this engraving (fig. 3.9).[54] One reader of Plantin's 1568 Dutch edition, noting the same problem with the fourth illustration to book VI, was more succinct in his general remark, written on the preceding image: "These figures are all reversed and consequently represent things incorrectly. In Vesalius they are correct."[55]

Clearly, if Plantin wanted to claim that this work made a valuable scholarly contribution, these plates had to be corrected. The fact that he did have new plates made indicates that he also still believed (or at least hoped) that new editions of this text would be profitable, some ten years after he had first conceived of the project around 1561 and five years after the publication of his first Latin edition in 1566. But the ultimate fate of his three subsequent editions suggests that Plantin was overly optimistic and had misjudged the market. Recall that a Spanish edition begun by 1576 was never completed, while a Latin edition begun in 1572 was not finished until 1579. Although there are various plausible explanations for the disruption of work on these editions – a more pressing (and lucrative) demand for enormous quantities of new liturgical editions in the early 1570s, for example, or the increased difficulties of the war in and around Antwerp around 1576 – it is also clear from archival documents that both the 1568 Dutch edition and the later Latin edition simply did not sell as well as Plantin's initial Latin edition from 1566.[56] For example, according to a 1602 inventory of Jan Moretus I's current stock of books, the following were still on hand, some twenty-three (in the

53 The two engravings concerned are the third and fourth illustrations (Tab. III and Tab. IIII) to the sixth "book" (Lib. VI), or chapter of Plantin's de Valverde editions. Huys was paid for making one new engraving on October 21, 1571 and for another on March 24, 1572 (see MPM Arch. 31, fol. 64 rht, for these payments). These two plates are correctly oriented in the 1559/1560 Italian edition that served as the basis for Plantin's illustrations.

54 For this annotated copy, see MPM (A 1358). The original Latin note (written on "Tab. IIII. Lib. VI", p. 135) reads: "In hac et sequenti Tabula male sculptor posuit in latere sinistro, quae dextro conveniebant, et contra: quod alibi etiam frequenter accidit. Sed hoc lectorem semel monitum non turbabit."

55 For this copiously annotated copy, see MPM (R 7.9). The original Dutch text noted on "Tab. III Lib. VI" reads: "dees figueren staen alle averecht ende wysen daer om al qualyck. In Vesalio staense wel." The most obvious problem with this plate is that the spleen is incorrectly shown on the right. The remark concerning "Tab. IIII Lib. VI" reads: "dees figuer is everecht, waer door dat den truncus van de crom omgebooghde arteri, ten rugge waerts loopende, haeren situs en gelegentheyt verliest geteeckent i. gelyck oock doet het beginsel van de groote arteri geteeckent A." (This figure is reversed. Consequently, the trunk of the artery bent in a curve, going towards the back, loses its [correct] place and position [and is] marked "I," while the start of the large artery is marked "A.")

56 The production and illustration of the new liturgical editions will be discussed at greater length in chapter 4. Although there are no complete records of the sale of Plantin's 1566 Latin edition, the fact that he appears to have begun a new Latin edition in 1572 suggests that it was sold out by that time (or at the very least by 1579, when Plantin's next Latin edition was finally published, thirteen years after his first).

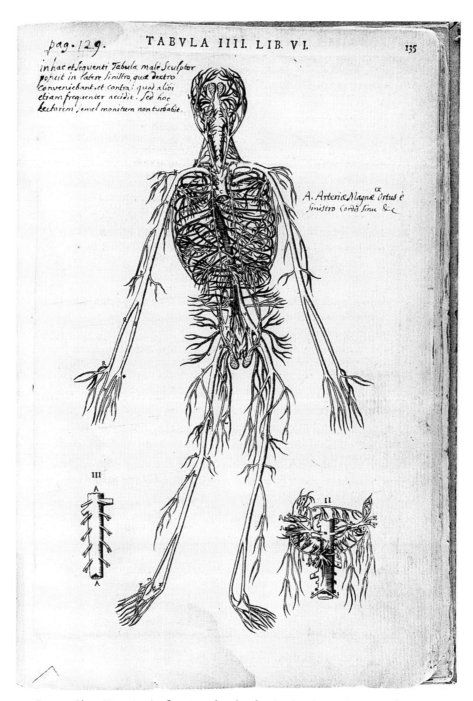

3.9 Frans or Pieter Huys, *Arteries*, from Juan de Valverde, *Vivae imagines partium corporis humani* (Antwerp: Christopher Plantin, 1566; 4°), p. 135, engraving, 238 × 142 (Antwerp, Museum Plantin-Moretus, A 1358).

case of the Latin edition) to thirty-four years (in the case of the Dutch edition) after Plantin had printed them:

> fifty copies of the 1568 Dutch edition, without illustrations, forty-two valued at 10 st. per piece, eight at 5 st.;
> twenty-one copies of the same, but with illustrations, valued at 30 st. per piece; and
> two copies of a Latin edition, with illustrations, valued at 3 fl. (or 60 st.) per piece.

Of these, only the two Latin copies were listed as *vendibiles* (saleable). All seventy-one copies of the Dutch edition – with or without illustrations – were listed as *minus vendibiles*, or less saleable.[57] In addition to these unsold copies, others were in the possession of Jan Moretus's in-laws, as part of the settlement of Plantin's estate in 1589. Jan Moretus periodically repurchased these, along with other remainders from Plantin's old stock. Consider, for example, the following record from 1 February 1607:[58]

Receu de Jan Spirinx et ma tante Catherine (Received from Jan Spirinx and my aunt Catherine [= Plantin's daughter Catherine and her husband])

> 20 *Monumenta* Montani 4to [PP 590; the *quarto* edition of Arias Montano's *Humanae salutis monumenta*, discussed in chapter 5] (fl. 3) . . . fl. 60
> 5 Anatomie met figuren [5 "Anatomie" with illustrations] (fl. 3) . . . fl. 15
> 9 Idem sonder figuren [9 of the same, without illustrations] (st. 30) . . . fl. 13 st. 10.

Regrettably, it is not certain whether Dutch or Latin copies (or both) were purchased.

Finally, in 1623, Balthasar Moretus I paid the Galle workshop for printing seventy-five complete sets of the illustrations.[59] These impressions from the old plates were presumably used to illustrate the last remaining (unillustrated) copies of the text that they had on hand, as there is no evidence that sets of the illustrations were sold separately. The lack of references to copies of the "Anatomie" in subsequent records of the Moretuses' stock of books, including one made in 1630, suggests that the last remaining copies of Plantin's ambitious first attempt to produce a text with engraved illustrations had finally been sold by that time, fifty-five or more years after they had been printed.[60]

What would have caused this apparently unanticipated decrease in interest in these editions? Had Plantin simply misjudged the market for anatomical editions in general following the initial success he appears to have enjoyed with his 1566 edition? Or had his editions become outdated and unappealing in comparison with other contemporary publications? The latter hypothesis seems the most likely, for while other publishers continued to produce new anatomical editions, Plantin's editions remained a pirated combination of de Valverde's 1556 illustrations and Grévin's 1564 adaptation

---

[57] For these records, see MPM Arch. 490, fols. 1v, 2v, 13v, and 14r, respectively. Here the Dutch editions are referred to as copies in "duyts," which was commonly used for Dutch at the time.

[58] MPM Arch. 179, fol. 20r.

[59] For the payment to the Galle workshop, see MPM Arch. 123, fol. 60v. All of the plates used to illustrate Plantin's various editions of the *Vivae imagines*, including both the incorrect and correct versions of the third and fourth illustrations to book VI, are still preserved at the Plantin-Moretus Museum (under KP 241 C–258 C, 284 C–291 C, 296 C–311 C, 315 C, 320 C, and 321 C). See also appendix 4, p. 383.

[60] For the 1630 inventory of their stock of books, see MPM Arch. 109bis.

of Vesalius's *Epitome*. Moreover, the known copies of Plantin's 1572/1579 Latin edition demonstrate that, despite having incurred the expense of commissioning new, corrected plates, Plantin did not use them right away, but rather continued to rely upon impressions of the old, incorrect plates for the illustration of a number of copies of this edition.[61] In other words, financial concerns and economy – satisfied through the conscious use of old, inaccurate impressions that Plantin most likely had on hand, before paying to have new corrected ones printed – won out over the ideal of producing the best scholarly aid possible, despite Plantin's boastful assertions in his foreword to this book.

And what of the other implied goals, in particular, demonstrating that Antwerp's craftsmen could also produce a book with superior engraved illustrations? Plantin's initial 1566 edition clearly reflects his attempt to imitate the true integration of typographically printed text and engraved illustrations, as found in his model publication. But the fact that he relinquished that goal in the production of his subsequent editions and reverted to the more conventional and technically simpler insertion of groups of separately printed illustrations at the end of each chapter suggests that there were objections to working this way. Were readers dissatisfied with the interspersed illustrations? Or was this shift necessitated by such practical considerations as what the engraver, Pieter Huys, was willing and able to arrange for the printing of the illustrations? Regardless of the precise cause, Plantin's first great independent venture in the world of producing books with engraved illustrations ended up being akin visually to *La pompe funèbre*, namely, an independent series of prints accompanied by a typographically printed text.

Was, then, the huge sum that Plantin invested in the illustrations of the first edition of this book – nearly 600 fl. out of the approximately 788 fl. spent on producing the edition – worth the effort? Despite having begun his production of books with engraved illustrations well with a clearly successful type, an anatomical work, problems emerged with two of the plates and sales evidently slowed. The circumstances around the execution or printing of the engraved illustrations could also not have been fully satisfactory. Otherwise, why (as discussed at the beginning of this chapter) would Plantin have declined to take on the well-backed inquiries from the Italian authors Onufrio Panvinio and Fulvio Orsini to print their texts with engraved illustrations in the following year? And yet, these were clearly difficulties that Plantin decided to work on. Indeed, just five years after the appearance of his first edition of the *Vivae imagines*, when he had the pleasure of working with the Spanish theologian Benito Arias Montano, Plantin produced a series of highly original publications with engraved illustrations. In contrast to his imitative production of de Valverde's anatomical work, these new projects – a polyglot bible, a book of hours, and a theological emblem book – would all be innovative in terms of the fundamental decision to illustrate these texts with engravings. In addition, the latter two texts would exhibit a new degree of technical proficiency in the combination of intaglio illustrations and letterpress. Together, these

---

[61] For examples of the 1572/1579 edition with the original (i.e., faulty) engravings, see, e.g., Cambridge, Gonville and Caius College Library (K.5.1); KBR (VH 7423 C LP); MPM (A 2003); SBA (J 11395); and Washington, D.C., National Library of Medicine (WZ 240 V215v 1572a).

publications helped set the stage for the revolutionary role Plantin would play in the production of books with intaglio illustrations in the following decades. The first of these that Plantin began (shortly after his initial publication of the *Vivae imagines*) was his Polyglot Bible. Produced with the financial support of Philip II, this project brought Plantin lasting fame.

A ROYAL POLYGLOT BIBLE

Imagine conceiving of the production of an extraordinarily detailed bible in several large folio volumes, with four ancient languages printed side by side, so as to enhance scholars' probing examination and comparison of these holy texts. Imagine conceiving of such a thing at a time and in a place where unqualified adherence to the Vulgate Bible, St. Jerome's Latin translation of the text, was not simply advisable, but fought over.

These were the circumstances in which Plantin found himself when he first devised the printing of his great Polyglot Bible by 1566, the year in which the first edition of his *Vivae imagines* appeared.[62] Even though this publication did feature engraved title-pages and frontispieces, in addition to the unprecedented use of engravings as text illustrations in a biblical work, Plantin had not envisaged the project as an opportunity to produce an exemplary, finely illustrated book. Rather, he was inspired primarily by the idea of printing a new scholarly polyglot bible to replace that which was printed in Alcalá de Henares, Spain, in 1514–1517.[63] As of 1558, Plantin had periodically published bibles (or parts thereof) in Latin, Hebrew, Greek, Dutch, and French; thus, he would have been familiar with the publication of this genre of text in general.[64] Furthermore, the need for a new polyglot bible was clear. The Alcalá Bible was difficult to obtain now and, perhaps of greater significance, did not reflect the important advances that had been made in biblical scholarship since its appearance. A new, authoritative version was also essential and appropriate given the recent Protestant upheavals and challenges to the old Catholic standard. However, Plantin may also have been inspired by factors other than an abstract scholarly interest in the project. For, at this point in his career (around 1566–1567), he was desperately endeavoring to distance himself from anti-Spanish, pro-Protestant initiatives supported by his then business partners, members of the Van Bomberghen family, and portray himself as a staunch supporter of

---

[62] Of the numerous accounts of Plantin's Polyglot Bible (PP 644), the following are basic, useful sources. Rooses 1880 (which regrettably has no footnotes) provides perhaps the best, detailed account of Plantin's production of his Polyglot Bible, from its inception, through the printing of each gathering, to its distribution and the costs incurred along the way. For a revised French version of the original Dutch text, see Rooses 1914, pp. 71–93. Clair 1960, pp. 57–86, and Voet, GC, I, pp. 56–64, offer more concise overviews of this project in English. Two valuable and complementary bibliographic accounts of this book are provided in PP 644 and Darlow and Moule 1963, II.1, pp. 9–12. Finally, for a detailed examination of the history of biblical scholarship to which this publication made a major contribution, see Basil Hall's essay, "Biblical Scholarship: Editions and Commentaries," in Greenslade 1963, pp. 38–93.

[63] For basic bibliographic accounts of this work, which is also referred to as the Complutensian Bible, see Darlow and Moule 1963, II.1, pp. 2–6, and Norton 1999, cat. 27A. For a recent and detailed account of its production, see, e.g., Martin Abad 1999.

[64] See PP 644–725.

3.10 Pieter van der Heyden after an anonymous artist, title-plate to *Biblia sacra* (Plantin's Polyglot Bible) (Antwerp: Christopher Plantin, 1568–1573; f°), vol. I, engraving, *c.*378 × 245 (Antwerp, Museum Plantin-Moretus, B 65).

Catholicism. Owing to the increasing pressures in the Low Countries against those with Protestant sympathies, the dissolution of this successful partnership seemed imminent. Consequently, Plantin had to find a new financial backer for his business. While he clearly was seeking to win the favor of the Antwerp magistrates with his dedication in the 1566 *Vivae imagines* edition, if he could entice a wealthy, Catholic-inclined patron to support him with this project, he might be both free from suspicion and financially secure again. What better target was there for this scheme than the Catholic sovereign of the Low Countries, Philip II himself?

To this end, Plantin had sample pages of the text printed and made a prospectus for it, in the hope of convincing potential patrons of the value of the project and his ability to execute it.[65] Finally, he inundated various adherents of the Spanish court with letters attesting to his own faith in the Catholic church and his great regard of Philip II. Ultimately, thanks to the help of Plantin's longstanding friend, Gabriel de Çayas – Philip II's secretary and a regular recipient of Plantin's letters – Philip II agreed to lend his support to the project, with the provision that a scholar of his choosing would supervise it. The man Philip II sent to oversee Plantin's work (and to convey the essential promised funds) was a learned Orientalist and renowned biblical scholar, Benito Arias Montano (or Benedictus Arias Montanus), who had gained recognition through his participation in the third session of the Council of Trent (1562–1564). Philip subsequently named him his personal chaplain in 1566 and sent him to Antwerp in 1568.[66] What resulted was an unexpectedly successful working relationship between Plantin and Arias Montano that quickly evolved into a firm and lasting friendship.[67]

While Plantin saw to the technical and practical aspects of having the Polyglot Bible printed (in addition to some sixty to seventy other publications per year), Arias Montano devoted himself to supervising, preparing, and even enlarging its content – and, consequently, the financial burden of the project to all involved.[68] Their shared responsibility for the production of this book is even represented on the title-page (fig. 3.10) through the symmetrical inclusion of Plantin's printer's device and an image of Achilles (alluding to Arias Montano) in the corners of the base supporting the visualization of the project.[69] But, as Arias Montano acknowledged in an introductory text to the first volume, many others made invaluable contributions to this project as well. These included linguists, who saw to the correct transcription and interpretation of the Syriac, Chaldean, and Hebrew texts, including the compilation of special dictionaries and grammars; censors, who carefully read and commented on all of the texts; Plantin's

[65] Philip II was not the only one with whom Plantin discussed this project. For example, Duke Augustus of Saxony, whom he saw at the Frankfurt book fair in the spring of 1566, was another potential sponsor (cf. Rooses 1880, p. 5).

[66] On Arias Montano, see Rekers 1972.

[67] For examples of Plantin's great admiration of Arias Montano see, e.g., *Corr.*, I, no. 127 (pp. 277–280) (a letter Plantin wrote to de Çayas on June 11, 1568; see p. 278 in particular); and no. 131 (pp. 284–286) (a letter Plantin wrote to the abbot Jean Moflin on June 13, 1568). For an example of Arias Montano's great personal regard for Plantin, see, e.g., his letter of January 3, 1590 to Plantin's son-in-law, Jan Moretus I, upon learning of Plantin's death (*Corr.*, VIII–IX, no. 1515, p. 620).

[68] For an overview of Plantin's production in the period 1568–1572, see Voet 1984, p. 365.

[69] For detailed iconographic analyses of the title-plate and the "Pietas regia" image, see Coppens 1989, pp. 190–200.

own learned proofreaders, who were responsible for checking the Greek and Latin texts; and many others, ranging from cardinals to other printers and even an English refugee, John Clemens, who generously provided the manuscripts and printed works needed for producing the definitive texts.[70] Ironically, in this period of life-and-death fighting in the name of one's faith, the successful completion of this immense project for the adamantly Catholic King of Spain, Philip II, was achieved thanks to a great cooperative scholarly effort in which rank and faith were ignored.[71]

In a letter written on November 14, 1572, Plantin admitted to de Çayas, "Now that this bible is finished, I am astounded at what I undertook, a task I would not do again even if I received 12,000 escudos [= 24,000 fl.] as a gift."[72] Nevertheless, Plantin's basic scheme had succeeded with far better results than Plantin himself could have imagined. His Polyglot Bible – also referred to as the *Biblia regia*, or Royal Bible, because of Philip II's support of the project – became the new standard for such works. It was known in particular for the unprecedented addition of the Peshitta (or simple) version of the Syriac New Testament and the concluding three volumes of dictionaries and commentaries. In addition, Plantin's ability to complete this mammoth eight-volume work in such an exemplary visual and scholarly fashion rightfully made him famous throughout Europe and earned him the approbation of Philip II that he sought. By 1570–1571, when the printing of the bible was still underway, Philip began to favor Plantin with an unforeseen bounty of, often huge, commissions for liturgical editions and books of hours. These frequently included, in turn, an unprecedented number of works with engraved illustrations. Was it just a coincidence that Plantin's Polyglot Bible was also exceptional in terms of its illustration with engravings?

Deciding to illustrate

It was not a foregone conclusion that illustrations should be added to this publication. The Alcalá Bible was not illustrated, and illustrated Latin bibles, such as the Estienne 1540 *Biblia sacra*, discussed below, were exceptional. Images were much more common to bibles printed in the vernacular.[73] Rather, the basic principle behind the decision to illustrate this work is related in Arias Montano's forward to the entire publication, in which he states:

[70] The most complete transcription of the individuals acknowledged in Arias Montano's introduction is given in Darlow and Moule 1963 (II.1, p. 9, under "Editors"), while Rooses offers a detailed account of precisely what most of these people did (Rooses 1880, pp. 18–20). Additional details, including extra bibliographic references, are found in Voet, GC, I, *passim* (listed by name in the index); de Clercq 1956, pp. 162–168; Rekers 1972, pp. 45–55, *passim*; and Dequeker and Gistelinck 1989, pp. 9 and 23 (for those connected with Leuven).

[71] On the unorthodox beliefs of many of those working on this project, see Shalev 2003, p. 59.

[72] Translation from Mathiesen 1985, introduction to cat. no. 15. The original text reads: "tel œuvre à chef que la voyant ores parachevée je m'espovante et m'esmerveille de telle entreprinse laquelle je n'oserois maintenant entreprendre de refaire encores qu'on me donnast en pur don douze milles escus." (*Corr.*, III, no. 432, p. 227.) Clair incorrectly suggests that this letter was written on June 9, 1572 (see Clair 1960, p. 76).

[73] For examples of illustrated French editions, see, e.g., Mortimer 1964, nos. 68, 69, and 71; Chambers 1983 contains only occasional, exceptionally brief remarks on the illustration of these books. See Rosier 1997 (for the illustration of sixteenth-century Netherlandish bibles), and Schmidt 1962 for Lutheran bibles.

So that you would not think that anything pertinent to the splendor of this fully regal work had been omitted, illustrations, artfully engraved in copper, have been included in the appropriate places. Although limited in the space it occupies, the explanation of the various texts and the divine mysteries that are concealed in them is dealt with in the plates in a long and fully divine account, as all who are interested will note.[74]

Among the thousands of pages that make up the eight volumes of Plantin's Polyglot Bible, six engravings were included as either a title-page or a frontispiece to four of the eight volumes, while sixteen additional engravings – fifteen full page and one small plate – were added as text illustrations to the last volume.[75] Given the latter concentration of the illustrations, it is appropriate that Arias Montano returned to the theme of how the illustrations can help clarify divine mysteries in his discussion of the content of the last three volumes of this publication, the so-called *Apparatus*, or tools for understanding the Bible – in this case, dictionaries and explanatory texts:

At the end [in volume VIII], we provide an assessment of weights, the result of in-depth research, and of sacred architecture, well embellished with rules and examples that are thoroughly attractive and worth being learned by all. For the clarification of the secret and hidden meanings of the divine oracles, nothing could be more suitable or appropriate to be sought or desired than these tracts. For it will never happen by any method that anyone may grasp the true knowledge of the accounts that you will find here, superbly engraved, suitably and aptly brought together at the right place, as noted above, concealed under the images themselves and somehow lying hidden (as it were), if the artful and fully divine structure of the image is not known and clear to him first.[76]

Consequently, the illustrations in the *Apparatus* were meant to complement the text and thereby contribute to the underlying goal of clarifying hidden divine mysteries.[77]

In addition, both of these passages clearly reveal that Arias Montano valued highly the good quality, as well as the decorous appearance and placement, of the illustrations, and unabashedly cited these merits in his explicative remarks to the reader. Given this

---

74 "Ne vero quidquam, quod ad regii plane operis splendorem pertinere videbatur, praetermissum existimes: singulae tabulae, aere artificiose celatae, suis locis insertae sunt. Quibus tabulis singulorum textuum, ac divinorum mysteriorum, quae sub eis latent, explicatio, licet exiguo loco contenta, longo tamen ac divino prorsus argumento tractatur, ut studiosus quisque animadvertere poterit." *Biblia sacra* (Antwerp: Christopher Plantin, 1568–1573), I, fol. ✱✱ 6v.

75 For a list of all of the subjects included in the eight volumes, see Voet, PP, I, pp. 311–312, notes on the illustrations to PP 644. Many of these images are discussed in greater detail below. Hänsel argues that an additional engraving of the *Temple of Jerusalem* that Plantin published independently in 1576 was originally meant to be included in the Polyglot Bible. See Hänsel 1991, p. 50, and PP 584 for this broadside.

76 "Sub finem, ponderum aestimationem diligenter examinatam, ac sacrae architecturae praeceptionibus, atque exemplis iucundis omnino, & dignis quae ab omnibus perdiscantur, concinne exornatam exhibemus. Quibus nihil ad arcanos & occultos divinorum oraculorum sensus explicandos, aut aptius, aut magis accommodatum requiri, aut desiderari potest. Nulla enim ratione unquam fiet, ut veram cognitionem earum historiarum, quas hic egregie caelatas, apteque, & apposite, ut supra admonuimus, suo loco collocatas, conspicies, sub ipsis imaginibus absconditam, & quodammodo (ut ita dicam) latentem, quis recte assequatur, nisi prius artificiosa, ac divina plane imaginum structura ei cognita, ac perspecta sit." *Biblia sacra* (Antwerp: Christopher Plantin, 1568–1573), I, fol. ✱✱✱ 1r.

77 In his remarks in *Chaleb*, on the division of Israel into tribal lands, Arias Montano similarly states that a map was included to facilitate the understanding of the text and its divine significance. See Shalev 2003, p. 63.

stance and Arias Montano's own immersion in directing the production of the Bible, as well as writing most of the concluding commentaries, it should not come as a surprise to note that, in most cases, Arias Montano was involved (to varying degrees) in determining the subjects of the illustrations. For example, in Plantin's commentary on the three symbolically complex images used to mark the start of the first volume – an all-encompassing title-page for the entire Polyglot Bible (fig. 3.10), an allegorical image of Philip II, referred to as the "Pietas regia" (fig. 3.11), and an allegorical image demonstrating the veracity of the Pentateuch – Plantin clearly states that the second plate, the "Pietas regia," was "determined by Arias Montano in order to demonstrate the piety of King Philip and his fervor for the Catholic faith."[78] While Plantin is silent about Arias Montano's possible involvement in the designing of the remainder of the title-pages and frontispieces, the plates for the text illustrations speak for themselves, in that thirteen of the sixteen engravings included in the last volume of the Apparatus bear inscriptions containing a phrase indicating Arias Montano's involvement (compare figs. 3.13–3.17).[79] Comparable allusions are only missing from the engravings of the Israelites' camp (which is essentially a copy of a standard representation of this subject that was commonly included in earlier bibles), the map of Jerusalem (which appears to have been based upon a recently published map of the area by Peter Laickstein), and Philips Galle's small engraving of the shekel (fig. 3.12), perhaps, as is discussed below, because it was his own work.[80]

Such an arrangement was not unusual for the production of this type of book. In 1540, for example, the Parisian printer Robert Estienne openly acknowledged the assistance of François Vatable, a recognized professor of Hebrew at the Sorbonne, in preparing certain illustrations for his new edition of the Latin bible.[81]

Thus, not only did Arias Montano admire the visual benefits of the engraved illustrations and their value as a means to understanding the divine mysteries concealed in the text, but he also played an active role in determining the subjects of the majority of the images included. Some authors go on to argue that Arias Montano was actively involved in determining the depiction of specific subjects.[82] Before we can consider this issue, however, we need to examine exactly which subjects were portrayed and how the resulting selection fits in with traditional biblical illustrations, as well as in the history of using engravings for book illustrations as a whole.

---

[78] "Haec tabula a Benedicto Aria posita est, ad Philippum Regis pietatem significandam, & studium erga Catholicam Religionem ostendendum." Biblia sacra (Antwerp: Christopher Plantin, 1568–1573), I, fol. [flower] 8r. Contrary to what is suggested by Hänsel, Plantin's identification of Arias Montano's direct involvement in determining a subject is clearly limited to just the second image and did not apply to the other two engravings introducing the first volume (cf. Hänsel 1991, pp. 27–32).

[79] The following phrases were used on some of these plates: "ex descriptione Benedicti Ariae Montani" (from Benito Arias Montano's description) or "ex descriptione Mosis A Bened. Aria Montano observatum [or] expositor [sic]" (from Moses' description as observed [or] explained by Benito Arias Montano).

[80] Cf. Mortimer 1964, fig. to cat. 83, for a comparable image of the Israelites' camp and Shalev 2003, p. 61, on the map of Jerusalem.

[81] The illustrations in this bible are discussed at greater length below.

[82] See Hänsel 1991, pp. 24–51, passim, and pp. 35, 42, and 44 in particular, and Shalev 2003.

3.11 Pieter van der Heyden after Crispin van den Broeck, *Pietas regia*, frontispiece to *Biblia sacra* (Plantin's Polyglot Bible) (Antwerp: Christopher Plantin, 1568–1573; f°), vol. I, engraving, c.376 × 246 (Antwerp, Museum Plantin-Moretus, B 65).

3.12 Philips Galle after an anonymous artist, *Shekel*, from *Biblia sacra* (Plantin's Polyglot Bible) (Antwerp: Christopher Plantin, 1568–1573; f°), vol. VIII, p. [20] of the section "Thubal-Cain, sive, de mensuris sacris liber," engraving, 90 × 67 (Antwerp, Museum Plantin-Moretus, A 5).

Distinguishing the illustrations in Plantin's Polyglot Bible

As noted above, Plantin's Polyglot Bible comprises twenty-two engraved illustrations. One title-page and five frontispieces were commissioned to mark the start of four of the eight volumes. The subjects represented in the three illustrations used to introduce the first volume are strikingly complex and unusual, and are consequently clarified in an introductory note. Given that Arias Montano is credited with determining the subject of at least the second of these illustrations in this text, it seems likely that he may also have contributed to this commentary and that it was not simply written by Plantin, despite his name appearing alone at the end of it. The images concerned are the title-page for the entire Polyglot Bible (fig. 3.10), with visual allusions to the languages represented in the book and to all the rulers of Christian lands and their joint commitment to the Christian faith; the "Pietas regia" allegory of Philip II (fig. 3.11), in which he is represented as the new Joshua, the renewer and protector of the Catholic church and faith; and an allegorical image demonstrating the veracity of the Pentateuch. The remaining engraved frontispieces – images of the Crossing of the Red Sea, the Parable of the Workers in the Vineyard, and the Baptism of Christ – were ordinary representations of biblical subjects that had been illustrated (and thereby highlighted) by earlier publishers in their bibles, although not as frontispieces,

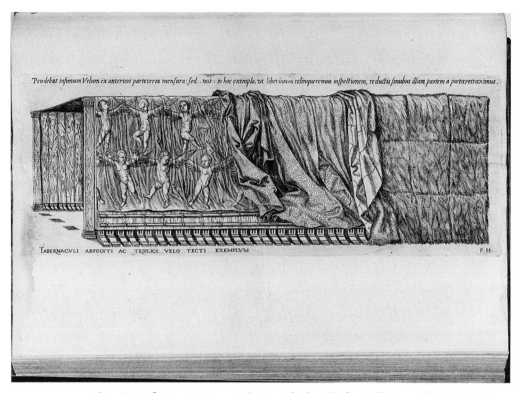

3.13 Pieter Huys after an anonymous artist, *Covered Tabernacle*, from *Biblia sacra* (Plantin's Polyglot Bible) (Antwerp: Christopher Plantin, 1568–1573; f°), vol. VIII, inserted at the end of the section "Exemplar, sive, de sacris fabricis liber," engraving, *c.*140 × 390 (Antwerp, Museum Plantin-Moretus, A 5). Compare this image with fig. 3.18.

per se.[83] According to Sylvaine Hänsel, all of these frontispieces are united by the underlying theme of demonstrating the veracity of God's work.[84] Regardless of the significance of what they represent, the use of an engraved title-page (or frontispiece) to introduce a book was still a rarity in most of Europe. The inclusion of a fully engraved title-page dates at least as far back as an edition of Thomas Aquinas's *Della purita della conscientia* that was published in Florence in 1512. Nevertheless, it was not until the mid-sixteenth century that printers in several European cities began to publish works featuring them. While numerous examples are known among Italian books and print series, the title-page to Plantin's Polyglot Bible is among the earliest known examples from the Low Countries and is the first example we know of for a biblical edition or liturgical work.[85]

[83] These images introduce vols. II, IV, and V, respectively. For examples of them in sixteenth-century Netherlandish bibles, see Rosier 1997, nos. 130, 427, and 381, respectively, of his iconographic index.

[84] Hänsel 1991, p. 35.

[85] For remarks on the 1512 Thomas Aquinas edition, see, e.g., Bland 1969, pp. 121 and 142, and Hofer 1934, pp. 299–301. Both Bland and Hofer go on to assert that the use of engraved title-pages had become commonplace by the mid-sixteenth century. While this is attested to in A. F. Johnson's study of

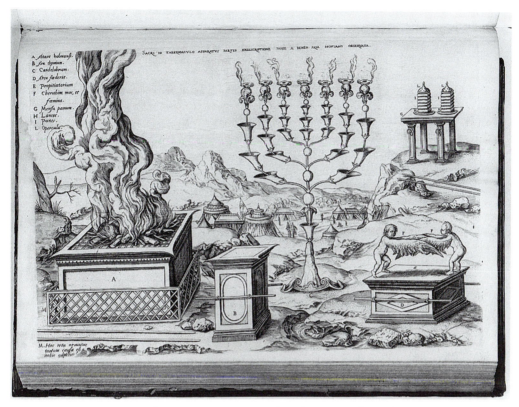

3.14 Pieter Huys after an anonymous artist, *Tabernacle apparatus*, from *Biblia sacra* (Plantin's Polyglot Bible) (Antwerp: Christopher Plantin, 1568–1573; f°), vol. VIII, inserted at the end of the section "Exemplar, sive, de sacris fabricis liber," engraving, c.240 × 370 (Antwerp, Museum Plantin-Moretus, B 65).

All of the remaining sixteen engravings in Plantin's Polyglot Bible illustrate commentaries in the final volume that were written by Arias Montano. With the exception of Galle's image of the shekel, the basic subjects represented were, themselves, not unusual. Comprising images of Noah's Ark, Aaron, the Tabernacle, the Temple at Jerusalem, and several maps, there are numerous precedents for the inclusion of most of these subjects in biblical texts. The essential sources for most of these images were the woodcuts originally used to illustrate Robert Estienne's 1540 Latin bible (figs. 3.18–3.19). As observed above, these were designed, at least in part, with the advice of the Hebrew scholar François Vatable, upon whom Estienne had relied for textual commentary in some of his earlier bible editions. Based themselves upon illustrations derived from fourteenth- and early fifteenth-century manuscripts, the Estienne-Vatable woodcuts became the standard representations for many of the subjects shown and

Italian engraved title-pages (cf. Johnson 1936), it is not clear that the practice was as widespread elsewhere as Bland and Hofer suggest. In the Low Countries, Hubertus Goltzius in Bruges was the primary printer to make use of engraved title-pages prior to and simultaneously with Plantin. See the discussion of his works in ch. 5.

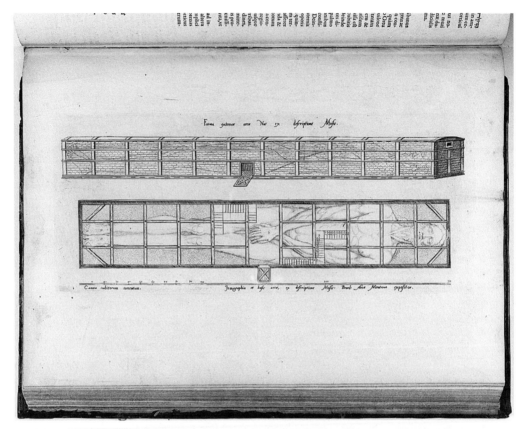

3.15 Pieter Huys after an anonymous artist, *Noah's Ark*, from *Biblia sacra* (Plantin's Polyglot Bible) (Antwerp: Christopher Plantin, 1568–1573; f°), vol. VIII, inserted at the end of the section "Exemplar, sive, de sacris fabricis liber," engraving, *c*.138 × 346 (Antwerp, Museum Plantin-Moretus, A 5).

were widely copied.[86] Nevertheless, there are several significant differences between the illustrations in the Polyglot Bible and those found in other contemporary bibles, from the way in which the familiar subjects are depicted, to the function they serve, and the medium used – woodcut or engraving.

Generally, with the exception of just one of the sixteen text illustrations (the Israelites' camp, see above), the way in which the images in Plantin's Polyglot Bible were depicted is more often decidedly distinct from than similar to the Vatable woodcut designs (compare, for example, figs. 3.13 and 3.18). Some feature unusual, iconographically supplemented representations of such traditional subjects as Noah's ark (which is discussed in greater detail below; see fig. 3.15). In yet other illustrations, new, supplementary views of conventional subjects were added. Some of these (see, for example, fig. 3.17)

---

[86] See Mortimer 1964, no. 68, for both the remarks on Vatable and the Estienne editions. On the textual significance of Estienne's 1540 Latin bible, see, e.g., Armstrong 1954, pp. 72–75. See also Schreiber 1982, cat. 59. For the pervasiveness of these subjects in bibles produced in the Low Countries, see the iconographic index in Rosier 1997, nos. 67, 70, 71, 74–76, 91–93, 97, 98, 106, and 192–194. Similar arguments can be made for books printed in France and Germany (cf. Hänsel 1991, pp. 41–51).

3.16 Pieter Huys after an anonymous artist, *Aaron*, from *Biblia sacra* (Plantin's Polyglot Bible)
(Antwerp: Christopher Plantin, 1568–1573; f°), vol. VIII, inserted at the end of "Aaron . . . ,"
engraving, *c.*358 × 245 (Antwerp, Museum Plantin-Moretus, A 5). Compare this image with fig. 3.19.

recall diagrams of rationalized, precisely measured architectural structures that are
completely foreign to conventional biblical illustrations.[87] Finally, a few completely
new subjects were also added, like the maps of the world and Jerusalem, and the small
image of an ancient Jewish coin called a shekel (or the Holy Shekel; see fig. 3.12).[88]

---

[87] Hänsel discusses possible sources for this conception of the Temple, including a Spanish edition of the
work of Sebastiano Serlio (see Hänsel 1991, pp. 47–48). See also Rosenau 1979, p. 94.

[88] See Delano-Smith and Ingram 1991, esp. the introduction, pp. xxi–xxix, for an overview of which types
of maps appeared when and their significance in relation to the text. We are not convinced by the
authors' arguments that the inclusion of maps in bibles should be associated primarily with Protestant
bibles (as opposed to, e.g., vernacular bibles). The small engraving (89 × 66 mm) of the shekel is
signed by Philips Galle and catalogued in *New Holl., Galle,* II, no. 226, but is erroneously dated 1582
instead of 1572. It was not included in all copies of this bible (cf. version A of PP 644). Although Sellink,
Rosier, and Hänsel mention this engraving, none notes a precedent for it. See Sellink 1997, I, p. 26;
Rosier 1997, I, p. 45, and II, fig. 326; and Hänsel 1991, p. 36.

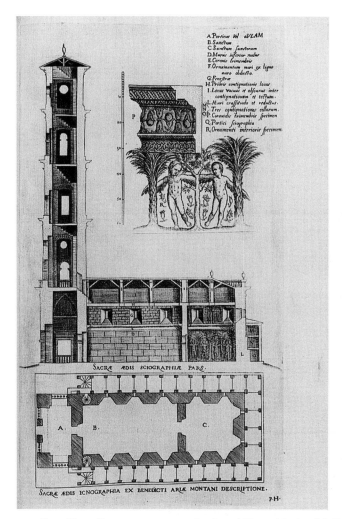

3.17 Pieter Huys after an anonymous artist, *Ground Plan and Section of the Temple at Jerusalem*, from *Biblia sacra* (Plantin's Polyglot Bible) (Antwerp: Christopher Plantin, 1568–1573; f°), vol. VIII, inserted at the end of the section "Exemplar, sive, de sacris fabricis liber," engraving, *c*.368 × 215 (Antwerp, Museum Plantin-Moretus, A 5).

The generally distinctive appearance of these illustrations is underscored both by their unusual placement within the text and by the medium in which they were made – engravings instead of the usual woodcuts. Rather than being inserted amid the relevant narrative context within the body of the biblical text (as was common among illustrated bibles), all of these images appear in a supplementary volume of the Polyglot Bible that is dedicated to providing scholarly aids and commentary. This might explain both the additions to the standard representations of these subjects and the presence of extra, uncommon subjects. For example, Galle's engraving of the shekel was printed (in some copies) at the end of a new treatise on Hebrew weights, measures, and coinage,

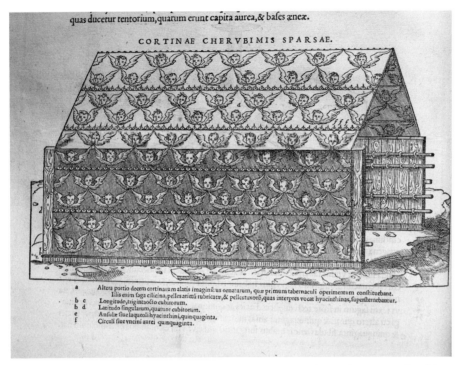

3.18 Anonymous artist, *Covered Tabernacle*, from *Biblia sacra* (Paris: Robert Estienne, 1540; f°), fol. 27v, woodcut, 115 × 215 (Leuven, Katholieke Universiteit, Maurits Sabbebibliotheek, P22.053.2/F0 BIJB 1540). Compare this image with fig. 3.13.

titled *Thubal-Cain sive de mensuris sacris* . . . , while the maps may have been intended as academic tools, as well as meditative aids.[89]

Another significant, underlying difference between the illustrations in the Polyglot Bible and those in other bibles is, as alluded to above, the uncommon decision to have these biblical illustrations engraved instead of cut in wood. Aside from the obvious implications in terms of cost and printing, this switch in medium also influenced how the illustrations were combined with the accompanying text and the general impression the entire publication would have given in the context of illustrated works as a whole.

As already observed, the illustrations in the Polyglot Bible were removed from their normal narrative contexts and used instead to complement scholarly commentary on specific aspects of the original biblical narrative. Although this shift could have been made independent of the medium used for the illustrations, the use of engravings instead of woodcuts would have encouraged and underscored this. First, as was the case

[89] For Shalev's detailed, interpretative examination of these maps as examples of "sacred geography," see Shalev 2003. R. Shirley gives a similar assessment of the world map, claiming that it was "inserted principally for theological reference" (see Shirley 1984, no. 125). For additional references to the other maps included in the Polyglot Bible, see Laor 1986, no. 45 (for the map of Canaan), no. 46 (for the map of Israel), and no. 945 (for the map of Jerusalem).

3.19 Anonymous artist, *Aaron*, from *Biblia sacra* (Paris: Robert Estienne, 1540; f°), fol. 30r, woodcut, 222 × 108 (Leuven, Katholieke Universiteit, Maurits Sabbebibliotheek, P22.053.2/FO BIJB 1540). Compare this image with fig. 3.16.

with some of the plates engraved for Plantin's editions of de Valverde's *Vivae imagines*, images that were previously, in their woodcut form, real text illustrations, inserted in columns of text wherever appropriate, were now either enlarged to fill an entire full-page engraving (as with the Tabernacle illustrations, compare, for example, figs. 3.13 and 3.18), or else grouped together on one plate, as with the illustration of the cult objects associated with the Tabernacle (fig. 3.14). This last image is particularly reminiscent of the phenomenon observed for some of the de Valverde plates. For, in the Plantin image, the five essential devotional objects are grouped together and are artificially displayed in a single open landscape, instead of being included one by one, following their independent textual description in diverse chapters of Exodus, as was the case with their woodcut counterparts.[90] The same arguments made above, concerning the potential extra costs and technical complications of trying to execute several smaller individual plates, apply here as well. Second, if one returns to the general realm of books with engraved illustrations, it is clear that, up until this time, engravings had been used to illustrate a variety of texts, including portrait series, emblem books, and various scientific studies, such as cartographic works, architectural studies, and the Vesalius and de Valverde anatomical editions discussed above. However, religious texts in general and biblical editions in particular were not usually among them. Thus, the novel appearance here of a series of engravings including maps, an archaeologically appealing display of cult objects, as well as architectural sections, floor plans, and elevations would have underscored this text's separation from standard religious works and strengthened its association with the more exclusive realm of finely illustrated scholarly studies for a wealthy, learned public.

Who was responsible for the conception and production of the illustrations?

The question to ask now is: who was responsible for the decision to illustrate this text in such a novel way, in terms of both the content of what was represented and the medium favored for the illustrations? Although it is impossible to resolve this question conclusively, all of the evidence points to Arias Montano. Not only did he openly endorse the practice of using illustrations to further one's understanding of the divine mysteries concealed in texts, but he was also associated with the selection and determination of the majority of the images included. Finally, in addition to clearly stating his aesthetic appreciation of the engraved images contained in this publication, Arias Montano would continue to be involved in the production of exceptional publications with engraved illustrations throughout his sojourn in Antwerp. When considered together, these various projects – ranging from annotated editions of print series to his own texts – consistently attest to his own strong personal preference for this medium.[91]

That said, the tempting follow-up question is: to what degree did Arias Montano specify the content of each image? This remains a quagmire, however, that only leads to more questions and speculations than it resolves, owing to the highly ambiguous relationship between the illustrations in the Polyglot Bible and the obvious pictorial sources, on the one hand, and Arias Montano's accompanying texts, on the other. Specifically, despite the references to Arias Montano in the inscriptions on most of the illustrations in Volume VIII of the Polyglot Bible, these images differ

[90] For evidence of this, consult the iconographic index in Rosier 1997, II, nos. 67, 69, 70, 72–76, in particular. Similarly, in other bibles like the 1540 Estienne edition, for example, the illustrations of these five main items are dispersed among fols. 26v, 27r, 29r, and 31r.

[91] Of the various editions of Arias Montano's texts published by Plantin, one contains a simple woodcut diagram, his *De optimo imperio sive in lib. Iosuae* of 1583 (PP 579), while the remainder were either unillustrated (see PP 577–578, 581–583, and 585–587) or illustrated with some number of engravings (see PP 580, 584, and 588–591). The majority of the latter group will be discussed in the course of this book. For Arias Montano's contributions to the projects of the Antwerp print publisher Philips Galle, see Sellink 1997, I, pp. 25, 48–53, and 87–94; Hänsel 1991, pp. 90–129; and appendix 5.

widely in how faithful to and original they are from common visual precedents. For example, while the exterior view of the Tabernacle differs primarily in its detailing from possible precedents, the floor plan and interior view of the Temple at Jerusalem (fig. 3.17) are completely new. Do these inscriptions simply indicate, then, who decided which models should be followed for the given subjects? One cannot argue that Arias Montano was responsible for a similarly consistent degree of innovation in all of the comparably inscribed illustrations. Moreover, if Arias Montano was responsible for the iconographic innovations in these illustrations, one might expect that the particularly unusual aspects would feature in the accompanying commentaries, thereby fulfilling the presumably desired complementary functions of the texts and images. This is not the case, however.

Consider the illustration of Noah's ark (fig. 3.15), with the striking inclusion of a faintly drawn image of the crucified Christ in both the exterior and interior views. This engraving underscores the typological connection between the ark and the crucified Christ as a means of salvation, whereby the ark functions as the Holy Sepulcher. The potential sources for this view range from early printed editions of Nicolas of Lyra's *Postilla super totam bibliam* to St. Augustine's analysis of Noah's ark in his treatise *De civitate Dei*, or *The City of God*, in which he states: "The very measurements of the ark's length, height, and breadth symbolize the human body, in the reality of which it was prophesied that Christ would come to mankind, as, in fact, he did . . . And as for the door that it received on its side, that surely is the wound that was made when the side of the crucified one was pierced by the spear."[92] And yet, in Arias Montano's accompanying commentary on Noah's ark, he simply asserts that the dimensions of the ark (300 cubits long, 50 cubits wide, and 30 high) were based upon the proportions of a dead man lying on the ground, with no reference to Christ at all.[93] Was it an anonymous male cadaver (as suggested in Arias Montano's commentary), or was it the crucified Christ, as suggested by other sources, including the illustration itself? If Arias Montano was responsible for determining the content of the images in addition to the text in this last volume, why did he not reinforce the essential aspects of the illustrations in the accompanying text? Was it Arias Montano's intent, perhaps, to inspire reflection through such open questions, posed by an unexplained, faintly drawn figure of Christ or by equally faint and unidentified, but nevertheless persistently present ghostly faces in the wooden elements of the Tabernacle (see fig. 3.13)? Did he want to suggest visually what he dared not in a text that had to pass a potentially contentious and conservative censor's approval? Or did other factors or individuals play a role in determining the visual program?

[92] We would like to thank Dr. Walter Melion of Emory University for his suggestion of editions of the *Postilla super totam bibliam* as a source for this image. See Hänsel 1991, pp. 41–42, for her discussion of St. Augustine's text. For the translation of St. Augustine's text cited here, see Levine 1966, p. 567. Finally, see Shalev 2003, pp. 71–73, for his interpretation of this image as "sacred architecture."

[93] See p. 7 of "Noah, sive, de arcae fabrica, et forma, volumen I," a subsection of the "Exemplar, sive, de sacris fabricis liber. Benedicto Aria Montano Hispalensi auctore," in Volume VIII of the Polyglot Bible, for the following quotation: "Arcae longitudo ex divino praescripto cubitorum fuit trecentorum . . . Latitudo fuit quinquaginta cubitorum. Altitudo ad rectos angulos quadrata fuit cubitorum triginta: ita ut sextuplo longior esset quam pro latitudinis modo; decuplum autem longitudo altitudinem superaret. Haec autem hominis in terra iacentis & mortui secundum longum, latum, & altum observata mensurarum ratio est."

The answers to these questions remain frustratingly unclear and consequently defy arriving at a definitive resolution to the issue.

Regardless of the degree to which Arias Montano was involved in the conception of the images, the credit for organizing the production and printing of the illustrations should, presumably, go to Plantin, whose payment records reveal something of the process by which this text was illustrated. While the designs were executed, at least in part, by Crispin van den Broeck and Plantin's favorite draftsman, Peeter vander Borcht, at least four engravers of diverse ages and experience – Pieter van der Heyden, Jan Wierix, Philips Galle, and Pieter Huys – were employed to make the plates.[94] The known payment records for the execution of the engravings indicate that the timing of the work on the illustrations was generally coordinated with the printing of the text itself. For example, van der Heyden was paid for his engravings for the first volume between February and June 1569 (while the printing of the bulk of the text for the first volume was finished concurrently in March 1569); payments to him for maps included in Volume VIII, however, did not begin until January 1571 (and ran through at least November 1571), while the text itself was printed intermittently in 1571 and 1572. Similar observations can be made for the timing of the payments made to Jan Wierix and Huys for their contributions. Regrettably, no payment records for Galle's engraving of the shekel are known.[95]

Thus, while Plantin's staff worked on the composition and printing of the text, at least three engravers were paid irregularly over a period of more than three years, from February 1569 through March 1572, to execute the twenty-one full-page engravings used to decorate the Polyglot Bible. This is in striking contrast with the production of the illustrations for Plantin's editions of the *Vivae imagines*, where thirty-nine slightly smaller plates were executed largely by one engraver, Pieter Huys, in just one and a half years. There is no firm evidence indicating why a group of artists was employed in one case and primarily one engraver in the other. Plantin used both approaches to having the illustrations for his publications executed in the years to come.[96] The variety of engravers employed is also reflected in the wages they received for their work. For example, while van der Heyden was periodically paid smaller sums of money that amounted to approximately 30 fl. per plate (for both the single-page frontispieces and the two-page maps), both Wierix and Huys received single, lump sums upon the completion of a plate. Although both executed full-page engravings, Wierix was always paid approximately 12 fl. per plate, while Huys received differing amounts, ranging from 10 to 22 fl., depending upon the image. Clearly, each artist was paid (or negotiated) his own wage in function of the work executed (and his reputation) and independent of what other artists working on the same project were receiving.[97]

---

[94] See ch. 2 and appendix 1 for more on these artists and their work for Plantin, including records of payment for their work on this project, among others, and their place in Antwerp's world of print production. See also ch. 6 for more on Galle and Plantin's working relationship.

[95] Plantin may have just borrowed the plate from Galle (cf. appendix 1, p. 334). For other examples of Plantin borrowing engravings from Galle, see, e.g., the discussion of A. Barlandus's *Hollandiae comitum historia et icones* (Leiden: Christopher Plantin, 1584) (PP 625) in ch. 6.

[96] See ch. 2 for more on which artists Plantin hired when.

[97] See Bowen and Imhof 2003 for how an artist's wage may have been determined (at least in part) by his reputation.

Another important component of this process that changed significantly between Plantin's production of his 1566 and 1568 anatomical editions and the completion of the Polyglot Bible was the way in which the illustrations were printed and incorporated into the text. When Plantin was ready to have sets of illustrations added to copies of his 1566 and 1568 editions of de Valverde's text, he arranged to have these printed by Pieter Huys, the artist who had engraved the majority of the plates concerned.[98] When it was time to illustrate copies of his Polyglot Bible, however, Plantin then employed the independent print-seller and colorist Mynken Liefrinck, who was, perhaps not coincidentally, the widow of Pieter Huys's brother Frans.[99] Regrettably, only one payment to Liefrinck is known for this work, namely, one made on July 24, 1572 (just before Plantin began the second printing of the *Apparatus*) for the printing of 2,500 sheets with illustrations at a rate of 1 fl. per hundred sheets printed (or 25 fl. total).[100] It is not clear precisely how many copies were illustrated among the more than 600 that were completed by this time, but the following example does provide some perspective on the matter. If one added up all of the pages on which engraved images appear throughout all eight volumes of the Polyglot Bible, one could arrive at twenty-five pages if all six frontispieces, twelve single, full-page illustrations, and Galle's small engraving of the shekel were counted once and each of the three two-page maps was counted twice. If this was the way in which these sheets were counted – other scenarios are also possible – this would imply that Liefrinck was paid for printing the illustrations for a hundred complete copies of the Polyglot Bible. While this is far from the total number of copies that we know were ultimately illustrated, it does provide a useful example of how the completion of this book may have been arranged and at what cost. This was, in fact, not the first instance when Plantin employed Liefrinck for such work and it was far from the last. For, Liefrinck continued to serve as Plantin's favored printer of engraved illustrations for the remainder of his career.

Thus, while Arias Montano was responsible for the selection of most (if not all) of the images, Plantin saw to the practical execution of the illustrated copies. Distinct in approach from his production of de Valverde's *Vivae imagines*, this very diversity – a sort of case-by-case approach for each book – would continue to characterize his production of works with engraved illustrations. But, while Plantin was resolving the technical side of this production, he was still experimenting with the market side of the equation. For, as the concluding examination of the impact of his Polyglot Bible will reveal, technical success did not always make the book popular or profitable.

The impact of Plantin's Polyglot Bible

In retrospect, the Polyglot Bible was a royal, scholarly project through and through, from the unabashed presence of Philip II, as the great Catholic king, in the introductory

---

[98] See under Pieter Huys in appendix 1 for these records.
[99] See ch. 2 and appendix 1 for more on Liefrinck and her work for Plantin.
[100] See MPM Arch. 16, fol. 177 rht, for the following payment: "p[our] f° 2500 de la bible a 1 fl. le cent. val. _ fl. 25 st. _."

images, to Arias Montano's determination to include scholarly commentary and translations despite others' fears that it would pave the way for challenges to the official Vulgate text. It is no wonder, then, that the publication in general, and Arias Montano in particular, met with some irate detractors and criticism. These ranged from the pope, to censors from the theological faculty of Leuven (Augustinus Hunnaeus and Cornelius Reyneri Goudanus), along with the Jesuit Johannes Harlemius, and, the most tenacious of all, prelate Willem van der Linden (or Lindanus), bishop of Roermond, and Leon de Castro, a professor at Salamanca, who brought his case against Arias Montano and the Polyglot Bible before the Inquisition, but ultimately to no avail.[101] Moreover, slow sales of the Polyglot Bible and Philip II's tardy and incomplete payment of the sums he had promised to support the project meant that financially it was a source of great concern rather than profit.[102] Nevertheless, the Polyglot Bible did firmly establish Plantin's reputation as a printer and it remained the essential text for studies in the field, including serving as a model for the production of two later "great" polyglot bible projects – one published in Paris by Antoine Vitré between 1629 and 1645, and the other published in London by Thomas Roycroft between 1655 and 1657.[103]

And what of the illustrations? Many of the plates were reused for two other publications of the *Officina Plantiniana*, namely, Plantin's folio Latin bible of 1583 and a 1593 work titled *Antiquitatum Iudaicarum libri IX*, which comprised many of Arias Montano's commentaries from the *Apparatus* of the Polyglot Bible. In Plantin's 1583 bible, the illustrations were now either included among the preliminary texts or inserted, like the traditions of old, as simple text illustrations wherever appropriate in the body of the text.[104] The *Antiquitatum iudaicarum libri IX* was published in Leiden by Plantin's son-in-law Franciscus Raphelengius I (who had himself assisted with the production of the Hebrew dictionaries and the Chaldee translation in the Polyglot Bible). It comprised Arias Montano's large diagram of the Temple, as well as all of the text illustrations from the Polyglot Bible except for Galle's engraving of the shekel.[105] The anticipated publication of this book may explain why all of the plates for the Polyglot Bible were at the Leiden branch of the Plantin Press when Plantin died in 1589.[106] As they were not returned when that branch of the Press ceased its operations in 1619, these illustrations did not appear in subsequent publications of the Antwerp-based *Officina Plantiniana*.

---

[101] On the criticism of this work, see Dequeker and Gistelinck 1989, pp. 9–10 and 23–24; Rooses 1880, pp. 21–23 and 30–33; and Clair 1960, pp. 76–81. For a more recent summary of these matters, see, e.g., Rekers 1972, pp. 55–66; and Morocho Gayo 1998, pp. 190–194.

[102] See Rooses 1880, pp. 27–29, and Clair 1960, pp. 83–85, on these problems and the discussion below of the financial assistance provided by the Spanish merchant Luis Perez.

[103] For a detailed description of both of these polyglot bibles, including references to their dependence on Plantin's, see Darlow and Moule 1963, nos. 1442 and 1446, respectively. See also Miller 2001 for the Parisian polyglot and Barker 2002 for the London edition.

[104] For the 1583 bible, see PP 690. See ch. 5 for more on the illustration of this work.

[105] See TB, I, no. 284, for this work and PP 584 for the extra image of the Temple. Several of the plates from the Polyglot Bible had been reworked and/or cut and trimmed by this time. For an example of this, see, e.g., fig. 91 of Rosenau 1979, taken from the Raphelengius edition, in which the floor plan of the temple had been cut from the bottom edge of one plate (that labeled "N" in Raphelengius's publication) and was printed sideways next to the exterior view of the structure (on plate "M"). See appendix 1, p. 334, for the replacement of Galle's engraving with an anonymous copy.

[106] See appendix 4 for listings of these plates in Plantin's estate inventories.

3.20 Anonymous artists, *Aaron*, from *Biblia* (the Parisian Polyglot Bible) (Paris: Antoine Vitré, 1629–1645; f°), vol. I, fol. KKIV, engraving, 304 × 257 (Leuven, Katholieke Universiteit, Maurits Sabbebibliotheek, P Plano 52 BIJB). Compare this image with figs. 3.16 and 3.19.

Aside from the simple reuse of the plates in these two publications, few imitations of the compositions are known. For example, in Augustinus Torniellus's *Annales sacri*, published by Plantin's successors in 1620, Torniellus recommends Arias Montano's essay on Noah's ark from the Polyglot Bible in his own discussion of the dimensions of the ark. In the woodcut of Noah's ark that was made for this publication, an anonymous male is portrayed filling the ark, exactly as is described in Arias Montano's text. Notably absent, however, are the traits of Christ that were evident in the comparable illustration in the Polyglot Bible.[107] Thus, even though Torniellus praised Arias Montano's

107 See vol. I, p. 150, of Torniellus's work for this woodcut and its accompanying text. For more on Torniellus's publication, see, e.g., Imhof 1996a, cat. 27a.

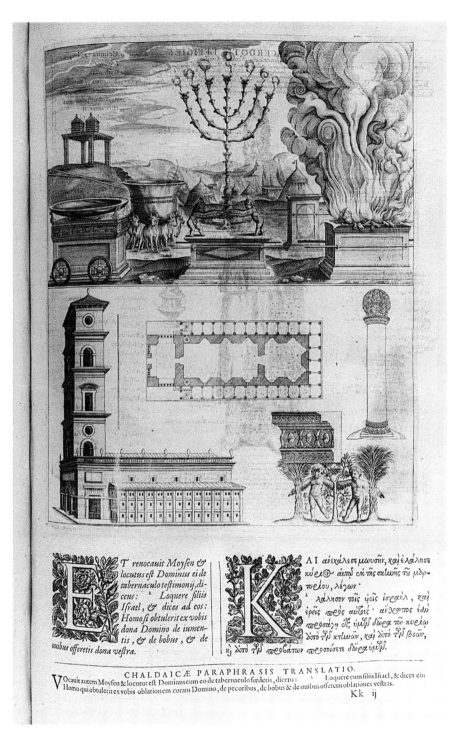

3.21 Anonymous artists, *Tabernacle "apparatus" and the Temple at Jerusalem*, from *Biblia* (the Parisian Polyglot Bible) (Paris: Antoine Vitré, 1629–1645; f°), vol. 1, leaf Kk2r, engraving, 295 × 243 (Leuven, Katholieke Universiteit, Maurits Sabbebibliotheek, P Plano 52 BIJB). Compare with figs. 3.14 and 3.17.

text, the distinctive and defining elements of the accompanying image in the Polyglot Bible were not worth alluding to. Even in the case of the two later polyglot bibles, very selective replications of Plantin's illustrations are present just in the Parisian edition. In particular, the general conception of the composite image of the Tabernacle "apparatus" (but not the descriptions of the individual elements) was imitated (compare figs. 3.14 and 3.21), while the exterior view, floor plan, and sample details of the Temple were copied. The image of Aaron, however, clearly depends more on the old woodcut designs of the subject (compare figs. 3.16, 3.19, and 3.20), while the remainder of the illustrations in the Parisian polyglot (two dedicatory engravings and a selection of maps) bear no resemblance to the plates in Plantin's Polyglot Bible. And as with Plantin's own 1583 bible, the placement of the subjects reflected the old narrative traditions and not Arias Montano's innovative scholarly presentation.[108] Even the basic concept of illustrating a bible with engravings as seen in Plantin's Polyglot Bible, or in the more traditional form of Plantin's 1583 folio bible, was not immediately replicated in the sixteenth century. Only the practice of having an engraved title-page was imitated fairly quickly, but that could also easily be attributed to the distinct and broader-based tradition of distinguishing a book with an engraved title-page.

Although the illustrations as they appeared in the Polyglot Bible may not, consequently, have exerted much influence themselves, the publication as a whole did play an essential role in determining Plantin's future production of books with engraved illustrations. On the one hand, it provided him with a positive introduction to many individuals at Philip II's court, which resulted in orders for thousands of books with engraved illustrations within one or two years of the Polyglot Bible's completion. On the other hand, work on the Polyglot Bible helped establish Plantin's good working relationship with Arias Montano, which paved the way for at least one of Plantin's groundbreaking publications with engraved illustrations, his *editio princeps* of Arias Montano's *Humanae salutis monumenta*, published in 1571. Indeed, Plantin had clearly begun to order the plates for this and his related project – a 1570 *Horae beatissimae Virginis Mariae* – in 1569, some three years prior to the completion of the Polyglot Bible itself, and only two years after his unfruitful negotiations with the Italian authors concerning publications with engraved illustrations.[109] What had changed in this brief period to alter Plantin's dissenting attitude into one full of daring and willingness to take on the financial burdens and technical difficulties inherent in printing texts with engraved illustrations? It could not simply have been the inspiration of Arias Montano, but must also have included some shrewd business planning. For, what was not accomplished with the Polyglot Bible in terms of creating a popular work with engraved illustrations, was achieved unequivocally with the next two publications.

---

[108] Although in Darlow and Moule 1963 (II.1, p. 21) the "preparation" of the plates for the Parisian polyglot is attributed to Jacques Sanlecque, in the copy we examined (KULG [P Plano 52 BIJB]), we noted the following names: Sébastian Bourdon (a designer), Gilles Rousselet, and "Hé Le Roy" (both engravers). The London polyglot was also illustrated, but with an independent series of etchings by Wenceslaus Hollar, in addition to some woodcut illustrations and diagrams.

[109] The first known payment for illustrations used in both Plantin's 1570 book of hours and his 1571 edition of Arias Montano's *Monumenta* (images of the four Evangelists) was made on October 22, 1569 to Jan Wierix (see appendix 1, under Wierix, for this and related records).

DEVOTIONAL LITERATURE FOR THE DELECTATION OF THE LEARNED
AND WEALTHY: BENITO ARIAS MONTANO'S *HUMANAE SALUTIS
MONUMENTA* AND A *HORAE BEATISSIMAE VIRGINIS MARIAE*

On the basis of their content alone, any objective reader would argue that Plantin's
1570 *Horae beatissimae Virginis Mariae* and his 1571 edition of Arias Montano's *Humanae
salutis monumenta* were independent publications. The latter has been described as a
theological work printed in the form of an emblem book, complete with a lemma (or
motto, identifying the subject), an icon (or image), and an epigram (a short poem
providing an allegorical interpretation of the image). Consisting of a series of complex
Latin poems on a selection of subjects from the Old and New Testament, this text was
clearly intended for a learned public, offering them meditative study and repose in a
visually appealing form.[110] The former was a conventional book of hours, comprising
prayers dedicated to the Virgin (among other saints) that would have been so familiar
that many readers would have known them by heart.[111] This book was styled in the
old manuscript tradition of sumptuous, conspicuously costly copies for display or
ostentatious personal devotion.

The decision to print each of these texts can be readily accounted for on the basis of
Plantin's prior production. During the preceding thirteen years, Plantin had printed as
many as twenty-two distinct editions of books of hours in three different languages –
French, Latin, and Spanish. These editions were all illustrated with a selection of
woodcut illustrations (and an occasional set of woodcut borders or cast fleurons) that
he had ordered specially for this purpose.[112] Although Plantin's editions of emblem
books do not date back as far, Plantin quickly established himself as the leading printer
of emblematic literature in the Low Countries in the 1560s.[113] Amounting to no fewer
than twenty-one editions of emblem books in three different languages – Latin, French,
and Dutch – printed between 1561 and 1570, Plantin's publications consisted of various
editions of the work of Andreas Alciati, Adrianus Junius, Claude Paradin and Gabriel
Symeon, and Joannes Sambucus.[114] Each edition was illustrated with a selection of four
different sets of woodcuts, supplemented occasionally with borders.

And yet, despite their clearly distinct content and literary traditions, Arias Montano's
1571 *Monumenta* and the 1570 *Horae* are visually very much alike. Indeed, a comparison
of the illustration of these two works (see figs. 3.24–3.25) immediately reveals that
these two editions have more in common with one another than with any of Plantin's

---

[110] See, for example, Landwehr 1976, p. 1, Chatelain 1992, p. 329, and Melion 2005, p. 73, in particular.
Contrary to what the first two authors suggest, this was not the first time that a religious emblem book
was printed. That honor goes to the first edition of Georgette de Montenay's popular Christian
(Protestant) emblem book, *Emblemes, ou devises chrestiennes* (Lyon: J. Marcorelle, 1567), which is
illustrated with prints in a combination of etching and engraving (cf. Adams 2000; and Adams et al.
2002, II, F.437, pp. 177–181). For Plantin's production of Arias Montano's text, see Bowen 2003.

[111] For general information on the content and use of books of hours, see Wieck 1988.

[112] For an overview of these editions and their illustration, see Bowen 1997a, pp. 94–111.

[113] On the production of emblem books in Antwerp and Plantin's part in it, see Landwehr 1988 and Meeus
2000.

[114] For these editions, see PP 22–24 (Alciati); PP 1476–1479, 1482, and 1484–1486 (Junius); PP 1949–1953
(Paradin and Symeon); and PP 2168–2170 and 2173–2174 (Sambucus). This excludes the later
(post-1571) editions of these texts printed by Plantin and his successors in Leiden and Antwerp.

3.22 Title-page of *Horae beatissimae Virginis Mariae* (Antwerp: Christopher Plantin, 1570; 8°), with Philip II's coat of arms, engraving, 73 × 72, by Jan Wierix after an anonymous artist (Antwerp, Museum Plantin-Moretus, 8–595).

earlier publications. The connection between them is not simply a reflection of the switch from woodcut to engraved illustrations. Rather, there are two other essential factors at play: (1) a comparable general layout of the illustrated pages in both books, in which an engraved border frames the main engraved illustration and an accompanying text; and (2) the use of many of the same plates (for both the main illustrations and the borders) for the illustration of both books. For example, ten of the seventeen text illustrations and twelve of the sixteen borders known to have been used to embellish copies of the 1570 *Horae* were used to illustrate copies of Plantin's first edition of the *Monumenta*. Other plates from the 1570 *Horae* were used to illustrate later editions of the

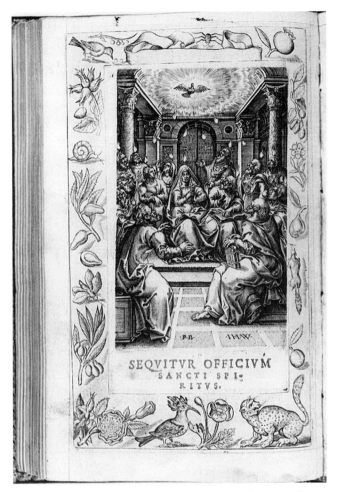

3.23 Jan Wierix after Peeter vander Borcht, *Pentecost*, from *Horae beatissimae Virginis Mariae* (Antwerp: Christopher Plantin, 1570; 8°), fol. C8v, engraving, 115 × 73 (Antwerp, Museum Plantin-Moretus, 8–595). This page exhibits a rare example of how the main illustration overlaps the border slightly in the upper right.

Monumenta (in addition to other texts). Given the number of illustrations and borders that appear in both books and the fact that they were printed and illustrated within a year of one another, Plantin – and perhaps Arias Montano as well – must have come to envision the illustration of both editions as a single large project.[115] Work on them clearly overlapped. In particular, while payment records indicate that the *Horae* was completed first, the same sources reveal that the illustrative program for the *Monumenta* must have been determined before the illustrations had been added to the bulk of the

---

[115] See Bowen 1997b, pp. 147–150, and Bowen 2003 for a more detailed account of the printing and illustration of these books.

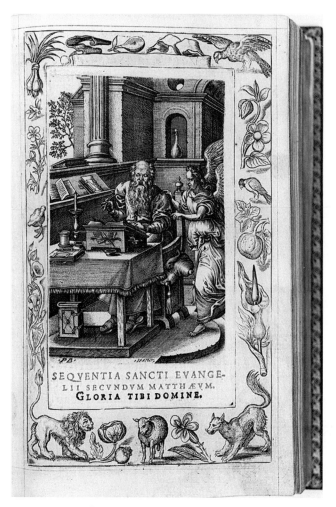

3.24 Jan Wierix after Peeter vander Borcht, *St. Matthew*, from *Horae beatissimae Virginis Mariae* (Antwerp: Christopher Plantin, 1570; 8°), fol. d3r, engraving, 113 × 73 (Antwerp, Museum Plantin-Moretus, 8–595). Compare this page with that in fig. 3.25.

copies printed of the *Horae*. For, some of the engravings used to illustrate the *Monumenta* were finished in or before the same month (October 1570) when Plantin paid for the delivery of the first batch of illustrated copies of the 1570 *Horae*.[116] With the virtually simultaneous appearance of these two textually distinct editions bearing comparable, technically challenging decorative schemes, Plantin demonstrated his ability to produce exceptionally richly illustrated printed books with unexpected positive results. But before we turn to that topic, we must first clarify the significance of what Plantin (and his intaglio printer) achieved technically with the illustration of these books.

[116] See Bowen and Imhof 2003, pp. 188–189, under Hieronymus Wierix, for these early payments for engravings for the *Monumenta*. For the contemporaneous payments made to Mynken Liefrinck for printing the illustrations in copies of the *Horae*, see MPM Arch. 16, fol. 136 rht.

3.25 Jan Wierix after Peeter vander Borcht, St. Matthew, from Benito Arias Montano, Humanae salutis monumenta (Antwerp: Christopher Plantin, 1571; 8°), fol. E1r, engraving, 113 × 73 (Leuven, Katholieke Universiteit, Maurits Sabbebibliotheek, R 38 T ARIA HUM 1571). Compare with fig. 3.24.

The technical challenge and success

Combining letterpress with any number of decorative woodcut or cast elements – such as illustrations, borders, special enlarged initials, fleurons, or tail-pieces – was a routine operation by the early sixteenth century, common to books of hours and emblem books (among others), as all of these elements could be set and printed together on one press. The addition of engraved decorative elements, however, complicated this process on several fronts, including the way in which the illustrations were to be combined with the sheets of text and by whom. While Plantin had turned to professional print publishers and printmakers already involved in the production of his first two projects with intaglio illustrations for the printing of those illustrations, he now turned to the print seller and colorist Mynken Liefrinck for the work on the 1570 Horae and the 1571 Monumenta. However, Plantin did not ask Liefrinck simply to print an independent series of engravings, as Hieronymus Cock had done for La pompe funèbre, for example. Rather, as Pieter Huys had done for the main illustrations for Plantin's 1566 edition of the Vivae imagines, Liefrinck had to print the engravings on pages with typographically printed text. While the careful registration of an engraved image on to a sheet with letterpress was itself complex enough to deter many other sixteenth-century printers, Plantin raised the technical challenge one level further by deciding to subdivide the copies of both the 1570 *Horae* and the 1571 *Monumenta* into two separate issues, one with borders and one without.[117] For, the addition of engraved borders to some copies required an extra, even more precise registration of the engravings on the sheet of text, as well as additional runs through the intaglio press. That separate printing runs were needed for the main illustrations and the borders is evident from at least one copy of the 1570 *Horae* where, on one page (fig. 3.23), the impression of the main illustration and the border overlap slightly in the upper right. It is a high credit to Liefrinck and those she employed that examples of overlapping images and borders are few and far between.[118]

In 1565, Plantin had similarly manipulated the borders included around a set body of text in order to produce what appeared to be two distinct editions of a book of hours with a minimal amount of effort. Specifically, by framing one block of text with a set of wider woodcut borders for one printing and a set of thinner fleurons for the second, Plantin was able to produce an *octavo* and a 12° book of hours simultaneously with the same basic text within the differing border elements.[119] The most difficult part in this case was most likely simply devising the scheme, for all of the decorative elements were either woodcuts or fleurons. Thus, the entire process of setting and printing both editions could easily have been arranged by Plantin's own compositors and with Plantin's immediate supervision, if need be.

Performing the same trick with engraved illustrations instead of woodcuts was another matter, however. To the best of our knowledge, earlier printers had rarely dared such a technically complicated feat of combining so many separate printings of text and engraved (or etched) illustrations and borders for the embellishment of just one side of a sheet of paper making up the book. The best (and only) precedent that we know of is Francesco Sansovino's *L'historia di casa Orsina* (Venice: Niccolò Bevilacqua [pt. 1] and Domenico Nicolini [pt. 2], for Bernardino and Filippo Stagnino, 1565). This work contains a series of twelve portraits of the Orsini family, each with a border around the central image. In eight cases, the border was printed from a separate plate, while in four cases, the portrait and a border were engraved or etched together on a single plate. Among Italian editions in particular, the latter approach of engraving the

---

[117] See PP 1365–1368 for these two distinct issues of Plantin's *Horae*. Payments made to Mynken Liefrinck for the printing of these illustrations indicate that (initially, at least) approximately 65 copies were printed with borders, while approximately 300 copies were not. See MPM Arch. 16, fol. 136 rht, for these payments, where she charged 4 fl. (= 80 st.) per hundred sheets illustrated with borders and 13 st. per hundred sheets for copies without. See Bowen 2003 for a detailed account of the printing of the *Monumenta* and p. 25 in particular for the records indicating that Liefrinck produced 379 copies with borders and 175 copies without.

[118] Mauquoy-Hendrickx was similarly of the opinion that the borders and main illustration were printed separately, although she simultaneously erroneously suggests that the letterpress was added last (see Mauquoy-Hendrickx 1971, p. 74). A comparison of when payments were made to Plantin's compositors and pressmen as against those responsible for the addition of the engraved illustrations for a given edition always clearly documents that the text was printed first and the illustrations second (see appendix 5 and Bowen 2003, p. 8).

[119] For more on the printing of both of these books, see Bowen 1997a, pp. 74–75 and 222–223, under PP 1351 and PP 1352, and figs. 33 and 50 for the related results.

border and the main image together on one plate was a common means of satisfying the desire to have the main image embellished with a border, without the extra technical complication of having to print and align two separate intaglio plates.[120]

But eight full-page illustrations, with little or no accompanying letterpress text, remain far less of a challenge than the seventeen and seventy text illustrations found in Plantin's editions of the *Horae* and *Monumenta*, respectively, where typographically printed text and intaglio illustrations were printed within millimeters of one another. The technical prowess of these editions is most evident in the placement of a title in a banderole that was consistently outlined at the top of each engraved border and left open for the appearance of typographically printed text. Once again, the basic concept – this time, the inclusion of letterpress within a decorative frame for a title-page or a decorative border – was common to sixteenth-century publications in general, and books of hours (especially early French editions) in particular. But what was a relatively simple operation in relief techniques (once correctly set by the compositor), became a significant challenge to two individuals – the compositor and the intaglio printer – working in separate quarters, at different moments in time, to align both the printed text and the intaglio elements correctly. While this admirable technical feat clearly deserves to be praised, it was most likely not a goal in itself. It was, rather, a means to create a visually stunning product, beyond the ordinary realm of printed books. That this was Plantin's fundamental goal is suggested by the books themselves. For, the sumptuous appearance of the 1570 *Horae*, with its large red and black type and exceptional engraved illustrations, as well as the uncommonly magnificent, complementary pages of the *Monumenta*, with its poems in elegant italic type on the left and distichs and finely engraved images on the right, was left as undisturbed as possible. Even such basic typographical conventions as the use of catchwords were omitted and the systematic signing of the pages in the lower right was reduced to just the printing of the first letter of each new gathering along the outer edge of the framing border (see fig. 3.25). Plantin's 1570 *Horae* and 1571 *Monumenta* were, thus, novel masterpieces. But for whom were they produced? For whom was all the effort made, all the time and money invested in resolving a new, self-imposed technical challenge of printing both engraved illustrations and borders? The answer seems to lie in both the texts and the visual traditions evoked by their embellishment.

The prospective audiences for Plantin's 1570 Horae *and 1571* Monumenta

If one were to read a description of the visual enrichment of the 1570 *Horae*, one might easily think that the work being discussed was a luxurious manuscript illuminated by one of the numerous workshops active in Ghent and Bruges around the turn of the

---

[120] For a more detailed description of this book, see Mortimer 1974, no. 460. We examined copies in the BL (c.80.c.9) (the source for the remarks here) and Cambridge University Library (T*.1.35 and Acton.b.28.204). The portraits appear in Book 4 of part 2. There are also an additional five pages here on which only the borders were printed and not the portraits. For other examples of illustrations with borders already engraved around the illustration itself, see, e.g., Mortimer 1974, nos. 30, 136, 319, 343–344, and 446, nearly all from the 1580s.

fifteenth century. For, the borders printed in some copies of this *Horae* (see figs. 3.22–3.24) feature individually, realistically described insects, fruits, vegetables, and animals – designs that characterized and helped establish the fame of those illumination workshops. In addition, the title-pages of most copies of Plantin's *Horae* bear an engraving of the coat of arms of one of three prominent officials – King Philip II (fig. 3.22), the duke of Alva, or Cardinal Granvelle. The inclusion of an individual's coat of arms on the title-page goes back to the days of personalized, hand-made books of hours and suggests that the individual thus represented was a special patron. However, when the 1570 *Horae* was printed, these men's favor was no certain thing; it was, rather, what Plantin hoped to consolidate, perhaps with the exceptional embellishment of the title-page of this special edition.[121] Finally, some copies were even printed on parchment, while several buyers requested that their copies be specially bound with gold tooling, and others had their copies hand-colored as if they were indeed precious manuscripts.[122]

Thus, the 1570 *Horae*, the first of Plantin's projects with engraved illustrations to appear following his 1566 and 1568 anatomical publications, may well represent the epitome of what Philip Hofer repeatedly argued was required if books illustrated with engravings were to become popular enough to make them feasible ventures for printers. According to Hofer, wealthier collectors would have to regard books illustrated with engravings as a substitute for illuminated manuscripts: a new type of luxury item in book form.[123] The price alone that was charged for this book – 1 fl. (or 20 st.) for ordinary copies without borders, or 6–7 fl. (120–140 st.) for copies with borders – would certainly have precluded its purchase by people with an ordinary budget.[124] Plantin's 1565 *Horae* in *octavo*, which was also embellished with borders, but illustrated entirely with woodcuts, cost just 8 st. per copy, or a day's wages or less for some laborers working in Antwerp at that time.[125]

An examination of the sales records for the first full year of sale of this book reveals three important markets for it, which similarly distinguish it from other books of hours that Plantin had produced in the past. They were (1) Paris; (2) a selection of dealers elsewhere in Europe (and beyond the Southern Netherlands); and (3) individuals connected with Philip II or his court in Brussels.[126] Of these, shipments to Paris were the most frequent and continued into 1575, at least. These generally range from six to twenty-five copies per shipment (among numerous other books) and were most likely intended for Plantin's bookshop in Paris. The single largest shipment of copies of the

---

[121] For more on these coats of arms and arguments that some copies were adorned with that of Cardinal Granvelle, see Bowen 1997a, pp. 116–117 and n. 60, in particular.

[122] See, for example, the reference to three copies sent to de Çayas with "dor sur le cuir" (gold on the leather) (MPM Arch. 49, fol. 67r). For one copy on parchment, with a hand-painted coat of arms of the houses of Gonzaga and Lorrain on the title-page and carefully colored illustrations, see ONB Vienna (CP.I.E.22).

[123] Hofer 1934, pp. 295 and 306.

[124] These prices are derived from the sales records discussed below. They exclude the extra costs of having a book bound or specially finished in any other way.

[125] See Scholliers 1976, pp. 163–166, for the wages earned by skilled and unskilled masons in this period. For the selling price of Plantin's 1565 *Horae* in *octavo*, see, e.g., Bowen 1997a, pp. 118–119.

[126] Printed in the summer of 1570, the first batch of illustrated copies was not available for sale until late October 1570. See Bowen 1997b, pp. 132–133, for references to this work. Thus, the following remarks are based upon sales records dating from November 1570 through December 1571.

Horae (fifty-five in one order) made in the first year of its sale was sent to a certain Daniel Format in Lille and may also have been destined for distribution in Paris.[127] Other dealers throughout Europe – Job Mattheeus in Utrecht, Georg Willer in Augsburg, Mathias Gast in Salamanca, and Pietro and Francisco Tini in Milan, for example – usually purchased one or two copies as part of a larger order of books. Only Gaspar de Portonariis, a bookseller in Spain, purchased significantly more – twelve copies in one order.[128] When private individuals are named, most are influential figures linked to Philip II's entourage. Of these, the most prominent are Cardinal Granvelle (who had eight copies sent to Rome), Gonçales Gante, the secretary of the duke of Alva, and de Çayas, to whom Plantin sent eight copies, including one on vellum and several others with goffered edges and bindings. All of these specially finished copies were presented as a gift, six for de Çayas, and one each for two other Spanish officials, including Francisco de Villalva, a Spanish priest who was to play an active role in supervising Plantin's subsequent, large-scale production of religious texts for Spain.[129]

Thus, Plantin's 1570 *Horae* appealed to the Parisian market for richly illustrated books of hours, as well as to a much broader, more international audience than was usual for Plantin's books of hours.[130] In addition, however, this book also served an important function as a sort of presentation copy for powerful individuals whom Plantin sought to impress. This extra, self-promoting function of the 1570 *Horae* is evident to an even greater degree among the sales records of the 1571 *Monumenta*, even though the general market for this book is strikingly different from that for the 1570 *Horae*.

Finished a little less than a year after the 1570 *Horae*, copies of the *Monumenta* generally cost 70 st. (= 3 fl. 10 st.) if printed with the borders, and 60 st. (= 3 fl.) without.[131] The first completed copies of this work were not simply sent to members of Philip II's entourage or directed to Plantin's bookshop in Paris. Rather, they were sent, in the first place, to the Frankfurt book fair, other theologians, and high-placed church officials, in addition to what appear to have been a number of Arias Montano's personal acquaintances. The following sample of names from the first year of sales is impressive to read: "le confesseur de son Exc[ellence]," Abraham Ortelius (the cartographer and a good friend of Plantin and Arias Montano), a certain Bishop "Tydensis," Jacobus de Zeelandre (a canon of Ghent), Cardinal Granvelle, the Spanish merchant Luis Perez (another important friend of Plantin and Arias Montano, who will be discussed in greater detail below), de Çayas, Joachim Hopperus (a high-placed legal advisor for

---

[127] Although these books, together with a number of bibles, were sent to Format in Lille, the exceptional size of this order, along with the inclusion of a package of clothes for the Parisian bookseller Michel Sonnius, suggests that Format may have been serving as an intermediary for the transport of these books to Paris. See MPM Arch. 49, fol. 125v for this shipment. For clearly marked shipments to Paris, see MPM Arch. 48, fol. 180v, and MPM Arch. 49, fols. 17v, 45v, 46v, 47r, and 120v. For an example of copies of this book being sent to Paris in 1575, see, e.g., MPM Arch. 53, fol. 32r.

[128] For sales to these dealers, see, e.g., MPM Arch. 49, fols. 37v (Mathius), 30r (Willer), 26r (Gast), 6ov (Tini), and 89r (de Portonariis).

[129] For this sampling of sales to private individuals, see, e.g., MPM Arch. 48, fol. 175r (Granvelle), and MPM Arch. 49, fols. 48r (Gante), and 67r (de Çayas).

[130] For the localized sale of two other books of hours Plantin produced, see Bowen 1997a, pp. 118–120.

[131] For this difference in price, compare the records of sales of this book to Gerard de Jode in MPM Arch. 49, fol. 159v (six copies at 3 fl. each), and MPM Arch. 50, fol. 64r ("1 Monumenta . . . cum vignettes" for 3 fl. 10 st.).

Philip II in Madrid), the abbot of Ninove (in the Low Countries), Francisco de Villalva, Johannes Harlemius (a theologian from Leuven who assisted with the Polyglot Bible), the bishop of Tournai, the bishop of Cordoba, Adrianus Junius (the celebrated author of emblem books), Mattheus Contarellus (a datary connected to the papal court), and Benedictus Sirgosus (a representative of Philip II to the pope). While Plantin once again gave copies to de Çayas and Villalva, as well as to the Bishop "Tydensis" and the bishop of Cordoba for example, the majority of such gifts were made to lesser known individuals, including several theologians. Beyond these personal sales and gifts, there were two large shipments to Frankfurt (one of twenty-five copies in August of 1571 and one of twelve copies in February of 1572, presumably for the respective fall and spring book fairs), one large shipment of twenty copies to Paris, and only an occasional sale to a bookseller. Some of the last group are the same as those who bought copies of the 1570 *Horae* – the Tini brothers in Milan and Gaspar de Portonariis in Spain, for example. There is one notable addition to this list, however, namely, the Antwerp print dealer Gerard de Jode, who made two relatively large purchases of six copies each of the *Monumenta* several months after it had been published, perhaps owing to its pure visual appeal.[132]

In his second explanatory text to the reader included in the *Monumenta*, Plantin describes why this work was admired by the learned, ecclesiastic elite:

As soon as our recently published work, the *Humanae salutis monumenta*, which is written by Benito Arias Montano, a man of lofty intellect, in a poetical form that is no less refined than it is learned, came in the hands of many very learned and important men, they could do nothing else but be astonished to the utmost by the impressive erudition of the author, by his superb knowledge of religious matters, and by his treatment of this serious subject with such admirable poetical beauty and dignity.

And yet, Arias Montano's book could not fully satisfy its readers on the basis of its content alone, for, as Plantin continues:

They conveyed to me personally that no one has treated the succession and totality of all those subjects in the Holy Scriptures that are regarded as essential for our salvation – even from Adam himself down to the Last Judgment of our Lord Christ – with such certainty and ease that they are shown to have been dealt with here, with such brilliance and learning, as by this excellent man. Nevertheless, many of these same men could not conceal their sorrow from me. Indeed, these wise men perceived that this treatment of these Holy subjects – which was not only useful and pleasurable, but also fully essential for all types of educated people – would not be so easily understood by everyone due to the lofty treatment of these topics. The text required, they continued, a learned, pious and above all attentive reader who was experienced in the Holy Scriptures and piety. When I realized this, I could do nothing else than satisfy this honorable wish from these learned and important men mentioned above (because I believe that my soul is inclined towards the world of learning). I thought that it would be worthwhile for me to write a series of brief notes in which I would highlight and explain in some way the

---

[132] For the sales and presentation copies referred to here, see MPM Arch. 49, fols. 88v, 96v, 101r, 105v, 113v, 115r, 116r, 119r, 126r, 127v, 130v, 131v, 133v, 134r, 135r, 136r, 136v, 138r, 139v, 140r, 141r, 142r, 142v, 150v, 152r, 153r, 158v, 159v, 162r, 163v, and 169r; and MPM Arch. 50, fols. 3r, 5r, 22r, 24r, 24v, 42r, 52r, 53r, 57r, 64r, 77v, 82v, 84v, 104v, 105v, and 114v.

subjects and significance of the seventy-one odes, in which the mysteries of human salvation have been described in such an exemplary fashion. I did not assume this task because I feel that I can achieve more with my intellectual capacities than others. Rather, I had no doubt that in most of the passages which, in the opinion of many, did appear to be difficult, I could convey the spirit and meaning of the author, with whom I am on intimate terms in accord with the faculties of the character with which he is endowed. Make use, then, reader, of my efforts and if you think that anything has been made available here which will promote your studies, give all praise and honor to all-knowing God, to whose honor everything is to be credited. Antwerp, August 1, 1571.[133]

Thus, this book was not only intended for a learned and prestigious public, but it was written in such a way that only those with a detailed knowledge of the Holy Scriptures could fully understand it, which resulted in the addition of a series of brief explanatory remarks at the end of the book. If this was the case, then the success that this publication did enjoy and the influence it exerted on the formulation of future publications, like the new literary form of the learned, pious emblem book,[134] could not have been based upon its content alone. The group of its potential readers would have been far too limited. Rather, as is suggested by the extra effort put into its embellishment with both engraved borders and illustrations, its visual aspect was also of great importance. It certainly must have been so for Arias Montano, who, as noted above, periodically participated in the production of engraved print series with Philips Galle when in Antwerp and demonstrably preferred engraved illustrations for Plantin's publication of his work.[135]

[133] We are indebted to Prof. Jan Ziolkowsky of Harvard University and Prof. Dirk Sacré of the Katholieke Universiteit Leuven for their advice on the translation of this text. Both noted that the quality of the Latin here was exceptional, which raises the question of whether Plantin actually wrote it himself, or if he was assisted by someone else, perhaps even Arias Montano himself. Composed for Plantin's first edition of this text (printed in 1571), this introduction also appears in each of the subsequent editions Plantin produced, including that in *quarto* from 1583 (PP 590). See, e.g., MPM (A 387) (a copy of Plantin's 1575 edition), fol. A1r = p. [1] of the second part of the book, for the following transcription of this text: "Christophorus Plantinus lectori s. Simulac ea, quae a nobis nuper excusa sunt, Humanae salutis monumenta, a Benedicto Aria Montano excelsi ingenii viro, non minus eleganti quam docto poëmate conscripta ad multorum doctissimorum & amplissimorum hominum manus pervenerunt, non potuerunt illi summam hominis doctrinam, rerum divinarum cognitionem clarissimam, & gravissimum illud argumentum admirabili carminis suavitate, & dignitate tractatum summopere non admirari. Eorum enim omnium, quae vel ab ipso Adamo ad Christi D. N. postremum usque iudicium, in sacris libris ad nostram salutem necessaria habentur, seriem & summam, tanta certitudine & facilitate complectitur, ut a nemine unquam tanto splendore ac doctrina, atque a praestantissimo hoc viro tractatam esse mihi suis verbis sint testati. Plerique tamen ex iis non potuerunt suum animi dolorem ita continere, quin eum quoque mihi patefacerent. Videbant quippe homines sapientissimi, fore, ut sancti illius argumenti tractatio, eaque non solum utilis & iucunda, verum etiam omni literatorum generi plane necessaria, propter rerum quae in ea continentur, celsitudinem, non a quovis ita facile intelligeretur. Doctum enim (aiebant) pium & valde attentum, beneque in sacris libris & pietate exercitatum lectorem ea desiderat. Quod cum animadverterem, nec possem, pro eo quo me esse sentio erga rem literariam propenso animo, studiosorum, atque etiam clarissimorum hominum, quos dixi, honestissimo desiderio non satisfacere; operae pretium me facturum existimavi, si unius & septuaginta illarum odarum, quibus humanae salutis mysteria elegantissime descripta sunt, argumenta, & sensum brevibus aliquot annotationibus indicarem, & aliquo modo explicarem. Hanc vero provinciam non ideo suscepi, quod meo ingenio fretus aliquid a me prae ceteris praestari putem, sed quia non dubito quin plerisque in locis, qui multorum sententia difficultate carere non videntur, mentem ac sensum auctoris, quo quidem, pro ea qua praeditus est morum facilitate, familiariter utor, non sim assecutus. Hisce igitur laboribus, lector, fruere & si quid, quo tua studia promoveri posse existimes, hic a nobis praestitum esse cognoveris, Deo sapientissimo, ad cuius gloriam omnia sunt referenda, totam laudem & honorem tribue. Vale Antverpiae, Calend. Augusti MDLXXI."

[134] See, e.g., Chatelain 1992, pp. 329–331. [135] See n. 91 above.

As revealed in the discussion of the illustration of the Polyglot Bible, Arias Montano clearly appreciated a finely executed engraving. Thus, it appears that Arias Montano's 1571 *Monumenta* was also meant to be appreciated visually, like the remarkable 1570 *Horae* it resembled, only now, as revealed by its distinctive initial distribution, for the delectation of the learned, religious elite.

It is in this context, namely, the creation of sumptuous books for an intellectual and devout public through the use of engravings, that the *Monumenta* and the 1570 *Horae*, in particular, were revolutionary on several counts. Representing a great technical coup, Plantin's manipulation of separately engraved borders and text illustrations in these books also constituted a novel application of conventional means of incorporating and manipulating woodcut illustrations. Even more fundamental, however, was Plantin's basic decision to illustrate a book of hours with engravings. For, while some emblem books, including Georgette de Montenay's popular Protestant emblem book, *Emblemes, ou devises chrestiennes*, had recently appeared with engraved or etched illustrations, the same was not true for common religious or devotional works like a book of hours.[136] As with the combined printing of separate engraved borders and illustrations, precedents are few and far between. The best example documented thus far among a variety of standard religious and liturgical works is a copy of Domenico Lupi's *Figurae ad devotionem excitantes de passione Christi cum alia figura rosarii virginis gloriose et carminibus* (Bruges: Hendrick de Valle, March 10, 1503). Although this work was successfully illustrated with a series of twenty-three engravings printed together with typographically printed text, it was not imitated.[137] This is in striking contrast to Plantin's 1570 *Horae*, however. As discussed above, this work was particularly well received in Paris and – of inconceivable significance for Plantin's future production of works with intaglio illustrations – among influential members of the Spanish court. For example, Francisco de Villalva, to whom Plantin had sent special complimentary copies of both the 1570 *Horae* and the 1571 *Monumenta*, specifically recommended the illustrations, borders, and type of the *Horae* as models for the composition and decoration of some of Plantin's subsequent editions of books of hours.[138] The timing of Plantin's production of the 1570 *Horae* was fortuitous – or perhaps perfectly planned. For, by the spring of 1571 – a few months before fully illustrated copies of Arias Montano's *Monumenta* were ready – Plantin was granted the coveted (and financially propitious) right to print the recently reformed breviary and missal for all Spanish domains. A year later, Plantin began on the mass production of books of hours for Spain as well. All produced in various formats and systematically

---

[136] For de Montenay's emblem book, see n. 110 above. For a selection of Italian emblem books with engraved or etched illustrations printed in or before 1571, see Landwehr 1976, cat. nos. 10 and 604–606, and Mortimer 1974, nos. 76 and 449.

[137] In Lupi's *Figurae . . . de passione Christi*, the illustrations were printed on the verso of pages of printed text. For a copy of this work, see BN Paris (Rés. D. 18421). It is described under NK 3448, where it is made clear that references to similarly illustrated publications by Lupi from the same year – referred to as a *Meditationes* and a *Rosarium Virginis Mariae* – are actually this same work (see Hofer 1934, pp. 296–297, for examples of this confusion). See also the discussion in the introduction of the Würzburg and Eichstätt service books with one or two intaglio illustrations.

[138] Cf. MPM Arch. 122, pp. 55 and 503, for examples of de Villalva's commendation of Plantin's 1570 *Horae* (often referred to as the Alva *Horae*, presumably thanks to a copy bearing the coat of arms of the duke of Alva).

illustrated with engravings, as well as woodcuts, these trend-setting devotional and liturgical works will be the focus of the next chapter.

CONCLUSION

Plantin's unexpected achievements with the 1570 *Horae* and the 1571 *Monumenta* are all the more astounding if we recall his reticent responses a few years before to the propositions Granvelle forwarded from his Italian acquaintances, asking Plantin to print their texts with engraved illustrations. What do these publications teach us that can help explain Plantin's striking change in stance toward producing works with engraved illustrations? Was it, for example, simply a reflection of Plantin's distinct relationships with the people concerned? While Granvelle was clearly a valuable ally to have and hence well worth accommodating – with an engraving of his coat of arms printed on the title-pages of some copies of the 1570 *Horae*, for example – Arias Montano was a revered and respected friend, who may have been able to inspire Plantin to risk and endeavor more. But, however valuable, personal contacts cannot always pay the bills or attend to the essential practical matters of production. Rather, the decisive factors were more likely something so banal but essential as finding either the funds needed to cover the extra exceptional costs associated with producing engraved illustrations or the appropriately skilled staff to assist with such projects.

Clearly, one could not produce books with costly engraved illustrations if one did not have appropriate financial resources or backers. For Arias Montano's publications, at least, this problem appears to have been solved through the assistance of Luis Perez, a wealthy Spanish merchant in Antwerp, who established close, enduring friendships with both Plantin and Arias Montano. Although Perez is often cited as one who helped Plantin periodically when he was in dire financial circumstances in the mid-1570s and 1580s,[139] his role as a financial backer of Arias Montano's publications is not as well known. The evidence of this system of support is best documented for the period when Jan Moretus I was managing the Press following Plantin's death. In these instances, Perez would advance a sum of money and then Jan Moretus would provide him with an equivalent sum in the form of copies of the resulting publication, valued at 40 percent of the normal selling price.[140] In a letter to Jan Moretus from January 3, 1590, however, Arias Montano indicated that similar practices had occurred under Plantin.[141] Although it is not certain when Perez began to support the publication of Arias Montano's works, records of his personal purchases of books begin on October

---

[139] See, e.g., Kingdon 1963, pp. 306, 310–311, and 314.

[140] Occasionally, Perez would purchase extra books, in addition to the initial "exchange." See MPM Arch. 126, fols. 44, 127, and 175, for examples of these transactions. They are discussed in Dirk Imhof's forthcoming dissertation on the publications of Jan Moretus I (Imhof 2007–2008).

[141] See *Corr.*, VIII–IX, no. 1515, p. 621, for the following excerpt: "*Commentaria in librum Iudicum, id est, de republica varia, ante annum absolvi. Ea in mundum descripta servo quoad hominem reperiam cui tuto credere possim ad vos transmittenda. Ad eorum vero impressionem interim nummos aliquot quaesiturus qui vobis subsidio esse possint, quibuscum iisdem cogito conditionibus agere quas cum parente vestro (illo animi mei dimidio) tenui ut, videlicet, quae ego dederim non mihi sed vobis usui evadant, praeter exemplaria aliquot quae amicis donanda remittetis, qua de re iam ad Perezium nostrum longius quae tecum conferret, scripseram.*" (I completed the *Commentaria* a year ago. I am keeping the neatly written manuscript until I can find someone whom I can trust to bring it safely to

18, 1571, when he acquired one copy of the 1571 *Monumenta* (in addition to a few other books). Purchases of additional copies of Arias Montano's publications soon followed, as well as Plantin's gift of a specially bound copy of the *Monumenta* with goffered edges.[142] By March 1572, concurrent with these indisputable examples of his interest in Arias Montano's work, Perez also negotiated a means of helping Plantin out of the serious financial difficulties he incurred through his production of the Polyglot Bible. Perez's solution was to purchase 400 copies of the mammoth publication – one-third of all the copies printed – for the grand sum of 16,800 fl. and see to their distribution himself (on the condition that Plantin would not start to reprint the text or undersell him while his copies remained). In addition, at the end of May 1572, Perez also arranged to have at least twenty-seven (if not forty-nine) copies of the Polyglot Bible sent to Arnold Mylius, an agent of the well-known Birckman family of booksellers in Antwerp and Cologne. Finally, in April 1584, Perez, together with his son-in-law Martin de Varron, agreed to buy an additional 260 copies of the Polyglot Bible, once again for resale elsewhere. Thus, Perez helped Plantin by ultimately relieving him of approximately 700 of the 1,200 copies printed of the Polyglot Bible. For Plantin, Perez's initial large purchase in particular meant that he could enjoy the benefit of ready cash without having to take out an interest-based loan.[143]

There is, consequently, ample evidence of a special relationship between Perez, Plantin, and Arias Montano that may have facilitated the unexpected appearance of two exceptionally richly illustrated publications within a year of one another. Nevertheless, this cannot account for the great technical feat that was achieved with these books or the subsequent sale and general success of Plantin's 1570 *Horae*. While sufficient financial resources clearly eased the production of costly editions with engraved illustrations, such funding was worthless without the essential means of having the illustrations printed and finding an extensive enough market for the resulting books. Recall, for example, that even though Onufrio Panvinio had offered to split the costs (and profits) of his project, Plantin did not accept his proposal, at least in part because Hieronymus Cock did not want to work on it. Plantin's contemporary employment of Pieter Huys for the printing of the illustrations of his de Valverde editions appears to have been similarly unsatisfactory. For, Plantin did not hire him again to print illustrations for his own subsequent projects, even though he continued to employ him as an engraver for several years to come. Did Huys refuse to print plates executed by other engravers, or

---

you. In the meantime, I will look for some money for the printing of it, that will help you financially. I would like to do this with the same conditions as I did with your father [the other half of my soul], namely, that what I would give, would not be for my own advantage, but for yours, except for a few copies that you would send to me to give to my friends. I have already written to our Perez about this extensively, and he will discuss it with you.)

[142] See MPM Arch. 16, fols. 183 lft and 228 lft, for these purchases and Plantin's gift.

[143] For the records of Perez's bulk purchases of the Polyglot Bible and the terms of his agreement with Plantin, see MPM Arch. 19, fols. 19 (rht and lft) and 180 (rht and lft). For Perez's arrangements in conjunction with Arnold Mylius, see MPM Arch. 50, fol. 61v (under May 29, 1572), for the initial record concerning 27 copies. This is continued on fol. 63v (under June 2, 1572), where the shipment of the remaining parts of the original 27 copies and an additional 22 complete copies of the bible is recorded. Rooses also notes an entry indicating that Plantin delivered 400 copies of the Polyglot Bible to Perez on June 23, 1572. Presumably, these were the 400 copies mentioned in his and Plantin's agreement (see Rooses 1880, p. 25).

was Plantin displeased with Huys's work? Was he too expensive, or was he, for example, unable or unwilling to combine the engraved illustrations with the letterpress to the degree that Liefrinck did?

The 1570 *Horae* and the 1571 *Monumenta* succeeded, on the one hand, precisely because Plantin had found a print workshop where technically superior effects could be achieved. This was, notably, that run by Mynken Liefrinck, the widow of Frans Huys, the first engraver Plantin hired to work on his first independent publication with engraved illustrations, the *Vivae imagines*. Liefrinck was clearly the key to the success of Plantin's great breakthrough in the production of books with engraved illustrations. Having proved the skill with which her workshop could satisfy Plantin's complex printing demands, she would continue to serve Plantin as the primary supplier of his engraved illustrations for the remainder of his career. These publications also succeeded because enough buyers were interested in them both to warrant Plantin reprinting them and to inspire other printers to imitate them. The initial sales of Plantin's 1566 de Valverde edition, 1570 *Horae*, and 1571 *Monumenta* edition are telling. For they already reveal in this first, experimental stage of Plantin's production of works with intaglio illustrations which markets Plantin would be able to rely on for regular sales of these editions – Paris and then the Frankfurt book fair – and how he would always have to supplement these sales with a significant, but diverse complement of other buyers who vary according to the book. The continuing importance of both these considerations – the practical feasibility of producing such a book and its subsequent market appeal – will emerge in the course of the next chapters, as we continue to explore the further evolution of Plantin's burgeoning career as a publisher of precious books adorned with engravings. No longer the occasional, willing and unwilling dabbler in the realm of engraved book illustration, Plantin had definitively entered the field with his pair of stellar publications, throwing down the gauntlet to his competitors, challenging them, wittingly or not, to match his works.

CHAPTER FOUR

LITURGICAL EDITIONS AND THE SPREAD OF ENGRAVED BOOK ILLUSTRATIONS

Humanist texts and vernacular classics garnered prestige for the bookmen, but liturgical manuals paid the bills.[1]

Paul Grendler's practical observation concerning the prosperous sixteenth-century Italian family of printers, the Giunti, and their reliance on sales of liturgical editions to build and sustain their extensive family business, can readily be applied to Plantin as well. Indeed, the opportunities for profiting from the sale of liturgical editions were greater than ever in the early 1570s owing to a series of influential decisions made concerning the reform and controlled publication of the essential revised texts. These events were set in motion by a decision taken on the last day of the Council of Trent (December 4, 1563), authorizing the pope to see to the revision of the catechism, missal, and breviary, in addition to other texts, as part of the Council's design to purify and rectify the practice of the Catholic faith.[2] Subsequent papal decrees, stating that the new authorized editions had to be used to the exclusion of all others, immediately created an immense demand for these books in all Catholic countries from which numerous printers (including Plantin) wished to profit. While Plantin may have initially sought the rights to print these texts for simple financial gain, he also took advantage of the huge demand for them to experiment with his production of books with engraved illustrations.

Consequently, our examination of Plantin's production of thousands of copies of these texts will not be a conventional study of religious book illustrations. Rather, we will combine a consideration of the illustration of these books with a study of archival records pertaining to their printing and sale to reveal several essential aspects of how Plantin systematized the incorporation of engravings in his publications. In particular, in this chapter we will focus on the following topics: Plantin's formation of a stock of engravings and etchings; how he went about reusing and supplementing his collection

---

[1] Grendler 1977, p. 170.
[2] For a transcription and translation of this and a related decree, see Tanner 1990, II, fols. 797 and 723–724, respectively.

of plates to maximize its potential use; how he calculated the costs (at least initially) for the inclusion of engraved illustrations; the markets to which Plantin directed these specially illustrated books; and the degree to which his novel production of liturgical editions influenced his competitors. Thus, while our analysis focuses on Plantin's production of liturgical and devotional books, it will also elucidate how he organized the mass production of editions with engraved or etched illustrations to make it a viable, profitable venture with a wide market appeal.

THE REVISED LITURGICAL EDITIONS AND THEIR PRINTERS

In order to appreciate fully Plantin's production of these texts, we need to sketch the context in which they were printed. As indicated above, this great production of liturgical and devotional editions was instigated by a decision taken at the Council of Trent to have texts essential for the practice of the Catholic faith reformed. This was in response to challenges to the faith posed by the Reformation and spread by the unchecked printing of unauthorized versions of these texts.[3] Only certain texts were cited specifically in the Council's decrees. Chief among these were the Vulgate, the only acceptable Latin translation of the Bible; the catechism, a popular manual for Catholic instruction; the breviary, the primary book used by clerics for their personal devotion, derived from the Divine Office; and the missal, the text used by priests to perform the mass. Books of hours, which will also be discussed below, were not named explicitly. The actual revision of these various texts took several years and was completed piecemeal. Of the works cited above, for example, the catechism was completed first (and promulgated in September 1566), while a definitive version of the Vulgate was not completed until 1590.[4]

Inspired, perhaps, by the Council's complaints concerning the lax standards of earlier printers regarding the proper content of these books, the pope also endeavored to control the production of the new authoritative versions of these texts. Each newly revised text was first officially sanctioned, and then recommended to all members of the Catholic community; all previously published versions of the text were banned. The pope thereby created an immediate, immense need for thousands of copies of the given work throughout Europe that numerous printers were eager to satisfy, for their own profit. Nevertheless, the pope typically entrusted the privilege to print each of these newly revised books to just one printer in Rome, who was allowed to negotiate the subdivision of the work among other printers, subject to papal approval. Initially, Paulus Manutius was persuaded to come to Rome and take on this work.[5] All printers who did

---

[3] The Council's concern with printers' free publication of potentially corrupt or dissenting versions of important Catholic texts is most clearly stated in its decree concerning the revision and ultimate exclusive interpretation of the Vulgate bible (see Tanner 1990, II, fols. 664–665, and fols. 723–724).

[4] For a brief description of these texts and their reform, see, e.g., NCE, III, pp. 225–232 (for the catechism), II, pp. 791–792 (for the breviary), and IX, pp. 897–900 (for the missal). For an overview of the reformed bible, see the discussion of the 1590 and 1592 editions of the *Biblia sacra* in Darlow and Moule 1963, II.2, pp. 958–963.

[5] For Manutius and his production of these books, see Barberi 1985. For a detailed study of the arrangements for the printing of the first editions of the new missal, see Duval 1998.

not abide by these arrangements and dared to print unauthorized editions of these texts were liable to fines and excommunication. And yet, with the promulgation of each new text – the catechism in 1566, the breviary in 1568, and the missal in 1570, for example – the prompt appearance of unauthorized editions and official challenges to the papal privileges throughout Europe made it readily apparent that the papal system could not be sustained. Each printer's desire for part of the profits from the numerous guaranteed sales of these books evidently outweighed any fear of sanction. The definitive end to the pope's attempts to maintain exclusive privileges for the printing of these texts came with the promulgation of the new book of hours in 1571 and the subsequent challenges to that privilege made in important printing centers such as Venice, Paris, Lyon, and Antwerp. By 1573, most of these centers had an independent printer authorized by a local authority to print all of the reformed texts, and not just the new book of hours.[6] In Italy, production was typically dominated by the Giunti presses. In France, Jacob Kerver, son of the successful French printers Thielman Kerver and Yolande Bonhomme, had garnered the rights for the initial production of liturgical editions. And in the Netherlands, Plantin (as will be discussed in greater detail below) won the day. Many of the challenges to the exclusive papal privileges reflected longstanding political battles – that between Rome and Venice – and battles of might and right between the kings of France and Spain and the papacy, where the kings challenged the papal right to determine fully and independently who would print liturgical works in their countries.

These challenges also reflected the practical side of things, namely, that the demand for these books was so great that it was impossible for any one printer or simple partnership of a few printers to satisfy alone. For example, once the Venetian printer Dominicus Basa had obtained from Manutius the right to print the new breviary, he then went on to form a sort of consortium with Luc'Antonio Giunti and four other Venetian printers, where the six commanded a total of fourteen presses.[7] In this regard, Plantin had a great advantage over his fellow printers. For, by 1569, when he began printing the reformed breviaries, he alone had ten presses, and that number subsequently increased, hovering between fifteen and sixteen in the years 1574–1575. It was not until the end of 1576, following the sack of Antwerp by Spanish troops, that this number dropped back to just a few working presses and Plantin's initial, immensely productive phase of printing the revised Catholic texts came to an end.[8] Plantin was, in fact, one of the printers Paulus Manutius had asked to come to Rome to help him with his work printing the reformed texts and (as of March 1567) with the printing of the new breviary in particular. Plantin declined, but did, by June 1567, ask Cardinal Granvelle – then in Rome, assisting Philip II's representatives there[9] – to help him obtain the rights to print the new breviary, and then the other liturgical books, for sale in the Low Countries and

[6] For the situation in Italy, see Grendler 1977, pp. 169–181; for France, see Pallier 1982, pp. 329–332; for the Low Countries (i.e., Plantin and his competitors), see Voet, GC, I, pp. 65–67, and Witcombe 1991, pp. 133–140; and for Spain, see Voet, GC, I, pp. 67–68, and Moll 1990.

[7] Grendler 1977, p. 172. For similar arguments that the great demand for these books resulted in the formation of companies that jointly produced the required publications, see Pallier 1982, pp. 331–332 (a brief overview of Pallier 1981).

[8] See Voet, GC, I, pp. 437–438, for the number of presses in use at the *Officina Plantiniana* per year from 1564 through 1765.

[9] On Granvelle, see NBW, I, cols. 566–572.

other neighboring countries. Granvelle succeeded in this task for each of the three primary texts concerned, namely the new breviary, the new missal, and the new book of hours. Nevertheless, Plantin soon encountered local challenges to these privileges.[10]

Of even greater importance, however, at least in terms of the quantity of copies concerned, was the prospect of sales of specially modified versions of the missal and breviary for use in Spanish domains. Philip II, who assumed his traditional right as the king of Spain to govern churches in his territories, took advantage of the general reform of the liturgical editions to petition the pope for the right to have special adaptations of these texts prepared for use in Spanish churches. The pope granted Philip II his wish and thereby created yet another distinct, but large market for missals and breviaries. Plantin readily garnered the first large orders for these books for the Spanish market thanks to Arias Montano, who had written to Philip II, praising Plantin (in contrast with other printers) for both the high quality of his work and his ability to print the large number of books that Philip needed.[11] Officially extended in February 1571 (and ratified by the pope in April of that year), Philip's preference for Plantin was also logical. Plantin was then working on the Polyglot Bible for him and the king had appointed him as his chief printer in the Netherlands ("prototypographus") in 1570, above Plantin's local competitor, Willem Silvius, whom Philip had named as his royal printer in the Netherlands in 1560.[12] Although it has been asserted that Plantin had some sort of monopoly agreement for the production of these books for Philip II, this was not the case in practice.[13] Rather, Plantin was simply the favored, primary provider of the revised liturgical books for the Spanish market until it was no longer possible, practically, for him to do so following the Spanish Fury in 1576. Then, the hieronymite friars at the Escorial, whom Philip had entrusted with the distribution of the reformed texts – the "nuevo rezado" – as of 1573, turned to other publishers, primarily associates of the Giunti. Regardless of how Plantin's initial production of liturgical and other devotional editions for Spain (and elsewhere) is viewed, it provided him with the opportunity to sell more than 50,000 such books to Philip II alone in just four and a half years (from October 1571 through April 1576). As is documented below, thousands of copies of these texts were also sold elsewhere, all in addition to Plantin's other (albeit then more limited) production and sales.[14] Not only did these sales help sustain Plantin's great expansion in the period 1572–1576 (and, presumably, help pay more than a few bills), they also, as argued above, provided him with the opportunity to test out a broader market for works with engraved illustrations.

---

[10] On Plantin's privileges for these books and challenges to them, see Witcombe 1991, pp. 134–140, and Voet, GC, 1, pp. 65–67.

[11] See, for example, Robben 1989, p. 404, and Clair 1960, pp. 91–92.

[12] On Plantin's and Silvius's titles, see Voet, GC, 1, pp. 68–71, and ch. 3, n. 11.

[13] See, e.g., Voet, GC, 1, p. 68, for the traditional view of Plantin's "virtual monopoly" for the printing of the Spanish editions. For the dissenting view, see, e.g., Moll 1987, Moll 1990, and Robben 1989, pp. 404–406.

[14] For an overview of Plantin's sales to Spain in this period, see Imhof 1992, cat. 96 (pp. 229–230), and transcriptions (although occasionally incomplete and misleading – see n. 65 below) in Bécares Botas 1999, pp. 325–346. For an overview of Plantin's general production in these years, see, Voet 1984, pp. 365–366; and the chronological lists of Plantin's publications in PP, VI, pp. 2472–2484.

Determining the appearance of Plantin's liturgical editions

When Plantin published his first editions of the revised breviary in 1569 (PP 805–808), he was in the midst of ordering engraved illustrations for other religious texts: grand title-plates and full-page illustrations for his Polyglot Bible (figs. 3.10–3.11), as well as numerous text illustrations and borders for his 1570 *octavo* book of hours (figs. 3.23–3.24).[15] Nevertheless, these first editions of the reformed breviary were illustrated with only a selection of small woodcuts. Given the text's function as an essential but basic tool for daily prayer for clerics, this is not surprising and is fully consistent with the conventionally sober decoration of breviaries, whereby many earlier editions (including one of Plantin's) bore no illustrations at all.[16] Plantin did not start to illustrate any of his breviary editions with engravings until 1575 (see PP 822–823). Matters were different with Plantin's production of missals, however. Plantin was granted the right to print the reformed missal for the Netherlands, Hungary, and part of Germany in July 1570 and several months later (in February 1571) Philip II awarded him the initial large contracts for the Spanish market. Consequently, Plantin's editions of the reformed missal (published as of 1571; see PP 1675) were destined for both the local and Spanish markets from the start. These were, notably, the first of Plantin's editions of the reformed liturgical texts to have some copies illustrated with engravings: namely, an engraved title-page vignette of the *Last Supper* and occasionally an engraving of the Crucifixion, with and without an engraved border printed around the facing page of text, to mark the start of the canon (see figs. 4.1–4.3). Why did he introduce these illustrations? Although Georg Reyser occasionally included an intaglio image of the *Crucifixion* in his missals, it seems unlikely that Plantin sought to mimic these works specifically.[17] A more logical explanation is that Plantin was seeking to satisfy wishes for engraved illustrations expressed by authorities supervising the printing of the new liturgical editions. Among these figures (who will all be discussed in more detail below) was Benito Arias Montano, who was most likely behind the decision to include engraved illustrations in the Polyglot Bible and whose first text to be illustrated with numerous engravings (his *Humanae salutis monumenta* from 1571) was being printed by Plantin at this time.[18] Plantin may also have decided to include them as part of a calculated marketing ploy. A more detailed examination of the illustration of his editions of these texts in comparison with those printed by his competitors sheds some light on this matter.

It is clear from all accounts of Plantin's acquisition of the rights to print the new liturgical editions from the chosen Roman printers that he always printed his first editions of these texts from sample books (or gatherings thereof) sent from Rome. But the editions of the new breviary printed by Paulus Manutius and the new missal

---

[15] For examples of payments for these illustrations, see appendix 1, under Pieter van der Heyden, Pieter Huys, Jan Sadeler I, and Jan Wierix, in the period 1569–1572.

[16] For Plantin's pre-reform breviaries, see PP 801–803, where PP 802 has no illustrations and both of the others have just one woodcut.

[17] For an example of such missals, see the discussion of Reyser's 1484 *Missale Herbipolense* in BMC, II (1912), p. 570. For more on Reyser's exceptional editions, see the introduction.

[18] On Arias Montano's clear personal preference for engravings, see ch. 3.

4.1 Title-page of *Missale Romanum* (Antwerp: Christopher Plantin, 1571; f°), with the *Last Supper* by Jan Wierix after Peeter vander Borcht, engraving, 103 × 103 (Ghent, Universiteitsbibliotheek, Kostbare werken, Res. 403).

printed by an association of printers in Rome and Venice are illustrated with only a limited selection of woodcuts.[19] Consequently, these works are unlikely candidates for Plantin's inspiration to illustrate his books with engravings. There are also no indications in Plantin's correspondence that someone connected with his work after the Roman models had suggested that he consider including engraved illustrations.

[19] We examined a *Breviarium Romanum* (Rome: Paulus Manutius, 1568) in *octavo* (MPM [R 43.3]), which is cited in a 1592 inventory of the books in Plantin's collection (cf. MPM M 121, fol. 89r) and excerpts from the *editio princeps* of the new *Missale Romanum* (Rome: Successors of Bartolomeo Faletti, Giovanni Varisco, and Associates, 1570) in folio, as well as a *quarto* missal from the same consortium, but printed in Venice in 1571 (MPM [R 40.8] and MPM [B 1223], respectively). For the identification of the excerpts of the *editio princeps* of the new missal, see Duval 1998, p. 164.

4.2 Philips Galle after Maarten van Heemskerck, *Crucifixion*, from *Missale Romanum* (Antwerp: Christopher Plantin, 1572; f°), extra fol. 2v°, engraving, 255 × 179 (Augsburg, Staats- und Stadtbibliothek, 2° Th. Lt K 44).

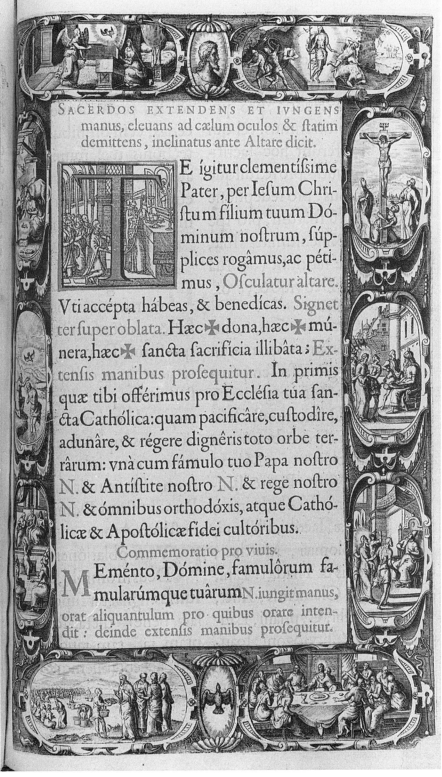

manus, eleuans ad cælum oculos & statim
demittens, inclinatus ante Altare dicit.

TE igitur clementíssime
Pater, per Iesum Chri-
stum filium tuum Dó-
minum nostrum, súp-
plices rogâmus, ac péti-
mus, Osculatur altare.
Vti accépta hábeas, & benedícas. Signet
ter super oblata. Hæc ✠ dona, hæc ✠ mú-
nera, hæc ✠ sancta sacrifícia illibâta ; Extensis manibus prosequitur. In primis
quæ tibi offérimus pro Ecclésia túa sancta Cathólica: quam pacificâre, custodîre,
adunâre, & régere dignêris toto orbe ter-
rârum: vnà cum fámulo tuo Papa nostro
N. & Antístite nostro N. & rege nostro
N. & ómnibus orthodóxis, atque Cathó-
licæ & Apostólicæ fidei cultóribus.

Commemoratio pro viuis.

MEménto, Dómine, famulôrum fa-
mularúmque tuârum N. iungit manus,
orat aliquantulum pro quibus orare inten-
dit : deinde extensis manibus prosequitur.

4.3 Jan Wierix after Peeter vander Borcht, border with scenes from the *Life of Christ*, from *Missale Romanum* (Antwerp: Christopher Plantin, 1572; f°), p. [277], engraving, 310 × 197 (Augsburg, Staats- und Stadtbibliothek, 2° Th. Lt K 44).

When Plantin took on the task of printing the new liturgical editions for Philip II, he did so, apparently, with the understanding that a group of Spanish officials would send instructions as to how these books should be printed (in addition to sample pages and model books). Given Philip's determination to have independent versions of the new liturgical editions composed specially for the Spanish market, as well as his earlier insistence that someone from his court supervise Plantin's printing of the Polyglot Bible, it is not surprising that he made such demands for the printing of these texts. The primary figures at Philip II's court in Madrid who were charged with overseeing Plantin's work in this period were the royal chaplain and tutor to the young Philip II, Francisco de Villalva (or Villalba), Philip's secretary for international political affairs, Gabriel de Çayas (or Zayas), and Philip's keeper of the crown jewels ("guardajoyas del rey"), Hernando de Virbiesca (or Birbiesca).[20] The diversity in the occupations of these individuals is striking, as it ranges from a learned cleric to a political administrator and one entrusted with caring for, protecting, and acquiring some of Philip's costliest possessions – at one time, the keeper of the crown jewels was also responsible for the Burgundian Library.[21] As such, this selection of individuals places Philip II's orders of these books in a much more significant, broader context, with links to otherwise diverse branches of his court. Plantin (initially, at least) did not receive his instructions from this committee directly, but rather via Arias Montano, upon whom he clearly relied for the definitive word as to how he should proceed in this work.[22] The highly detailed nature of these instructions attests to the freedom felt by those charged with supervising Plantin's printing of these texts to dictate, among other aspects, the layout of the text and its visual appearance, from the use of red and black ink, to the type of letters and decorative initials used and the selection of the illustrations. These instructions are, consequently, a logical source for Plantin's new approach to illustrating at least some copies of these texts with a selection of engravings. Nonetheless, one cannot ignore the potential, unspecified input of Arias Montano, whose decided, personal preference for engraved illustrations had already manifested itself in the contemporaneous decision to illustrate both the Polyglot Bible and his own *Monumenta* with engravings.

The single best record of the Spanish advisors' views on the printing and illustration of the new liturgical editions is a set of instructions concerning the printing of the new missal.[23] Although not dated, this text must have been written between February 1, 1571, when Phillip II officially agreed to have Plantin print the new missals and breviaries for Spain, and July 1572, when another missive from Spain was sent to Plantin complaining that he had not yet addressed some of the points in the earlier correspondence, including a couple of the items highlighted below.[24] In the original 1571/1572 document, six of

---

[20] For the identification of these men as the primary advisors in Spain, see Moll 1990, p. 17. For more information on de Villalva, see Dávila Pérez 2002, I, p. 36, and Bécares Botas 1999, p. 277; for de Çayas, see Bécares Botas 1999, p. 244; and for de Virbiesca, see Bécares Botas 1999, pp. 113 and 140.

[21] For the tasks of the keeper of the crown jewels, at least at the court in Brussels in the sixteenth and seventeenth centuries, see Aerts et al. 1995, I, pp. 172–177.

[22] For Arias Montano's role as intermediary, see a letter Plantin wrote in August 1572 to the Spanish government (*Corr.*, III, no. 412).

[23] MPM Arch. 122, pp. 1–15.

[24] See MPM Arch. 122, pp. 87–94 and pp. 97–104, for two copies of this letter of complaint, a transcription of which is printed in *Corr.*, III, no. 407. The date of this text, which was added to one version of it (see

some twenty-five items in total (nos. 10–15) addressed the illustrations. Among these, four of the six (nos. 10–13) were concerned with detailing a sort of hierarchy of the feast days and having that reinforced visually by determining which sections of the text should be marked with an introductory image (and possibly a border) and, if so, how large that image should be. The subjects of these images were never specified, but were supposed to be "appropriate to the feast."[25] In the remaining two items, one (no. 14) emphasized that the introit of the remaining feast days and the start of the gospel lessons should be marked not with an image or with gothic letters, but rather, with "illuminated cases" ("casos illuminados") – historiated initials, perhaps – like the ones included in the sample sheets sent with these instructions – but regrettably no longer accompanying this document. In the last item (no. 15) the illustration of the title-page is discussed. Here, the Spanish advisors state that either there should be no image at all on the title-page, or else, if one had to be included, a representation of SS Peter and Paul, as in the missal of "His Holiness" (that is, the pope), or else a portrait of the pope would be acceptable.[26] This is the only time that the subject of the preferred image was noted.

In a separate letter from Francisco de Villalva from February 18, 1573, it appears that similar decorative conventions – namely, that images and possibly borders were to mark the "principal feasts" of the book – were to be applied to Plantin's production of the new breviaries as well – just as was done already in his books of hours.[27] However, the preferred technique for the illustrations (woodcuts, engravings, or etchings) was never stated explicitly in any of the instructions sent from Spain concerning the printing of these editions. Only a preference for some of the engravings included in some of

p. 87), is, in turn, confirmed by Plantin's response to it, in which he notes that the letter was sent in July 1572 and that he had received it on August 7 of the same year (see MPM Arch. 122, pp. 79–81, pp. 83–85, and pp. 588–589, for three separate copies of this letter; and MPM Arch. 8, fols. 13v–14v, for the original draft of it, which, on fol. 13v, bears a similarly written note regarding the dating of the letter of complaint). The transcription of Plantin's response in *Corr.*, III, no. 412, consists of a selection of excerpts from the various versions of the letter cited above.

25 For such a reference, see, e.g., item 12: "en todos los suso dictios dias se pongan imagenes grandes al principio de los Introitos de las missas al proposito de la fiesta del tamaño que van en las hojas que se le embian . . ." (on all the above cited days there must be large images at the start of the introit of the masses appropriate to the feast, of the size shown in the pages that are sent to you . . .) (MPM Arch. 122, p. 5). See item 13 (MPM Arch. 122, p. 5) for a similar remark.

26 "En la primera hoja del Missal se ponga el titulo de la mesma forma y manera q.' [que] va enel missal de su sanctidad y ono se ponga alli ymagen alguna sino solas las letras del titulo grandes o si se vbieren de poner imagines sean sanct Pedro y Sanct Pablo como van enel missal de su sanctidad y podran si quisieren poner alli el retracto del papa como va enel missal q' [que] de aca se embia . . ." (On the first page of the missal the title should be placed in the same form and manner as in the missal of His Holiness [the Pope] and either no images at all but only the large letters of the heading or, if one must put an image there, it must be one of SS Peter and Paul, as in the missal of His Holiness and they may, if they wish, put here the portrait of the pope, as it appears in the missal that was sent to you from here . . .) (MPM Arch. 122, p. 6, item 15.)

27 "En estos breviarios de camera ansi en los de pergamino, como en los de papel se podran poner algunas imagines y orlas y viñetas, en algunas fiestas principales, como se ponen en las horas, y se han de poner en los missales conforme a la muestra de las imagines y estampas que aca han venido." (In these breviaries "de camera," both those in parchment and in paper, some images and borders and vignettes can be placed by some principal feasts as they are placed in the Horae, and they must be put in the missals according to the models of the images and prints that have arrived here.) (MPM Arch. 122, pp. 532–533.)

Plantin's books of hours is expressed in letters from 1572–1573 from two of the Spanish advisors, Hernando de Virbiesca and de Villalva.[28]

To what extent, then, were these directives followed by Plantin? The easiest and most obvious "tests" for the application of the instructions concerning the illustration of Plantin's missals are the last two items noted, namely, the decoration of the title-page and the omission of extra illustrations prior to either non-specified introits or the gospel excerpts. In both cases, there is a clear break between Plantin's first missal editions from 1571 and 1572 and those from 1573–1576, when Plantin's sales of these editions were dominated by shipments to Spain. Specifically, in his first few missal editions (PP 1675–1678), Plantin, like all the other printers publishing the newly reformed missals – the Faletti–Varisco consortium in Rome and Venice, the Giunti Press in Venice, and Jacob Kerver in Paris – set small woodcut images in the text, marking many of the gospel excerpts.[29] Plantin alone ceased this practice, such that of the twenty missal editions he is credited with publishing as of 1573, only one *octavo* missal from 1577 (PP 1697) is known to have such extra small inserted woodcut illustrations. Plantin's own views regarding this type of decoration are conveyed in his August 1572 letter, written in response to a list of complaints from the Spaniards supervising his production of missals. Here he states: "We will subsequently omit, with great pleasure, the images at the start of the gospels. In this case, we followed only the recommendation from Rome."[30]

Plantin's selection of an image for the title-page of his missals follows a similar pattern. Namely, while Plantin occasionally printed an image of the *Last Supper* on his first missal editions (as in fig. 4.1), he consistently used an image of SS Peter and Paul (one of the options specified in the Spanish instructions) for the illustration of all of his missals (known to us) printed between 1573 and 1585 (PP 1680–PP 1699; as in fig. 4.6). As suggested by the instructions from Spain, some of the first missals printed by the Faletti–Varisco consortium in Rome and Venice, working under the direction of the Vatican, also had an image of SS Peter and Paul on the title-page.[31] Plantin's other

---

[28] Consider, for example, MPM Arch. 122, p. 503, part of a letter from 1572 or 1573 from de Villalva in which he asks that "Que en todo caso haga una impression de las Horas de la gran letra en que imprimio las dela Duquesa de Alva, y que te[ng?]an las mismas estampas y orlas, y sean de la misma forma y manera." (That in all cases the "Horas" [i.e., books of hours] must be printed with the letter used in that of the Duchess of Alva (PP 1367) and with the same prints and borders and be made in the same form and manner.) Or see MPM Arch. 122, pp. 526–527, part of a set of instructions from de Virbiesca from October 20, 1573 concerning the printing of the missals, breviaries, and books of hours, which reads: "El yndice de los Himnos, psalmos y canticas que esta antes del psalterio y . . . de poner una plancha de cobre de las Horas grandes. Que sea una muy buena ymagin. de Nuestra Señor o de Nuestra Señora lo que alla mejor Paresciere queste en la pagina antes del psalterio que le corresponda." (That the index of the hymns, psalms, and canticles must be removed from its place before the Psalter and . . . one must place a copper plate from the "grandes Horae" [PP 1769] [there] that must be a very attractive image of Our Lord or Our Lady that will relate to the adjacent page of the Psalter better [than the indices].)

[29] For examples of this common practice among Plantin's competitors, see, e.g., MPM (B 1223), a 1571 *quarto* Faletti–Varisco edition, BS Munich (8° Liturg. 843), a 1574 *octavo* Giunti edition, and BL (845.e.3), a 1577 *octavo* Kerver edition.

[30] "Figuras in principiis Evangeliorum libentissimè praetermittemus posthac. Nos verò hac in re sequuti fueramus consilium Romanum." (MPM Arch. 122, p. 80, item 6, transcribed in *Corr.*, III, no. 407, pp. 170–171.)

[31] See, e.g., MPM (R 40.8), which comprises excerpts from a folio edition printed in Rome in 1570, and MPM (B 1223), a *quarto* edition printed in Venice in 1571.

competitors for the production of liturgical editions, however, did not consistently use such an image on the title-page of their missals. Rather, a full range of subjects, as well as the respective printers' personal devices, appear instead. Thus, once again, following the receipt of various sets of instructions from Spain between 1571 and July 1572, Plantin altered his initial practices for the illustration of this text in order to apply specific wishes expressed in these directives that would, in turn, distinguish his editions from his primary competitors in this field.

Another aspect of the embellishment of Plantin's missals that changed between his first folio editions from 1571–1572 (PP 1675–1678) and all the editions he is known to have printed thereafter was the selection of text illustrations. Aside from the numerous small woodcuts marking, for example, the start of readings from the gospels, Plantin's first folio editions bore only a couple of full-page images marking the start of the body of the text and the canon. By contrast, all of Plantin's subsequent missals featured a greater selection of larger text illustrations marking the start of various essential subdivisions of the text, in addition to specific feast days, and none of the smaller woodcuts marking the gospel readings. While Plantin's omission of the smaller inserted illustrations can (as noted above) be attributed to an effort to follow instructions sent from Spain, matters are not as clear cut in terms of the array of larger text illustrations.

The use of larger woodcuts of various sizes to mark the start of certain feast days was a common practice among other printers of the new liturgical editions – Jacob Kerver in Paris, and the Giunti Press in Venice, for example.[32] It was an established convention for the visual definition of texts that can readily be traced back to the illustration of manuscripts, where decorative elements of various sizes were used to mark and simultaneously underscore a relative hierarchy among selected components of the text.[33] Such a hierarchical use of illustrations (and occasionally borders) was also outlined in detail in the instructions sent from Spain.[34] Nevertheless, the specific selection of texts that were ultimately highlighted in Plantin's missals, and the relative scale of the related images, do not agree fully with what was set out in the Spanish missives. For example, Plantin's missals from 1573 onwards do not have nearly as many full-page (or relatively large) images with borders as was advocated in the Spanish instructions.[35] In addition, other feasts and even, occasionally, entire sections of the missal (for example, the *Commune sanctorum*) that were not mentioned in the Spanish directives, are illustrated in Plantin's missals from 1573 onwards. The influence of other individuals in determining the decorative program of Plantin's missals is clearest in an annotated copy of one of his *quarto* missals from 1573.[36] For while the relative size of the woodcuts used to decorate this book largely agree with the stipulations in the Spanish instructions, someone has gone through this copy and periodically noted

[32] There are numerous examples of this practice among Kerver and Giunti editions. See, e.g., MPM (B 1087), a 1571 folio missal from Kerver that was also cited in the 1592 inventory of Plantin's books (cf. MPM M 121, fol. 88r); and BL (C.35.d.19), a 1576 *octavo* Giunti missal.

[33] See, e.g., Toubert 1982, p. 97.   [34] MPM Arch. 122, pp. 3–6, items 10–13.

[35] For this point, compare the list of subjects in MPM Arch. 122, pp. 4–5, item 12, with the selection of full-page illustrations in Plantin's 1574 folio missal (Cambridge, Trinity College Library (E.3.56)).

[36] MPM (R 54.26); PP 1682.

alterations in scale for many of the illustrations. In a couple of cases, the image of *All Saints* accompanying the November 1 feast day for All Saints in the *Proprium missarum de sanctis* (fol. k3v), for example, the annotation indicates that the image should be larger and fill an entire page ("heel page"). More often than not, however, the relevant image was to be made smaller ("klein"), as was the case, for example, with an image of the *Adoration of the Magi*, marking the text for "In epiphania domini" (fol. C8r) of the *Proprium missarum de tempore*. Notably, while both of these changes do not follow what was stipulated in the Spanish directives, they would both (along with other images) distinguish the appearance of all Plantin's subsequently printed missals from those printed by his competitors.

Thus, aspects of the characteristic appearance of Plantin's missals can be traced back both to instructions sent from Spain and to other unknown advisors. The influence of Spanish wishes is clearest in the placement of an image of SS Peter and Paul on the title-page and the omission of numerous smaller inserted woodcuts. While Plantin's shift to featuring a selection of main text illustrations in assorted sizes may also have been inspired by the Spanish directives, the ultimate selection of subjects and their relative scale was determined by other, potentially local advisors, such as theologians from the University of Leuven or Antwerp clerics. Of all the possible sources of influence, the original Roman models now seem the least likely. For, with the exception of the subject of the title-page vignette – suggested, in fact, by Plantin's Spanish advisors – all the other essential traits of the illustration of those texts were clearly disregarded and altered in the final conception of the illustrations in Plantin's books.

And what of Plantin's decision to illustrate at least some portion of his editions with engraved illustrations, the most striking difference of all between his editions of the new liturgical texts and those printed by his competitors? While a preference for some of the engravings seen in Plantin's books of hours was occasionally expressed in letters from his Spanish advisors, there is no indication that they suggested Plantin consistently illustrate his books in this fashion. Did Plantin venture into this untried realm of illustration at the suggestion of Arias Montano or some local advisor, or was it his own initiative? The evidence of when Plantin started to acquire the necessary copper plates, the way in which he used them, and the way in which he calculated the charges for including engravings in these books suggests an answer to this question. Namely, while Arias Montano may have encouraged him to include engraved illustrations, Plantin's cost-effective, profit-minded use of them reflects his own business-minded approach to introducing engraved illustrations on such an unprecedented scale.

PLANTIN'S COMPILATION OF HIS STOCK OF ENGRAVED PLATES

When Plantin began to print the newly revised Catholic texts, he already had some engraved plates that could (and would) serve to illustrate these works, namely those ordered for the illustration of his 1570 *Horae* in octavo, as well as some of the plates ordered for the embellishment of his 1571 edition of Arias Montano's *Humanae salutis monumenta*.[37] But these plates were not always the right size – cut for the illustration of *octavo* books, they could not be used readily as full-page illustrations for larger books – nor did they comprise all of the subjects Plantin needed for the embellishment of missals, the first of the newly reformed texts that he printed with engraved images. Thus, many of the illustrations in these first editions constituted a new, additional investment. Both the extant copies of these first editions and the archival records of their sale indicate that Plantin initially ordered relatively few new plates for these books. The first image that is known to have been used is an engraving of the *Last Supper*, present on the title-pages of some copies of the first missal edition he printed in 1571 (fig. 4.1). In the next two years, Plantin acquired a few more single plates for the illustration of his folio and *quarto* missals. These included at least one full-page illustration of the *Crucifixion* and an accompanying border to highlight the start of the canon in some of his folio missals from 1572 (figs. 4.2 and 4.3). This part of the text was traditionally embellished with such an image (but then a woodcut) even when other sections of the missal were left without comparably scaled illustrations.[38] Also significant was an image of St. Jerome for the Spanish offices, an engraved version of which was included in some missals by at least 1573.[39]

It was not with his first missal editions, but rather, with editions of the new book of hours that Plantin appears to have taken the plunge in terms of commissioning large numbers of engravings for the illustration of his books.[40] For, in 1573, Plantin published several editions of books of hours in a variety of formats (large *octavo*, ordinary *octavo*, 12°, and 32°), where each edition was subdivided into a number of copies with woodcuts and a number of copies with engravings.[41] Although a few of the plates used to illustrate the large *octavo* edition are dated 1570 or 1571 (see fig. 4.4) – a year or more prior to Plantin's receipt of the official papal permission ("licentia") to print the reformed book of hours in March 1572 – many of the engravings used to illustrate these editions were not completed until 1573 (see fig. 4.5).[42] Consequently, what is known about the execution of these plates confirms what is suggested by the books themselves, namely, that while Plantin was already engaged in commissioning some

---

37 See the discussion of the 1585 *quarto* missal below for examples of the reuse of these plates.

38 Cf., e.g., the Faletti–Varisco missals cited in n. 31 above.

39 Although no copies of the 1573 folio missal with the engraved illustration of St. Jerome are known (see PP 1680 for a basic description of this edition and the archival references to the inclusion of this image in some copies shipped to Spain), the image may have been comparable to (or even the same as) that present in a 1574 folio Plantin missal preserved in Trinity College, Cambridge (E.3.56; cf. PP 1685) (see fig. 4.10).

40 While the Latin title for a book of hours (devoted to the Virgin) is often best known as a *Horae Beatae Mariae Virginis*, following the reform of the text, the Latin title was altered to the *Officium beatae Mariae Virginis* (BMV). In order to avoid confusion, in the following discussion we will generally simply refer to books of hours and not use one of these specific titles.

41 For basic descriptions of these editions, see PP 1769–1773. See under the same numbers in Bowen 1997a, pp. 235–241, for more information concerning the timing of the printing and illustration of each edition. Given the evidence of sales of 32° books of hours with engravings as of January 1573 (see appendix 3, figure A.3.1), it appears that the suggestion in Bowen 1997a that only the second edition in 32° (PP 1773) was illustrated with engravings is wrong.

42 See Bowen 1997a, pp. 236–237, for the three 1570–1571 engravings. See Bowen 1994, pp. 291–293, for the 1573 dating of a set of engravings used to illustrate a book of hours in 12°. See appendix 1, p. 344, for Pieter Huys's work on illustrations for a book of hours in 32°. Regrettably, no payments are known to date the production of the remaining plates.

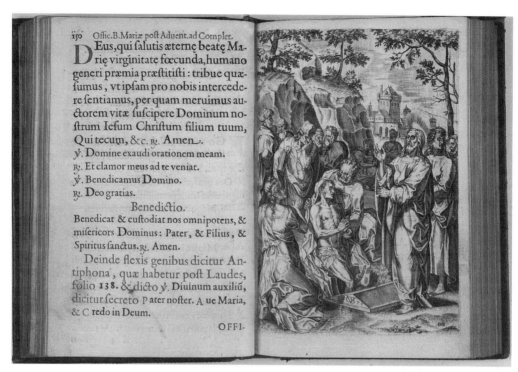

4.4 Abraham de Bruyn after Crispin van den Broeck, *Raising of Lazarus*, from *Officium B. Mariae Virginis* (Antwerp: Christopher Plantin, 1573; 8°), fol. K4r, engraving, 171 × 116 (Antwerp, Museum Plantin-Moretus, 8–604).

engravings for the illustration of his books of hours by 1571, his full-scale investment in this venture did not begin until 1573 (or 1572, if one allows for the time lag between the commissioning of the plates and their completion), once he was more certain of his rights to print them.

In 1574, within a year of the appearance of this assortment of richly illustrated books of hours, Plantin began to apply a similar approach to the illustration of his missals, whereby editions in a variety of formats (folio, *quarto*, and *octavo*) were printed with either a complete series of woodcut illustrations, or a series of engravings of the same subjects.[43] Once again, a number of new plates had to be made in order to complete the expected series of illustrations for these texts (see, for example, figs. 4.6–4.9 and 4.11). In 1575, Plantin rounded out his ventures in the new world of engraved book illustrations that he had created by similarly producing copies of breviaries (in folio and in *quarto*) with a full series of engraved text illustrations (see figs. 4.12 and 4.13).[44] As in

[43] See PP 1685, 1686, and 1688, for these books. While no copy of the *quarto* edition is known (with woodcuts or engravings), copies of the other editions have come to light since the publication of Voet, PP, IV: see Cambridge, Trinity College (E.3.56) for the folio edition, and MPM (8-637) for the *octavo* edition. Another copy of the latter is preserved in the Cultura Fonds in Dilbeek, Belgium (see Sorgeloos 1990, cat. 331).

[44] See PP 822 and 823 for these two editions.

4.5 Jan Wierix after Peeter vander Borcht, *Annunciation*, from *Officium beatae Mariae Virginis* (Antwerp: Christopher Plantin, 1573; 12°), p. 32, engraving, *c*.55 × 55 (MPM Arch. 1230, fol. 619v). Compare fig. 4.23, where the same engraving is used to illustrate a missal Plantin printed in 1585.

all the preceding cases, this also entailed the purchase of extra engravings, although the lack of surviving copies of the *quarto* edition makes it impossible to determine precisely how many. Plantin did not introduce engraved or etched illustrations to other essential Catholic books until the later 1580s when, for example, he began to produce editions of Petrus Canisius's *Manuale catholicorum* with etched and engraved illustrations (see chapter 5).

How many intaglio plates did Plantin commission between 1570 and 1575 in this initial, large-scale immersion in the illustration of these texts? Various factors make it difficult to determine this exactly. Chief among these is the lack of copies of some of the editions under consideration, which impedes learning precisely which subjects were used to illustrate the given text. Two essential characteristics of Plantin's purchases

4.6 Title-page of *Missale Romanum* (Antwerp: Christopher Plantin, 1574; f°), with SS *Peter and Paul* by Jan Wierix after an anonymous artist, engraving, 116 × 125 (Cambridge, Trinity College Library, E.3.56).

and use of his stock of copper plates complicate the matter further. The first is his habit of reusing plates not only for later editions of the text for which a particular plate was first ordered, but also for other texts, which happen to have the same subject among their illustrations. For example, one engraving of the *Annunciation* that was first used for the illustration of Plantin's luxury book of hours from 1570 (fig. 4.14) was subsequently reused to illustrate some copies of Benito Arias Montano's *Humanae salutis monumenta* (fig. 4.15), and most likely some of Plantin's missals and breviaries, in which this same subject, if not the exact same engraving, regularly appeared (see figs. 4.16 and 4.20). This is all in addition to the appearance of this same plate in copies of other editions of Plantin's books of hours.[45]

---

[45] On the reuse of plates in Plantin's books of hours, see Bowen 1997b, pp. 145–150, and p. 147 under M-H 2181, copy c, for the reuse of this specific plate.

4.7 Anonymous artist after Gerard van Groeningen, *Adoration of the Shepherds*, from *Missale Romanum* (Antwerp: Christopher Plantin, 1574; f°), fol. B5v, engraving, 294 × 199 (Cambridge, Trinity College Library, E.3.56).

The second essential feature of Plantin's handling of his stock of copper plates is the contemporaneous existence (and use) of two or more plates made after the same composition. It is logical to imagine ordering a new plate of an acceptable composition once the original could no longer provide satisfactory impressions. This appears to have been done, for example, for several of the folio plates that were first used to illustrate Plantin's 1574 folio missal (PP 1685). As missals and breviaries were often illustrated with several of the same subjects, when Plantin planned to embellish some copies of his 1575 folio breviary with engravings, it made good economic sense to reuse whichever plates he could from the 1574 folio missal. But, by the time he was ready to have nearly 130 copies of his 1575 breviary illustrated with engravings for Philip II, he had already sent Philip 1,000 copies of the 1574 folio missal, as well as 322 copies of his 1575

4.8 Anonymous artist (Peeter vander Borcht?), border with scenes from the *Passion of Christ*, from *Missale Romanum* (Antwerp: Christopher Plantin, 1574; f°), fol. Dd6r, etching, 295 × 191 (Cambridge, Trinity College Library, E.3.56).

folio missal, illustrated with engravings.[46] These shipments alone – excluding sales of copies of these books with engraved illustrations to other clients – clearly exceeded Plantin's contemporary best estimate of 1,000 impressions, as the number of usable images that normally could be pulled from a copper plate.[47] Thus, if only one plate was used for the printing of a given image in the 1574 missal, it should have been, according to Plantin's estimates, mostly worn out and in need of being replaced. It is, therefore, not surprising to see that at least two of the six images common to Plantin's

46 See MPM Arch. 22, fols. 70r–70v, and 74v, for the shipments of the breviary; fols. 61v–62r, for the 1575 folio missal; and fols. 45v–49v, for the 1574 folio missal. Regrettably, no copy of the 1575 folio missal is known to compare with copies of the other editions.

47 See appendix 2 for a transcription and translation of this estimate, which is part of a summary of the costs of printing texts with engraved illustrations that will be discussed in greater detail below.

4.9 Anonymous artist after Peeter vander Borcht, *Marriage at Cana*, from *Missale Romanum* (Antwerp: Christopher Plantin, 1574; f°), fol. EE7v, engraving, 72 × 72 (Cambridge, Trinity College Library, E.3.56). See fig. 4.26 for copy of this engraving.

1574 folio missal and 1575 folio breviary were printed from different plates after the same subjects.[48]

For smaller engravings of common subjects that could more easily be added to books in a variety of formats, like the *octavo* image of the *Annunciation* highlighted above, it is logical that numerous plates had to be made of that image in order to illustrate all the editions of the various texts in which it might be used. For example, thus far, we have been able to trace five distinct plates made after this one composition for the

[48] The two subjects that were repeated between these two books, but with different plates are the images of the *Adoration of the Shepherds* (fig. 4.7) and *Pentecost* (see Holl. *Dutch & Flemish*, LXX, nos. 20.2 and 15.7). It is also possible that two different engravings of the *Resurrection* (*New Holl.*, *Van Groeningen*, II, no. 264) were used in these two books, but the original of this image is missing from the only known copy of Plantin's 1574 folio missal (see Cambridge, Trinity College [E.3.56]). We compared the Cambridge missal with a copy of the 1575 folio breviary in the Escorial (1.IV.14).

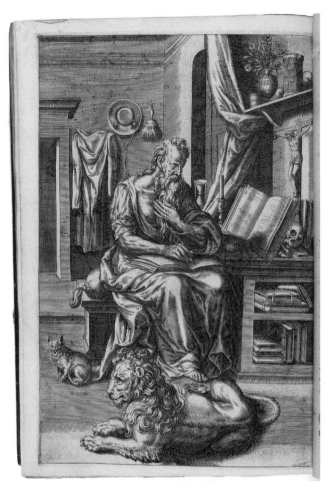

4.10 Anonymous artists, *St. Jerome*, from *Missale Romanum* (Antwerp: Christopher Plantin, 1574; f°), fol. †8v, engraving, 306 × 207 (Cambridge, Trinity College Library, E.3.56).

illustration of books printed at the *Officina Plantiniana* (compare figs. 4.14 and 4.17–4.20). What is notable – not to mention particularly frustrating if one is trying to determine how many plates Plantin had in use at any one time – is that most of these plates were used contemporaneously with one another. Indeed, it appears that the plates featured in figs. 4.14 and 4.17 were both made for Plantin by 1570–1571 and were then reused simultaneously, together with yet another plate after the same composition (fig. 4.18), in 1575 (as well as in later years, as is seen in figs. 4.15 and 4.16).[49]

Consequently, however much contemporary cataloguers of book illustrations are inclined to discuss a particular "set" of illustrations for a specific book, this was clearly not how Plantin (or the printer of his illustrations) thought about the matter. Rather,

[49] For evidence of the reuse of these plates, see Bowen 1997b, p. 147, and Bowen 2003, graph 3.1 under the *Annunciation* and M-H 2181.

4.11 Anonymous artists, *Ascension of Christ*, from *Missale Romanum* (Antwerp: Christopher Plantin, 1574; 8°), fol. BB6r, engraving, 72 × 72 (Antwerp, Museum Plantin-Moretus, 8–637). See fig. 4.22, where the same engraving is used to illustrate a larger missal Plantin printed in 1585.

Plantin maintained a general stock of plates from which he could draw as needed for the illustration of these books. This attitude is also reflected in the inventory made of his copper plates in which some plates were grouped together as, for example, "25 diverses figuras in 8° pour Hora, Breviarium et Missale."[50] The illustration of Plantin's 1585 *quarto* missal (PP 1699) clearly attests to this "mix-and-match" approach. This was the first missal Plantin had printed since 1577, when the war in the Low Countries, the new Protestant government in Antwerp, and the resulting difficulties in being associated with the Catholic, Spanish king, all made the production of the reformed liturgical works an impractical, less profitable activity. Aside from a few images that were common to Plantin's *quarto* missals – the woodcut border around the start of the

50 See appendix 4 for this and other comparable entries.

4.12 Pierre Dufour after Crispin van den Broeck?, *King David*, from *Breviarium Romanum* (Antwerp: Christopher Plantin, 1575; f°), fol. ∗∗∗∗4v, engraving, 287 × 183 (Biblioteca Nacional de España, Madrid, ʀi/3).

4.13 Anonymous artists, *King David*, from *Breviarium Romanum* (Antwerp: Christopher Plantin, 1575; 4°), fol. ****6v, engraving, 171 × 116 (Antwerp, Museum Plantin-Moretus, A579).

canon on p. 215, for example – the majority of the engravings in this book had previously been used to illustrate either completely distinct texts or else missals in other formats. The following images demonstrate the variety of the alternative uses of the illustrations present in copies of this book.[51] Specifically, some of the *quarto* (full-page) images used here, like the image of *King David* (fol. **** 4v), had previously appeared in Plantin's large *octavo* book of hours from 1575 (PP 1776, p. [213]) and his *quarto* breviary from the same year (fig. 4.13). Others, like the engraving of the *Crucifixion* (fol. O3v), had already been used in Plantin's 1583 *quarto* edition of Arias Montano's *Humanae salutis monumenta* (PP 590, fol. R1r) and 1583 folio Latin bible (PP 690, fol. G7v). Illustrations that were one size smaller had appeared in Plantin's *octavo* books of hours and, occasionally, in *octavo* editions of Arias Montano's *Monumenta* (see fig. 4.21).[52] Some of the 1585 missal illustrations were also common to missals printed in other formats (see figs. 4.22 and 4.11).[53]

---

[51] These observations are based upon the copy of this missal in MPM (4–207). Other copies have a different selection of plates (but the same series of subjects). Such variation is not unusual among Plantin's devotional and liturgical editions with engraved illustrations. For other examples of this see, e.g., Bowen 2003 and the discussion of Plantin's 1575 *Officium BMV* in Bowen 1997b.

[52] This plate was trimmed (primarily along the bottom edge) before being printed in the 1585 missal. See Bowen 1997b, p. 147, and Bowen 2003, graph 3.1, under M-H 2184, copy a, for the earlier use of this engraving of the *Nativity* in Plantin's books of hours and the *Monumenta*.

[53] This same plate was also included in, for example, Plantin's 1574 folio missal (Cambridge, Trinity College [E.3.56], fol. Bb5v).

4.14 Anonymous artist after Peeter vander Borcht, *Annunciation*, from *Horae beatissimae Virginis Mariae* (Antwerp: Christopher Plantin, 1570; 8°), fol. g8v, engraving (M-H 2181 c, state I), 116 × 74 (Antwerp, Museum Plantin-Moretus, R 55.27). Figs. 4.14–4.16 exhibit three states of the same engraving, as used over a period of more than twenty years, while figs. 4.14 and 4.17–4.20 represnt five different engravings, all made after the same composition and used to illustrate publications of the *Officina Plantiniana* for at least twenty years.

4.15 Anonymous artist after Peeter vander Borcht, *Annunciation*, from Benito Arias Montano, *Humanae salutis monumenta* (Antwerp: Christopher Plantin, 1581; 8°), fol. E6r, engraving (M-H 2181 c, state II), 116 × 74 (Antwerp, Museum Plantin-Moretus, R 55.23). See the remarks appended to fig. 4.14.

4.16 Anonymous artist after Peeter vander Borcht, *Annunciation*, from *Missale Romanum* (Antwerp: Jan Moretus I, 1594; 8°), fol. ✳✳✳✳8v, engraving (M-H 2181 c, state III), 116 × 74 (Antwerp, Museum Plantin-Moretus, A 1641). See the remarks appended to fig. 4.14.

4.17 Abraham de Bruyn after Peeter vander Borcht, *Annunciation*, from Benito Arias Montano, *Humanae salutis monumenta* (Antwerp: Christopher Plantin, 1571; 8°), fol. E6r, engraving (M-H 2181 b, state I), 116 × 74 (Leuven, Katholieke Universiteit, Maurits Sabbebibliotheek, R 38 T ARIA HUM 1571). See the remarks appended to fig. 4.14.

4.18 Jan Wierix after Peeter vander Borcht, *Annunciation*, from *Officium B. Mariae Virginis* (Antwerp: Christopher Plantin, 1573; 8°), fol. B8v, engraving (M-H 2181 "Original," state I), 112 × 75 (Antwerp, Museum Plantin-Moretus, 4–228). See the remarks appended to fig. 4.14.

4.19 Anonymous artist after Peeter vander Borcht, *Annunciation*, from *Officium B. Mariae Virginis* (Antwerp: Christopher Plantin, 1575; 8°), fol. B8v, engraving (M-H 2181 a, state I), 113 × 75 (Antwerp, Museum Plantin-Moretus, 4–232). See the remarks appended to fig. 4.14.

4.20 Anonymous artist after Peeter vander Borcht, *Annunciation*, from *Breviarium Romanum* (Antwerp: Jan Moretus I, 1590; 16°), vol. I, fol. K8v, engraving and etching (M-H 2181: unknown version), 93 × 62 (Antwerp, Museum Plantin-Moretus I, A 1284). See the remarks appended to fig. 4.14.

4.21 Abraham de Bruyn after Peeter vander Borcht, *Nativity*, from *Missale Romanum* (Antwerp: Christopher Plantin, 1585; 4°), fol. B2r, engraving, 95 × 63 (Antwerp, Museum Plantin-Moretus, A 802).

4.22 Anonymous artists, *Ascension of Christ*, from *Missale Romanum* (Antwerp: Christopher Plantin, 1585; 4°), fol. Q4r, engraving, 72 × 72 (Antwerp, Museum Plantin-Moretus, A 802). See fig. 4.11 for an earlier use of this same engraving.

Finally, many of the smallest illustrations came either from plates made for Plantin's 12° books of hours (see figs. 4.23 and 4.5) or editions of his 24° *Sanctorum kalendarii Romani* and *Evangeliorum* (see figs. 4.24 and 6.2). Although the number of possible sources for the illustrations of this book – seven or more – may be unusually high for Plantin's editions, the practice of reusing plates in diverse texts in various formats was not. Indeed, such puzzles of plates of diverse origins are common to the illustration of Plantin's liturgical and devotional editions, as they were illustrated with so many of the same subjects. For, in this system of illustration, only the subject and the size of the plate mattered and not the concept of neat, stylistically consistent sets of images for individual editions.

Having identified Plantin's guiding principles for the acquisition and use of his copper plates, it is now possible to return to the original question of how many plates Plantin may have had, initially, for the illustration of his liturgical editions, and make an educated estimate. To this end, we will focus on the period 1573–1575, when Plantin

4.23 Jan Wierix after Peeter vander Borcht, *Annunciation*, from *Missale Romanum* (Antwerp: Christopher Plantin, 1585; 4°), fol. CC4v, engraving, 55 × 55 (Antwerp, Museum Plantin-Moretus, A 802). See fig. 4.5 for an earlier use of this same engraving.

was commissioning all the plates (and woodcuts) he needed to illustrate each of the texts most actively sought at the time – books of hours, breviaries, and missals – in a full range of formats. By following the basic principles Plantin himself applied to selecting plates for the illustration of each of these editions – namely, the subject represented and the relative scale of the image – we can make a rough estimate of the minimum number of plates that he must have had by 1575 in order to illustrate all of these publications.

Let us begin with Plantin's books of hours, the first of the texts under consideration that he illustrated with engravings. Between 1570 and 1575, Plantin published books of hours with engraved illustrations in large *octavo*, *octavo*, 12°, 24°, and 32°, where each of these formats required a set of illustrations in a different scale from the rest in order to satisfy the preference, evident in his editions, for illustrations that would essentially fill an entire page.[54] Editions in each of these five basic formats typically had at least seventeen distinct text illustrations and one image on the title-page, amounting to a

---

54 As we will discuss below, Plantin illustrated books in an ordinary 12° and 16° format with the same size illustrations.

4.24 Paul Uten Waele after Peeter vander Borcht, *St. John the Baptist*, from *Missale Romanum* (Antwerp: Christopher Plantin, 1585; 4°), fol. Z6r, engraving, 58 × 39 (Antwerp, Museum Plantin-Moretus, A 802). See fig. 6.2 for an earlier use of this same engraving.

minimum of ninety different plates.[55] Plantin's richly illustrated missals from 1574 in folio, *quarto*, and *octavo* also comprised various numbers of images and borders, depending upon the format. While the lack of a copy of Plantin's 1574 *quarto* edition makes it impossible to know how many extra plates were needed to illustrate all of these books, we can still estimate a minimum number of additional plates that Plantin most likely ordered for the basic illustration of these editions. Specifically, he had thirty plates made, all measuring c.71/75 × 71/75 mm (a size of plate that does not occur in Plantin's books of hours) for the illustration of various feast days. He would also have had to order eight full-page plates for the main text illustrations of his folio editions, and four additional full-page *octavo* and *quarto* plates – images of the *Last Supper* and *All Saints* – that were not part of the typical series of images present in his books of hours.[56] Finally, Plantin would have found all the plates he needed for the illustration

---

[55] For examples of such series of subjects, see Bowen 1997a, pp. 236–237 and 244–248.

[56] The following is based upon the illustration of Plantin's 1574 folio missal in Trinity College, Cambridge (E.3.56) and the MPM (8–637) copy of his 1574 *octavo* missal. Plantin usually included

of his 1575 folio and *quarto* breviaries among the plates commissioned for his books of hours and missals except one, namely, a full-page image of *King David* for his folio edition (fig. 4.12).[57]

All told, Plantin must have ordered a minimum of 133 plates for the basic illustration of these texts. This estimate excludes a variety of extra single images that were occasionally included in specific copies, like that of *St. Jerome* found in some of Plantin's missals for Spanish use (see fig. 4.10). It also omits various borders that were used to mark the primary images in some of Plantin's missals and books of hours (see figs. 4.8, 4.18, and 4.19). Thus far, we know of eight distinct borders ordered for the decoration of Plantin's folio missals and thirty or more in copies of Plantin's *octavo* books of hours.[58] Finally, the above minimum estimate of Plantin's initial investment in copper plates also lacks all of the duplicate plates he ordered. Two copies of the folio engravings he used for his missals and breviaries are cited above, and at least another thirty-eight copies are known among the *octavo* plates Plantin used for the illustration of his books of hours in 1573 and 1575.[59] There is no evidence of any significant number of duplicate plates being made of Plantin's other illustrations at this point. Adding all of these extra plates to the earlier "minimum" suggests that Plantin ordered at least 210 plates for the decoration of the new liturgical and devotional editions he published between 1573 and 1575.

On its own, 210 plates seems like a large number. However, if one compares it with Plantin's other investments in intaglio plates, it appears that it was roughly equivalent to the sum of all the other plates Plantin had made by 1575. Specifically, by 1573, Plantin already owned the forty-three plates needed for the illustration of de Valverde's anatomical editions, the twenty-one plates he had commissioned for the illustration of the Polyglot Bible, and the extra sixty-six plates he needed to complete the illustration of Arias Montano's *Humanae salutis monumenta* (which he used together with six engravings that he had for the illustration of his 1570 book of hours). By 1574, Plantin had also acquired an exceptionally large engraving (247 × 386 mm) of an ancient Roman calendar for a broadside and a series of sixty-six full-page folio etchings and a title-plate for his 1574 edition of Joannes Sambucus's *Icones veterum aliquot ac recentium medicorum*, which was essentially a print album of portraits of scholars and physicians.[60]

All together, this amounts to 198 additional plates completed between 1566 and 1574 for the illustration of five publications for a learned public, two of which – de Valverde's

---

full-page illustrations of the following subjects in his missals: the *Annunciation, Nativity, Crucifixion, Resurrection, Pentecost, Last Supper, Assumption,* and *All Saints.*

[57] These two breviary editions (PP 822 and PP 823) both bore the following subjects: *King David,* the *Nativity, Resurrection, Pentecost, Last Supper, Assumption of the Virgin,* and *All Saints.* The *quarto* edition (PP 823) also had an image of the *Annunciation,* which would be common to Plantin's subsequent breviary editions.

[58] For examples of the folio missal borders, see, e.g., the copy in Trinity College, Cambridge (E.3.56). For examples of the borders used in Plantin's *octavo* books of hours – in addition to some copies of Arias Montano's *Monumenta* (see Bowen 2003, table 2, pp. 32–33) – see, e.g., copies of his 1573 edition (PP 1770: e.g., MPM [4–228]), and of his 1575 edition (PP 1775: e.g., MPM [4–232]).

[59] For the *octavo* plates Plantin used for his books of hours in 1573 and 1575, see Bowen 1997b, pp. 147–150.

[60] For the Roman calendar, see PP 863 and Voet, PP, 11, fig. 2. It appears that while Plantin retained the etchings for Sambucus's work (PP 2175) (see appendix 4, p. 391), he himself did not actually pay to have the plates made (see ch. 5).

anatomical work and Arias Montano's *Monumenta* – would be reprinted once by 1575. It is this last observation – the number of text editions that Plantin was able to illustrate with a group of approximately 200 plates – that indicates the essential distinct value (and relative cost) of the groups of plates concerned.[61] For, as indicated above, the plates Plantin ordered for his liturgical editions were not book-specific, like the other plates cited above, but the opposite. They were multifunctional plates that, together, served to illustrate some ten distinct editions of books of hours, six editions of missals, and two editions of breviaries in the period 1573–1575 alone.[62] Although the exact number of books that were illustrated with these plates in this period is not known, it must have been close to 10,000. Philip II alone purchased more than 5,000 copies of these texts with engraved illustrations (see below). In addition, as the sample of sales recorded in appendix 3 reveals, 782 copies of only four of the approximately eighteen liturgical editions Plantin produced with engraved illustrations between 1573 and 1575 were sold to Plantin's other clients in just one year. Sales of the other editions Plantin printed with engraved illustrations in this period – de Valverde's anatomical texts, the *Monumenta*, and the Polyglot Bible, for example – were much more limited. Records of the printing of each of these editions reveal that initially (between 1566 and 1572) 1,050 copies of de Valverde's texts, 554 copies of the 1571 edition of the *Monumenta*, and 416 copies of the 1575 edition were illustrated in this period, while 1,213 copies of the Polyglot Bible were printed in total.[63] Together, this amounts to 3,233 copies printed, but not necessarily sold, which is still less than the known – but far from complete – sales of the liturgical editions cited above.[64]

Such extensive returns on his investments in illustrations for his liturgical editions were made possible, in part, by Plantin's "mix-and-match" approach to the formation of his stock of plates, as well as his exhaustive use and reworking of the plates concerned. Another essential factor that supported Plantin's extensive use of his stock of engraved and etched illustrations was the great, widespread demand for the texts concerned. As we will demonstrate below, Plantin not only sold thousands of missals and breviaries to the Spanish court, but he also benefited from significant sales of these books elsewhere, thanks to his diversified approach to the production of these books, with three different types of texts, for three different types of readers, printed in various formats, for distinct prices. Such a success would have been impossible to

---

[61] Unfortunately, not enough records of payments for the execution of these plates are preserved to allow us to calculate precisely how much Plantin spent on having the plates in these two groups made.

[62] See the discussion of PP 1769–1777bis, and PP 1778 in Bowen 1997a, pp. 235–249, for the books of hours Plantin may have printed with engravings in this period. The exact number of editions printed with engravings is uncertain owing to the lack of known copies and imprecise payment records for the printing of the illustrations. See PP 1685, 1686, 1688, 1689, 1690, and 1691, for the missal editions Plantin is known to have illustrated with more than one or two engravings between 1573 and 1575. See PP 822–823 for the two breviaries Plantin printed with engravings in 1575.

[63] See appendix 1 for the payments made to Pieter Huys for printing the illustrations for de Valverde's text; see Bowen 2003, pp. 25–26 for the number of copies illustrated of the *Monumenta* editions; and see PP 644, n. 5, for the printing of the Polyglot Bible. No production figures are known for either Sambucus's *Icones . . . medicorum* or the Roman calendar.

[64] Copies of the Dutch edition of de Valverde's text (printed in 1568) and of the Polyglot Bible, for example, are noted in Jan Moretus's 1602 stock inventory (see MPM Arch. 490, fols. 1v, 2v, and 13v [for the former] and fol. 5r [for the latter]), while as many as 302 copies of Sambucus's text had not been sold by 1603 (see MPM Arch. 112, fol. 121 lft, and MPM Arch. 113, fol. 44 lft).

obtain with book-specific illustrations for a learned public that were, by design, limited in their potential market. But with Plantin's multifunctional, conventional illustrations for texts with a widespread demand, matters were clearly different.

THE SALE OF PLANTIN'S LITURGICAL EDITIONS WITH ENGRAVED ILLUSTRATIONS TO PHILIP II

Who wanted to buy Plantin's luxuriously illustrated copies of the reformed liturgical and devotional texts and what did they have to pay for them? The single greatest buyer by far was Philip II. This is not surprising given the total number of books the king and his representatives ordered in the period 1571–1576 for further distribution in Spanish domains. It was a market that Plantin was understandably eager to have and satisfy. As discussed above, as of the mid-1560s Plantin had been endeavoring to distance himself from his earlier Protestant associations and win the favor of Philip II. He had also tested out the market for devotional works with engraved illustrations in 1570 and 1571 with his richly illustrated editions of a conventional book of hours and Benito Arias Montano's sophisticated theological work, *Humanae salutis monumenta*. Notably, both of these books had clear Spanish connections. On the one hand, the *Monumenta* was written by the man Philip II had sent to Antwerp to oversee Plantin's production of the Polyglot Bible. On the other hand, the book of hours was adorned with title-pages bearing the coat of arms of either King Philip II of Spain, his local military commander, the duke of Alva, or Plantin's great advocate in Catholic circles in Spain and Rome, Cardinal Granvelle, each shown within Plantin's device of a pair of compasses (see fig. 3.22). The visually highlighted link between Plantin and these men – none of whom was generally popular locally owing to the revolt in the Low Countries against the rule of Philip II – underscores the international focus of Plantin's decoration of the title-page. Whether Plantin's production of either of these texts was of particular importance in his efforts to win Philip's approval for the large-scale production of the newly reformed texts is not clear. Nevertheless (as discussed above), in February 1571, shortly before the publication of Arias Montano's *Monumenta*, Plantin did succeeded (largely as a result of Arias Montano's staunch support) in garnering Philip II's initial huge orders for the reformed missals and breviaries.

Records of Plantin's shipments of the reformed texts to the Spanish court were carefully kept and are still preserved in several forms that enable one to track not only which books were sent in which quantities, but, often, which type of paper was used for which copies, how the books were decorated, and what was charged for them as a result. The details of the shipments themselves – which books were sent and how – were kept simultaneously in two documents, one in French and one in Spanish.[65] While

---

[65] See MPM Arch. 22 and 6, for the French and Spanish record books, respectively. Most of the shipments recorded in MPM Arch. 22 are transcribed, at least in part, in Bécares Botas 1999, appendix IV, pp. 325–346. The transcriptions here are misleading, however, for while they appear to be complete, they are not. Many contain abbreviations not present in the original document and seemingly randomly omit some details, such as an occasional reference to the price of a book or its illustration. Moreover, all records of how the books were shipped are omitted, while lists of individual books are often omitted here and included elsewhere in Bécares Botas's book.

the French version has one more (last) shipment noted under April 6, 1576 than the Spanish version, the Spanish record book is often more detailed and definitive in form – lacking, for example, items that were noted and then crossed out in the French record book.[66] The costs of the shipments and payments for them were simultaneously noted in three record books. All three were begun to chart the costs of and payments for the work on the Polyglot Bible. One, kept in Latin, ends in July 1574, nearly two years before records of the shipments themselves would cease to be kept in April 1576. Its pages periodically bear Arias Montano's signature, as if a record of his checking and approval of the financial accounts. The other two account books were kept in Spanish. Although these are virtual copies of one another, the records in one stop with August 1574, while the other continues through February 1575.[67]

In addition, there is a separate, undated document in Latin in which the charges for printing the texts and including engraved illustrations are outlined.[68] The charges for the text were based upon the type of paper and letters used and were expressed as a certain number of sheets to be printed for a given quantity of stuivers. The charges for the illustrations were calculated in terms of the relative scale of the images and whether they were printed directly on to the sheet of paper, together with the text, or were printed separately on plain white paper. No separate charge was made for the inclusion of woodcut illustrations. Rather, the costs for printing texts with woodcut illustrations were simply calculated at the basic text-printing rate based upon the letters and paper used. Several remarks in this document concerning which books had been or were being printed or illustrated help date the text to early 1574. This date coincides with the clear application of these principles for calculating the costs of printing and illustrating some missals and a breviary with engravings, in the records of books shipped to Spain in 1574 and 1575. The characteristic trait of the use of this system in each of these cases is the subdivision of the costs into two parts, one for the printing of the text and one for the addition of engraved illustrations.[69]

The archival records outlined above reveal the following about the initial huge orders for liturgical and devotional works by the Spanish court in the period from October 1571 (when the first shipment was sent) through December 1575 (the last full year of shipments to be recorded).[70] In this period of a little more than four years, the books sent in the greatest quantities by far were breviaries (15,505 copies total, including 8,739 in *octavo* alone and approximately 2,000–2,400 copies each in folio, *quarto*, and

---

[66] For the last entry in the French record book, see MPM Arch. 22, fol. 75v. For examples of items that were first listed and then crossed out in MPM Arch. 22 and then not noted at all in MPM Arch. 6, compare Arch. 22, fol. 63v, and Arch. 6, fol. 59v.

[67] For the Latin account book, see MPM Arch. 24. See MPM Arch. 5, for the Spanish account book ending in August 1574, and MPM Arch. 5bis for the one ending in February 1575. This last record book is the one relied upon here.

[68] See appendix 2 for a full transcription and translation of this document.

[69] The dating of this document is discussed in appendix 2. See MPM Arch. 5bis, fols. 29 rht, 30 rht, and 32 rht, for examples of the application of this price-calculating system.

[70] Although a few shipments of books in 1576 are noted in MPM Arch. 22 (fols. 75r–v) and Arch. 6 (fols. 69r–72r), none of these contains references to the type of illustrations contained in the books sent and are, consequently, not as useful for the present study.

16°) and missals (c.14,875 copies total, including c.9,660 in quarto, 3,915 in folio, and 1,300 in octavo). Approximately 9,520 books of hours were also sent (c.3,800 in 12°, 2,100 in 32°, 2,000 in 16°, 1,500 in 24°, 100 in quarto, and 20 in octavo), along with more than 10,000 other assorted texts, including diurnals, offices of specific saints, indices for missals, and so on, as well as extra, imperfect copies of many of the missals, breviaries, and books of hours sent.[71]

Of these nearly 50,000 books, only a selection were illustrated with engravings. Notably, although more breviaries were sent than any other type of text, relatively few of these copies (300 of the 1575 quarto and 129 of the 1575 folio edition) were illustrated with engravings.[72] It was, rather, copies of the missals that were most frequently purchased with engraved illustrations: at least 3,781 out of the approximately 14,876 copies shipped, or around one-quarter of all of the missals sent.[73] The 3,781 copies comprised at least 1,746 copies of various folio editions, 1,735 copies of various quarto editions, and 300 copies of Plantin's 1574 octavo edition.[74] As discussed above, folio missals were the first of all of the reformed texts that Plantin began to print with, albeit limited, numbers of engravings. Following the missals, books of hours were the next most frequently purchased text with engraved illustrations. This seems logical given the periodic favorable references to the illustrations in Plantin's 1570 book of hours in his correspondence with Philip II's advisors on his production of the reformed texts mentioned above. Nevertheless, the total number of copies sent with engravings (833) is strikingly less than the total number of missals sent with engraved (or etched) illustrations (3,781) and comprises relatively few copies (112) of the editions that were closest to Plantin's original 1570 book of hours. Rather, the bulk of the books of hours sent with engraved illustrations were either in 32° (400 copies) or 12° (321 copies), while the most richly illustrated books of hours in larger formats (12 copies in octavo and a few in large octavo) were, more often than not, exceptional copies destined for specific individuals, like Philip II, Gabriel de Çayas, and Hernando de Virbiesca.[75] The only other type of text, beyond the breviaries, missals, and books of hours described above, that was sent to Spain with engraved illustrations was "del canto despana in 4°," 226 copies of which were shipped in June 1575. This may have been intended to accompany a quarto missal from 1575 (PP 1690), 226 copies of which had been sent a

---

[71] These totals are based upon the shipments to Spain listed in MPM Arch. 22, fols. 1–74r.

[72] For shipments of breviaries with engraved illustrations, see MPM Arch. 22, fols. 55v–56v, 70r–70v, and 74r; or MPM Arch. 6, fols. 54v–55r, 64r–65v, and 68v.

[73] The uncertainty in the total here is owing to a discrepancy in the notation of precisely how many copies were shipped (sixty or eighty-four) with an engraving of St. Jerome, as listed in MPM Arch. 22, fols. 25v–26r as against MPM Arch. 6, fol. 24v.

[74] For these shipments, see MPM Arch. 22, fols. 10v–11v, 17v–18r, 23v, 25v–26r, 37v–38r, 41r–41v, 42v–43r, 44v, 45v–49v, 61v–62r, 63r, and 68v–69r; or MPM Arch. 6, fols. 8r–8v, 14v, 22r, 24v, 38r–38v, 41v–42r, 43r–43v, 45r, 46r–49v, 58v–59v, and 63r.

[75] For examples of references to copies of Plantin's 1573 octavo book of hours (PP 1770) and 1573 large octavo book of hours (PP 1769) being shipped to these figures, see, e.g., MPM Arch. 22, fol. 23r. For the larger shipments of Plantin's smaller books of hours with engraved illustrations, see MPM Arch. 22, fols. 18r, 22v, 23r, 25v, and 69v; or MPM Arch. 6, fols. 14r, 20v, 21v, 28v, and 63v. For the editions concerned, cf. PP 1771–1773 and 1776bis, as described in Voet, PP, and Bowen 1997a, pp. 239–241 and 247–248.

few months earlier in April 1575.[76] We have yet to trace a copy or find a description of this "canto" and its illustration.

Thanks to the various cost-accounting documents kept for these shipments, we can also determine what Plantin charged for the majority of the books sent, from the first missals with engraved illustrations (shipped in April 1572) to the shipments of his folio breviary with engraved illustrations in December 1575. This series of records provides a highly informative overview of Plantin's various approaches to calculating (and charging for) the addition of engraved illustrations.

Three distinct practices are documented in Plantin's shipments to Spain. The first and most unexpected is that in which Plantin did not appear to charge anything extra for the inclusion of one or two engravings in editions of his missals. This practice is evident in the first shipment of missals in which the inclusion of engravings (an image of the *Crucifixion*) was noted, namely, in copies of a folio missal (PP 1676–1678) sent in October 1572. Here, 216 copies printed on ordinary paper ("communi pap.") were noted as having "la croix de cuivre" (the engraved cross [or crucifixion]), while 100 printed on "grand pap. de Lyon" (a better quality paper) contained "canon de cuivre et la croix de cuivre," presumably the engraved border around the start of the text of the canon and the engraved cross (as in figs. 4.2 and 4.3). In the cost-accounting documents, the copies of this edition were not listed according to the type of decoration included in them, but rather, according to the type of paper upon which the copies were printed. Thus, 600 copies on ordinary paper are listed (216 with an engraving of the *Crucifixion* and 384 with a woodcut of the same subject), and *all* were charged at the rate of 3 fl. 5 st. per book, while 100 copies on "grand pap. de Lyon" were all charged at the rate of 4 fl. per book.[77]

One might argue that the price of the last group of 100 copies was higher because of the inclusion of two engravings and not just the type of paper used. Nevertheless, other contemporary sales to Philip II of missals with just one or two engraved illustrations support the premise that, at this point, when few engravings were involved, Plantin had decided to supply the engravings free of charge – or simply as part of the general, base charge for the book. Consider, for example, copies of another folio missal (PP 1680) that Plantin shipped to Spain in November 1573. Of the 420 copies sent, 32 were printed "avec la croix en cuivre et le S. Hierosme en bois" (with the engraved cross and woodcut of St. Jerome), 16 were printed "avec la croix en cuivre et le S. Hierosme en cuivre" (with the engraved cross and engraving of St. Jerome), and at least 60 were printed "cum S. Hieron. en cuivre" (with the engraved St. Jerome).[78] Despite the variation in which engravings were printed in these 108 (or more) copies, the entire group of 420 copies sent – the remaining copies were listed without any reference to illustrations – were all

[76] For the shipment of the "canto despana," see MPM Arch. 22, fol. 63v; or MPM Arch. 6, fol. 59v. For the earlier shipment of a similar quantity of *quarto* missals, see MPM Arch. 22, fols. 61v and 63r; or MPM Arch. 6, fols. 58v and 59v. A potentially comparable text (but in folio) is included at the end of the copy of Plantin's 1574 folio missal in Trinity College, Cambridge (E.3.56).

[77] MPM Arch. 24, fol. 11 lft, and MPM Arch. 5bis, fol. 23 rht.

[78] For records of the first two groups of missals, see MPM Arch. 22, fol. 23v; or MPM Arch. 6, fol. 22r. For the last group of sixty, see MPM Arch. 22, fols. 25v–26r; or MPM Arch. 6, fol. 24v, where there is the above-mentioned unresolved discrepancy in the notation of precisely how many copies were shipped with this engraving (sixty or eighty-four).

charged at the same rate of 3 fl. per book, regardless of which (if any) engravings were included.[79] Similarly, Plantin does not appear to have charged anything extra for the occasional printing of a single engraving in some of his small *quarto* missals (PP 1681), sent to Spain in April of 1573.[80]

Regrettably, it is difficult to determine whether this "give-away" pricing policy was something that Plantin generally applied to all his sales of these books at this time or just to Philip II's exceptionally large orders. For while an occasional sale of a missal with an engraved illustration appears in his ordinary account books (his Journals) for this period, the paper on which the given copy was printed is not noted. Rather, the entries simply read as follows: "1 Missale Romanum f° cum fig. aeneis fl. 4 st. 10" (1 Missale Romanum [in] folio with an engraved figure 4 fl. 10 st.).[81] Other folio missals sold in this period, but without a reference to engraved figures, were typically sold at just 4 fl. per copy.[82] Does the difference in price reflect the addition of an engraved illustration, or better paper, or both? If Plantin's own price listing for a folio missal can be applied to these copies, then the answer would be clear: 4 fl. was the standard price for copies on ordinary paper, while 4 fl. 10 st. was that for copies on better paper, regardless of the illustration.[83] While this is tempting to accept as evidence supporting the general rule observed among the missals sent to Philip II in 1571 and 1572, the argument must remain hypothetical. If Plantin had applied the pricing schema that he worked out by 1574 to these first editions, he would certainly have earned more money on these initial sales. In the case of the 1572 folio missal discussed above, for example, he "lost" 43 fl. by not charging for the additional engravings. This amount was equivalent to the price of at least four copies of the same missal printed on better paper, or thirteen printed on ordinary paper.[84] Perhaps Plantin's "give-away" pricing of these early missals was actually a sort of discount or else a ploy to whet Philip II's and his advisors' appetites for more. If the latter hypothesis is true, then one could argue that Plantin's marketing strategy paid off, for the costs of small books of hours with a full series of engraved illustrations that were shipped to Philip in the spring of 1573 were calculated according to an entirely different standard.

The second pricing practice evident in the sales to Philip II is that whereby the price of books with engraved illustrations was simply double that of ordinary copies of the same text with woodcut illustrations. This was applied to editions of smaller (32° and 12°) books of hours with numerous illustrations that were printed and shipped

---

79 MPM Arch. 24, fol. 13 rht, and MPM Arch. 5bis, fol. 26 rht.

80 For the shipment records for this missal, with 175 copies with an engraved crucifixion and the remaining 825 without, see MPM Arch. 22, fols. 17v–18r, and MPM Arch. 6, fol. 14v. For the uniform pricing of all of these copies, see MPM Arch. 24, fol. 12 lft, and MPM Arch. 5bis, fol. 24 rht.

81 MPM Arch. 50, fol. 104v, sale to a certain "Mattheo Contarello" on October 22, 1572. This most likely represents the sale of a copy of one of Plantin's folio missals from 1572 (see PP 1676–1678).

82 See, for example, MPM Arch. 50, fols. 65v and 132r.

83 See MPM M 296, fol. 11v, for this price list. Voet asserts (without justification) that this "very likely refers" to Plantin's 1571 folio missal (see PP 1675, n. 8).

84 One can calculate the money that Plantin "lost" by multiplying the number of copies sent by the price he would have charged for adding the illustrations in later editions, namely, 2.5 st. for every illustration of the *Crucifixion* in the 216 copies on ordinary paper, and 5 st. for every paired engraved border and image of the *Crucifixion* in the 100 copies on better paper. As noted above, for this edition, Plantin charged the Spanish court 4 fl. per missal on better paper and 3 fl. 5 st. per missal on ordinary paper.

to Spain in 1573. Specifically, copies of the 32° book of hours with engravings cost 6 st. (instead of the 3 st. charged for the basic copies of the text) and copies of the 12° edition with engravings cost 12 st. (instead of 6 st.).[85] Records of sales of Plantin's large *octavo* book of hours from 1573 to the Italian merchants Giovanni Antonio and Raphael Brunelli in Milan suggest that this book was similarly treated, with copies with woodcut illustrations costing 1 fl. and copies with engraved illustrations costing 2 fl.[86] It is difficult, however, to compare this example with sales to Spain, for only copies with engraved illustrations were sent to Spain and these were priced at just 34 st. per book (as opposed to 40 st, or 2 fl.).

Was the price increase for both of the smaller books of hours simply an educated guess, or was it based upon some sort of system? If Plantin had applied the pricing schema that he worked out by 1574 to these books (see appendix 2), the costs would have been slightly different. Consider the 32° books of hours. Presumably, the seventeen engravings Pieter Huys made for a book of hours in 32° by February 1573 were used to illustrate these books.[87] According to Plantin's pricing schema, he would charge 1 st. per five small engravings, which would amount to approximately 3$^1/_2$ st. for all seventeen illustrations. This is already $^1/_2$ st. more than the extra 3 st. Philip II was charged for the copies of these books with engraved illustrations above the basic price for copies with woodcut illustrations. Because we do not know exactly which type and paper were used to print Plantin's 32° books of hours, nor what was used as the basis for his pricing schema for books such as these, it is difficult to calculate what he would have charged for the base price of printing the text (according to his pricing schema) to compare with the 3 st. that was actually charged in this case. Independent of this problem, the dating of the two shipments to Spain of copies of 32° books of hours (one in April 1573 and the other in November 1573) suggests that these may have been copies from two distinct editions, the first completed in December 1572, and the second completed in August 1573.[88] These two editions have distinct signatures, whereby the first (PP 1772) needed approximately two and a half more sheets of paper to print than the second (PP 1773). If we were to calculate the cost of printing this text according to Plantin's pricing schema, this would most likely have resulted in it costing around 1 st. more to print per copy than the other. Such a difference in the base price of the 32° books of hours sent is not evident in the charges for these shipments. Like the diverging costs for the inclusion of the engraved illustrations, the evidence here similarly suggests that the prices of these copies were not based strictly upon Plantin's 1574 pricing schema. Perhaps a more rudimentary system was used instead to provide provisional cost estimates for the first more richly illustrated editions sent to Spain.

The third pricing practice, Plantin's detailed pricing schema from 1574, was clearly used to calculate the price of the majority of the remaining books for which the cost was noted in the shipment records, namely, Plantin's *octavo*, folio, and large *quarto*

---

[85] For the pricing of the 32° book of hours (PP 1772–1773), see MPM Arch. 5bis, fols. 24 rht and 26 rht. For the 12° book of hours (PP 1771), see MPM Arch. 5bis, fol. 25 rht.

[86] See MPM Arch. 51, fol. 61v, under May 8, 1573, for these sales.

[87] See appendix 1 under Huys for the full reference to and transcription of this payment.

[88] See Bowen 1997a and the discussion of PP 1772–1773 (p. 241) for the evidence of the date at which each edition was completed and the distinct signatures of these editions.

missals from 1574 (PP 1688, 1685, and 1686, respectively), and his *quarto* breviary from 1575 (PP 823).[89] Of these texts, the *quarto* breviary provides the clearest example of the application of this system. It took 160 sheets of paper to print each copy of this edition.[90] According to Plantin's pricing schema, he could print the text for a *quarto* breviary at 2 st. for every seven sheets. At this rate, one comes to slightly less than 46 st. for each book printed. In the cost accounting for the shipments of this edition to Philip II, the printing of the text for all the copies sent (with engraved illustrations or not) was indeed calculated at 46 st. per copy.[91] In this same shipment record, it was noted that 300 of the copies sent bore one small ("pequena") engraving – presumably on the title-page – and eight larger figures ("figuras grandes") – presumably for the text illustrations. The smaller engraving was charged at a rate of $^1/_2$ st. per image, while the larger engravings were charged at 1 st. per image.[92] Returning to Plantin's pricing schema, one can see that the $^1/_2$ st. rate was applied to the fourth group of illustrations noted, namely, smaller illustrations used to illustrate the "minores festa" (minor feast days) in Plantin's *quarto* and folio missals. The 1 st. per image rate agrees with what was charged for illustrations included in Plantin's books of hours with larger type, like his large *octavo* editions. The link between the illustrations in the *quarto* breviary and Plantin's large books of hours is logical, simply a result of the comparable formats of the books concerned. It is also underscored by the one engraving present in the only known copy of this breviary, namely, an image of *King David* (fig. 4.13) that was also used to illustrate copies of Plantin's 1575 edition of his large *octavo* book of hours.[93] Combined, this comes to $8^1/_2$ st. extra per copy for the addition of engraved illustrations.

The cost accounting of the missals that Plantin shipped to Philip II in 1574 exhibits a comparable, typifying subdivision of the costs of each book into that for the printing of the text and that for the addition of engraved illustrations.[94] This system, devised for calculating the costs of illustrating his books with engravings, highlights, once again, how Plantin evidently regarded and used the engravings for his liturgical and devotional editions. They were, namely, subjects to be grouped (and charged) according to the size of the plate, which could, in turn, be used for the illustration of several different texts of diverse formats, depending upon the need. It was a practical, systematic approach, devoid of all "artistic" concerns for "series" of illustrations or the stylistic unity of the plates that were ultimately printed together.

Although there is no evidence indicating whether Plantin continued to apply this pricing schema to the calculation of the costs of his subsequent liturgical and devotional

---

[89] See appendix 2 for this schema. The only books with engraved illustrations that were sent to Spain and do not fit clearly into any of these pricing practices are the hundred copies of Plantin's large *octavo* book of hours and the twelve individually directed copies of his *octavo* book of hours.

[90] The number of sheets of paper needed to print this book can be calculated on the basis of its signature: *-***[8], ****[6], A–Z[8], Aa–Zz[8], AA–TT[8], VV[10], a–k[8]. It is also given in Plantin's own listing of this edition and its price in MPM M 164, fol. 3v, and MPM M 296, fol. 2r, transcribed in PP 823, n. 5.

[91] MPM Arch. 5bis, fol. 32 rht.   [92] MPM Arch. 5bis, fol. 32 rht.

[93] Consider, for example, the following copies of this book of hours: BL (c.66.c.16), and Chicago, The Newberry Library (Case c 8653.575), p. [213] in both cases.

[94] See MPM Arch. 5bis, fol. 29 rht, for the calculation of the costs of both the large *quarto* and *octavo* missals, and fol. 30 rht, for the folio missal.

editions, he did continue to pursue his "mix-and-match" approach to the illustration of the books themselves, as was demonstrated with the illustration of his 1585 *quarto* missal discussed above. Thus, he must have been satisfied with the reception of his works, illustrated as they were. And, as the following sampling of sales will demonstrate, while Plantin's editions with engraved illustrations may have been conceived with the Spanish market in mind, they were also popular elsewhere.

SALES OF PLANTIN'S EDITIONS WITH ENGRAVINGS ELSEWHERE

Predictably, Plantin's sales of thousands of liturgical and other devotional works to Philip II in the period 1571–1575 cannot be matched by his sales to any other single market. This was particularly true of the editions he had illustrated with engravings in this period, as Philip II and his advisors ordered hundreds of copies of most of these novel illustrated works. The main lacunae among their orders were copies of books of hours with engraved illustrations. Indeed, of all the editions of books of hours that Plantin printed with engraved illustrations between 1573 and 1575 – eleven, perhaps, in total – copies of only six editions were sent to Spain.[95] The evident preferences for specific texts (illustrated with engravings) in specific formats that are discernible in these sales to Philip II are all the more striking in the sales of these same books elsewhere.

In order to learn more about the general distribution of the numerous editions Plantin printed with engraved illustrations during his initial, large-scale production of these texts between 1573 and 1575, we traced the sale of a sample of these texts. We selected editions with engraved illustrations that, owing to the format in which the given text was printed, would be more readily distinguished from other editions of the same text in Plantin's sale records. Consequently, we chose the first missal he printed in *octavo* (PP 1688, from 1574), the first breviary he printed in *quarto* (PP 823, from 1575), and the first book of hours he printed in large *octavo* (also referred to as a *quarto* in the sales records) (PP 1769, from 1573). Because the records of the last are occasionally difficult to distinguish from another book of hours in *octavo* that Plantin similarly published with engraved illustrations in 1573 (PP 1770), we also decided to examine the sale of copies of his first 32° books of hours to be illustrated with engravings (PP 1772 and 1773, both from 1573) which, perhaps because of their smaller size and lower price, enjoyed a much greater distribution than the larger books of hours. We traced the first year of sales of copies with engraved illustrations for each of these editions. To this end, we consulted the sales records from Plantin's local shop in Antwerp, as well as the records kept in his Journals. The former comprise a very rudimentary list of which books were sold within a given period (for example, blocks of one to three weeks),

---

[95] No copies with engraved illustrations were ordered of the following books of hours: PP 1774 (16° edition from 1574), PP 1775 (octavo edition from 1575), PP 1776 (large *octavo* edition from 1575), PP 1777 (12° edition from 1575), and PP 1778 (24° edition from 1575). See Bowen 1997a, pp. 242–249, for arguments that some copies of each of these editions may have been illustrated with engravings. See n. 75 above for which of Plantin's books of hours were sent to Philip II.

without mention of who purchased them – although the buyers here are presumed to be local individuals. Plantin's Journals, on the other hand, provide much more detailed information, listed per day, of (among other items) who bought (or returned) which books. Rather than representing the local (Antwerp) market, the sales here document Plantin's national and international contacts.

The results of our research are striking. Among the sales to the local market made via Plantin's own shop in Antwerp (examined from January 1573 through May 7, 1576, when the records end), only two books from the sample group could be identified with any certainty: the 1573 large *octavo* book of hours (with one copy clearly sold between May 1573 and May 1574, and possibly seven more in the same period) and the *quarto* breviary from 1575 (with possibly two copies sold in the course of 1575).[96] In all other cases, only copies of these texts with woodcut illustrations appear to have been sold.

Sales at the Frankfurt book fair – a large international marketing opportunity – are also notably limited. While Plantin (or a representative of his Press) was recorded at the fair in all the years under consideration here (1573–1576), the only copies of the liturgical and devotional editions discussed here that he sent for possible sale at the fair were six of the *quarto* breviaries (shipped in February 1575).[97] Although Plantin had sent some 262 books of hours with woodcut illustrations (100 in 32°, the rest in *octavo*) to Frankfurt in 1573, it was not until 1576 that various copies of books of hours with engraved illustrations were shipped.[98]

If Plantin's local Antwerp clients and his expected contacts in Frankfurt were not interested in his liturgical editions with engravings, who was? Although the precise sales figures vary, naturally, from edition to edition, the most frequent destination for most of the editions considered was Italy (see appendix 3, fig. A3.1, for references to all of these sales). Specifically, of the 161 copies of Plantin's large *octavo* book of hours sold between mid-April 1573 and mid-April 1574, 68 went to Italian clients, while Henricus Bouchaut, a bookseller in Naples, bought an additional 200 copies of a large octavo book of hours with engravings in December 1574.[99] Of the 594 copies of his 32° book of hours sold in the first year, 54 copies went to Italian buyers, 29 of which were sold to a certain dealer in Milan, Giovanni Antonio d'Antoni.[100] Of the 73 copies of Plantin's

96   See MPM Arch. 43[III], fols. 48r, 49v, 51r, and 52v, for the sales of the book of hours; and fols. 63v and 70v, for the sales of the breviary. It is occasionally difficult to determine definitively whether copies were illustrated with engravings or woodcuts because the type of illustrations is often not noted and the otherwise indicative price of each copy was not always specified.

97   For records of Plantin's representation at the Frankfurt fair, see Schwetschke 1850, pp. 10–13. See MPM Arch. 53, fol. 20v, for shipment of breviaries.

98   For Plantin's initial large shipment of books of hours in 1573, see MPM Arch. 51, fol. 26r. For examples of his later shipment of copies with intaglio illustrations, see MPM Arch. 54, fols. 9r and 141v.

99   Although sales to Philip II are included in fig. A3.1, they are omitted from the figures cited here. See MPM Arch. 52, fol. 194v, for the sale to Bouchaut, and *Corr.*, IV, p. 249, for the identification of him as a bookseller. It is not certain, however, which edition, specifically, he purchased – PP 1769 from 1573, or PP 1776, which was completed in November 1574. The question remains as to whether the illustrations could have been added to that many copies of the book in such a short period of time. See Bowen 1997a, pp. 244–245, for notes on the printing and illustration of PP 1776.

100 D'Antoni is identified in Plantin's sale records and in MPM Arch. 19, fol. 22 lft, in the accounts kept with the shipper of these books, Raphael Brunelli.

octavo missal sold between May 1574 and April 1575, 15 went to Italian clients. Among these buyers was one merchant, Michiel de Wesel, who would purchase an additional 25 copies in the coming months. De Wesel appears to have at least arranged for the transport of books between Antwerp and Rome, if he did not deal in books himself.[101] Finally, of the 120 copies of Plantin's 1575 *quarto* breviary sold between mid-December 1574 and mid-December 1575, 57 copies went to Italy, with Michiel de Wesel once again taking the most (30).

Aside from the few individuals noted above who took significant amounts of the editions under consideration, the majority of the other Italian purchasers of Plantin's editions were booksellers or merchants located in a variety of Italian cities. Chief among these were the brothers Benedictus and Bernardus Bonvisi, bankers and merchants in Lucca, who bought twenty-four copies of the large *octavo* book of hours, four copies of the *octavo* missal, and one copy of the *quarto* breviary.[102] Other Italian dealers made more isolated purchases of one or the other of the books under consideration here. These include Julio Cesare Talignani, a bookseller in Genoa, and Pietro and Francisco Tini, booksellers in Milan who regularly purchased books from Plantin.[103] This distribution to his Italian bookseller clients may also help explain why Plantin did not bother taking many of these books to the Frankfurt fairs. For, no representatives from any of these cities were noted as being at the Frankfurt fair in the period under consideration. Rather, sellers from Venice, a city with a strong tradition in woodcut prints and book illustrations, predominate among the Italian dealers present.[104] Notably, most of the other copies of these books that were sent to Italy were sent as gifts, either from Plantin or from other individuals. For example, Plantin sent several copies of his *octavo* missal and *quarto* breviary (among other books) to Alanus Copus (or Cope), an English priest who had been in Leuven around 1560 and had settled in Rome as of 1572, where he was the attendant of Cardinal Hesius. Plantin published two editions of a collection of his diatribes against Protestant reformers.[105] Jacques Buysset, the registrar ("greffier") of the "grande conseil" in Mechelen, had several copies of the *quarto* breviary sent to his brother, Jean Buysset, a Jesuit in Rome with whom Plantin often corresponded. And

---

[101] For the subsequent sale to de Wesel, see MPM Arch. 53, fol. 157r. Although de Wesel's name appears periodically in Plantin's records (e.g., MPM Arch. 16, fols. 118 and 133, and MPM Arch. 18, fols. 61, 139, and 343), his place of residence and profession are never given. Our identification of him is based upon sale records in which de Wesel was responsible for the transport of items to Rome for Henrico d'Ardenna (the "lieutenant" of the Italian postmaster in Antwerp, Antoine de Tassis). For these records, see MPM Arch. 53, fols. 131r and 160r. For the identification of d'Ardenna and de Tassis, see, e.g., *Corr.*, IV, p. 224, n. 4.

[102] For the identification of the Bonvisi brothers, see, e.g., MPM Arch. 53, fols. 7v and 120v. In Bécares Botas 1999, p. 150, he mentions just two members of this family, Ludovico (active in the first half of the sixteenth century) and "Benedetto," who is presumably the same as the "Benedictus" mentioned in the Plantin records.

[103] For the identification of Talignani and his purchase of ten large *octavo* books of hours, see MPM Arch. 51, fol. 95v. For a summary of Plantin's accounts with the Tini brothers, see MPM Arch. 17, fol. 154. For their purchase of six copies of the 32° book of hours, see MPM Arch. 51, fol. 205r. See also *Rivista italiana di musicologia*, 12 (1977), pp. 231–251, for more information on the Tini brothers.

[104] See Schwetschke 1850, pp. 10–13.

[105] For this identification of Copus and his publications with Plantin, see Voet, PP, II, pp. 687–692. For Plantin's shipment of these books free of charge (indicated by the word "dono," Latin for gift), see MPM Arch. 52, fol. 201v.

the Leuven theologian Joannes Harlemius similarly had some of these books sent to someone else in Rome under his name.[106]

Only in the case of Plantin's 32° book of hours from 1573 were the purchases made by his Italian clients significantly surpassed by buyers elsewhere. In this case, a surprisingly large number of these books – probably 108 copies in the first year of sale and 200 more a few months later (in May 1574) – went to the Iberian peninsula, primarily through two businessmen. A certain Piedro de Molina, brother of the Lisbon bookseller Joannes de Molina, took 250 of these books, where one batch of 200 copies was sold at the significantly discounted price of 3 st. per book instead of the 7 or 8 st. usually charged.[107] This sale is also intriguing because Plantin's primary contact with Joannes de Molina was for the printing of other small books of hours (then with woodcut illustrations) for sale in Spain, via de Molina.[108] Another 50 of the 320 copies were sold to Marten de Varron – an Antwerp businessman of Spanish descent and son-in-law of Louis Perez – who later signed a contract with Jan Poelman in September 1581 for the sale of books in Salamanca.[109] Thus, while the specific destination of these copies remains uncertain, they were probably sent to Spain. The other main (but much smaller-scale) buyer of this work in Portugal was the Franciscan Franciscus de Canto in Lisbon (seven copies).[110] In comparison with the remarkably large number of copies of the 32° book of hours that were sold to Spanish businessmen, strikingly few of the other books discussed here were bought. Specifically, only three copies of the large *octavo* book of hours, fifteen copies of the *octavo* missal, and three copies of the *quarto* breviary were sold in the months considered (see fig. A3.1). The primary buyers were Piedro de Molina, once again, who bought ten of the fifteen missals sold, and Hortensio Magnacavalli, an Italian bookseller who had settled in Toledo, who purchased two of the three breviaries and four of the remaining five missals sold.[111]

Shipments to Plantin's shop in Paris, then run by his son-in-law Gillis Beys, represented, nevertheless, an even more significant (and reliable) destination for these books than the exceptional sales described above, destined for the Iberian peninsula (see

---

[106] For Plantin's contact with Jean Buysset, see, e.g., *Corr.*, IV, p. 12. See MPM Arch. 53, fol. 8r, for Buysset's shipments. For Harlemius, see BN. vol. 28, col. 238, under Willemsz. For a shipment of both missals and breviaries to a certain "Egidio de Cavalcantibus" in Rome under his name, see MPM Arch. 53, fol. 215v. Other examples of purchases made in the name of others or as pure gifts for others can be found among the other sales of these books cited in fig. A3.1.

[107] For the discounted sale to de Molina, see MPM Arch. 52, fol. 71v, under May 25, 1574. For an earlier sale of fifty copies of the same text to de Molina at the usual price of 7 st. per copy, see MPM Arch. 52, fol. 1r. For de Molina's identification as Joannes de Molina's brother, see MPM Arch. 16, fol. 156 lft. We have not been able to determine where Piedro de Molina himself was based. In Brulez 1959, p. 26, a certain Pieter de Molin is cited as a representative of the businessman Robrecht van Eeckeren in Seville, while a "P. a Molinos" is linked with a Spanish edition of Terence's comedies published in 1577 in Zaragoza (= Saragossa); see the entry under Terentius, for *Las seis comedias de Terencio*, in STC Europe (pre-1601), p. 92.

[108] For these editions, see PP 1354, 1355 (perhaps), and 1357–1362, where the last group consists of a series of title-pages for Latin books of hours with de Molina's name in the imprint.

[109] See appendix 3, n. 5, for more on de Varron and this sale. See ch. 3 for more on Plantin and Perez's special contacts.

[110] For the identification of de Canton, see MPM Arch. 18, fol. 54 rht, which includes a reference to a payment made via Pierre Mourentorf (the brother of Plantin's son-in-law, Jan Moretus [Mourentorf]), who was active as a diamond merchant in Lisbon (1570–1577); see Voet, GC, I, p. 162.

[111] For the identification of Magnacavalli, see, e.g., Bécares Botas 1999, p. 159.

fig. A3.1). They also represented Plantin's virtually exclusive outlet for these editions for all of France, at least during their first year of sale.[112] Of the above sample of books, only the *quarto* breviary from 1575 did not feature prominently in Plantin's regular and large shipments to this shop. By contrast, 192 copies of his 32° book of hours were sent, along with at least 40 copies of his large *octavo* book of hours and 24 copies of his *octavo* missal. Given Paris's longstanding association with the production of books of hours, the large anticipated sales of these texts in particular is not surprising.

The remaining three main potential markets for Plantin's editions were individuals associated with Philip II's courts in Brussels or Spain – Cardinal Granvelle and Benito Arias Montano, for example – booksellers and private individuals in the Low Countries (roughly, present-day Holland and Belgium), and Germany. The only sales of these books beyond these general markets that we found were to English buyers, in particular a certain Nicolas Jude, who bought seven copies of the 32° books of hours (see fig. A3.1).

Plantin usually sold fifteen or more copies of these various texts to his group of "Spanish contacts," with Arias Montano and Granvelle – both known bibliophiles – appearing the most frequently in these records.[113] Other figures associated with Philip II's court who periodically purchased (or were given) copies of these books include Gabriel de Çayas, the "confessaire de son excellence" (and this man's "socius" or "compagnon," that is, associate), and Hernando de Torres, a representative of Philip II in Rome, who, for example, sent Plantin a copy of the new reformed book of hours.[114] Plantin's sales to individuals in the Low Countries and Germany varied more, dependent upon the book concerned.

Plantin's clients in the Low Countries were often a mix of private individuals and booksellers. Of the booksellers, the names that appear the most often are Job Mattheus from Utrecht, the widow of the Ghent bookseller Gheeraert van Salenson, John Fowler (identified in these records as Joannes [or Jan] Foulerus Anglus), then active in Leuven, Andreas Sassenus, in Leuven, Paul de Beaufeu, in Liège, and Pierre de la Tombe, in Brussels.[115] But all of these booksellers typically bought just one or two copies of these books at a time, suggesting that they were isolated items, perhaps for particular clients,

---

[112] On Beys and Plantin's shop in Paris at this time, see, e.g., Voet, GC, I, pp. 77 and 80. See also Renouard 1979, pp. 312–373, and Rouzet 1975, pp. 14–15, on Beys.

[113] On Granvelle's interest in amassing Plantin editions for his libraries, see, for example, Clair 1960, p. 94. Arias Montano's interest in books is evident in his theological training and work on the Polyglot Bible, as well as in the role he played in forming the library of the Escorial (on this topic, see, e.g., Beer 1905).

[114] "Son Excellence" could refer to either the duke of Alva or Cardinal Granvelle: see Corr., III, p. 106, for the former association, and p. 264, for the latter. For examples of sales to this and related individuals, see MPM Arch. 51, fol. 210r, MPM Arch. 52, fols. 26v, 44r, and 145v, and MPM Arch. 53, fols. 55r and 176r. For Plantin and de Torres's contacts in connection with this book of hours, see, e.g., letters Plantin wrote to de Torres and Arias Montano in June 1572 (Corr., III, nos. 191 and 192, respectively). See fig. A3.1 for examples of these books going to de Çayas and de Torres.

[115] For basic information on all of these booksellers except Mattheus, see Rouzet 1975, p. 197 (for the widow of van Salenson), pp. 64–65 (for Fowler), pp. 197–198 (for Sassenus), p. 7 (for de Beaufeu), and p. 119 (for de la Tombe). Fowler and his widow, Alice, are discussed in greater detail in ch. 5. For the identification of Mattheus see Gruys and de Wolf 1989, p. 119, and MPM Arch. 17, fols. 28, 153, 219, and 361, for summaries of his dealings with Plantin in this period.

among much larger purchases of other books – either other texts or else copies of the same books but with woodcut illustrations instead of engravings. Such was the case, for example, with the Leuven dealer John Fowler and his purchases of Plantin's 32° books of hours. For while he bought only isolated copies of this book with engraved illustrations, he made more regular purchases of it with woodcut illustrations.[116]

The private individuals in the Low Countries who purchased (or were given) Plantin's luxurious copies of these editions had a range of backgrounds. There were politicians, like the governor of Hoogstraten or a "mons. le gouverneur," members of the clergy or other religious groups, like Jacobus de Zeelandre, a canon in Ghent, Henricus Dungheus, a canon at Antwerp cathedral, and David Regius of the Beghards in Antwerp, humanists, like Stephanus Pighius, and several others whose professions are not known.[117] But, as with the booksellers from the Low Countries, these people also rarely obtained more than an isolated copy of any of these books.[118]

Plantin's German sales were dominated by what the Augsburg bookseller Georg Willer and the Cologne-based Birckman firm bought of the books under consideration (see fig. A3.1).[119] Willer's purchases ranged from just two copies of the large octavo book of hours, to four copies each of the quarto breviary and the octavo missal, and twenty-four of the 32° book of hours. The Birckmans' most striking purchase consisted of eight copies of Plantin's large octavo book of hours. Only Plantin's 1573 32° book of hours attracted the attention of other Germany-based booksellers and printers, namely Jehan Aubri and Claude de Marne – a Frenchman and Englishman active in Frankfurt and related by their marriages to daughters of the Parisian printer André Wechel – who purchased six copies of this book in December 1573, and Joannes Gymnicus III in Cologne, who appears to have bought two copies.[120]

Looking back on this sample of sales, several important points have emerged concerning the market for Plantin's luxuriously illustrated liturgical editions and devotional works. The first essential point is that these were primarily sold to an international audience, in particular to clients in Italy, France, and (at least in the case of books of hours) the Iberian peninsula. The demand for these books in Italy is logical given the well-established market for the sale and production of engravings there. But this, like the requests Plantin received from Italian authors to print their works with engraved

---

[116] For examples of Fowler's larger purchases of books of hours with woodcut illustrations (each with usually twelve copies or more), see, e.g., MPM Arch. 51, fols. 109v, 141r, 162v, and 192r; and MPM Arch. 52, fol. 63r.

[117] While examples of most of these sales are noted in fig. A3.1, the following fell slightly beyond the first year of sales recorded there, namely sales of the quarto 1575 breviary to the governor of Hoogstraten and David Regius (see MPM Arch. 54, fols. 72r and 7r, respectively).

[118] The three main exceptions here were Jacobus de Zeelandre, who obtained three copies of the quarto breviary with engravings, Dungheus, who bought four copies of Plantin's 32° books of hours, and the nine copies of the large octavo book of hours that were purchased by "mons. le gouverneur" (see fig. A3.1).

[119] On Georg Willer, see Künast and Schürmann 1997, pp. 31–40. For the Birckmans, see Rouzet 1975, pp. 16–18.

[120] For the identification of all three men, see Benzing 1963, pp. 120 and 230, respectively. Gymnicus also purchased ten other small books of hours with engraved illustrations on April 24, 1573 (see MPM Arch. 51, fol. 54r), but it is not clear which editions, specifically, were sold.

illustrations, then begs the question (which we will consider below) why Italian print-ers were not producing such texts as well. It is less obvious why these books were so popular in the Iberian peninsula. As Plantin's early works with engravings indicate, he knew of a Spanish interest in engravings, at least among certain circles connected with Philip II, that was just waiting to be tempted and satisfied. Perhaps his friend Arias Montano, who himself clearly preferred engraved illustrations, had encouraged him to try out this market.[121] The dealers in the Low Countries with whom Plantin regularly did business were not among the most avid purchasers of these books, nor were clients in Germany, where Catholic texts were not universally welcome and there was a strong tradition and preference for woodcut illustrations instead of engravings.[122]

Plantin's far-flung, international distribution of these specially illustrated books to Italy and Spanish domains fits in perfectly with the characterization of Antwerp in the early to mid-sixteenth century as a center, not only for the production of books and prints, but also for trade in luxury products.[123] The presence in Antwerp of hundreds of merchants from numerous European cities, whose business entailed arranging for and financing the purchase, transport, and sale of goods to and from Antwerp, must have facilitated Plantin's ability to sell these books so widely. For, as noted above, many of the larger purchases of these books were made in the name of international merchants, businessmen, and bankers and not always booksellers per se.

The more than 5,000 books with engraved illustrations sold in Philip II's name between 1572 and 1575 far outweighs the sales of approximately 780 books elsewhere, as documented in fig. A3.1. However, if one reduces the sales to Philip II to just those books seen in our sample of sales elsewhere – Plantin's 1573 books of hours in 32° and large octavo, his octavo missal from 1574, and his quarto breviary from 1575 – the total number of copies of these books with engraved illustrations that were sold to Philip II (1,100) is much closer to the first year of sales to all the other markets combined (approximately 780). And if one added some of the extra, large sales of these and comparable editions made in the coming months, such as the Naples dealer Henricus Bouchaut's purchase of 200 copies of a large octavo book of hours with engravings in December 1574 (see above), these totals would be even closer still. Thus, while Philip II's orders did provide Plantin with an easy, large market for his newly illustrated texts, it was not his only sales option. Rather, Italian-based dealers or merchants, Plantin's own shop in Paris, and occasional, isolated buyers elsewhere counterbalanced Philip II's purchases.

There is, nevertheless, one essential difference between these two groups of buyers, namely, the price each paid for their books. In the sample of editions discussed above, this difference is most obvious in the prices charged for Plantin's 1574 missal in octavo and his 1575 breviary in quarto. As discussed above, the price that Philip had to pay for copies of each of these editions was calculated on the basis of Plantin's detailed pricing schema. Specifically, each octavo missal with engraved illustrations that Philip II purchased cost him 17 st. for the printing of the text and 13$^1/_2$ st. for the addition of

---

[121] See ch. 3 for Arias Montano's preference for engravings.
[122] See Kunze 1993, pp. 118–119, on the German preference for woodcuts.   [123] See ch. 2.

the engraved illustrations, or $30^1/_2$ st. (= 1 fl. $10^1/_2$ st.) per book. Each *quarto* breviary with engraved illustrations cost Philip 46 st. for the printing of the text and $8^1/_2$ st. for the addition of the engravings, or $54^1/_2$ st. (= 2 fl. $14^1/_2$ st.) per book.[124] The significant differences in the charges for printing the text and adding the illustrations to these editions reflect the differing quantities of paper needed to print the text and the divergent number of illustrations used to illustrate each text: the breviary was a larger book and the missal had more illustrations. Both of these rates were nearly a third less than what Plantin's regular customers paid for the same books, including, for example, the businessman Michiel de Wesel, who was an important buyer-shipper for the Italian market, and Plantin's own son-in-law Gillis Beys, who ran Plantin's shop in Paris. Both of these men, for example, paid as much as 42 st. (= 2 fl. 2 st.) per copy of the *octavo* missal with engravings (against Philip's $30^1/_2$ st.), while de Wesel (and others) paid a full 80 st. (= 4 fl.) for each *quarto* breviary with engraved illustrations he purchased (as opposed to Philip's $54^1/_2$ st.).[125] These consistent, significant price differences make it clear that Plantin's pricing schema was intended not for general use, but rather for the specific case of large shipments of these editions to the Spanish court.

Philip II received similar, but less significant discounts on the two books of hours considered here. He paid only 34 st. per copy of the large *octavo* book of hours (rather than the standard base price of 40 st. [= 2 fl.] charged to Plantin's other clients), and 6 st. per copy of the $32°$ book of hours (not the standard 7 st. per copy charged).[126] In both cases, this amounts to essentially just a 1 st. discount for every 7 st. in the standard price. And, as noted above, Plantin even sold 200 copies of the $32°$ books of hours with engraved illustrations to Piedro de Molina at the much lower rate of just 3 st. per copy – 3 st. less per copy than what Philip II was charged. It is not clear why there was such a difference between the relative pricing of Plantin's books of hours, on the one hand, and his *octavo* missal and the *quarto* breviary, on the other. Perhaps it was related to the fact that Philip II tended to buy far more missals and breviaries in general than books of hours. Regardless of these distinctions, the fact remains that while Plantin would have been more secure in being able to sell larger quantities of his editions with engraved illustrations to Philip II, his profit margins were greater in his sales of the same texts to his other clients. Thus, the question alluded to above remains important, namely, if Plantin was enjoying profits from his sales of books with engraved illustrations in other countries, to what extent did the local printers respond to this infringement upon their potential sales?

THE PRODUCTION OF THE REFORMED LITURGICAL AND DEVOTIONAL EDITIONS WITH ENGRAVINGS ELSEWHERE

As discussed above, the first printers to garner the rights to print the revised liturgical and devotional editions were (aside from Plantin) Jacob Kerver in Paris, the Giunti in

---

[124] See MPM Arch. 5bis, fols. 29 rht and 32 rht, respectively, for these figures.
[125] See the records of sales to each person listed in fig. A3.1 for examples of such purchases.
[126] See the sales to Philip II and to Plantin's shop in Paris in fig. A3.1 for examples of these prices.

4.25 Anonymous artists, *Visitation*, from *Officium B. Mariae Virginis* (Venice: Aldus Manutius II, 1576; 12°), fol. A11v, engraving, *c.*102 × 55 (Antwerp, Museum Plantin-Moretus, B 1657).

Italy, and those associated with the Vatican press in Rome – Paulus Manutius and the Faletti–Varisco consortium, in particular. To the best of our knowledge, none of these printers (or their successors) published missals or breviaries with engraved illustrations as Plantin did during his lifetime, even though some of them did publish other works with engraved illustrations in this period.[127] Only an occasional competing book of hours – the first liturgical or devotional work Plantin printed with engravings – appeared with engraved illustrations. For example, in 1576, Aldus Manutius II published a book of hours in 12° with woodcut illustrations for the calendar section and engravings of a common selection of subjects for the body of the text (fig. 4.25). There are some parallels between this book and the composition of Plantin's 1573 and 1575 *octavo* books of hours (PP 1770 and PP 1775 – both of which had some copies illustrated with engravings) in terms of the inclusion of accompanying biblical excerpts below most of the main illustrations. However, the number of divergences between Plantin's books of hours and Manutius's in the selection of the accompanying text and its formulation,

---

[127] For example, as early as 1553 and 1558, Paulus Manutius was involved in printing the text for a couple of publications with engraved illustrations, namely, an edition of Antonio Zantani's *Omnium Caesarum verissimae imagines ex antiquis numismatis desumptae*, with plates by Enea Vico (Mortimer 1974, no. 557) and an edition of Enea Vico's *Augustarum imagines* (trans. by N. Conti) (Mortimer 1974, no. 533). By the 1580s, some branches of the Giunti presses had also begun to print a selection of other texts with engraved illustrations (see, e.g., Mortimer 1974, nos. 41, 83, and 223), including several editions of Juan de Valverde's *La anatomia del corpo humano*, with the plates used to illustrate the 1560 edition of the text published by A. Salamanca and A. Lafreri, which had inspired Plantin's 1566 edition, discussed in ch. 3. For the Giunti editions of de Valverde's text, see, e.g., Cushing 1962, pp. 148–150. For an overview of the Giunti family of printers and publishers, see, e.g., Perini 1980.

in addition to the series of images featured, suggest that Plantin's editions of books of hours could not have served as direct models for this book. At most, his use of engravings since 1570 to illustrate this type of text could have inspired the general conception of this edition. Similar arguments can be made concerning the illustration of Blanche Marentin's (Jacob Kerver's widow) 1584 book of hours with an independent series of engraved illustrations.[128] Consequently, if one of Plantin's initial motivations for producing these types of texts with engraved illustrations was to distinguish himself from the other primary producers of the reformed texts, he would have been successful in that goal.

Why none of these other printers – particularly the Giunti in Italy, where engravings had long been popular – attempted to illustrate their liturgical editions like Plantin remains a mystery. Was it simply owing to the technical difficulties of printing engravings on to pages already largely filled with letterpress text? This might well have been a discouraging prospect for the Giunti, whose missals typically boast an abundant array of small, inset woodcut illustrations that would have been difficult to replace with engravings. Or was it a matter of finding artists (and printers of engravings) who could do the work? Or did these printers simply not have the financial capacity to invest in the stock of plates needed to produce such an array of publications? Certainly in France and Italy, where the printers of the revised liturgical editions were often compelled to work together with others, the acquisition and subsequent difficult subdivision (in the event of the dissolution of the partnership) of a large, interdependent group of plates would also have been a daunting prospect.[129]

Despite this array of possible impediments to following Plantin in the production of liturgical editions with engraved illustrations, two other printers did imitate his editions to some degree in the later 1580s. One is the French printer Jean (or Jamet) Mettayer. Active from 1573 to 1605, he had the title of "Imprimeur du Roy" for several years and was one of the printers who gained the right to print the revised liturgical editions in France in the 1590s.[130] Mettayer produced a few mammoth (and consequently highly impractical) liturgical and devotional editions with engraved illustrations in the mid-1580s. These include a grand (but bulky) *quarto* book of hours printed in 1586 and two editions of a folio breviary printed in 1587 and 1588.[131] Mettayer's *quarto* book of hours was printed with exceptionally large letters, like Jan Moretus I's own large *quarto* book of hours made for the local rulers, the archdukes Albert and Isabella, in 1600–1601.[132] Nevertheless, in contrast with Moretus's later, extensively illustrated edition, Mettayer's book of hours contains a conventional series of illustrations that is comparable – although not identical – to series of illustrations in Plantin's known

[128] For a copy of this book, see MPM K 32.

[129] See Grendler 1977, pp. 172–173, for an example of Italian printers working together to print these texts, and Pallier 1981, for the case of France.

[130] For a brief summary of Mettayer's work, see Renouard 1965, pp. 306–307. For his acquisition of the right to print the reformed texts, see, e.g., Pallier 1981, pp. 262–263.

[131] For the copies we examined, see MPM (R 30.12) for the book of hours, and BL (c.66.k.2) and MPM (K 8²), for the 1587 and 1588 breviary editions, respectively.

[132] For Jan Moretus's large *quarto* book of hours, see, e.g., Imhof 1996a, cat. 11a.

books of hours. Mettayer's breviaries were printed on a similarly grand scale and were subdivided into a winter and summer volume. Much larger, physically, than Plantin's folio breviaries from 1573 and 1575 (PP 818 and 822), Mettayer's 1588 edition also comprised more illustrations generally and a few specific subjects that were not common to Plantin's known breviaries – the image of the *Ascension*, for example.[133] Given the unusual, impractical size of all of these books – which would, presumably, have also priced them beyond the reach of most buyers – and the lack of a clear repetition of the series of illustrations in Plantin's own editions, it seems unlikely that Mettayer was trying to emulate the latter's approach to the illustration of these texts. Rather, these works probably represent specific royal initiatives. A logical assumption, given Mettayer's title of "Imprimeur du Roy," this is also suggested, for example, by the remark printed on the title-page of the breviaries, noting that the rubrics had been translated into French "par le commandement expres du Roy, pour l'usage de ses religieuses congrégations" (by express decree of the king for the use of his religious congregations).

The second printer whose publications are reminiscent of Plantin's is the Frenchman Guillermo Foquel, who was active as a printer in Salamanca in the period 1585–1593.[134] Foquel's publications differ from all the preceding examples in several essential ways. Not only did he imitate aspects of Plantin's general approach to the illustration of these editions, in addition to having some of the images themselves copied, but he also had several different types of liturgical texts illustrated with engravings in a relatively brief time span (c.1587–1591).[135] Consider, for example, a copy of his 1589 *octavo* breviary in the British Library, which comprises some gatherings with woodcut illustrations and some with engraved illustrations. Although not certain, this subdivision does recall some Plantin editions where two issues were produced, one with woodcut illustrations and one with engraved illustrations whereby, in some copies, gatherings from these two issues were mixed.[136]

Foquel's missals provide evidence of an even more careful imitation of not only specific compositions, but also the basic visual structure of Plantin's missals in terms of

---

[133] The illustrations in the copy of Mettayer's 1587 folio breviary in the British Library (c.66.k.2) (STC French [1470–1600], p. 268) were typically independently published engravings that were subsequently pasted into this volume. Consequently, it is difficult to speak about the intended series of images of this particular edition.

[134] For a brief summary of Foquel's work, see, e.g., Ruiz Fidalgo 1994, I, pp. 117–119.

[135] See, e.g., Ruiz Fidalgo 1994, III, nos. 1218, 1249, 1269, 1284, 1309, 1329, and 1330.

[136] For this copy of Foquel's 1589 breviary (only the *pars aestivalis*), see BL (473.a.7) (STC Spanish, p. 111). For a complete description of both volumes of this edition, see Ruiz Fidalgo 1994, III, no. 1269. A complete copy of this edition is in the Cambridge University Library (G.4.39) (Adams L 889 and 890), where the *pars hiemalis* is illustrated exclusively with woodcuts. For an example of the possible mixing of issues in some copies of Plantin's editions, see, e.g., MPM (A 579), a copy of Plantin's *quarto* breviary from 1575 (PP 823), and the discussion of a copy of Plantin's 1573 large *octavo* book of hours (PP 1769) in Bowen 1997a, pp. 235–238. See ch. 1, n. 43, for our differentiation between copies with woodcut illustrations and those with engraved (or etched) illustrations as distinct issues of the same edition. Plantin was not the first printer to subdivide an edition between copies with woodcut and engraved illustrations. Consider, for example, two copies of Joost de Damhoudere's *Practique judicaire es causes criminelles* (Antwerp: Joannes Bellerus, 1564) (BB, II, p. 27, D 41): MPM (R 24.22, with engraved illustrations pasted in on blank spaces left open for the illustrations) and MPM (R 47.21, with woodcut illustrations printed together with the text).

4.26 Anonymous artists, *Marriage at Cana*, from *Missale Romanum* (Salamanca: Guillelmus Foquel, 1589; f°), fol. Eee7r, engraving, 84 × 84 (Antwerp, Museum Plantin-Moretus, K 120). This engraving was copied from that in fig. 4.9.

the general distribution of full-page and smaller illustrations throughout the text.[137] For example, several of the illustrations in his large folio missal from 1589 are copies in reverse of plates Plantin had used to illustrate his folio missal from 1574 (compare, for example, figs. 4.26 and 4.9). However, the inclusion of characteristically Italian subjects, like the *Disputation over the Sacrament*, that were not part of Plantin's stock of plates, and the use of full-page illustrations to mark sections of text that Plantin did not highlight to the same degree, make it clear that Foquel's editions were not simple, routine copies.[138] They were thought-out imitations, with some modifications,

---

[137] See in particular copies of both a large *quarto* missal Foquel published in 1587 (Ruiz Fidalgo, III, no. 1218, where the format is incorrectly given as a small folio) – BL (468.c.2), see STC Spanish, p. 113; and Cambridge University Library (A*.4.30 [C]), and Trinity College Library, Cambridge (D.16.90 [I]), see Adams L 1157–1158; and a large folio edition from 1589 (Ruiz Fidalgo, III, no. 1284) – MPM (K 120), and Trinity College Library, Cambridge (E.2.3). Although similar in size, both books were illustrated with a distinct series of plates.

[138] See MPM (K 120), p. [380], and BL (468.c.2), p. [398], for two distinct (but similar) engravings of the *Disputation over the Sacrament*, present in Foquel's large and small folio missals. See MPM (K 120),

presumably in consideration of the market for which they were intended. We would have to know more about Foquel's total production and the distribution of his editions in order to determine the degree to which he was able to replicate and compete with Plantin's (and his successors') own editions of these texts. The relative brevity of his years of activity, however, would have made it difficult for him to establish himself as a printer of luxurious editions like Plantin.

CONCLUSION

Few could have imagined what the revision of essential Catholic texts in the years following the Council of Trent would lead to. What began as a project to defend and strengthen the practice of the Catholic faith, in the face of challenges raised during the Reformation, had far more diverse implications. Printers, eager to profit from the huge, immediate demand for the new texts, dared to challenge papal attempts to maintain a strict control of the production of the revised texts. Kings and local governments exerted their own authority and rights to govern the production of these books in conjunction with, if not above, the Vatican. Philip II even gained permission to have special versions of what were to be uniform, authoritative texts, prepared for use in Spanish domains. And Christopher Plantin, one of a few, select group of printers who won a part of the market for the production of the new texts, took advantage of his virtually guaranteed sales of thousands of copies of these books to experiment with the use of engravings as book illustrations in them.

We can now already offer at least part of an answer to one of our essential questions here, namely: what, specifically, led Plantin to venture into this new area of book illustration? Plantin's editions of missals were designed, at least in part, to satisfy the wishes of Philip II's advisors on the production of the new liturgical editions, his initial, primary market for these books. Recall, for example, Plantin's alteration of the subject of the title-page vignette to an image of SS *Peter and Paul* and his elimination of the small inset images at the beginning of sundry gospel readings. And while no records remain containing a specific request from these Spanish authorities to illustrate copies of these texts systematically with engravings, Plantin did receive positive responses to the engravings he had included in his 1570 *octavo* book of hours. His friend and important middle-man for exchanges with Philip II and members of his court, Benito Arias Montano, also clearly had a strong personal preference for engravings. However, the great, ever-present sense of competition for these large, lucrative sales may also have encouraged Plantin to risk the investment in engravings and test out the market for more luxuriously illustrated copies of these books, in the hope of distinguishing his own editions further. For, as demonstrated above, while large potential sales to Philip II may have initiated Plantin's production of most of his liturgical editions, individuals in other countries – in particular Italy – also bought significant quantities of his books with engraved illustrations. Plantin's "mix-and-match" approach to the

pp. [544]–[545] (fols. Ll8v and Mm1r), for a full-page image of St. *Laurence* and an accompanying border, marking the start of a feast day that Plantin marked with a smaller, inset image at most (compare with a copy of Plantin's 1574 folio missal in Cambridge, Trinity College: E.3.56, fol. h1r).

compilation and use of his basic stock of plates for the illustration of these books must have contributed to his ability to satisfy what were ultimately numerous distinct markets for different types of texts – missals, breviaries, or books of hours – in different formats, as economically – and, hence, with the greatest profit margin – as possible. Although other publishers were slow to imitate Plantin's liturgical editions, they did, with time, begin to confront him and his successors with competitive, comparably illustrated texts – the repercussions of Plantin's revolution in book illustration.

In the meantime, while Plantin was learning about the potential markets for his novel illustrated liturgical editions, he was also learning about the costs and limits of using engravings as book illustrations. This process is reflected in his evolution from nominally not charging anything extra at all for the inclusion of one or two engraved illustrations, or simply doubling the price of the basic text when an entire series of engraved illustrations was added, to the compilation of his detailed pricing schema around 1574 for the books sent to Philip II. With this document, one could both estimate the basic cost of having a text printed and calculate the cost of adding any engraving of any size. As we have shown above, the prices in this document were clearly set to calculate the discounted rates Philip II was granted for the books he ordered and not Plantin's standard selling prices for the same texts. It is not known whether Plantin used a similar schema to calculate his usual selling prices. It is clear, however, from records of what he charged Philips Galle for the printing of texts, for example, that comparable formulations for the cost of printing the text were used, namely, a number of stuivers per ream or sheet of paper printed.[139]

In addition to having established a system for calculating the cost of adding any engraving to a printed text, Plantin also cited several essential practical considerations for the printing of books with engravings in this pricing schema, including: (1) that there was a limit to the number of usable impressions (a thousand) that one could pull from a single plate before it had to be reworked or replaced; (2) that while the incorporation of woodcut images did not add to the cost of having a text printed, the inclusion of engraved illustrations did, significantly, because if the work was not done well, it implied not only the loss of the cost of printing that one image, but also the loss of the entire sheet of text on which it was printed; and (3) that it was not always easy, even in a printmaking center such as sixteenth-century Antwerp, to find reliable engravers to make the plates required.[140] The first clearly affected how many copies of an edition or a reprint thereof could be illustrated with a group of plates and, consequently, how great an investment would have to be made in the engraving of plates in order to complete the illustration of a specific project. The second underscores the technical difficulties in incorporating engraved illustrations and the unexpected cost and production complications if errors were made in this process. Above all else, however, the third observation underscores a fundamental underlying problem, namely, if Plantin could not find reliable engravers who were willing to make engravings for him, then none of his projects with engraved illustrations could be continued, regardless of the extent to which the plates could be

---

[139] See ch. 6.
[140] See appendix 2 for a full transcription and translation of these remarks. See chs. 2 and 5 for more on the issue of artist availability.

printed and the funds Plantin had available. In the next chapter, we will move on to the 1580s and examine the next phase in Plantin's novel production of editions with intaglio illustrations. These were difficult times in which to do business of any sort because of the war with Spain. In addition, this period was also marked by the absence of Plantin's Spanish clients – his single greatest market for his liturgical editions – and by an unpredictable, diminishing pool of artists who could (and would) make his engravings. We shall see how Plantin persisted, nevertheless, in meeting these challenges by producing works with intaglio illustrations for new markets.

CHAPTER FIVE

THE 1580s AND PLANTIN'S ETCHED BOOK ILLUSTRATIONS

In addition, one must consider that the plates for such illustrations [engravings] can give no more than one thousand copies of the illustration before the plate is worn, with the result that one must begin again to have another plate cut, which is very expensive for us and causes innumerable problems to find and keep engravers who are often depraved, pernickety, difficult, and do not keep their promises.[1]

Such are the concluding remarks in the cost-calculating schema that Plantin composed around 1574 for the Spanish court for their exceptionally large orders of liturgical editions, discussed in the preceding chapter. These liturgical editions represented Plantin's great breakthrough in the use of engravings as book illustrations. With these texts, he was able to apply a basic investment in costly engraved plates to a large spectrum of editions that, as a group, satisfied a diverse demand for books with such illustrations. However, as the remark above indicates, while Plantin may have devised a cost-effective use of engraved plates, the medium itself had its own inherent restrictions. First, there were only so many impressions that one could make from an engraving before it had to be reworked or replaced for an additional, significant sum of money. Second, finding a competent artist who was willing (and able) to produce the engravings required was not always simple. The second point in particular recurs periodically in Plantin's correspondence from the 1580s, when he was endeavoring to find artists who would engrave the plates for Jerome Nadal's (or Hieronymus Natalis) series of Catholic meditations, *Evangelicae historiae imagines*.[2] In his letters concerning his search for artists, Plantin repeatedly observes that the well-known engravers active in the area at that time – Philips Galle, the Sadelers, Hendrick Goltzius, and the Wierix brothers – either did not want to take on the project (Galle, Goltzius, and the Sadelers) or could not be relied upon to do the work (the Wierix brothers).[3] In one letter from October 22, 1586,

---

[1] See appendix 2, pp. 361 and 363. The "depraved, pernickety, [and] difficult" artists referred to in this text are probably Jan and Hieronymus Wierix. For more on them, see ch. 2 and appendix 1 in particular.

[2] For a basic study of this publication, see, e.g., Wadell 1985.

[3] For an example of Galle's refusal to work on the project, see the introductory excerpt to ch. 6, p. 248. For an example of Goltzius's similar refusal to take on the project, as well as the problems of working with

he laments generally: "These days, I find that the engravers are much more pernickety and unjust in the prices that they set than I have ever found before."[4]

Are these, then, the reasons why, in the 1580s – particularly as of 1583 – the vast majority of the intaglio plates Plantin ordered for his new illustrated editions were etchings instead of engravings?[5] Or did other factors play a role? As will be discussed in greater detail below, by the mid-1570s – when Plantin's first independent editions with etchings appeared – etchings had already been used for the illustration of a range of texts produced in various European cities, including works that Plantin himself bought and sold, so he would certainly have been aware of this technique as a viable option for book illustrations.[6] Etchings also had certain qualities that may have made them preferable to engravings. To start with, the very way in which the composition was laid down in an etching – a free drawing made with a light needle through a protective layer on top of the copper plate – readily lent itself to a much less calculated, more sketch-like appearance of the resulting image. In engraved images, by contrast, harder, sharper lines were often systematically laid in accord with conventions for creating light and dark effects with hatched lines (compare figs. 5.14 and 5.15). These visual distinctions may have made etchings more appealing for the depiction of certain subjects, such as those featuring landscapes. Similarly, the way in which the design drawn on to the plate was commonly etched in the sixteenth century – by having all of the exposed lines of bare metal simultaneously bitten down deeper into the plate through a single immersion of that plate into an acid bath – also implied that an etching could be completed more quickly and less expensively than an engraving.[7] For both of these reasons, etchings may also have been preferred to engravings for the illustration of some specific types of publications with numerous illustrations, where the cost, speed, and ease of execution were essential.[8]

In the course of this chapter we will examine all of these issues – matters of artist availability, visual aspects that were associated with specific subjects, cost, and speed of execution – and consider the extent to which each may have contributed to Plantin's

the Sadelers and the Wierixes, see Plantin's letter to the Jesuit Jacobus Ximenez of October 22, 1586 (Corr., VIII–IX, no. 1160). For a brief discussion of Plantin's correspondence concerning this topic, see Wadell 1985, pp. 15–16. See Rooses 1888 for an overview of Plantin's involvement in finding engravers for this project, in addition to transcriptions of eight key letters. For more recent transcriptions of these same letters with some notes, see Corr., VII, nos. 1044, 1106, and 1108; and Corr., VIII–IX, nos. 1160, 1182, 1188, 1193, and 1194.

4 "Hoc tempore quo experior celatores morosissimos esse et iniquiores in preciis postulandis quam hactenus expertus fuerim." See Plantin's letter to the Jesuit Jacobus Ximenez (Corr., VIII–IX, no. 1160, p. 71). See ch. 2 for more on this issue.

5 This excludes all projects discussed in ch. 6 and appendix 5, where Plantin worked together with or for someone else as just the printer of the text, as well as his few late reprints of his missals (PP 1699–1702), breviaries (PP 828–835), and books of hours (Bowen 1997a, PP 1783–1788ter, pp. 251–258), which usually bear a mixture of old and new engravings. It is not known to what degree Plantin ordered new engravings for them in the 1580s.

6 Consider, for example, La pompe funèbre (PP 939; ch. 3), Hubertus Goltzius's antiquarian texts (discussed below), and Edward de Dene's De warachtighe fabulen der dieren (see ch. 6).

7 On the time needed to complete an etching as opposed to an engraving, see, for example, Landau and Parshall 1994, pp. 30–31; see Reed and Wallace 1989, p. xix, for sixteenth-century treatises in which etchings are described as being easier to make than engravings. See below for a discussion of the relative costs of executing etchings and engravings.

8 See Riggs 1977, pp. 148–149, for his observations of how Cock typically used etchings either for large series of plates or for specific genres, like landscapes.

evident shift from engravings to etchings for the illustration of most of his publications during the last decade of his life. In order to evaluate this transition properly, we will trace Plantin's shift to etched book illustrations in the 1580s from his final new projects with engraved illustrations in the early 1580s through his increasing reliance upon etched illustrations in the latter part of the decade. By the time of his death in 1589, the selection of texts Plantin had illustrated with etchings would be the most diverse sample of his publications to bear intaglio illustrations considered thus far. Nevertheless, were etchings ultimately a satisfactory medium for book illustrations? Given the clear dominance of engraved (instead of etched) illustrations in the works of most seventeenth-century publishers, including Plantin's successors, the Moretuses, the answer seems obvious. But why was this the case? Relying upon the visual evidence of the books themselves, in addition to archival records of the printing and reworking of these plates for both initial and subsequent editions, we will provide a better documented answer to this question than has been provided thus far. Finally, in addition to considering these specific topics, we will also periodically examine the sales of a selection of the editions discussed in order to determine which buyers were interested in Plantin's new publications. In this way, we will highlight all of the primary aspects of Plantin's last great experiment with intaglio book illustrations. While he may have been forced into this new terrain by assorted circumstances beyond his control, his new venture did enable him to maintain a place for himself in the world of luxury books with intaglio illustrations that he had so successfully fostered with his liturgical editions from the 1570s. Nevertheless, we will also reveal some of the reasons why this was not the way forward for future profit-minded producers of books with rich intaglio illustrations.

PLANTIN'S LAST GREAT PROJECTS WITH ENGRAVED ILLUSTRATIONS

In 1580 and 1583, Plantin published his last projects with a significant number of new engraved illustrations. These consisted of a small (24°) calendar and evangeliary printed in 1580 (and reprinted in 1584) (PP 865 and 867 and PP 1152–1153, respectively), with more than 270 small engraved illustrations (see figs. 6.1–6.3), as well as a folio bible (PP 690), a new *quarto* edition of Arias Montano's *Humanae salutis monumenta* (PP 590), and a lengthy poem by Jan-Baptist Houwaert, advising ladies on love and courtship (PP 1412), all published in 1583 and featuring more than a hundred engravings between them (see figs. 5.1–5.6a).[9] While distinct in content from his liturgical editions, Plantin still tried to apply his cost-minimizing, mix-and-match reuse of engravings to each of these publications as well. This was, perhaps, most successfully done with the 1583 folio bible and *quarto* edition of Arias Montano's *Monumenta*.

Plantin's 1583 *Biblia sacra* (figs. 5.1, 5.2, 5.4, and 5.5) was unique in the history of sixteenth-century bibles printed in the Low Countries, if not in Europe as a whole, as

---

[9] Beyond these engravings and those used in the texts cited in n. 5 above, Plantin generally ordered only solitary engraved title-plates, an occasional author's portrait, or coat of arms. These are not discussed here, as they did not represent the same significant financial or practical investment as the production of a text with a full series of intaglio text illustrations.

a result of Plantin's unprecedented use of engravings for an otherwise common series of text illustrations.[10] Plantin's account of his plans for this publication in a letter he wrote to Arias Montano on July 1, 1580 provides important information concerning the illustration of this book.[11] First, Plantin's remarks indicate that the bulk of the text illustrations were conceived of for this project, and not a previously agreed upon new edition of Arias Montano's *Monumenta*, even though the images were (in Plantin's words) similar to those that had appeared in Arias Montano's earlier *Monumenta* editions. Second, Plantin boasts, "If I am not mistaken, this work will please the curious and those who wish to ornament their libraries with rarities."[12] In another letter written in October 1582 to the classicist Joachimus Camerarius, Plantin repeats his idea that this bible, which he characterizes by its extra large type and engraved illustrations, will appeal to those who enjoy richly embellished books to adorn their libraries.[13] It appears that Plantin also succeeded in garnering Philip II's interest in this project. For, albeit somewhat belatedly on January 1, 1584, Philip did authorize Alessandro Farnese to pay Plantin 9,000 fl. for the printing of a bible, a copy of which was sent to the Hapsburg Cardinal-Infant Albert, a dedication to whom is present in some copies of the 1583 folio bible.[14] It is possible that this payment was also inspired, in part, by Plantin's repeated complaints that Philip had yet to compensate him fully for other significant investments – stocks of special paper, for example – that Plantin had purchased in the 1570s for the printing of liturgical editions for the king.[15] The initial sales of this book, discussed in greater detail below, attest to Plantin's success in appealing to both of these special categories of buyers, namely, a broad-based, presumably wealthier, buying public and, exceptional for his illustrated editions from the 1580s, individuals of Spanish and Portuguese descent.

Given Plantin's clear intent from the start to make this an appealing luxury item, it may come as a surprise to note that in fact probably only one-quarter of the engravings used to illustrate this work were newly made just for its embellishment.[16] Rather, like Plantin's successful liturgical editions from the 1570s – and contrary to what he suggests in his letter to Arias Montano cited above – most of the images included here had been or would be used to illustrate other texts, in particular, a new (and

---

[10] Cf. Rosier 1997, I, p. 48. Although Plantin's Polyglot Bible also bears engraved illustrations these are not, as discussed above (see ch. 3), conventional text illustrations, like the images in Plantin's 1583 bible.

[11] See MPM Arch. 10, fols. 18v–19r, for this letter, a transcription of which is in Dávila Pérez 2002, II, no. 74.

[12] ". . . quod opus, ni fallor, placebit curiosis et illis qui raris cupiunt ornare suas bibliothecas" (Dávila Pérez 2002, II, no. 74, p. 456).

[13] *Corr. supplément*, no. 176, p. 200: "Biblia Latina maximis typis cum figuris in aere sculptis [*sic*] pro iis qui talibus delectantur ad ornandas bibliothecas."

[14] See Lefèvre 1953, no. 941.

[15] See, e.g., a letter written to de Çayas on September 5, 1581 in which Plantin complains at length about his financial situation and briefly inquires as to whether the 1583 bible would not appeal to Philip (*Corr.*, IV, no. 940).

[16] Consider, for example, the illustrations on fols. A4v, A6v, A7v, A8r, B1r, B3r, B4v, B6v, C4r, D8v, E6r, E6v, E7r, E7v, E8r, F6r, G1r, G1v, G3v, G4v, O8r, P1r, and P3r of the bible.

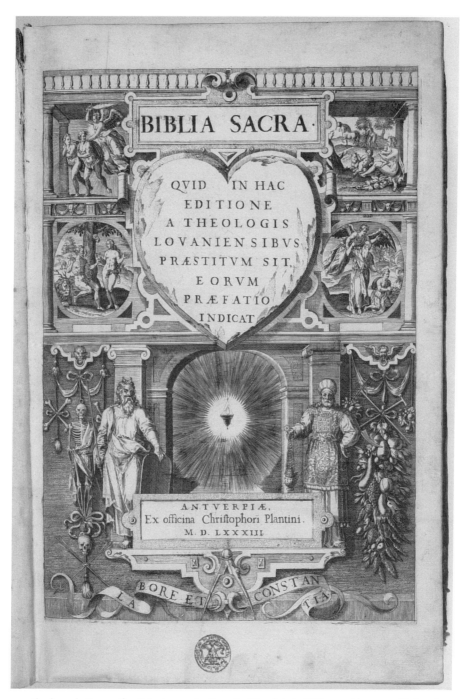

5.1 Abraham de Bruyn after Crispin van den Broeck, title-plate to *Biblia sacra* (Antwerp: Christopher Plantin, 1583; f°), engraving, 357 × 249 (Antwerp, Museum Plantin-Moretus, R 39.6).

5.2a Jan Sadeler I after Crispin van den Broeck, *St. John the Evangelist*, from *Biblia sacra* (Antwerp: Christopher Plantin, 1583; f°), fol. F4r, engraving (state I), 167 × 115 (Antwerp, Museum Plantin-Moretus, R 39.6).

5.2b Detail of St. John's knees. See fig. 5.3b for an example of the reworking of this plate for the illustration of Arias Montano's *Monumenta*, similarly published in 1583.

Plantin's final) edition of Arias Montano's *Humanae salutis monumenta*.[17] Specifically, of the ninety-four engravings in the 1583 *Biblia sacra*, twelve of the thirteen folio (or larger) plates came from earlier Plantin editions – eleven from his Polyglot Bible (PP 644) and the floor plan of the Temple at Jerusalem from Arias Montano's broadside on the Temple (PP 584).[18] Only the engraved title-page was new, executed by Abraham de Bruyn in 1582 after a design by Crispin van den Broeck (fig. 5.1).[19] Of the remaining *quarto*-scaled text illustrations, some forty-six of the plates would also be used to illustrate the *Monumenta* (compare figs. 5.2 and 5.3), while a few others were taken from Plantin's pool of illustrations for his liturgical editions. Consider, for example, the image of the *Raising of Lazarus* (fig. 5.4), where a comparable engraving was used to illustrate Plantin's 1573 large *octavo* book of hours (fig. 4.4) and a later state of this plate was used to illustrate a 1591 *octavo* book of hours published by Jan Moretus I.[20] Thus, while one might initially imagine that Plantin had ordered a total of 166 plates for the illustration

[17] For more on this text, see ch. 3.

[18] Specifically, all of the illustrations to vol. VIII of the Polyglot Bible were included except the images of the shekel, Noah's ark, the floor plan of the Tabernacle, the map of Jerusalem, and the elevation of the Temple.

[19] See appendix 1, under van den Broeck and de Bruyn. The iconography of this new title-plate is discussed in Coppens 1989, pp. 200–208.

[20] See MPM (O.B. 4.2) for a copy of the 1591 *Officium B. Mariae Virginis*. Owing to Plantin's practice of simultaneously using different engravings of the same compositions for his liturgical editions

5.3a Jan Sadeler I after Crispin van den Broeck, St. John the Evangelist, from Benito Arias Montano, Humanae salutis monumenta (Antwerp: Christopher Plantin, 1583; 4°), fol. I4r, engraving (state II), 167 × 115 (Antwerp, Museum Plantin-Moretus, R 54.20). See fig. 5.2 for an earlier state of this engraving.

of the 1583 bible and the 1583 Monumenta (with 94 and 72 illustrations, respectively), the actual total of newly commissioned plates (such as fig. 5.5) was probably closer to just 100, a much more manageable sum for two conspicuously, richly illustrated editions. Moreover, it is also important to note here that the majority of these "new" plates – some 60 of the 70 illustrations needed to illustrate the Monumenta, for example – had already been completed by 1576, seven years prior to the printing of these books. This fact is documented by the inclusion of many of these engravings in a commemorative album of illustrations from Plantin's editions that Jan Moretus I prepared for Plantin

(see ch. 4), it is possible that the exact number of old, reused plates may vary between some copies of the 1583 bible and Monumenta. Differing states of the same plate have already been observed among some copies of this edition of the Monumenta (cf., e.g., three copies in the Bibliothèque de l'Arsenal, Paris: 4° T 582; 4° T 583; 4° T 267).

5.3b Detail of St. John's knees. Compare with fig. 5.2b.

as a New Year's present for January 1, 1576.[21] Because these engravings were pasted in largely in the order in which they would appear in the *Monumenta*, it seems that at that point in time (around 1576) work was geared towards illustrating the *Monumenta* and not the bible, as Plantin wrote to Arias Montano later on in 1580. Regardless of this question of "priority," work on the plates for these two last, large projects with engravings was clearly well underway by the mid-1570s, when Plantin was routinely ordering engravings for other editions, and was not begun five or more years later (as one might think from the date of publication) when Plantin's purchase of new engravings had become more of an anomaly.

The interchangeability of these plates for the illustration of distinct texts – a bible, the *Monumenta*, and books of hours, as well as, potentially, other liturgical editions – is underscored in the inventories of Plantin's stock of plates made up after his death. Here, there are references to 113 figures for the folio bible, the *Monumenta* in *quarto*, and *quarto* books of hours combined and 18 separate plates just for the *Monumenta* in *quarto* (the plates for the Polyglot Bible were always listed separately for that specific project).[22] Despite Plantin's cost-minimizing reuse of plates between the bible and the *Monumenta*

---

[21] See MPM Arch. 1228 for this album (dated in Jan Moretus's introductory text), and fols. 239r–248r for the early impressions of many of these engravings.

[22] See appendix 4, p. 385, for the following listings: "113 figure p[our] la Bible in f° et monumenta 4° et horae 4° [and] 18 tot Monumenta 4°, etc." The eighteen separate *Monumenta* plates could have comprised the title-plate, the six Old Testament subjects that were included in the *Monumenta*, but not the bible (see, e.g., *New Holl.*, *Van Groeningen*, 11, nos. 373, 380, and 381), and other New Testament

5.4 Jan Wierix after Crispin van den Broeck, *Raising of Lazarus*, from *Biblia sacra* (Antwerp: Christopher Plantin, 1583; f°), fol. G3r, engraving, 167 × 112 (Antwerp, Museum Plantin-Moretus, R 39.6).

in particular, it is evident that ultimately priority was given to the illustration of the bible, as it was the first of the two to be illustrated. For plates that were printed in both books always appear in stronger, earlier states in the bible and in weaker, occasionally reworked, later states in the *Monumenta*, as is the case, for example, in figs. 5.2 and 5.3, where St. John's robes and the eagle bear rough extra hatching lines in the impression in the *Monumenta*. Moreover, what is visually apparent is also supported by what is known concerning the timing of the printing of the illustrations in these books. Specifically, while the earliest known payments for the printing of illustrations in the 1583 bible date from July 1581, the only known payment that may pertain to the illustration of the 1583

subjects from the *Monumenta* that were not common to either the bible or Plantin's books of hours (see, e.g., M-H 2253 and 2254).

5.5 Abraham de Bruyn after Crispin van den Broeck, *Gathering Grain on the Sabbath*, from *Biblia sacra* (Antwerp: Christopher Plantin, 1583; f°), fol. A6v, engraving, 168 × 113 (Antwerp, Museum Plantin-Moretus, R 39.6).

Monumenta in *quarto* dates from September 1582.[23] This corroborates what is suggested in Plantin's letter to Arias Montano cited above, namely that producing this illustrated bible was (or at least had become) the primary project. If so, the *quarto* edition of the *Monumenta* would have been an extra, lavishly illustrated book that would have been relatively inexpensive for Plantin to produce, as its illustration would have cost little more than the investment in making some eighteen additional plates and printing the lot. Whichever project was "first," Plantin's mix-and-match reuse of engravings here, a continuation of his earlier cost-minimizing use of engravings across his religious texts, was an effective way, once again, to make the most out of his engraved plates.

Although Plantin applied similar tactics to the selection of plates used to illustrate his two other major projects with engraved illustrations from this period, namely his

[23] See MPM Arch. 18, fol. 430 rht, and Bowen 2003, p. 8, n. 13, respectively, for these payments.

5.6a Jan Wierix after an anonymous artist, *Jan-Baptist Houwaert*, from Jan-Baptist Houwaert, *Pegasides pleyn ende den lust-hof der maeghden* (Antwerp: Christopher Plantin, 1583; 4°), vol. I, fol. ++++2v, engraving, 160 × 124 (Antwerp, Museum Plantin-Moretus, R 54.19).

Sanctorum kalendarii Romani . . . imagines and *Evangeliorum dominicalium summaria* from 1580, on the one hand, and his publication of Houwaert's *Pegasides pleyn ende den lust-hof der maeghden* (Pegasus's Square and the Pleasure Garden of Virgins) on the other, his options for reusing the plates included in these works were much more limited. Of the 273 small plates illustrating the calendar and evangeliary, only 13 were old plates (all previously used to illustrate Plantin's small books of hours – see fig. 6.1) and just a few others were subsequently reused in other texts he published, such as a missal in *quarto* from 1585 (see figs. 6.2 and 4.24).[24] And, of the 18 plates used to embellish Houwaert's poem, only Houwaert's portrait (fig. 5.6) and an engraving of his coat of arms were reused in another work, namely, Houwaert's moralizing poem on how to live virtuously, *De vier wterste, van de doot, van het oordeel, van d'eeuwich leven, van de pyne der hellen* (The Four Last Things: Death, the Last Judgment, Heaven, and Hell), which Plantin

[24] For more on the plates used to illustrate Plantin's 1580 calendar and evangeliary, see ch. 6. For the subsequent reuse of a few of them in his 1585 missal, see ch. 4.

5.6b Detail of the outer frame and a piece of armor (on the left side). Compare this detail with fig. 5.7b for an example of the different effects achievable with engraving (here) and etching (there).

similarly published in 1583 (PP 1413). In each of these cases, the subjects portrayed implied a more limited use (and potential reuse) of any investment in decorative matter. Consequently, if the general prices for engravings were increasing by the late 1580s, as Plantin suggests in one of the letters cited above, that would have been an extra incentive to use less expensive media for the illustration of his subsequent projects with more subject-specific (and hence restrictive) images.

What of Plantin's other recurring complaint from the 1580s concerning the difficulty in finding competent artists who were willing to make engravings for book illustrations? As was the case with all of his earlier projects with engraved illustrations, Plantin employed various artists to make the necessary engravings for these works.[25]

[25] Each of these artists is discussed in greater detail in ch. 2 and appendix 1.

For the illustration of the bible and the *Monumenta*, the vast majority of the truly "new" plates – ones that were not included in Jan Moretus's 1576 album – were either anonymous works, or else engravings signed by the designer Crispin van den Broeck and the engraver Abraham de Bruyn, both of whom had occasionally worked for Plantin before. Plantin's calendar and evangeliary are noteworthy as they document the best known occasion when the engraver Paul Uten Waele worked for him, as well as Plantin's exceptional reliance upon Philips Galle's workshop for more than fifty engravings for that one project.[26]

Of all of these artists, none is known to have made an engraving for Plantin after 1583.[27] Plantin himself moved to Leiden by January 1583, where he had established a new printing business, working in part for the University of Leiden and hedging his bets, as it were, during the intensification of the war around Antwerp. His sons-in-law, Jan Moretus I and Franciscus Raphelengius I, stayed in Antwerp to manage the business there as best they could.[28] Once Antwerp surrendered to Alessandro Farnese on August 17, 1585, following a prolonged campaign to starve out Antwerp's citizens, those with Calvinist sympathies who did not wish to remain under Catholic rule had four years to leave and others who had fled during the period of Calvinist rule and Farnese's siege could return. While Plantin was among those who returned – he is known to have been back in Antwerp by October 1585 – several of the artists with whom he had worked up until that time were among those who left. Specifically, of the people named above, Abraham de Bruyn returned definitively to Cologne (where he died around 1587) and Crispin van den Broeck moved to Middelburg (where he remained until 1587). Nothing is known about Paul Uten Waele's whereabouts in this period, in particular when, if at all, he was in Antwerp.[29] Thus, of the figures named above, this only left Philips Galle, who was clearly not interested in becoming a regular supplier of engravings for other publishers' projects, Jan Wierix, whom Plantin repeatedly cites as an unreliable artist, and Peeter vander Borcht, who was on good personal terms with Plantin and who had already supplied him with hundreds of drawings and numerous etchings by this time.[30]

This general dispersion of the pool of engravers Plantin had relied upon in the early 1580s bears out at least one of his laments cited above concerning the difficulties he experienced, particularly in the late 1580s, in finding artists who could and were willing to make engravings for him. Regrettably, there are not enough payments known for the work on these projects to determine whether Plantin's complaint from 1586 concerning artists' "unjust" prices is as justifiable. This is of particular interest in the case of Jan Wierix, who remained in Antwerp and was, thus, theoretically available to work, but whose skill and growing reputation may have induced him to raise his prices beyond what Plantin could and wanted to pay. The few indications that there are of Jan

---

[26] See ch. 6 for more on Uten Waele's and Galle's workshops' contributions to the calendar and evangeliary.

[27] Plantin's only known publications from the later 1580s in which engravings by these artists are present are a few of his breviaries (PP 829 and 832–834) and missals (PP 1699–1702), but these all appear to be printed from older plates.

[28] For a general survey of Plantin's work in Leiden, see Voet, GC, I, pp. 105–113.

[29] See Holl. *Dutch & Flemish*, LV, p. 7.

[30] See ch. 2 for more on these artists' working relationship with Plantin.

Wierix's prices for engravings do substantiate this hypothesis. For, even in 1570–1571, the wages he received as a young engraver, just twenty-one or twenty-two years of age, were on the upper end of Plantin's pay scale for comparable work. And while we do not have sufficient data to chart the evolution of his wages, payments made by Plantin and his successors to his brother Hieronymus Wierix between 1570 and 1616 indicate that he, at least, was able to raise his fees to exceptional levels thanks to his reputation, which was comparable to that of his brother Jan.[31] It is even possible that Jan Wierix's noteworthy presumed production of all sixteen of the text illustrations for Houwaert's *Pegasides pleyn ende den lust-hof der maeghden*, as well as two portraits of Houwaert (see fig. 5.6), may have come about only because Houwaert himself apparently was subsidizing the cost of having the illustrations made.[32]

Plantin's final, large-scale projects with engraved illustrations from the early 1580s thus appear to support at least one of his complaints about having engravings made for his publications, namely that competent engravers who were willing to work became increasingly difficult to find. His other complaint, concerning the relative increase in the cost of having engravings made, may also have been true to some extent. Particularly if the pool of available artists was diminishing, the prices charged by those remaining may well have gone up if the demand for engravings was constant or on the rise. Thus, when his now limited production and sales options for his previously successful liturgical editions forced him to try out new types of texts with intaglio illustrations, Plantin may have found the extra investment in engraved illustrations too great an added risk. Did etchings, particularly those made by his ready and willing companion Peeter vander Borcht, offer the best solution? In order to address this question properly we will consider the essential characteristics of etchings and their initial use as book illustrations first, before delving into Plantin's own immersion in this technique for his new line of works with intaglio illustrations.

ETCHINGS AS BOOK ILLUSTRATIONS: INITIAL ATTEMPTS

The first etched prints were probably made around 1500 in the workshop of Daniel Hopfer in Augsburg, some sixty to seventy years after the emergence of engraving as a viable print technique.[33] Etchings were originally made on steel and iron plates, which had the disadvantages of rusting easily and not being suitable for engraving. Copper plates, however, could be used for both etchings and engravings and, thus, a combined technique of the two, in which, for example, the first part of the composition was

---

[31] For more information on the Wierixes' wages, see Bowen and Imhof 2003.

[32] Houwaert's assistance with the payments to Jan Wierix for these illustrations is documented in one record from January 15, 1583, which reads "Ledit [January 15, 1583] recue de Monsieur Jan Battista Houwaert la somme de florins 51 et 6 patars lesquels sont florins 30 pour bon compte des livres quil prendra et xxi florins et 6 patars a compter a Hans Wierickx quand il livrera les deux planches, valent fl. 51 st. 6." (Received the following from Monsieur Jan Battista Houwaert, the sum of 51 florins and 6 stuivers, which are 30 florins for the books he will take and 21 florins and 6 stuivers for the account of Jan Wierix, when he delivers the two plates.) (MPM Arch. 61, fol. 9v; also transcribed in M-H *Wierix*, III.2, p. 541, no. 36.) See Holl. *Dutch & Flemish*, LXVIII, nos. 2102 and 2103 (for two portraits of Houwaert), and LXX, book no. 35, for the text illustrations. Only Houwaert's coat of arms was engraved by Abraham de Bruyn (see PP 1412, n. 8).

[33] Landau and Parshall 1994, pp. 27 and 323.

etched and then supplemented with engraved lines. The first copper-plate etchings were probably made in Italy and the Netherlands around 1515–1520, after which the technique developed and was used in Italy more than in northern Europe.[34] In theory, etchings are easier to make than engravings: once the metal plate was prepared and covered with a material that was impervious to acid, all the artist had to do was draw the desired composition lightly through the protective layer with a needle and then immerse the plate in an acid bath, whereby the lines drawn on to it were bitten out, ready, then, to be filled with ink and printed. It did not require the years of training needed to learn to engrave a plate or carve a woodblock and was, consequently, open to many more aspiring printmakers. However, in the early sixteenth century, when the basic techniques of making engravings and woodblocks had already been mastered, etching was still in a highly experimental state, technically. One of the primary and most unpredictable difficulties arose when the protective ground loosened when in the acid – either because it had not been properly laid or because lines had been drawn too close together – and resulted in random "overbite." Early etchings also often suffered from "underbiting," when the plate was not left in the acid bath long enough, thereby resulting in too shallow lines that would print too weakly and produce fewer serviceable impressions. Perhaps because of these potential difficulties, sixteenth-century etchings were most often "bitten" just once, after which the composition was reinforced or complemented with lines engraved with a burin to provide a richer array of tones. Federico Barocci, active in Urbino, and Hieronymus Cock of Antwerp are the only two better known sixteenth-century etchers who are credited with applying multiple bitings to their plates.[35] These early technical complications may have discouraged people initially from using etchings for book illustrations instead of the more predictable engravings or woodcuts.

The earliest known book to be illustrated with etchings is Augustin Hirschvogel's model book *Ein eigentliche und gründliche Anweisung in die Geometria*, published anonymously in Nuremberg in 1543, approximately seventy years after the earliest known examples of engravings being used as book illustrations.[36] By the 1560s, however, etchings were being used to illustrate various types of books throughout Europe. A few of the better known examples include Gabriello Faerno, *Fabulae centum* (Rome: [Paulus Manutius for] Vincenzo Luchino, 1564), with a hundred full-page etched illustrations;[37] Georgette de Montenay's popular emblem book, *Emblemes, ou devises chrestiennes*, ed. by P. de Castellas (Lyon: Jean Marcorelle, 1567), which comprises a hundred illustrations exhibiting a mix of engraving and etching;[38] Wenzel Jamnitzer's *Perspectiva corporum regularium* ([Nuremberg s.n.]: 1568), with forty-three etched text

---

[34] Landau and Parshall 1994, pp. 28 and 327–328.

[35] See Reed and Wallace 1989, p. xxii, and Riggs 1977, pp. 128–132, respectively.

[36] See the Introduction for an overview of the early use of engravings and etchings as book illustrations. Although Mortimer 1964 and Mortimer 1974 provide informative accounts of sixteenth-century illustrated books from France and Italy, they also contain numerous errors in the discernment of etchings versus engravings and consequently are not useful when trying to compile an overview of early editions with etched illustrations.

[37] See Reed and Wallace 1989, cat. no. 178, which gives examples of several other contemporary Italian editions with etched illustrations.

[38] See Adams 2000 and Adams et al. 2002, II, F.437, pp. 177–181, for this and later editions of this text.

illustrations and seven ornamental borders;[39] and in the Low Countries, Edward de Dene's *De warachtighe fabulen der dieren* (Bruges: Pieter de Clerck for Marcus Gheeraerts I, 1567), with a series of 107 etched text illustrations by Gheeraerts, and Hubertus Goltzius's various editions of the *Vivae omnium fere imperatorum imagines*, the texts for which were printed in Antwerp by Gilles Coppens van Diest I, in Latin, German, Italian, French, and Spanish, between 1557 and 1560, each with approximately 150 etched plates printed over chiaroscuro woodcuts. Plantin bought and sold copies of at least the last two works.[40]

Why might etchings have been chosen for the illustration of these (and other) works? Various factors could have contributed to these decisions. Assuming those who executed these etchings had mastered the technical uncertainties of the medium, then the general advantages of the relative ease and lower cost of producing etchings compared with engravings would certainly have been attractive to those publishing books with large numbers of illustrations, as was the case with most of the editions cited above. For some of these texts, in particular Faerno's and de Dene's editions of fables, which usually featured images of animals in a landscape setting, the characteristic sketchy, spontaneous appearance of etchings may also have been preferred, visually, to the harder, more controlled and systematized lines of engravings for the rendering of such subjects. In de Montenay's emblems and Jamnitzer's perspective constructions, along with other works featuring series of architectural images,[41] the intrinsic sketchy appearance of etchings was subdued and supplemented with engraving such that the resulting lines appear finer and sharper, as a rule. For these works, another common advantage of etchings may have influenced the decision to use the medium, namely the facility of laying out a basic composition quickly and easily (perhaps with use of a ruler for scientific and architectural studies), which could then be finished off by hand with a burin to give the resulting appearance of an engraving without all the time and work usually required to produce one. One final advantage of working with etchings as opposed to engravings is evident in Hubertus Goltzius's editions, that is, the opportunity etchings provided to those not trained as engravers to make their own prints. For while Goltzius did receive some training as an artist, it was not as an engraver. Thus, etchings would have enabled him to retain personal control over the renditions of the ancient coins that were essential to his publications.[42] The question remains as to which of these factors (if any) may have influenced Plantin in his decision to employ etchings.

39 See Seelig et al., 2001–2003, *Book Illustrations*, II, pp. 132–138, no. 44; May 1985, and cat. nos. 756–757 in the same publication; and a 1973 reprint of the original edition by Graz Publishers.
40 See ch. 6 for de Dene's text. For an overview of Goltzius's publications with etched illustrations, see Le Loup 1983. Although Le Loup identifies the title-pages of Goltzius's later publications (from 1562–1576) as etchings, these are actually all engravings. For a detailed discussion of Goltzius's *Vivae omnium fere imperatorum imagines*, see Bialler 1993. See MPM Arch. 16, fols. 74 and 75, for examples of Plantin's purchases of this work.
41 See, e.g., Antonio Labacco's *Libro appartenente a l'architettura*. First printed in Rome in 1552 and reissued in 1557 and 1559, this work consisted primarily of a brief introductory text and then a series of twenty-seven plates (see Mortimer 1974, no. 245, and Reed and Wallace 1989, n. 1 to cat. 37).
42 For Goltzius's training and personal interests, see Le Loup 1983, pp. 9–12. Although not documented conclusively, it is generally assumed that Goltzius made the etchings for his publications.

5.7a Peeter vander Borcht, *Andreas Vesalius*, from Joannes Sambucus, *Icones veterum aliquot, ac recentium medicorum, philosophorumque* (Antwerp: Christopher Plantin, 1574; f°), fol. G2r, etching, 198 × 180 (Brussels, The Royal Library, Rare Books Department, VB 13.263 C LP).

PLANTIN'S FIRST EDITIONS WITH ETCHINGS

As noted above, Plantin was certainly aware of the possibilities of using etchings as book illustrations early on in his career. His and Hieronymus Cock's 1559 co-publication of *La pompe funèbre* featured a series of etched and engraved plates executed by two of the then great practitioners of the medium in the Low Countries, namely, Joannes and Lucas van Doetecum – although in this case Plantin was probably not directly or solely responsible for the selection of the medium or the artists behind the illustrations.[43] Indeed, it was not until the mid-1570s that Plantin himself began to produce works with etched illustrations. The two main examples among his publications from this period are

---

[43] On the van Doetecums' etching technique, see Riggs 1977, pp. 36, 133, and 140–142, and the introductory text to *New Holl., Van Doetecum*, I, pp. xi–xxi. See ch. 3 for more on *La pompe funèbre*.

5.7b Detail of the outer frame and part of Vesalius's face. Compare with fig. 5.6b.

Joannes Sambucus's *Icones veterum aliquot, ac recentium medicorum, philosophorumque*, with a series of sixty-seven portraits of ancient and recent physicians and philosophers, which Plantin published in 1574, and Laurentius Gambara's *Rerum sacrarum liber*, a collection of religious poems embellished with fifty-three etchings, published in 1577.[44] And yet, in neither of these cases was Plantin personally responsible for providing the illustrations. The plates for Gambara's collection of poems were made in Italy, at least in part by the Roman artist Bernardino Passari (whose name appears on the title-plate), and were then shipped to Antwerp for inclusion in the text.[45] While the illustrations for Sambucus's portrait series appear to have been made locally by Peeter vander Borcht (who was then in Antwerp, having fled the fighting in Mechelen in 1572), a letter Sambucus wrote to Abraham Ortelius on September 2, 1573 indicates that Sambucus himself was paying for the execution of the illustrations.[46] The fact that Plantin did not order many more etchings from vander Borcht for the next seven to eight years (while he did order engravings from other artists, as discussed above) suggests that, at least at this point in time, he generally preferred engravings to etchings for the illustrations of his publications. A comparison of a portrait of Andreas Vesalius from Sambucus's text with Jan Wierix's portrait of Jan-Baptist Houwaert, made nearly a decade later (cf. figs. 5.6 and 5.7), readily reveals how vander Borcht's etching could not compete with

[44] For Sambucus's work, see PP 2175 (and the bibliography cited there), as well as Visser 2004. For Gambara's text, see PP 1235. Plantin also had at least four full-page borders etched for the illustration of his 1574 folio *Missale Romanum* (PP 1685; copy in Trinity College Library, Cambridge [E.3.56], fig. 4.8), to complement the approximately fifty engravings illustrating the text.

[45] See the notes to the illustrations in PP 1235, and figs. 1–2 of Voet, PP, III, for reproductions of the title-page and one sample illustration.

[46] For the attribution of these etchings to vander Borcht, see PP 2175, n. 6. For Sambucus's role in paying for the illustrations, see Visser 2004, p. 305, in which he cites the following letter (in n. 18), published in Hessels 1887, no. 44, p. 105: "Oro te cohortere, eum qui Museolum nostrum prae manibus habeat, ut urgeat opus: ubi ad extremum erit, munus illi denuo mittam." (I beg you to encourage the one who had our "Museolum" to get on with the work. When the work is completed I will send him a reward.)

Wierix's engraving in the clear, precise rendition of varying tones and textures. But was this the reason behind Plantin's preference for engravings? While one might like to attribute such quality-based reasoning to Plantin, the evidence from his subsequent use of etchings to illustrate his publications in the 1580s makes it seem unlikely that this was the primary motivating factor. Moreover, as suggested above, the decision to have Jan Wierix make the engravings for Houwaert's publication may not have been Plantin's, but Houwaert's, as he was evidently willing – perhaps because of such artistic concerns – to help subsidize the cost of employing Wierix. By contrast, in Sambucus's letter to Ortelius cited above, it appears that Sambucus was anxious to have his already delayed publication appear. Hence, the relative speed with which etchings could be completed, in addition, perhaps, to potential cost advantages, may have led Sambucus, at least, to advocate using etchings for his publication despite the visually less sophisticated result.[47] What would change, then, in the coming seven years to induce Plantin to switch from the one technique to the other?

In 1581 and 1582, when he was still working on his last new projects with engraved illustrations, Plantin produced his first independent publications with etched illustrations. The first of these to appear were two new editions of Ludovico Guicciardini's description of the Low Countries – one printed in Italian in 1581 and one in French, published in 1582.[48] Guicciardini was a Florentine nobleman who settled in Antwerp around 1540 and started dealing in fabrics there with his brother. The reasons why he chose to write an account of the Low Countries are unclear, although he was paid for his efforts by the city of Antwerp and his text did earn him some recognition, as it was the first detailed description of the principalities and cities of the Low Countries to be produced.[49] Plantin was not the first to print Guicciardini's text, however. Rather, in 1565, Plantin's local competitor, Willem Silvius, received a ten-year privilege for the production of this text and proceeded to publish editions in Italian (in 1567) and in French (in 1567 and 1568).[50] Each of these editions was illustrated with fifteen wood-cuts, while two oversize intaglios – an etched map of the Low Countries as a whole, signed by Cornelis de Hooghe, and (depending upon the edition) an engraving or an etching of the city hall of Antwerp – were inserted in some, if not all copies of these books. The 1565 dating of the prints of the city hall, together with the inclusion of a publisher's address along the lower edge, suggest that they were initially issued separately when the town hall was completed in 1565 and were not designed for inclusion in these publications.[51] Then in 1580, just when Plantin was planning his own edition of

---

47 See Visser 2004, pp. 304–305, for Sambucus's impatience to have this work published and his failed attempts to have it completed elsewhere first.
48 For these two editions, see PP 1277 (his *Descrittione di tutti i Paesi Bassi*) and PP 1278–1279 (his *Description de touts les Pais-Bas*), respectively. Plantin also printed a second Italian edition in 1588 (PP 1280). For an overview of all of the editions printed of Guicciardini's account of the Low Countries, see Guicciardini 2001. For what little is known of Guicciardini, see Voet, PP, III, pp. 1054–1055 (and the additional references there), as well as Guicciardini 2001, pp. 9–24.
49 See PP 1277, n. 6, for his remuneration from the city of Antwerp.
50 See Guicciardini 2001, pp. 27–31, for these editions. Here, the authors incorrectly identify the intaglio plates that were occasionally inserted in these books as "kopergravures," or engravings; at least one was an etching.
51 See Guicciardini 2001, p. 139, for these two prints: Antwerpen-Stadhuis-1 (an engraving) and 2 (an etching).

this text – Silvius's original privilege for the text had expired in 1575 – a German edition with numerous woodcut illustrations was printed in Basel by Sebastian Henricpetri.[52] Consequently, all of the earlier editions of this text were clearly conceived of as projects with woodcut illustrations with only an occasional "extra" intaglio print added to them.

When Plantin decided to reprint Guicciardini's text, his visual conception of the publication was significantly different from that of his predecessors. In fact, when he wrote to Silvius on February 16, 1580, offering to buy his stock of woodblocks, Plantin was unequivocal about his plan to illustrate his edition entirely with intaglio illustrations, thereby making it grander than Silvius's own ("encores que je ne m'en veuille servir veu que je fays faire le tout en cuivre en autres grandeurs que les vostres").[53] He asserted, with dubious good will, that he simply wanted to compensate Silvius for his impending loss, as the latter would no longer be able to use his own woodblocks once Plantin's edition was on the market. However, Plantin was most likely interested in Silvius's woodblocks as a sort of preventative measure, intended to impede Silvius from bringing out a new edition with his old illustrations that might compete with his own. Silvius did not accept Plantin's offer, as he was himself apparently endeavoring to gather additional city views for a new edition of the text.[54] But he died soon hereafter and, by July 1, 1580, Plantin had garnered a privilege for the production of the text in any language for the next twelve years. Plantin did, at some later date, acquire the woodblocks and two copper plates that Silvius had used for his first editions, presumably from Silvius's widow.[55]

Plantin's illustration of Guicciardini's text was of a completely different order than Silvius's, his primary local competitor in this regard. Plantin had not only changed the medium of the illustrations, but also their number. Where Silvius's editions were introduced with a conventional title-page with woodcut frame, Plantin had four full-page introductory engraved (not etched) images of: (1) an allegorical portrayal of the Low Countries; (2) an allegorical title-frame, featuring images of agriculture and a horn of plenty or abundance on the left, and Neptune and the fruits of the sea on the right (fig. 5.8); (3) a frame with the coats of arms of the seventeen provinces of the Low Countries, with (often, but not always) the coat of arms of Philip II inserted in the middle; and (4) an allegory of the Arts and Sciences, with, in most copies, a portrait of Philip II inserted in the middle.[56] Where Silvius had just fifteen woodcut views and potentially two extra inserted intaglio prints, Plantin's first edition had fifty-five etched illustrations, comprising maps, city views, and some extra images of Antwerp (see fig. 5.9), only a selection of which were copied from Silvius's illustrations. It is not known who was responsible for the bulk of these illustrations. A few were made locally in some of the portrayed cities, such as the image of Leiden. Speculation concerning

---

52 See Guicciardini 2001, p. 32.   53 For this letter, see Corr., VI, no. 864, and Corr. supplément, no. 149.

54 See Guicciardini 2001, p. 36.

55 See the summary of these events, documented by various sources, in Guicciardini 2001, p. 36. Contrary to what is suggested here and in PP 1277, n. 2, it is not certain (only conjectured) that Silvius's widow sold Plantin the blocks in 1583 (see Rooses 1914, p. 224).

56 Of these engraved plates, only that of the allegorical image of the Low Countries is signed (by the designer Crispin van den Broeck and the engraver Abraham de Bruyn). Their signatures here have led some to assume that they were also responsible for designing and engraving the remaining introductory images, although there is no evidence to support this.

5.8 Anonymous artists, title-plate to Ludovico Guicciardini, *Descrittione di tutti i Paesi Bassi* (Antwerp: Christopher Plantin, 1581; f°), engraving, 270 × 187 (Antwerp, Museum Plantin-Moretus, A 1342).

the remaining plates focuses on Peeter vander Borcht, the circle of Frans Hogenberg of Cologne, and his assistants Ferdinand and Ambrosius Arsenius.[57] All of Plantin's text illustrations were scaled to fit in the format of the book (thereby avoiding the difficulty in Silvius's editions of the oversize inserted etchings). But, while all of the illustrations were printed directly into the book in Plantin's first (Italian) edition of Guicciardini's text in 1581, for each of his subsequent editions (two French versions from 1582 and another Italian edition from 1588) the illustrations were printed separately and inserted later on, thereby enabling Plantin to sell copies with and without the accompanying illustrations. The price difference between these two variants was significant: 7 fl. (or 140 st.) for the illustrated text and just 2 fl. 10 st. (or 50 st.) for the text alone. As we will discuss in greater detail below, a surprising number of copies of Plantin's

[57] See Guicciardini 2001, pp. 38–39, and PP 1277, n. 3, for summaries of these views. Each of these images is described in Guicciardini 2001.

5.9 Anonymous artist, *View of Antwerp*, from Ludovico Guicciardini, *Descrittione di tutti i Paesi Bassi* (Antwerp: Christopher Plantin, 1581; f°), pp. 88–89, etching, 235 × 321 (Antwerp, Museum Plantin-Moretus, A 1342).

French edition were sold without the accompanying illustrations with which Plantin sought to distinguish his editions. Evidently, he was right to be concerned about the possible competition of a cheaper edition of the same text, with or without Silvius's old woodcuts.

Plantin's first edition of Guicciardini's text was produced in 1581, when he clearly still had access to some engravers whom he was employing to make the plates for his 1580 calendar and evangeliary project and 1583 bible and *Monumenta* projects. Why, then, did Plantin decide to have the text illustrations etched and not engraved like the four introductory images? One important factor may have been the textual genre and contemporary expectations of its illustrations. Specifically, it was not uncommon among the popular cartographic, geographic works with maps and city views that were being produced at this time to have etched maps and views instead of engravings. Indeed, of the important contemporary publications in this field – Abraham Ortelius's atlas, the *Theatrum orbis terrarum*, Philips Galle's pocket derivative thereof, Georg Braun and Frans Hogenberg's *Civitates orbis terrarum*, and Gerard de Jode's *Speculum orbis terrarum*, all of which Plantin would have known – only the maps included in Ortelius's original folio atlas were consistently engraved.[58] Thus, etchings must have been accepted, if not

---

[58] For Ortelius's and Galle's atlases, see ch. 6 and appendix 5. For a basic description of Braun and Hogenberg's *Civitates orbis terrarum*, and de Jode's *Speculum orbis terrarum*, see Koeman 1967–1971, II, pp. 10–25 and 205–212, respectively. See Denucé 1912–1913 for Plantin's active involvement in this world of cartographic publications.

preferred, for the rendition of city views and maps for the illustrations for these types of publications. Plantin's decision similarly to rely on etchings might simply reflect his recognition of this practice. Significantly, even the distinction between engraved frontispieces and title-pages and etched text illustrations found in Plantin's Guicciardini editions is also present in some of the publications cited above, in particular Braun's and Hogenberg's *Civitates orbis terrarum*. While the title-plate to de Jode's *Speculum orbis terrarum* is primarily engraved, it does contain some etched elements – the inner frame around the title, for example. Galle's pocket atlases are noteworthy for their more conventional title-pages with ordinary printed text and only one of Plantin's woodcut printer's marks for decoration – a less expensive option appropriate, perhaps, for a work conceived of as a cheaper alternative to a full-fledged atlas. These diverse solutions to producing a suitable title-page suggest that an additional order of association and subdivision among print media was at play. Specifically, while etchings were, indeed, favored for the execution of certain series of text illustrations, other traditions for the execution of the title-page were continued independent of the medium chosen for the text illustrations, be it the printing of a conventional typographically set title-page or the inclusion of independent engraved title-pages and frontispieces.[59]

Thus, in the case of his editions of Guicciardini's description of the Low Countries, two separate traditions probably governed Plantin's choice of medium for the illustration of this book simultaneously but independently of one another: namely, that of introducing texts with an engraved title-page or frontispiece and that of illustrating cartographic works with etchings. Plantin's other main project from this period that bears primarily etched illustrations, his illustrated account of the 1582 state entry of the duke of Anjou into Antwerp – exhibits a similar mix of media. However (as we will argue below), this is the result of other distinct traditions and expectations for the illustration of such a publication. Plantin's initial switch to etched illustrations was, thus, not a simple, single across-the-board decision, as it might appear, but rather, one made on a case-by-case basis, where various factors were at play.

On February 19, 1582, the fleet of the duke of Anjou – the fifth son of Henry II and Catherine de' Medici of France – landed at the mouth of the River Schelde near Antwerp (see the cover illustration). It was here that his ceremonial and politically charged installation as the duke of Brabant, the replacement of Philip II as the sovereign of the Low Countries, took place. For many in Europe, this represented an unlawful rebellion against a legitimate ruler (Philip II). For many in the Low Countries – in particular those who supported William of Orange's fight against Spanish rule – it represented their best chance to free themselves from Spanish domination. Little did the organizers of this event know that the existing tensions raised by Anjou's active observance and support of the Catholic faith, as well as his relative inexperience in military matters, would soon thereafter be coupled with financial difficulties and disagreements between him and the States General (the local, collective governing body of the Low Countries) concerning

---

[59] This same phenomenon is also evident in various other editions with etched illustrations. For example, such works as Faerno's *Fabulae centum*, Sambucus's *Icones medicorum* (see, for example, the copy in KBR [VB 13.263 C]), and Goltzius's antiquarian publications from the 1560s and 1570s (all cited in full above).

how the war against Spain should be funded.[60] The deterioration of relations was such that just one year later, Anjou was party to an attempted (but unsuccessful) sack of Antwerp by his French troops on January 17, 1583, which is commonly referred to as the "French Fury."[61] The final demise came a year and a half after that, with the deaths of Anjou and William of Orange in the summer of 1584 and the success of Spanish forces, lead by Alessandro Farnese, in steadily winning back all of the major cities in the Southern Netherlands.

But, at the beginning of 1582, the future turn of events was not known and the organizers of this event, William of Orange and the States General, focused on their immediate objective of providing themselves with a legitimate alternative to Philip II who would assist them militarily and politically in their effort to force out Philip and his troops. They endeavored to do this by first installing Anjou as their new sovereign outside Antwerp's city gates before representatives not only of Anjou's entourage and the States General, but also of Elizabeth I of England (who had expressed some sympathy for the rebels' cause), William of Orange, and the troops fighting the Spanish forces. Once Anjou was declared the new duke of Brabant, the organizers were then able to follow established traditions for official state entries ("Blijde Inkomsten") of rulers of the Low Countries, thereby further legitimizing their daring act. Several aspects of official state entries were important here, in particular, the exchanging of oaths of respect and obedience between the new sovereign and the representatives of the cities he entered. Also significant was the pageant held in each of the cities the sovereign entered in which various influential groups in the city set up triumphal arches and wagons and put on theatrical pieces, each with its own symbolic message, reflecting the hopes for the ruler and themselves. Given Antwerp's influential position in the Low Countries at the time, with its established potential for commerce and trade via the Schelde, it was logical that this city was the site for the ceremonial transfer of power to Anjou and his first state entry as the duke of Brabant.

Once the state entry had taken place, it was not uncommon to have a written account of it produced soon thereafter to help publicize and record the event in a more permanent manner.[62] In this case, the published account appears to have been written by Pierre Loyseleur de Villiers, the head chaplain and advisor to William of Orange.[63] The task of printing the definitive account of Anjou's entry logically fell to Plantin, who was then the official printer of the States General and the city of Antwerp, and who would become "the duke's printer" as of April 17, 1582, although he dropped this title following the scandal of the French Fury in January 1583.[64] The text appeared in three distinct forms:

---

[60] For these issues, see, e.g., Holt 1986, pp. 170–177.

[61] For an account of this event, see, e.g., Holt 1986, pp. 181–185.

[62] See ch. 3, notes 10 and 13, for references to publications of state entries and other related events in the Low Countries.

[63] This attribution is based upon a little-known payment to a certain "minister Villiers" "omdat hij in geschrift gestelt heeft de historie van de komst van Zijne Hoogheid binnen deze landen en namelijk binnen deze stad, en den triomf daarover geschied" (because he put in writing the history of the arrival of His Highness in these lands and, namely, in this city [Antwerp] and the resulting triumph that took place), as cited in Gielens 1940, p. 94, with the following source "Fl. Prims, *Stadswijnen en andere giften, 1583–1585* (Antwerp: 1937), p. 287." For Villiers, see, e.g., Boer 1952.

[64] Voet, GC, I, pp. 65–66.

one illustrated edition in French in folio, which exists in two editions, as it was set and printed twice in the months following Anjou's entry; and two editions in *quarto* without illustrations, one in French and one in Dutch.[65] As Plantin's own editions indicate, such texts were not necessarily illustrated. When they were, woodcuts were usually used. The main exception to this rule, as discussed earlier, is Plantin and Hieronymus Cock's joint publication of *La pompe funèbre*, which boasted a series of etchings (with some supplementary engraving). Although a record of Charles V's commemorative funeral procession and not a state entry per se, this work may still have served as a model for Plantin for what type of prints (namely, etchings) could be used to illustrate his publication of Anjou's entry. The speed and relative ease with which etchings could be completed would also have been an advantage, as one presumably would want to have this type of commemorative publication available as soon as possible after the event. In this case, Hans Vredeman de Vries, the man responsible for the general conception of the decorations for the state entry in Antwerp, as well as the design of specific elements, also designed the illustrations in Plantin's commemorative album at the city's expense.[66] We do not know who made the plates or who paid for them, although they did end up in Plantin's possession, like those used to illustrate *La pompe funèbre*.[67] Sales of the completed, illustrated text by the end of April 1582, just two months after the event itself, confirm that the production of this edition was completed very quickly indeed.[68] Whatever the reason(s) behind the choice of etchings for the bulk of the images used to illustrate this work, it was presumably a conscious one, for this publication was produced at a time when Plantin was engaging artists to execute engravings for the 1583 bible and *Monumenta*. It also appears to have been a satisfactory decision, for the next two state entries published by Plantin's successor, Jan Moretus I, were similarly illustrated with etchings, at a time when Moretus was simultaneously employing other artists, like Hans II and Adriaen Collaert, for the execution of engravings for his publications.[69]

Aside from providing a visual record of some of the events that took place and displays that were exhibited during Anjou's entry into Antwerp, the illustrations in Plantin's publication are also intriguing because of the often ignored mix of etchings

---

[65] See PP 1211 for the illustrated French edition. See Purkis 1973, p. 30, on the existence of two distinct versions of this text, although she does not characterize the differences between them. For the records of the original composition and printing of the folio edition by April 14, 1582, see MPM Arch. 33, fols. 41 lft and 46 rht. For the reprinting of at least eight formes (for sheets D2, E1, F1, and F2), see MPM Arch. 33, fols. 40 rht and 50 rht. For a facsimile edition of the folio edition with an extensive introduction detailing the significance of the entry and the themes represented in the displays in Antwerp, see Purkis 1973. For the unillustrated *quarto* editions, see PP 1212 and 1213, respectively.

[66] Vredeman de Vries 2002, p. 81 and n. 10. Vredeman de Vries is also credited with making some of the etchings (see Holl. *Dutch & Flemish*, XLVII and XLVIII, nos. 460–469), but this is not evident from the same archival sources.

[67] See appendix 4, p. 392, for the listing of twenty of the twenty-two plates used to embellish this publication.

[68] For the first recorded sale of this book on April 23, 1582 (to the London dealer Ascanius de Renialme), see MPM Arch. 60, fol. 68r.

[69] Both written by Joannes Bochius, these were the *Descriptio publicae gratulationis . . . in adventu . . . Ernesti archiducis Austriae . . .* of 1595 (see, e.g., BT 344, STC Dutch and Flemish [1470–1600], p. 36, and Adams 1967, I, B 2208), and the *Historica narratio profectionis et inaugurationis . . . Alberti et Isabellae . . .* of 1602 (see Simoni 1990, B 195). See *New Holl., Collaert*, VII, for several examples of the Collaerts' work for Jan Moretus.

5.10 Anonymous artist after Hans Vredeman de Vries?, *Duke of Anjou on Horseback*, from [Pierre Loyseleur de Villiers?], *La ioyeuse et magnifique entrée de Monseigneur François . . en sa tres-renommée ville d'Anvers* (Antwerp: Christopher Plantin, 1582; f°), plate V, engraving, 240 × 260 (Antwerp, Stadsbibliotheek, K 7624 [C2-537a]).

and engravings present. Specifically, of the title-plate and twenty-one text illustrations used to embellish this work, the title-plate and two of the text illustrations (see fig. 5.10) were fully engraved while all of the remaining text illustrations were primarily, if not fully etched (see fig. 5.11). The title-plate was actually the same as that used to introduce Plantin's editions of Guicciardini's description of the Low Countries (see fig. 5.8). The image itself was not inappropriate. As argued by Helen Purkis, the allusions to a wealth of produce from the land could symbolize the general prosperity that would come to the country if peace returned under Anjou. The figure of Neptune could allude to Antwerp, which was often associated with river gods given the importance of the River Schelde for its economic success – consider, for example, Philips Galle's 1586 engraving of *Scaldis*, which has a view of Antwerp in the back left.[70] And, as argued above, the use of an

[70] See Purkis 1973, p. 27; and *New Holl.*, *Galle*, no. 428, and Delen 1930, no. 168, for Galle's print.

5.11 Anonymous artist after Hans Vredeman de Vries?, *Festivities on the Grote Markt of Antwerp*, from [Pierre Loyseleur de Villiers?], *La ioyeuse et magnifique entrée de Monseigneur François . . . en sa tres-renommée ville d'Anvers* (Antwerp: Christopher Plantin, 1582; f°), plate XXXI, etching (with some engraving), 286 × 388 (Antwerp, Stadsbibliotheek, K 7624 [C2-537a]).

engraved title-plate for a work with otherwise only etched illustrations was not uncommon and might be clarified by the independent traditions for the production of engraved title-pages. The two exceptionally engraved text illustrations are another matter.

The first (plate V; fig. 5.10) is a close-up image of Anjou in regal attire, riding a white charger under a gold canopy held aloft by six men, capturing the moment when Anjou entered the gates of Antwerp, following his installation as the duke of Brabant. This is the only image of Anjou included in this book in which his face was clearly portrayed; as such, it may have functioned as a sort of official portrait of the new sovereign. The second engraved text illustration (plate XIII) depicts a float with Neptune riding a whale. In traditional religious processions in Antwerp, the whale, the seahorse, and a ship were all regularly used to refer to Antwerp as a port city that depended upon the sea for its prosperity.[71] In all of the illustrations in Plantin's edition of Anjou's entry into Antwerp, only the whale and the seahorse are featured prominently. On this occasion, however, the seahorse was combined with an image of Concord, carrying the arms of Anjou, thereby emphasizing Anjou's ability to bring back peace (plate XV). The float with the whale, however, was not only ridden by Neptune (already featured on the title-plate), but was also combined with figures representing Commerce (with a horn of plenty), Navigation (holding a ship), and a river god, alluding to the Schelde. The interpretation of this group as an image of Antwerp's prosperity as a port city is supported by the commentary on this image in the text itself, which reads: "Neptune nud tenant en main son trident; signifiant les grandes commoditez que reçoit la ville d'Anvers par la navigation de la Mer & de la Schelde." (Neptune, naked, holds his trident in his hand, signifying the great comforts that the city of Antwerp receives via the navigation of the sea and the Schelde.)[72]

Thus, the two exceptionally engraved text illustrations in this publication are the only images of the two essential protagonists in this event, namely the duke of Anjou and the city of Antwerp. Was this the reason why these images alone were engraved? If so, it would suggest that while etchings were accepted as a viable medium for book illustrations, there was still a hierarchical preference for engravings for the most important images. Such an attitude is documented for another text produced by Jan Moretus I that is similarly illustrated primarily with etched text illustrations, but also contains engraved portraits of important figures. The book concerned is Thomas Sailly's *Guidon, et practicque spirituelle du soldat chrestien*, a small devotional book intended for soldiers in the field, which Jan Moretus published in 1590. Sailly was concerned about the illustration of his text. Not only did he correspond with Moretus about it, but he also had a model book with sample illustrations made up to be used as a guide for the execution of the illustrations for his book.[73] In both this model book and his correspondence with Moretus about the composition and illustration of this text, Sailly singled out one of the two engraved images, namely the portrait of Alessandro Farnese. For this image, Sailly recorded in his model book how Farnese should be portrayed (wearing armor and

---

[71] Purkis 1973, p. 19.

[72] *La ioyeuse et magnifique entrée de Monseigneur Françoys . . . en sa tres-renommée ville d'Anvers* (Antwerp: Christopher Plantin, 1582), in folio, p. 32.

[73] See BT 4210 for this edition. See MPM (M 393) for Sailly's model book.

kneeling before a crucifix) and that this image should be handsomely engraved.[74] Sailly also repeated his request that Farnese's portrait should be well made in a letter that he wrote to Moretus on July 27, 1590.[75] Farnese was an important figure for Sailly because Farnese had awarded him the position of head chaplain for his troops, which would account for Sailly's wish that this image be especially well made, that is, engraved and not etched. Sailly did not specify explicitly how the other engraved image in this book, a portrait of St. Ignatius, was to be executed (beyond a general indication of the desired scale of the image). However, in Sailly's model book for this publication, the sample image of St. Ignatius stands out as the only image for which an existing engraving was used as the model instead of a general drawing of the subject. Adjacent to this print – an independent engraving by Jan Wierix – Sailly did note that it was to be copied, albeit on a smaller scale. Perhaps this is why Jan Moretus had this image engraved as well, while all of the remaining text illustrations, which Sailly clearly regarded as mere decorative filling to please the reader, were etched.[76]

Thus, as in Plantin's illustrated edition of Anjou's entry into Antwerp, the most important subjects in this book were engraved while all of the remaining images were etched, consequently implying a hierarchy whereby engravings were superior to etchings. This hierarchy agrees with the few known sixteenth-century accounts of etchings and engravings. For example, when the Florentine artist Benvenuto Cellini describes how to make etchings in a 1568 manual, he concludes "this technique is very easy [but] it is all the less satisfactory than burin engraving." Similarly, in his description of the work of Marcantonio Raimondi in his 1568 edition of *The Lives of the Artists*, Giorgio Vasari observes: "Nor is the invention [of etching] to be considered less than commendable whereby prints are made more easily than with the burin, although they do not come out as clean."[77] Thus, when deciding which medium – etching or engraving – to employ for the illustration of a given text, one not only had to consider technical issues relating to which medium was better and more predictable, as well as the associations between certain mediums and certain publications, but one also had to weigh questions of which medium was acceptable visually to those commissioning the book and to its potential buyers.

Looking back on this transitional period, 1580–1583, we have seen Plantin use both engravings and etchings for the embellishment of his primary new illustrated editions. Engravings continued to be preferred for his religious publications, including his

[74] See MPM (M 393), p. 3, for Sailly's request that "Debet autem haec imago puchre sculpi." (This illustration must be engraved beautifully.)

[75] MPM Arch. 93, p. 13: "Dixi P. Guilielmo de sculpenda imagine celsitudinis suae ad vivum, quam desidero bene fieri." (Father Guilielmus and I have discussed the engraving of the portrait of the duke of Parma from life, that I wish be done well.)

[76] For the original Wierix print, see *Holl. Dutch & Flemish*, LXV, no. 1528 (not in M-H, *Wierix*). This entry contains a confusing note about the copy of this print in Sailly's book, as it states that the copy was engraved by Peter vander Borcht and that it was etched. The copy is engraved and is not necessarily by vander Borcht. For Sailly's views on the remaining text illustrations, see his postscript to the same letter cited in n. 75 above, which reads: "D.V. bene faciet si in tertia operis parte . . . interserat aliquot pias imagines quarum formas habet in precibus Canisii vel aliunde iam factas, ita erit liber gratior etiam idiotis." (It would be advantageous if you could include a few devout illustrations in the third part of the book. You could use such images as have already been made for Canisius's prayers and other works [e.g., the *Manuale catholicorum* discussed below]. In this way, the book will be more pleasant for the laity.)

[77] See Reed and Wallace 1989, p. xix, for both of these excerpts.

great bible project, designed for those who sought beautiful books to adorn their libraries. He used etched illustrations for new publications where, in earlier editions of comparable texts, etched illustrations had already been used. Nevertheless, as both the engraved introductory images to Plantin's Guicciardini editions and the engraved text illustrations to his account of Anjou's entry into Antwerp demonstrate, even when he had decided to illustrate a text with etchings, other traditions, including the association of engravings with the finer, most important images, still prevailed in specific instances in these same publications. This contrast within a single work makes the distinct import and function of the respective illustrations all the more clear.

Having thus determined some of the reasons why Plantin illustrated these editions as he did, the question remains as to what extent these books were a success: who ultimately bought them? In order to answer this question, we examined the first year of sales of four of the books discussed above: Plantin's 1581 and 1582 editions of Guicciardini's description of the Low Countries, the illustrated account of Anjou's entry into Antwerp, and Plantin's 1583 folio bible. As one might expect, with Plantin's and Antwerp's altered fortunes in the early 1580s, the primary buyers are strikingly different from those who featured in the sample of sales examined for Plantin's liturgical editions in chapter 4. As we will see later on when we consider the sales of some of his last editions to be illustrated with etchings, some of the new markets evident here became Plantin's primary markets by the time of his death in 1589.

SALES OF PLANTIN'S EDITIONS WITH INTAGLIO ILLUSTRATIONS FROM THE EARLY 1580S

Plantin's hefty Latin bible, descriptions of the Low Countries in Italian and French, and his commemorative edition of a daring political venture, are notably diverse in their subject matter, language, the type and medium of their respective illustrations, and cost. Indeed, the selling price for these works ranged from usually 15 fl. per copy of the bible, to 7 fl. per illustrated edition of Guicciardini's text, to just 1 fl. 10 st. (a tenth of the cost of the bible) for a copy of the illustrated account of Anjou's entry. One might justifiably assume, then, that the primary buyers of these books were as diverse as the books themselves. While this is borne out to some extent, as we will discuss in greater detail below, two important exceptions to this general premise are evident in the first year of sales. First, there is the Parisian printer and bookseller Michel Sonnius I, who regularly bought at least a quarter to a third of the copies sold of each of these editions within the first year of sales, whereby his shop in Paris was regularly Plantin's single greatest selling point for these and other editions.[78] A close second in general importance among these initial sales were the shipments of these books to the biannual book fair in Frankfurt, for further distribution to the international array of buyers present there.[79]

[78] See the data for fig. A3.2 in appendix 3 for Plantin's sales to Sonnius. For evidence of Sonnius's systematic, large purchases of Plantin's publications, see the records of his purchases in MPM Arch. 19, under "Michiel Sonnius."

[79] See the data for fig. A3.2 in appendix 3 for these shipments.

Sonnius had been one of Plantin's favored clients since the late 1570s. This special business relationship was solidified on August 22, 1577 when Plantin sold his bookshop in Paris to Sonnius for the sum of 7,500 fl. Done to the great annoyance of his son-in-law, Gillis Beys, who had been managing the shop until then, Plantin is thought to have taken this step because he desperately needed ready cash to meet his debts following the plundering of Antwerp during the Spanish Fury in November 1576.[80] Along with the sale of his Parisian bookshop, Plantin also granted Sonnius significant discounts on his publications. According to the agreement they signed on August 22, Sonnius was to receive a 40 percent discount on purchases of up to fifty copies of books in folio and up to a hundred copies of books in other formats. This was comparable to the discounts Plantin granted to other important booksellers. It is clear, however, from the purchases documented here by other Parisian dealers that while Sonnius bought by far the most from Plantin, he did not enjoy a true, full monopoly for the sale of his editions in Paris.[81] Although Plantin's shop in Paris had also been an important outlet for some of his liturgical editions in the early 1570s when run by Beys (see fig. A3.1), it did not provide Plantin with the regular, large-scale sales that were made to Sonnius. And, as we will see below in our concluding look at the sales of some of Plantin's last editions to be illustrated with etchings, this advantage that Sonnius offered Plantin – a mixed blessing, if one is to believe the latter's letters on the topic – only grew as the years passed.

The shipments to the Frankfurt book fair, particularly when compared with the meagerness of this market for Plantin's liturgical editions with engraved illustrations from the early 1570s, represented a new, potentially significant outlet for his editions with intaglio illustrations. But, as will be discussed in more detail below, as the decade progressed, Frankfurt turned out to be a more variable market, with sales fluctuating significantly depending upon the type of text. Thus, while Sonnius provided Plantin with a crucial, regular outlet for his editions with intaglio illustrations, the Frankfurt book fairs offered him a variable, but occasionally significant outlet for specific editions. What were the other markets for these publications? As suggested above, as each text differed from the other, so did the remainder of its buying public.

Of Plantin's two Guicciardini editions – the Italian one from 1581, which was offered only with etched illustrations, and his French edition from 1582, which could be bought with and without the etched illustrations – the French edition sold much better in the first year than the Italian.[82] While Plantin's customers purchased at least 150 copies of the Italian edition, more than 260 of the French edition were sold with illustrations and nearly 100 copies were sold without. For the Italian edition, the most important markets (following the two cases discussed above) were local (anonymous) buyers

---

[80] See Voet, GC, I, pp. 87 and 159.

[81] For Plantin and Sonnius's special agreement, see Corr., V, no. 774 (from August 1577), and Corr., VI, no. 803 (a letter from July 30, 1578). Voet erroneously states that Plantin had granted Sonnius a monopoly on the sale of his editions in Paris (see Voet, GC, II, p. 401). For other booksellers' discounts with Plantin, see Voet, GC, II, pp. 442–444. And for sales to other buyers in Paris, see below and appendix 3, figs. A3.2 and A3.3.

[82] Please note that all of the figures cited here are minimums. For while we did succeed in identifying most of the buyers cited, some individuals remained elusive and these sales are consequently not included in the discussion below. See fig. A3.2 in appendix 3, for the sources for all of the sales noted here.

who bought copies through Plantin's shop in Antwerp (at least nineteen copies), then other customers in the Low Countries (sixteen copies), Germany, and London (with approximately ten copies going to buyers in each of these countries in the first year), and then five copies each to clients from Italy and Spain. Among these buyers were the Birckmans – with their main office in Cologne and branch offices in Antwerp and London – the London dealer Ascanius de Renialme, and Plantin's son-in-law, Franciscus Raphelengius I, who was also working independently as a bookseller; each purchased several copies, while almost all of Plantin's other clients bought just single copies of this work.[83]

Predictably, sales of Plantin's French edition featured many buyers based in France, who purchased numerous copies of this book (twenty-six with the etchings and fifteen without). Significant here are a certain Jean de Burdigale, "sieur de la Chabossiere de la Rochelle," and Pierre Porret, a long-time, intimate friend of Plantin's in Paris, who helped him with both personal and business matters there.[84] Booksellers based in the Low Countries also bought significant numbers of copies in the first year (thirty-one with the illustrations and seventeen without). But, as was the case with Plantin's Italian edition, they usually took just one or perhaps two copies at a time, with the exception of Franciscus Raphelengius and the Amsterdam dealer Cornelis Claesz.[85] Finally, a number of additional buyers in Germany and London also bought several copies each, including Hans Spierinck, another of Plantin's sons-in-law, who was then serving as Plantin's agent in Hamburg, the Birckmans, Georg Willer, who was the primary German purchaser of Plantin's liturgical editions with engraved illustrations from 1573 to 1575, Arnold Mylius in Cologne, who, like Sonnius, would purchase (if not commission) large numbers of books from Plantin in the years to come, de Renialme and Hercule François in London, and William Herle, a diplomat and spy for Elizabeth I, who specialized in the Low Countries.[86]

Thus, while the specific numbers relating to how many copies of which publication went where vary between these two editions, the primary markets for both were the same, namely, primarily western Europe – the Low Countries (especially dealers located in present-day Belgium), France, and Germany – and London, with buyers typically purchasing just single copies (with the exception of the notably large orders for Sonnius and Frankfurt). Plantin's sales of his French edition of Guicciardini's text are also noteworthy for the unexpectedly large quantity (nearly 100 out of the more than 350 copies bought during the first year) that were sold without the text illustrations. The

---

[83] For a general overview of the Birckmans' activities, see Rouzet 1975, pp. 16–20. Plantin dealt regularly with them. On de Renialme and his purchases from Plantin in general, see Roberts 2002, pp. 157–160. For a passing reference to Raphelengius's independent activities as a bookseller, see Voet, GC, I, p. 83.

[84] For the identification of Jean de Burdigale (or Bourdigalle), see MPM Arch. 20, fol. 108. In the legends of Plantin's youth, Porret is cited as his brother, although there is no evidence to collaborate this. For more on his and Plantin's personal connections, see Voet, GC, I, pp. 4, 7–12 passim, 24, 37–39, 50, 53, 60, 77, 154, 157, 159, and 161. See Voet, GC, II, pp. 27, 71, 90, 164, and 275, for examples of Porret's help with Plantin's business concerns.

[85] On Claesz, see Schilder, VII (2003). See n. 83 for Raphelengius.

[86] On Spierinck's work in Hamburg, see, e.g., Voet, GC, I, pp. 155–156. On Georg Willer, see ch. 4, n. 119. On Arnold Mylius, see Rouzet 1975, pp. 157–158, and for Voet's hypothesis that Mylius had Plantin print editions largely for him, see Voet, GC, I, p. 91, and Voet, GC, II, pp. 11–12. On François and his purchases from Plantin in general, see Roberts 2002, p. 158. On Herle, see DNB 1993, p. 305.

copies without illustrations did not go just to local buyers, but also to Frankfurt (fifty) and France (fifteen), where the buyers would not necessarily have been familiar with the appearance of towns in the Low Countries, but apparently found the extra visual complement to the text unnecessary – or at least not worth the extra 4 fl. 10 st. Plantin asked for it above the basic 2 fl. 10 st. selling price.[87] Notably poorly represented here, even for the Italian edition of Guicciardini's text, are Italian, Spanish, and Portuguese buyers. This is in striking contrast to the selection of clients who played an important role in the sale of Plantin's liturgical editions with engraved illustrations from 1573 to 1575. The predominance of western European buyers for Plantin's first editions with etched illustrations recurs in the sales of a sample of his last editions with etched illustrations discussed below. Only in the case of Plantin's 1583 folio bible (discussed below) are there more purchases from Italian, Spanish, and Portuguese clients. But the significance of these sales out of the total remains far below the importance of these markets in the 1570s for his liturgical editions with engraved illustrations.

The purchases of Plantin's illustrated edition of Anjou's entry into Antwerp differ significantly from those of Guicciardini's description of the Low Countries, reflecting the distinct political, commemorative, and visual value customers placed on this text, as well as, perhaps, its price tag. While it is impossible to judge from mere sales records why, specifically, someone purchases a particular book, the striking differences within Plantin's conventional distribution of sales reveal, nevertheless, exceptional interest in specific books. This is the case with this richly illustrated, yet relatively inexpensive commemorative text – 1 fl. less than an *unillustrated* copy of Plantin's French edition of Guicciardini's text, the 30 st. price of this book was the equivalent of one and a half day's work by a skilled laborer working in Antwerp at this time.[88]

In the first year of sale (from April 1582 through March 1583), an exceptionally high figure of 158 copies of this illustrated work were sold via Plantin's shop in Antwerp (in addition to numerous copies of his French and Dutch editions without illustrations). Indeed, a remarkable 95 copies were bought in the course of May 1582 alone, attesting to the great, timely, local demand for this work. These purchases represent the largest single group of sales for this book – greater even than the 76 copies sent to Frankfurt and the 52 copies bought by Sonnius, the usual "high buyers" of Plantin's illustrated editions from this period. The city of Antwerp also ordered a significant number of copies (74) in addition to a few extra copies sold later on to specific members of the local government. Predictably, given Elizabeth I's support of Anjou and the number of her representatives who took part in his state entry into Antwerp, a notably large number of copies were also purchased by English buyers. These included Elizabeth I's ambassador William Herle (eighteen), and the booksellers Ascanius de Renialme (thirteen), and Hercule François (eight). Several customers throughout the Low Countries saw to the sale of an additional forty-four copies. The primary buyers were Job Mattheeus from Utrecht (four copies), Louis Elsevier in Leiden (three), Cornelis Claesz in Amsterdam (six),

---

[87] For another example of a contemporaneous cartographic work that was sold with and without illustrations, see McKitterick 2003, p. 87. An unillustrated German edition of Guicciardini's text was also published contemporaneously with Plantin's (see Guicciardini 2001, p. 33).

[88] See Scholliers 1976, p. 165, for the contemporary wages of skilled masons.

Franciscus Raphelengius in Antwerp (three), and the cartographer Abraham Ortelius (ten). Other dealers in the Low Countries and Antwerp in particular are generally poorly represented, perhaps reflecting a decision Plantin took to save the local sale of the illustrated version of this text primarily for himself. All of these purchases by clients in the Low Countries can be readily explained by the political interest in these cities in the naming of Anjou as their new ruler. In addition, however, a surprising number of copies were also bought by German dealers (thirty in total), in particular by Hans Spierinck in Hamburg (eight), Georg Willer in Augsburg (three), Wernard Coleman in Königsberg in the former German Empire (what is now the Russian city of Kaliningrad near Poland) (ten), and Hans Gundlach in Nuremberg (six). Another surprisingly large number of purchases (thirty-seven in total) were made by local figures active in the print world, thereby attesting to the visual appeal of the series of twenty-one plates illustrating this text. The primary buyers here included Philips Galle (nine copies), Mynken Liefrinck (nine), Abraham de Bruyn (three), and Edward van Hoeswinckel, who bought fifteen copies before he died during the so-called "French Fury" of January 1583, when Anjou's troops attempted to sack Antwerp.[89] Thus, while there may be evidence within this very publication of an occasional hierarchical preference for engravings over etchings, the suite of (mostly etched) illustrations was still of enough interest to warrant these exceptional purchases by local print dealers and artists. All told, some 560 copies of this text were sold in the first year of sale, leaving just 100 or so of the original group illustrated by Liefrinck.[90] As we will see with the other examples of the sales of Plantin's illustrated editions discussed later on, this was a remarkably high "success rate" in terms of the percentage of the illustrated copies that were sold within a year. This would have been all the more important in terms of this text, given its nature as a commemorative volume of a political event that soon lost all of its significance – or even became treacherous to praise openly – once Antwerp was back in Spanish hands in little more than three years' time. Perhaps not coincidentally, the plates for this edition were not kept in Antwerp, but around 1590, were noted in the Leiden stock of copper plates, at a politically safe distance.[91]

Plantin's grand, 1583 bible, designed to serve as an ostentatious object as much as a text, had, as such, yet another function and type of illustration distinct from the preceding works, and consequently appealed to a completely different market. Of the works considered here, this is the only one that is at all reminiscent of Plantin's liturgical editions from the early 1570s, in terms of both its religious content and the abundant series of engravings used to embellish it. Similarly, the buyers most interested in this text are also closest to the selection of buyers who figured most prominently in Plantin's sales of his liturgical editions in the period 1573–1575. Nevertheless, as is common

---

[89] On Hoeswinckel's death, see Rouzet 1975, p. 96. On the "French Fury," see n. 61 above.

[90] See MPM Arch. 20, fol. 119 rht, for the following record: "pour limpression des entrees de cequelle a imprimé 148 cents a xij patt le cent val in Ns. la somme de fl. 96 st. 4" (for the printing of the Entrees, of which she printed 148 hundred at 12 [error for 13, according to the final payment noted] st. per hundred is the sum of fl. 96 st. 4). Dividing the total number of sheets printed by twenty-two (the title-plate plus the twenty-one text illustrations) results in at least 672 complete copies. Recorded in September 1582, this is clearly part of a lengthy summary of various old charges that had, presumably, been submitted in the course of the preceding months.

[91] See appendix 4, p. 392.

to each of the texts from the early 1580s whose sales are discussed here, purchases by Sonnius – with a noteworthy 106 copies of the approximately 270 sold of this bible in the first year going to him – and shipments to Frankfurt – for a total of 57 copies to be sold at the spring and fall book fairs held there in 1583 – dominate here as well. The striking difference with the sales above is the group of buyers that comes next, namely Spanish and Portuguese clients (taking twenty-four copies all together), who rarely featured in the sales of any of the preceding texts. Prominent here are Ferdinand Ximenes, a Portuguese merchant in Antwerp who bought six specially bound and decorated copies, Blas de Roblas, a bookseller in Madrid who had helped Plantin with the transport of liturgical editions to Philip II in 1576–1577, who purchased six copies of this bible, and Paul van Assche, a bookseller in Medina del Campo, who bought five.[92] Similarly, the Roman bookseller Girolamo Franzini's purchase of twelve copies of this book represented an exceptional purchase from an Italian dealer.[93] For, Italian buyers, like their Spanish and Portuguese counterparts, are otherwise notably absent among the purchasers of Plantin's other editions from the 1580s despite having been well represented among the buyers of his liturgical editions from the early 1570s. And, while local sales, or copies bought by other dealers in present-day Belgium, were important for the other publications discussed above, they were, as with the earlier sales of Plantin's liturgical editions, of little significance here, constituting just occasional, solitary purchases. Perhaps this work, by far the most costly, at 15 fl. (300 st.) per copy, was beyond the means of most buyers in the war-weary Low Countries. Other booksellers who did purchase several copies of this bible, as well as copies of the other illustrated editions discussed above, include Ascanius de Renialme in London (with seven copies) and Hans Gundlach in Nuremberg, who bought five copies of this book.

What is unclear here is whether the exceptional interest in this bible among Spanish, Portuguese, and Italian dealers was a result of the type of text (religious) or the type of illustrations (engravings as opposed etchings). As we will discuss in greater detail below, the sales of a sample of Plantin's last editions with etched illustrations suggest that while both may have been contributing factors, the medium of the illustrations included could have been the primary one. The other significant observation that is evident from this group of sales is that local buyers in the Low Countries generally did not constitute Plantin's best market for his costly illustrated editions. This is supported by the sales of his later editions with etched illustrations (discussed below), where it appears that the Dutch speakers, in particular, often did not purchase these more expensive illustrated copies of an edition. Was this a matter of taste or financial necessity following so many years of a draining war that left towns half empty and lacking much of their former human and financial resources? Regardless of the reasons behind the weak local market for Plantin's more costly illustrated editions, this scant demand may also have been a motivating force behind his decision to switch to the cheaper medium

---

[92] For the Ximenez family, see Pohl 1977, pp. 79–82 and 357. For de Roblas, see, e.g., Plantin's correspondence with him c.1576–1577 (*Corr.*, V, nos. 706, 713, 722, and 759). For the identification of van Assche, see MPM Arch. 19, fol. 164; see also Robben 1993, pp. 63–64, and other references in the index.

[93] On Franzini, see *Dizionario dei tipografi*, I, pp. 460–461.

of etchings. In order to address this issue, however, we will need to examine more of Plantin's editions with etched illustrations and consider what motivated him to rely on etchings ever more exclusively for his specially illustrated books.

PLANTIN'S ILLUSTRATED EDITIONS IN LEIDEN

Just as the sale of his grand 1583 folio bible began in December 1582, Plantin left Antwerp to take up a position as printer for the University of Leiden and start up a new business there. Spanish troops received much needed reinforcements throughout the summer of 1582, thereby enabling Alessandro Farnese to make significant new military gains. This was also a period of increasing tension and division among the rebel forces. Anjou and his French troops were increasingly dissatisfied with their situation which, in January 1573, led to their attacks on some of the towns they were supposed to protect from Spanish troops, including Antwerp – the so-called "French Fury" discussed above. Plantin had evidently (and with some foresight) decided that the war with Spain had made his business in Antwerp precarious enough to warrant a move to the Protestant north in an effort to safeguard his options.[94] He did not return to Antwerp until October 1585, once the city had fallen to Farnese and restoration under a new Catholic leadership was underway. The few independent projects with any significant number of illustrations that he completed while in Leiden – series of biblical images and illustrated editions of Justus Lipsius's Neo-Latin studies – were all illustrated with etchings and thereby constitute a true break with his production of illustrated works in Antwerp up until 1583.

The first of these projects begun in Leiden were two series of biblical illustrations etched by Peeter vander Borcht (who signed many of the plates). These are commonly identified as the *Imagines et figurae bibliorum* – a group of ninety-eight images and an introductory title-plate in oblong folio (fig. 5.12) – and the *Bibelsche figuren* – a group of eighty-three images in a slightly smaller format (oblong *quarto*), with no introductory title-plate.[95] As several of the etchings in the first group are dated 1582, in addition to one etching from the latter, work on both sets appears to have begun by that time. The only known payments to vander Borcht that appear to pertain to the execution of these prints were recorded between April 16 and May 28, 1583.[96] In this period, vander Borcht was periodically paid 4 fl. per image for the completion of eight illustrations for the Gospel of St. Luke and three for the book of Machabees. As there are exactly eight illustrations for Luke's Gospel in the *Bibelsche figuren* (see pp. 12–13 = fols. b2v–c2r), these payments probably pertain to prints in this book. It is less clear for which of these two projects the Machabees illustrations were intended. A reference to "Bybelsche figuren in coper gebeten door P. V. Borcht" in one of Plantin's own lists of works from his Press that were ready for sale by 1584 suggests that at least one of these series was completed by

---

[94] For a general overview of this period of Plantin's career, see Voet, GC, II, pp. 105–113.

[95] For a basic description of each etching in these two series, see *New Holl.*, Van der Borcht, Book Illustrations, I, nos. 235–334, and nos. 335–422, respectively.

[96] See MPM Arch. 61, fols. 47v, 51v, 54v, 56v, 62v, and 66v, for these payments.

5.12 Peeter vander Borcht, *Adoration of the Golden Calf*, from Hendrik Jansen van Barrefelt, *Imagines et figurae bibliorum* (Leiden: Franciscus Raphelengius I, 1592?; oblong 4°), opposite text fol. 47, etching, 187 × 241 (Antwerp, Museum Plantin-Moretus, A 1169).

that time.[97] One collection of the *Imagines* series without any accompanying text, not even in the open cartouches in the title-plate, supports the hypothesis that at least some of these images were sold separately as an independent print series, as the preceding archival reference suggests.[98] Less clear is when the accompanying commentary for the *Imagines* series was printed. Although Voet dates a completed publication of the first group of images (with an accompanying text attributed to Hendrik Jansen van Barrefelt) to 1584, more recent studies of these images have convincingly argued that the text edition comprising the first series of illustrations was not produced until around 1592, several years after Plantin's death, and then under the direction of Franciscus Raphelengius I in Leiden.[99] References to groups of a hundred folio and eighty oblong *quarto* etched biblical illustrations in the list of plates at the Leiden branch of Plantin's business in 1590, one year after his death, probably refer to these plates and suggest that Plantin had abandoned these projects when he returned to Antwerp in 1585.[100] This is understandable given the contentious nature of the author of the commentary for the *Imagines* series – Barrefelt was known as the leader of the spiritualist sect, the Family of Love, which was not welcomed by either Protestants or Catholics.[101] This fact may also account for the fake date (1581) of publication and fake names given to the author and printer of the text (Renatus Christianus and Jacobus Villanus, respectively) when the *Imagines et figurae bibliorum* finally did appear.

Regardless of the issue of when these publications were completed and under which circumstances, the decision to etch the series of illustrations instead of having them engraved was a logical one for several reasons. To start with, most of these images feature a landscape setting for which, as noted above, etching was an accepted, if not a preferred medium. In addition, given the large number of sizable plates desired for these projects, etchings would also have been a sensible choice technically and financially. Requiring less time to complete than engravings or woodcuts, etchings, as we will discuss below, also appear to have been significantly cheaper to make than engravings. Finally, given vander Borcht's close ties with Plantin, he would probably have been a relatively willing and compliant person to employ, in contrast with the Wierix brothers or other engravers who may have been available to work at the time. Known to have been active as an etcher by 1560,[102] and apparently the one who made the illustrations for Sambucus's series of medical scholars in the mid-1570s, vander Borcht should also have been a proficient etcher by the early 1580s when he began work on this project.

Were these considerations – the relative technical ease and financial advantage of etchings and the facility of working with a trusted artist – the reasons why Plantin also

---

[97] See MPM M. 321, fol. 9r, for this reference. In Voet's discussion of the first group of plates (see PP 631), he states that two of the plates (nos. 8 and 30) are dated 1584, while Ursula Mielke, the compiler of *New Holl., Van der Borcht*, has read the dates as 1582.

[98] For this copy, see the Bibliothèque de l'Arsenal in Paris, in a volume titled "œuvre de Van de Borcht," fols. 1–50, Est. 1011 (as cited in Hamilton 1981a, p. 273, n. 10).

[99] See PP 631 for Voet's commentary. See, e.g., Visser 1988 for the later dating of this work.

[100] See appendix 4, p. 391.

[101] For a recent summary of the beliefs of this sect and references to bibliography on the movement and Barrefelt in particular, see Dekoninck 2004, pp. 49–63, and pp. 53–55 in particular.

[102] For vander Borcht's earliest known dated etching, *Skating Feast at Mechelen* from 1559, see *New Holl., Van der Borcht*, no. 169.

chose etchings for the illustrations of his other main independent projects from his Leiden period, the Neo-Latin studies of Justus Lipsius? It is not obvious that this was the case, as circumstances were clearly different with Lipsius's publications. Not only were there no established visual precedents for these types of illustrations, but vander Borcht, perhaps still occupied with the biblical illustrations, does not seem to have been responsible for the bulk (if any) of the illustrations for Lipsius's editions at this stage.

Justus Lipsius was born in 1547 in Overijse, near Leuven.[103] In 1568, following his studies in Leuven, he went to Rome and thereby began a period in which he traveled regularly, finally settling in Leiden from 1578 to 1591. Hereafter, Lipsius gradually made his way back to Leuven, where he lived until his death in 1602. His first publication, *Variarum lectionum libri IIII*, which was primarily a collection of critical studies of texts by ancient Latin authors (PP 1547), was printed by Plantin in 1569, when Lipsius was still in Italy. Lipsius became a learned classical scholar, who, true to the concept of a Renaissance humanist, studied not only the languages, but also the culture, history, literature, and philosophy of Greek and Latin societies. His numerous publications were widely read throughout Europe in his lifetime and were, consequently, an important, reliable source of income and fame for Plantin and his successors, as the favored publishers of his texts. None of these editions was truly illustrated until both Lipsius and Plantin were in Leiden in the early 1580s.[104]

These first illustrated editions were thematically related and represented Lipsius's first cultural-historical publications, rather than conventional textual commentaries or editions of his letters. They comprised a revised edition (from 1585) of his 1582 unillustrated study of Roman gladiators, the *Saturnalium sermonum libri duo, qui de gladiatoribus*, now bearing sixteen etched illustrations, and a follow-up study of the amphitheaters in which the gladiators fought, his *De amphitheatro liber* and *De amphitheatris quae extra Romam libellus*, both published for the first time in 1584, with eight etchings between them.[105] Of these texts, most is known about the illustration of the *Saturnalia* and Lipsius's attitudes toward these images.

When Plantin printed the second edition of Lipsius's *Saturnalium sermonum libri duo* in 1585, the inclusion of textual revisions and intaglio illustrations was announced on the title-page: "Noviter correcti, aucti, & formis aeneis illustrati" (newly corrected, augmented, and with illustrations on copper). However, Lipsius himself was concerned enough about the historical accuracy of at least one image (the procession of the gladiators in the amphitheater) that he insisted on including warnings to the reader about excessive artistic license, either in the related commentary, or else, in the 1588 edition of this text, in his general foreword to the reader.[106] Lipsius's concerns about these illustrations are all the more interesting because the designs, at least (see fig. 5.14),

---

[103] The basic sources on Lipsius are far too numerous to cite here. For an overview of Lipsius's life, see, e.g., NBW, X (1983), cols. 403–416.

[104] Of Plantin's first editions of his work, only Lipsius's 1581 commentary on Tacitus, *Ad annales Corn. Taciti liber commentarius* (PP 1561), bore a single small woodcut of a Roman ring.

[105] See PP 1557 (for the *Saturnalia*) and PP 1530 and 1531 for the *De amphitheatro* editions, as well as Lipsius Antwerp 1997, cat. nos. 30 and 33, and Lipsius Leuven 1997, cat. nos. 20 and 21, for these texts.

[106] For these remarks see either chapter 19 of Book II of Lipsius's text (see, e.g., p. 150 of the 1585 edition [PP 1530]), or else fol. *iv of the 1588 edition (PP 1558).

LORICAE SEGMENTATAE

CATAPHRACTAE

5.13 Peeter vander Borcht, Roman Soldiers, from Justus Lipsius, *De militia Romana* (Antwerp: Jan Moretus I, 1596; 4°), p. 212, etching, 131 × 203 (Antwerp, Museum Plantin-Moretus, A 570).

5.14 Otto van Veen?, *Two Gladiators Fighting*, from Justus Lipsius, *Saturnalium sermonum libri duo, qui de gladiatoribus* (Antwerp: Christopher Plantin, 1585; 4°), p. 116, etching, 116 × 177 (Antwerp, Museum Plantin-Moretus, A 371). See fig. 5.15 for an engraved copy of this composition.

are attributed to Otto van Veen in Aubertus Miraeus's 1609 biography of the author, where he notes in his discussion of the *Saturnalia* that Lipsius was "assisted by the elegant hand and brush of Otto Venius, by far the greatest of our painters" (venusta Othonis Vaenii, nostratium pictorum facile principis, manu ac penicillo adiutus).[107] And, as is indicated in a letter he wrote to Dominicus Lampsonius in Liège in May 1584, Lipsius was normally pleased with van Veen's depictions of ancient subjects for him and consequently regretted his departure from Leiden around this time.[108] Payment

[107] See Aubertus Miraeus, *Vita Justi Lipsii sapientiae et litterarum antistitis* (Antwerp: David Martin, 1609) (Simoni L-71; MPM [A 2392]), p. 20. The designs for all of the illustrations to this text (but not the actual etching) are also attributed to van Veen in Holl. *Dutch & Flemish*, XXXII, nos. 203–215 – although the presentation of the illustrations there is misleading. Two distinct sets of prints were made after the one set of designs, one etched (for the 1585 and 1588 editions [see PP 1557 and PP 1558]) and one engraved for the 1604 edition (BB, III, pp. 1072–1073, L 509). In the Hollstein entry for this book, pieces of information about these two sets of illustrations are repeatedly interspersed. For example, while the sample illustrations and page numbers for the images are taken from the engravings included in the 1604 edition (which are different from the 1585 edition), the measurements of most of the plates are taken from the etchings used in the 1585 edition.

[108] For this letter, see ILE, II, no. 350 (84 05 31), pp. 123–124, lines 23–25, which read: "Otto Venius a nobis abit, sed invitis, insignis moribus et arte adolescens et cuius manus usui mihi esse poterat ad multa Antiquitatis illustranda." (Otto Venius has left against his will. He has an extraordinary character and gains in his skill. His hand could have been useful to me for many images from antiquity.) For

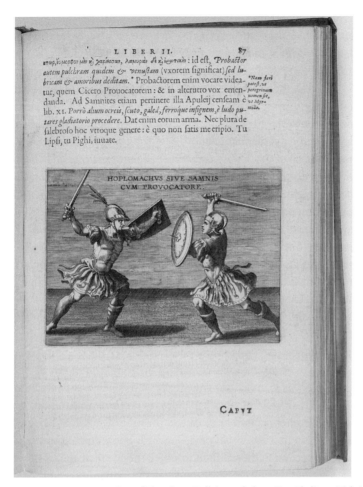

5.15 Anonymous member of Theodoor Galle's workshop, *Two Gladiators Fighting*, from Justus Lipsius, *Saturnalium sermonum libri duo, qui de gladiatoribus* (Antwerp: Jan Moretus I, 1604; 4°), p. 87, engraving, 102 × 138 (Antwerp, Museum Plantin-Moretus, A 973). See fig. 5.14 for the original etched version of this composition.

records kept by Jan Moretus I indicate that van Veen did design some illustrations for Lipsius's *De militia Romana* and/or *Poliorceticon sive de machinis, tormentis, telis, libri quinque*, both of which were printed for the first time in 1595–1596. The same records indicate that vander Borcht etched at least some, if not all of these same illustrations.[109] An examination of the illustrations in Lipsius's *De militia Romana* (fig. 5.13) confirms the attribution of these etchings, at least, to vander Borcht. For, the depictions of the main figures exhibit his characteristically poor sense of human proportions, three-dimensional form, and movement in space, whereby, for example, legs and body trunks are twisted and drawn flatly on the picture plane. Comparing this image with that of the

further evidence of Lipsius's admiration of van Veen, see his entry (from June 2, 1584) in van Veen's *Liber amicorum* (see KBR [HS II 874] for the original album and ode XX in the Gheyn 1911 facsimile edition).

[109] See BB, III, pp. 1002–1003 (L 369) and pp. 1037–1038 (L 424), respectively, for these editions. See Imhof 1999a, p. 70, for the records of the payments to van Veen and vander Borcht.

two gladiators fighting from Lipsius's Saturnalia (fig. 5.14), the differences are striking and unmistakable, as these two gladiators, in contrast with vander Borcht's soldiers, are round, muscled men, moving through a three-dimensional space. There is, thus, no sign of vander Borcht's hand in this etching, or others in the Saturnalia.

Whoever did etch the illustrations for Lipsius's 1585 edition of the Saturnalia was proficient with the technique and took full advantage of it to create a vibrant, moving image. There is no sign of foul biting, despite the use of closely laid hatching lines, and the depiction of the gladiators and the moving pleats of their skirts suggests a quickly drawn sketch of black lines on a white background that adds life and vigor to the image. It is precisely these vibrant effects that one misses in the engraved version of this same composition (fig. 5.15), made for a later edition of Lipsius's text. Working from the same composition, the later artist made full use of the possibilities of precisely laid engraved lines to detail, shade, and highlight the figures, their clothes, and the background – now a semi-defined space with a floor and back wall. The result is that the figures themselves appear frozen in their fight and not, as in the early, etched image, caught in a momentary glimpse of their action. Firm, fixed, and superbly detailed versus a fleeting, changeable instant, such is the characteristic contrast of finely made engravings and etchings, seen here in the form of book illustrations.

Was a desire for such evocative images of gladiators in action what motivated Plantin (or Lipsius?) to choose etchings for the illustrations for these editions, or were these illustrations simply a fortuitous result and not the sought-after effect? Arguments for the use of etchings based upon the relative ease with which they could be made for less money than engravings carry less weight here, as far fewer illustrations were involved than in any of the other projects with etched illustrations undertaken by Plantin thus far. There were also no clear visual precedents for these illustrations that could have influenced the selection of the medium in which they were made. It is always possible that Plantin simply did not have much choice in the matter, if the only artists available and willing to work on these illustrations when he was in Leiden were draughtsmen and etchers. Nevertheless, it cannot be pure coincidence that all of Lipsius's subsequent illustrated editions, first published by the Antwerp Plantin Press in the 1590s when under the direction of Jan Moretus I – the De militia Romana and Poliorceticœn sive de machinis, tormentis, telis, libri quinque cited above and the De cruce edition discussed at the end of this chapter, for example – were similarly illustrated with etchings. For, when Jan Moretus commissioned these plates he was simultaneously having engravings made for the illustration of other projects.[110] This pattern, rather, suggests that a positive choice for etched illustrations for these books was made, perhaps by Lipsius himself, who was clearly concerned about the illustration of his works. It seems unlikely, however, that he was attracted to the vibrant visual effects possible with etchings and seen in the Saturnalia illustrations, for the majority, if not all, of the etchings made for Lipsius's later editions were executed by vander Borcht in a more staid style (recall fig. 5.13). Perhaps Lipsius simply enjoyed the possibility of working with vander Borcht directly

[110] For examples of engravings made by Julius Goltzius for Jan Moretus, see Bowen and Imhof 2001, pp. 276–277, and for work by the Collaerts, see n. 69 above.

and taking advantage of the fact that he could send him to work from sources in other people's collections and then have him transfer these images first hand on to copper plates. Such was the case, for example, when Lipsius was working on his *Poliorceticωn*. In September 1595, he wrote to Abraham Ortelius to ask if he might have a suitable model for vander Borcht to draw.[111] Once again, while the specific reasons why etchings may have been favored instead of engravings for any one project are as varied as the distinguishing advantages of etchings themselves, the net effect on Plantin's production in the 1580s was the same, namely, the striking dominance of this medium among his new independent publications.

PLANTIN'S FINAL WORKS WITH ETCHED ILLUSTRATIONS

When Plantin returned to Antwerp in the fall of 1585, the city was definitively back in Catholic hands and released from Farnese's campaign of starvation, but its future was still far from assured. For, despite Farnese's success, the mouth of the Schelde remained under rebel control, which brought an end to Antwerp's former wealth and prosperity as a city of trade. Thousands of inhabitants left, not only out of religious convictions, but also for simple economic considerations, as all trade and work dependent upon the waterways became much more difficult and significantly more costly to pursue as a result of the heavy taxes the rebel forces placed on the use of the river. The result was a much smaller, poorer population facing the difficult task of reconstruction. For Plantin, Antwerp's return to a government supportive of the Catholic, Spanish king Philip II meant that he could revive his printing of missals, breviaries, and books of hours – his former "bestsellers" – although the illustrations were usually printed from old engravings or some new, often cruder, anonymous variants thereof. It would take another thirty years, however, before the *Officina Plantiniana* was asked to print large quantities of these books for Spain again.[112] But etchings were ordered for all of Plantin's new projects with any significant number of new illustrations. The main new projects from these last four years of Plantin's life were: (1) several editions of Petrus Canisius's Catholic handbook, printed in Latin, Dutch, and French in smaller formats (12° and 16°) in 1588 and 1589, with a series of twenty-two text illustrations; like Plantin's liturgical editions, these were systematically printed with two versions, one with woodcut illustrations and one with intaglio illustrations (fig. 5.16);[113] (2) Franciscus Costerus's series of fifty meditations on Christ's Passion, printed in Dutch

---

[111] See Hessels 1887, no. 277, p. 663, for the following excerpt: "In re machinarum [= *Poliorceticωn*] sum totus, et scriptum hoc iam peregi: sed figurae et iconismi restant, in quibus possit me fortasse bibliotheca tua iuvare. Vide sodes, siquid habes. Puto in Columna Traiani carrobalistam expressam me vidisse: si ita est, Vander Burchtius [= vander Borcht] quaeso deliniet, et ad me mitte." (I am fully occupied with the instruments [of war] and I have completed the text. The illustrations remain and perhaps your library can be of assistance there. Would you please see if you have something. I think that I saw that one can see a "carrobalistam" on Trajan's column. If this is the case, will you have vander Borcht draw it and send it to me?)

[112] For Plantin's last editions of these books, see PP 832–835 and 1699–1702, and Bowen 1997a, PP 1786sexies–PP 1788ter, pp. 254–258. The plates used to illustrate a small (24°) book of hours Plantin printed in 1588 (PP 1788) are etchings and not engravings. See Voet, GC, I, pp. 213–215, for the return of the Spanish market around 1615.

[113] For all of these editions, see PP 890–896.

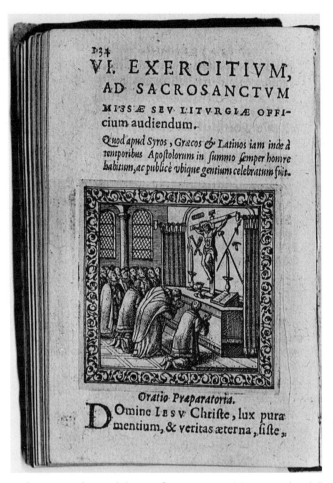

5.16 Peeter vander Borcht?, *Mass*, from Petrus Canisius, *Manuale catholicorum* (Antwerp: Christopher Plantin, 1588; 16°), p. 134, etching, 58 × 58 (Antwerp, Museum Plantin-Moretus, A 1282).

and French in *octavo* in 1587, and illustrated with an optional series of fifty accompanying etchings by Peeter vander Borcht (fig. 5.17);[114] (3) a series of fifteen etchings for prayers to accompany a rosary, with French captions, printed in *quarto* in 1588;[115] and (4) a selection of twenty-five chapters of Epiphanius of Constantia's study of animals, *Ad physiologum*, with an etching marking the start of each chapter (fig. 5.18).[116] While Plantin's use of etchings for the illustration of these works simply appears to be a consistent continuation of his approach to illustrating new editions in the 1580s, which, of the numerous considerations highlighted above, may have motivated him here? In order to answer this question, we need to examine what type of publications these were and the markets to which they appealed.

Characteristic of Plantin's production at this time, most of these books were devotional or instructive works on the Catholic faith, indicative of the new trend of

---

[114] See PP 1048 and 1049 for the Dutch and French editions, respectively.
[115] See PP 1138 for this edition.   [116] See PP 1126 for this edition.

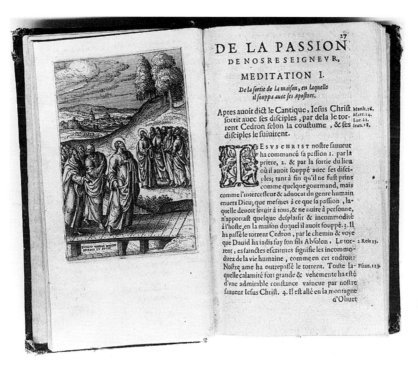

5.17 Peeter vander Borcht, *Christ and his Apostles*, in Franciscus Costerus, *Cinquante meditations . . . de la Passion de Nostre Seigneur* (Antwerp: Christopher Plantin, 1587; 8°), plate no. 1 in the series, inserted between pp. 26 and 27, etching, 105 × 70 (Antwerp, Museum Plantin-Moretus, R 55.35).

Jesuit-supported, Counter-Reformation texts. For example, the Jesuit Petrus Canisius (born in Nijmegen in the Low Countries, but most active in Germany and Switzerland) was one of the leading figures in the Catholic Counter-Reformation and was known in particular for his catechisms, which prevailed as the most popular and successful basic instructive manual for the Catholic faith.[117] Although serving a different function than Canisius's catechism, with just 16 "exercises" instead of a long series of 124 questions to be studied and answered, the *Manuale catholicorum* (or Catholic handbook) was also a highly popular work on Catholic doctrine. While editions of Canisius's catechism – by Plantin or by other printers – were rarely illustrated, Plantin systematically embellished each of his editions of Canisius's handbook with twenty-two text illustrations.[118]

Franciscus Costerus was also a Jesuit, but was more active as an author of devotional literature. Better known than Canisius locally for his activities as a preacher, as well as a writer, Costerus served as a provincial in Germany and the Low Countries from 1565 to 1589. During this period he also helped establish various sodalities in the name of the Virgin, to whom several of his devotional works were dedicated.[119] Costerus's fifty

[117] On Canisius, see, e.g., NNBW, v, cols. 91–98. For a recent study of Canisius and his catechism, see, e.g., Filser and Leimgruber 2003.

[118] The one striking exception to this pattern among Plantin's editions is his and Philips Galle's joint publication of a sort of pictorial catechism (with more than a hundred etchings), based upon Canisius's own (see PP 884 and ch. 6).

[119] On Costerus, see, e.g., NBW, 1, cols. 333–341. See PP 1039–1051 for Plantin's editions of his texts devoted to sodalities throughout the Low Countries.

5.18 Anonymous artist, *De formica* (Ants), from Epiphanius of Constantia, *Ad physiologum* (Antwerp: Christopher Plantin, 1588; 8°), p. 71, etching, 70 × 70 (Antwerp, Museum Plantin-Moretus, R 55.37).

meditations on Christ's Passion, which Plantin printed simultaneously in Latin, Dutch, and French in 1587, is a case in point. While the Dutch edition was dedicated to the sodality of the Virgin in Antwerp, the French and Latin editions were dedicated to the sodality of the Holy Sacrament in Douai.[120] Of these three editions, only the Latin text was printed in a smaller format (16°) and left unillustrated (except for a small vignette on the title-page). Both the Dutch and French editions, however, were printed in a larger format (*octavo*) and were sold either as a plain text edition with no illustrations (not even woodcuts) for 6 or 7 st. per copy or, for a much greater sum of 2 fl. 5 st. (= 45 st.), with a series of fifty pertinent images appropriately inserted among the pages of text. But, as will be discussed in greater detail below, copies of Canisius's and Costerus's

120 See n. 2 to PP 1048.

religious texts with etched illustrations did not go primarily to the local market, but rather to Michel Sonnius in Paris and dealers in Douai.

Plantin's small publication of images for the devotion of the rosary, *Les XV mysteres du rosaire de la Sacrée Vierge Marie*, fits in thematically with the increased interest in devotional works, demonstrated by the great success that Costerus's editions enjoyed. Nevertheless, this work remains an odd, exceptional publication among Plantin's editions from this period. It is essentially just a series of fifteen prints with only brief accompanying verses composed in French by Michel d'Esne ("seigneur de Bétencourt" and a soldier turned priest) that were engraved on to the plates themselves.[121] Plantin had very few copies of this booklet printed – just 170 – and sold (or gave away) only 16 copies in the first year following its completion.[122] All this suggests that this edition was actually printed for someone else, but we have yet to determine for whom. While d'Esne is the most likely candidate, the general accounts with him in one of Plantin's "Grand livres" only record the fact that Plantin gave him six copies of the book, in exchange for his work on the translation of the text.[123]

Plantin's edition of Epiphanius's *Ad physiologum* obviously differs from the preceding group of texts, but does fit in with Plantin's earlier editions of classical authors.[124] This text was, in fact, a reprint of an edition that was printed a year earlier (in 1587) in Rome by Francesco Zanetti and Giacomo Ruffinelli, but then with woodcut illustrations.[125] The etchings in Plantin's publication were roughly based upon the woodcuts in the Roman edition. As we will discuss below, of the four books with etched illustrations from the later 1580s highlighted here, Plantin had the greatest expectations for the sale of this edition with etchings.

Thus, of all of Plantin's new projects from the late 1580s, only the Epiphanius edition had an obvious visual (woodcut) antecedent. For the other texts, there were few, if any, direct precedents for the illustration of them generally and for the use of intaglios in particular, beyond independent print series of, for example, the Passion of Christ and the devotion of the rosary. Plantin was, consequently, free in his choice of medium for the illustration of each of these texts. Why did etchings prevail? Only in the case of Epiphanius's work on animals could one argue that the subject matter may have lent itself more readily to the sketch-like characteristic of etchings, particularly if one associated this work with the various series of animal fables published with etched illustrations that Plantin knew.[126] In each of the other publications considered here, figural compositions dominate and all are executed in vander Borcht's staid style, more

[121] See PP 1138 for references to Michel d'Esne.

[122] For the number of copies printed, see MPM Arch. 20, fol. 308 rht, for the following payment made to Mynken Liefrinck on July 13, 1588 for printing the illustrations for this book: "Ad 13 Julij [1588] vijf sorten vande Rosaire de nostre dame op elckx hondert & 70 beloopt 850 bladeren tot 30 st. t'hondert fl. 12 st. 15." (On July 13 [1588] five sorts of the Rosary of Our Lady on each one hundred and 70, amounts to 850 sheets at 30 st. per hundred fl. 12 st. 15.) For Plantin's few initial gifts and sales of this book, see MPM Arch. 65, fols. 101v, 107r (another record of the six copies given to d'Esne), 116r, and 119r.

[123] See MPM Arch. 20, fol. 318.

[124] For an overview of Plantin's editions of classical authors or other Neo-Latin studies, see Voet, PP, VI, pp. 2657–2669.

[125] For the Italian edition, see, e.g., Mortimer 1974, no. 171.

[126] See the discussion of de Dene's *De warachtighe fabulen der dieren* and related books in ch. 6.

reminiscent of an engraver's approach to defining and shading forms than a (seemingly) spontaneously drawn etching.[127] Indeed, the etchings used to illustrate Canisius's text were, in fact, supplemented with some engraving. In these cases, etchings (particularly if simply executed by the favored local artist) may have been chosen as an easy, less costly means to test out the market for Plantin's new Catholic devotional texts with intaglio illustrations.

SALES OF PLANTIN'S LAST INDEPENDENT PROJECTS WITH ETCHED ILLUSTRATIONS

To which markets, then, did this sample of Plantin's last editions with etched illustrations appeal?[128] When we examined the sale of Plantin's last large-scale project with engraved illustrations, his 1583 folio bible, as well as his first independent editions with etched illustrations – his Guicciardini editions from 1581 and 1582, and the 1582 commemorative album of Anjou's entry into Antwerp – we observed that the two primary markets for these publications were buyers at the Frankfurt book fair and the Parisian printer and bookseller, Michel Sonnius I. At that time, Sonnius usually took a quarter to a third of all the copies sold in the first year of sales. The shipments to Frankfurt usually comprised fewer books than Sonnius bought up in a year, but nevertheless often represented the next single most important destination for these editions.

While shipments to both Sonnius and the Frankfurt fair are prominent in these later sales as well, the import of each had changed. The Frankfurt fair was no longer a reliable, consistent component of the total sales spectrum. Rather, its importance varied significantly, dependent upon the text concerned. Specifically, of the works considered here, not one copy of Canisius's *Manuale catholicorum* – either with woodcut illustrations or with intaglios – or of the Dutch edition of Costerus's fifty meditations on Christ was sent to Frankfurt in the first year of its sale.[129] The lack of sales of the latter may well have resulted from the language in which it was printed, for fifty (albeit unillustrated) copies of the French version of the text were shipped to Frankfurt in November 1587, soon after it was completed. The lack of interest in Canisius's work, printed in Latin, the international language that usually sold easily at Frankfurt, must be a result of other factors. One possible explanation is that Plantin's potential market for Canisius's work at Frankfurt was pre-empted by the existence of other editions of the same text printed closer at hand. Specifically, the first editions of the *Manuale catholicorum* were printed in Ingolstadt and Freiburg the year before (in 1587). Thus, it is plausible that there was a local preference, if not an official privilege, for these

---

[127] Although none of the rosary images or the plates used to illustrate Canisius's *Manuale catholicorum* is signed, the figures in both works recall vander Borcht's conventional elongated figures with small heads. The etchings in Epiphanius's work are not signed and are harder to link to vander Borcht stylistically.

[128] Regrettably, owing to the lack of records of sales of books via the Leiden branch of the Plantin Press, it is impossible to make a similar study of the sales of the Lipsius editions considered here. See appendix 3, fig. A3.3, for references to all of the sales discussed below.

[129] Given the paucity of copies sold of the rosary print series, this work will only be mentioned in a few specific instances below.

first editions in German-speaking territories.[130] Sales of Epiphanius's *Ad physiologum* represent the other extreme, with 300 of the more than 450 copies sold in the first year going to Frankfurt in one large shipment sent out in August 1588, the first month that completed copies of the text were available for sale.

Purchases of these texts by Michel Sonnius had, by contrast, not become more erratic, but now tended to assume an even greater percentage: as much as 50 percent or more of all the copies sold in the first year. Sonnius often bought the majority of these copies within the first month that the book concerned was available for sale. Specifically, of Costerus's French edition on Christ's Passion, Sonnius took 212 of the approximately 500 copies sold without accompanying illustrations and 50 of the 90 or so copies sold with the accompanying set of etched illustrations. Understandably, Sonnius did not buy any copies of the Dutch edition of Costerus's text. Of Canisius's *Manuale*, Sonnius similarly bought 300 of the c.475 copies sold with woodcut illustrations and 125 of the c.200 copies sold with the intaglio illustrations. He also purchased 100 copies of Epiphanius's work, but this represented a lower percentage of the total sold in the first year (slightly less than a quarter) than was common for Sonnius in this period.

Beyond the regular sales to Sonnius and an occasional shipment to Frankfurt, where else did these late editions with etched illustrations go? When we examined the sales of Plantin's first projects with etched illustrations from 1581–1582, buyers in western Europe – Germany, France, and especially the Low Countries – dominated, along with regular sales of a number of copies to dealers in London, in particular Ascanius de Renialme. Now, some six to seven years later, the range of markets for Plantin's late editions was even more limited. As before, purchases by Spanish, Portuguese, and Italian buyers – which had previously represented a significant portion of Plantin's sales of his liturgical editions with engraved illustrations – are virtually non-existent here. Only copies of Canisius's *Manuale catholicorum* with intaglio illustrations were sold in any quantities, and then just six copies each to two solitary buyers: one anonymous figure in Spain and another for Alessandro Farnese's library.

The primary cause behind this phenomenon is probably the general decline in the number of Italian, Spanish, and Portuguese booksellers with whom Plantin dealt in this period.[131] There are two important exceptions to this pattern: Jan Poelman in Salamanca and Georgio Piscatori (or Joris de Visser) in Rome. As of 1586, Poelman had an agreement with Jan Moretus I, whereby he was designated as Plantin's primary contact for sales in Spain, which would clarify, at least in part, the latter's otherwise significantly limited contact with other dealers there. That said, although Poelman regularly purchased large quantities of books from Plantin worth hundreds of florins, these purchases rarely contained significant numbers of either liturgical editions with engraved illustrations or this selection of Plantin's late editions with etched illustrations. Other

---

130 Our warm thanks to Dr. Thomas Jahn of the Bayerische Staatsbibliothek in Munich for informing us that copies of these first editions in his collection (Asc. 3038 and Asc. 944) do not contain any privileges.

131 These observations are based upon those listed in Plantin's primary account book for foreign booksellers in this period (MPM Arch. 19). His contact with such dealers at the Frankfurt book fair also appears to have been limited (see Lauwaert 1972, pp. 170–171).

publishers, like the Giunti, may have satisfied this demand.[132] Thus, while the basic decline in interest in Plantin's late illustrated editions in southern Europe may be largely associated with the general decline in his contacts with dealers in these countries, it appears that there was also simply not a big demand for them.

Matters were slightly different with Piscatori. Not only did he lack Poelman's special status as a particular sales contact in a foreign country, but he also maintained an exceptional interest in Plantin's liturgical editions with engraved illustrations. The Piscatori family was buying such editions as early as 1574 and continued to do so into the late 1580s.[133] In contrast with other dealers' purchases of Plantin's liturgical editions from this period, which usually consisted of a mix of copies, some with woodcut illustrations and some with engravings, Piscatori almost exclusively bought large quantities of copies with engraved illustrations.[134] This suggests that, at least in the case of Plantin's potential Italian clients where there still was a market for his liturgical editions with engravings, the paucity of sales of these late editions with etched illustrations may also have been caused in part by the subject matter of the books and the medium of the illustrations. In this regard, it is worth recalling the mixed praise of etchings as easy alternatives to engravings, but ultimately not as clean or satisfactory, given by the sixteenth-century Italian artists Benvenuto Cellini and Giorgio Vasari.[135] For, it suggests that in some Italian circles, at least, works with etched illustrations would not have been as well received as those with engravings. Such aesthetic dissatisfaction with etchings is not as evident in northern Europe. For example, Karel van Mander, known for his northern counterpart to Vasari's account of primarily Italian artists, praises Marcus Gheeraerts for his etched illustrations to *De warachtighe fabulen der dieren*.[136] Rather, as we will argue below, in this case, financial concerns appear to have influenced clients in the Low Countries more at this time.

Buyers from German cities are also notably absent from the sales of Plantin's late editions with etchings. In most cases, it was probably owing to the texts under consideration – the French and Dutch editions of Costerus's meditations may well not have appealed to German-speaking buyers and, as suggested above, Canisius's editions may have been spread independently by German printer-publishers. But even Epiphanius's work, which Plantin shipped in such great quantities to the Frankfurt fair, was not bought separately by a single German bookseller in the first year of its sale. Similarly, while de Renialme did buy four copies of Epiphanius's *Ad physiologum*, as well as some copies of Canisius's *Manuale catholicorum* (four with woodcut illustrations and four with

---

[132] On Poelman's special arrangements with Plantin, see Voet, GC, II, pp. 402–403, and Robben 1993, pp. 57–65. Although most preserved records of Poelman's transactions with the Plantin Press only indicate the total value of the shipments concerned (see, e.g., MPM Arch. 19, fol. 162, and MPM Arch. 117, pp. 7–78), some inventories of the books at his shop indicate that he did not deal in the standard liturgical editions of the Press (see, e.g., MPM Arch. 117, pp. 415–442, p. 423 in particular). See Moll 1990 for alternative suppliers for this market.

[133] See MPM Arch. 52, fol. 16r, under January 27, 1574, for the sale of two large *octavo* books of hours with engraved illustrations to a certain Gillis Piscatori in Rome. For evidence that he and Georgio were related and of Georgio's large purchases of books from Plantin as of 1581, see MPM Arch. 18, fol. 212 lft.

[134] See MPM Arch. 65, fol. 167v, for such an order.

[135] See p. 206 above for the full citation of these remarks.

[136] See Van Mander 1994–1999, I, p. 290, and IV, p. 178. See ch. 6 for more on this publication.

etched), his purchases were small in comparison with those from the early 1580s. This was presumably because of the Catholic content of the works considered here and not necessarily the medium of the illustrations included, or the language in which they were printed, as he regularly bought works in French and Latin, some of which, like those documented in fig. A3.2, bore etched illustrations. Nevertheless, no other buyers with a direct connection with England appear in these accounts – not even for Epiphanius's work, which would not have posed any difficulties in terms of its content – except Hans Wouteneel (or Wanteneel), a Dutchman who was then active as a bookseller in London, who similarly bought copies of Canisius's *Manuale catholicorum* (six with woodcut illustrations and six with etchings).[137]

With these reductions in the markets for the illustrated texts Plantin was printing at the end of his life, only clients in France and the former Low Countries remained to support his production. While the booksellers in the Low Countries bought notably more copies of these works in total than others in France (beyond Sonnius), this was largely down to a few specific customers. Philippus Zangrius in Leuven, and Hieronymus Verdussen, Jan van Keerberghen I, and Peter van Tongheren in Antwerp were, for example, all important buyers of the Dutch edition of Costerus's meditations (but always without the accompanying illustrations).[138] Of greater general significance among this sample of sales, however, were those made to booksellers in Douai. Then a part of the Low Countries (but now part of northern France), Douai was known as a center for English Catholic refugees. While many of this group initially went to Leuven and studied there, this role was taken over by Douai once a university was opened there (to serve this community, in particular) in October 1562.[139] Consequently, many booksellers with connections in Leuven also endeavored to establish themselves in Douai to take advantage of the growing need for books there.[140] Two such bookseller families who are significant here are those of Jan Bogard I and II and Alice Fowler, the widow of John Fowler, who was previously an important client of Plantin's when in Leuven.[141] For example, of the 162 copies of Canisius's *Manuale catholicorum* with woodcut illustrations sold to booksellers in the Low Countries, 100 went to Bogard alone, while he bought 12 of the 52 copies sold with etched illustrations. Booksellers in Douai similarly feature more prominently in the sales of the French edition of Costerus's meditations on the Passion than others in the Low Countries. Specifically, of the approximately 250 copies

[137] On Wouteneel, see Clair 1959, especially pp. 29–30 (for "Wanteneel").

[138] For these purchases of the Dutch edition of Costerus's work (not included in fig. A3.3), see MPM Arch. 64, fols. 58v and 70r, and MPM Arch. 65, fols. Iv and 54r (all for Zangrius); MPM Arch. 64, fols. 59r, 85r, 113v, 122v, 125v, 138r, and MPM Arch. 65, fol. 46v (all for Verdussen); MPM Arch. 64, fols. 102v and 136r, and MPM Arch. 65, fols. 5v, 8v, 44v, 48v, 50r and 56r (all for van Keerberghen); and MPM Arch. 64, fols. 103v and 145v, and MPM Arch. 65, fol. 46v (all for van Tongheren). For a basic overview of the activities of each, see, e.g., Rouzet 1975, pp. 252 (for Zangrius), 233–234 (for Verdussen), 107 (for van Keerberghen), and 222–223 (for van Tongheren).

[139] On this topic see Guilday 1914. This university is distinct from the English college in Douai, which was expelled from the city in 1578 following conflicts with local Calvinists and did not return until 1593 (see Guilday 1914, pp. 45, 76–77, and 84).

[140] On Douai booksellers and printers in this period, see Labarre 1985.

[141] For Jan Bogard I and II, see Persoons 1989, pp. 619–623. For Alice Fowler, see Rouzet 1975, p. 64. For more on John Fowler and his importance as a printer of books for English refugees, see Southern 1977, pp. 342–344, and Coppens 1993, pp. 18–20.

sold (all but 18 without the accompanying illustrations), 149 (including 3 illustrated copies) went to booksellers in Douai. In this case, Alice Fowler bought the most (80 copies), followed by Bogard (45 copies, including the 3 illustrated ones), while a certain bookseller, Jacques Utens, purchased the remaining 24. Presumably the exceptionally large quantities of these texts bought by these booksellers in Douai must be accounted for by the university and the large population of English Catholics there, for while both Bogard and Alice Fowler also purchased some copies of Epiphanius's work on animals, the quantities – six and two copies, respectively – were not nearly so exceptional. Were the hundreds of copies of Catholic works meant for local use at the university, or were they intended, perhaps, for clandestine export? It is regrettably impossible to know. Whatever the reason, these booksellers remain an important, unexpected outlet for Plantin's new Catholic editions.

Of this sample of late illustrated editions, Costerus's French edition of his meditations on Christ was, predictably, the most appealing to Plantin's French clients (beyond Sonnius). Striking here is that while sales of Plantin's editions with intaglio illustrations generally lagged behind sales of the same books with just woodcut illustrations (or none at all), these French buyers – in particular, two dealers in Paris, Abel L'Angelier and Guillaume Bichon – were primarily interested in copies with the accompanying set of etched illustrations and not just the text.[142] Buyers from the Low Countries apparently had just the opposite taste or – perhaps more to the point – budget for this group of books. For Costerus's meditations, for example, a copy without illustrations typically cost 6 st. (if in Dutch) and 7 st. (if in French). Copies with the accompanying etched illustrations cost 40–50 st. (depending upon the buyer and the language). Evidently, while many French buyers were willing and could afford to pay the extra 34 st. for these illustrated copies (nearly six times the cost of the original text), most buyers in the Low Countries were not.

Specifically, Parisian customers bought thirty-six illustrated copies (while Nicolas Lescuyer in Rouen purchased just twelve copies of the plain text). In contrast, booksellers in the Low Countries bought (all told) 230 copies of this book within the first year of sale, only 8 of which were illustrated. Sales of Costerus's Dutch edition to booksellers in the Low Countries yield similar results: 223 copies sold in total in the first year, 12 of which were illustrated – and all 12 of which were sold to Christopher Raphelengius, the son of Plantin's son-in-law, Franciscus Raphelengius, who was then running Plantin's shop in Leiden, a town with better economic prospects at that time than most of its war-ravaged counterparts in the southern Low Countries.[143] In the case of Canisius's *Manuale catholicorum*, this difference in buyer preference was not as pronounced, perhaps because the difference in price between copies with woodcut illustrations (typically 5 st. per book) and copies with etched illustrations (typically

[142] For L'Angelier, see Balsamo and Simonin 2002. For Bichon, see Renouard 1965, p. 33.
[143] For the sale of the illustrated copies (in addition to thirteen copies without illustrations) to Raphelengius, see MPM Arch. 65, fol. 93r. For sales of this text to Zangrius, Verdussen, van Keerberghen, and van Tongheren, see n. 138 above. For sales to other customers in the Low Countries, see MPM Arch. 64, fols. 59r, 60v (2x), 61r, 62r, 62v, 65v, 66v, 74v, 75v, 100r, 106r, 114r, 114v, 115r, 121r, 125v, 127v, 128r, 129r, 139v, 141r, 144r, 146v, 151v, and 159v; and MPM Arch. 65, fols. 5r, 6v, 25r, 35r, 37r, 39r, 42v, and 53v.

10 st. per book) was not nearly as significant. Indeed, for this edition, approximately a quarter of all the copies bought by Sonnius, on the one hand, and booksellers in the Low Countries, on the other, were illustrated with etchings instead of woodcuts. The main difference between these two groups – as was usually the case – was the relative quantities involved: while Sonnius purchased 300 copies with woodcut illustrations and 125 with etchings, the local booksellers bought half as many, just 162 copies with woodcuts and 59 with etchings. Or, if one discounts the unusually large purchase of 112 copies of this book by Jan Bogard II, other local buyers bought just 62 copies with woodcuts and some 47 with etchings, or just a quarter of Sonnius's purchases. For the Epiphanius edition (typically sold at 10 st. per copy), the difference between Sonnius's purchases and those of booksellers from the Low Countries was even greater, with Sonnius buying 100 copies, while just a third of that amount (34) was sold in small, individual purchases to various customers in the Low Countries.

Thus, Plantin's market for his books with etched illustrations in the late 1580s appears to be the most limited yet of all the periods examined. Dominated clearly by what the Parisian dealer Michel Sonnius purchased (in addition to other French clients), it notably lacks a reliable group of local buyers interested in these illustrated editions. Consequently, it appears that Plantin's luxury editions with intaglio illustrations, with which he made a name for himself internationally in the early 1570s with his liturgical editions, were still most popular in an international market, but an ever narrower one.

Plantin's late editions of his missals, breviaries, and books of hours with engraved illustrations were purchased in greater quantities than these other illustrated editions, but were also similarly limited in their main markets. This is clear from a sample study of the primary, "large-scale" buyers of these editions in 1588, namely, people who bought ten or more copies of various liturgical texts with engraved illustrations.[144] The striking paucity of such clients in Italy and Spain for these late editions has already been discussed above. Rather, the primary, reliable markets were Frankfurt – but now supplied through Plantin's agent, Jan Dresseler, who appears to have specialized in the sale of his liturgical editions there – and Michel Sonnius in Paris.[145] There was, however, one noteworthy local addition to this group of repeat purchasers of Plantin's specially illustrated liturgical editions, namely, the Antwerp bookseller Jan Cordier.[146] These recurring sales to a few specific clients were occasionally supplemented by single significant purchases of these liturgical editions by other booksellers. In this sample year, we noted Guillaume Bichon, who also bought some of the illustrated editions discussed above, and Sébastien Nivelle, both in Paris, Petrus Bellerus in Antwerp, and Georgio Piscatori in Rome. The Cologne-based dealer Arnold Mylius also bought large quantities of Plantin's liturgical editions, but then primarily with woodcut illustrations

---

144 For this case study, we used the sales recorded in Plantin's 1588 Journal (MPM Arch. 65), supplemented with the lists of sales to Jan Poelman cited in n. 132 above.

145 See Voet, GC, II, pp. 404–405, for Plantin's arrangements with Dresseler, and MPM Arch. 65, fols. 4v, 74r, 76r, 108r, and 172v, for large shipments of liturgical editions to him. For Sonnius's regular, large-scale purchases of these books, see, e.g., MPM Arch. 65, fols. 24v, 29v, 49r, 58r, 66r, 82v, 97r, 109v, and 151v.

146 On Cordier, see Rouzet 1975, p. 47. For a sample of his purchases of these liturgical editions, see MPM Arch. 65, fols. 18v, 131v, 135v, 168v, and 173r (see also MPM Arch. 65, fols. 30r, 70r, 114r, and 164r).

and not engravings.[147] Considered as a whole, the following pattern emerges concerning Plantin's sales of his liturgical editions with engraved illustrations. Sonnius was, once again, by far the single largest purchaser of these books. When this is considered in conjunction with the dominating weight of his purchases among Plantin's late editions with etched illustrations, it clarifies Plantin's regular complaints in letters written toward the end of his life that he was now only serving as a mercenary, working for others, like Michel Sonnius I.[148] While Dresseler also bought large quantities of Plantin's liturgical editions in general, the relative percentage of copies with engraved illustrations was lower. Piscatori's purchases, by contrast, are striking owing to the predominance of copies with engraved illustrations. These observations reinforce the general impression of a stronger interest in Italy for works with engraved illustrations than in a German-based market, like Frankfurt, even if it did serve an international community. A number of these sales are also noteworthy for the fact that they consisted exclusively (or nearly so) of liturgical editions, thereby suggesting that these books were regarded as a category apart. Finally, among all the breviaries, missals, diurnals, and books of hours purchased with engraved illustrations, small books of hours for personal devotion were by far the most popular, which agrees with the findings of our initial study of the sales of Plantin's liturgical editions from the 1570s (see appendix 3, fig. A3.1).

PLANTIN'S ESTIMATIONS OF THE DEMAND FOR HIS ILLUSTRATED EDITIONS FROM THE 1580S

To what extent did the first year of sales of these illustrated editions from the 1580s meet Plantin's own expectations for purchases of these books? What was the relationship between the number of copies sold and the total number of copies illustrated? Thanks to the accounts kept with Mynken Liefrinck, there are clear indications of the number of illustrated copies produced for each of the editions discussed here except those printed while Plantin was in Leiden (for which there are simply no pertinent records) and Guicciardini's description of the Low Countries. While there are records of Liefrinck's work on the illustration of Guicciardini's texts, it is impossible to calculate exactly how many impressions were printed of either the French or the Italian edition, specifically, because she printed the illustrations for them in irregular, vaguely specified batches, largely dependent upon the demand for the illustrated copies.[149]

When we examined the printing and sale of the commemorative album of Anjou's entry into Antwerp, we observed that Plantin had estimated the initial interest in that book well, selling approximately 560 of the 670 or so copies illustrated in the first year. Plantin's initial sales of his grand folio bible were less successful in this regard.

---

[147] For these sales, see MPM Arch. 65, fols. 43v (for Bichon), 152r–v (for Nivelle), 48v (for Bellerus), 167v (for Piscatori), and MPM Arch. 65, fols. 30r, 70r, 114r, and 164r (for Mylius). See n. 142 above for Bichon. For Nivelle, see Renouard 1965, pp. 324–325. For Bellerus, see Rouzet 1975, pp. 11–12. And for Piscatori and Mylius, see n. 133 and n. 86, respectively, above.

[148] See ch. 6 for a discussion of these letters.

[149] For transcriptions of a sample of payments made to Liefrinck for this work, see Denucé 1912–1913, I, pp. 161–162. See pp. 25–26, for a discussion of the various advantages of Liefrinck's usual practice of illustrating limited numbers of copies at any one time.

For while a comparable number of copies were printed (around 650), Plantin only sold about 270 copies in the first year, or slightly less than a third of the total printed.[150] This implies that Plantin was left with a much greater, lingering, uncompensated investment in the paper and illustration costs of the large folio bible. Naturally, he could also count on being able to sell copies of the bible for a longer period of time (until the text itself was modified by papal decree in 1590[151]) than a commemorative work of contentious, potentially ephemeral political import, thereby making the estimation of the sales of the Anjou edition all the more critical. But still, unrecouped costs remained significant, particularly in financially difficult periods of war. As the records for the printing and initial sale of Plantin's last illustrated editions indicate, the relatively high initial sales of the illustrated copies of the Anjou edition were more the exception than the rule.

Aside from the unusual case of the mere 170 illustrated copies printed of *Les XV mysteres du rosaire*, discussed above, the number of illustrated copies printed of each of the remaining books considered here varied notably from the 650 copy average for the two earlier editions. The text with the largest number of known illustrated copies out of all the books considered here is Epiphanius's *Ad physiologum*, with 835 copies completed by July 23, 1588.[152] This is not entirely surprising given the large number of copies (300) shipped to Frankfurt and Sonnius's own purchase of 100 copies soon after the illustrations were added. With these large initial shipments, Plantin ultimately sold approximately 470 copies (well over half) of the 835 copies printed in the first year. However, subsequent sales were evidently slow, for Plantin's successors still had copies of this text as late as 1642, as it was included in a list of the books they had for sale that year.[153] Plantin had fewer copies illustrated of Costerus's and Canisius's texts, perhaps because he knew that they would not sell as well (or at all) at Frankfurt and he was still uncertain as to how the local market would respond to these new illustrated publications. Specifically, while he had approximately 500 copies of Canisius's *Manuale catholicorum* printed with etched illustrations, he had only 306 sets of the accompanying illustrations for Costerus's meditations on the Passion printed in the course of the first seven months in which the illustrated copies were sold.[154] In the first year of sale of these books, Plantin sold 213 (or nearly one-half) of the approximately 500 illustrated copies of Canisius's handbook, and 104 copies (92 French and 12 Dutch) of Costerus's text with the accompanying illustrations, thereby using approximately one-third of the sets of illustrations Liefrinck printed. While it is also possible that Plantin sold sets of the Passion illustrations separately, as an independent print series, we have yet to find examples of this.

---

[150] The estimated number of illustrated copies of this bible is based upon several records of payment to Liefrinck in which she was regularly paid for adding illustrations to 650 copies each of the cited sheets of the text (see MPM Arch. 18, fol. 430 rht for such records).

[151] See ch. 4 for more on the revision of essential Catholic texts in the latter sixteenth century.

[152] See MPM Arch. 20, fol. 308 rht, for Plantin's payment to Liefrinck for the illustration of this text.

[153] For their 1642 *Index librorum* (Antwerp: Balthasar Moretus II, 1642), see, e.g., MPM (R 27.3), p. 10.

[154] See MPM Arch. 20, fol. 308 rht, under September 15, 1588, for the payment to Liefrinck for illustrating 514 copies of Canisius's text. Between October 19, 1587 and May 22, 1588, Liefrinck typically delivered batches of fifty or a hundred copies of the accompanying illustrations for Costerus's *octavo* editions on the Passion, all charged at 6 st. per hundred images printed (see MPM Arch. 20, fols. 288 rht and 308 rht).

Thus, for each of these three works with etchings, Plantin succeeded in selling approximately a third to a half of the copies illustrated within the first year, as was the case with the initial sales of his 1583 folio bible. In the case of Epiphanius's *Ad physiologum*, the text illustrated in the greatest quantity out of all these editions, Plantin had, nevertheless, overestimated its popularity. The extra accompanying illustrations for Costerus's meditation on the Passion also do not appear to have been such a success. Aside from the relatively small number of copies with these illustrations sold in the first year – 104 for all of Plantin's markets combined – no subsequent, comparably illustrated edition of this text appears to have been published by the *Officina Plantiniana*, only an unillustrated edition in Dutch from 1597.[155] Consequently, if Plantin had chosen etchings for the illustration of these last editions, at least in part because he was looking for a less expensive means to test out the market for new types of richly illustrated editions, his reasoning would have been wise given the ultimately limited sales of three of the four publications considered here. Matters were different with Canisius's *Manuale*, however, as both Plantin and Jan Moretus I regularly reprinted it in a variety of formats with both intaglio and woodcut illustrations, just as if it was one of their liturgical editions.[156] But how suitable were etchings – instead of the engraved illustrations common to Plantin's liturgical editions – for this purpose? In order to evaluate this last, critical consideration for the use of etchings as book illustrations, we will need to jump a few years ahead in time to when Jan Moretus I was running the *Officina Plantiniana* following Plantin's death in 1589. For, only then are the implications evident of the pattern of events set into motion by a few of Plantin's last editions with etched illustrations.

THE RELATIVE COST AND "LIFE" OF ETCHED AND ENGRAVED PLATES

In the course of this chapter, we have periodically alluded to the presumption that etchings were not only easier and faster to make than engravings, but also cheaper. Beyond this basic initial outlay, however, is another important, closely related issue that Plantin raised in his evaluation of the costs of including engraved illustrations cited at the beginning of this chapter, namely: how many serviceable impressions could be made from a plate before one had to invest in either reworking the existing plate or replacing it entirely? What is the evidence of these relative costs for etchings and engravings? For the presumption that etchings were easier and faster to make, we can only rely on occasional, passing remarks in contemporary artists' accounts of etchings, such as those of Benvenuto Cellini and Giorgio Vasari cited above, or logical arguments by modern scholars concerning the time needed to complete an etching or an engraving.[157] Even with the great archival sources in the Plantin-Moretus Museum concerning the production of etchings and engravings for the illustration of

---

[155] See BB, I, p. 882, C 548, and BT 5525 for this text.
[156] For Plantin's subsequent editions of Canisius's text, see PP 892–896. For examples of Jan Moretus's editions of this text, see: BCNI nos. 4161, 4285, 4380, 4515, 5040, 5188, and 5391; as well as BT 6534 and 6535.
[157] Consider, for example, Landau and Parshall 1994, pp. 30–31, and Griffiths 1996, pp. 56–57. See p. 206 for Cellini's and Vasari's remarks.

their books, we cannot penetrate into the daily working world of engravers and etchers in sixteenth- and seventeenth-century Antwerp to determine precisely how long it took them to complete a single plate. For, even if you can bracket the time needed to complete one or a group of plates by the date when the plates were commissioned and the date when they were completed, you still will never know, for example, whether the artist concerned worked only on the required plates or also completed other jobs simultaneously.

The books and bookkeeping of the Plantin-Moretus Press do offer more valuable information on the other questions raised here, namely, the relative costs of etchings and engravings and how many impressions an etched or engraved plate could yield before it needed to be replaced. Although the best examples of such information date not from Plantin's life-time, but from the decade thereafter, this was still a critical transitional period for the illustrated editions of the *Officina Plantiniana*. For in the 1590s, Jan Moretus I vacillated between the two mediums, before ultimately shifting from Plantin's concluding reliance on etchings for the majority of his new projects and his own arrangements as of 1600 to work nearly exclusively with Theodoor Galle's workshop of engravers. Hereafter, engravings once again became the medium of choice for the intaglio illustrations of all the Moretuses' publications. By examining these records from the 1590s, we can, as it were, consider some of the evidence that Jan Moretus I must have had when evaluating for himself, shortly after Plantin's death, which medium was best for the illustration of his books.

Let us begin with the relative costs of executing etchings and engravings. When endeavoring to find payments for both etchings and engravings that were made relatively close in time to one another (to avoid any added complications of altering monetary values, for example), we were limited by the few records known for the completion of etchings for the Plantin-Moretus Press. Specifically, the best sources of such payments are (albeit incomplete) records of vander Borcht's work on the 180 plates needed for the illustration of Jan Moretus's 1591 edition of Ovid's *Metamorphoses* in oblong 16°.[158] Each of the text illustrations was c.70 × 85 mm, while the title-plate was somewhat larger. Vander Borcht's role as the etcher of these plates is confirmed by the payment records. One plate (no. 176) is also signed "PETRUS VANDER BORCHT INVENIT ET FECIT," thereby indicating that he was responsible for designing these images as well. Vander Borcht received 2 fl. on average for every plate he is known to have delivered.[159]

Payments for engravings made in this period are also scarce. The best source for such records is a small account book kept by Jan Moretus II, in which various matters pertaining to the production of books are noted, including the costs for some illustrations. According to the first line of this notebook, the entries were compiled in 1602, when Jan II was living with his family in Leuven. But all of the notes for the illustrations appear to date from the 1590s. For example, among the accounts for Adriaen Collaert, there is a payment for a vignette for Caesar Baronius's *Annales ecclesiastici*, which was

---

[158] See, for example, Adams 1967, II, O 504 and BT 3913.
[159] For examples of such payments, see MPM Arch. 66, fols. 134r, 147r, 162r, and 171r; and MPM Arch. 67, fol. 2r. In each case he was paid 10 fl. for delivering five plates.

used for the first time in 1594 in the fourth volume.[160] This series of payments made to Collaert offers the best sample of what contemporary engravings would have cost. As we have argued elsewhere, the prices charged by engravers working in Antwerp in the sixteenth and seventeenth centuries were a function of various factors, including the reputation or relative fame of the artist concerned, the level of difficulty of what was to be engraved, and the size of the plate.[161] By this time, Collaert was a recognized engraver: he had his own pupils and had been appointed to several important administrative positions in the St. Luke's guild of Antwerp.[162] Consequently, he (or any members of his workshop who may have done the actual work) may not have been the cheapest engraver available at the time. However, it is clear from the Plantin-Moretus account books from this period that he was one of the few engravers the Moretuses are known to have periodically employed in the 1590s. Thus, expensive or not, his rates were one of the accepted alternatives to what vander Borcht might have charged for making the same plates.

All of the fees listed in Jan Moretus II's account book confirm the general assumption, namely, that engravings were more expensive than etchings. Two payments are of particular significance in comparison with vander Borcht's charges noted above. They are, on the one hand, a payment of 2 fl. per plate for a series of images used to decorate the calendar section of a small book of hours in 24°, and, on the other hand, a payment of 4 fl. per plate, for the main text illustrations for a slightly larger book of hours in 12°.[163] Because of the lack of precise dates in these records and the scarcity of copies of Jan Moretus's small books of hours from this period, it is not possible to link these payments with specific illustrations in one of Jan Moretus's books. Nevertheless, known copies of such texts printed by him in the 1590s still indicate how large, generally, these illustrations must have been. Specifically, calendar illustrations for a book of hours in 24° were often only 18 × 30 mm, essentially three times smaller than the text illustrations for the *Metamorphoses*, for which vander Borcht was similarly paid 2 fl. per plate.[164] The text illustrations for a book of hours in 12° were, predictably, larger than the preceding calendar illustrations, but were, nonetheless, probably no bigger than c.53 × 55 mm, the size of the woodcut illustrations used to illustrate other copies of the same edition.[165] This being the case, Collaert was paid twice as much (4 fl. per plate) for the execution of engravings that were still notably smaller than the approximately 70 × 85 mm text illustrations for Ovid's *Metamorphoses*, for which vander Borcht received only 2 fl. per plate. The pay scales for Collaert and vander Borcht

---

[160] MPM Arch. 1079, fol. 12v, the third item. For this volume of the *Annales*, see Adams 1967, I, B 238 and BT 7849.

[161] See Bowen and Imhof 2003.   [162] See *New Holl.*, *Collaert*, I, pp. lv–lxii.

[163] See MPM Arch. 1079, fol. 12v, for the following records: "Pour la taille des 12 mois des heures en 24° fl. 24" and "Pour figures des heures en 12° la piece fl. 4."

[164] For an example of such a book of hours with calendar illustrations this size, see the *Officium BMV* in 24°, published by Jan Moretus I in 1592 (Wroclaw: University Library [455246]).

[165] See London, Lambeth Palace (H2080) for one such book of hours in 12° from 1593 with woodcut text illustrations (c.53 × 55 mm). No copies of Jan Moretus's books of hours in 12° with intaglio illustrations are known. But, given Plantin's and the Moretuses' habit of setting the text of a book of hours once and just replacing the woodcut illustrations with intaglios, the intaglios must have been of comparable scale to the woodcut illustrations (or smaller), or else they would have printed over the text.

were clearly and consistently distinct. Some of the divergence between their two rates of pay may reflect a difference in their reputation, or a general worth associated with engravings rather than etchings. But whatever the cause, the net result is the same, namely, a confirmation of the common assumptions that etchings were generally less expensive than engravings.

And what of the issue raised by Plantin concerning the number of impressions an intaglio plate could provide before the plate had to be reworked or replaced? In order to address this question, we sought two publications, one with engraved illustrations and one with etchings, that were initially printed (with a new set of plates) and then reprinted in roughly the same period of time, once again in the hope of minimizing the number of possible contingent factors that could inadvertently influence the findings. The best examples that we found for this case are: several new engravings, possibly executed by 1590 by Adriaen Collaert's brother Hans (or Jan) Collaert II after designs by Maarten de Vos for the illustration of a missal (but which were not used for the first time until 1596); and the set of etchings (presumably executed by vander Borcht) for the illustration of the *quarto* editions of Justus Lipsius's *De cruce liber tres*, a detailed study of crucifixions in the ancient and early Christian periods, first published in 1593/1594.[166] In both cases, the text for which the new set of plates was made was reprinted enough times that both sets of illustrations highlighted here not only had to be reworked in the course of the reprinting, but ultimately replaced. The number of times that the plates were reworked and the resulting number of impressions pulled from them differ, however, between the two media.

In the case of the engraved missal illustrations, five of these plates – the *Crucifixion*, the *Resurrection*, *Pentecost*, the *Last Supper*, and the *Assumption of the Virgin* (fig. 5.19) – were used to illustrate at least five, if not all six, of the Moretuses' folio missal editions printed between 1596 and 1613.[167] Following the publication of the Moretuses' 1613 missal, the de Vos plates do not appear to have been used again for the illustration of this text. Rather, the Moretuses used a new set of plates designed by Peter Paul Rubens and engraved at Theodoor Galle's print workshop.[168] Records of the illustration of these missals reveal that as many as 4,071 impressions were made of each of the five plates used from 1596 to 1613. The individual amounts per edition are as follows: 646 impressions for the 1596 missal,[169] probably 425 for the 1599 edition,[170]

---

[166] For more on the missal illustrations, see Bowen and Imhof 2001, pp. 259–275. For Lipsius's *De cruce* editions, see Lipsius Antwerp 1997, cat. 37, Lipsius Leuven 1997, cat. 22, and BB, III, pp. 918–925, L 200–L 212. We will be focusing on the three editions Jan Moretus printed in *quarto*, namely, in 1593/1594 (L 200), 1599 (L 205), and 1606 (L 207).

[167] For precisely which plates were used in which edition (when known), see Bowen and Imhof 2001, pp. 259–275 and 288–289.

[168] For a discussion of Rubens's and Galle's execution of these plates (some of which were first used to illustrate the Moretuses' 1614 *Breviarium Romanum*, but later reused for their folio missals), in addition to some borders used to illustrate the same missal editions, see, e.g., Judson and van de Velde 1977, I, nos. 6–9 (pp. 85–101) and nos. 20–28 (pp. 126–150), and II, payment records 5–11 (pp. 451–453), and payment records 17 and 20, pp. 455–456.

[169] See Bowen and Imhof 2001, p. 264 and n. 17.

[170] Bowen and Imhof 2001, p. 269 and n. 29. Although no copy is known of this missal, it is highly likely that the same plates were used here as well given the consistency with which this group of plates was used to illustrate all the other known copies under consideration.

5.19a Hans Collaert II after Maarten de Vos, *Assumption of the Virgin*, from *Missale Romanum* (Antwerp: Jan Moretus I, 1596; f°), p. 478, engraving (state I), 275 × 185 (Brussels, The Royal Library, Rare Books Department, RP 3365 C). See fig. 5.20 for the last state used of this engraving.

5.19b Detail of section of clouds below the Virgin's feet in 5.19a.

550 impressions for the 1605 missal,[171] 800 impressions for the 1606 missal,[172] 875 impressions for the 1610 edition,[173] and 725 impressions for the 1613 missal (see fig. 5.20).[174] The engraving of the *Assumption of the Virgin* featured here was reworked at least four times in the course of the printing of these six missal editions.[175] Thus, this example reveals that around 1600 an engraving could be periodically reworked in order to yield some 4,000 impressions before having to be replaced – a full 3,000 more than Plantin indicated in his *c.*1574 estimation cited at the start of this chapter.

The etchings for Lipsius's *De cruce* editions, by contrast, appear to have been reworked just once and were used to illustrate fewer copies of this text. Specifically, following the illustration of the initial run of 1,500 copies of the 1593/1594 edition of this text (fig. 5.21), the plates were reworked prior to printing another 1,500 copies of the 1599 edition.[176] The poor state of the etchings by the end of the illustration of the 1599 edition must have led Jan Moretus to order new plates (a set of engravings after the compositions seen in the etchings) for the illustration of his 1606 edition of this text. Apparently, however, the new engravings were not all ready by the time the text was printed in 1606 and an additional 100 impressions were made from the old etchings in June 1606, in their worn state (fig. 5.22) to cover, presumably, an initial group of sales. Theodoor Galle's workshop was not paid for the new engravings until September 1606 and did not finish printing the new illustrations in the remaining 1,400 copies of this edition until July 21, 1607.[177] A similar pattern is evident in the reprinting of the

[171] Despite records indicating that as many as 750 copies of this edition were printed with engraved illustrations (see Bowen and Imhof 2001, p. 269 and n. 31), the Galle workshop was paid for printing illustrations for only 550 copies (see MPM Arch. 123, fol. 13r, under March 5 and April 2, 1605).

[172] Bowen and Imhof 2001, p. 271 and n. 45.

[173] Bowen and Imhof 2001, p. 275 and n. 52.

[174] Judson and van de Velde 1977, I, p. 453, number 11.

[175] See Bowen and Imhof 2001, pp. 269–275 and 288–289, for more on when each of these plates was reworked.

[176] The illustration of both editions was undertaken by a certain Lynken van Lanckvelt (see MPM Arch. 21, fol. 219 rht, under February 22, 1594, and fol. 362 rht, under March 16, 1599, respectively). It is not known who reworked these plates or when.

[177] See MPM Arch. 123, fols. 15r (for the initial illustration of two batches of fifty copies of this text), 15v (for the engraving of the new plates and reworking others), and 16r (for the illustration of the remaining copies). The staggered printing of the 1606 edition is also discussed in Imhof 1999a, p. 75.

5.20a Hans Collaert II after Maarten de Vos, *Assumption of the Virgin*, from *Missale Romanum*
(Antwerp: Jan Moretus II and Balthasar Moretus I, 1613; f°), fol. tɪv, engraving (state ɪv), 275 × 185
(Antwerp, Museum Plantin-Moretus, ᴀ 1546). See fig. 5.19 for the original state of this engraving.

5.20b Detail of section of clouds below the Virgin's feet in 5.20a.

illustrations for Lipsius's *De militia*, initially published by Jan Moretus I in 1595/1596. Once again, the original set of etchings was used to illustrate the first run of 1,500 copies, then reworked and reused to illustrate all 1,500 copies of the next edition of the text (from 1598) and then replaced (after the printing of just 200 copies) with a set of engravings that was used to illustrate the remaining 1,300 copies of Moretus's third edition of the text (from 1602).[178]

Hence, vander Borcht's etchings from the mid-1590s appear to have been capable of being reworked at least once and illustrating a little more than 3,000 copies of a text. What is noteworthy when one examines copies of these books (see figs. 5.21b and 5.22b) is how the etched quality of the images – their rich, fuzzy, drawn appearance – disappears within the first 1,500 impressions made, leaving only thin traces of the original etched lines and the extra engraved lines added during the reworking. The net effect then, in the second set of 1,500 impressions, was one of a sloppily executed, patched-up, and fading engraving, instead of a true etching. Thus, if anyone had decided to use etchings instead of engravings for book illustrations specifically because of the characteristic visual features of etchings, the potential, saleable run of such books (from the sixteenth century, at least) would probably have been limited to fewer than 1,500 copies. Books in which etched illustrations were chosen primarily for their ease and speed of execution and were combined with burin work from the start – like many etched cartographic plates – would not have been thus restricted. Their original visual effects were closer to engravings and would thus not have been altered as significantly with use as the purely etched illustrations in Lipsius's editions. Naturally, the question remains as to how many of the publications illustrated with etchings in the sixteenth century had print runs of 1,500 copies each. Of all of the Plantin editions with etchings considered above, the number of copies illustrated with etchings ran from a mere 170 copies of

178 For this book, see, e.g., Lipsius Antwerp 1997, cat. 40, Lipsius Leuven 1997, cat. 24, and BB, III, L 369–L 371, pp. 1002–1004. For the number of copies of both the 1595/1596 edition and the 1598 edition that were printed with etched illustrations, see the citation of these editions in MPM M 39 (the fourteenth item under the listings for 1595 and the fifteenth item for the listings under 1597). Finally, for the printing of the illustrations in the first 200 copies of the 1602 edition, see MPM Arch. 123, fol. 7r. For payments for the engraving of new plates to illustrate this work, see MPM Arch. 123, fols. 7r–8r. For the printing of the illustrations in the remaining 1,300 copies (in batches of 200–250 copies per payment record), see MPM Arch. 123, fols. 8r–8v.

5.21a Peeter vander Borcht?, *Christian Martyr*, from Justus Lipsius, *De cruce liber tres* (Antwerp: Jan Moretus I, 1593; 4°), p. 81, etching (state I), 108 × 57 (Antwerp, Museum Plantin-Moretus, A 1187 B). See fig. 5.22 for the last state used of this etching.

Les XV mysteres du rosaire to 835 copies of Epiphanius's *Ad physiologum*, also printed in 1588 – all still notably under the 1,500 maximum suggested above, for reasonable, characteristic impressions of an etching.[179] As another of Plantin's late projects with etched illustrations was also limited to approximately 875 copies, it is possible that the actual practical restriction in the number of reasonable impressions that could be made from an etching was closer to this number.[180] Thus, the issue of the relative "return" on these plates in terms of the number of satisfactory impressions that could be pulled

[179] See above for the number of copies illustrated of each of these editions. It is possible that as many as, if not more than 800 impressions were printed of the plates used to illustrate the three editions of Guicciardini's text that Plantin printed between 1581 and 1588 (see PP 1277–1280). But, as noted above, the records of payment to Mynken Liefrinck for the illustration of these texts are too imprecise to determine exactly how many sets of illustrations were printed.

[180] See ch. 6 for the discussion of Plantin's and Galle's co-edition of Petrus Canisius's *Institutiones christianae, seu parvus catechismus catholicorum*.

5.21b Detail of smoke along left side. Compare this detail with fig. 5.22b for an example of how this etching was modified with time.

from them may not have come to a head until exceptionally popular publications, like editions of Canisius's *Manuale catholicorum* and Lipsius's treatises, were illustrated with etchings. Was it then such a coincidence that Plantin never ordered complete sets of etched illustrations for any of his most popular liturgical editions? This drawback, particularly for publishers of popular illustrated works with thousands of copies, could well have been known at the time. If this was the case, it would have represented an additional, important criterion, next to that of subject matter and considerations of the relative cost and speed of the execution of the plates, when determining which books were to be thus illustrated. If a high print run (or large number of reprints) was anticipated, etched illustrations were simply not a sensible choice.

Although the difference in the total number of impressions (of good or poor quality) that could be pulled from engravings and etchings in the later sixteenth century is not as great as one may have imagined – as many as 4,071 impressions of the engravings and 3,100–3,200 of the etchings – it was also not to be ignored. For, 1,000 extra impressions before the plates absolutely had to be replaced was still significant, particularly for profit-minded publishers like Plantin and Jan Moretus, who clearly endeavored to obtain as many impressions as possible from every plate, no matter how weak the result (as in figs. 5.3, 5.20, and 5.22). Moreover, if one places the 4,000 or so impressions of

5.22a Peeter vander Borcht?, *Christian Martyr*, from Justus Lipsius, *De cruce liber tres* (Antwerp: Jan Moretus I, 1606; 4°), p. 67, etching (state II), 108 × 57 (Antwerp, Museum Plantin-Moretus, A 573). See fig. 5.21 for the original state of this etching.

the engravings (made between 1596 and 1613) in the spectrum of what is known about the number of impressions that could be pulled from engravings used to illustrate the books of the *Officina Plantiniana* – 1,000 impressions per plate around 1574; 4,000 impressions per plate c.1596–1613; and more than 10,000 impressions in the course of the seventeenth century – the returns on being able to rework plates effectively and being able to pull ever more impressions from them were growing with time. It was a valuable advantage that buyers of intaglio plates at the time knew could not be achieved with etchings.[181]

[181] For the 1,000 print-per-plate estimate, see n. 1 above. For the even greater potential of the number of impressions that could be pulled from copper plates later on in the seventeenth century, see Bowen and Imhof 2005. For remarks concerning the importance that the plates be engraved and not etched for certain estimates of the number of impressions that could be pulled from them, see Bowen and Imhof 2005, p. 266.

5.22b Detail of smoke along left side. Compare with fig. 5.21b.

If one combines these results with those detailed above concerning the relative cost of etchings and engravings, it becomes clear that a dilemma would have arisen between saving money on the initial purchase of the intaglio plate and the degree to which the original image would last and the plate could be satisfactorily reworked to yield the greatest number of impressions possible. When were the savings on the cost of the initial plate and the time needed to complete it outweighed by the advantage of being able to reuse the original plate longer? Clearly, this depended in part on the expected run of the work in question. The greater the anticipated sales, the greater the concern for the number of serviceable impressions that would result from the original investment. These considerations must have been of primary concern for the Moretuses, as the number of copies of their popular texts that were illustrated with intaglio illustrations steadily grew, presumably as a result of an ever increasing demand for them.[182] Is it then so surprising that in the seventeenth century, the great century for the production of etchings throughout Europe, the Moretuses opted instead for engravings for the illustration of the vast majority of their publications?

---

[182] Evident in their production as a whole, the Moretuses' shift to producing ever more copies of illustrated texts with engraved illustrations is most readily documented among their liturgical editions (see, e.g., Imhof 1996a, p. 39 and table D, p. 181).

CONCLUSION

Although Plantin's shift to ordering etched illustrations for the majority of his new projects in the 1580s may initially appear to represent a single, consistent decision, it was actually probably the result of many diverse impulses. Indeed, the choice of etchings instead of engravings for the illustration of his first major publications bearing this medium – *La pompe funèbre* (1559), Sambucus's *Icones . . . medicorum, philosophorumque* (1574), and Gambara's collection of poems (1577) – may all well have been made by other individuals involved in the production of these works, namely, Hieronymus Cock, for the first, and the authors of the last two texts. When Plantin's own independent publications with etched illustrations first appeared around 1581–1582 with his new editions of Guicciardini's description of the Low Countries and the commemorative account of the state entry of the duke of Anjou into Antwerp, other considerations may have influenced him. There were, for example, visual precedents for the illustration of these types of texts with etchings and the advantage of the relative speed with which etchings could be made. By the late 1580s, however, when Plantin was illustrating a new series of religious texts – devotional works and instructive manuals on the Catholic faith – he was not subject to the expectations aroused by visual precedents and the wishes of associated authors or business partners. If anything, financial concerns and an ever decreasing pool of artists to choose from would have encouraged him to opt for staid etchings by his reliable designer-etcher, Peeter vander Borcht, instead of engravings. These were the very matters he expressed concern about in his correspondence from this period, as indicated at the beginning of this chapter. The question of cost must have been especially important given the generally difficult economic situation in Antwerp and other major cities in the southern Low Countries at this time, following the years of war and the resulting flight of people and capital. It must also have been of particular concern to Plantin, as his records suggest that he was trapped in an ever narrowing market for the sale of his illustrated editions. On the one hand, he had to cater to what his single greatest client, the Parisian bookseller Michel Sonnius, thought he could sell; and, on the other hand, Plantin had to consider what his diverse clients in the Low Countries could afford. As these buyers – and Sonnius in particular – were still interested in Plantin's editions with etched illustrations, one must assume that the medium itself was accepted as a viable alternative for book illustrations in these markets, at least.

Thus, while Plantin's movement toward etchings as book illustrations may have been instigated by other individuals and visual precedents, he probably continued the practice for additional reasons. Primary among these must have been the paucity of other viable alternatives – artists who were willing to make engravings for book illustrations at an affordable price – and the appeal of a less costly medium for the intaglio illustrations of his new, untried publications for a buying public that accepted, if not welcomed, this cheaper alternative. Etchings may, consequently, have offered Plantin the best means in troubled times to maintain his name in the luxury market for works with intaglio illustrations that he had entered so successfully in the 1570s. For these were not, by and large, artful etchings, but mundane, cheaper, quick-to-make replacements for engravings. This shift in medium was not reversed until the increased demand for works with intaglio illustrations exceeded the capacity of etchings to yield enough satisfactory impressions and other alternatives became available again. For the *Officina Plantiniana*, this moment arrived by the beginning of the seventeenth century when it became evident that well-made engravings could provide an ever increasing (and greater) number of serviceable impressions than etchings and when Theodoor Galle was prepared to have members of his workshop execute numerous book illustrations for Plantin's successors. While the distinguishing visual qualities of both etchings and engravings may also have played a role in these decisions – for example, in the preference given to etchings for landscape subjects and Jan-Baptist Houwaert's possible request for engravings by Jan Wierix for his publications – such cases remain the exceptions rather than the rule. For, much as one would like to clarify the choice of book illustrations on aesthetic grounds,[183] the evidence of Plantin's and his successors' movements between these two media suggests otherwise. Financial and practical considerations appear to have led the way.

[183] See, e.g., David Becker's remarks in his discussion of Gabriello Faerno's *Fabulae centum*, in Reed and Wallace 1989, cat. 37.

CHAPTER SIX

PLANTIN PRINTS FOR OTHERS' EDITIONS WITH INTAGLIOS

Veni Antverpiam, conveni Gallaeum qui prorsus negavit se nullum opus suscepturum cuius non esset absolute futurus dominus. (I went to Antwerp and met with Galle. He definitively declined [the offer] because he did not want to undertake any work over which he would not have full control in the future.)[1]

In the above excerpt, taken from a letter Plantin wrote to the Jesuit Michael Hernandez on May 28, 1586, Plantin reports back on Philips Galle's firm decision not to make the plates for the illustration of Jerome Nadal's *Evangelicae historiae imagines*. According to Plantin, it was simply a matter of who had control of the project and Galle not wanting to relinquish it. His observation thus appears to support Manfred Sellink's view that Galle "cherished his independence and tried to remain in control over all the work his studio produced."[2] Galle was not alone in this stance, as Plantin makes a similar remark regarding both him and Jan Sadeler I in a letter he wrote to the Jesuit Ludovico Tovardus on November 5, 1585, apparently concerning this same project: "Reliqui vero novitii vel Gallaeo vel Sadelero sunt obligati qui plures desiderant neque quicquam suscipere volunt quod apud se non maneat." (The other novices are bound to either Galle or Sadeler, who want more and are unwilling to take on any project that will not remain under them.)[3] And yet, when seeking to produce and publish works in which typographically printed text and engraved illustrations were combined, the desire to retain full control of the project – and, more to the point, the plates – had to be reconciled with the necessity of entering into some sort of cooperative arrangement in order to complete it. For practical and financial reasons that will be discussed at greater length below, the tasks of printing text and producing engraved or etched illustrations were usually led by different individuals working in separate locations. Consequently, the production of works in which the two media were combined required some degree

---

[1] *Corr.*, VII, no. 1106, p. 23.   [2] Sellink 1997, I, p. 11.

[3] *Corr.*, VII, no. 1044. For more on Galle, Sadeler, and other artists who similarly distanced themselves from making book illustrations, see ch. 2. For a detailed examination of Nadal's *Evangelicae historiae imagines*, see Wadell 1985. See also the ongoing translation of this text (Homann and Melion 2003).

of cooperation, negotiation, or simple (but also potentially significant) financial outlay in order to achieve the desired results. Moreover, in sixteenth- and early seventeenth-century Europe, the profession of "publisher" – the one responsible for overseeing the production and distribution of a work – was not so clearly defined, or practiced to the exclusion of other activities.[4] Indeed, the work that a typographical printer, a "pictorial printer," an engraver, and a publisher took on often merged. And while some might specialize in one task or the other, people also dabbled or even regularly engaged in other work that is too often regarded as distinct by definition. Thus, although one can examine the activities of a printer, printmaker, or publisher primarily from the perspective of the projects known to have been under his or her control – a view one is sometimes required to take, owing to a lack of other sources – the results would almost certainly be incomplete. They would lack a potential treasure trove of information that not only enriches but also corrects conventional views of the "great master." Thanks to the exceptionally wealthy stores of archival documents and typographical materials in the Plantin-Moretus Museum, we are able to provide this rarely documented, yet essential, supplementary perspective on Plantin.

Thus far, we have discussed cases in which Plantin was the one actively organizing and financing the production of texts with engraved or etched illustrations. In this chapter, we will turn the tables and consider publications in which Plantin printed the text, but neither owned the plates used to print the illustrations, nor assumed the sole, leading role in having the illustrated work produced. Amounting to fifty-two distinct publications, the vast majority of these projects were published by print publishers based in Antwerp.[5] The dominant person here was Philips Galle, who employed Plantin to work on twenty-nine projects between 1574 and 1589. Varying widely in their subject matter and in the disposition of text and illustrations, these publications consist of print series and maps with accompanying text, richly illustrated emblem books and pocket atlases, as well as verses and indulgences. Between 1585 and 1589, the print publisher Adriaen Huberti similarly engaged Plantin to print the text for at least seven of his publications. These range from Richard Verstegen's controversial book on Catholic martyrs to indulgences and verses. Another leading Antwerp print publisher, Gerard de Jode, appears to have employed Plantin to print three editions of moralizing, emblematic texts for him: one in 1579 and two in 1584. Even Plantin's favorite intaglio printer, Mynken Liefrinck, commissioned Plantin to print texts for some unspecified figures for her. The remaining illustrated projects on which Plantin worked were all published by independent authors who provided the plates. The leading figure here is Abraham Ortelius, the "father" of the modern atlas, for whom Plantin printed five editions of his *Theatrum orbis terrarum* and four editions of his *Additamentum* between 1579 and 1587. Beyond this body of work, only a few solitary publications remain, namely, maritime atlases, for which Plantin printed the texts in Leiden in 1584

---

[4] For discussions of the diversity of activities and arrangements in which "print publishers" were engaged in this period in both the Netherlands and Italy – the two main centers for the production of engravings and books illustrated with them at this time – see, e.g., Bury 2001, pp. 9–10 and 68; Orenstein 1996, pp. 12–13; and Van der Stock 1998, pp. 143–145.

[5] See appendix 5 for the full citation of or source for each of the projects cited.

and 1585 for Lucas Janszoon Waghenaer and for Albert Hayen, as well as a grand fable book Plantin printed for Etienne Perret in 1578.

We will focus initially on Plantin's richly documented working relationship with the print publisher Philips Galle. Because their dealings with one another were so extensive, we will break this study down into four main topics: (1) Plantin employing Galle (or members of his workshop) to engrave plates for Plantin's own projects; (2) Galle employing Plantin to print texts for his projects; (3) Galle and Plantin working together as co-publishers; and (4) Plantin's and Galle's supplementary business transactions. This analysis will provide a novel view of the surprisingly varied and overlapping working worlds of a letterpress printer and printmaker who were similarly interested in producing works in which typographically printed text and engraved or etched images were combined. We will then examine how the other projects in which Plantin was involved fit into the model of his and Galle's working world. Why did Plantin either enter into joint projects with print publishers or (as was the case for most of the publications that will be discussed) simply hire himself and his staff out for the printing of potentially competitive texts for third parties? The following examination of these diverse publications and the decisions that were made on a project-by-project basis will shed some light on this complex topic. For, as will become evident, while the issue of who controlled the project and who was the "hired hand" was of fundamental importance, it was not the only factor at play.

PLANTIN'S EMPLOYMENT OF GALLE AS AN ENGRAVER

Philips Galle was born around 1537 and began his career working in Haarlem. As early as 1557, however, he also periodically engraved prints that were then published by Hieronymus Cock in Antwerp. Galle appears to have moved to Antwerp either late in 1569 or early in 1570, some months prior to Cock's death in the latter year.[6] Galle and Plantin's earliest recorded business transaction dates to June 27, 1571, a year or more after the former's arrival in Antwerp. At this time, Plantin purchased "diverses protraictures [sic]" (various images) from Galle for 9 fl. 3$^{1}/_{2}$ st. Plantin then shipped them, together with other "protraictures" from Gerard de Jode and the widow of Hieronymus Cock, on July 3, 1571 to Georg Willer, a bookseller in Augsburg.[7]

Within a year of this initial purchase, however, Plantin had also engaged Galle to produce at least one, if not two engravings for the illustration of his books. Plantin thus began what would evolve into some eighteen years of mutual employment for the production of works in which engraved or etched illustrations were combined

---

[6] See appendix 1 for more on Galle. He was certainly in Antwerp by May 23, 1570, when he was present at the baptism of his godchild, Jeanne de Jode, the daughter of Gerard de Jode, another Antwerp printmaker and publisher (see Sellink 1997, I, p. 19). J. Denucé's suggestion that Galle was active in Antwerp as early as 1564 is based on an erroneously dated draft of a dedicatory text for his 1574 publication, *Fontium puteorumque iconicas delineationes* (see appendix 5).

[7] For Plantin's initial purchase of prints from Galle, see MPM Arch. 16, fol. 171 rht. For the subsequent shipment of these prints to G. Willer, see MPM Arch. 49, fol. 88r. Plantin's purchase of goods from Galle (and Galle's purchases from Plantin) will be discussed at greater length below. See ch. 2 for Plantin's activities as a dealer in prints.

with typographically printed text. One of the engravings Plantin commissioned from Galle is an image of the *Crucifixion* (see fig. 4.2), dated 1572 and designed by Maarten van Heemskerck, a Haarlem-based artist whose work Galle had engraved on several occasions before.[8] The other is an engraving of a shekel (see fig. 3.12) that is similarly signed by Galle and is datable to around 1572, when the book in which it was used, the eighth volume of Plantin's Polyglot Bible, was printed and illustrated.[9] We have not found records documenting Galle's production of either engraving for Plantin. However, Plantin's frequent reuse of the *Crucifixion* to mark the start of the canon in various *quarto* and folio missals that he published between 1572 and 1589 – including at least one reworked state of the plate in which Galle and Van Heemskerck's signatures were removed – suggests that he owned the plate and had full control over it.[10] As the engraving of the shekel is not listed individually in any of the inventories of Plantin's copper plates at the time of his death (see appendix 4), it seems less likely that he actually owned it. There are no known records of Plantin ever paying Galle for the delivery of such a plate and it alone of all of the plates included in the Polyglot Bible was never used again in any of the publications of the Plantin Press. Rather, an anonymous engraved copy of it was subsequently used together with other original engravings from the Polyglot Bible.[11] If anything, the lack of references to this engraving leaves open the possibility that Plantin may not have owned it, but may have borrowed it from Galle, as he did with other plates in Galle's possession.[12]

According to the most recent publications on Galle's production, these are the only engravings he made for the illustration of Plantin's books – or anyone else's, for that matter.[13] As Plantin's remark cited at the start of this chapter suggests, although Galle did provide Plantin with a couple of engravings early on in his career in Antwerp, he was not interested in devoting his or his workshop's time to producing book illustrations for third parties in general. Nevertheless, several payments to Galle noted in the Plantin archives indicate that Galle and/or members of his workshop did provide Plantin with fifty-five illustrations for a *Sanctorum kalendarii Romani . . imagines* and *Evangeliorum dominicalium summaria* that the latter published in 1580 (see fig. 6.3) and, in 1583, a map of the area over which the Antwerp magistrates had full judicial and administrative authority (see fig. 6.4).[14]

---

[8] See ch. 4 for more on this engraving. For Galle and van Heemskerck's working relationship, see Sellink 1997, I, pp. 17–19.

[9] See ch. 3 for more on this engraving.

[10] For the missals bearing this engraving, see PP 1676, 1678, 1685, 1690, 1695, and 1702. For a copy of the 1589 edition in which Galle and van Heemskerck's signatures were removed, along with the 1572 date (PP 1702), see MPM (O.B. 6.5), p. [260] (= fol. Z1 v). This state is not described in *New Holl., Galle*, 11, no. 171.

[11] See p. 334.

[12] See the discussion below of A. Barlandus's *Hollandiae comitum historia et icones* (Leiden: C. Plantin, 1584) (PP 625).

[13] See *New Holl., Galle*, IV, p. 255. All of these (except for the two used by Plantin) were either included in a compendium of prints (as with G. de Jode's "picture bible," the *Thesaurus sacrarum historiarum veteris testamenti*), or else they were independent prints that other publishers subsequently included in their books (as in the publications of Jan Philipsz. Schabaelje, for example).

[14] Literally, the title of the map reads: "Bescriivinge vande paelen der vriiheiit van Antwerpen," or "Description of the boundaries of the 'Vrijheid' [Freedom] of Antwerp." The term "Vrijheid van

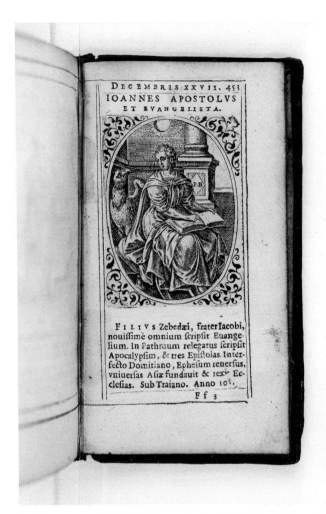

6.1 Anonymous artist after Peeter vander Borcht, *St. John the Evangelist*, from *Sanctorum kalendarii Romani . . . imagines* (Antwerp: Christopher Plantin, 1580; 24°), p. 453, engraving, c.57 × 38 (Antwerp, private collection).

Even though Plantin's 1580 editions of the *Sanctorum kalendarii Romani* and *Evangeliorum* were printed with independent title-pages, they were conceived of as a single large project.[15] Both works are essentially picture books with little accompanying text. While the *Sanctorum kalendarii Romani* features illustrations of saints and other subjects described in the New Testament that were celebrated on fixed days throughout the year, the *Evangeliorum* features scenes from the Life of Christ that are arranged and celebrated according to the movable liturgical calendar. All of the plates needed for the illustration of both of these books were, however, grouped together in a single listing

Antwerpen" refers to the legal freedoms enjoyed by those living in the areas defined as belonging to some cities or towns, in contrast with, e.g., a lord ruling over the people living on his property.

[15] See PP 865 and PP 1152, respectively, for these editions. As noted by Voet, Plantin's catalogue references to these texts also indicate that they were usually sold together, as a single unit (see the notes to PP 1152).

6.2 Paul Uten Waele after Peeter vander Borcht, St. John the Baptist, from *Sanctorum kalendarii Romani . . . imagines* (Antwerp: Christopher Plantin, 1580; 24°), p. 169, engraving, 58 × 39 (Antwerp, private collection). See fig. 4.24 where the same engraving is used to illustrate a mussial Plantin published in 1585.

of "275 Figuerckens Calendarii Romani" (275 small figures for the Calendarium Romanum) in an inventory of Plantin's copper plates.[16] This total (275) is only two more than the number of plates used for the illustration of Plantin's 1580 edition of these texts and probably reflects the reuse and redistribution of these and comparable plates for the illustration of other books.[17] The original set of plates can be grouped as follows: 207 new plates for the illustration of the *Sanctorum kalendarii Romani* (9 of which

---

[16] See appendix 4, p. 387.

[17] Plantin reprinted these texts in 1584 with a slightly modified series of illustrations (see PP 867 and PP 1153) and then reused some of the plates for other Plantin editions, such as his missals and books of hours (see ch. 4). Consequently, it is impossible to determine precisely which plates were among the 275 listed in the 1590 inventory.

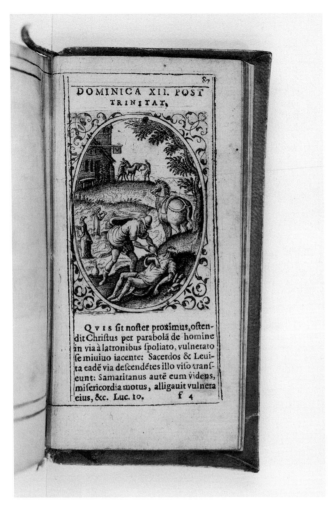

6.3 Philips Galle's workshop?, *Good Samaritan*, from *Evangeliorum dominicalium summaria* (Antwerp: Christopher Plantin, 1580; 24°), p. 87, engraving, c.57 × 38 (Antwerp, Museum Plantin-Moretus, B 2016).

were printed twice), 53 new plates for the *Evangeliorum*, and 13 old plates (2 of which were printed twice) that were originally designed, if not engraved, for the illustration of Plantin's books of hours. Thus, as with Plantin's other religious editions, while one might imagine that the illustrations for a new project would be uniform in their design and execution, this was not the case. Not only was there the common mix of old (see fig. 6.1) and new (see figs. 6.2 and 6.3) plates, but even among the latter illustrations that were, presumably, engraved specifically for the illustration of these books, inconsistency reigns. Many (but not all) bear the initials of the designer, Peeter vander Borcht and/or the engraver Paul Uten Waele (see fig. 6.2).[18] In addition, many, but not all, of the plates bear crudely inscribed dates, but even these do not consistently overlap

[18] See appendix 1 for more on these artists and their work for Plantin.

6.4 Philips Galle's workshop?, *Bescriivinge vande Paelen der vriiheiit van Antwerpen*, from *Rechten ende costumen van Antwerpen* (Antwerp: Christopher Plantin, 1582; f°), inserted following p. [392], engraving, 247 × 450 (Antwerp, Stadsbibliotheek, E 2927, ex. 2 [C2-514b]).

with those plates bearing either of these artists' signatures. The motley, "patched-up" impression left by the illustrations in this book is reinforced by the few payments made to Galle for this project. First, Plantin received fifty completed engravings from Galle in May 1579. Then in September 1580, nearly sixteen months later, Galle delivered an additional five engravings (executed by Galle's "homme" [man] – an assistant, perhaps) and at least seven (and possibly as many as twenty-seven) extra copper plates.[19] Galle appears to have been helping Plantin fill in the gaps in his supply of engravings for this project. But which plates did Galle deliver? Regrettably, this is difficult to determine, as no signatures or other inscriptions are present to help distinguish the groups of fifty and five engravings Galle delivered. Nevertheless, some of the engravings (see fig. 6.3) can be singled out as possible candidates for the Galle workshop plates owing to their notably distinctive design – a greater interest in portraying the scene in depth – and fine execution, when considered in comparison with the majority of the illustrations in these books.

The engraving of the legal boundaries of the city of Antwerp (fig. 6.4) is much easier to place. This map was included in a publication by the government of Antwerp, titled *Rechten, ende costumen van Antwerpen* (Rights and Customs of Antwerp), which was the result of several years of research compiling the common law of the city.[20] Although we will never know for certain why Plantin turned to Galle for the execution of this plate

---

[19] See appendix 1, under Galle, for transcriptions of these records.
[20] See PP 569 for a detailed description of the history of this publication and the arrangements made between Plantin and the Antwerp government for printing it. See MPM KP 68 E for the original copper plate.

and why Galle agreed to do so, it was a logical arrangement. For this elegant description of the area fits in with the latter's independent production of maps at this time.[21] Was Galle, once again, simply helping Plantin, who was, by this time, a close friend of his? Did the project just appeal to him, as one who was clearly interested in the production of maps? Or did someone else from the Antwerp government, for example, serve as an influential intermediary? While the last option is possible, given the active role the Antwerp government played as both author and distributor of this publication, Plantin was the one who paid for and retained the plate. Specifically, on April 28, 1583, he paid Galle 28 fl. "pour la platte des confines d'Anvers" (for the plate of the boundaries of Antwerp). Then, between April 5 and June 10, 1583, he paid Mynken Liefrinck 4 fl. 15 st. for printing "488 palen van Antwerpen tot 20 st." (488 boundaries of Antwerp at 20 st.), and on October 22, 1587 he paid her an extra 2¹/₂ st. for printing an additional "12 bladeren van palen van Antwerpen" (12 sheets of the boundaries of Antwerp).[22] These last two payments are particularly intriguing. According to Voet's account of Plantin's negotiations with the Antwerp government concerning the production of this publication, Plantin was forbidden to sell or distribute any copies of the text beyond those he printed for and delivered to the city government. While the number of copies was originally set at 300, Plantin was ultimately paid for delivering 400 copies of this text.[23] Thus, either Plantin sold as many as 100 extra independent impressions of Galle's map, or else he was distributing some 100 extra copies of the text on the sly.

Regardless of which were the determining factors behind the arrangements for both of these projects, Plantin did end up employing Galle (or members of his workshop) for the execution of book illustrations in both cases. Thus, despite Galle's evident desire to avoid executing engravings for someone else's publications, he could still be persuaded to do so. While we have only demonstrated this for Plantin's production, the possibility still exists that Galle (or members of his workshop) performed similar work for other printers whose production is not as well known.

GALLE HIRES PLANTIN TO PRINT TEXTS FOR HIS PROJECTS

Although Plantin clearly initiated business relations with Galle through his purchases of the latter's independent prints and commissions of plates for the illustration of his publications, it was Galle's subsequent hiring of Plantin for the printing of texts for his own publications that would prove to be the most common form of their mutual employment for the production of illustrated works. The concept of a letterpress printer being hired to print text for a third party was familiar enough. Plantin would certainly have been aware of the practice from his period of training in France, where independent printers were regularly hired by publishers to print texts for them.[24] And, as of 1555, the

---

[21] See Schilder, II (1993), pp. III–122, Denucé 1912–1913, I, pp. 221–260, and the discussion below of Galle's numerous editions of a pocket atlas derived from Abraham Ortelius's trend-setting *Theatrum orbis terrarum*.

[22] For these payments, see MPM Arch. 20, fol. 57 rht (for Galle), and fols. 186 rht and 288 rht (for the two payments to Liefrinck).

[23] See PP 569, nn. 1 and 3.   [24] See, e.g., Parent 1974, pp. 126–132.

very year that he established his own business printing and publishing books, Plantin was printing books for or together with other Antwerp printers.[25]

Galle began to produce illustrated works together with other printers soon after he had settled in Antwerp. As early as 1572, for example, he published the *Arcus aliquot triumphal. et monimenta . . . in honor . . . Jani Austria*, by the Hungarian humanist Joannes Sambucus. This is an illustrated series of allegories of triumph, composed in honor of Don Juan of Austria's victory over the Turks at Lepanto, Greece, in 1571.[26] But, despite having had some business contacts with Plantin by June 1571, as shown above, Galle did not employ him for the printing of this text, but rather, it seems, Gillis Coppens van Diest I (who had died by September 5, 1572) or his successor, Anthonis Coppens van Diest. For some of the decorative initials used in the accompanying text are identical to ones present in other earlier publications by Gillis Coppens van Diest.[27] The Coppens van Diest family was a logical choice for such work, as Gillis Coppens van Diest I regularly printed texts for other printer-publishers and authors. Moreover, he was also known for printing impressive works with engraved illustrations, like Abraham Ortelius's atlas, the *Theatrum orbis terrarum*, the first edition of which appeared in 1570. Following the death of Gillis Coppens van Diest I, Anthonis Coppens van Diest inherited his father's print shop and all the materials belonging to it. This fact is important because it is often the typographic materials used to print the texts accompanying Galle's publications that offer the only indication of which printer was responsible for this work. Although it is always possible that close copies of certain decorative letters existed and were used by other printers, the association of Anthonis Coppens van Diest with some of Galle's contemporary publications supports the tentative attribution of this and other publications to Anthonis (or Gillis I) Coppens van Diest as well.[28] Specifically, if one examines Manfred Sellink's list of Galle's most important publications from the period 1572–1575, Anthonis Coppens van Diest's name appears in the colophon of Galle's 1573 and 1574 editions of *Divinarum nuptiarum conventa et acta* and *Christi Jesu vitae admirabiliumque actionum speculum* – two series of devout emblematic engravings on forms of sacred matrimony and the *Life of Christ*, respectively. In addition, Galle's publication of ancient coins in the possession of Abraham Ortelius, his *Deorum dearumque capita* from 1573, bears distinctive decorative initials that duplicate ones found in texts printed by Gillis Coppens van Diest I.[29]

---

[25] For examples of such works from 1555, see G. M. Bruto, *La institutione di una fanciulla nata nobilmente* (PP 842), which Plantin printed for J. Bellerus in 1555, and P. Belon du Mans, *Les observations de plusieurs singularitez et choses memorables* (PP 637), which Plantin appears to have published jointly with J. Steelsius. For more on this topic in general, see Voet, GC, II, pp. 10–12.

[26] For this publication, see BT 4239, *New Holl.*, Galle, IV, R 24, and Sellink 1997, I, pp. 21 and 27.

[27] Specifically, the decorative 33 mm initial "T" marking the start of the introductory text on leaf C4r (see, e.g., MPM [A 1357]) is exactly the same as the "T" found on fol. D1r of Gemma Frisius's *De radio astronomico & geometrico liber*, which Gillis Coppens van Diest I printed in 1545 for Gregorius Bontius in Antwerp and Petrus Phalesius in Leuven (BT 1258; we examined a copy in MPM [R 34.9]). For more on the Coppens van Diest family of printers, see Rouzet 1975, pp. 45–46.

[28] For a more extensive discussion of the value of and difficulties with the analysis of typographical materials for the identification of printers, see the introductory remarks to appendix 5.

[29] For more on these editions, see appendix 5, under the 1580 edition of the *Divinarum nuptiarum conventa et acta* and the 1582 edition of the *Deorum dearumque capita*. For the attribution of the 1573 edition of the *Deorum dearumque capita* to Coppens van Diest, we examined a copy in MPM (R 12.2). Consider the 10 mm

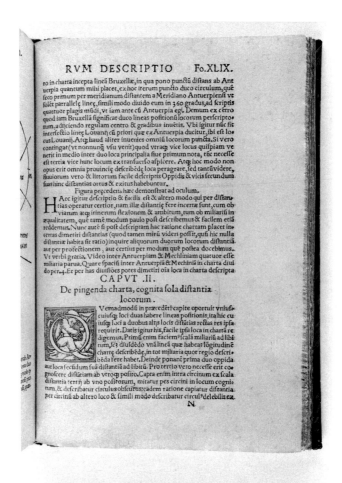

6.5 Letter "Q" from Petrus Apianus, *Cosmographia per Gemmam Phrysium* (Antwerp: Gillis Coppens van Diest I, 1540; 4°), fol. NIr, 29 × 29 (Antwerp, Museum Plantin-Moretus, A 3486). See fig. 6.6 for the same initial "Q" in a different publication.

The import of the identification of the typographical materials used is perhaps most significant in the case of Galle's renowned series of portraits of scholars, the *Virorum doctorum de disciplinis benemerentium effigies XLIIII*, originally published in 1572. As observed by Sellink, two versions of this series exist. These are most easily distinguished by the treatment of the verses engraved on to a selection of the plates that were actually old plates, which Galle had previously used for the illustration of another series of portraits,

italic "P" initial used to mark the start of the introduction to the reader (fol. Aiii r). This same initial is present in several publications by Gillis Coppens van Diest I, including Melchior Barlaeus, *De vetustissima Brabanticae gentis origine . . . libri V* (Antwerp: G. Coppens van Diest, 1562), fols. E7r and K8v (BT 252; we saw MPM [A 3008]); and Cornelius Grapheus, *La tresadmirable, tres magnificque . . . entrée du . . . Philipes . . . filz de . . . Charles V* (Antwerp: G. Coppens van Diest for P. Coecke van Aelst, 1550) (BT 1328; we saw MPM [A 2955]), fols. B1v and F4r.

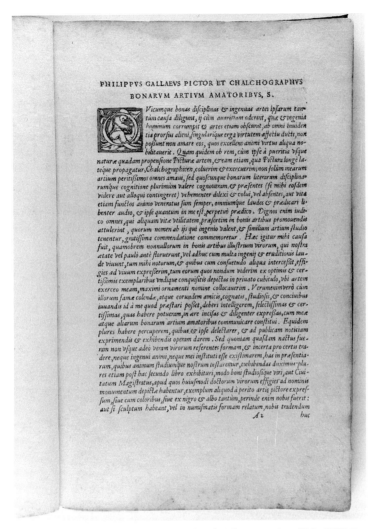

6.6 Letter "Q" from *Virorum doctorum de disciplinis benemerentium effigies XLIIII* (Antwerp: Gillis I or Anthonis Coppens van Diest for Philips Galle, [1572]; f°), fol. A2r, 29 × 29 (Antwerp, Museum Plantin-Moretus, 4–97). See fig. 6.5 for the same initial "Q" in another publication.

published in Haarlem around 1567.[30] In one version, the verses engraved on to the old plates were covered up with pieces of paper to allow for the printing (typographically) of new verses composed by Benito Arias Montano. In the other version, all of the old verses were removed and Arias Montano's verses were themselves engraved on to the plates. Attributing the printing of the text in both cases to Plantin, Sellink dates the former first and hypothesizes that the second version may have been printed around

---

[30] For Sellink's discussion of both the 1572 series and the original 1567 series, see Sellink 1997, II, appendix 2A (for the 1567 series) and 2B (for the 1572 series). See Arias Montano 2005 for a reprint of this text.

6.7 Letter "Q" from *Virorum doctorum de disciplinis benemerentium effigies XLIIII* (Antwerp: Christopher Plantin for Philips Galle, [1586]; f°), fol. Aij r, 39 × 39 (Antwerp, Museum Plantin-Moretus, Prentenkabinet: R 115).

the time that Galle's complementary "follow-up" series of portraits of learned men, his *Imagines L. doctorum virorum*, was published in 1587.[31]

A consideration of the typographical materials used to print these series in conjunction with archival evidence clarifies this situation. On the one hand, the decorative letters used to mark the introductory texts in the two versions of Galle's 1572 series indicate that, while Plantin did print the text for the second version, in which all of the verses were newly engraved, Gillis I or Anthonis Coppens van Diest saw to the printing of the text for the first version. Specifically, the 29 mm "Q" initial with a boy in the middle that appears in the original 1572 edition of this text is the same as that found

---

[31] For the 1587 series, see appendix 5.

in another text printed by Gillis Coppens van Diest in 1540 (compare figs. 6.5 and 6.6).[32] The 39 mm decorative "Q" initial present in the later issue (fig. 6.7) was, in contrast, part of a set of letters that Plantin frequently used. The decorative "P" that marks the start of the introductory text in Galle's complementary series of portraits from 1587 similarly comes from this same set.[33] On the other hand, archival records confirm Sellink's theory that Galle reissued the 1572 series with texts printed by Plantin close to the completion of his complementary series of portraits in 1587. According to Galle's accounts with Plantin, first Galle was charged 4 fl. 10 st. for the printing of "1 rame [ream] doctorum virorum" on July 3, 1586. Then, sometime between October 2, 1587 and April 13, 1588, the following charge was noted under Galle's accounts: "gedruckt int boeck vande geleerde de twee eerst bladeren 3 riemen tegen 2 gulden ... fl. 6" (printed in the book of the scholars, the two first sheets, 3 reams, at 2 guilders ... 6 fl.).[34] Given that the timing of the second record coincides perfectly with the dating of Franciscus Raphelengius I's introductory text to Galle's complementary series of portraits, this payment likely pertains to this edition, leaving the earlier one as a possible record of Plantin's reprinting of the texts for Galle's 1572 series.

Thus, while Plantin did not originally help Galle with the printing of texts, he did assume this role. This transition appears to have occurred in the course of 1574, the year in which Anthonis Coppens van Diest died. Like Coppens van Diest's work for Galle, Plantin's is attested to both by the appearance of his name on an assortment of Galle's editions as of 1575 – his *David, hoc est virtutis exercitatissimae probatum Deo spectaculum*, an exemplum of commendable behavior for contemporary rulers, for example[35] – and by the typographical materials used for additional, otherwise anonymously printed editions that Galle published as of 1574. For examples of the latter, consider Galle's *Fontium puteorumque iconicas delineationes*, or suite of "small wells," designed by Hans Vredeman de Vries, and his *Libellus varios regionum tractus continens*, a series of landscape etchings after Hans Bol. Both of these works bear decorative initials that were commonly used by Plantin.[36] Only in the case of Galle's 1572 portrait series of popes, *Pontificum maximorum XXVII effigies*, is the identity of the printer still uncertain. The dedicatory text to this work begins with a c.30 mm *criblé* letter "R," which we have been unable to link specifically with any printer. While this type of letter was not commonly used by

---

[32] We examined the following copies of the "1572" series, namely MPM (4–97), for the former, and MPM PK (R 115), for the latter. For the earlier use of the 29 mm "Q" initial by Gillis Coppens van Diest, see P. Apianus, *Cosmographia per Gemman Phrysium* (Antwerp: G. Coppens van Diest I for A. Birckman, 1540) (NK 126), fol. N1r. We examined the copy in MPM (A 3486). Who, precisely, was responsible for printing the texts for Galle's 1572 edition depends on when the texts were actually printed in relation to Gillis Coppens van Diest's death.

[33] For this set of 39 mm initials, see Harvard 1974, cat. 10. The woodblocks for both the "Q" and the "P" are also still preserved in the Plantin-Moretus Museum under MPM HB 12,254 and HB 12,252, respectively. We examined the following copies of Galle's 1587 portrait series: KBR (VB 13.266.1 RP) and MPM PK (R 115). Additional copies are listed in both *New Holl., Galle*, IV, p. 28, and Sellink 1997, II, p. 229.

[34] For the 1586 charge, see MPM Arch. 20, fol. 228 lft; for the 1587/1588 record, see MPM Arch. 20, fol. 307 lft. In fact, the printed text in the associated book appears on leaves A1r, A2r, and A2v, which, in a book in *quarto*, represents the recto and verso of the first sheet and not two separate sheets. Galle's editions with portraits of scholars are also discussed in appendix 5.

[35] See appendix 5 for many other such examples.

[36] See the discussion of both of these publications in appendix 5.

Plantin, Gillis Coppens van Diest I often included such letters in his publications.[37] Thus, it seems more likely that this text was printed by Coppens van Diest (or yet another printer) than by Plantin.

Once Plantin began to print texts for Galle in 1574, he continued to work regularly for him until he died some fifteen years later in 1589. As we have already observed, the resulting list of twenty-nine projects for which Plantin printed the text is varied. For in addition to the predictable (for a print publisher) print series and maps with accompanying texts, Galle also published pocket atlases, emblem books, and a catechism, as well as such mundane, smaller works as verses and indulgences. The following is an abbreviated list of these publications, each of which is described in greater detail in appendix 5.

> *Fontium puteorumque iconicas delineationes,* after Hans Vredeman de Vries (1574);
> *Libellus varios regionum tractus continens,* after Hans Bol (1574);
> *David, hoc est virtutis exercitatissimae probatum Deo spectaculum* (1575);
> B. Furmerius, *De rerum usu et abusu* (1575) (see fig. 6.11);
> Galle's pocket atlas, the "Epitome," with editions in 1577 (Dutch), 1579 (French) (see fig. 6.13), 1583 (French), 1583 (Dutch), 1585 (Latin), 1588 (French), and 1589 (Latin);
> text for an unspecified map (1578);
> M. Vosmerus, *Principes Hollandiae et Zelandiae, domini Frisiae* (1578) (see fig. 6.14), in addition to a French translation by Nicolas Clément de Trêles, published in 1583 and 1586;
> A. Freitagius, *Mythologia ethica, hoc est moralis philosophiae per fabulas brutis attributas traditae amoenissimum viridarium* (1579) (see fig. 6.22);
> text for a map of Maastricht (1579);
> text for a map of France (1579);
> unspecified typographic work (1579);
> *Divinarum nuptiarum conventa et acta* (1580);
> *Deorum dearumque capita . . . ex musaeo Abrahami Ortelii* (1582);
> *Prosopographia sive virtutum, animi, corporis . . . delineatio* (c.1585–90);
> *Virorum doctorum de disciplinis benemerentium effigies XLIIII* (1586) (see fig. 6.7);
> verses (unspecified) (1586);
> *Imagines L. doctorum virorum* (1587);
> *D. Seraphici Francisci totius evangelicae perfectionis exemplaris, admiranda historia* (1588);
> indulgences (1588);
> P. Canisius, *Institutiones christianae seu parvus catechismus catholicorum* (1589) (see fig. 6.12);
> P. Galle, *Instruction et fondements de bien pourtraire* (1589).

---

[37] See Harvard 1974, cat. 44, for the only woodblocks that Plantin is known to have had with *criblé* letters (i.e., a white initial set against a black ground that is speckled with white dots and potentially other fine forms). Of these, only the 18 mm letters "N" and "P" are known to have been used in two of Plantin's publications, both dating from 1571. For references to Galle's series of popes, see BT 1214 and Sellink 1997, II, appendix 2F. We examined a copy in KBR (VH 9080 A RP).

The above represent all but one of Galle's known publications with letterpress from the period 1575–1589.[38] While all of these editions – except the 1575 publication of Furmerius's *De rerum usu et abusu* – bear Galle's name, Plantin's name was not consistently included.[39] Although it is impossible to determine whether this was Plantin's or Galle's decision, there is a logical pattern for when Plantin's name appears. The critical factor seems to have been the degree to which the engravings and the letterpress were integrated. In all of the publications where the engraved illustrations were printed adjacent to or in combination with letterpress text and, consequently, resembled an illustrated book, Plantin is cited as the printer of the text on the title-page.[40] In those publications in which the typographical work was limited to a brief introductory text and the illustrations appeared more as an appended series of prints, Plantin's name generally does not appear at all. The main lacunae in these observations are Galle's publications of single maps, verses, and indulgences with letterpress printed by Plantin, for which there are no known copies. While it is tempting to associate these with Galle's "print series" publications (and assume that Plantin's name would not have appeared on them), that remains pure, tentative speculation, particularly for the single maps, as Plantin was clearly interested in publishing collections of maps and selling individual ones.[41]

Having established what Plantin did and did not print for Galle, it is important to note that his decision to buy copies of one of Galle's publications was not consistently related to whether or not his name actually appeared on it, or even if he had printed it. On the one hand, it is true that Plantin regularly bought back copies of Galle's publications that bear his name. However, he also bought back copies of works that he had printed anonymously for Galle, as well as copies of publications that Anthonis Coppens van Diest had printed for Galle. For example, although his name does not appear on Galle's 1586 reissue of his 1572 series the *Virorum doctorum ... effigies*, or on the 1587 publication *Imagines L. doctorum virorum*, Plantin continued to buy copies of these series into 1588.[42] Similarly, among the works he did not print for Galle, Plantin occasionally bought copies of his portraits of popes, Sambucus's *Arcus aliquot triumphal. et monimenta*, and Ortelius's *Deorum dearumque capita*, while he regularly bought copies of Galle's original 1572 edition of the *Virorum doctorum ... effigies* and the *Divinarum nuptiarum conventa et acta*. Each of these editions was included in Plantin's own list of Galle's publications, which also reveals what most of these editions cost, namely, 9 st. for Sambucus's text, 16 or 18 st. for Ortelius's, 16 st. for the *Virorum doctorum ... effigies*, and 35 st. for the *Divinarum nuptiarum conventa et acta*, or roughly one to three days' work for masons working in Antwerp then.[43] On the other hand, printing the text for someone else's publication did

---

38 The one exception, Galle's 1578 publication *Esbatement moral des animaux* (translated by Pieter Heyns), was printed for him by the Antwerp printer Gerard Smits (BT 8489). This work is discussed in greater detail below.

39 Plantin's original Latin edition of Furmerius's *De rerum usu et abusu* and his 1585 Dutch translation of it (see PP 1228–1229) are discussed in greater detail below.

40 These works are *David, hoc est virtutis*, Furmerius's *De rerum usu et abusu*, all of the editions of Galle's pocket atlas, the three editions of Vosmerus's account of the counts of Holland and Zeeland, the *Mythologia ethica*, and Canisius's catechism.

41 See Denucé 1912–1913, *passim*.   42 See below and in appendix 5 for examples of these sales.

43 See MPM M 296, fol. 388r (fig. 6.8) for this list. See below for a sample of contemporary wages for day-laborers to compare with these prices. For examples of Plantin's purchases of these publications in

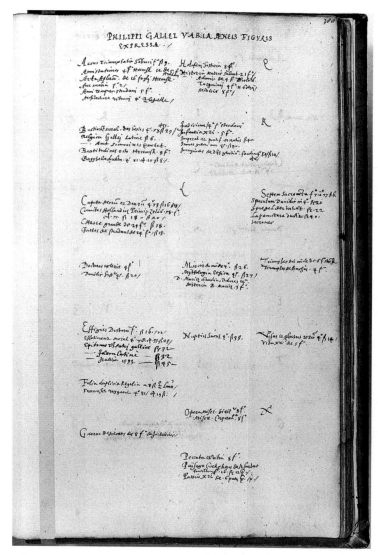

6.8 Christopher Plantin's list of Philips Galle's publications, which Plantin had for sale (Antwerp, Museum Plantin-Moretus, M 296, fol. 388r).

not automatically imply, by association, a certain professional commitment to it. For, excluding the portrait series of popes and scholars noted above, there are no records indicating that Plantin purchased copies of Galle's other independent print series for which he had printed a brief introductory text – like the Bol landscapes or Vredeman de Vries's images of wells. Similarly, even though his name does appear on the title-page of Galle's 1580 edition of the *Divinarum nuptiarum conventa et acta*, Plantin rarely bought

the early 1570s, see, e.g., MPM Arch. 16, fol. 171 rht (for the *Virorum doctorum*, series of popes, and Sambucus's text); MPM Arch. 16, fol. 172 rht (for the *Divinarum nuptiarum*); and MPM Arch. 18, fol. 64 rht (for the *Deorum dearumque capita*).

a copy.[44] Plantin clearly stuck by his own independent assessment of what he did and did not want to sell.

Given that Galle employed Plantin so consistently as of 1575 – at least for his better-known publications – one must assume that Galle was generally satisfied with these arrangements. But how much did such work cost? We do not always know how much Plantin charged for particular jobs – for Bol's landscapes and Vredeman de Vries's series of wells, for example. Nor do we know how he calculated each sum – occasionally, as with the unspecified work he did for Galle in 1579, only a total amount is noted. Nevertheless, there are enough similar examples to establish what Plantin's standard fees were in two distinct blocks of time (1575–1579 and 1584–1589) and to determine what the exceptions to these general rules were.

The first known record of Plantin's fees for printing texts for Galle is recorded in his summary of the production costs for the 1575 edition of Furmerius's *De rerum usu et abusu* (see figs. 6.9 and 6.10). Here, the costs for the composition and printing of the text were calculated at 18 st. per ream, or 500 sheets of paper.[45] Plantin similarly charged 18 st. per ream for printing the text for Galle's first edition of his pocket atlas in 1577. He charged slightly more (20 st. per ream) for the printing of Galle's first edition of Vosmerus's account of the counts of Holland and Zeeland in 1577 and for the 1580 edition of his *Divinarum nuptiarum conventa et acta*.[46] Only the costs for the printing of Galle's first French edition of his pocket atlas and for the text for the map of Maastricht (both completed in 1579) were significantly higher, at 30 st. per ream and 70 st. per ream, respectively.[47] It is not clear why Plantin would have charged so much more for these two projects. Perhaps, at least in the case of the map of Maastricht, the setting of the text was exceptionally complicated.

In the period 1584–1589, the most common rate that Plantin charged for the setting and printing of texts was 40 st. per ream – twice as much as he had charged five to ten years earlier.[48] In order to put this shift in some sort of perspective, we compared these rates with the daily summer wage paid to skilled and unskilled masons who were, along with Plantin's compositors and pressmen, among the better paid day-laborers in Antwerp in this period.[49] Between 1575 and 1584–1589, the daily summer wages paid to an unskilled mason had increased from 8 st. in 1575 to 12 st. in 1584 (where it would remain for most years until 1589) – an increase of 50 percent. The wages paid to a skilled mason had similarly risen approximately 50 percent in the same period: starting at 12 st. in 1575 and rising to 20 st. in the years 1580–1584, these wages would go back down to 18 st. for the rest of the 1580s. Thus, Plantin's printing fees increased twice as much as the wages paid to Antwerp's better-paid day-laborers in the same

---

44 Plantin's purchase of this work is discussed in appendix 5.
45 See MPM Arch. 18, fol. 143 lft, under April 13, 1575.
46 For these printing rates, see MPM Arch. 18, fol. 253 lft, under November 9, 1577, for both the work on the atlas and Vosmerus's text; and fol. 282 lft, in May 1579, for the work on the *Divinarum nuptiarum*.
47 See MPM Arch. 18, fol. 282 lft, in May 1579, for both of these charges.
48 For examples of this, see MPM Arch. 20, fol. 146 lft, under August 31, 1584 (accounts for Galle's pocket atlas in Latin); fol. 307 lft (work on indulgences, Galle's 1587 edition of portraits of scholars, and the texts for the print series on St. Francis, all recorded between October 2, 1587 and April 13, 1588); and fol. 356 lft (for the printing of Canisius's catechism in May 1589).
49 For this assessment, see Scholliers 1976, p. 162.

period. This suggests that Plantin's increase in fees did not simply reflect general wage increases in Antwerp. Was he trying to price himself beyond the routine performance of such work, or had he incorporated some "added value" as well. Indeed, his 40 st.-per-ream fee was actually at the low end of the charges he entered into Galle's accounts for setting and printing text in the period 1584–1589. In July 1586 he charged Galle 85 st. per ream for the printing of the second French edition of Vosmerus's text – more than four times what Plantin had charged for the printing of the original Dutch edition in 1577. Immediately thereafter, Galle was charged 90 st. for the printing of just one ream of text for his 1586 reissue of the 1572 publication *Virorum doctorum . . . effigies*.[50]

How significant were the resulting sums that Galle had to pay Plantin for his part in the production of these editions?[51] Ranging from 3, 6, or 7 fl. to as much as 48 fl. (for the 1584 Latin edition of Galle's pocket atlas), the smaller amounts would have been the equivalent of a few copies of such illustrated works as Galle's pocket atlas, or his *Mythologia ethica* – clearly not that significant in the grand scheme of Plantin's business concerns. But even the occasional larger amounts that Galle had to pay – ranging from 19 to 48 fl. – were still just a drop in a bucket when considered in comparison with the sums that Plantin paid Galle on an annual basis for maps and print series or, as will be detailed below, to compensate Galle for his part in one of their joint ventures. Thus, simple financial gain could not have been Plantin's primary incentive when serving as the hired hand for Galle's productions. Thus, in order to gain a better understanding of the potential motives for Plantin to engage in such work, we need to examine his working relationship with Galle in greater detail and reconsider the issues of who invested in a project, who maintained the control over it, and who profited from the distribution of the resulting works.

PLANTIN AND GALLE'S EVER VARYING WORKING RELATIONSHIP: SHARING CONTROL OF A PROJECT

While most of the twenty-nine works listed above constituted simple cases of a print publisher hiring a printer to work for him, five do not, as they represent, rather, carefully worked out cooperative arrangements in which the control over the project was shared. The two best-known examples of Plantin and Galle's "joint ventures" are their 1575 edition of Bernardus Furmerius's *De rerum usu et abusu* (PP 1228; fig. 6.11) and their 1589 edition of Petrus Canisius's *Institutiones christianae, seu parvus catechismus catholicorum* (PP 884; fig. 6.12). While the former was published soon after Plantin had begun to print texts for Galle, the latter was completed shortly before Plantin's death. A comparison of the arrangements made for these two publications reveals what was essential for both projects, namely, who provided and who retained the plates used for the illustrations.

Illustrated with twenty-five engravings, executed at least in part by Jan Wierix, Furmerius's *De rerum usu et abusu* was a moralizing text on justice and injustice, set

---

[50] See MPM Arch. 20, fol. 228 lft, under July 3, 1586.
[51] Whenever known, the final amount Plantin charged for the printing of a particular text is noted in the discussion of that work in appendix 5.

in the form of an emblem book.[52] Although only Plantin's name appears on the title-page of this work, his accounts with Galle make it clear that they shared the costs of producing the book and the resulting copies equally.[53] The accounts for the production of it were begun on April 13, 1575. What Plantin contributed (or paid out) was recorded on the left, the "debit" side under Galle's name (fig. 6.9), while what Galle contributed (or paid for) was recorded on the right, the "credit" side under Galle's name (fig. 6.10). Because this was a joint project in which all of the costs were to be shared, the two columns, left and right, had to be equated. Apparently, the original arrangement was a logical one in which Galle provided the plates, printed them, and had the text engraved on to the title-page vignette, while Plantin provided the paper and saw to the printing of the text. Thus, the following sums were noted on Galle's side of the costs (the right side; fig. 6.10):

[under April 13, 1575]

156 fl.   For the twenty-six illustrations of this book (= the twenty-five text illustrations and the title-page vignette), at 6 fl. per plate.

26 fl.   5 st.   For printing the illustrations, at 15 st. per hundred sheets, where a total of 3,500 sheets were printed.

5 st.   For engraving the letters on the title-page vignette.

182 fl. 10 st.   Total of these three items.

[under July 30, 1575]

31 fl. 10 st.   For printing an additional 3,500 impressions of the illustrations, now at 18 st. per hundred sheets.

5 st.   For (re-engraving?) the letters on the title-page vignette.

31 fl. 15 st.   Total of these two items.

In addition, Galle's periodic deliveries of illustrated copies to Plantin were also noted here. Dating from March 17, 1575 to June 25, 1576, these amounted to 265 copies, 17 of which Plantin returned to Galle on July 30, 1576, leaving Plantin with 248 of the 500 copies that comprised the entire edition (as indicated immediately below this tally of copies).

In Leon Voet's presentation of this data, he asserts that the 6 fl. charged per plate (noted above) was "very likely half of their price."[54] This seems unlikely to us for two reasons. First, the whole system of Plantin noting his and Galle's cost separately and then equalizing them at the end would not work if half of the cost of having the plates made was deducted in advance from one side, while, for example, the full cost of the paper needed to print the entire edition was noted on the other (see below). Second, the few known records of what Jan Wierix was paid for engravings made for Plantin's projects between c.1570 and c.1582 indicate that he received a comparable wage of 6, 7,

---

[52] See the discussion of this work in appendix 5 for more on the authorship of the text and the illustrations.
[53] See MPM Arch. 18, fol. 143 lft and rht (figs. 6.9 and 6.10), for these records.
[54] PP 1228, n. 2.

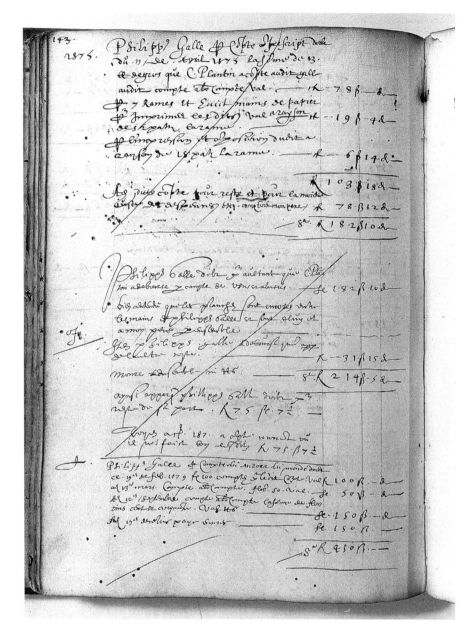

6.9 Costs for the production of Bernardus Furmerius's *De rerum usu et abusu* (Antwerp: Christopher Plantin and Philips Galle, 1575), debit side (Antwerp, Museum Plantin-Moretus, Arch. 18, fol. 143 lft).

or 8 fl. for engravings of a similar size.[55] The two records concerning the printing of the illustrations – each for a total of 3,500 illustrated "fueilles" (*sic*) (sheets) most

[55] Consider, for example, the following payments noted in M-H *Wierix*, 111.2: document no. 13: a payment of 8 fl. for an engraving of "unes nopes" = the *Marriage at Cana* (M-H 2194), noted under October 20, 1570; document no. 21: a payment of 6 fl. for an engraving of "Dominus palmarum" = *Christ's Entry into Jerusalem* (M-H 2198), noted under April 4, 1570; and document no. 35, a payment of 7 fl. for "la derniere figure en cuivre pour le livre de Houwaert" (the last figure in copper for Houwaert's book [the 1583

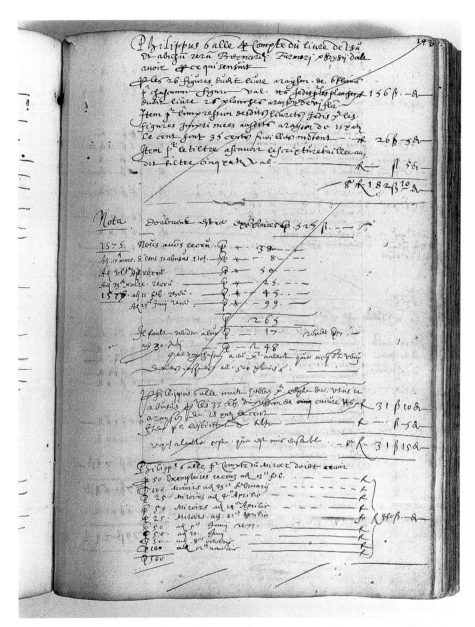

6.10 Costs for the production of Bernardus Furmerius's *De rerum usu et abusu* (Antwerp: Christopher Plantin and Philips Galle, 1575), credit side (Antwerp, Museum Plantin-Moretus, Arch. 18, fol. 143 rht).

likely represent the costs for printing the illustrations in two groups of 250 copies: one completed *c*. April 13, 1575 and the other completed *c*. July 30, 1575. For each book was

publication *Pegasides pleyn ende den lust-hof der maeghden*]) (see M-H 2315–2330 and PP 1412; this book is discussed in greater detail in ch. 5). The first two engravings noted are approximately 115 × 74 mm and those in Jean-Baptist Houwaert's publication are approximately 152 × 110 mm, while those in Furmerius's work are approximately 109 × 102 mm.

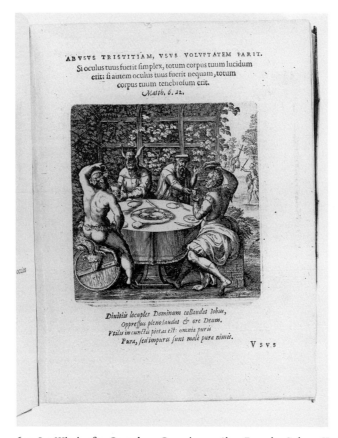

6.11 Jan Wierix after Gerard van Groeningen, *Abuse Engenders Sadness, Use Brings Forth Joy*, from Bernardus Furmerius, *De rerum usu et abusu* (Antwerp: Christopher Plantin and Philips Galle, 1575; 4°), p. 7, engraving, 110 × 105 (Antwerp, Museum Plantin-Moretus, R 55.18).

made up of seven sheets of paper, with two engravings printed on each side of each sheet. Thus, if the cost of printing the illustrations was calculated on the basis of the number of times a sheet of paper went through a press for the addition of illustrations, seven sheets run through the press twice (once for each side) for 250 copies comes to 3,500 impressions of these sheets. We do not know why there are two separate payments for the (engraving of?) letters for the title-page, unless either too little was noted the first time, or else the letters had to be re-engraved.

On Plantin's side of the costs (the left side; fig. 6.9), the following sums were recorded:

[under April 13, 1575]

78 fl.　　　 A cash advance from Plantin to Galle for the balancing of the accounts.

19 fl. 4 st.　 For seven reams and eight quires of paper, needed for printing at least 500 copies of the book, at 52 st. per ream.

6 fl. 14 st.　 For the composition and printing of the text, at 18 st. per ream.

103 fl. 18 st. Total of these three items.

78 fl. 12 st. An extra amount of cash paid to balance the accounts with Galle for the production of this book.

182 fl. 10 st. New total cost of the project to Plantin, which now equals the total cost to Galle noted on the right side under April 13, 1575.

31 fl. 15 st. Cash compensation for Galle for the extra costs noted on his side of the accounts under July 30, 1575 for the printing of the second group of 3,500 sheets of illustrations and for (re-engraving?) the text on the title-page.

The final sum noted among Plantin's outlays, 75 fl. 7½ st., "que Philippus Galle doibt pour reste de sa part" (what Philips Galle must [have] for the remainder of his share) has no counterpart on the right side of Galle's accounts. This was, in fact, noted a couple of years later, between June 20 and July 31, 1577, on another page of Galle's and Plantin's accounts, with a reference back to this page, the original summary of their accounts for the production of this book.[56] There is no indication on either page, however, of what this large sum was for. It is all the more perplexing because all of the costs for the original project appear to have been settled in July 1575 and work on the next edition of this text – a Dutch edition published in Leiden in 1585 – was probably not yet underway.[57] The answer to this puzzle may lie in the change in location (and ownership) of the plates between 1575 and 1590.

On Plantin's side of the accounts (the left side), the following was noted once the initial balancing of accounts had been completed on or shortly after April 13, 1575 and prior to the final balancing in July 1575, once Galle had completed the illustration of the second set of copies: "bien entendu que les planches sont encores entre les mains de Philippus Galle et sont de luy et a mon pere p[ar?] ensemble" (note that the plates are still in the possession of Philips Galle and belong to both him and my father [i.e., Plantin]). Thus, while the plates were officially their joint property, physically they could only be in one place and at this time – the spring or early summer of 1575 – Galle had them. In 1590, however, when inventories of Plantin's possessions in both Antwerp and Leiden were written up for the final settlement of his estate, the following entry was made in the list of plates at the Leiden branch of the Plantin Press: "26 Usus et abusus rerum."[58] It is not surprising to find the plates listed among Plantin's belongings in Leiden, for the last work to be illustrated with them at the Plantin Press was the 1585 Dutch edition of the text mentioned above, although it should be noted that the illustrations were clearly printed separately, together with the old accompanying Latin verses, and were added only to some copies. Thus, the plates could have been printed anywhere – it is not known where or by whom – and then appended, as desired, to the separately printed texts. But, regardless of where the plates were actually printed, the question remains: what was done about Galle's joint ownership of them? For all

[56] See MPM Arch. 18, fol. 187 lft, for the notation of this sum in the summer of 1577.

[57] See PP 1229 for the 1585 Dutch edition, which appeared under both the original Latin title and the Dutch title, *Recht ghebruyck ende misbruyck*. We will discuss this edition below.

[58] MPM Arch. 99, fol. 33, transcribed in appendix 4. These plates would ultimately be sold by Franciscus Raphelengius II sometime after May 12, 1602, when he offered to return them to Jan Moretus I, along with others that had once belonged to Plantin (see MPM Arch. 92, p. 141). Hereafter, the plates would be reused a few times between 1609 and 1620 for new editions of this text published in Arnhem and in Amsterdam (*New Holl.*, G. van Groeningen, II, p. 24).

of the archival records pertaining to the printing and sale of the 1585 Dutch edition suggest that Galle had nothing to do with it. There are no records indicating that there was a similar cooperative arrangement, as was undertaken for the 1575 Latin edition of the text, and no records of Galle being paid either to print the illustrations for the 1585 edition or for delivering completed copies. Rather, it is Galle who occasionally purchased copies of the text from Plantin following its publication.[59] Is it not possible, then, that Plantin's unilateral, large payment of 75 fl. 7½ st. to Galle in June or July 1577 for something related to the original 1575 project was actually a record of him buying up Galle's share in the plates? Recalling that the plates originally cost 156 fl. when new, the 75 fl. 7½ st. was only 5 fl. 5 st. less than half of the original amount. It may have been accepted as a reasonable compromise for plates that had been used once and were, hence, less valuable in terms of the number of impressions that could still be made from them.

Thus, what began as a joint project, with all of the original production costs, the resulting copies, and the plates being shared equally, ended up (in the following edition) being a project in which Plantin bore all of the costs, had sole possession of the plates, and was free to gain all of the possible benefits from sales. But, as the examination of Plantin and Galle's subsequent joint projects will show, this was not a model for their cooperative arrangements, but rather just one of several forms that they could take.

Plantin and Galle's other well-known cooperative venture in which they shared the costs and the resulting copies equally is their 1589 edition of Petrus Canisius's *Institutiones christianae, seu parvus catechismus catholicorum* (fig. 6.12). Although associated with Canisius, this work was essentially only a pictorial embodiment of Canisius's catechism.[60] Featuring 101 etched illustrations (two of which were printed twice), there was little typographical text to divert one from the images. In May 1589, Galle and Plantin made the following contributions to the production of this edition:[61]

Plantin:

252 fl. 10 st.	For 101 illustrations, at 2 fl. 10 st. per plate.
13 fl. 10 st.	For the copper, including having it cleaned, etc.
48 fl.	For the printing of twenty-four reams of the text, at 2 fl. per ream.
314 fl.	Total of costs thus far.

Galle:

45 fl. 12 st.	For twenty-four reams of paper that Galle provided, marked with a "P," at 38 st. per ream.
15 fl.	For reworking the illustrations with a burin.

---

[59] See, e.g., MPM Arch. 20, fol. 228 lft, for Galle's purchase of three copies of the "Recht gebruyck ende misbryck" on February 11, 1586. Galle also bought copies of the "Usus et abusus" in 1586 and 1587 (see MPM Arch. 20, fol. 228 lft), but it is not clear whether these were old copies of the 1575 Latin edition, or copies of the new Dutch edition, noted under the Latin title.

[60] See pp. 97 and 113, for the same etching of Joab killing his cousin Amasa, and pp. 59 and 107, for the same etching of Cain killing Abel. For a recent examination of this work in comparison with another of Canisius's catechisms, see Dael 2004.

[61] See MPM Arch. 20, fol. 356 lft (for Plantin) and rht (for Galle), for these accounts.

6.12 Peeter vander Borcht, *Crossing of the Red Sea*, from Petrus Canisius, *Institutiones christianae, seu parvus catechismus catholicorum* (Antwerp: Christopher Plantin and Philips Galle, 1589; 8°), p. 109, etching, 80 × 70 (Antwerp, Museum Plantin-Moretus, A 1400).

275 fl.   For the printing of 11,000 sheets of illustrations, at 2 fl. 10 st. per hundred sheets.

335 fl. 12 st. Total of costs thus far.

Plantin's illness and death a few months later apparently complicated the conclusion of these accounts, for it was not until January 2, 1590 that Jan Moretus I advanced Galle the difference between the initial totals noted above, namely 21 fl. 12 st. Matters were not settled definitively until May 1590, however, when Jan Moretus paid Galle an extra 12 fl. 10 st. for printing the illustrations for an additional twenty-six copies.[62] But what of the plates? Even though it was Plantin who had provided the plates for this project, it appears that Galle stored them, once again. For the following was noted in 1590 in one of the numerous lists of outstanding debts and debts paid, which were compiled for

[62] Both of these concluding payments are noted in MPM Arch. 21, fol. 34 rht.

the settlement of Plantin's estate: "pour les 50 figures du Catechismus que Philippus Galle a entre ses mains estimes a fl. 25 st." (for the 50 figures of the catechism that Philips Galle has possession of, estimated at 25 fl. [or 10 st. per plate]).[63] Only 50 of the 101 plates Plantin had originally provided are listed, most likely because the goal of this document was to establish the value of all of Plantin's possessions. As Plantin and Galle were sharing the costs (and possession) of all parts of this project, Galle was entitled to the value of the other 50 (and one half) plates. Given that the original 101 plates had cost 252 fl. 10 st. (or 50 st. per plate) when new, it is clear that they had decreased significantly in their value following the illustration of the approximately 876 copies printed of this one book. Whether this was owing to the medium – etchings instead of the usual engravings – or the circumstances – making bulk estimates of plates for the settlement of Plantin's estate – is impossible to determine on the basis of this information alone. However, the use of etchings instead of engravings was probably at least a contributing factor. For, as is discussed in chapter 5, etchings were much more susceptible to wear than engravings and appear to have produced fewer useful impressions. Indeed, as is documented in chapter 5, a run of around 875 copies was on the high end for Plantin's editions with etched illustrations from the later 1580s. This valuation of fifty of these plates is the last known reference to them. They do not appear to have been used again by either the Moretuses or the Galles and there are no clear references to them in later inventories of their respective stocks of plates.[64]

Despite these last uncertainties concerning the final valuation and "resting place" of the plates used for this book, the information presented here remains highly instructive, particularly when compared with what is known about Plantin and Galle's first joint venture. Both projects share some predictable, profession-ordained divisions of labor, namely, Plantin saw to the printing of the text while Galle saw to the printing of the illustrations. Beyond these two elements, however, the precise division of the work – or, perhaps more to the point, the division of the costs – varied, particularly in terms of who was responsible for providing the paper and who was responsible for providing the plates – the two greatest costs in any project with intaglio illustrations. Although we do not know how the precise allotment of tasks was made in each case, these two examples suggest that the two most significant expenditures, the acquisition of the paper and the plates, were balanced against one another, perhaps in the hope of minimizing the amount of cash that would have to be exchanged in the final balancing of the accounts. Perhaps simply the one with the best contacts with the artist needed to make the plates took on this responsibility; obtaining the plates could not have been a goal in itself. For, regardless of who actually provided them, in both cases, Plantin and Galle shared the rights to (and value of) the plates equally, even though Galle, alone,

[63] MPM Arch. 99, p. 123.
[64] For later inventories of the Moretuses' copper plates, see MPM Arch. 124. For a transcription of the inventory of the plates in the possession of Philips Galle's daughter-in-law, Catharina Moerentorff (Plantin's granddaughter), the wife of Galle's successor, his son Theodoor Galle, at the time of her death in 1636, see Duverger, IV (1989), no. 893, pp. 18–24; and Denucé 1927, pp. 1–16. The only possible allusion to the catechism plates in this inventory is, for example, a general reference to "Drijhondert vyffendertich heel cleijn plaetkens" (335 very small plates) (Duverger, IV [1989], p. 22).

6.13 Anonymous artist, *The Bishopric of Salzburg*, from Pieter Heyns, *Le miroir du monde* (Antwerp: Christopher Plantin for Philips Galle, 1579; oblong 8°), p. 22, map no. 28, etching, c.78 × 107 (Antwerp, Stadsbibliotheek, 10122). See fig. 6.17 for Ortelius's original, larger map of this area.

stored them. In the case of the 1575 edition of Furmerius's *De rerum usu et abusu*, Galle, despite having arranged to have the plates made, evidently decided to relinquish his right to them, perhaps, for the considerable sum of 75 fl. 7¹/₂ st. In the case of their 1589 edition of Canisius's catechism, the timing of Plantin's death and subsequent prolonged negotiations over the division of his estate may have helped determine the fate of those plates. Evidently plates that no one found worth using again, they were still shared fifty-fifty by the two families when last mentioned in the Plantin archives, but were left de facto in Galle's possession.

The last three projects for which Plantin and Galle had a special cooperative arrangement were the three French editions of the latter's pocket atlas, which appeared in 1579 and 1583 under the title *Le miroir du monde*, and in 1588, under the title *Epitome du theatre du monde d'Abraham Ortelius*. This last title is, perhaps, the most accurate as the maps often were derived from Ortelius's successful *Theatrum orbis terrarum*. Reworked in a reduced, compact format, the smaller maps and condensed text offered the buyer a more portable version of Ortelius's large folio atlas (compare figs. 6.13 and 6.17).[65] It appears, however, that Ortelius himself was not entirely satisfied with the quality of the maps in Galle's editions of this pocket atlas. For, in a letter Ortelius wrote on October 5, 1589 to G. Camden about the making of maps, in which he recommended

[65] Galle's pocket atlases and Plantin's editions of Ortelius's are described in greater detail in appendix 5.

the work of one of the van Doetecum brothers – the brothers were not clearly distinguished from one another in Ortelius's mind at the time – Ortelius remarked that "hic multo elegantius tibi ista elaborabit, quam ille, qui epitomen mei Theatri" (the remaining brother [Joannes] will execute much finer work than he who worked on the epitome of my *Theatrum* [= Galle's pocket atlases]).[66]

Despite this criticism, Galle's pocket atlases (or the "*Epitome*," as they are commonly referred to) were very popular. When Galle published his first edition in 1577 under the title *Spieghel der werelt* (Mirror of the World), with accompanying texts in Dutch by Pieter Heyns, his arrangements with Plantin were straightforward and standard. Galle simply paid Plantin (21 fl. 3 st.) to print the accompanying texts and once Galle had added the illustrations, Plantin then bought back an occasional copy for resale.[67] The arrangements for the printing of the next edition – the first French edition, published in 1579 – appear to be the same as before, for Plantin entered a charge (now 33 fl.) under Galle's accounts for the printing of the text. This time, however, instead of buying back only an occasional copy, Plantin bought back all 500 copies of the atlas that were printed. While he shipped some copies to Frankfurt, for sale at the book fair there, his single largest consignment of copies (200) went to Michel Sonnius I, the bookseller in Paris who had recently taken over Plantin's shop there and enjoyed significant discounts on his editions.[68] A similar distinction is evident in the arrangements made for the printing of all of the following editions of Galle's pocket atlas. While Plantin served simply as the "hired hand" and an occasional buyer for all of the Dutch and Latin editions, he acted as the sole distributor for both the 1583 and 1588 French editions, once Galle had compensated him for printing the text. Although 600 copies were printed of the 1583 edition, only 250 appear to have been printed of the 1588 edition, thereby suggesting an anticipated decrease in the potential market for the publication.[69] Despite these arrangements, the imprint on the title-page of each of these editions reads (with slight variations in the spelling) "A Anvers, de l'imprimerie de Christofle Plantin, pour Philippe Galle" (At Antwerp, from the Press of Christopher Plantin, for Philips Galle), thereby suggesting that, as was the case for each of the Dutch and Latin editions of his *Epitome*, Galle had simply hired Plantin to print the text for him. And yet, as documented above, this was clearly not the case.

Why, then, would they have entered into such a deliberately deceptive cooperative arrangement for the French editions? One can only speculate. The most significant cost to Galle for these projects was the extra wear on his plates, which would have affected their state when he published his Latin editions of the *Epitome* in 1585 and 1589. In exchange for this cost, Galle not only retained full control over his plates, but he also could enjoy the renown of having appeared to bring out yet another edition of his atlas without the extra work and worry of sales. In addition, Galle would also,

---

[66] This letter is cited in Denucé 1912–1913, I, p. 202. See *V. cl. Gulielmi Camdeni et illustrium virorum ad G. Camdenum epistolae* (London: Richard Chiswell, 1691), no. XXIX (pp. 35–36), for the complete, original text. Lucas van Doetecum died sometime before 1589 (see appendix 1, pp. 331–332).

[67] See the notes on this edition in appendix 5.

[68] See the notes on this edition in appendix 5 and ch. 5, for more on Sonnius and Plantin's business relations.

[69] See the notes on these editions in appendix 5.

presumably, have made some calculated profit on the sale of the illustrated copies to Plantin, although the lack of information on Galle's costs makes it impossible to determine this precisely. As for Plantin, these arrangements would have enabled him to publish these French editions of Galle's pocket atlas without having to invest time or large sums of money in having a comparable set of seventy or more maps made and risk competing openly with a good friend and business associate. Indeed, Plantin and Galle may have agreed that Plantin was best suited to distribute an edition for the French market because of his connections in Paris. This theory is supported by the large number of copies that Plantin was able to send to Michel Sonnius. Plantin must have been assured from the start of a favorable market for the sale of these books there – although still less certain than Galle's calculated profit from the sale of all of the copies to Plantin.

To see how this may have worked in practice, let us consider the original 1579 edition of the *Miroir du monde*. While Plantin bought back all 500 copies from Galle for a sum of 450 fl., or 18 st. per copy, he then sold nearly 200 of these copies to Sonnius by early June 1579 at a price of 26 st. per copy.[70] Although Galle was permitted to buy back six copies in August 1579 at the extra discounted price of 23 st. per copy, 26 st. was generally the best price Plantin offered to favored booksellers and the value he gave to copies shipped out for sale at the Frankfurt fair.[71] Other individuals paid as much as 30 or even 36 st. per copy.[72] Consequently, if Plantin was able to sell all 500 copies at 26 st. or more (on average) – which he presumably did prior to engaging in the production of 600 more copies of the text in 1582 – this would have amounted to a profit of at least 200 fl. Plantin's profit margins for the 1583 and 1588 French editions of the *Epitome* were most likely less, because the best price he offered Sonnius was closer, if not identical, to the price he paid to Galle for the same books. Specifically, for the 1583 edition, Plantin bought back the copies from Galle at a rate of 21 st. per copy, while he sold large numbers of copies (at least 250 in December 1582 alone) to Sonnius at just 23 st. per copy. This would have represented only a 2 st. per copy profit margin as opposed to the previous 8 st. per copy price difference.[73] For the 1588 edition, the price Plantin paid to Galle for copies – 32 st. – was the same as the price he charged Sonnius for copies of the same book. Consequently, these sales, at least, would have provided Plantin with no direct financial gain.[74]

[70] See the discussion of this edition in appendix 5 for these sales.
[71] For Galle's extra discounted purchase of six copies of this edition, see MPM Arch. 18, fol. 321 lft. When Galle bought back an additional twelve copies of this text in September 1581, he had to pay the usual low price of 26 st. per copy (see MPM Arch. 18, fol. 394 lft). For examples of other booksellers buying copies at this same discounted price of 26 st. (or 1 fl. 6 st.) per copy, see, e.g., MPM Arch. 57, fol. 32r (to Adrian Barentzoon of Amsterdam); fol. 36r (to Robert Cambier in London); and fols. 108r and 118v (both sales to Plantin's son-in-law Franciscus Raphelengius). Finally, for shipments of copies of the 1579 *Epitome* to Frankfurt, similarly valued at 26 st. per copy, see, e.g., MPM Arch. 57, fols. 28v and 95r. In an initial shipment of twenty-five copies to Frankfurt, made on February 23, 1579, the books were valued at 25 st. per copy instead of 26 st. (see MPM Arch. 57, fol. 20v).
[72] For examples of these higher prices, see, e.g., MPM Arch. 57, fol. 37r, a sale of one copy of the *Miroir du monde* at 36 st. (or 1 fl. 16 st.) to a certain Jan Sandi on March 23, 1579; and fol. 89r, for a sale of one copy to the bookseller Daniel Rundtvleisch for 30 st. (or 1 fl. 10 st.) on June 21, 1579.
[73] See the discussion of this edition in appendix 5 for these sales.
[74] See the discussion of this edition in appendix 5 for these sales.

Thus, in addition to working as full, equal partners, dividing the costs and resulting copies between them, Galle and Plantin also agreed to other forms of cooperative arrangements. While neither the costs nor the copies were shared, Plantin was able to benefit from the use of Galle's plates without owning them and Galle was able to benefit from the production of an edition without having to concern himself with its distribution and sale. According to Michael Bury's analysis of cooperative arrangements made for the production of prints in Italy in the period 1550–1650, those entering into special short-term agreements were "driven by the need to share costs and risks."[75] That does not seem to be the case here, however, particularly for Plantin and Galle's two clear "joint ventures" – the 1575 edition of Furmerius's *De rerum usu et abusu* and their 1589 edition of Canisius's catechism. The former was illustrated with 25 engravings ($c.110 \times 105$ mm), while the latter bore 103 small etchings ($c.80 \times 70$ mm). Both Galle and Plantin, however, periodically produced illustrated publications on their own in which the costs of purchasing the paper and having the illustrations made – the two largest single costs, as observed above – would have been comparable to, if not greater than, those noted above. Recall, for example, Galle's 1572 and 1587 publications of the *Virorum doctorum . . . effigies* and *Imagines L. doctorum virorum*, with 44 and 50 engraved portraits of scholars ($c.170$–177 $\times$ 118–124 mm), respectively. Or consider Plantin's 1571 edition of Arias Montano's *Humanae salutis monumenta*, with 70 engravings ($c.112 \times 72$ mm) and his investment in more than 240 etchings (all $c.200 \times 265$ mm or larger) in the early 1580s for the illustration of Ludovico Guicciardini's description of the Low Countries and Hendrik Jansen van Barrefelt's biblical editions.[76] Thus these projects do not demonstrate how two independent businessmen were occasionally "driven" to join forces. Rather, they reveal the flexible interaction that two businessmen with overlapping interests in illustrated publications engaged in as part of their everyday working world. This view supports our introductory, cautionary remarks against oversimplified accounts of the activities of letterpress printers and print maker-publishers in sixteenth-century Europe. As will become evident when we examine the remaining aspects of Galle and Plantin's working relationship, the unexpected merging of and variations in what many regard as their "independent" activities is what prevails. Thus, the picture of this working world can only be completed when a fluid rather than a divided realm is imagined.

COMPLEMENTARY ASPECTS OF PLANTIN AND GALLE'S WORKING RELATIONSHIP

As noted at the beginning of our discussion of Galle and Plantin's working relationship, their earliest known business transaction dates to June 27, 1571, a little more than a year after Galle's arrival in Antwerp. At that time, Plantin purchased "diverses protraictures" (*sic*) (various images) from Galle and then shipped them, together with

---

[75] Bury 2001, p. 73.
[76] Both of Galle's publications are discussed above and in appendix 5. Plantin's editions of the *Monumenta* are discussed in ch. 2, while his editions of Barrefelt's and Guicciardini's works are discussed in ch. 5.

other "protraictures" (sic) from Gerard de Jode and the widow of Hieronymus Cock, on July 3, 1571 to Georg Willer, a bookseller in Augsburg.[77] This one purchase represents the proverbial "tip of the iceberg" for Plantin and Galle's future transactions. For, up until his death in 1589, Plantin bought large quantities of prints, maps, and illustrated books (or print books) from Galle on an annual basis. His purchases were such that they dominated their accounts – including their respective charges for printing texts and illustrations – and resulted in Plantin always being in debt to Galle and never the reverse.[78] This is essential to bear in mind, because while this chapter is dedicated to Plantin's work as a printer of accompanying letterpress texts for others, this was not always Plantin's primary (financial) concern in his dealings with the same individuals.

Of all the works that Galle had for sale, Plantin spent the most on a selection of Galle's print books, namely his *Virorum doctorum . . . effigies*, the *Divinarum nuptiarum conventa et acta*, *David, hoc est virtutis*, Vosmerus's account of the counts of Holland and Zeeland, copies of Galle's pocket atlas, the *Mythologia ethica*, and its French counterpart, the *Esbatement moral des animaux*.[79] In addition, Plantin also regularly purchased numerous copies of Georg Braun and Frans Hogenberg's *Civitates orbis terrarum* (Cities of the World) or "Het Steden Boek" (Book of Cities), as Hogenberg (then in Cologne) had apparently granted Galle the right to sell this book in Antwerp.[80] As suggested by his first purchase from Galle, Plantin was also interested in buying independent prints, either singly or in sets, as well as many independent maps, and would continue to do so until just before his death. Although the vast majority that Plantin purchased are simply listed as sheets of unspecified prints, occasionally a series is listed by a general title, for example, a series of the Passion (without texts), a series of the Four Last Things, images of hunts, etc.[81] Similarly, aside from a selection of maps of "Belgia" or "Belgiques" or "Belgicae" and one map of Denmark, most of the maps purchased are simply identified as maps by Mercator.[82]

---

[77] See ch. 4, n. 119

[78] These observations are based upon an examination of Plantin's and Galle's accounts, as noted in the following summary record books called "Grand livre" or "Grootboek" (Large Book): MPM Arch. 16, fols. 171 and 172; MPM Arch. 18, fols. 64, 143, 187, 253, 282, 321, and 394; and MPM Arch. 20, fols. 57, 129, 146, 228, 307, and 356.

[79] Except for the *Esbatement moral des animaux* (BT 8489) (discussed below) and Galle's initial issue of the *Virorum doctorum . . . effigies* (discussed above), each of these publications was printed by Plantin for Galle and is described in greater detail in appendix 5. These accounts include examples of Plantin's purchases of the works concerned.

[80] For Hogenberg and Braun's "Steden Boek," see BT 392, 393, 5296, 5297, 7969, and 7970; Denucé 1912–1913, I, pp. 266–281; and Elliot 1987, pp. 26–37.

[81] For examples of Plantin's purchases of prints, see, e.g., MPM Arch. 16, fol. 172 rht (for the Passion series); MPM Arch. 18, fols. 64 rht (for the Four Last Things), 282 rht (bulk prints), and 394 rht (for prints of hunts); and MPM Arch. 20, fols. 146 rht and 228 rht (for many bulk prints). According to Van der Stock, it was not uncommon that, among dealers in prints, bulk rates per ream would be charged (see Van der Stock 1998, pp. 59–60). Some of Plantin's purchases are also transcribed in Delen 1932, pp. 17–20.

[82] For examples of Plantin's purchases of maps of "Belgica" (many of which Schilder identifies as Galle's 1578 map of the Netherlands; see Schilder, II (1993), pp. 119–121), see, e.g., MPM Arch. 18, fol. 282 rht. For the map of Denmark, see MPM Arch. 20, fol. 228 rht. Finally, for examples of Plantin's purchases of Mercator's maps via Galle (all of which were noted between 1583 and 1587), see MPM Arch. 20, fols. 57 rht, 146 rht, 228 rht, and 307 rht. On Plantin's purchases of Mercator's cartographic publications, see Imhof 1994b.

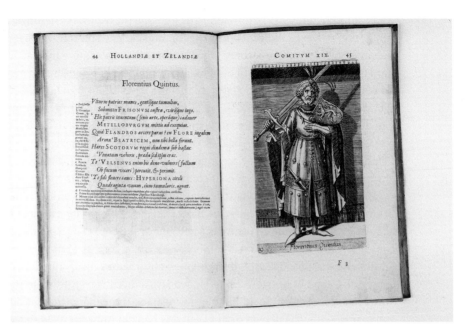

6.14 Anonymous artists, *Floris V*, from Michael Vosmerus, *Principes Hollandiae et Zelandiae, domini Frisiae* (Antwerp: Christopher Plantin for Philips Galle, 1578; f°), p. 45, engraving, 205 × 120 (Antwerp, Museum Plantin-Moretus, A 1558). In fig. 6.15, this same engraving appears in another, competing publication.

In addition to these primary purchases, Plantin also owed Galle for several other services that were occasionally rendered: the engraving of plates (as discussed above), having two Mercator globes painted for 36 fl.,[83] and, of great importance in this context, for the printing and loan of some of Galle's plates for the illustration of one of his publications. Galle's charge to Plantin for not only the printing but also the use (wearing down) of some of his copper plates was made in conjunction with Plantin's production of Adrianus Barlandus's *Hollandiae comitum historia et icones* in the fall of 1583 (PP 625).[84] In his dedication to the States of Holland and of Utrecht, Plantin describes how he came to establish a press in Leiden and notes that this description of the counts of Holland and Zeeland was his first publication to be printed there. The plates concerned were ones that Galle had already used for the illustration of his first two editions of M. Vosmerus's own (briefer) accounts of the counts of Holland and Zeeland, published in 1578 in Latin and in 1583 in French (see figs. 6.14 and 6.15). Plantin had printed the text of these editions for Galle and afterwards bought back numerous copies once they had been illustrated.[85] It is, thus, all the more remarkable

[83] See MPM Arch. 62, fol. 1r, under January 1, 1584.
[84] Unknown to Voet, there are two variants of the first two leaves of the text, most easily distinguished from one another by the title-page vignette used and the setting of the text on leaf *2. MPM (A 1554), the only variant known to Voet, has a vignette featuring a seated woman with four coats of arms, while MPM (2–157) has a more conventional printer's device (compare the reproductions of these vignettes [nos. 45 and 40, respectively] at the end of Voet, PP, VI).
[85] Both are discussed in greater detail in appendix 5.

6.15 Anonymous artists, *Floris V*, from Adrianus Barlandus's *Hollandiae comitum historia et icones* (Leiden: Christopher Plantin, 1584; f°), p. 43, engraving, 205 × 120 (Antwerp, Museum Plantin-Moretus, A 1554). See fig. 6.14 for the original use of this engraving.

that Plantin undertook his edition of Barlandus's text and that Galle agreed to loan his plates for it. Barlandus's text (although written in Latin) might well have been regarded as a rival publication for Vosmerus's editions and Galle clearly wanted to remain free to reissue his plates himself – as he would do in 1586, in a second French edition of Vosmerus's text.[86]

The calculations for the loan and the printing of Galle's plates for Plantin's Barlandus edition were noted in two separate entries in October 1583. The first is a charge of 56 fl. for the printing of the illustrations in 400 copies of the text.[87] This was calculated in a conventional manner, namely, at a fixed rate (in this case 14 st.) per hundred sheets printed with illustrations, where all thirty-four illustrations fit on to twenty sides (recto and verso) of the sheets of paper used to make up the book, each of which was printed 400 times for all the illustrated copies desired.[88] The second entry is a charge of

[86] See appendix 5 for more on this edition.
[87] "Philippus Galle doibt avoir pr. compte de comites Hollandiae Barlandi comme sensuit 400 tot 14 st. het hondert ende syn 20 bladeren van elck 4 hondert dat is te samen 80 hondert tot 14 st. maken fl. 56." (Philips Galle must have for the account of the Comites Hollandiae [by] Barlandus as follows 400 [copies] at 14 st. per hundred [sheets] and there are 20 sheets, 400 of each, that amounts to 8,000 at 14 st., which makes 56 fl.) (MPM Arch. 20, fol. 129 rht.)
[88] Because this book was printed in folio, in each gathering the first and fourth leaves are joined, as are the second and third leaves, where the recto of the third leaf is on one side of the original sheet and the recto of the second leaf is on the opposite side. Thus, if there are illustrations on leaves A2r and A3r, one would have been printed on each side of the sheet. Similarly, illustrations on the rectos of the first and fourth leaves also appear on opposite sides of the original sheet of paper. This implies that, because of the setting of the text and placement of the illustrations in Plantin's edition of Barlandus's text, the following pairs of plates were printed together on either side of one of the sheets of paper making up

one "negenmanneken" (or a "duit," a coin equaling one-eighth of a stuiver) for each impression of each plate in all 400 copies of the text.[89] With 34 illustrations printed in each of the 400 copies Plantin had illustrated, this came to 13,600 figures, or 1,700 st. or 85 fl. total., a full 29 fl. more than the cost of having the plates printed into all 400 copies of the book. This type of transaction was not unique. Manfred Sellink mentions, for example, that Galle may have leased plates from Hieronymus Cock and leased out some of his own to Gerard de Jode.[90] And Philips Galle's son Theodoor similarly charged Plantin's successor, Jan Moretus I, for the loan of plates for some of his publications, like Laevinus Torrentius's edition of the works of Horace, from 1608.[91] Rather, the loan of plates between print publishers and letterpress printers underscores, once more, the degree to which their working worlds overlapped, as each sought to produce and distribute comparable, yet independent, illustrated publications.

Indeed, while Plantin turned to Galle for the purchase of his publications and the rendering of services as an engraver and pictorial printer, Galle went to Plantin with similar requests for goods and services. Perhaps the most significant in these accounts – both in terms of the quantity of items concerned and the money spent – were Galle's purchases of a great variety of books from Plantin. Begun by September 22, 1571, a few months after Plantin had started to buy prints from Galle, these purchases consisted primarily of a varied selection of Plantin's own publications. Galle bought large quantities of only a few items: some 145 small books of hours (primarily, if not all, in 24°) with engraved illustrations; 25 copies of an unillustrated Latin grammar book by Cornelius Valerius; 30 copies of a work referred to simply as "Acolastus," which most likely refers to Gulielmus Gnapheus's theatrical work, *Acolastus de filio prodigo*, published in Antwerp by Jan van der Loe in 1562; and, finally, between September 1571 and 1583, he periodically bought a few copies of Clemens Perret's virtuoso engraved calligraphy book (both with and without borders).[92] Beyond these works, Galle tended

the book: plates 1 and 2; plates 4 and 7; plates 5 and 6; plates 8 and 11; plates 9 and 10; plates 12 and 15; plates 13 and 14; plates 16 and 18; plates 19 and 20; plates 21 and 23; plates 24 and 26; plates 29 and 32; plates 30 and 31; and plates 34 and 35 (amounting to fourteen sheets in total). The remaining illustrations (plates 3, 17, 22, 25, 27, and 33) were all printed alone on one of the sheets (amounting to six additional sheets). Thus, all of the thirty-four illustrations were printed on twenty separate sheets of text. Although the illustrations are numbered 1–35, the plate numbered 28 (an image of John of Bavaria) was omitted from Plantin's publication of Barlandus's text. See pp. 54–55 for more on the rates Plantin usually paid for having intaglio illustrations printed.

[89] "Philippus Galle doibt avoir pr. compte de comites Hollandiae Barlandi comme sensuit . . . p. 34 figuren die daer in comen tot een negenmanneken de figure maken 13600 figuren voor de 400 ende souden bedraghen fl. 85 is geaccordert naer de rekeninghe van Phil. Galle fl. 84 st. 8." (Philips Galle must have for the account of the Comites Hollandiae [by] Barlandus as follows . . . for 34 figures that are included there, one "negenmanneken" [or duit] for each figure, makes 13,600 figures for the 400 [copies] and should amount to 85 fl., and is agreed to for the account of Philips Galle . . . 84 fl. 8 st. [a reduction of 12 st. or 96 "negenmannekens"). (MPM Arch. 20, fol. 129 rht.)

[90] See Sellink 1997, II, n. 113, for the example of Cock; and Sellink 1997, I, p. 34, for that of de Jode.

[91] See Simoni 1990, H-180, and BB, III, p. 503, H-243. See MPM Arch. 123, fol. 17r, under September 20, for the following charge: "vande plaeten te lenen te weeten effigies Torentius en Horatius beyden te samen 8 gul." (for the loan of the plates, namely, portraits of Torrentius and Horatius, both together 8 fl.).

[92] For these purchases, see MPM Arch. 18, fol. 282 lft (for books of hours bought in September 1578 – see the account of PP 1780 in Bowen 1997a, pp. 250–251) and fol. 253 lft, under May 26, 1578, for purchases of both Valerius's grammar book (perhaps PP 2381; see also Voet, PP, V, pp. 2288–2289 on this edition) and the "Acolastus" edition (see BT 8390). See MPM Arch. 16, fol. 171 lft, and MPM Arch. 18, fol. 64 lft, for Galle's purchase of Perret's calligraphy book (PP 1961; discussed on pp. 65–66 above).

to make isolated purchases of a great variety of texts, illustrated and otherwise, and most (but not all) of which were printed by Plantin. Too numerous to enumerate here, these ranged from ordinances and political pamphlets, to herbals and pharmaceutical works, historical texts, editions of classical authors, works of music, and a selection of Plantin's own richly illustrated publications, featured in the preceding chapters, including one copy of de Valverde's anatomical treatise, a few copies of one of the *octavo* editions of Arias Montano's *Humanae salutis monumenta*, ten copies of Plantin's 1582 publication *La joyeuse et magnifique entrée de . . . Françoys, fils de France . . . en . . . d'Anvers* (on the state entry into Antwerp of Francis, duke of Anjou), and one copy of J. B. Houwaert's *Pegasides pleyn ende den lust-hof der maeghden* from 1583.[93] Regrettably, it is impossible to determine which (if any) of these sporadic, isolated purchases were intended for his own personal use and which were intended for resale.

The other item that Galle regularly purchased from Plantin was paper. Galle bought both new paper and reams of "maculatures," paper that had been spotted with ink or was otherwise misprinted and then sold cheaply. While Galle's purchases of the latter were concentrated in the period September 1575–1576 – with only an occasional purchase of such paper in the period 1577–1580 – he purchased ordinary, new paper for a longer period of time, ranging from 1575 through 1584, and then intermittently in 1586 and 1589.[94] Galle was not the only one to buy paper from Plantin. Indeed, the purchase of reams of "maculatures" was common to other printer-booksellers well known to Plantin, including his son-in-law Franciscus Raphelengius I, who, by the late 1570s, was working as an independent bookseller, Guillaume Rivière, a relative of Plantin's who had worked for him as a printer (and occasionally a compositor) before establishing himself as an independent printer, and another well-known Antwerp printer-publisher, Hieronymus Verdussen.[95] Once again, the worlds of letterpress printers and pictorial printers like Galle overlapped.

Finally, in addition to these more standard offerings from a book printer-publisher, Galle also occasionally purchased independent prints, maps, and even a set of plates of the Acts of the Apostles from Plantin.[96] Galle also occasionally paid Plantin for the

---

93 For this sample of purchases, see MPM Arch. 16, fol. 171 lft (for ordinances); MPM Arch. 20, fol. 57 lft (for a few political pamphlets, including an *Afgheworpen brieven van den cardinael van Granvelle en andere* [PP 1931] and *Discours sur la blessure de . . . le Prince d'Orange* [PP 1925]); MPM Arch. 18, fol. 64 lft (for a copy of de Valverde's anatomical treatise – which edition is not specified; and for a purchase of Arias Montano's *Monumenta* [probably his 1575, see Bowen 2003, pp. 26–27 in particular]); MPM Arch. 18, fol. 321 lft (for Valerius Cordus's pharmaceutical treatise [PP 1024] and a French edition of St. Augustine's *De civitate Dei*, which was definitely not printed by Plantin); MPM Arch. 20, fol. 57 lft (for nine copies of the folio edition of the state entry of the duke of Anjou and for one copy of the *quarto* edition [see PP 1211 and PP 1212]); MPM Arch. 20, fol. 146 lft (for a copy of a "Chroniques de Flandres" [possibly PP 1841], a copy of Houwaert's *Lusthof der maeghden* [PP 1412], and an herbal by Dodoens [possibly PP 1101]); and MPM Arch. 20, fol. 307 lft (for a few musical scores, none of which appears to have been printed by Plantin).

94 See MPM Arch. 18, fol. 187 lft, for examples of such purchases.

95 For examples of these other purchases of "maculatures" in the randomly chosen year of 1579, see MPM Arch. 57, fols. 4r and 24r (for Raphelengius), fols. 9v and 29v (for Rivière), and fol. 39v (for Verdussen). For summaries of each of these figures' activities as independent printer-publishers, see Rouzet 1975, pp. 183–184 (for Raphelengius), pp. 189–190 (for Rivière), and pp. 233–234 (for Verdussen).

96 For examples of these purchases, see MPM Arch. 18, fol. 64 lft (for two "figures de la bible 8to"); MPM Arch. 18, fol. 321 lft (for some maps); and MPM Arch. 20, fol. 307 lft (for Galle's purchase of "de plaeten van werken der apostolen wegen 35 lb. fl. 3 st. 10" [the plates of the Acts of the Apostles, weighing 35 lb. 3 fl. 10 st.]).

transport of certain items. These shipments included copies of Hogenberg's *Civitates orbis terrarum* (sent from Cologne), an unspecified number of plates sent from Rome, eight plates that had originated in Hamburg (and were sent via Frankfurt?), as well as the puzzling shipment of twelve "peerdekens" (small horses) that had to be picked up in the city of Gravelines in northern France.[97]

Each of these categories of purchases is of interest in its own right for the enrichment they lend to our understanding of Galle and Plantin's transactions. The occasional sales and transport of plates are particularly tantalizing for the evidence they provide that such things were done. They are simultaneously frustrating, however, because of the difficulty in identifying specifically which plates are cited. The records of Galle's and Plantin's purchases of each other's publications provide a more valuable source of information in the context of this study, for they indicate which of the two men had the ultimate control over the distribution of a particular work. In most cases, this evidence is primarily corroborative in nature, confirming what is known from other sources. It is not surprising, for example, that Galle would appear to be the primary distributor of books for which Plantin had simply been paid to print the text – as with his editions of Vosmerus's account of the counts of Holland and Zeeland and the *Mythologia ethica*, for example. Plantin subsequently bought back copies of these texts bit by bit, presumably as needed. It is similarly to be expected that Plantin would sell Galle copies of his own illustrated publications – like Arias Montano's *Humanae salutis monumenta* or the state entry of the duke of Anjou – and not the reverse.

In the case of Plantin's editions of Galle's 1579 publications *Een cort verhael van de gedincweerdichste saken . . . in de XVII Provincien vande Nederlanden* and *Sommaire annotation des choses plus memorables advenues . . . és XVII provinces du Pais Bas* (A brief account of the most memorable events in the XVII provinces of the Netherlands) (PP 1230–1231C), accounts here of Galle's purchases of these texts from Plantin further our understanding of the production of these works. Although not illustrated, these publications are commonly regarded as the translations of a Latin text that Plantin originally printed for Galle in 1578, in conjunction with his map of the Netherlands.[98] According to Plantin's and Galle's accounts, between April 10 and June 1, 1579, Plantin delivered a total of 525 copies of the Dutch and French editions of this text to Galle, often in large batches of 50 or 100 copies, in addition to 90 extra copies in the months thereafter.[99] While the value of all of these copies was systematically noted, Galle was ultimately charged for just 325 of the first group of 525 (for a total of only 11 fl. 14 st., or 7.2 st. per 10 copies).

---

[97] For these shipments, see MPM Arch. 18, fol. 321 lft, in November 1579, for a charge of 2 fl. for "35 lb. pesantes des Theat. Civitatum, etc. venus de Cologne . . ." (for 35 lb. weight of the "theat. Civitatum," sent from Cologne); MPM Arch. 20, fol. 228 lft, under June 18, 1587, for a charge of 11 fl. 2 st. for "le port des plates venues de Rome pesantes 20 lb." (the transport of plates sent from Rome, weighing 20 lb.); MPM Arch. 20, fol. 307 lft, in March or April 1588, for both a charge of 4 fl. for "Acht plaetkens comende uit Hamborch, Francfort" (eight small plates coming from Hamburg, Frankfurt); and for a charge of 3 fl. 12 st. for "la port de 12 peerdekens gezonden naer [Rouen?] ende aengehaelt te Grevelingen" (the transport of 12 small horses sent to [Rouen?] and picked up in Gravelines).

[98] For more on this work, see the discussion of Plantin's printing of a text for a map for Galle in 1578 in appendix 5.

[99] See MPM Arch. 18, fol. 321 lft.

Apparently, they had agreed that Galle was to receive 200 copies free of charge.[100] Such accounting practices (the only ones of this kind found amid Galle's purchases of books from Plantin) suggest that this was some sort of cooperative venture, although the precise nature of the arrangements remains unclear. On the one hand, there is no obvious charge to Galle for the printing of this text, as was usually noted for the publications that Plantin printed for him, regardless of whether it was one of their joint publications or not. On the other hand, there is an ambiguous note amid the items that Galle had delivered to Plantin, indicating that the two men had agreed to a sum of 30 fl. "p[ou]r les Discours imprimes depuis le commencement quils sont venues en lumiere iusques a present p[ou]r 5 impressions tant francois que flameng a 1 lb. p[ou]r impression que ledit Galle a p[ar] accord avec C. Plantin sans quil debourse rien de limpression ou papier etc. . . . fl. 30" (for the Discours printed from the beginning up until the present day, for five impressions of both the French and the Dutch [text] at 1 Flemish pound per impression, which Galle has agreed to with C. Plantin, without him [Galle?] having to pay anything for the printing or the paper, etc.).[101] Voet identifies this as the amount that the latter was to pay Plantin for the printing of this edition.[102] However, it not only seems like an unrealistically large amount for the printing of what was such a small, inexpensive publication, but it was also noted on the right side of their accounts, namely, along with the other sums that Plantin owed Galle for what the latter had delivered and not the reverse. Perhaps this agreement pertains to copies of Galle's map with which this text is associated, although no copies of this publication are known with the map bound into the booklet. Regardless of the precise significance of this record, the evidence of Plantin's independent sale of almost a thousand additional copies of this booklet in the course of 1579 indicates that Plantin – and not Galle, as suggested by both Voet and Sellink – was the primary distributor of both the French and Dutch editions of this text.[103] Thus, as is the case with the French editions of Galle's pocket atlas, this publication does not constitute what is indicated on the title-page, namely, a simple case of Plantin printing for Galle, but rather, a more obtuse and still unresolved form of a cooperative arrangement.

Plantin and Galle's working relationship, begun in the second half of 1571 and lasting until Plantin's death in July 1589, was clearly a complex and ever varying one. It began conventionally when Plantin sought out Galle as a potential source for engraved plates for his own publications and printed images for his longstanding independent sale of prints, while Galle turned to Plantin as a source of publications to complement his own

---

[100] See MPM Arch. 18, fol. 282 lft. The fact that no final amounts for the initial batches of copies delivered to Galle between April 10 and May 15, 1579 were noted in the column on the far right of this page indicates that Galle was not charged immediately for these. The final settlement concerning which copies had to be paid for was noted further down on this same page, under June 1, 1579.

[101] MPM Arch. 18, fol. 282 rht.   [102] PP 1230, n. 4.

[103] For Plantin's independent sales of this text (which amount to approximately 490 copies each of the French and Dutch editions) to people other than Galle, see MPM Arch. 57, fols. 37v–40r, 45r, 46v, 47r, 48r, 48v, 52r, 53r–54r, 55r–56r, 57r, 59r, 59v, 60v, 61v, 63r, 64v, 66r–67r, 69r, 71v, 74v, 77r, 78r, 78v, 80r, 83r, 88v, 89v, 92r, 93r, 97r, 98r, 99v, 100r, 102r, 105v, 109v, 110r, 112v, 120r, 133v, 145r, 147v, and 166v. For Voet's and Sellink's association of Galle with these editions, see PP 1230–1231C and Sellink 1997, I, p. 32.

stock. But within a few years – by 1575 – it had grown to include a variety of arrangements that supported their mutual interest in the production of richly illustrated works. Perhaps not coincidentally, by this time – and potentially several years earlier – the two men had also become close friends. One essential group of artist-printer-humanist friends to which they both belonged is periodically alluded to in Plantin's and Jan Moretus I's correspondence with Arias Montano. For in these numerous letters, greetings are routinely exchanged between not only Plantin, Arias Montano, and Galle, but also several other figures, in particular: "Paludanus" (the artist Crispin van den Broeck), Theodorus Pulmannus (a cloth merchant by day, humanist-scholar by night), Paul van Quickelberghe (Kikelberg) (an old friend of Plantin's and a witness, for example, at the wedding of Franciscus Raphelengius I and Marguerite Plantin), Arnold Mylius (a representative of the Cologne-based Birckman printer-publisher business), and Abraham Ortelius.[104] Portraits were exchanged, entries made in each other's *Libri amicorum*, and Galle even chose Plantin as the godfather of his fifth child, Philip Galle, who was baptized at Antwerp cathedral on May 30, 1581.[105] Plantin and Galle's friendship was likely fueled by mutual interests in art, prints, and texts, as well as their less strict Catholic sentiments – sentiments that were dangerous to admit to openly in this period of wars fought in the name of faith.[106] But whatever the source of their obvious mutual regard, the Plantin archives make it abundantly clear: business was business and financial matters continued to be noted faithfully, regardless of any bonds of friendship or family ties. Thus, while their close friendship may have encouraged their reliance upon one another for so many diverse business matters, it did not necessarily imply that the forms of cooperation and self-employment documented here represented some sort of exclusive, exceptional arrangements between friends. Rather, as we will demonstrate in the following pages, many of the arrangements entered into by Plantin and Galle have their counterparts in the former's dealings with other authors and print publishers.

PLANTIN'S DEALINGS WITH OTHER PRINT PUBLISHERS AND AUTHORS: ABRAHAM ORTELIUS

Of all the remaining people for whom Plantin worked, Abraham Ortelius (fig. 6.16) was the most significant, in terms of both the number of projects concerned – five

[104] For just a few examples from this abundant correspondence, see, e.g., *Corr.*, IV, no. 643 (a letter from Plantin to Arias Montano, dated August 13–14, 1575); *Corr.*, IV, no. 638 (a letter from Arias Montano to Jan Moretus, dated July 7, 1575); *Corr.*, V, no. 652 (a letter from Plantin to Arias Montano, dated September 18, 1575); *Corr.*, V, no. 745 (a letter from Jan Moretus to Arias Montano, dated November 1576); *Corr.*, V, no. 754 (a letter from Jan Moretus to Arias Montano, dated February 13, 1577); and *Corr.*, VI, no. 947 (a letter from Plantin to Arias Montano, dated September 15–18, 1581).

[105] See *Corr.*, VI, no. 947 (cited above) for Plantin's receipt of a portrait of Ortelius engraved by Galle, perhaps comparable to fig. 6.16. Both Plantin and Galle, from 1574, contributed, for example, to Ortelius's *Liber amicorum*, which is now preserved in Pembroke College, Cambridge (MS 2.113). See Puraye 1968 for a reprint of it. For Plantin's entry, see vol. I, fol. 73, and vol. II, pp. 58–59. For Galle's entry, see vol. I, fol. 14, and vol. II, p. 23. Finally, see Génard 1859, p. 201, and SAA, *Doopregister van O. L. V. Kerk, Antwerpen, Parochieregister 9* (begun on December 1, 1580), p. 36, for Plantin's status as the godfather of Philip Galle II.

[106] On Plantin and his circle of friends involved in this spiritual movement, commonly referred to as the "Huis der liefde" or the "Family of Love," see, e.g., Voet, *GC*, I, pp. 21–30, Hamilton 1981b, Sellink 1997, I, pp. 25, 90–91, and Rekers 1972, ch. 4 in particular.

6.16 Philips Galle after an anonymous artist, *Abraham Ortelius*, from Abraham Ortelius, *Theatrum orbis terrarum* (Antwerp: Christopher Plantin for Abraham Ortelius, 1579; f°), fol. B4v, engraving, 327 × 218 (Antwerp, Museum Plantin-Moretus, R 60.1).

editions of his atlas and four editions of his *Additamenta* (a separate publication of only his most recently published maps) – and the hundreds of florins that exchanged hands in the process. The first known reference to Ortelius in the Plantin archives dates back to January 13, 1558, when Ortelius – identified as a "paintre des cartes" (painter of maps) – bought a copy of the writings of Virgil, in Latin and bound in parchment.[107] At this time, Plantin had been working as a printer-publisher for only a few years, while Ortelius was active as a colorer of maps, as well as a dealer in maps and antiquities. Ortelius also had a clear interest in curiosities and works of art, which soon gained him entry into various humanistic and artistic circles, including that to which Plantin and Galle belonged, resulting (as noted above) in all three becoming life-long friends. Above all, however, Ortelius is known for the essential role he played in formulating the atlas as we know it today, namely, as a collection of maps, all printed uniformly in one format, and published together as a single unit (fig. 6.17).[108]

As was the case with Plantin's dealings with Galle, Plantin and Ortelius's initial business transactions consisted of numerous purchases of their independently produced goods and services.[109] As noted above, Ortelius began buying books from Plantin as early as 1558, just three years after the latter had begun to work as a printer in Antwerp. Ortelius would continue to buy a variety of books from Plantin for years to come. Similarly in 1558, Plantin began to pay Ortelius for coloring maps and soon thereafter (in the 1560s), for purchases of independent maps that Ortelius had for sale. This balance of purchases would change significantly once Ortelius began to publish editions of his atlas, the *Theatrum orbis terrarum* (Theatre of the World), in 1570, as Plantin then began to buy large quantities of Ortelius's atlases for further distribution.

Reminiscent, once again, of his transactions with Galle, Plantin did not print the texts for Ortelius's initial editions of his atlas, despite his and Ortelius's established business relations and burgeoning friendship. Rather, for those editions published between 1570 and 1575, Ortelius (like Galle) employed Gillis I and Anthonis Coppens van Diest, and then, upon the latter's death in 1574, Gilles van den Rade.[110] Thus, while Plantin started printing texts for Galle in the course of 1574, perhaps following the death of Anthonis Coppens van Diest, Ortelius delayed this switch-over until after the completion of the 1575 edition of his atlas – the only one to be printed by van den Rade. Although Ortelius did not publish another edition of his atlas until 1579 (and then with the assistance of Plantin), it is clear from archival records that he had decided to employ Plantin for this project by January 1577, when he began to stock the necessary paper in the latter's shop.[111] The actual production of the atlas was not begun until December 1578, when Ortelius had returned from a prolonged period of travel away from Antwerp to avoid the troubled times following the Spanish Fury. The 1579 edition

---

[107] See MPM Arch. 35, fol. 4v, for the following entry: "A Abraham paintre des cartes 1 Virgilius Latin rel. en parchemin" (For Abraham, colorer of maps, 1 Virgilius in Latin, bound in parchment). The following is drawn from Imhof 1999b, pp. 79–89.

[108] For an overview of the editions of Ortelius's atlas and his related publications, see Koeman 1967–1971, III, under Ortelius.

[109] Many, but not all, of these purchases are transcribed in Denucé 1912–1913, II, pp. 149–214.

[110] For more on these printers, see, e.g., Rouzet 1975, pp. 45–46 (for G. and A. Coppens van Diest) and pp. 182–183 (for van den Rade).

[111] See Imhof 1999b, pp. 82–83.

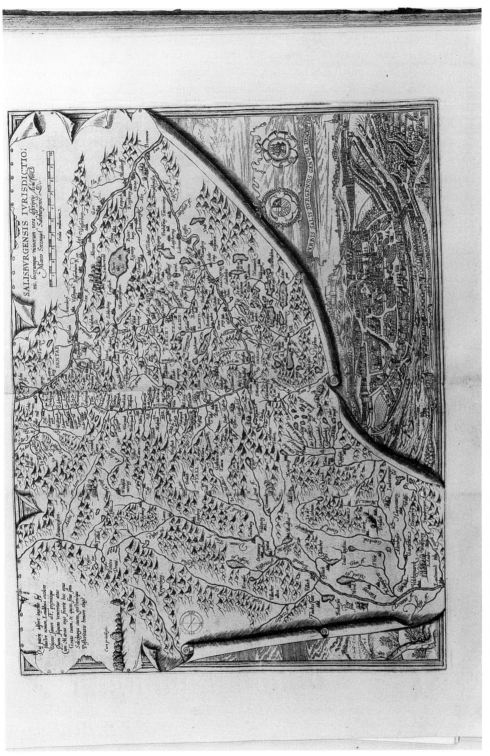

6.17 Anonymous artist, Bishopric of Salzburg, from Abraham Ortelius, *Theatrum orbis terrarum* (Antwerp: Christopher Plantin for Abraham Ortelius, 1579; f°), map no. 51, etching and engraving, 344 × 443 (Antwerp, Museum Plantin-Moretus, R 60.1). See fig. 6.13 for a smaller etched version of this map.

of Ortelius's *Theatrum* is also noteworthy as the first edition to bear an introductory portrait of Ortelius engraved by Philips Galle (fig. 6.16). Manfred Sellink asserts that this portrait was engraved by Galle at Plantin's request.[112] Although Plantin may have suggested this, we know of no records indicating that he either paid Galle for the engraving of this portrait or had such a plate in his possession. Given that this portrait was also included in Jan Baptist Vrints's editions of the atlas, it seems most likely that Ortelius, himself, owned the plate. For these atlases were illustrated with Ortelius's own plates, which Vrints acquired following Ortelius's death in 1598.[113] Ortelius's 1579 *Theatrum* was the first of what would evolve into a succession of five editions of the main atlas and four editions of the *Additamenta*, all printed for him by Plantin between 1579 and 1587. In each of these cases, Ortelius served as the publisher, paid Plantin to print the text, and then sold varying quantities of the fully illustrated copies back to Plantin, who resold them via his established network of markets and to individual buyers.[114]

In addition to these works, Plantin printed one Spanish edition of Ortelius's atlas in 1588 under the title: *Theatro de la tierra universal de Abraham Ortelio*.[115] Contrary to all other known editions of the atlas, Plantin, and not Ortelius, initiated the project, paid all of the costs, and saw to its distribution. This entailed having the texts for the atlas translated into Spanish (at a total cost of 100 fl.), then seeing to the printing of the text (which was completed in April 1588), and then paying Ortelius to add the maps. For this work, Ortelius charged him 6 fl. per copy, which was significantly below the 16 fl. per copy rate that Plantin had paid Ortelius for fully illustrated copies of his 1587 French edition of the atlas, the *Theatre de l'univers*, published just one year earlier. The significant difference between these two prices must reflect the difference between who paid for the paper and printing of the accompanying text: Plantin in the case of the Spanish atlas and Ortelius in the case of the French edition. Between April 1588 and January 2, 1590 – a good six months after Plantin's death – Ortelius delivered 255 illustrated copies (at a total cost of 1,530 fl.), which appears to have been the entire edition. Thus, the arrangements were, in essence, the same as those Plantin made for any of his other illustrated publications. The main difference is that here he had Ortelius provide the engraved illustrations, just as Galle had done for Plantin's 1584 Barlandus edition on the counts of Holland and Zeeland discussed above. Both are examples of how Plantin paid Ortelius and Galle to print impressions of plates for him, where the plates remained in the possession (and under the control) of Ortelius and Galle, respectively. Ortelius's charges to Plantin for this work only lack the distinction between the cost of "borrowing" the plate and that of printing it, which was so clearly made in Galle's charges. While it is tempting to liken the production of this Spanish edition of Ortelius's atlas to Plantin and Galle's production of the French editions of Galle's pocket atlases, there is one significant difference between them. This is the fact that Plantin charged Galle for printing the text for each of the French pocket atlases. Galle

---

[112] *New Holl.*, *Galle*, IV, no. 659.

[113] For an example of one of Vrints's editions with Galle's portrait of Ortelius, see, e.g., the Spanish edition from 1602 (Koeman 1967–1971, III, no. Ort 34) and the Latin edition from 1603 (Koeman 1967–1971, III, no. Ort 36). It is not known when or how, precisely, Vrints obtained these plates.

[114] Each of these editions is described in appendix 5.

[115] See Imhof 1999b, p. 88, and Voet's extensive notes to PP 1822 for more on this edition.

consequently bore some of the costs, as well as the responsibilities for the production of these books. Ortelius, however, did not pay anything and remained a simple hired hand for this one edition.

Plantin may have decided to publish this atlas as part of a campaign to persuade the Spanish court and its adherents that he was still loyal to them, despite his sojourn in the anti-Spanish, Calvinist city of Leiden between April 1583 and October 1585.[116] For the atlas contained a dedication to the future king, Philip III, which was signed by Plantin, but actually written for him by Arias Montano. Once Ortelius started to deliver illustrated copies to him by the end of April 1588, Plantin then began to organize the shipment of several "presentation" copies for Philip III and others in his court.[117] Plantin's death a little more than a year later (and before Ortelius had finished delivering all 225 copies) prevented him from ever determining whether this costly gesture had the desired affect.

Having ascertained the degree to which Plantin and Ortelius worked together on the production of illustrated books, it is important to put these observations in the broader context of their general working relationship. As noted at the start of this discussion, the two men actively bought and sold publications from one another throughout their careers. As was the case with Galle's early publications, although Plantin did not always print the texts accompanying Ortelius's atlases, this did not discourage him from buying copies of the finished books. Indeed, Plantin played an extremely important role in the distribution of the editions of Ortelius's atlas from the very start, purchasing tens to hundreds of copies annually.[118] Because these atlases were exceptionally expensive – the earliest editions cost Plantin 6 fl. 10 st. per copy, while the enlarged French edition from 1587 cost 16 fl. per copy – they also comprised the single most significant part of Ortelius and Plantin's balance of accounts. Even though the amounts Plantin charged for printing the atlas were notably large, ranging from 120 to around 200 fl. per edition (compared with the c.45–48 fl. maximum that he charged Galle for printing work), these fees were, nonetheless, soon eclipsed by what he paid out in return when buying back the illustrated copies.[119] Consider, for example, Ortelius's 1579 edition of the *Theatrum*, the first edition that Plantin printed. While Plantin charged Ortelius 120 fl. for printing the text, he then proceeded to buy back 239 copies between 1580 and 1584, at 12 fl. per copy, for a total of 2,868 fl.[120] Similar conclusions can be drawn concerning the overwhelming weight of Plantin's purchases in comparision with his printing charges for Ortelius's 1581 French and 1584 Latin editions of his atlas. The two exceptions to this pattern are Ortelius's 1580 German atlas and his 1587 French atlas. While Plantin bought as few as thirty-nine copies of the latter between 1587 and 1589, he does not appear to have purchased any of the former.[121]

The parallels between Plantin's working relationship with Ortelius and that which he maintained with Galle are striking. Despite already having business contacts with Plantin, both Galle and Ortelius began by hiring Gillis I and Anthonis Coppens van

---

[116] On this period, see Voet, GC, I, pp. 105–113.
[117] See PP 1822, n. 5.   [118] See Imhof 1999b, pp. 81–87.
[119] See the entries for Ortelius's atlases and Galle's pocket atlases in appendix 5 for these relative fees.
[120] See Imhof 1999b, pp. 83 and 85, for these figures.   [121] See Imhof 1999b, pp. 85–87.

Diest for the printing of the texts for their publications. We will consider why this was the case later on. In addition, it is clear from Plantin's accounts with Galle and Ortelius that, both prior to and during the periods in which they employed him for the printing of text, his independent purchases of their publications – be they prints, maps, or illustrated books – were far and away the most significant component of their transactions. Are these features common only to special relationships between friends, or were they typical of Plantin's business transactions generally? In order to answer this question, we will have to consider Plantin's remaining work as a printer for other people's illustrated editions.

PLANTIN'S WORK FOR OTHER AUTHORS: ALBERT HAYEN, LUCAS JANSZOON WAGHENAER, AND ETIENNE PERRET

The most obvious examples that break with the patterns of Plantin's transactions with Galle and Ortelius are his projects for certain independent authors. It was not uncommon for authors to approach Plantin and negotiate a deal in which he would print their manuscript at their own expense.[122] Similar arrangements were also made with a few authors whose publications included engraved or etched illustrations. Aside from Ortelius's atlases, the most obvious examples of this are Etienne Perret's grand publication of a selection of famous animal fables, his *XXV fables des animaux*, from 1578 (see fig. 6.19); Lucas Janszoon Waghenaer's influential editions of his maritime atlas, *Teerste deel vande spieghel der Zeevaerdt* (fig. 6.18) and *Het tweede deel vanden spieghel der Zeevaert* published (with several variants) by Plantin in Leiden in 1584 and 1585; and Albert Hayen's complementary *Amstelredamsche zee-caerten*, which was similarly published in Leiden in 1585.[123]

Little is known about Plantin's production of the maritime atlases for Hayen and Waghenaer (both experienced pilots), largely because they were printed in Leiden and no records of their production survive. However, the imprints of these publications – indicating that Plantin had printed the texts for the authors – as well as the lack of references in the inventories of Plantin's estate to the plates used to illustrate either work, suggest that both publications were printed at the expense of the author and that the author would have seen to the addition of the illustrations and assumed the primary role in distributing the books. Of these two works, Waghenaer's was included in Plantin's own catalogues of his publications, while Hayen's was not.[124] Nevertheless, for the subsequent editions of Waghenaer's text, Cornelis Claesz of Amsterdam appears to have assumed the role of publisher and the control of the plates, hiring a variety of other printers, including Plantin's successor at the Leiden branch of the Plantin Press, Franciscus Raphelengius I, to print new editions of these texts.[125] This reinforces the impression that the manager of the Leiden branch of the Plantin Press – be it Plantin or

---

[122] See, e.g., Plantin's production of Esteban de Garibay y Zamalloa's history of the Iberian peninsula, *Los XL libros d'el compendio historial de las chronicas y universal historia de todos los reynos de España* (PP 1238).
[123] Richard Verstegen's *Theatrum crudelitatum haereticorum nostri temporis* is discussed below, together with Plantin's work for the print publisher Adriaen Huberti. See also appendix 5 for each of these editions.
[124] For the citations of Waghenaer's editions, see PP 2480, n. 7.
[125] See Koeman 1967–1971, IV, pp. 469–470, and *New Holl., Van Doetecum*, III, pp. 230–232.

6.18 Anonymous artists, title-plate of Lucas Janszoon Waghenaer, *Teerste deel vande spieghel der zeevaerdt* (Leiden: Christopher Plantin for Lucas Janszoon Waghenaer, 1584; f°), etching and engraving, 324 × 238 (Antwerp, Museum Plantin-Moretus, R 45.2).

Raphelengius – simply took on the occasional job of printing the texts for Waghenaer (and Hayen) and did not own the plates or organize the production of these publications himself.

More is known about the production of the *XXV fables des animaux* by Etienne Perret, an author and political activist from Brabant. Although Plantin's charge to Perret for printing this book was initially phrased in terms of a (not specified) fixed rate per number of sheets of paper printed, as was usually the case with his work for both Galle and Ortelius, it was not ultimately calculated this way. Rather, on May 6, 1578, the fee was formulated in terms of the number of illustrated copies that Perret was to give to Plantin in return, namely 104: "Et est accordé quil liverat p[ou]r cela p[ieces] 104 des fables imprimees avec les figures." (He had agreed that he would deliver for this 104 copies of the fables printed with the figures.)[126] Although no value is noted for the completed copies in Plantin's accounts with Perret, records of Plantin's sales of this text in his daily account book ("Journal") from 1579 indicate that he charged 18 or 20 st. per copy, which would amount to a minimum of 93 fl. 12 st. for all 104 copies (if all had been sold at 18 st. per copy).[127] This seems like a large amount for a thin folio book comprising fifty-two pages, only twenty-seven of which bore any typographically printed text. Unfortunately, we do not know how many copies were printed and whether Plantin also had to be compensated for providing the paper. Regardless of these additional questions, it appears that Plantin never even received his full payment, for his accounts indicate that Perret delivered only 70 of the 104 copies agreed to.[128] Plantin's accounts with Perret also notably lack the extra dealings in other items that are so striking in his transactions with Ortelius and the print publishers discussed here.

Perret's elegant book of fables (see fig. 6.19) is also significant in terms of Plantin's working relationship with Galle. As noted above, once Plantin began to print the texts for Galle's illustrated publications, he appears to have done so for nearly all of Galle's works containing letterpress up until 1589, when Plantin died. The one exception to this pattern is Galle's 1578 publication of the *Esbatement moral des animaux* (see fig. 6.21), for which Galle hired the Antwerp printer Gerard Smits to print the accompanying texts.[129] This exception to the "general rule" of Galle's employment of Plantin is all the more striking because the following year he did pay Plantin to print the text for a Latin edition of a comparable work, published under the title *Mythologia ethica hoc est moralis philosophiae per fabulas brutis attributas traditae amoenissimum viridarium* (see

---

[126] See MPM Arch. 18, fol. 142, for this agreement and notes on the delivery of the promised copies.

[127] For examples of sales of this book, identified as "Fables des animaux [in] f°," at 20 st., see MPM Arch. 56, fol. 62v (two copies to Michel Sonnius in Paris on May 12, 1579) and fol. 68r (one copy to Gerard van Kampen on May 24, 1579). For examples of the sale of this book at 18 st. per copy, see MPM Arch. 56, fol. 121v (two copies to Franciscus Raphelengius on October 1, 1578) and MPM Arch. 57, fol. 20v (five copies that were shipped to Frankfurt for sale at the book fair there, noted under February 23, 1579).

[128] See MPM Arch. 18, fol. 142, and MPM Arch. 56, fol. 60v, under May 12, 1578, for another record of Plantin's receipt of this group of seventy copies. Plantin's accounts with Perret are continued in MPM Arch. 20, fol. 85, where a note on the left side stating that Perret still owed Plantin thirty-four copies of the book lacks any corresponding acknowledgment of the receipt of them, which suggests (as noted by Voet, see PP 1962 n. 3) that the remaining copies were never delivered.

[129] See BT 8489 for this edition and Rouzet 1975, p. 204, for Smits.

I I.

De l'Aigle, & Limaſſon.

Celuy qui cerche à trop haut s'exalter,
L'on voit ſouuent bien bas precipiter.

LE Limaſſon faiché de ſe traîner par terre,
Promet de fort grans dons à celuy qui voudroit
D'ici bas l'eſleuer enuers le ciel tout droit:
Et qu'en outre feroit touſiours ſon tributaire.
L'Aigle oyant ces propos, pour de luy prouſit raire,
Haut il l'a eſleué, dont a eſté ioyeux:
Et bien luy a ſemblé tel eſtat valloir mieux,
Qu'en ce monde mener vie ſi ſolitaire.
Le Limaſſon en l'air menoit ioyeuſe vie,
Penſant qu'ici bas, plus ſur terre ne viendroit:
Mais l'Aigle luy a dit, Paye-moy or-endroit
Ce que tu m'as promis, auant que trop m'ennuie.
Dont la Limaſſé eut peur: & bien fort l'Aigle ſie
De le vouloir quitter dequoy par trop faché,
Entre ſes ongles vif l'a par piece eſtaché.
Promettre lon ne doit, ce que lon pouuoir denie.

ALLVSION

LE cas pareil ſouuent à pluſieurs il aduient,
Qui par ambition cerchent de s'exalter,
Ne pouuans leurs deſirs par raiſon contenter:
Parquoy tresgrand malheur tout à coup leur furuient
Mais qui en ſon eſtat bien content ſe maintient,
Et rend graces à Dieu de ce qu'il luy enuoye,
Iceluy à ſon cœur en repos plain de ioye.
A l'orgueilleux touſiours quelque malheur aduient.

LVCÆ XII.

CELVY qui eſt contens de ſa vocation,
Et par orgueil ne cerche à trop ſoy exalter,
En certes & en bien-le verra augmenter,
Et pourement finir, qui cerche ambition.

6.19 Anonymous artists, The Eagle and the Snail, from Etienne Perret, XXV fables des animaux (Antwerp: Christopher Plantin for Etienne Perret, 1578; f°), p. [7], opposite fable II, engraving, 212 × 280 (Antwerp, Museum Plantin-Moretus, R 26.6). This engraving was based upon the etching shown in figs. 6.20–6.22.

6.20 Marcus Gheeraerts I, *The Eagle and the Snail*, from Edward de Dene, *De warachtighe fabulen der dieren* (Bruges: Pieter de Clercq for Marcus Gheeraerts I, 1567; 4°), p. 160, etching, 95 × 112 (Antwerp, Stadsbibliotheek, H 49887). Compare figs. 6.20–6.22 for three different appearances of the same etching.

fig. 6.22). Galle's exceptional employment of Smits for the production of his 1578 French edition of the text may simply have been owing to Plantin's having a prior commitment for the printing of Perret's text. Moreover, Perret's *XXV fables des animaux* may have been regarded as a rival publication for Galle's *Esbatement moral*. Not only were both works moralistic accounts of animal fables written in French, but both clearly drew upon an earlier, trend-setting publication of fables featuring animals, namely Edward de Dene's *De warachtighe fabulen der dieren* (fig. 6.20). Printed in 1567 in Bruges by Pieter de Clerck for Marcus Gheeraerts I, the etcher responsible for the text's 107 illustrations, this work is now famous for the early use of etchings as true text illustrations and for the significant repercussions it had on later editions of animal fables produced in the Low Countries.[130]

Before summarizing the relationship between the four works concerned – *De warachtighe fabulen der dieren* from 1567, Perret's *XXV fables des animaux* from 1578, and Galle's 1578 and 1579 publications, the *Esbatement moral des animaux* and the *Mythologia*

---

[130] We examined a copy of this work in SBA (H 49887). See de Dene 1978 for a reprint of it with commentary. For other authors' assessment of this book and its significance for the illustration of later works like Perret's and Galle's publications, see, e.g., Bland 1969, p. 163; Harthan 1981, p. 75; Hodnett 1971, pp. 31–41; and Scheler 1968, pp. 350–355.

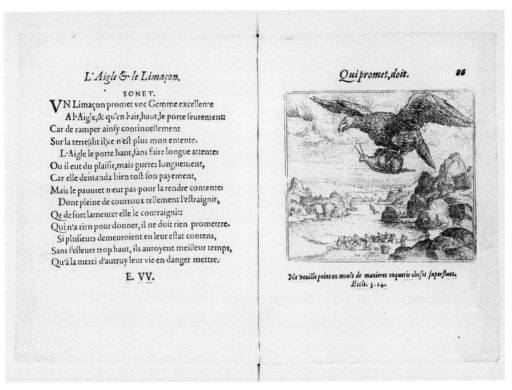

6.21 Marcus Gheeraerts I, *The Eagle and the Snail*, from Pieter Heyns, *Esbatement moral des animaux* (Antwerp: Gerard Smits for Philips Galle, 1578; 4°), fol. 86r, etching, 95 × 112 (Ghent, Universiteitsbibliotheek, kostbare werken, BL 1189). See the comment appended to fig. 6.20.

ethica – we first need to examine their illustration, the discussion of which has often been confused in earlier studies.[131] The original 107 text illustrations (but not the title-page vignette) etched by Gheeraerts for *De warachtighe fabulen der dieren* were all reused (albeit reworked), together with 18 new etchings, possibly executed by Gheeraerts, for the illustration of Galle's 1578 French and 1579 Latin editions of these fables. However, the order in which the original Gheeraerts etchings appear in Galle's editions is completely different from that in de Dene's text. In addition, the 18 extra illustrations are noteworthy for the introduction of an occasional image of nature alone, without a figural component, or scenes featuring men without animals.[132] Galle's publications also differ from their obvious visual precedent in the layout of the pages and in the selection of accompanying biblical references (compare figs. 6.20–6.22). Thus, while the plates were largely the same, it appears as though Galle was endeavoring to produce a textually distinct publication.

[131] See the discussion of Galle's *Mythologia ethica* from 1579 in appendix 5 for examples of this, in addition to opinions regarding the attribution of these plates and arguments as to who actually possessed them when Galle published his editions.

[132] In Galle's *Mythologia ethica*, the new etchings appear on pp. 3, 5, 7, 9, 11, 27, 33, 43, 45, 49, 51, 57, 93, 115, 127, 131, 135, and 235.

6.22 Marcus Gheeraerts I, *The Eagle and the Snail*, from Arnoldus Freitagius, *Mythologia ethica, hoc est moralis philosophiae per fabulas brutis attributas traditae amoenissimum viridarium* (Antwerp: Christopher Plantin for Philips Galle, 1579; 4°), p. 171, etching, 95 × 112 (Antwerp, Museum Plantin-Moretus, A 385). See the comment appended to fig. 6.20.

Perret's *XXV fables des animaux* is, in many ways, the opposite of Galle's publications. Here, the illustrations consist of a (in relative terms) fairly limited selection of twenty-four subjects that had appeared in *De warachtighe fabulen der dieren* – although, once again, in a clearly independent order – together with one introductory image of man as king over the animal world. In addition, while the main compositional elements present in each of the animal fables shown are clearly taken from Gheeraerts's original set of illustrations, the compositions are reversed and the main elements are stretched out vertically and enlarged upon in the creation of each grand, full-page engraving. No longer set within a page of text – as is the case in both *De warachtighe fabulen der dieren* and Galle's publications – Perret's illustrations appear as sumptuous, independent engravings to be enjoyed in their own right, as compared with the other, smaller, overtly textual illustrations produced by Gheeraerts (compare figs. 6.19 and 6.20). In Perret's publication, the accompanying text, typically a reduced selection of what one finds in *De warachtighe fabulen der dieren*, is limited to the facing, left-hand page. The absence of even commonplace pagination or signatures of leaves enhances the similitude of this work with a print book and strengthens the distance between it and ordinary illustrated books. Thus, while Perret's selection of illustrations and presentation of them is highly independent from its model, *De warachtighe fabulen der dieren*, its textual component and, in particular, the selection of accompanying biblical verses, was clearly a simple reduction of what was found in de Dene's work.

The distinctions in visual appearance and textual content between these works suggest that the authors and publishers involved were aiming at satisfying the preferences of different markets. While de Dene's and Galle's works both have a much more substantial textual grounding – albeit different in content and language – Perret's work may have been more appealing for those wanting a quick, visually pleasurable "read." Plantin bought and sold numerous copies of all four publications, despite the fact that he printed the accompanying text only for two – Perret's *XXV fables des animaux* from 1578 and Galle's *Mythologia ethica* from 1579. Specifically, between February 12, 1569 and May 1571, some two to four years following the publication of *De warachtighe fabulen der dieren*, he purchased a hundred copies of the book from Hubertus Goltzius, the bookseller in Bruges to whom Gheeraerts had dedicated the publication. Plantin was able to buy these copies at a reduced rate of 10 st. per copy (instead of the originally stated 12 st.), for a total of 50 fl. Although this agreement was noted on August 7, 1569, Goltzius was paid in installments, over the period from February 1569 to May 1571, via the intermediary of another bookseller in Bruges, Jacobus Plantius.[133] As noted above, in May 1578, Plantin received 70 copies of Perret's publication (of a promised 104) in exchange for printing the text. In addition, he also periodically purchased copies of both of Galle's editions up until his death in 1589. Usually buying two to six copies at one time, these isolated purchases would amount to approximately fifty copies of each publication by August 1589.[134]

Although tracing the buyers of all of the copies of these publications in Plantin's possession would be akin to trying to locate 270 needles in twenty haystacks, an examination of his initial sale of each work is itself of interest. Plantin arranged to buy his large consignment of a hundred copies of *De warachtighe fabulen der dieren* in 1569, some ten years prior to the publication of the other three works under consideration. An examination of his sales from this year reveal that the biggest sales (of twelve copies each) were made to people familiar to us here, namely, Hieronymus Cock, Gerard de Jode, and Abraham Ortelius. Only a few isolated copies were shipped to other individuals – all living in the Northern Netherlands, Amsterdam, or The Hague, for example – and not one was included in Plantin's shipments of books for the Frankfurt fair. While Ortelius and a certain Peeter Quertkens in Amsterdam paid a specially discounted price of only 12 st. per copy – the price that Goltzius was originally going to charge Plantin for each of his hundred copies – de Jode paid 14 st. per copy and the remaining buyers paid a full 15 st.[135] A sample of records of sales from 1578 and 1579 – the first two years in which the remaining three publications appeared – reveals the following about these works.

[133] For this transaction, see MPM Arch. 16, fol. 16, under "Fabulen der dieren."
[134] For records of these purchases, see MPM Arch. 18, fols. 282 rht, 321 rht, and 394 rht; and MPM Arch. 20, fols. 146 rht, 228 rht, and 307 rht.
[135] For sales of thirteen copies to de Jode in the course of 1569, see MPM Arch. 16, fol. 15 lft, under May 9, 1569. These records also reveal that de Jode had already purchased nine copies of this book (then at 15 st. per copy) in 1568. For the remaining sales, see MPM Arch. 47, fol. 31r (three copies to Peeter Peeterssen "alias Sweertkens?" for a certain "Marie" in The Hague); fol. 45v (twelve copies to Hieronymus Cock); fol. 58v (one copy to Waulter Janssen in The Hague); fol. 126r (twelve copies to Ortelius); and fol. 153r (one copy to Peeter Quertkens? in Amsterdam).

Although a couple of shipments of Perret's book to the Frankfurt fair are known, the majority of the copies sold – forty-four in 1578 alone, valued at 18 or 20 st. per copy – went to a great variety of booksellers and some private individuals.[136] This is in striking contrast to Galle's *Esbatement moral des animaux* (typically listed at 25 st. per copy) and his *Mythologia ethica* (typically listed at 27 st. per copy). For most of Plantin's initial purchases of these editions indicate that the vast majority of these copies were, in fact, bought for immediate shipment to Frankfurt for sale at the fair there.[137]

Thus it appears that, in contrast with his sale of Perret's text, Plantin's initial purchases (and resale) of Galle's editions were more limited in quantity and market, being destined mainly for the Frankfurt fair as opposed to the local market and his regular buyers. It would, indeed, be logical if these markets were left to Galle as the publisher of these books. Galle was able to benefit, in turn, from Plantin's international distribution network via the Frankfurt book fair even on the rare occasion that he did not involve Plantin in the production of the work. Plantin's initial sale of *De warachtighe fabulen der dieren* also seems to have been limited, but then either to a few local buyers interested in prints, or to a few individuals further away in the Northern Netherlands. This peculiar distribution may have been influenced by the fact that the book had been available for sale for two years before Plantin acquired his group of a hundred copies. All of these sales also confirm what has already been observed, namely, that whether Plantin himself had actually printed the accompanying text does not appear to have affected his decision as a bookseller as to whether or not he would actively distribute the work. These were clearly distinct and independent components of Plantin's business activities.

PLANTIN'S WORK FOR THE PRINT PUBLISHERS ADRIAEN HUBERTI AND GERARD DE JODE

The last two figures who are known to have occasionally employed Plantin (in addition to other local printers) for the printing of letterpress for their independent publications are Adriaen Huberti and Gerard de Jode. De Jode, a friend of Philips Galle, made his name as a publisher of maps and prints in Antwerp in the 1550s, just when Plantin was beginning to work as a printer-publisher of books. Huberti, who was the son-in-law of Mynken Liefrinck, the person Plantin employed to print the majority of his intaglio book illustrations, was younger and did not establish himself as an engraver and print publisher in Antwerp until the 1570s. Huberti would similarly employ Plantin's successor, Jan Moretus I, for the occasional printing of texts for his publications.[138] Of

---

[136] For a sample of these sales, see MPM Arch. 56, fols. 60r, 61r, 62r, 62v, 63r, 65r (2x), 68r (2x), 70v, 73v, 75r, 79v, 80r, 92v, 96v, 121v, and 139v.

[137] For examples of this, see, e.g., MPM Arch. 57, fol. 11v (under January 27, 1579) for the initial purchase of six copies of the *Esbatement moral des animaux*, and fol. 12r (under January 28, 1579) for the inclusion of six copies of the same in a shipment destined for Frankfurt. See MPM Arch. 58, fol. 9r (under January 22, 1580) for an initial purchase of twenty copies of the *Mythologia ethica*, and then, just below in another entry, the inclusion of a group of twenty copies of the same in a shipment bound for Frankfurt.

[138] For a brief overview of de Jode's activities, see Rouzet 1975, pp. 105–106. Huberti's activities are also discussed in appendix 1, pp. 341–342. That de Jode and Galle were friends can be inferred from the fact

the two, Huberti's transactions with Plantin are closest to Galle and Plantin's exchange of activities, despite their brief concentration in the later 1580s.[139]

As was the case with Galle, Huberti engaged Plantin to print some of his better known (and most likely more costly) publications – Latin and French editions of Richard Verstegen's *Theatre of the Cruelties of Heretics of our Time* – as well as some of his lesser known and ephemeral works – indulgences, verses, and a series of the seven sacraments, with St. Francis.[140] Although we have not been able to identify specifically which indulgences Plantin printed for Huberti, examples of such texts published by the latter reveal that these, at least, were not necessarily illustrated.[141] In addition – and, once again, reminiscent of Galle – Huberti also occasionally saw to engraving work for Plantin. For example, Huberti was compensated for having letters engraved on to a title-plate used for one volume of Caesar Baronius's *Annales ecclesiastici*. Finally, Huberti also sold Plantin some copper plates, whose only specification was that they were old.[142] Despite these numerous similarities in the sorts of transactions Plantin had with both Huberti and Galle, the production of Richard Verstegen's controversial text on Catholic martyrs does provide an example of yet another distinct set of arrangements made for the production of books with engraved illustrations.

Richard Verstegen, alias Richard Rowlands, fled England sometime prior to 1580 and, following a period in Paris, settled in Antwerp in the 1580s. Once there, Verstegen was an important figure among the English Catholic refugees. Although he himself did not have a printing press, he saw to the publication of a number of works defending the Catholic church.[143] Among these works are nine editions of his *Theatrum crudelitatum haereticorum nostri temporis*, or *Theatre de(s) cruautez des hereticques de nostre temps*, eight of which were published by Huberti between 1587 and 1607. Of these, two Latin and three French editions appeared in 1587 and 1588 alone.

As is documented in appendix 5, Plantin first printed the text for the 1587 Latin edition (which was then reissued in 1588 with a newly dated title-page), after which he printed the shorter of the two French editions Huberti published in 1588 (see fig. 6.23). The typographical materials used to print the two remaining French editions from 1587 and 1588 indicate that Plantin was not involved in either of these publications. Although the other French edition from 1588 – often characterized as the expanded edition with

---

    that Galle was the godfather of de Jode's daughter, Jeanne de Jode (see Sellink 1997, II, p. 154, n. 62). For more on Huberti and Jan Moretus's on/off working relationship, see Imhof 2007–2008.

[139] Although the works that we will be discussing are all datable to 1587–1588, one record (MPM Arch. 20, fol. 259 lft) indicates that Huberti's accounts were carried over from another record book called the "memoriales," which may have comprised earlier accounts that are no longer preserved.

[140] Each of these is described in appendix 5. Verstegen's editions are also discussed in greater detail below.

[141] See Huberti's (1) *Aflaeten van . . . Sixtus de vijfste ghegunt die artbroederschap der coordedraghers S. Francisci* (BT 6744; MPM [R 63.8 II: 28]); (2) *Indulgencias concedidas, por . . . Sisto Quinto, especialmente a la archiconfradia del cordon del padre san Francisco* (BT 6747; MPM [R 63.8 II: 27]); and (3) *D'inhoudt des aflaets van woordt tot woorde, d'aertsbroederschaps van S. Franciscus coorde* (BT 6038; MPM [R 63.8 II: 16]). Regrettably, it has not been possible to determine whether or not Plantin printed these specific works.

[142] See MPM Arch. 20, fol. 259 rht, for the charge of 12 st. for "escripture quil a taille in frontispicio Annalium f°" (the writing that he engraved in the frontispiece [of the] *Annales* [in] folio); and for the record that Plantin owed Huberti 24 fl. because "quil a . . . vendu quelques vieles planches de cuivre a mon pere et sont d'accordt pour le dit prix" (he had sold a few old plates of copper to my father [Plantin] and [they] agreed to the stated price).

[143] On Verstegen and his publications, see Rombauts 1933; Rombauts 1934; Petti 1963; and Arblaster 2004.

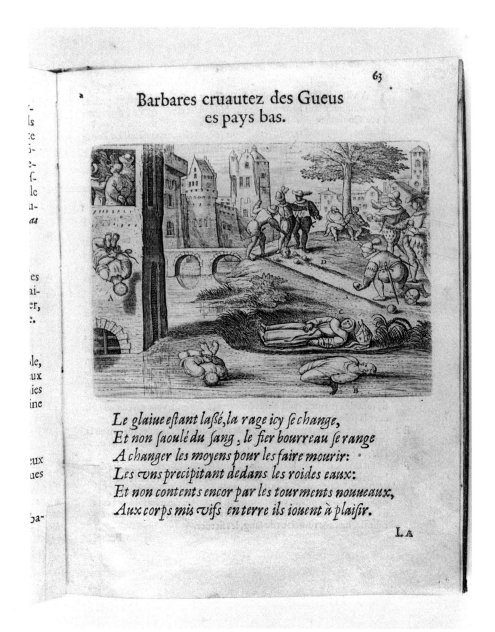

6.23 Anonymous artists, *Barbaric Cruelties Inflicted by the "Geuzen" on the Priests in Oudenaarde, Flanders*, from Richard Verstegen, *Theatre des cruautez des hereticques de nostre temps* (Antwerp: Christopher Plantin for Adriaen Huberti [and Richard Verstegen], 1588; 4°), p. 63, engraving, 99 × 133 (Antwerp, Museum Plantin-Moretus, R 16.4).

a "fuller commentary" – bears the same illustrations as those found in the editions printed by Plantin, the illustrations in the 1587 French edition are what Anthony G. Petti terms "poor copies" of the presumed originals. This has resulted in the 1587 French edition being called "piracy," while other editions are identified as "genuine"

Huberti editions.[144] Beyond this question of copies and originals, it is clear from the Plantin archives that the production and publication of these texts was not a simple case of Huberti organizing matters, as one might expect from the title-pages of the editions concerned, where simply the place of publication (Antwerp) and the publisher (Huberti) are cited. Rather – at least for the 1588 French edition which Plantin printed – Verstegen, and not Huberti, was charged for the work of printing the text. Moreover, Verstegen (and not Huberti) was the one who sold Plantin copies of both Latin and French editions of this text.[145] Thus, while the imprints on the title-pages of all of these editions indicate that the text was published by Huberti, this was not, in fact, the case. Verstegen, not Huberti, filled the role of publisher (at least on occasion), organizing the production of the book, distributing at least some of the copies, and paying some, if not all, of the accompanying costs.[146] Huberti's main contribution may simply have been serving as a front for Verstegen. This unexpected (and clandestine) organization of the production of these books may help clarify the variation noted above in both their content and the selection of who would print them, or who might secretly copy them. Once again, occasional work as the printer of some else's text was no guarantee of more.

Plantin's scant, infrequent transactions with Gerard de Jode provide the most telling contrast with Plantin's extensive and multifaceted working relationship with Galle. Like Galle, de Jode dealt in maps and independent prints, which he sold primarily as independent sheets, but also occasionally in book form. His single most ambitious cartographic project was his *Speculum orbis terrarum*. This atlas was first printed for de Jode in two volumes in 1578 by the Antwerp printer Gerard Smits, who also printed the text for Galle's edition of the *Esbatement moral*, which was published in the same year.[147] Hereafter, however, it appears that de Jode employed Plantin (and his sons-in-law, Franciscus Raphelengius and Jan Moretus, when Plantin was in Leiden in 1584) to print the accompanying texts for his next print-book publications. Instead of cartographic works, these were all moralizing, edifying texts, namely, the 1579 (and possibly the 1584) edition of the *Parvus mundus*, a 1584 edition of the same in Dutch, titled *De cleyn werelt*, and a 1584 publication of Jan Moerman's *Apologi creaturarum*, which is the only one of the four to bear Plantin's name as the printer.[148] Although the emblematic combination of text and image in all of these works is similar to Galle's fable books, discussed above, the illustrations in de Jode's editions are clearly distinct in both subject matter and composition (see figs. 6.24 and 6.25).

---

[144] For this identification of the second set of plates, see Petti 1963, p. 89, no. 4e. For the subsequent description of the 1587 French edition as piracy and others as genuine Huberti editions, see, e.g., Allison and Rogers 1989, nos. 1301–1303. Allison and Rogers do not include the expanded 1588 French edition in either of these groups, simply describing it as "A different French translation" (see no. 1304).

[145] See MPM Arch. 20, fol. 298 lft, for the charge to Verstegen at an unspecified date in 1588 for "limpression de 18 rames en . . . son livre en françois a 30 patt la rame" (the printing of 18 reams in . . . his book in French at 30 st. per ream). See fol. 298 rht for records of Plantin's purchases of copies of both French and Latin editions of this text in the course of 1588.

[146] Although Petti even attributes the execution of the plates to Verstegen (Petti 1959, p. 81), it is not clear if this was, in fact, the case.

[147] For more on de Jode's *Speculum orbis terrarum* (BT 5577), see Denucé 1912–1913, I, pp. 181–198. For Smits, see n. 149.

[148] See appendix 5 for more on each of these editions.

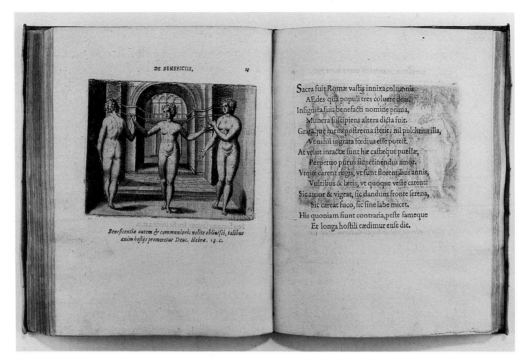

6.24 Anonymous artists, *De beneficiis*, from Laurentius Haechtanus, Μικρόκοσμος. *Parvus mundus* (Antwerp: Christopher Plantin for Gerard de Jode, 1579; 4°), fol. E3v, engraving, 93 × 118 (Antwerp, Museum Plantin-Moretus, 55.18).

6.25 Marcus Gheeraerts I?, *Superborum ruina*, from Jan Moerman, *Apologi creaturarum* (Antwerp: Christopher Plantin for Gerard de Jode, 1584; 4°), fol. A1r, etching, 76 × 121 (Antwerp, Museum Plantin-Moretus, R 55.18).

While it is impossible to know for certain, de Jode's switch to Plantin as the printer of the accompanying typographical texts for his publications may have come about simply because Smits appears to have stopped working as a printer by 1579 and may have died soon thereafter.[149] The increasingly difficult situation in Antwerp in 1584 resulting from the siege by the Spanish troops may also have led Plantin (and his sons-in-law), as well as de Jode, to think differently about working together on such projects. It seems unlikely that these arrangements were made because of a particular bond with Plantin, as one might argue in the case of Galle or Ortelius. De Jode's transactions with Plantin were remarkably irregular, both in their timing and in terms of the quantity of items involved.[150]

Generally, de Jode made only occasional purchases of richly illustrated books, like Arias Montano's *Humanae salutis monumenta* and de Dene's *De warachtighe fabulen der dieren*.[151] These sales amounted to approximately 30–40 fl. per year and were often fairly evenly balanced by Plantin's own purchases of independent prints, as well as many colored and varnished maps, from de Jode. Plantin also did not always grant de Jode the same discounts that he gave to Ortelius and his circle of favored booksellers.[152] In addition to these rather limited transactions, however, de Jode did buy four copies of Plantin's Polyglot Bible by June 3, 1572, for a total of 240 fl. And, in 1583 and 1587, he made three remarkably large purchases of books that are striking for the great variety of titles listed and the lack of the richly illustrated copies that otherwise characterize his purchases. The last and largest of these sales, recorded on August 5, 1587, was for a total of 519 fl. 12 st., which Plantin reduced to 472 fl., to be paid within four months. Extra notes here indicate that de Jode had, in fact, bought these books for other individuals in Danzig, Poland: a certain Salomon Bisset and a bookseller, Stephen Schultzen. Most likely, de Jode's two other exceptional purchases made in 1583 were similarly for third parties.[153]

As for de Jode's publications in which Plantin (or his sons-in-law) were involved, there is only evidence of Plantin buying back copies of two of them: de Jode's 1579 *Parvus mundus* edition and his 1584 *Apologi creaturarum*. The former is the only one of the four de Jode editions that Plantin noted in his own list of publications of Antwerp printers and the latter is the only one of the four publications that bears Plantin's name as the printer.[154] Nevertheless, as Plantin's general accounts with de Jode make clear,

---

[149] See Rouzet 1975, p. 204.

[150] See MPM Arch. 16, fols. 15, 31 and 196, MPM Arch. 18, fols. 66 and 414, and MPM Arch. 20, fols. 63 and 206, for de Jode's accounts with Plantin, and Denucé 1912–1913, I, p. 165, for a summary of their transactions, and pp. 210–220 for some transcriptions of these records.

[151] See, e.g., MPM Arch. 16, fol. 31 lft, under December 2, 1570, for de Jode's purchase of six copies of the *Monumenta*, and fol. 15 lft, for purchases made between August 22, 1568 and May? 1569 of twenty-two copies of a work identified as the "fabulen der dieren 4°."

[152] Consider, e.g., the remarks above concerning de Jode's purchases of *De warachtighe fabulen der dieren*.

[153] For these purchases, see MPM Arch. 16, fol. 196 lft (for the copies of the Polyglot Bible) and MPM Arch. 20, fol. 63 lft (under June 2, 1583 and October 4, 1583) and fol. 206 lft (under August 5, 1587). Each of the larger purchases is transcribed in greater detail in other record books. For the first two from 1583, see MPM Arch. 61, fols. 67v–68v and fol. 131r, respectively; for the one from 1587, see MPM Arch. 64, fols. 101v and 102r.

[154] For this reference to the 1579 edition of the *Parvus mundus*, see MPM M 296, fol. 389r, where it is listed under its Greek title, Μικρόκοσμος, with a selling price of 28 st.

such purchases were more the exception than the rule. For example, in the two and a half years between September 14, 1584 and January 14, 1587, Plantin bought just eight copies of the *Apologia creaturarum*, each at 22 st. per copy.[155] This is in stark contrast, for example, with his purchases of nearly thirty copies each of Galle's *Esbatement moral* and *Mythologia ethica* in the first couple of years following their publication.[156]

Could the buying publics for de Jode's and Galle's publications have been so different as to justify such a difference in Plantin's buying interest, or were there other factors at play? As observed above, the vast majority of Plantin's initial purchases of Galle's *Esbatement moral* and *Mythologia ethica* editions were sent on to Frankfurt for sale at the fair there, almost immediately after Galle had delivered the copies. De Jode may have sought to prevent Plantin (and other booksellers) from distributing his publications there because he had his own stand at the Frankfurt fair. This was run by a German merchant, Cornelis Caymockx, who served as de Jode's representative there and who, presumably, endeavored to work as the one and only marketer of de Jode's publications at the fair.[157] Thus, one of the important facets of Plantin's working relationship with both Galle and Ortelius, namely, as an important international distributor of their publications, may have been beyond Plantin's grasp for de Jode's work. Would this, in turn, have influenced both de Jode and Plantin when considering whether or not they should work for one another, either occasionally or systematically? It is one option that we will have to consider in our concluding examination of the potential motives behind the mutual engagement of letterpress printers, pictorial publishers, and authors.

CONCLUSION: TO WORK FOR ANOTHER OR NOT?

In the mid-1580s, shortly after his return to Antwerp from Leiden in October 1585, Plantin regularly wrote letters to friends and, in particular, potential patrons, in which he lamented the sorry state of his business and his bleak prospects. In these letters, Plantin regularly refers to himself as a "slave" or "le simple loyer du labeur comme mercenaire" (a simple hired hand, like a mercenary).[158] Plantin simultaneously referred to his business as one that was "riche de presses et de characteres mais pauvres pour les employer autrement qu'au plus grand profict d'autruy que de moymesmes" (rich in presses and type, but too poor to employ them except to the great profit of others).[159] Were these self-pitying letters in part just a show, put on by Plantin in order to garner extra sympathy and work? Or did Plantin enter into such arrangements simply for the additional income, while viewing himself meanly as just a hireling? Or were these arrangements for all concerned, something that was done simply out of pure necessity, at some expense, and with the implied loss of some degree of control over the resulting project? While Plantin cited his work for other publishers of books when making these

---

[155] See MPM Arch. 20, fol. 266 rht, for these purchases of the *Apologi creaturarum* and MPM Arch. 57, fol. 103r, under July 16, 1579, for Plantin's purchase of a few copies of the *Parvus mundus*.
[156] See MPM Arch. 18, fols. 282 rht, 321 rht, and 394 rht, for these purchases.
[157] On de Jode's representative in Frankfurt, see Denucé 1912–1913, I, p. 166.
[158] For this particular excerpt, see *Corr.*, VII, no. 1047, p. 219.
[159] See Voet, GC, I, p. 117, n. 2 for this excerpt, which is cited without a specific source.

remarks, it is worth considering whether this was his attitude towards his work for print publishers and authors of richly illustrated works as well.[160]

When employed to print the text for another's illustrated work, Plantin typically charged a set number of stuivers per ream of sheets printed. The few more detailed records that we have for the rates that he paid to the individual compositors and pressmen engaged to execute this work indicate that usually the single greatest component of Plantin's fees was that of having the text set.[161] Occasionally Plantin also provided and charged for the paper used. Generally, however, the person commissioning the work appears to have provided the paper himself. The paper was, usually, the single greatest cost in the production of a work, alongside the cost of having intaglio illustrations made.[162] In only one case – Etienne Perret's *XXV fables des animaux* – did Plantin accept a specified number of copies of the finished work in lieu of a set payment. While this practice may have been more common among editions without intaglio illustrations, it remained a gamble – both in terms of whether Plantin would actually receive all of the promised copies and whether or not he would be able to sell them for his calculated profit once they were delivered.[163]

Regardless of how Plantin was compensated, printing texts for others' illustrated works did not represent a significant money-making component of his business. Not only were the fees that he charged relatively small in comparison with other sums that he would have earned through sales, but these occasional commissions represented a relatively small percentage of his work on an annual basis.[164] Consider, for example, the period 1578–1589, when Plantin was hired to print accompanying texts for three or four illustrated publications on average per year.[165] In this same period, he printed approximately eighty to one hundred editions of his own annually, ranging from one-page announcements to books comprising hundreds of pages.[166] Thus, Plantin's work for others' illustrated editions was but a small part of his total output. Moreover, as was observed in the discussions of his dealings with Galle and Ortelius, Plantin's charges to them for the printing of text were always significantly outweighed by what he owed for the illustrated books and independent images he bought from them. Thus, in these cases, at least, Plantin may have regarded his work not as a money-making venture, but rather as a means of offsetting some of the purchases he wanted to make and thereby lessening how much he himself would have to pay out to others.

---

[160] For this reference to his work for other booksellers, see Voet, GC, I, p. 118. Voet observes that Plantin used these phrases with "monotonous regularity" from this time onward, and usually in letters to those who might be able to assist him (Voet, GC, I, p. 117, n. 2, and p. 118).

[161] See, e.g., the discussion of Galle's *Mythologia ethica* from 1579 in appendix 5.

[162] For examples of the dominating cost of paper among Plantin's publications, see Voet, GC, II, pp. 379–385, as well as Plantin and Galle's production of Furmerius's *De rerum usu et abusu* and Canisius's catechism, discussed above. The only possible exceptions to this general rule would be cases in which a large number of impressions were made of a relatively inexpensive plate (see also Bury 2001, p. 44).

[163] See Voet, GC, I, p. 118, for examples of Plantin receiving copies of books that he printed for other printer-publishers.

[164] See above for a discussion of the relative value of Plantin's fees.

[165] These figures are calculated on the basis of the projects cited in appendix 5.

[166] See Voet 1984, pp. 367–368, for these figures.

It is also important to recall that agreements to print texts for another do not appear to have come with extra guarantees. There are two essential aspects of this "no guarantee policy," both of which are particularly clear from Plantin's dealings with Galle and de Jode. First, established business connections, degrees of personal friendship, and even a regular habit of employing Plantin for the printing of accompanying texts did not guarantee that the same individuals – Galle or Ortelius, for example – would always hire him. The occasional examples of these publishers turning to another printer may reflect an active, positive choice on their part owing to, for example, another printer simply offering a better price for the given project. They could also reflect a necessary switch because of Plantin's refusal to help with a particular project. Plantin may have had too much work at that time – as may have been the case in the early 1570s when Galle and Ortelius employed other printers – or competing commitments – as may have been the case in 1578 when Plantin printed Perret's *XXV fables des animaux* and Galle turned to another Antwerp printer, Gerard Smits, for the printing of his *Esbatement moral des animaux*. Second, Plantin's decision to purchase another publisher's work for resale was not simply linked to whether or not he had printed the text for it. While Plantin did regularly buy back fully illustrated copies of the texts he printed, he did not do so invariably. Apparently, he was not always interested in (or permitted to, perhaps, in the case of de Jode's works) selling copies of the publications he printed for others. One agreement in one branch of Plantin's business (that of printing texts) did not necessarily imply an agreement in another branch (sales).

The above observations provide little support for the hypothesis that Plantin agreed to work as the printer for these projects for simple, predictable financial gain. While he presumably would have been sure that he made a profit when charging others for printing texts, the amounts that he ultimately earned in this fashion were not that significant when considered in the broader context of his business operations and production as a whole.

The timing of Plantin's engagement in this type of work is also significant when considering the question of whether or not his professed feeling of being a hireling can be associated with his work on these illustrated publications. The list of these publications in appendix 5 reveals that Plantin agreed to take on such work periodically from 1574 to 1589. Thus, he started to execute such commissions once his business was on a firm footing and he had demonstrated that he could organize the production of striking publications with engraved illustrations on his own. While it is tempting to relate the timing of his acceptance of these extra printing commissions to periods of greater financial difficulties owing to the war with Spain, the majority of them – in particular, those from 1574, 1575, and the late 1580s – fall beyond these dates. Thus, the timing of Plantin's work on these projects similarly provides little support for the association of them with his self-proclaimed status as a mere hireling for others.

Was Plantin, then, a generally interested, engaged figure when assisting others with their production of publications with engraved and etched illustrations? Looking back over the list of his work on others' illustrated editions, it is evident that the majority of these projects were for those with whom he had the most extensive extra business dealings, namely, Galle and Ortelius. Was this purely coincidental, did this work simply represent an exchange of favors between friends, or, to return to our original question, were there yet other (non-monetary) factors influencing Plantin's willingness to print for others? What were the advantages of such arrangements for all concerned?

Why was it common for these two sets of printers – letterpress and copper-plate printers – to maintain separate businesses and employ one another from time to time? The obvious, logical argument is that it was advantageous in both practical and economic terms to specialize in just one of the two crafts. Nevertheless, Plantin found it worth his while to acquire the necessary materials for printing intaglio images and to maintain one employee, Jacques vander Hoeven, for the occasional printing of his copper plates in the period 1571–1584 and in 1589. Plantin did so while he also regularly turned to independent print shops – in particular, that run by Mynken Liefrinck – for the printing of the bulk of his intaglio book illustrations.[167] Why did such figures as Galle, who clearly maintained a large, active business, not do the reverse? The answer lies in a simple analysis of the costs associated with working as a letterpress printer.

If one totals all of the amounts that Plantin is known to have charged Galle for the addition of letterpress to the latter's own, independent publications (as detailed in appendix 5), this amounts to approximately 236 fl. for the entire thirteen-year period, 1577–1589. This amount is, by necessity, an underestimated minimum for two reasons: first, we do not know what Plantin charged for all of the work that he executed for Galle – consider the texts he added to Galle's early 1574 print series of Bol's landscapes and Vredeman de Vries's series of wells, for example; and second, it also excludes the printing costs of five major projects in which Plantin was also involved and, hence, helped defray the costs. These are, namely, Galle and Plantin's two joint projects – their 1575 edition of Furmerius's *De rerum usu et abusu* and 1589 edition of Canisius's illustrated catechism – and the three French editions of Galle's pocket atlas that were ultimately bought up in full by Plantin. If one were to add half of the printing costs of their two joint publications – 3 fl. 7 st. for the *De rerum usu et abusu* and 24 fl. for the catechism – and all of the printing costs for the three French Epitome editions – 33 fl. for the 1579 edition, 34 fl. for the 1582 edition, and 45 fl. 10 st. for the 1588 edition – the new minimum of what Galle owed Plantin for the printing of texts would be approximately 376 fl. Plantin charged Ortelius more than twice this amount – at least 782 fl. – for his work on five editions of Ortelius's atlas, produced between 1579 and 1587 (see appendix 5). Even so, the conclusions would be the same, for the costs of establishing and maintaining a print shop for typographical text were higher still.

While a basic typographical printing press that could be maintained for decades might cost only 50–60 fl.,[168] the annual payments Plantin made on extra accessories, type, and the staff necessary to work a press – usually at least one compositor, one pressman, and an assistant for the pressman – were much more. For example, just replacing the parts of a press (the linen and parchment found in the tympans and friskets, for example), as well as the leather and wool filling of the ink balls that would wear out in the course of a year, could amount to as much as approximately 20 fl. per

---

[167] See ch. 2 for more on copper-plate printers generally and Plantin's employment of vander Hoeven and Liefrinck in particular.

[168] See Voet, GC, II, p. 133.

press in use per year.[169] The minimum wages that Plantin paid to his staff on an annual basis were, on average, approximately 68 fl. for a compositor, 124 fl. for a pressman, and 76 fl. for the pressman's assistant.[170] Naturally, these costs would most likely have been less if a press was only used intermittently and the staff needed to man it hired on a daily basis, for example. The main unavoidable expense, however, was for the type used. Costing as much as 70–86 fl. per font, type wore out readily and had to be replaced regularly.[171] If one wanted to combine different fonts in different sizes, as was commonly done, the costs for all of the fonts used, together with the other expenses incurred, would exceed even our largest estimate of 782 fl. for Plantin's charges to Ortelius. Thus, the advantage to Galle and Ortelius – and other authors and print publishers like them – in employing a letterpress printer like Plantin for the printing of the accompanying text in their publications is clear. But what of Plantin? What were the advantages to him of entering into such agreements?

If Plantin was, indeed, endeavoring to earn a reputation for himself as a leading figure in the production of texts with engraved illustrations, one relatively inexpensive way to increase his association with this type of publication was to appear as their printer. In this way, he could benefit from some "free publicity" won by the distribution of these works by their publisher, if not by himself. The pattern of the appearance of Plantin's name in these publications offers some support for this theory. For he is named in the vast majority that were, in essence, illustrated books (as distinct from a series of prints with only an introductory note to the reader or a dedication).[172] This holds true, notably, for Galle's and Ortelius's publications – the men for whom Plantin worked the most – as well as for Hayen's, Waghenaer's, and Perret's texts. The main exceptions to this pattern are de Jode's editions of the *Parvus mundus* and Verstegen's texts on Catholic martyrs. In terms of the Huberti–Verstegen publications, if Verstegen's roles as author and financier were deliberately concealed, why not Plantin's role as the printer? As for de Jode's editions, we can only speculate. Perhaps the absence of Plantin's name was symptomatic of de Jode's wishing to appear as their exclusive publisher, or else, simply their limited working relationship, which did not flourish as did Plantin's dealings with Galle and Ortelius.

Another possible incentive for Plantin may have been the resulting extra contact with others in Antwerp who were actively engaged in the production and publication of engraved or etched images in combination with an accompanying letterpress text. As observed above, the majority of Plantin's commissions for the printing of texts came from men with whom he had significant supplementary dealings in the sale of prints, maps, and illustrated (print) books, in addition to occasional transactions involving copper plates. Perhaps Plantin's performance of these extra, often relatively

---

[169] See Voet, GC, II, pp. 148–151, for his estimates of the additional outlays that Plantin made for these accoutrements in the period 1563–1567, when Plantin was operating five presses annually, on average.

[170] For examples of the wages Plantin paid to his compositors and pressmen in the period 1563–1567, see Voet, GC, II, pp. 336–337. In some years (1566, for example), Plantin employed, on average, at least two pressmen and more than two compositors per press (see Voet, GC, II, p. 335).

[171] For examples of the amounts Plantin paid for some of his type fonts, see, e.g., Voet, GC, II, pp. 106 and 122. On the need to replace type regularly and the resulting significant cost of type for a printer, see, e.g., Voet, GC, II, p. 113, and Febvre-Martin 1990, pp. 110 and 114.

[172] See appendix 5 for the editions which actually bore Plantin's name.

small printing jobs was also part of an effort to foster favorable business relations with these people, supported, potentially, by an underlying willingness to help out friends, albeit for a nominal fee? Regrettably, we will never know for sure owing to the lack of records of their terms of agreement.

These questions aside, a few essential points are clearer now. First, even well-known Antwerp businessmen like Plantin and Galle were willing to work together to produce common, ephemeral works such as verses or indulgences, in addition to their more famous publications. Second, most of the individuals considered did deal in objects usually believed to be beyond their "official" job description – recall, for example, how Plantin, Galle, Ortelius, and Huberti would sell and lend copper plates to one another, or Galle's numerous purchases of paper, as well as a variety of illustrated and unillustrated books from Plantin, and the reams of prints and maps that Plantin bought in exchange. And third, by way of this work – and especially those editions bearing his name as the printer – Plantin did manage to embed himself all the more thoroughly and prominently in the world of producing costly and technically demanding publications featuring engraved or etched illustrations. With the worlds of print maker, print publisher, pictorial printer, letterpress printer, publisher, and dealer in books, maps, prints, paper, and plates perpetually overlapping, Plantin was clearly in the thick of it all. Only the evidence of who owned which kind of printing press and its accessories provides the primary and constant distinguishing factor. Thus, while the control and possession of the plates used for these publications were, indeed, carefully guarded rights, the arrangements made to print and publish the resulting images were surprisingly supple and varied.

CONCLUSION

Ite procul reliqui commercia vilia libri,
    Caetera Plantino cedite praela meo.
Ite libri, cunctaeque simul sordescite chartae,
    Quae non haec prima nomina fronte gerant:
Christophorus toto Plantinus cognitus orbe,
    Excudit propriis hoc opus ille typis.

(Be gone, crass trade in other books!
    Give way, other presses, to my Plantin!
Go, books, and grow shabby at once, all texts
    that do not bear these words on the title-page:
Christopher Plantin, known throughout the whole world,
    printed this work with his own type.)[1]

Plantin's last years were trying both physically and professionally, as he endeavored (when aged and ailing) to rebuild his business following the subjugation of Antwerp in 1585.[2] Ravaged by years of war, the city was no longer the burgeoning, prosperous place Plantin had described a decade earlier in his letter to Pope Gregory XIII.[3] Rather, the resources and manpower required to run a business were scarce and the local buying public more prudent in their purchases. Nevertheless, when Plantin passed away on July 1, 1589 his printing house was still one of the largest in Europe, maintaining a respected, enviable place in the contemporary world of printing. What neither he nor his descendants could have imagined at the time is how his achievements as a printer and publisher would be recorded and honored in histories of printing for centuries to come. Leaving their mark on a variety of fields, these accomplishments included irrevocably altering the earlier, century-old domination of woodcuts for book illustrations. Admittedly, this was most likely not something Plantin had set out to

---

[1] Excerpt from the sixth verse of Joannes Bochius's *Epigrammata funebria* (Antwerp: Jan Moretus I, 1590) (see BB, I, p. 305, B 387; BT 345; and STC Dutch and Flemish [1470–1600], p. 36). Our warm thanks to Dr. Jan Ziolkowski for his advice on the English translation of this verse.

[2] See Voet, GC, I, pp. 113–121.   [3] See the introductory remarks to ch. 2.

achieve. Rather, it is a remarkable example of the right person taking advantage of being in the right place at just the right moment in time.

That the time was ripe for such a change is evident from the progress that had already been made in the production of books with intaglio illustrations in the decades prior to Plantin's immersion in the medium around 1570. The essential technical difficulties of combining the relief technique of printing text with the intaglio technique of printing engravings and etchings had been resolved, and printers throughout Europe were discovering pockets of interest in these elegantly illustrated editions that justified the occasional production of a costly, special edition. Although few editions with intaglio illustrations are known to have been produced in the city prior to the appearance of Plantin's own, mid-sixteenth-century Antwerp excelled in all of the businesses necessary to support such a production: the printing of texts and (independent) images, finance, and international trade. The key was Plantin's fortuitous contacts and successful entrepreneurial skills. For, on the one hand, it was Plantin's strong personal contacts – with figures like Arias Montano, de Çayas, and Cardinal Granvelle – that both encouraged and supported his original large-scale use of engraved illustrations and then helped him garner a significant portion of the new market for liturgical and devotional works. But, on the other hand, only Plantin's shrewd business skills could have enabled him to profit so fully from these circumstances and accommodate the wishes of a large, but disparate body of buyers interested in and willing to pay for luxuriously illustrated copies of these new texts. Through his economic reuse of his stock of plates for the illustration of various liturgical texts, Plantin made the essential transition from earlier sixteenth-century printers' production of isolated editions with intaglio illustrations to a viable, large-scale production of more costly, but still sought-after illustrated texts. While the markets for these books and the artists needed to produce the necessary illustrations were often unpredictable or unreliable, Plantin's subsequent production of a greater variety of texts with intaglio illustrations in the 1580s demonstrates the durability and pervasiveness of this general shift in buyers' interests. Plantin's earlier successful production had been decisive in providing the final impetus for change in both buyers' and printers' perspectives on the feasibility and desirability of fostering the production of these specially illustrated editions. What had been a limited specialty market ten to twenty years earlier was, by the end of Plantin's life, a market worth catering to and making one's name in.

Clearly, Plantin's achievements in this field were recognized and most readily imitated by his immediate successors. His legacy was considerable. To start with, there were the physical remains of his production: unsold copies of the books he had printed with intaglio illustrations and, above all, the implements for printing that he had acquired over the years, including an extensive collection of copper plates. While Plantin's stock of unsold books was dispersed among his various heirs, his printing materials were subdivided between the two *Officinae* he had founded, at least in part, simply on the basis of what had been left where.[4] This was certainly the case for the

---

[4] See Voet, GC, I, pp. 162–168, and Imhof 2007–2008 for a discussion of the dispersal of Plantin's property following his death.

thousands of copper plates that Plantin had amassed and used to sustain his production of works with intaglio illustrations. According to the inventories of Plantin's possessions, compiled upon his death, the *Officina Plantiniana* in Leiden, run by Plantin's son-in-law Franciscus Raphelengius I, had a total of 461 of Plantin's copper plates, which had been commissioned for the illustration of just seventeen different publications. The Antwerp *Officina Plantiniana* had nearly four times as many of his original plates (some 1,536), which may have been used for the illustration of as many as a hundred distinct editions.[5] Ironically, however, neither collection was valued that highly in monetary terms in these inventories. Perhaps the plates appeared to be too worn to be of much use or perhaps the subjects represented could not be readily reused. Whatever the reason, it is telling to see that regardless of how important the accumulation and reuse of the necessary copper plates had been to Plantin's successful production of editions with intaglio illustrations, the plates themselves were not deemed particularly valuable per se.

A much more reliable and lasting form of Plantin's legacy for his successors was his creative, shrewd approach to the production of these luxuriously illustrated works, in addition to his reputation and connections to facilitate their sale. For, as we have determined in the course of this book, while the production of a work with engraved or etched illustrations was clearly possible, technically, as of the later fifteenth century, the ability to sustain a significant production of such works was a completely different matter. Clearly, one had to start with a text for which there would be a large enough market to make the use of intaglio illustrations worthwhile. In the first place, this implied finding enough buyers to help cover the extra costs of purchasing intaglio plates instead of woodcuts. But this could also be interpreted in terms of whether one could make full use of the intaglios by reusing them for subsequent editions of the same text or other publications. As observed above, Plantin made an essential breakthrough in this regard by finding an extensive new market for Catholic liturgical and devotional works with engraved illustrations, whereby various distinct texts could be illustrated with a limited selection of plates. By the end of the sixteenth century, other printers finally began to challenge the near exclusive production of such illustrated works by the *Officina Plantiniana*. Once underway, the challenges came from all directions – the Giunti, Parisian printers of the reformed editions, printers at the Vatican Press in Rome, and even local Antwerp competitors. Nevertheless, the managers of the Antwerp *Officina Plantiniana* persisted in endeavoring to dominate this successful area of production with which Plantin had first made his name, despite the ever-changing make-up of European demand and supply for these illustrated editions.[6]

---

[5] See appendix 4 for the inventories of Plantin's copper plates. The estimate of the number of projects the cited plates may have illustrated is based upon the number of distinct titles mentioned in the inventories, as well as the number of editions of certain frequently reprinted works (missals, breviaries, books of hours, and P. Canisius's *Manuale catholicorum*) that Plantin may have produced with intaglio illustrations. For Plantin's books of hours, see Bowen 1997a, pp. 228–229 (PP 1365–1368), and pp. 233–258. For all of the other editions, see the relevant entries in Voet, PP.

[6] On Plantin's successors' fight to dominate the production of liturgical editions in general, including the more luxurious forms of them, see Imhof 2007–2008. Obviously, given the Calvinist bent of the northern Low Countries at this time, Catholic service books could not represent an important part of the production of the Leiden *Officina Plantiniana*.

Once the type of illustrated text had been selected, one then had to find (time and again) artists who were willing to make the necessary plates at an affordable price. Rarely did a desire to have a uniform set of plates executed by a single artist for a specific project appear to guide Plantin's practical decision-making process. In addition, many better known engravers were not willing to divert either their own time or that of their assistants with commissions for someone else's projects and potential profit. This appears to be one of the reasons why Plantin had so many etched illustrations made in the 1580s when competent, willing engravers were increasingly hard to find. However, by switching media, he also encountered and had to resolve new issues concerning the relative life of the plate, namely, the number of suitable impressions that could be made from it, the degree to which it could be reworked, and whether buyers would be as satisfied with well-used etched illustrations as engraved.

Finally, in addition to determining the market viability of an illustrated text and having the desired plates made, one also had to find technically competent intaglio printers who would agree to take on the low-paying charge of printing the desired illustrations on to the sheets with letterpress text. Individuals seeking to earn their living as print publishers did not always agree to perform such work. Nevertheless, this seems to have been the easiest aspect of all for Plantin to resolve, as he succeeded in finding two people who met his requirements for an intaglio printer and who were willing to work for him continuously for eighteen to twenty years. While Plantin's successors at the Antwerp *Officina Plantiniana* initially worked with the same individuals, they ultimately succeeded in improving upon Plantin's system. For, as of 1600, Jan Moretus I entered into an almost exclusive working relationship with the Galle family of engravers and print publishers that would be maintained until the late 1670s. The result was that the members of the various Galle print workshops active in the course of the seventeenth century saw to all of the Moretuses' primary needs for the execution, reworking, and printing of their book illustrations.[7] In this way, Plantin's successors finally resolved a significant stumbling block to the production of works with intaglio illustrations, namely, the seemingly perpetual search for artists who would make the required plates.

Plantin's fame in the realm of book illustration is much more broadly based, because his works simultaneously served as models for other printers and potential competitors throughout Europe. Perhaps not surprisingly given that Plantin's initial burst of production of books with intaglio illustrations was dominated by liturgical and devotional works, the most obvious, immediate examples of the influence of this production are explicit and implicit imitations of these books. Consider, for example, French editions. In their study of the work of Abel L'Angelier and his widow, Jean Balsamo and Michel Simonin specifically cite the arrival of Plantin's books of hours in Paris as a turning point there in the evolution from woodcut to engraved book illustrations.[8] The records of Plantin's sales to his bookshop in Paris in the early 1570s and to Michel Sonnius I in the 1580s support the notion that his books of hours (with woodcut as well as

---

[7] Karen Bowen is currently studying the working relationship between the Moretuses and the Galle family of engravers and print publishers. At the moment, little is known about the Raphelengii's production of works with intaglio illustrations.

[8] Balsamo and Simonin 2002, p. 128.

engraved illustrations) were extremely popular in Paris. Examples of French imitations of Plantin's books of hours with engraved illustrations are evident as of the mid-1580s.[9] It is a logical continuation of Paris's renown as the center for the production of books of hours in the early sixteenth century. The increased production of works with intaglio illustrations in France (and Paris in particular) was also helped by the arrival of numerous artists and other craftsmen escaping from the intensification of the war in Flanders generally and in Antwerp in particular. Hence, in various publications on the rise of engraving in Paris in the later sixteenth and the seventeenth century, one reads about the influential influx of Flemish artists as of the mid-1570s, although the introduction of roller presses was probably earlier, given the number of Parisian publications from the 1560s that bore engraved illustrations.[10]

But the impetus Plantin gave to the production of works with intaglio illustrations was not limited to just this one country. As is discussed above, many of Plantin's competitors in the production of the reformed liturgical editions in Italy and Spain (in addition to France) also began to imitate his editions, in terms of the general use of engraved decorative elements, as well as in specific compositions.[11] Indeed, one of the earliest known imitations of Plantin's books of hours with intaglio illustrations was one printed by Aldus Manutius II in Venice in 1576 (see fig. 4.25). Published six years after Plantin's first book of hours with engraved illustrations from 1570 (PP 1365–1368), it appeared just three years after the start of Plantin's extensive production of such works.

Nevertheless, while the clearest examples of the direct influence of Plantin's editions are liturgical or devotional works, the impact of his illustrated editions was far greater. For, as argued in the course of this book, an essential aspect of Plantin's success was his ability to adapt his production to an ever changing market. The amorphous "market" alluded to in studies of other editions with intaglio illustrations has a much clearer (albeit malleable) form in terms of Plantin's editions, as his sales records help determine the basic destination of hundreds of copies of the books concerned. Though these sales vary according to the subject of the book and the period, they reveal, nonetheless, the regions of reliable demand for such texts, and confirm how widespread and varied was the reach of Plantin's editions. This, in turn, supports the conclusion suggested by the production of comparable texts elsewhere, namely, that thanks to the extensive distribution of Plantin's editions (in addition to what publishers elsewhere were producing), buyers throughout Europe were becoming accustomed to this kind of work and were demanding more. Even in Germany, where a general preference for woodcuts still prevailed, some artists and publishers – like the Frankfurt-based family of Theodore de Bry – also came to specialize in the production of works with intaglio illustrations. Although one cannot emphasize enough the unprecedented speed with which Plantin prepared thousands of copies of these books for European-wide distribution, the ramifications of his production were not as readily evident. Rather, like the waves

---

[9] See, e.g., a 12° *Officium BMV*, published by Jacques Kerver's widow Blanche Marentin in Paris in 1584 (e.g., MPM [K 32]) and a 1586 *L'office de la vierge Marie* . . . in *quarto*, published in Paris by Jamet Mettayer, the official printer to the king (e.g., MPM [R 30.12]), both of which are discussed in ch. 4.

[10] See, e.g., Balsamo and Simonin 2002, p. 128; Grivel 1986, pp. 6 and 377–379; and Martin 1954, pp. 258–260.

[11] See ch. 4.

of an incoming tide, the influence of his publications was less visible, but nevertheless persistent in supporting the ever more common publication of works with intaglio illustrations in the last decades of the sixteenth century and first of the seventeenth. The ever more frequent appearance of engraved illustrations evolved into a dominating trend within a diverse range of texts that went hand in hand with a corresponding decline in the production of new woodcuts, except for popular, cheaper editions.

And yet, having thus highlighted the importance of Plantin's editions in this evolution, we must also not lose sight of the significant, broader implications of this new understanding of his production for scholarship today. The detailed accounts of how, precisely, Plantin succeeded in making these books – and what the unanticipated pitfalls were – have revealed numerous unexpected aspects of this process. Clearly, engravings and etchings commissioned for the express purpose of illustrating a printed text were executed and used according to distinct book-related standards and cannot simply be evaluated as independent prints. We have discerned, for example, the conditions under which some artists agreed to make book illustrations for a third party and how other (often better known figures) would not. We have seen how the limited number of impressions that could be made from engraved and etched plates, and a publisher's financially prudent decision to illustrate copies of a text in discrete batches, as necessitated by demand, resulted in unexpected divergences in the appearance of different copies within a single edition. As a result, different copies might bear potentially distinct sets of engraved illustrations or reveal markedly varying states of wear of one and the same plate. With a heightened awareness of these issues, scholars will be able to assess more accurately both the illustrated books that have survived and the place of their intaglio illustrations in the œuvres of the artists concerned. In addition, the contingent, clearer appreciation of what we do and do not know about the earliest editions with intaglio illustrations, and what it took to maintain such a production, will sharpen our historical perspective on this important transitional period in the history of book illustration. Consequently, what is, on one level, an in-depth study of Plantin's editions will also further the work of researchers in a variety of fields – from bibliography and book illustration to the study of independent prints. For we can now apply new perspectives when endeavoring to understand how one specific example of an illustrated edition came to look the way it did, as well as the market for which it may have been intended. Internationally influential at the time, Plantin's editions also thus inform research today.

APPENDICES

THE ARTISTS WHO WORKED ON PLANTIN'S INTAGLIO ILLUSTRATIONS

This overview and the accompanying tables were compiled with two primary goals in mind. One is to provide a brief summary of the activities of each person known to be connected with the production of intaglio book illustrations for Plantin, as well as general bibliographic references. As is evident from the examples of Bartholomeus Weerts and "Gil Hor" included below, it was not always possible to identify each artist found via either payment records or prints in the books under consideration. Similarly, while this list documents all of the figures Plantin is known to have employed, the possibility remains that some additional artists whose work was not signed and for whom there are no known payment records have inadvertently been omitted. Thus, what is presented here must be regarded as the essential minimum of Plantin's contacts and not necessarily the full spectrum.

The second essential goal here is, for every year Plantin may have employed a given artist, to cite at least one example of a project or a payment record that indicates the general volume of the work involved – that is, whether just a few isolated prints, or a large series of images were produced. When multiple sources document an artist's work on a particular project, the dating of that work is derived, in the first place, from the date of the associated payment record or one on the print itself. If no date can be deduced from such sources, then the date of the publication in which the image(s) were used may be suggested. However, as is evident below – see, for example, under Abraham de Bruyn, Jan Sadeler I, and Jan Wierix – and is discussed in chapter 1, some engravings were clearly ready a year or more before Plantin's ultimate publication of the work in which they were included. Thus, each listing of an artist's work for Plantin begins with the date in which the activity was most likely completed and is then followed by a brief identification of the project concerned (including its date of publication), the number of images involved, and the source(s) for the information, if the prints are not signed.

The list of examples of an artist's work for Plantin for any given year is, nevertheless, not complete. The lack of copies of some of Plantin's illustrated editions and the relative scarcity of payment records make that an impossible goal to attain. Not even all the known records of payments to an artist could be included here. Either it was not certain for what type of work the payment was made – for example, an unspecified payment to vander Borcht could represent the completion of an etching, a painting, or a preparatory drawing for a woodcut or an engraving – or else the dating of the payment and the identification of the subject were too uncertain to allow for a firm association of some payments with specific years or projects.[1] Lists of all of the subsequent reuses of the given plates are also not provided, as that goes beyond the immediate goals of this appendix, namely, to document when artists actually worked for Plantin. Examples of the reuse of some plates are given in the main chapters.

VANDER BORCHT, PEETER (MECHELEN OR BRUSSELS, C.1535–1608, ANTWERP)

Etcher, draughtsman, painter and dealer in paintings, possibly also a woodcutter. Vander Borcht was active making his own woodcuts, etchings, and designs for others from 1552 through the turn of the seventeenth century – or else, some authors specu-late,[2] there may have been at least two similarly named artists, one who made woodcuts and one who designed and made etchings. His brother Pauwels was active as a painter and dealer in paintings. Vander Borcht's works were published by several print pub-lishers, including Bartholomeus de Momper, Jan Baptist Vrints, Adriaen Huberti, and Philips Galle (all in Antwerp). Vander Borcht began to work for Plantin as early as 1565, designing woodblocks for a botanical edition by Rembert Dodoens that Plantin printed in 1566, the *Frumentorum, leguminum, palustrium et aquatilium herbarum* (PP 1095). Vander Borcht continued to design hundreds of woodcuts for Plantin between 1565 and 1567, as well as in the early 1570s, at which point he also designed more than a hundred engravings for Plantin's first rush of publications with intaglio illustrations. Vander Borcht fled to Antwerp with his family in October 1572, following the ransacking of Mechelen by Spanish troops. Plantin's account of the event in a letter from Novem-ber 1, 1572, which he wrote to the Spanish theological scholar Benito Arias Montano, makes clear that vander Borcht, Plantin, and Arias Montano were on good terms by that time.[3] Vander Borcht's first documented etchings for Plantin are the sixty-six por-traits used to illustrate J. Sambucus's 1574 publication, *Icones veterum aliquot ac recentium medicorum* (PP 2175). Although it is generally assumed that once vander Borcht had fled to Antwerp he always stayed there, one payment from November 19, 1583 for copper plates sent from Mechelen for use in Leiden suggests that vander Borcht was working for Plantin in Leiden at that time.[4] Vander Borcht, along with print publisher Philips

---

[1] For examples of payments that could not be included here, see, e.g., MPM Arch. 31, fol. 164 lft (additional payments to vander Borcht for drawings for either woodcuts or engravings) and fol. 49 rht (payments to Crispin van den Broeck).

[2] See Jetty E. Van der Sterre's entry in the *Grove Dictionary of Art*, vol. IV, p. 384.

[3] See ch. 2, n. 45 for this text.

[4] See MPM Arch. 61, fol. 149r (under November 19, 1583), for the following: "paye a Magdalena van Clef chez Pauwel vander Burcht la somme de 18 patt. pour rest de 6 plates de cuivre venus de Malines lesquels sont envoyes a Leyden montant fl. 7 st. 18 dont les 7 fl. [?] comptes a Leyden a P. vander Burcht p. mon

Galle and the cartographer Abraham Ortelius, was also responsible for compiling the inventory of Plantin's stock of copper plates in 1590, following Plantin's death in 1589 (see appendix 4). [Lit.: New Holl., Van der Borcht, 4 vols. (2004–2007), fully illustrated, with introduction (1, pp. xvii–xxvii); Saur (1996), XII, p. 677; Grove Dictionary of Art, IV, p. 384; Depauw 1993; Delen 1924–1935, II.1, pp. 79–88, 90–8, 101–2, 105–6, 108–9, 112, 114–5, 123, 126–7, 134–7, 139, 144–5, 147–8, 151, 155, 159, 162–3, 167, and 170; II.2, pp. 99, 103–4, 120–1, 130, 138, 140–1, 143–4, 164–5, and 171.]

Work completed for Plantin's editions with intaglio illustrations:

1569?: PP 1365–68: *Horae BVM*, 8°, 1570: at least four of the eighteen compositions for this book that bear vander Borcht's initials on one engraving of them or another, must have been completed in (or prior to) 1569, as Jan Wierix was paid for engraving them in November 1569 (see figs. 3.23, 3.24, and 4.14).[5] For work on the other engravings used to illustrate the various issues of this publication, see under Pieter Huys, Jan Sadeler I, and Hieronymus Wierix.

c.1569–1570: PP 644: *Biblia sacra* (= Polyglot Bible), f°, 1568–1573: at least one drawing for the *Encampment of Israelites*, engraved by Jan Wierix (M-H 2278). For work on this and other engravings for this publication, see under Crispin van den Broeck, Philips Galle, Pieter van der Heyden, Pieter Huys, and Jan Wierix.

1569–1573?: three? designs for books of hours in large 8° (or 4°), namely, the *Adoration of the Magi*, *Christ as a Man of Sorrows* (both signed PB) and the *Adoration of the Shepherds*, which is not signed, but stylistically comparable to his work. The first two engravings are attributed to one of the Wierixes (see M-H 2240 and M-H 2269).[6] The earliest known appearance of these plates is in an *Officium BMV* (PP 1769), published in 1573. The dating of vander Borcht's drawings is uncertain, however, as three other engravings used to illustrate this same 1573 edition are dated either 1570 or 1571, which suggests that vander Borcht's designs may also have been completed as early as 1569 or 1570.[7] For work on other related engravings, see under Crispin van den Broeck and Abraham de Bruyn.

1570–1571: PP 588: B. Arias Montano, *Humanae salutis monumenta*, 8°, 1571: some of the engravings made after the numerous compositions provided by vander Borcht for this book (prints executed by Jan Wierix, Pieter Huys, Abraham de Bruyn, and Hieronymus Wierix – see below) were completed in 1570 (see fig. 3.25), while

---

pere val. in NS fl. 7 st. 18" (paid to Magdalena van Clef at Pauwel vander Borcht's, the sum of 18 st. for the rest for the six copper plates that came from Mechelen which were sent to Leiden, amounting to 7 fl. 18 st., the 7 fl. were paid to P. vander Borcht by my father in Leiden).

5 For evidence of vander Borcht's association with the designs of these various images, see Bowen 1997b, pp. 147–150. See below for the payment to Jan Wierix for engraving the four evangelist portraits.

6 Although Mauquoy-Hendrickx states that the first (M-H 2240) actually bears Jan Wierix's initials, they are not present on any of the impressions of this print that we have seen. Perhaps this is an error resulting from the thick paint layers on the impression cited by Mauquoy-Hendrickx.

7 For a list of all of the plates used to illustrate this edition and any signatures or dates evident on them, see the discussion of PP 1769 in Bowen 1997a, pp. 235–238; for an additional copy see, e.g., that in Tübingen, Universitätsbibliothek, no. Gi 230ª R.

others were finished in 1571, indicating that the compositional drawings for these plates must have been made in these years or earlier.[8]

1571: M-H 2145: drawing for a vignette of the *Last Supper*, signed by vander Borcht and Jan Wierix and used for the title-page of several of Plantin's folio missals as of 1571 (fig. 4.1).

1572: drawing for a full-page border, bearing the initials of vander Borcht and Jan Wierix and included in several of Plantin's folio missals as of 1572 (fig. 4.3).

1573: fifteen drawings for engravings (executed by Jan Wierix) for books of hours in 16° and 12° (fig. 4.5).[9]

1574: PP 2175: J. Sambucus, *Icones veterum aliquot ac recentium medicorum*, f°, 1574: sixty-six etchings by vander Borcht.[10]

PP 1685: *Missale Romanum*, f°, 1574: at least one etched border and approximately twenty-eight drawings for new engravings (all c.71/74 × 71/74) used in this edition (see fig. 4.9).[11] For work on other engravings for this publication, see under Crispin van den Broeck, Pierre Dufour, Gerard van Groeningen, and Jan Wierix.

PP 1686: *Missale Romanum*, 4°, 1574: drawing for title-page vignette of SS Peter and Paul, bearing the initials of vander Borcht and Jan Wierix.

1575: PP 1776: *Officium BMV*, large 8°, 1575: at least one new design for an engraving of the *Assumption of the Virgin*, signed with vander Borcht's and Jan Sadeler I's initials. For work on other engravings for this publication, see under Gerard van Groeningen and Jan Wierix.

prior to January 1, 1576: five engravings in MPM Arch. 1228 for: PP 590: B. Arias Montano, *Humanae salutis monumenta*, 4°, 1583; PP 690: *Biblia sacra*, f°, 1583; and an as yet unidentified project. This archive contains three engravings designed by vander Borcht that appear in the two cited books: the *Entombment* and *Christ carrying the Cross* – both engraved by Jan Wierix (M-H 2262 and 2254, respectively) – in the *Monumenta*; and the same engraving of the *Entombment*, along with the *Flagellation*, an anonymous engraving after vander Borcht (cf. fol. G7r), in the bible. See also under Crispin van den Broeck, Abraham de Bruyn, Pierre Dufour, Gerard van Groeningen, Jan Sadeler, and Jan Wierix, for their work on other engravings for these publications that were similarly included in this album. In addition to these engravings are two loose prints – an image of the Assumption of the Virgin and a border of the adult life of Christ, both signed with the initials of vander Borcht and Jan Sadeler I. These were probably used for one of Plantin's small folio or large *quarto* missals published prior to 1576, but of which there are currently no

---

[8] See ch. 3 for more on this book. Of all the illustrations in Plantin's *octavo* editions of the *Monumenta*, only that of *Christ in the Temple* (fol. F5r) bears the name of another designer, namely Crispin van den Broeck (see below). The vast majority of the remaining seventy plates bear vander Borcht's initials. For payments dating the production of specific plates, see Bowen and Imhof 2003, pp. 170–171 and 185, under Abraham de Bruyn, and pp. 188–189, under Jan and Hieronymus Wierix; for their subsequent reuse, see Bowen 2003, esp. table 1, p. 30.

[9] See MPM Arch. 31, fol. 164 lft, for a payment to vander Borcht for making these designs. See the discussion of PP 1771 in Bowen 1994. In n. 33 the payment to vander Borcht for the drawings is erroneously dated 1572.

[10] See the discussion of this book in ch. 5.

[11] See *New Holl.*, *Van der Borcht*, Book Illustrations, II, nos. 553–586, *passim*.

known copies.[12] All five of these engravings, together with the vast majority of the other illustrations in the *Monumenta*, must have been completed prior to January 1, 1576 because the bundle in which they are found is a collection of title-pages and text illustrations from Plantin's publications that Jan Moretus I gave to him as a New Year's present that day.[13]

[**1577?:** PP 1335: L. Hillessemius, *Sacrarum antiquitatum monumenta*, 8°, 1577.] Although Voet states under the illustrations to PP 1335 that two plates were signed by vander Borcht, one (on p. 14) is actually signed by Crispin van den Broeck – in some impressions of this print the "CV" preceding the "B" are faint and difficult to read.[14] The other (on p. 44) is, contrary to what Voet states in his discussion of the illustration of this edition, a weak impression of Abraham de Bruyn's engraving of the prophet Nathan (but with his initials now removed) that was first used in the 1571 edition of Arias Montano's *Monumenta* (PP 588). Rather, for the production of Hillessemius's engravings, see under Crispin van den Broeck and Jan Sadeler I.

1579–1580: PP 865: *Sanctorum kalendarii Romani . . .*, 24°, 1580: 84 of the 230 or 50 illustrations are signed with vander Borcht's initials as designer (see figs. 6.1 and 6.2). In the accompanying *Evangeliorum dominicalium . . .*, 24°, 1580 (PP 1152), 34 of the 55 engravings are signed with vander Borcht's initials as designer. Some portion of these compositions were most likely ready in 1579, because Philips Galle was paid for delivering 50 engravings for these books in May 1579; he did not deliver others until September 1580 (see below). Most of the remaining plates were engraved by Paul Uten Waele (see below).

1581: PP 1278: L. Guicciardini, *Description de touts les Pais-Bas*, f°, 1582: at least one etching (that of Tournai) that was not included in Plantin's 1581 Italian edition of this text, but appeared for the first time in his 1582 French edition. None of the plates illustrating Guicciardini's text is signed (see fig. 5.9). The attribution of this plate to vander Borcht is based upon the following payment record: "Payé a Peeter vander Borcht pour la ville de Tournay tailler et protraire [*sic*] fl. 12." (Paid to Peeter vander Borcht for the city of Tournai, cut and portrayed.)[15] See under Crispin van den Broeck and Abraham de Bruyn for their work on an engraved title-plate for this publication.

1582–1583: (see PP 631) H. Jansen van Barrefelt, *Bibelsche figuren*, oblong 4°, 1592 or 1593: eighty-three etchings, one of which is dated 1582, and several of which were paid for in 1583.[16]

---

[12] For these two engravings, see MPM Arch. 1228, fols. 268r and 278v. For examples of larger missals printed by Plantin in 1574 and 1575 for which there are currently no known copies with engravings, see PP 1686, PP 1687, PP 1690, and PP 1691.

[13] See ch. 5 for more on this bundle (MPM Arch. 1228) and its implications for the dating of the work on the 1583 edition of Arias Montano's *Monumenta* and the 1583 folio bible (which includes many of the illustrations found in the *Monumenta*).

[14] For a copy of this book in which van den Broeck's "CVB" monogram is clear, see, e.g., KBR (VH 15.384 A LP).

[15] MPM Arch. 59, fol. 104r (under July 8, 1581).

[16] For a series of payments made between April 16 and May 28, 1583 of 4 fl. per subject for what are probably some of these plates, see MPM Arch. 61, fols. 47v, 51v, 54v, 56v, 62v, and 66v. The association of these payments with this work is discussed in greater detail on p. 213.

1582 and 1585: (see PP 631) H. Jansen van Barrefelt, *Imagines et figurae bibliorum . . .*, large oblong 4°, 1592: a hundred etchings, most of which are signed by vander Borcht (see fig. 5.12) and many of which are dated 1582, while one is dated 1585.[17]

1586: PP 2054: S. W. Pighius, *Hercules prodicius seu principis iuventutis vita et peregrinatio*, 8°, 1587: at least one or two etchings, for which vander Borcht was paid in October 1586.[18]

1588: several projects with numerous etchings signed by or attributed to vander Borcht, including PP 1138: M. d'Esne, *Les XV mysteres du rosaire de . . . Marie*, 4°, 1588 (fifteen etchings); PP 1048–1049: F. Costerus, French and Dutch editions of fifty meditations on the passion, 8°, 1588 (fifty etchings; see fig. 5.17); and PP 890: P. Canisius, *Manuale catholicorum*, 16°, 1588 (twenty-two etchings; see fig. 5.16).

1589: PP 884 and PP 2149: P. Canisius, *Institutiones christianae, seu parvus catechismus catholicorum*, 8°, 1589: 101 etchings (see fig. 6.12), one of which is signed by vander Borcht.

PP 1788: *Officium BMV*, 24°, 1588: at least six and possibly sixteen designs for anonymous engravings (not etchings, as stated by Voet) for the illustration of a book of hours.

VAN DEN BROECK, CRISPIN (ALIAS "PALUDANUS") (MECHELEN, 1524–1589/1591, ANTWERP)

Painter, draughtsman, and etcher.

Van den Broeck became a master in the Antwerp St. Luke's guild in the guild year 1555–1556 and a citizen of Antwerp in 1559. He is said to have married Barbe de Bruyn,[19] the daughter of the engraver Abraham de Bruyn, who engraved a strikingly large number of van den Broeck's compositions for Plantin. He worked actively with Frans Floris until the latter's death in 1570. He was most prolific making designs for engravings in the 1570s, when he started working for Plantin. Van den Broeck was active in Middelburg for an uncertain amount of time around 1584–1586? It is likely that he was back in Antwerp by the summer of 1587, as Plantin refers to him as present in letters that he wrote to Arias Montano at that time.[20] In *Hollstein Dutch & Flemish*, III, van den Broeck is credited with making 61 etchings and some 145 engravings, many of which were for Plantin's publications. Noteworthy here is that while Jan Sadeler I and Hieronymus Wierix regularly appear as the engravers of van den Broeck's designs in these listings and de Bruyn only once (see no. 8), it was de Bruyn (followed by Jan Wierix) who signed the most engravings after van den Broeck's designs for Plantin's book illustrations. This dichotomy underscores one key feature of the group of engravers Plantin employed to make his book illustrations, namely, they were often not the engravers who were

---

[17] See plate 39, *New Holl.*, Van der Borcht, Book Illustrations, I, no. 334, for the etching dated 1585. See also the discussion of this and the preceding edition in ch. 5.

[18] See MPM Arch. 63, fol. 97v (under October 14, 1586), for the following record: "paye a Peeter vander Borcht la somme de sept florins pour une planche de figures pour le livre de Pighius fl. 7" (paid to Peeter vander Borcht the sum of seven florins for one plate of figures for Pighius's book 7 fl.).

[19] Saur 1996, XIV, p. 322, and Delen 1920, p. 100. Both state this without citing a source.

[20] See *Corr.* VIII–IX, nos. 1263 and 1303.

successful independent engravers and print publishers, like Hieronymus Wierix and Jan Sadeler I (see chapter 2). [Lit.: Saur 1996, XIV, p. 322; *Grove Dictionary of Art*, IV, p. 839; Holl. *Dutch & Flemish*, III, pp. 223–226; Delen 1924–1935, II.1, pp. 133, 135, 138, 145, 148, 150, 155, 159–63, and 165; II.2, pp. 101–2, and 119.]

Work completed for Plantin's editions with intaglio illustrations:

1570: PP 644: *Biblia sacra* (= Polyglot Bible), f°, 1568–1573: at least one drawing for a frontispiece (the "Pietas regia," engraved by Pieter van der Heyden [PAME], fig. 3.11).[21] For work on other engravings for this publication, see under Peeter van der Borcht, Philips Galle, Pieter Huys, and Jan Wierix.

1571: PP 588: B. Arias Montano, *Humanae salutis monumenta*, 8°, 1571: one engraving bears van den Broeck's name and Abraham de Bruyn's monogram (*Christ in the Temple*, fol. F5). For work on other engravings for this publication, see under Peeter vander Borcht, Pieter Huys, Hieronymus and Jan Wierix.

1570–1573: three compositions for a book of hours in large 8° (or 4°), each signed by van den Broeck and Abraham de Bruyn, namely, the *Visitation*, the *Circumcision*, and the *Raising of Lazarus* (fig. 4.4), where the last two are also dated 1571. The earliest known use of these plates is in an *Officium BMV* published in 1573 (PP 1769), which also bears an engraving by Jan Wierix (M-H 2232) that, like the prints after van den Broeck, has a similarly early date of 1570.[22] For work on other related engravings, see under Peeter vander Borcht and Jan Wierix.

1574: PP 1685: *Missale Romanum*, f°, 1574; and PP 822, *Breviarium Romanum*, f°, 1575: three drawings for engravings of the *Annunciation* and SS *Peter and Paul* (for the missal) and *King David* (for the breviary) (fig. 4.12). The attribution of these designs to van den Broeck is based upon a record of payment to the engraver, Pierre Dufour, cited below under his work for 1574. While the engraving of SS *Peter and Paul*, as well as an image of *King David*, has consequently been attributed to Dufour, the only known related engraving of the *Annunciation* was done by Jan Wierix (see below). See under Peeter vander Borcht and Gerard van Groeningen for compositions they made for these books.

1575–1576?: PP 604: St. Augustine, *Opera D. Aurelii Augustini Hipponensis...*, f°, 1576–1577: Van den Broeck was paid 6 fl. for making two designs for the beginning of this work (for the title-frame and the author's portrait), neither of which is signed.[23] As work on this ten-volume publication was underway in 1575 (see the

---

[21] See MPM Arch. 31, fol. 165 lft, for a payment to van den Broeck in 1570 for "Pietas in Bibliis magnis" ("Pietas" in the large bible). Although the description of the subject clearly matches this composition, the year 1570 noted at the top of the list of payments made to the artist does post-date the series of payments made to van der Heyden for engraving this image. While problematic (as the drawing must have been completed before the engraver could make the plate based upon it), the unusually sloppy and abbreviated form of these records suggests that this may have simply been a brief summary of payments that had already been made to the artist.

[22] See n. 7 above.

[23] For a record of this payment, along with one to an unnamed engraver for making the two plates and to an unnamed printer for printing them, see MPM Arch. 9, fol. 66r, for following notes: "la portraicture des commencements de S^ti Aug.^tini p Crispin, fl. 6" (the designs for the beginnings to St. Augustine by

notes to PP 604), it is possible that van den Broeck completed his compositions then or in 1576, simultaneously with the stylistically related author's portrait of St. Jerome, which is dated 1576 and signed by van den Broeck (and Jan Sadeler I) (see below under 1576).

PP 1335: L. Hillessemius, *Sacrarum antiquitatum monumenta*, 8°, 1577: seven of the forty engravings included in this work bear van den Broeck's name as designer. All but one of these was engraved by Jan Sadeler I, including one that is dated 1575, thereby indicating that van den Broeck had started work on the compositions by then.[24] Twenty-nine drawings are associated with this project, although at least two of these attributions seem unlikely, as there are no subjects resembling an image of Calvary or the Presentation in the Temple in Hillessemius's work.[25] Despite these questions concerning a few specific drawings, it seems likely that van den Broeck was responsible for designing all thirty-nine of the new, stylistically homogenous group of plates used to illustrate this text (see also the remarks for this edition under vander Borcht and Jan Sadeler I).

prior to January 1, 1576: engravings in MPM Arch. 1228 for: PP 590: B. Arias Montano, *Humanae salutis monumenta*, 4°, 1583: twelve of the thirteen compositions in the *Monumenta* that were signed by van den Broeck and engraved by a variety of artists (Jan Wierix, Jan Sadeler I, and Abraham de Bruyn) were included in this bundle of title-pages and illustrations.[26] All but four of these compositions (those on fols. K3r, L2r, P4r, and S3r), together with engravings of the *Adoration of the Magi* and the *Raising of Lazarus* (fig. 5.4) by Jan Wierix (M-H 2239 and 2246, respectively) that were not used to illustrate the *Monumenta*, were also included in Plantin's 1583 folio *Biblia sacra* (PP 690) (see figs. 5.2 and 5.3). However, van den Broeck designed many additional compositions for this book at a later time, including in 1582 (see below).[27] Of the fourteen engravings after van den Broeck's designs present in MPM Arch. 1228 that were subsequently used to illustrate either the *Monumenta* or the bible, eight are noteworthy for being printed prior to the engraving of his name (or monogram) on to the plates.[28] See also under Peeter van der Borcht, Abraham de Bruyn, Pierre Dufour, Gerard van Groeningen, Jan Sadeler, and Jan

Crispin, 6 fl.); "p la taille desdittes deux planches avec le cuivre fl. 36" (for engraving these two plates, with the copper, 36 fl.); and "p. limpression desdittes planches p[?] 2000 que sont deux figures a 10 patt le cent, fl. 10" (for the printing of these plates, 2,000 sheets, which are two figures at 10 st. per hundred, 10 fl.). As there is no corresponding payment to Mynken Liefrinck for printing these illustrations, the work may have been done by Plantin's printer Jacques vander Hoeven.

[24] For the plates signed by van den Broeck, see pp. 4, 6, 8 (1575), 10, 14, 30, and 60.

[25] See Van Puyvelde 1942, nos. 4–39, for this set of drawings and nos. 38 and 39 for the questionable attributions. These drawings are not reproduced, however, which impedes the resolution of this matter.

[26] For the dating of this bundle, see the discussion of it under vander Borcht. For a list of the illustrations in the *Monumenta* that are signed by van den Broeck, see the list of illustrations to PP 590. Only that of the *Circumcision* (fol. L2r in the *Monumenta* and engraved by Jan Wierix [M-H 2235]) is not in MPM Arch. 1228.

[27] For an overview of which illustrations in the 1583 bible were designed by van den Broeck, see the list of illustrations to PP 690.

[28] For these rare impressions, see MPM Arch. 1228, fol. 244r, *Visitation* (M-H 2233); fol. 244v, *Adoration of the Magi*; fol. 245v, *Raising of Lazarus* (M-H 2246); fol. 246v, *Christ before Caiaphas* (M-H 2250); fol. 246v, *Christ before Herod* (M-H 2251); fol. 246v, *Christ before Pilate* (M-H 2252); fol. 247r, *Crucifixion* (M-H 2258); and fol. 248r, *Pentecost* (M-H 2264).

Wierix, for their work on engravings for these publications that were similarly included in this album.

1576: PP 1333: St. Jerome, *Opera divi Hieronymi Stridoniensis . . .*, ed. by M. Victorius, f°, 1579: one drawing for the author's portrait, signed by van den Broeck and Jan Sadeler I and dated 1576.

1581: PP 1277: L. Guicciardini, *Descrittione di tutti i Paesi Bassi*, f°, 1581: one design for the frontispiece with the allegorical representation of the Low Countries, which is signed by van den Broeck and Abraham de Bruyn. See also under Peeter vander Borcht for an etching for a later edition of this publication.

1581–1582?: PP 690: *Biblia sacra*, f°, 1583: van den Broeck completed at least twelve additional compositions (beyond the nine that were ready prior to January 1, 1576, discussed above) for text illustrations (some signed by Jan Wierix or Abraham de Bruyn [see fig. 5.5] – see below) and perhaps as many as two frontispiece designs for this publication in or prior to 1582 (see fig. 5.1). No payment records for the compositions for the text illustrations are known, but many of these plates must have been completed by July 1581, when payments to Mynken Liefrinck for the printing of the illustrations of this volume began.[29] One payment made to "Crispin painctre" on October 6, 1582 for "les deux commencemens lesquels sont pour le bible grande figures val. in NS fl. 10" (the two introductory images which are for the grand bible figures, is in currency 10 fl.) suggests that originally two frontispieces were planned for this volume. Abraham de Bruyn was paid for engraving at least one of these designs. As copies of this book were sold as early as November 1582, all of the illustrations must have been finished by then.[30]

DE BRUYN, ABRAHAM (ANTWERP, 1538/1540–1587, COLOGNE)

Engraver and print publisher.

Born in Antwerp, de Bruyn moved often during his career. He is known to have been active in or near Breda in 1570, in Cologne around 1576–1578, in Antwerp c.1579–1585, and then back in Cologne, where he died in 1587. In *Hollstein Dutch & Flemish*, IV, de Bruyn is credited with making some 536 engravings. His earliest dated prints are from 1565 (nos. 61–66). He also published several extensive series of his own prints while in Cologne c.1576–1578 (see nos. 139–192, 193–241, and 248–306), and while in Antwerp in 1583 and 1584 (see nos. 67–78 and 102–107). In addition, some 110 of these cited prints were for Plantin editions, many of which were designed by his son-in-law, Crispin van den Broeck (see above). [Lit.: Saur 1996, XIV, p. 614; *Grove Dictionary of Art*, V, p. 61; *Holl. Dutch & Flemish*, IV, pp. 4–10; and Delen 1924–1935, II.1, pp. 85–6, 150–1, 159–63; II.2, pp. 73, 112–4, 126, 146–7, and 170–1.]

---

[29] For this first payment, dated to July 14, 1581, see MPM Arch. 18, fol. 430 rht.

[30] For the payment to van den Broeck, see MPM Arch. 60, fol. 164v; for that to de Bruyn, see MPM Arch. 14, bundle 4, fol. 12 rht, under November 19, 1582: "pour Abraham de Bruyn taill^r p^r le com[mencement] de la g[rand] bible £ 3" (for Abraham de Bruyn, engraver, for the start of the large bible £ 3 [= 18 fl.]). A payment of 18 fl. to de Bruyn for engraving an unspecified plate for the bible is also recorded under the same date in MPM Arch. 60, fol. 190r. See ch. 5 and fig. A3.2 in appendix 3 for the sale of this book.

Work completed for Plantin's editions with intaglio illustrations:

1570–1571: PP 588: B. Arias Montano, *Humanae salutis monumenta*, 8°, 1571: de Bruyn signed twenty-nine of the seventy-one illustrations for this book (nearly all of which are also signed by Peeter vander Borcht – see above) and appears to have been paid for them between October 12, 1570 and February 4, 1571 (figs. 4.17 and 4.21, as used in a later book).[31] For work on other engravings for this publication, see under Crispin van den Broeck, Pieter Huys, Hieronymus and Jan Wierix.

1571?: three engravings for a book of hours in large 8° (or 4°), each bearing de Bruyn's and Crispin van den Broeck's name or monogram, namely, the *Visitation*, the *Circumcision*, and the *Raising of Lazarus* (fig. 4.4), where the last two are also dated 1571. The earliest known use of these plates is in an *Officium BMV* (PP 1769), published in 1573, which also bears an engraving by Jan Wierix (M-H 2232) that has a similarly early date of 1570, thereby reinforcing the impression that several, if not all, of the larger plates seen in this book of hours were made c.1571.[32] For work on other related engravings, see under Peeter vander Borcht and Jan Wierix.

prior to January 1, 1576: three engravings in MPM Arch. 1228 for: PP 590: B. Arias Montano, *Humanae salutis monumenta*, 4°, 1583: one engraving (*Christ on the Mount of Olives*, on fol. O4r); PP 690: *Biblia sacra*, f°, 1583: one engraving (*Christ's Entry into Jerusalem* on fol. B3v); and one engraving (the *Betrayal*; on fol. 246r of MPM Arch. 1228) for an undetermined use. All three engravings are signed with the monograms of de Bruyn and Crispin van den Broeck. See also under Peeter vander Borcht, Crispin van den Broeck, Pierre Dufour, Gerard van Groeningen, Jan Sadeler, and Jan Wierix, for their work on engravings for these publications that were similarly included in this album.[33]

1578: PP 1955: A. de Pasino, *Discours sur plusieurs poincts de l'architecture de guerre concernants les fortifications . . .*, 4°, 1579: de Bruyn was paid for executing at least two, if not all five, engraved illustrations for this text in November and December 1578 (and not December 1579, as noted by Voet in n. 2 to PP 1955).[34]

1581: PP 1277: L. Guicciardini, *Descrittione di tutti i Paesi Bassi*, f°, 1581: the engraved frontispiece with the allegorical representation of the Low Countries bears de Bruyn's monogram and Crispin van den Broeck's name. See also under Peeter vander Borcht for an etching for a later edition of this publication.

1581?–1582: PP 690: *Biblia sacra*, f°, 1583: the engraved title-plate (fig. 5.1) and seven text illustrations (see fig. 5.5) that were included in this work, but not in MPM Arch. 1228 by January 1576 (see above) were executed by de Bruyn after designs by Crispin van den Broeck, presumably at a later date. Each of the seven text

---

[31] For a discussion of de Bruyn's work for this publication, see Bowen and Imhof 2003, pp. 170–171 and 185, under de Bruyn.

[32] See n. 7 above.

[33] For the dating of this archive (and, hence, the images in it), see the discussion of this bundle under vander Borcht.

[34] For the payments for these plates, see MPM Arch. 14, bundle 1, fols. 29 rht (under November 15, 1578) and 30 rht (under December 13, 1578).

illustrations bears his monogram (see fols. A4v, A6v, B4v, E5v, E6v, Ee7v, and F2r), while payment records document de Bruyn's and van den Broeck's work on the title-plate in 1582. As copies of this book were sold as early as November 1582, the extra text illustrations must have been completed by then and perhaps as early as July 1581, when Mynken Liefrinck began to print some of the illustrations for this work.[35] Jan Wierix was also employed in this period to complete engravings for this project (see below).

PP 1412: J.-B. Houwaert, *Pegasides pleyn, ende den lust-hof der maeghden*, 4°, 1583: de Bruyn was paid for engraving Houwaert's coat of arms (used in this and another of his texts) on November 22, 1582.[36] See under Jan Wierix for the execution of the main text illustrations.

COLLAERT, HANS (JAN) II (ANTWERP, C.1561?–C.1620?, ANTWERP)

Engraver and print publisher.

Registered as a master in the St. Luke's guild of Antwerp in 1586, Hans Collaert II was part of the renowned Collaert family of engravers. Son of Hans I and brother to Adriaen I, Hans II also married the daughter of another famous Antwerp engraver and print publisher, Philips Galle (see below). Hans II periodically worked for Philips Galle and his son and successor, Theodoor, as well as for other Antwerp print publishers, like Jan Baptist Vrints. In addition, he also occasionally engraved book illustrations for Plantin and his successor, Jan Moretus I, as well as for other Antwerp printers, in particular Jan van Keerberghen. Perhaps reflecting the altered status of the Antwerp print world by the start of the seventeenth century, Hans Collaert II differed from many of the other engravers Plantin employed in that he continued to produce book illustrations for several local publishers even when he, himself, was an established, recognized engraver. [Lit.: *New Holl.*, *Collaert* (2005–2006), 7 vols., fully illustrated, with an introduction (I, pp. xxxix–xcvii); Diels 2005, pp. 27–28.]

Work completed for Plantin's editions with intaglio illustrations:

1588: On October 21, 1588, Hans Collaert II was paid for delivering two unspecified plates.[37]

VAN DOETECUM, JAN (JOANNES) (DEVENTER? – 1605, HAARLEM); LUCAS (DEVENTER? – PRIOR TO 1589, PLACE OF DEATH UNKNOWN)

Etchers and engravers. Jan was also a glazier and glass painter.

---

[35] See the discussion of these images under van den Broeck for these records.
[36] See Voet, PP, vol. III, p. 1203, n. 8.
[37] See MPM Arch. 65, fol. 144v, for the following record: "A Hans Collard tailleur la somme de trente huict florins pour deux plates quil a livrees a mon pere val. in NS fl. 38." (To Hans Collaert engraver the total of thirty-eight florins for two plates that he delivered to my father, is in currency 38 fl.)

From 1554 to c.1572, both Jan and Lucas van Doetecum worked primarily for such leading Antwerp print publishers as Hieronymus Cock, Gerard de Jode, and Philips Galle. They are known for their prints after compositions by Hieronymus Cock, Pieter Bruegel I, and Hans Vredeman de Vries. It was in this period that they were asked (most likely via Cock) to make the illustrations to Cock and Plantin's joint publication, *La pompe funèbre*, from 1559 (see below). The van Doetecums were renowned for their ability to etch neatly and finish their etchings with engraving in such a way that their prints (including many maps) closely resembled engravings, but with less work. It remains unclear as to where, precisely, Jan and Lucas van Doetecum lived when they were working for these Antwerp print publishers. In particular, there are no documents indicating that they were actually living in Antwerp at this time, while there are occasional references linking them to Deventer. In the later 1570s, Jan van Doetecum began to publish more prints with only his signature. Jan was clearly working in Deventer from 1583 to 1586, after which he was active in Haarlem until his death there in 1605. [Lit. (for both van Doetecums): *New Holl., Van Doetecum* (1998), 4. vols., fully illustrated, with an introduction (I, pp. xi–xxi).]

Work completed for Plantin's editions with intaglio illustrations:

1559: PP 939: *La pompe funèbre*, f°, 1559: thirty-three plates, both etched and engraved, at least some after designs by Hieronymus Cock (see fig. 3.1).[38]

DUFOUR, PIERRE (PETRUS FURNIUS); ALIAS "JALHEA" (LIÈGE, C.1545–C.1610, LIÈGE)

Engraver and painter.

Dufour is most often discussed as a pupil of Lambert Lombard. Relatively few prints by him are known – only some thirty-six distinct, independent prints are cited in *Hollstein Dutch & Flemish*, VII (under Furnius).[39] Among these are prints after well-known designers from the period, namely, Maarten van Heemskerck, Maarten de Vos, and Joannes Stradanus. Two sets of Dufour's prints (nos. 31–36, from 1570, and nos. 14–19, from 1573) were published by Hieronymus Cock, which suggests that he was a competent engraver at that time. Following his brief, intense period of providing Plantin with plates in 1574, however, little is known of his subsequent print production. It appears that he then focused more on painting. [Lit.: Saur, vol. XXX (2001), p. 364; *Holl. Dutch & Flemish*, VII (under Furnius), p. 44; and Delen 1924–1935, II.1, p. 164; II.2, pp. 90, 91, and 169.]

---

[38] *La pompe funèbre* is not an ordinary folio because the conventionally printed folio text (with vertical chain lines) is combined with a series of primarily horizontally (i.e., oblong) oriented images, printed on leaves with horizontal chain lines. See *New Holl., Van Doetecum*, nos. 84 and 117, for two exceptional, vertically oriented images. See ch. 3 for more on this project and Cock's involvement in it.

[39] Although forty-two items are, strictly speaking, listed under his name, a handwritten note in the copy of this catalogue in the Prentenkabinet affiliated with the Plantin-Moretus Museum indicates that nos. 31–36 are the same as nos. 37–42.

Work completed for Plantin's editions with intaglio illustrations:

1574: PP 590: B. Arias Montano, *Humanae salutis monumenta*, 4°, 1583; and PP 690: *Biblia sacra*, f°, 1583: in May 1574, Dufour was paid for executing four engravings at 6 fl. per plate, with the following old testament subjects: "Moysis se dechaussant, le presbtre Aaron, Manna, et Josueiens terram Israelitis . . ." (Moses removing his shoes, the priest Aaron, Manna, and Joshua dividing the land of the Israelites . . .).[40] We have associated this payment with the following 4 engravings: [*Moses removing his sandals before*] *The Burning Bush*; *Gathering of Manna*; the *Allotment of Land in the Promised Land*; and *Aaron* (the Old Testament Priest). The first three of these were used in both the *Monumenta* and the bible and are believed to have been designed by Gerard van Groeningen (see *New Holl.*, *Van Groeningen*, nos. 375, 379, and 382, and the discussion of van Groeningen's work below). The fourth engraving only appears in the *Monumenta* (fol. F3r). We are associating the reference to the plate of Aaron with the image of the Old Testament Priest in the *Monumenta* because of visual similarities between this figure and that of standard representations of Aaron in bibles.[41] See also under Peeter vander Borcht, Crispin van den Broeck, Abraham de Bruyn, Gerard van Groeningen, Jan Sadeler, and Jan Wierix, for their work on engravings for these publications.

PP 1685: *Missale Romanum*, f°, 1574; and PP 822, *Breviarium Romanum*, f°, 1575: in the fall of 1574, Dufour completed at least fourteen engravings for these two projects combined. Of these, only three subjects were specified, namely three compositions by Crispin [van den Broeck] of the *Annunciation*, *SS Peter and Paul*, and *King David*, which Plantin sent to Dufour by October 1574. According to the following payment record, Dufour completed all three plates by December 7, 1574.[42] While an engraving of *SS Peter and Paul* in the 1574 folio missal (fol. e8v) and an engraving of *King David* in the 1575 folio breviary (fig. 4.12) are most likely the plates referred to in these records, the only known, comparable engraving of the *Annunciation* in the 1574 folio missal was engraved by Jan Wierix (Holl. Dutch & Flemish, LXX, no. 82). For work on other engravings included in these books, see under Peeter vander Borcht, Gerard van Groeningen, and Jan Wierix.

GALLE, PHILIPS (HAARLEM, 1537–1612, ANTWERP)

Engraver, draughtsman, and print publisher.

Galle was a pupil of and strongly influenced by the Haarlem humanist-engraver Dirck Volckertsz. Coornhert. In the period 1557–1563, Galle (still in Haarlem) made engravings that were published by others, in particular Hieronymus Cock, as well as (but to

---

[40] For this payment, see MPM Arch. 31, fol. 79 rht, which is transcribed in Delen 1924–1935, II.1, p. 164, n. 3.

[41] Consider, for example, the illustration of the high priest, or Aaron, in a Latin bible (*Biblia*) published in Antwerp in 1563 under the name of Jan Steelsius (BT 5192), fol. E1r.

[42] See MPM Arch. 31, fol. 79 rht, for two payment records, one from October 12, 1574, for twelve unspecified plates, and one from December 7, 1574, for completing three additional plates. These records are transcribed in Delen 1924–1935, II.1, p. 165, end of n. 3 from p. 164.

a lesser degree) Martin Peeters, also of Antwerp. In this period, he worked primarily after designs by Pieter Bruegel I, Frans Floris, and especially his fellow Haarlem artist, Maarten van Heemskerck. As of 1563, Galle began to work as an independent engraver-print publisher in Haarlem, making engravings after his own designs and those of van Heemskerck, many of which bore accompanying didactic verses by Hadrianus Junius. By 1570, Galle had established himself in Antwerp and was registered in the St. Luke's guild there. Galle published large numbers of independent prints and print series in the next few years (c.1572–1575). When in Antwerp, he turned to other designers, including Johannes Stradanus, Maarten de Vos, Gerard van Groeningen, and Hans Vredeman de Vries. These engravings were, in turn, made by a variety of engravers besides himself, all of whom were or would become respected local engravers. This group included Jan Sadeler I, Hieronymus Wierix, and the van Doetecums, as well as (later on) Adriaen and Hans Collaert II and Carel de Mallery (each of whom had married into Galle's family). As of 1600, Galle let his son Theodoor manage his workshop. While Galle executed only a couple of engravings for Plantin personally, he was on close terms with him from the early 1570s onward. In 1590, following Plantin's death, Philips Galle, together with Plantin's favorite designer and etcher, Peeter vander Borcht (see above), and the cartographer Abraham Ortelius, helped make up the inventory of Plantin's stock of copper plates (see appendix 4). [Lit.: *New Holl., Galle* (2001), 4 vols., fully illustrated, with introduction (I, pp. xxxiii–lxxxi); Sellink 1997; *Grove Dictionary of Art*, XII, pp. 15–16.]

Work completed by Galle for Plantin's editions with intaglio illustrations:

c.1570: PP 644: *Biblia sacra* (= Polyglot Bible), f°, 1568–1573: one small engraving of a *Shekel*, signed by Galle, but not dated (fig. 3.12).[43] It is possible that Plantin did not, in fact, commission this plate, but had borrowed it from Galle. For it alone out of all the illustrations in the Polyglot Bible was not included in Franciscus Raphelengius I's 1593 republication of Arias Montano's commentaries from the bible's *Apparatus*, under the title of *Antiquitatum Iudaicarum libri IX* (TB, no. 284). Rather, it was replaced with an anonymous copy (see p. 126). For work on other engravings for this publication, see under Peeter vander Borcht, Crispin van den Broeck, Pieter van der Heyden, Pieter Huys, and Jan Wierix.

1572: PP 1676: *Missale Romanum*, f°, 1572: one engraving of the *Crucifixion*, signed and dated by Galle and the designer Maarten van Heemskerck (fig. 4.2).

Work completed by Galle's workshop for Plantin's editions with intaglio illustrations:

1579: PP 865: *Sanctorum kalendarii Romani . . .*, 24°, 1580, with 230 illustrations; and the joint publication PP 1152: *Evangeliorum dominicalium . . .*, 24°, 1580, with fifty-five illustrations: in May 1579 Galle was paid for delivering fifty plates for either or

---

43 See *New Hollstein, Philips Galle*, II, no. 226, for this engraving where it is incorrectly dated 1582 – presumably an error for 1572.

both of these texts (see fig. 6.3), some portion of which were most likely designed by Peeter vander Borcht (see above).[44] Paul Uten Waele engraved many other plates for this publication (see below).

1580: in September 1580, Galle was paid for delivering five additional engravings for either or both of the preceding publications, some of which may have been designed by Peeter vander Borcht.[45]

1583: PP 569: *Rechten, ende costumen van Antwerpen*, f°, 1582: in April 1583, Galle was paid for delivering one engraving of the boundaries of Antwerp (fig. 6.4).[46]

GOLTZIUS, HENDRICK (MÜLBRACHT [NOW BRACHT-AM-NIEDERRHEIN], 1558–1617, HAARLEM)

Painter, draughtsman, engraver, and print publisher.

Goltzius was a highly successful, influential artist, executing masterly works in a variety of media including metal point, pen and ink, chalk, engraving, and painting. After having moved several times while young, Goltzius settled in Haarlem in 1577. In the period 1577–1578, he executed many engravings for Philips Galle, then in Antwerp. In 1582, Goltzius started his own print workshop, which became very successful and included such pupils as Jacob Matham (his stepson) and Jan Saenredam. Goltzius executed hundreds of engravings of a wide range of subjects. While he composed many himself or copied ancient or contemporary Italian artists, other engravings were after such famous contemporary designers as Joannes Stradanus, Maarten de Vos, Bartholomeus Spranger, and Corneliusz. van Haarlem. Plantin corresponded with him in 1586 concerning the execution of the illustrations for Jerome Nadal's *Evangelicae historiae imagines*, a project which Goltzius consistently declined to take on.[47] Around 1600, Goltzius began to paint actively and essentially gave up producing engravings. [Lit.: Amsterdam 2003; *Grove Dictionary of Art*, XII, pp. 879–884.]

Work completed for Plantin's editions with intaglio illustrations:

1583: PP 2261: G. Stewechius, *Commentarius ad Flavi Vegeti Renati libros*, 4°, 1585: engraved author's portrait, signed by Goltzius and dated 1583.[48] It is possible,

---

44 See MPM Arch. 18, fol. 282 rht for the following delivery made in May 1579: "50 cleyn plaetkens van heylighen tot 12 st. . . . Item 36 plaetkens van coper daertoe gelevert tot 1 st. $\frac{1}{4}$ stuck . . ." (50 small plates of saints at 12 st. [per piece] . . . Idem 36 small plates of copper delivered for the same at 1 st. $\frac{1}{4}$ [per] piece).

45 See MPM Arch. 18, fol. 321 rht, for the following delivery made in September 1580: "5 figurettes petites de cuivre que son homme a tailles au Calend. 13^{1}/2 [st.] piece . . . 7 plaetkens copere voor sulcke figurkens 1 st. ^{1}/2 piece . . . 20 se?den tot 2 st. stuck in dieverse rey?ses . . ." (5 small figures in copper that were cut by his assistant for the Calend[er] [at] 13^{1}/2 [st. per] piece . . . 7 small plates of copper for such figures [at] 1 st. ^{1}/2 [per] piece . . . 20 [of the same?] at 2 st. [per] piece at distinct times . . .). See ch. 6 for more on the significance of this work.

46 See pp. 255–256 for this payment record and more on this project.

47 See *Corr.* VII, no. 1108, and *Corr.* VIII–IX, nos. 1160, 1182, and 1193, for Plantin's correspondence concerning Goltzius and this project.

48 See Strauss, I, no. 178, for this engraving.

given the earlier dating, that this print was originally executed as an independent engraving and only subsequently included in Plantin's publication.

GOLTZIUS, JULIUS (JULES) (ANTWERP, C.1550–C.1595, ANTWERP?)

Engraver.

Perhaps best known as the son of the Bruges antiquarian Hubertus Goltzius, Julius Goltzius was active making independent prints around 1575–1595. Originally based in Bruges, Julius Goltzius moved to Antwerp by 1586, although he is noted in Plantin's accounts earlier (in 1577), for the completion of unspecified engraving work (see below). Julius Goltzius is also known to have made some engravings that were published by Antwerp print publishers, in particular Hans Liefrinck II (in 1584, for example), Jan Baptist Vrints (in 1586), and Hans van Luyck. [Lit.: Bowen and Imhof 2001, pp. 275–279 and pp. 287–288; Le Loup 1983, p. 106; Holl. *Dutch & Flemish*, VIII, pp. 140–142; Delen 1924–1935, II.1, pp. 151 and 165–6; and II.2, pp. 121, 126, and 160; and Delen 1920, p. 120.]

Work completed for Plantin's editions with intaglio illustrations:

1577: one payment for an unspecified engraving project.[49]
1583: sixteen engravings for a book of hours in 24°.[50]
1584: one payment for reworking engravings of the twelve months (presumably for a small book of hours – see Bowen 1997a, p. 145) and a vignette of the Virgin.[51]

VAN GROENINGEN, GERARD (ACTIVE 1561–C.1575/1576 IN ANTWERP)

Etcher, draughtsman, and designer of glass windows.

Little is known for certain about van Groeningen beyond the evidence of the work he left behind, namely, drawings for glass windows, more than two hundred independent prints after his designs, and some two hundred designs for book illustrations. His prints were engraved by several artists, including Pierre Dufour, Herman Jansz. Muller, and, in particular, Jan Wierix. They were most often published by Gerard de Jode, Philips Galle, and Christopher Plantin (as illustrations to his books). Van Groeningen's work for Plantin is limited to a brief but intensive two-year period from 1574 to 1575, in which he drew nearly forty compositions for Plantin's own publications and twenty-five more for an edition Plantin published jointly with Philips Galle. [Lit.: *New Holl.*, *Van Groeningen* (1997), 2 vols., fully illustrated, with an introduction (I, pp. 11–19).]

---

[49] See MPM Arch. 14, bundle 1, fol. 18 rht (under December 6, 1577), which reads: "p. Julius Golsius pr. taillures de cuivre fl. 17 st. 18 . . ." (for Julius Goltzius for engraving copper, 17 fl. 18 st.).

[50] See MPM Arch. 61, fols. 108r (under August 11, 1583) and 125r (under September 13, 1583) for payments for this work.

[51] See MPM Arch. 62, fol. 10v (under January 25, 1584) for the following payment: "Payé a Julius Golsius pour les 12 mois et un fignette de nostre dame pour les figures de nostre dame lesquelles il a refaictes a 17 patt. la p. val. in NS. fl. 11 st. 1." (Paid to Julius Goltzius for the 12 months and one vignette of Our Lady for the figures of Our Lady, which he reworked at 17 st. per piece, amounts to in currency, 11 fl. 1 st.)

Work completed for Plantin's editions with intaglio illustrations:

1574: PP 1685: *Missale Romanum*, f°, 1574: designs for six or seven full-page illustrations, namely, the *Adoration of the Shepherds* (fig. 4.7), the *Resurrection*, *Pentecost*, the *Last Supper*, the *Assumption of the Virgin*, *All Saints*, and possibly the *Crucifixion*. For the attribution of the first six subjects to van Groeningen, see *New Holl., Van Groeningen*, nos. 216, 264, 218, 217, 219, and 220, all of which, except for the *Resurrection*, are present in a copy of PP 1685 in Trinity College, Cambridge (E.3.56), which was not known to the compilers of this Hollstein volume. Also present here is an engraving of the *Crucifixion* (p. [304]), which is stylistically similar to the other compositions attributed to Van Groeningen in, for example, the description of the figures. At least one engraving after each of these designs was made by Jan Wierix (see below). For work on other engravings included in this missal, see under Peeter vander Borcht, Crispin van den Broeck, and Pierre Dufour.

1575: PP 1228: B. Furmerius, *De rerum usu et abusu*, 4°, 1575 (published jointly by Plantin and Philips Galle): designs for twenty-five text illustrations, engraved at least in part by Jan Wierix (see fig. 6.11).

prior to January 1, 1576: engravings in MPM Arch. 1228 for: PP 590: B. Arias Montano, *Humanae salutis monumenta*, 4°, 1583: all twenty-two compositions in this work that are currently attributed to van Groeningen, except the image of the *Raising of Lazarus* (*New Holl., Van Groeningen*, no. 395 = M-H 2245), were included in MPM Arch. 1228, implying that they were all completed prior to January 1, 1576.[52] The engraving of the *Raising of Lazarus*, however, was used to illustrate some copies of Plantin's 1575 *Officium BMV* (PP 1776; cf. M-H 2245), indicating that it, too, was made prior to January 1, 1576. Several of these plates were engraved by Jan Wierix (see below) and others by Pierre Dufour (see above). See also under Peeter van der Borcht, Crispin van den Broeck, and Abraham de Bruyn, as well as under Jan Sadeler I and Jan Wierix, for their work on other engravings for these publications.

VAN HEEMSKERCK, MAARTEN (HEEMSKERCK, 1498–1574, HAARLEM)

Painter and draughtsman.

Van Heemskerck went to Haarlem in 1527 to join the studio of Jan van Scorel. After a four-year sojourn in Rome (1532–1536), van Heemskerck returned to Haarlem. In addition to being active as a painter, van Heemskerck was a prolific designer of prints, making some six hundred such designs throughout his career. Working as a designer in earnest as of 1547, van Heemskerck's compositions covered a wide range of subjects, but were often didactic or moralizing. Various professional engravers executed the prints after his designs. While several print publishers distributed his designs, the Antwerp-based publishers Hieronymus Cock and then Philips Galle published the most. Van Heemskerck's solitary drawing of an image of the *Crucifixion* for Plantin clearly does not fit into this pattern. Rather, given the close (artistic) ties between

---

[52] For the dating of this archive (and hence the prints in it), see the discussion of this bundle under vander Borcht.

van Heemskerck and Galle, the engraver of the print, it seems most plausible that Galle arranged for van Heemskerck to draw the image. [Lit.: *Grove Dictionary of Art*, XIV, pp. 291–294; *New Holl., Van Heemskerck*, 2 vols., fully illustrated.]

Work completed for Plantin's editions with intaglio illustrations:

1572: PP 1676: *Missale Romanum*, f°, 1572: one engraving of the *Crucifixion*, dated 1572 and signed by van Heemskerck and Philips Galle (fig. 4.2).

VAN DER HEYDEN, PIETER (ALIAS PETRUS A MERICA = PAME) (ANTWERP, C.1530–1576?, ANTWERP)

Engraver.

Although he was not registered as a master in the St. Luke's guild of Antwerp until 1557, van der Heyden was active as an independent engraver as of the early 1550s. He went on to produce numerous engravings for Hieronymus Cock between c.1551 and c.1570, in addition to some work for other Antwerp print publishers, like Hans Liefrinck I. He worked after designs by a variety of known artists, in particular Pieter Bruegel I, but also, for example, Hieronymus Bosch and Lambert Lombard. Van der Heyden's latest known prints date from around 1570. Consequently, the engravings van der Heyden made for Plantin were among the last engravings he is known to have executed. It is noteworthy that Plantin had him engrave at least two, if not all four of the maps included in the Polyglot Bible, for van der Heyden does not seem to have specialized in the engraving of cartographic images, as other artists, like the van Doetecums, did. It is regrettable that we do not know more about the two men's working relationship, for van der Heyden is said to have resided in Plantin's home in Berchem as of 1571 (when Plantin was still paying him for his work on the maps for the Polyglot Bible) until van der Heyden was supposedly killed in 1576 during the Spanish Fury. [Lit.: *Grove Dictionary of Art*, XIV, pp. 504–505; Riggs 1977, pp. 309–394, handlist of prints published by Cock, nos. 6, 12–15, 34–51, 93–95, 101–102, 129, 164–169, 180, 184, 185, 204, 239–241, 265, and 268; *Holl. Dutch & Flemish*, IX, pp. 26–32; for van der Heyden's work after Pieter Bruegel I for Hieronymus Cock, see, e.g., Orenstein 2001.]

Work completed for Plantin's editions with intaglio illustrations:

1569: PP 644: *Biblia sacra* (= Polyglot Bible), f°, 1568–1573: the engraved title-page and two engraved frontispieces to the first volume of this work, one of which, the "Pietas regia," was designed by Crispin van den Broeck (see figs. 3.10 and 3.11).[53]

---

[53] Both the title-page for this bible and the "Pietas regia" frontispiece are signed "PAME," for Petrus a Merica, the latinized name of the engraver Pieter van der Heyden. Van der Heyden's work on the "Pietas regia," in addition to the third frontispiece, the *Allegory of the Authority of the Pentateuch* (which comprises a landscape view with Moses), is confirmed by a series of payments made to van der Heyden between February 17 and June 4, 1569 for his work on "deux planches le Roij et la table en paysaige avec Moses . . . pour le grande Bible" (two plates, the King and the landscape with Moses . . . for the large Bible). See MPM Arch. 756, fol. 173 lft for these payments.

1571–1572: PP 644: *Biblia sacra* (= Polyglot Bible), f°, 1568–1573: two to four maps included in the eighth volume. Van der Heyden's engraving of at least two maps for this work, the "universele" (universe [most likely the two-page world map]) and the "terrae sancte" (holy land [most likely the map of Israel, as that map was to be included at the end of the text on Caleb, or the "terra promissa" (promised land) divided]) is documented by a series of payments made between January 1571 and March 28, 1572, for a grand total of 113 fl. $4^1/2$ st. However, according to these same records, the execution of the two cited maps cost only 66 fl, which means that van der Heyden was paid an additional 47 fl. $4^1/2$ st. for unspecified work. Of the remaining plates, most can be attributed to either Pieter Huys or Jan Wierix (see below). The two notable exceptions are the maps of Canaan and Jerusalem, also included in the eighth volume of this bible, which would fit in thematically with the other work for which van der Heyden was paid in these records.[54] For work on other engravings for this publication, see under Peeter vander Borcht, Crispin van den Broeck, Philips Galle, Pieter Huys, and Jan Wierix.

"GIL HOR"

Engraver.

Work completed for Plantin's editions with intaglio illustrations:

1575: An as yet unidentified engraver who signed three engravings used to illustrate at least two copies of Plantin's 1575 8° *Officium BMV* (PP 1775).[55]

VANDER HOEVEN, JACQUES

"Coper drucker" (copper printer).

Known only through the archives in the Plantin-Moretus Museum, this man was also occasionally referred to as Jacques de Berchem, or simply "Jacques." One payment to vander Hoeven in March 1579 for a ransom he paid (perhaps to marauding Spanish troops) for the copper plates in Berchem suggests that when he worked for Plantin, he was located there (and hence the name, "Jacques de Berchem"), where Plantin apparently had some or all of his copper plates.[56] Often, the records documenting his employment by Plantin consist simply of the payment either of a fixed wage for unspecified work or for the delivery of black ink for printing for "Jacques."[57] A payment

---

[54] See MPM Arch. 757, fol. 370 lft and rht for this series of payments similar to an "installment plan."

[55] See Bowen 1997b, p. 150, n. 80.

[56] See MPM Arch. 57, fol. 25v (under March 9, 1579), for the following record: "A Jacques vander Hoeven de Berchem la somme de fl. neuf pour rançonnement des planches de cuivre qui estoyent a Berchem etc. vall. fl. 9."

[57] For examples of irregular payments to Jacques of a fixed wage of 7 st. per day, see MPM Arch. 31, fol. 181 lft (for the period March 5–August 4, 1571) and MPM Arch. 32, fol. 27 rht (for the period August 18, 1571–June 21, 1572). For other payments made to him of a fixed sum of 3 fl. for unspecified work, see, e.g., MPM Arch. 57, fol. 69r (under May 13, 1579), and MPM Arch. 58, fols. 4v, 9v, 20r, 35v, 44r, and 53r

made in July 1584 – or potentially noted in 1585, as a back payment – for the delivery of black ink for printing ("druk swert") to a certain "Jacob de Leyden Imprimer [printer]" may also pertain to the same man. If so, the timing of the payment and the new reference to Leiden suggest that he may have followed Plantin to Leiden by that time.[58] There is, in any case, a notable lack of references to payments made to him specifically in summary accounts kept in Antwerp of outlays made between 1585 and 1588. Records from 1589 are ambiguous concerning his whereabouts. On the one hand, payments to him for printing illustrations for a new edition of Lipsius's *Saturnalia* (which was printed in Leiden in 1588 – see PP 1558) were noted in the Antwerp-based account books (see below). On the other hand, there is also a reference to a debt of 42 fl. owed to vander Hoeven in the inventory of Plantin's stock in Leiden, which was made up following the latter's death. This at least supports the theory that he did some work for Plantin's Press there, regardless of where he lived in the late 1580s.[59] Only rarely is the project on which vander Hoeven worked indicated in these payment records (see below). All of these records combined indicate that he was regularly employed by Plantin in Antwerp between 1571 and 1584 and then once again, at least, in 1589. This observation is supported by the complementary records of payment to Mynken Liefrinck (see below), Plantin's primary printer of his intaglio plates. For, as of 1585–1586, there are records indicating that Liefrinck printed the illustrations for virtually all of Plantin's publications with intaglio illustrations completed in this period, except for those works printed in Leiden.[60]

Work completed for Plantin's editions with intaglio illustrations:[61]

> **1577**: PP 1335: L. Hillessemius, *Sacrarum antiquitatum monumenta*, 8°, 1577: see MPM Arch. 32, fol. 298 rht (under September 28, 1577), for the following record:

(for payments made at irregular intervals between January 9 and April 29, 1580). For examples of the delivery of black printing ink (sold by the pound) for Jacques ("druck swart . . . a Jacques"), see MPM Arch. 16, fol. 214 rht (in 1572) and fol. 240 rht (in 1573); MPM Arch. 18, fol. 82 rht (in 1574), and fol. 158 rht (in 1575 and 1576). The fact that all of the payments for black printing ink were made to Mynken Liefrinck, Plantin's primary printer of his intaglio plates, reinforces the association of this ink with the printing of copper plates.

58 See MPM Arch. 20, fol. 194 rht (under July 7, 1584), for this payment.

59 See MPM Arch. 99, p. 90, for this debt in the Leiden inventory. MPM Arch. 14 is a collection of summaries of expenditures and receipts made between July 1576 and August 1589. There are occasional records of payments made to vander Hoeven in the years 1578 (see bundle 1, fol. 30 rht), 1579 (e.g., bundle 1, fols. 32 rht, 33 rht, and 36 rht), 1580 (bundle 2, fol. 8 rht), 1581 (bundle 3, fols. 5 rht, 6 rht, 9 rht, 10 rht, and 11 rht), 1582 (bundle 4, fols. 1 rht and 8 rht), 1583 (bundle 5, fols. 1 rht and 4 rht), and 1584 (bundle 5, fols 14 rht and 15 rht). But there are no such records for the years 1585–1589, suggesting that he may no longer have been working for Plantin in Antwerp in that period.

60 Specifically, we have yet to find records that clearly record the printing of the illustrations for the following editions published between 1585 and 1589: PP 830 (1585 *Breviarium Romanum* in 4°); PP 1786septies (1586 book of hours in 24°; see Bowen 1997a, p. 255); PP 1047 (F. Costerus, *De universa historia Dominica*, from 1587, with only one etching on the title-page); PP 1804 (1587 *Officium diurnum* in 8°); PP 1786novies (1587 book of hours in 24°; Bowen 1997a, pp. 255–256); PP 1788bis (1588 book of hours in 32°; Bowen 1997a, p. 257); and PP 1806 (1589 *Officium diurnum* in 16°). It is also possible that the illustration of some of these editions (in particular the small books of hours) may have been combined with the records of payment to Liefrinck for illustrating other comparable texts.

61 As recorded in notes 57 and 59 above, other records indicate that Plantin also employed vander Hoeven in the years 1571–1576 and 1578–1583.

"compte avec Jacques de Berchem quil avoir imprime: 100 Hilsonius vallant 500 feilles a 2 fl le cent font. . . . fl. 10." (account with Jacques de Berchem, who printed 100 [copies of?] Hillessemius, amounting to 500 sheets at 2 fl. per hundred [amounts to] 10 fl.)[62]

PP 1778quater: book of hours in 24°, printed in 1577 (see Bowen 1997a, p. 250). In the same record cited above for work completed by vander Hoeven by September 28, 1577, he was also paid 7 fl. for illustrating 200 books of hours in 24°, with seven illustrated sheets each, at 10 st. per hundred sheets ("200 Horae in 24 a 7 feilles pour chacunne font 1400 feilles a 10 patt le cent font fl. 7").

PP 1235: L. Gambara, *Rerum sacrarum liber*, 4°, 1577: by October 12, 1577 vander Hoeven was also paid for printing illustrations on 2,350 sheets of this book at 14 st. per hundred sheets.[63]

1582: PP 690: *Biblia sacra*, f°, 1583: a payment to Mynken Liefrinck from around October 27, 1582 for printing illustrations for this bible contains an allusion to work on the same book completed by vander Hoeven, namely: "p. les figures qlle a imprimes en la Bible oultre celles du Jacques Verhoeven . . ." (for the figures that she printed in the bible beyond those from Jacques Verhoeven).[64]

1584: PP 1786quater: book of hours in 24°, printed in 1584 (see Bowen 1997a, p. 254): in a payment made to Mynken Liefrinck on May 25, 1584 for printing illustrations for a book of hours in 24°, it is stated that she did one part of the work and "Jaques" did the other: "afgerekent dat de horas in 24° lesq'les elle a imprimés une p[ar]tie et une p[ar]tie Jaques . . ."[65]

1589: PP 1558: J. Lipsius, *Saturnalium sermonum libri duo*, 4°, 1588: see MPM Arch. 98, p. 499, for two payments made to vander Hoeven (one of 8 st. made in April 1589, the other for 5 fl. 2 st. made in May 1589) for printing illustrations for Lipsius's *Saturnalia*. Voet notes that this text was printed in Leiden and also observes that, contrary to the 1585 edition, all of the illustrations were now inserted (and, hence, printed separately on other sheets than those with the letterpress).

HUBERTI (HUYBRECHTS), ADRIAEN (ADRIANUS) (ANTWERP, C.1550–1614, ANTWERP)

Engraver and publisher of, as well as dealer in, prints and maps.
Huberti was registered in the Antwerp St. Luke's guild in 1573 as a dealer in art objects. Also active as an engraver and seeing to the coloring of printed images, Huberti is best known, however, as a publisher of and dealer in prints and maps. His publications include prints by the Wierix brothers (often after Maarten de Vos), Peeter vander Borcht, and Hans Collaert I, as well as illustrated works with accompanying printed texts, like Richard Verstegen's work on Catholic martyrs (see ch. 6). Huberti's marriage to Mynken

---

[62] This calculation of the number of sheets needed to illustrate a hundred copies of this book makes sense, as all of the illustrations are found on just five sheets (those with gatherings A–E).

[63] See MPM Arch. 32, fol. 298 rht, for this record, which reads "Le 12 Octobre 1577 pour 2350 folia Poematum Gambarae a 14 patt. le cent font fl. 16_ 9 [st.]."

[64] See MPM Arch. 20, fol. 119 rht.   [65] See MPM Arch. 20, fol. 194 rht.

Liefrinck's daughter Marguerite (by 1577) also reinforced his connections in this world. While Huberti dealt in books and prints with Plantin and his successor, Jan Moretus I, he was also employed by them as an engraver, in particular, of texts on copper plates engraved by others. [Lit.: Rouzet 1975, pp. 100–101; Delen 1924–1935, II.1, pp. 155 and 168; and II.2, pp. 119, 150, and 167.]

Work completed for Plantin's editions with intaglio illustrations:

1580: By October 22, 1580, Huberti was paid 2 Flemish pounds (= 12 fl.) for unspecified engraving work.[66] Given that Huberti was, in later years, paid for engraving letters on to plates, that may have been involved here as well.[67]

HUYS, FRANS (ANTWERP, 1522–1562, ANTWERP)

Engraver.
Huys was registered as a master in the St. Luke's guild of Antwerp by 1546. His earliest dated prints are from 1555. He is best known for the prints he engraved after Pieter Bruegel I for Hieronymus Cock, although he also made prints for other Antwerp dealers, e.g., Hans Liefrinck (his brother-in-law, see under Mynken Liefrinck) and Bartholomeus de Momper. His work for Plantin was limited by his own early death at the age of forty. [Lit.: *Grove Dictionary of Art*, xv, p. 43; Riggs 1977, pp. 88–89 and 119–120, and pp. 309–394, handlist of prints published by Cock, nos. 52–54, 96, 150, 266–267, and 268; De Ramaix 1968; Holl. *Dutch & Flemish*, IX, pp. 162–168; Delen 1920, pp. 102–103 and 105. For examples of his prints after Bruegel, see, e.g., Orenstein 2001.]

Work completed for Plantin's editions with intaglio illustrations:

prior to April 28, 1562: PP 2413: Juan de Valverde, *Vivae imagines partium corporis humani*, large 4°, 1566: three engravings, completed sometime prior to the public sale of Plantin's possessions on April 28, 1562 (possibly among figs. 3.6, 3.7, and 3.9). For work on the other engravings for this work, see under Pieter Huys and Lambert van Noort.

HUYS, PIETER (ANTWERP, C.1520–PRE 1586, ANTWERP)

Painter, draughtsman, and engraver.
In 1545, Huys became a master in the Antwerp St. Luke's guild. Only a small number of independent works are attributed to him with any certainty. These include some prints,

---

[66] See MPM Arch. 14, bundle 2, fol. 10 rht (under October 22, 1580), for the following record: "p. Adriaen Huybrechts a bon compte de tailleures £ 2" (to Adriaen Huberti for the account of engraving, £ 2).

[67] See MPM Arch. 65, fol. 73r (under May 28, 1588), for a payment to Huberti for engraving the letters ("pour la taillure de lescripture") on an independent engraving of St. Bruno, made by Crispijn van de Passe after a design by Maarten de Vos (see pp. 44–45).

a couple of which were published by his brother-in-law, Hans Liefrinck (see under Mynken Liefrinck), and a few paintings. Rather, most of what is known of his artistic activities, particularly as a graphic artist, stems from the Plantin archives. Huys began to work for Plantin by 1563, when Plantin paid him for designing sets of decorative letters.[68] For the next ten years, Huys served as Plantin's all-purpose artist. Not only did Huys continue to design woodcuts for Plantin, but he also executed a variety of engravings – from large, full-page compositions for Plantin's Polyglot Bible to small illustrations for a book of hours – and even printed some of the plates he made. Huys's last known work for Plantin was perhaps his most spectacular, namely, the engraving in 1578 of the large folio title-frame used for Plantin and his successors' large folio editions of music. Both Delen and Voet (following Delen) speculate that Plantin did not have much faith in Huys because of a note in one payment record in which Plantin admits that he is not sure whether Huys really delivered five plates for de Valverde's anatomical text, or just four.[69] However, as is evident from Voet's own discussion of the delivery of these plates, Plantin's records are themselves occasionally unclear as to exactly how many plates were delivered when.[70] Huys is presumed to have died by April 1586, as his possessions were then sold at public auction.[71] [Lit.: *Grove Dictionary of Art*, XV, pp. 42–43; *Holl. Dutch & Flemish*, IX, pp. 169–172; Delen 1924–1935, II.1, pp. 81, 84, 85, 103, 107, 112–115, 125, 134, 139, 140, 142, 144, 145, 148, 159, 162, and 167; and II.2, pp. 112–113; Delen 1920, pp. 102–105.]

Work completed for Plantin's editions with intaglio illustrations:

prior to September 1564–February 1566: PP 2413: Juan de Valverde, *Vivae imagines partium corporis humani*, large 4°, 1566: forty engravings, seven of which were completed by September 14, 1564, another eleven by April 10, 1565, nineteen more during the remainder of 1565, and the last two text plates and the title-plate by February 1566 (see figs. 3.2, 3.6, 3.7, and 3.9).[72] See also under Frans Huys and Lambert van Noort for their contributions to the illustration of this work.

1566 and 1567: PP 2413: Juan de Valverde, *Vivae imagines partium corporis humani*, large 4°, 1566: printed the illustrations for first 200 copies (paid for on March 19, 1566) and then 400 copies (paid for on August 22, 1567), in both cases at a rate of 20 st. per hundred sheets printed.[73]

---

[68] See MPM Arch. 3, fol. 2r, for this payment record. It is transcribed in Delen 1924–1935, II.1, p. 112, n. 2.

[69] See Delen 1920, p. 104, and Voet, GC, II, p. 198, n. 3.

[70] See PP 2413, n. 7.   [71] Delen 1920, p. 103.

[72] This timetable is derived from the payments for plates for this text recorded in MPM Arch. 4, fol. 81 lft, and (particularly for a clarification of the first ambiguous record concerning the delivery of the plates here) in MPM Arch. 3, fols. 17v, 23r, 29v, 30r, 34r, 36r, 41r, and 44r. The payment records in Arch. 3 replicate the payment summary in Arch. 4, with the exception of one payment for three plates that, according to Arch. 4, was supposedly made around December 11, 1565, but which is not noted in Arch. 3. See n. 7 to PP 2413 for transcriptions of most of these records.

[73] See MPM Arch. 4, fol. 81 lft, for both payments, which are transcribed in n. 8 to PP 2413. The first of these records is similarly recorded in MPM Arch. 3, fol. 46v, under March 18, 1566. The second is not.

between July 12, 1567 and July 12, 1569: PP 2416: Juan de Valverde, *Anatomie oft levende beelden vande deelen des menschelicken lichaems,* large 4°, 1568: printed the illustrations for 450 copies of de Valverde's text, probably primarily for this edition.[74]

1569?–1570: PP 1365–68: *Horae BVM,* 8°, 1570: engraved one border and possibly reworked eight, while two title-page vignettes and six text illustrations bear his initials. The last figures may represent the six "figures pour le livret de la Bible" (figures for the booklet of the bible) for which he was paid in November 1569 and January 1570.[75] For work on the other engravings used to illustrate the various issues of this publication, see under Peeter vander Borcht, Jan Sadeler I, Jan and Hieronymus Wierix.

1569?–1571: PP 588: B. Arias Montano, *Humanae salutis monumenta,* 8°, 1571: for this edition, Huys engraved and signed the title-plate, five borders (see figs. 3.25 and 4.17), and five to eight text illustrations (the number depending on the copy of this text), some of which may also have been the engravings referred to as the "figures pour le livret de la Bible," cited in the preceding entry.[76] For work on other engravings for this publication, see under Peeter vander Borcht, Crispin van den Broeck, Abraham de Bruyn, Hieronymus and Jan Wierix.

1571–1572: PP 644: *Biblia sacra* (= Polyglot Bible), f°, 1568–1573: while Huys was paid for engraving both parts of the image of Noah's ark (fig. 3.15) on or shortly after October 21, 1571, he was not paid for engraving seven of the eight remaining plates bearing his initials in this bible until at least March 24, 1572 (see figs. 3.13, 3.14, 3.16, and 3.17).[77] One additional engraving associated with the preceding group (the ground plan for the Tabernacle) is often attributed to Huys, although it is not signed and there are no clear records of payment for it. For work on other engravings for this publication, see under Peeter vander Borcht, Crispin van den Broeck, Philips Galle, Pieter van der Heyden, and Jan Wierix.

1573: PP 1772–1773: *Officium BMV,* 32°, 1573: at the end of February 1573, Huys was paid for delivering seventeen small engravings for a book of hours in 32°.[78]

---

74 See MPM Arch. 31, fol. 64 rht, for this payment, which is transcribed in n. 4 to PP 2416. Neither the rate of pay nor the total amount paid is given in this record. See ch. 3 for a discussion of the illustration of this and Plantin's subsequent editions of this text.

75 For the one border he signed himself by this time, see Bowen 2003, pp. 32–33, table 2. For the two title-page vignettes, see Bowen 1997a, figs. 60 and 61. For payments for the reworking of other borders and the possible payments for the text illustrations, see MPM Arch. 31, fol. 64 rht. For the text illustrations signed by Huys, see Bowen 1997b, pp. 147–150.

76 For the payment for the title-plate on October 21, 1581, along with eight borders, some of which may be the ones seen in this book, see MPM Arch. 31, fol. 64 rht. As is discussed in Bowen 2003, p. 14, n. 30, these payments most likely post-date the actual completion of these plates. For the variation in the illustration of this edition, see Bowen 2003, pp. 24–26, and the discussion of the Type A and Type B sets of illustrations. See Holl. *Dutch & Flemish,* IX, under Pieter Huys, nos. 17–26, for a listing (without reproductions) of ten possibly related borders "with animals, children and flowers."

77 See MPM Arch. 31, fol. 64 rht, for the payments to Huys for his work on these plates, which, aside from the images of Noah's ark and Aaron, consist primarily of views of the Temple of Jerusalem, the Tabernacle, and its accoutrements. All of these records are transcribed in Delen 1924–1935, II.1, p. 115, n. 1 (although the entry for March 24 is incorrectly dated 1571 here instead of 1572) and n. 3.

78 See MPM Arch. 31, fol. 142 lft, for the following payment "Dix sept figures petites pour les heures en 32 _ 17 [fl.]." See Bowen 1997a, p. 241, for these editions. As is discussed on p. 366, both of these editions may have been illustrated with engravings and not just PP 1773, as is noted in Bowen 1997a.

On May 23, 1573, Huys was paid for delivering eight newly engraved borders (see fig. 4.18) and for reworking four, possibly for PP 1770: *Officium BMV*, 8°, 1573.[79]

1574: on October 16, 1574, Huys was paid for delivering four unidentified plates and for reworking an image of the *Resurrection*.[80]

1578: PP 1306: G. de la Hèle, *Octo missae quinque, sex et septem vocum*, large f°, 1578: one large engraved title-plate, which is signed on the back "P 1578 H" (see MPM KP 70 E).

LIEFRINCK, MYNKEN (WILLEMYNE) (AUGSBURG OR ANTWERP?, ?–1593, ANTWERP)

Seller, printer, and colorer of printed images.

Mynken Liefrinck was part of a family of printmakers and publishers, including Willem Liefrinck (her father) and Hans Liefrinck I (her brother). She was also married to the engraver Frans Huys; soon after his death in 1562, she married the painter Pauwels van Overbeke. In the sixteenth-century print and book publishing world, wives and daughters often carried on a business once the male head had died, if there were no immediate male successors. It is, consequently, not surprising that Mynken Liefrinck did the same. Plantin's first recorded business contacts with Mynken Liefrinck date from October 4, 1567, when she purchased several maps from him. Soon thereafter (by January 1568) Mynken Liefrinck began to provide Plantin with hand-colored maps.[81] Plantin went on to employ her nearly continuously between 1568 – the last year in which he paid her brother-in-law Pieter Huys for printing engravings for him – and 1589, the year of Plantin's death. Liefrinck served Plantin in a variety of capacities: as a source for independent maps, for the coloring of books and prints, and, above all, for the printing of his intaglio plates. Although (as noted above) Plantin also regularly employed another intaglio printer, Jacques vander Hoeven, simultaneously, Liefrinck consistently illustrated the majority of Plantin's publications. [Lit.: Jan Van der Stock 1998, pp. 66–67 (where Liefrinck's first husband is erroneously identified as Pieter Huys instead of Frans Huys), and p. 95; Rouzet 1975, p. 126.]

Work completed for Plantin's editions with intaglio illustrations:

Because Liefrinck worked virtually continuously for Plantin from 1568 through 1589, printing illustrations for numerous projects, only a selection of these projects will be cited below. For all of the records of Plantin's dealings with Liefrinck, see MPM Arch. 16, fols. 7, 136, 177, 214, and 240; Arch. 18, fols. 82, 158, 235, 278, 381, and 430; and Arch. 20, fols. 119, 186, 194, 237, 255, 288, 308, 334, and 365. See ch. 2 for an overview of her work for Plantin.

---

[79] See MPM Arch. 31, fol. 142 lft, under May 23, 1573, for these payments. The extra borders cited in n. 76 may overlap with these.
[80] See MPM Arch. 31, fol. 142 lft, for this payment.
[81] For these first transactions between Plantin and Liefrinck, see MPM Arch. 16, fol. 7 lft and rht.

1568: PP 2413: Juan de Valverde, *Vivae imagines partium corporis humani*, large 4°, 1566 (see MPM Arch. 16, fol. 7 rht).

1570–1571: PP 1365–68: *Horae BVM*, 8°, 1570 (MPM Arch. 16, fol. 136 rht).

1571–1572: PP 588: B. Arias Montano, *Humanae salutis monumenta*, 8°, 1571 (MPM Arch. 16, fol. 177 rht; these payments are cited in greater detail in Bowen 2003, p. 25).

1572: PP 644: *Biblia sacra* (= Polyglot Bible), f°, 1568–1573 (MPM Arch. 16, fol. 177 rht).

1573: PP 1770 A: *Officium BMV*, 8°, 1573 (MPM Arch. 16, fol. 214 rht).

1574: PP 1772–1773: *Officium BMV*, 32°, 1573 (MPM Arch. 18, fol. 82 rht).

1575: PP 2175: J. Sambucus, *Icones veterum aliquot ac recentium medicorum*, f°, 1574 (MPM Arch. 18, fol. 158 rht).

1576: PP 1775 A: *Officium BMV*, 8°, 1575 (MPM Arch. 18, fol. 158 rht).

1577: PP 584: B. Arias Montano, *Sacri templi exemplum*, broadsheet, 1576; and PP 1697 A: *Missale Romanum*, 8°, 1577 (MPM Arch. 18, fol. 235 rht).

1579: PP 1253: H. Goltzius, *Thesaurus rei antiquariae huberrimus*, 4°, 1579 (MPM Arch. 18, fol. 278 rht).

1580: PP 1955: A. de Pasino, *Discours sur plusieurs poincts de l'architecture de guerre concernants les fortifications . . .*, 4°, 1579 (MPM Arch. 18, fol. 278 rht).

1581: PP 1277: L. Guicciardini, *Descrittione di tutti i Paesi Bassi*, f°, 1581 (MPM Arch. 18, fol. 381 rht).

1582: PP 1412: J.-B. Houwaert, *Pegasides pleyn, ende den lust-hof der maeghden*, 4°, 1583 (MPM Arch. 20, fol. 119 rht).

1583: PP 569: *Rechten, ende costumen van Antwerpen*, f°, 1582 (MPM Arch. 20, fol. 186 rht).

1584: PP 1786ter: *Officium BMV*, 12°, 1584 (MPM Arch. 20, fol. 194 rht; see Bowen 1997a, p. 253, for this edition).

1585: PP 1699 B: *Missale Romanum*, 4°, 1585 (MPM Arch. 20, fol. 237 rht).

1586: PP 1039: F. Costerus, *Libellus sodalitatis*, 8°, 1586 (MPM Arch. 20, fol. 237 rht).

1587: PP 1045: F. Costerus, *De cantico Salve Regina septem meditationes*, 16°, 1587 (MPM Arch. 20, fol. 288 rht).

1588: PP 1138: M. d'Esne, *Les XV mysteres du rosaire de . . . Marie*, 4°, 1588 (MPM Arch. 20, fol. 308 rht).

1589: PP 835 B: *Breviarium Romanum*, 16°, 1589 (MPM Arch. 20, fol. 308 rht).

VAN NOORT, LAMBERT (AMERSFOORT, *C.*1520?–SEPTEMBER 1570/JUNE 1571, ANTWERP)

Draughtsman, architect, and painter.

Although born in Amersfoort in the northern Low Countries, van Noort was in Antwerp by 1549, when he was registered as a master in the St. Luke's guild. He became a citizen of Antwerp on April 30, 1550 and, except for a short trip to Italy in 1558–1559, he remained there. Van Noort is best known for his designs for stained glass windows. Examples can be found in a variety of churches, including the Antwerp cathedral, St. Janskerk in Gouda, and King's College Chapel, Cambridge. However, he also made designs for engravings and other decorative art forms, like tapestries. He died just when Plantin began to commission large quantities of engravings for his publications. [Lit.: *Grove Dictionary of Art*, XXIII, pp. 200–201; Van Ruyven-Zeman 1995.]

Work completed for Plantin's editions with intaglio illustrations:

1566: PP 2413: Juan de Valverde, *Vivae imagines partium corporis humani*, large 4°, 1566: design for the title-plate (fig. 3.2).[82] See under Frans and Pieter Huys for the execution of the engravings for this work.

VAN DE PASSE, CRISPIJN I (ARNEMUIDEN, 1564–1637, UTRECHT)

Engraver, draughtsman, print publisher, and painter.
Van de Passe was in Antwerp by 1584–1585, when he was registered as a master in the St. Luke's guild there. He presumably left Antwerp around the time of its fall to Alessandro Farnese in August 1585 or soon thereafter, when the city was returned to Spanish (Catholic) hands. Van de Passe was in Aachen in 1588 and in Cologne in 1589, where he established himself as an independent engraver and print publisher. Van de Passe left Cologne in 1611 for religious reasons and settled in Utrecht, where he died in 1637. By the time of his death, he had produced thousands of prints and print books that were popular throughout Europe. Several of his children continued in his footsteps. His work for Plantin was limited primarily to works that were designed by, if not engraved through the mediation of Maarten de Vos (see below). [Lit.: Veldman 2001, especially pp. 13–31; *Grove Dictionary of Art*, XXIV, pp. 235–236; Holl. *Dutch & Flemish*, XV–XVI; Delen 1920, pp. 110 and 121; and Rooses c.1900.]

Work completed for Plantin's editions with intaglio illustrations:

1585: PP 1699?: *Missale Romanum*, 4°, 1585: on October 19, 1585, van den Passe was paid 2 fl. 14 st. for delivering one engraving of the *Entombment of Christ* for a missal in 4°.[83] This may refer to the anonymous, c.56 mm² engraving of the *Entombment* on fol. K5r of Plantin's 1585 4° *Missale Romanum*.

1587–1588: forty-six small engravings (c.90 × 70 mm), by van de Passe after designs by Maarten de Vos, who clearly served as the middle-man for the execution of these plates, as he was paid for delivering them after they had been engraved by van de Passe.[84] This group includes thirty-five subjects from the Passion of Christ

---

[82] See MPM Arch. 3, fol. 44r, for this payment, which is transcribed at the end of n. 7 to PP 2413.

[83] See MPM Arch. 62, fol. 143r, under October 19, 1585, for the following payment: "Paye a Crispinus van Pas pour une figure du missel in 4° l'enterrement etc. deux florins 14 patt. de la sepulture de Christ fl. 2 st. 14."

[84] See, for example, MPM Arch. 65, fol. 15v (under January 30, 1588), for the following payment record: "Paye a Marten de Vos painctre a compte de paincture et taillure de six pieces taillees par Crispin

(nos. 10–44 in Rooses c.1900) and eleven other plates executed in the same scale with subjects that are common to the illustration of Plantin's liturgical editions, such that both breviaries and missals could be illustrated with some selection of these extra plates in combination with some of the Passion subjects. Contrary to what is suggested by the title of Rooses's publication and in contemporary references to these plates, this group does not comprise all of the subjects that Plantin usually included in his books of hours.[85] In particular, this group of plates lacks images of the four Evangelists, which were typically used to mark the start of each gospel account of the Passion. Only as of 1609 were these sections of the books of hours printed by Plantin's successors illustrated with scenes from the Passion instead.[86] Thus, as Rooses observes himself, it is not clear for which publication(s) – or perhaps some series of independent prints? – these plates were originally intended.

SADELER, JAN (JOHANNES) I (BRUSSELS, 1550–C.1600, VENICE?)

Engraver, draughtsman, and print publisher.

Jan Sadeler I was in Antwerp by 1572, when he was both registered as a master in the Guild of St. Luke and married in Antwerp cathedral. His first work for Plantin dates to 1569 or 1570, however. When in Antwerp, Sadeler made engravings principally after the designs of Crispin van den Broeck (who also designed many of the prints he made for Plantin) and Michiel Coxcie. Some of these were published by the Antwerp publisher Gerard de Jode. Sadeler also worked after designs by Maarten de Vos. Around the year 1579, Jan Sadeler and his younger brother Raphael I went to Cologne, but records indicate that Jan Sadeler frequently returned to Antwerp between 1582 and 1586. However, he does not seem to have made any more book illustrations for Plantin in this period. Following the fall of Antwerp in August 1585, Jan Sadeler and Raphael I moved to Germany, where they worked in several different cities in turn. In 1593, Jan Sadeler then went to Italy, where he may have died. Shortly before his death, Jan Sadeler made up a list of plates that he and Raphael Sadeler had, which attests to their sizable production and the value they placed on their stock of plates. [Lit.: *Grove Dictionary of Art*, XXVII, pp. 501–502; de Ramaix 1992, especially pp. 10–13; Holl. *Dutch & Flemish*, XXI, pp. 83–190; XXII, pp. 97–165, for many reproductions.]

ascavoir six taillees par ledit Crispin et dix figures de celles que mon pere a faict paindre nouvelles in 16 pour les heures val. in NS flor. 51." (Paid to Maarten de Vos, painter, for the painting and cutting of six pieces cut by Crispin, namely, six cut by the said Crispin and ten figures which my father had painted again in 16° for a book of hours, valued in currency, 51 fl.) For other payment records pertaining to this collection of plates, see MPM Arch. 64, fols. 76v (perhaps), 84v, 120v, 133r, and 153v; and perhaps MPM Arch. 65, fols. 23r and 62r. Some of these records are transcribed in Veldman 2001, nn. 47–49, p. 381. For de Vos's original drawings, see MPM Tek. nos. 273–312, where Tek. 278 is identified as "Simon and Anna praise the Lord," but was most likely meant to represent the more common subject of the Purification of the Virgin, which Plantin regularly included in his books of hours.

[85] For contemporary identifications of these plates as illustrations for a book of hours, see n. 84 and Rooses c.1900, p. [4] of the introduction.

[86] For this shift in imagery, see Imhof 1996a, cat. 55, pp. 155–156.

Work completed for Plantin's editions with intaglio illustrations:

1570: PP 1367–68: *Horae BVM*, 8°, 1570: set of six borders.[87] For work on the other engravings used to illustrate the various issues of this publication, see under Peeter vander Borcht and Pieter Huys, as well as under Hieronymus and Jan Wierix.

1575: PP 1776: *Officium BMV*, large 8°, 1575: one new engraving of the *Assumption of the Virgin*, signed with vander Borcht's and Sadeler's initials. For work on other engravings for this publication, see under Gerard van Groeningen and Jan Wierix.

1575–1577?: PP 1335: L. Hillessemius, *Sacrarum antiquitatum monumenta*, 8°, 1577: twelve of the forty engravings are signed by Sadeler, seven of these bear the initials of Crispin van den Broeck as designer (see above).[88] However, in the discussion of these plates in *Hollstein Dutch & Flemish*, all thirty-eight of the stylistically homogenous text illustrations, as well as the introductory author's portrait, are attributed to Sadeler.[89] When, precisely, these plates were executed is uncertain. One (that of Seth on p. 8) is dated 1575, thereby indicating that Sadeler had at least started to make these plates in that year.

prior to January 1, 1576: engravings in MPM Arch. 1228 for PP 590: B. Arias Montano, *Humanae salutis monumenta*, 4°, 1583; PP 690: *Biblia sacra*, f°, 1583; and as yet unidentified publications.[90] All five engravings signed by Sadeler that are in the *Monumenta* (four Evangelist portraits on fols. I1r, I2r, I3r, and I4r, all designed by Crispin van den Broeck, and an engraving of the *Resurrection* [fol. R4r]) are present in MPM Arch. 1228. The four Evangelist portraits were also included in the 1583 bible and represent the only engravings signed by Sadeler in that work (see fig. 5.2). See also under Peeter van der Borcht, Crispin van den Broeck, Abraham de Bruyn, Pierre Dufour, Gerard van Groeningen, and Jan Wierix, for their work on engravings for these publications that were similarly included in this album. Beyond these engravings, there are three additional prints in MPM Arch. 1228 that are signed by Sadeler: a border with animals and vegetables, an image of the Assumption of the Virgin, and a border of the adult life of Christ, the last two of which also bear vander Borcht's initials as the designer. These were most likely used for one of Plantin's small folio or large *quarto* missals published prior to 1576, but for which there are currently no known copies.[91]

1576: PP 1333: St. Jerome, *Opera divi Hieronymi Stridoniensis . . .*, ed. by M. Victorius, f° 1579: an engraved author's portrait, signed by Crispin van den Broeck and Jan Sadeler and dated 1576.

---

[87] See Bowen 2003, pp. 32–33 and table 2, for a description of these plates and their use.

[88] For the plates signed by Sadeler, see pp. 4, 6, 8 (1575), 10, 14, 24, 30, 36, 60, 74, 78, and 80. For the plates signed by van den Broeck, see pp. 4, 6, 8 (1575), 10, 14, 30, and 60.

[89] See *Hollstein Dutch & Flemish*, XXI, nos. 72–110 and 598. Oddly, one subject included in this list (no. 108, an image of "Ezra") does not appear in Hillessemius's book.

[90] For the dating of the images in this archive, see the discussion of this bundle under vander Borcht.

[91] For these three engravings, see MPM Arch. 1228, fols. 269r, 268r, and 278v, respectively. See *Holl. Dutch & Flemish*, XXI (p. 189) and XXII (p. 165) for the engravings on fols. 268r and 269r. For examples of larger missals printed by Plantin in 1574 and 1575 for which there are currently no known copies with engravings, see PP 1686, PP 1687, PP 1690, and PP 1691.

UTEN WAELE, PAUL (PAULUS WTEWAEL) (UTRECHT?, BEFORE
1555–1611, HOORN)

Engraver, sealer, and medallist.

Uten Waele is believed to have been active mostly in the area of Utrecht from around
1570 to 1580 – although he completed at least one engraved border for Plantin prior to
January 1, 1576. He then made many small engravings for Plantin c. 1579–1580. Although
the vast majority of the prints attributed to him in *Hollstein Dutch & Flemish* consist of
(too many of) the small engravings found in Plantin's calendar and evangeliary from
1580,[92] Uten Waele also made many engraved portraits in the 1570s. In the later 1580s
and 1590s he is documented in Kampen, when he is credited with making some etched
maps. He is also said to have been active as a medallist in Hoorn around 1591. [Lit.:
Holl. *Dutch & Flemish*, LV, pp. 7–56.]

Work completed for Plantin's editions with intaglio illustrations:

prior to January 1, 1576: one engraving in MPM Arch. 1228 for an as yet unidentified
publication.[93] The engraved decorative border with Uten Waele's PVW initials that
is included here (fol. 269v) was most likely used for one of Plantin's small folio or
large *quarto* missals published prior to 1576, but for which there are currently no
known copies.[94]

1579?–1580: PP 865: *Sanctorum kalendarii Romani . . .*, 24°, 1580: 37 of the 230 or so
illustrations are signed by Uten Waele (fig. 6.2), while none of the 55 engravings illustrating the accompanying *Evangeliorum dominicalium . . .* (PP 1152) are.
Many of these plates were designed by Peeter vander Borcht (see above). Work on
the engravings for these publications was underway in 1579, when Philips Galle
delivered fifty engravings for these books (see above).

VAN VEEN, OTTO (OTHO VAENIUS) (LEIDEN, 1556–1629, BRUSSELS)

Painter, draughtsman, and author of numerous emblem books.

Often cited as the teacher of Pieter Paul Rubens, van Veen moved frequently: from Leiden
to Liège (where he studied under Domenicus Lampsonius), to Italy, back to Liège (where
he served as the court painter to Ernest of Bavaria) and then Leiden (where he knew
Justus Lipsius, around 1583–1584), then to Brussels, Antwerp (where he was registered
as a master in the St. Luke's guild in 1593 and subsequently taught Rubens), and back
(finally) to Brussels (where he worked for the archduke and duchess, Albert and Isabella,
as of 1604). Van Veen's production of emblem books dates from the first decade of the
seventeenth century, when his commissions for paintings declined. Plantin may have
employed van Veen exceptionally at the request of Justus Lipsius because Lipsius was

---

[92] See the discussion of these texts in ch. 6.

[93] For the dating of the images in this archive, see the discussion of this bundle under vander Borcht.

[94] For examples of larger missals printed by Plantin in 1574 and 1575 for which there are currently no
known copies with engravings, see PP 1686, PP 1687, PP 1690, and PP 1691.

both a friend and admirer of van Veen's work.[95] [Lit.: *Grove Dictionary of Art*, XXXII, pp. 114–116; *Holl. Dutch & Flemish*, XXXII, pp. 159–184.]

Work completed for Plantin's editions with intaglio illustrations:

1584?: PP 1557: J. Lipsius, *Saturnalium sermonum libri duo, qui de gladiatoribus*, 4°, 1585: van Veen is credited with designing the sixteen illustrations for this text (cf. fig. 5.14). It is not known who (if not van Veen) etched them.

DE VOS, MAARTEN (ANTWERP, 1532–1603, ANTWERP)

Painter and draughtsman.
De Vos was listed as a master in the St. Luke's guild of Antwerp in 1558 and had students registered there off and on from 1564 to 1599. He began to work as a painter in the 1560s and was still sought for the painting of altarpieces in the 1590s. As of the 1580s, he was also exceptionally active designing prints – some 1,600 all told. His prints were published by various Antwerp publishers, in particular Adriaen Collaert, Philips Galle, Gerard de Jode, and Jan Baptist Vrints. De Vos's designs were engraved by well-known engravers, in particular, the Wierix brothers, the Sadelers, Crispijn van de Passe I, and Adriaen and Hans Collaert II. [Lit.: Bowen and Imhof 2001; *Holl. Dutch & Flemish*, XLIV–XLVI, fully illustrated; *Grove Dictionary of Art*, XXXII, pp. 708–712; Zweite 1980.]

Work completed for Plantin's editions with intaglio illustrations:

1587–1588: designs for forty-six small engravings (c.90 × 70 mm), with images from the Life of the Virgin, the Life of Christ, and Christ's Passion, executed by Crispijn van de Passe. De Vos evidently served as the middle-man for the execution of these plates, as he was paid for delivering them after they had been engraved by van de Passe (see the discussion of these plates under van de Passe).

VREDEMAN DE VRIES, HANS (JOANNES) (LEEUWARDEN, 1526–1609, HAMBURG)

Painter, designer, architect, and engineer.
Vredeman de Vries was active in a number of areas, but exerted the most influence through the hundreds of engravings published after his designs of gardens, buildings, perspective views, decorative frames, as well as other useful or decorative objects. Prints after his designs were made by a wide variety of artists, although the most by far were executed by the van Doetecums. These prints were published primarily by the Antwerp print publishers Hieronymus Cock, Gerard de Jode, and Philips Galle, although Vredeman de Vries himself worked in various cities throughout the northern and southern Low Countries. In Antwerp, he was involved in devising the decorations

---

95 See ch. 5 for more information on Lipsius and van Veen.

for several triumphal entries. It was in this capacity that he came to design a series of images for one of Plantin's publications, namely, the commemorative album for the state entry of the duke of Anjou in 1582. [Lit.: Vredeman de Vries 2002, especially pp. 15–38 and 51–58 (for biographical information by Heiner Borggrefe); *Holl. Dutch & Flemish*, XLVII–XLVIII, fully illustrated, with an introduction (XLVII, pp. 9–14); *Grove Dictionary of Art*, XXXII, pp. 724–727.]

Work completed for Plantin's editions with intaglio illustrations:

> **1582:** PP 1211: [Pierre Loyseleur de Villiers], *La joyeuse et magnifique entrée de Monseigneur Françoys . . . d'Anjou . . .*, f°, 1582: designs for the twenty-one text illustrations (see figs. 5.10 and 5.11).[96]

WEERTS, BARTHOLOMEUS

Engraver.

Work completed for Plantin's editions with intaglio illustrations:

> **1581:** on May 24, 1581, a certain Bartholomeus Weerts was paid 3 fl. for an engraving of the mark of the "sigulle" (perhaps the "sigillum") of the University of Leiden.[97]

WIERIX, HIERONYMUS (JEROME) (ANTWERP, 1553–1619, ANTWERP)

Engraver and print publisher.

Hieronymus Wierix was a child prodigy, as he began to make engravings in 1565 at age eleven and superb copies after Dürer at age twelve. Hieronymus became a master in the St. Luke's guild of Antwerp in the guild year 1572–1573. Hieronymus (like Jan) Wierix regularly worked after compositions by Maarten de Vos, in addition to making prints after other popular designers, such as Johannes Stradanus and Crispin van den Broeck, and came to specialize in small devotional prints. In the period 1577–1580, Hieronymus Wierix made numerous engravings that were published by Willem van Haecht and his nephew Godevaard van Haecht. Philips Galle, Hans van Luyck, Gerard de Jode, and Jan Baptist Vrints (all working in Antwerp) were also important publishers of his engravings. Of the three brothers (Jan, Hieronymus, and Anton II), Hieronymus was the most active as a publisher of his own prints (around 650 in total, compared with Anton's 235 or so own publications and Jan Wierix's 125). Hieronymus Wierix worked only briefly for Plantin, executing some ten engravings in the period 1569–1571, just prior to his registration as a master in the St. Luke's guild. Plantin also

---

[96] See the discussion of this project in ch. 5. It is not known who made the plates.

[97] See MPM Arch. 59, fol. 78r (under May 24, 1581), for the following payment: "Ledit a Bartholomeus Weerts graveur en cuivre la somme de trois florins que luy ay paye pour la marque du sigulle de luniversite de Leyden fl. 3." For an example of what this may have looked like, see the recurring mark of the University of Leiden in Amsterdam 1975, and the discussion of it under no. A59, as it appears on the official seal of the university.

occasionally paid fines for Hieronymus. He was more dissolute than his brother Jan, and even killed a woman by accident in 1578 while drunk. Nevertheless, he succeeded in becoming a figure of high artistic repute and admiration in many circles.[98] [Lit.: Holl. *Dutch & Flemish*, LIX–LXX, fully illustrated, with introductions in LXIX, pp. xi–xlv, and LXX, pp. xi–xiv. See also Carl Van de Velde's biography of Hieronymus Wierix in M-H *Wierix*, III.2, pp. 518–522; a shorter version of which is in *Grove Dictionary of Art*, XXXIII, p. 169.]

Work completed for Plantin's editions with intaglio illustrations:

1569 or 1570?: PP 1365–1368: *Horae BVM*, 8°, 1570: one engraving (the *Death of the Virgin*; M-H 2218), is signed IRW, for Hieronymus Wierix, along with the PB initials of the designer Peeter vander Borcht (see above). Although no payment for this engraving is known, Jan Wierix was paid for completing four engravings for this project in November 1569 (see below). For work on other engravings used to illustrate various issues of this publication, see under Pieter Huys and Jan Sadeler I.

1570–1571?: PP 588: B. Arias Montano, *Humanae salutis monumenta*, 8°, 1571: Hieronymus Wierix signed eight of the engravings in this book (see M-H nos. 2173, 2175, 2183, 2191, 2195, 2201, 2202, and 2211), some of which were designed by Peeter vander Borcht (see above). At least two of these plates were paid for in October 1570.[99] For work on other engravings for this publication, see under Crispin van den Broeck, Abraham de Bruyn, Pieter Huys, and Jan Wierix.

WIERIX, JAN (HANS OR JOHANNES) (ANTWERP, 1549–C.1618/1620, BRUSSELS)

Engraver, draughtsman, and print publisher.

Like his brother Hieronymus, Jan Wierix was a remarkable engraver at an early age, making superb engravings after Dürer in 1563 and 1565 (at ages fourteen and sixteen). Registered as a master in the St. Luke's guild of Antwerp in the guild year 1572–1573, Jan Wierix was active in Antwerp until around 1576/1577. He then moved to Delft, where he worked until 1579, at which point he returned to Antwerp and began a particularly successful period as an engraver there. He worked after his own designs, as well as those by Frans Floris, Crispin van den Broeck, and, above all, Maarten de Vos. His prints were published by several Antwerp publishers, including Gerard de Jode, Philips Galle, Hans van Luyck, Adriaen Huberti, and Jan Baptist Vrints. Jan Wierix left Antwerp permanently some time after 1594. Following a brief period working in The Hague as an engraver and print publisher, he then settled in Brussels, perhaps around 1600, where he also began to sell his own drawings. He began to work for Plantin as of 1569, while Plantin began to pay his drinking debts as early as 1570–1571. Of the numerous artists

---

[98] On Hieronymus Wierix's great reputation as an engraver, see Bowen and Imhof 2003.
[99] For a discussion of these payments, see Bowen and Imhof 2003, p. 188, under Hieronymus Wierix.

Plantin employed during his initial active acquisition of copper plates in the period 1569–1576, Jan Wierix supplied him with by far the most engravings (at least 120). [Lit.: Holl. *Dutch & Flemish*, LIX–LXX, fully illustrated, with introductions in LXIX, pp. xi–xlv, and LXX, pp. xi–xiv. See also Carl Van de Velde's biography of Jan Wierix in M-H *Wierix*, III.2, pp. 514–518, a shorter version of which is in *Grove Dictionary of Art*, XXXIII, pp. 168–169.]

Work completed for Plantin's editions with intaglio illustrations:

1569–1570?: PP 1365–68: *Horae BVM*, 8°, 1570: one coat of arms for the title-page (fig. 3.22) and seven illustrations in this book (see fig. 3.23) (all after compositions by vander Borcht, see above) were signed by Jan Wierix. At least four of these were completed by November 1569 (see fig. 3.24).[100] For work on the other engravings used to illustrate various issues of this publication, see under Pieter Huys, Jan Sadeler I, and Hieronymus Wierix.

1570: PP 644: *Biblia sacra* (= Polyglot Bible), f°, 1568–1573: Jan Wierix signed two engravings found in this publication – the *Crossing of the Red Sea* (M-H 2275) and the *Encampment of Israelites* (M-H 2278). These may correspond to a couple of payments made to him in 1570 for work on "une grande planche . . . pour la bible" (a large plate . . . for the bible).[101] For work on other engravings for this publication, see under Peeter vander Borcht, Crispin van den Broeck, Philips Galle, Pieter van der Heyden, and Pieter Huys.

1570–1571: PP 588: B. Arias Montano, *Humanae salutis monumenta*, 8°, 1571: this edition comprises some twenty new engravings (depending on the variant) that had not already been used for the illustration of Plantin's 1570 *Horae*.[102] Despite the number of plates made, there are only a few known payments that may pertain to the execution of these engravings, some from 1570 and some from 1571.[103] For work on other engravings for this publication, see under Peeter vander Borcht, Crispin van den Broeck, Abraham de Bruyn, Pieter Huys, and Hieronymus Wierix.

1570–1573?: five engravings for books of hours in large 8° (or 4°), one of which, the *Annunciation*, is dated 1570. Although work on these plates was clearly underway by that time, their earliest known appearance is in an *Officium BMV* (PP 1769),

---

[100] For a list of all the subjects included in this book of hours and evidence of which were engraved by Wierix, see Bowen 1997b, pp. 147–150. On p. 149, the initials for the engraving of the *Death of the Virgin* should be IRW, for Hieronymus Wierix, and not IHW, for Jan Wierix. For the payment to Jan Wierix for engraving the four Evangelist portraits for this book (M-H 2222–2225), see MPM Arch. 756, fol. 180 lft, which is transcribed and translated in Bowen and Imhof 2003, n. 98.

[101] For these payments, see MPM Arch. 28, fols. 16 rht and 18 rht (under March 18 and April 1, 1570, respectively), which are transcribed in M-H *Wierix*, III.2, p. 534, doc. 13. These records are repeated in MPM Arch. 757, fol. 369 rht, and are also transcribed in M-H *Wierix*, II.2, p. 536, doc. 21, but with the wrong folio number cited for Arch. 757. Two additional engravings in this bible are attributed to one of the Wierixes on stylistic grounds: the *Parable of the Workers in the Lord's Vineyard* (M-H 2276) and the *Baptism of Christ* (M-H 2277).

[102] For a detailed discussion of which engravings were used to illustrate this book when, see Bowen 2003.

[103] For one from 1570, see MPM Arch. 28, fol. 64 rht (under October 20, 1570). For one from 1571, see MPM Arch. 29, fol. 39 rht (under June 16, 1571). Both are transcribed in Bowen and Imhof 2003, p. 189.

published in 1573.[104] For work on other related engravings, see under Crispin van den Broeck and Abraham de Bruyn.

1571: M-H 2145: one engraving of a vignette of the *Last Supper*, with the initials of Peeter vander Borcht and Jan Wierix, which was used for the title-page of several of Plantin's folio missals as of 1571 (fig. 4.1).

1572: one full-page border, with the initials of Jan Wierix and Peeter vander Borcht, which was included in several of Plantin's folio missals as of 1572 (fig. 4.3).

1573: fifteen engravings after Peeter vander Borcht for books of hours in 16° and 12° (see fig. 4.5).[105]

PP 1770: *Officium BMV*, 8°, 1573: nineteen new text illustrations and one title-page vignette, after old designs by Peeter vander Borcht (see fig. 4.18).[106]

1574: PP 1686: *Missale Romanum*, 4°, 1574: one title-page vignette of SS Peter and Paul, with the initials of Peeter vander Borcht and Jan Wierix.

1574–1575?: PP 1685: *Missale Romanum*, f°, 1574; and PP 822, *Breviarium Romanum*, f°, 1575: seven full-page text illustrations, one (the *Annunciation*; M-H 2280) after Crispin van den Broeck, and the remaining six after Gerard van Groeningen (cf. *New Holl., Van Groeningen*, nos. 216–220 and 264; M-H 2281–2286); and one title-page vignette of SS Peter and Paul (fig. 4.6). Of these, the engraving of the *Annunciation* and at least four of the text illustrations after van Groeningen, if not five – it is not clear when Wierix's engraving of the *Resurrection* (*New Holl.* no. 264) was first used – appear in the only known copy of Plantin's 1574 folio missal. The first known appearance of Wierix's engraving of the *Adoration of the Shepherds* (*New Holl.* no. 216) is in Plantin's 1575 folio breviary, while an anonymous version of the engraving appears in the 1574 missal (fig. 4.7).[107] For work on other engravings for the 1574 missal, see under Peeter vander Borcht and Pierre Dufour.

1575: PP 1228: B. Furmerius, *De rerum usu et abusu*, 4°, 1575 (published jointly by Plantin and Philips Galle): although only one plate (fig. 6.11) is signed, all twenty-five engravings here (after designs by Gerard van Groeningen, see above) are attributed to Jan Wierix.

PP 1776: *Officium BMV*, large 8°, 1575: five new engravings by Wierix (see M-H 2236–2238, 2242, and 2245). Stylistically, all five appear to have been composed by van Groeningen, although only three are included in *New Holl., Van Groeningen*.[108] For work on other engravings for this publication, see under Peeter vander Borcht, Gerard van Groeningen, and Jan Sadeler I.

prior to January 1, 1576: engravings in MPM Arch. 1228 for: PP 590: B. Arias Montano, *Humanae salutis monumenta*, 4°, 1583; and PP 690: *Biblia sacra*, f°, 1583: of the twenty or so engravings signed by Jan Wierix that are present in these two books (see fig. 5.4), only one (an engraving of the *Crucifixion* after Crispin van den Broeck;

---

[104] See n. 7 above and *Holl. Dutch & Flemish*, LXX, nos. 10.2 (the *Annunciation*), 10.3, 10.6, 10.7, and 10.12, for the plates signed by or attributed to Jan Wierix.

[105] See the discussion of these plates under vander Borcht.

[106] For a complete listing of these illustrations, see Bowen 1997b, pp. 147–150.

[107] See also *Holl. Dutch & Flemish*, LXX, book nos. 15 and 20.

[108] Specifically: M-H 2236 = *New Holl., Van Groeningen*, no. 399; M-H 2238 = *New Holl., Van Groeningen*, no. 400; and M-H 2245 = *New Holl., Van Groeningen*, no. 395.

M-H 2257) was not included in Arch. 1228 and was, perhaps, engraved closer to 1583 (see below).[109] See also under Peeter van der Borcht, Crispin van den Broeck, Abraham de Bruyn, Pierre Dufour, Gerard van Groeningen, and Jan Sadeler, for their work on engravings for these publications that were similarly included in this album.

1580: PP 1255: J. Goropius Becanus, *Opera*, f°, 1580: one engraving of Goropius Becanus, paid for (at least in part) on September 9, 1580.[110]

1581–1582?: PP 690: *Biblia sacra*, f°, 1583: only one new engraving by Jan Wierix (an image of the *Crucifixion* [M-H 2257] after Crispin van den Broeck – see above) appears to have been completed for this book after Wierix's initial run of plates was finished by January 1576 (see above). No payment records are known for this engraving, but many of these plates must have been completed by July 1581, when payments to Mynken Liefrinck for the printing of the illustrations of this volume began. As copies of this book were sold as early as November 1582, this extra engraving must have been completed by then.[111] Abraham de Bruyn was also employed in this period to complete engravings for this project (see above).

1582: PP 1466: J. de la Jessée, *Les premières œuvres françoyses*, 4°, 1583: Jan Wierix was paid for engraving the author's portrait on October 10, 1582.[112]

1582–1583: PP 1412: J.-B. Houwaert, *Pegasides pleyn, ende den lust-hof der maeghden*, 4°, 1583: Jan Wierix is credited with engraving the sixteen text illustrations and author's portrait (fig. 5.6) included in this work. He was paid for completing unspecified illustrations for Houwaert in 1582 and 1583.[113] See under Abraham de Bruyn for the execution of another engraving included in this publication.

---

[109] For an overview of which plates were used to illustrate these two books, see *Holl. Dutch & Flemish*, LXX, pp. 205–211.

[110] See MPM Arch. 14, bundle 2, fol. 9 rht, for this payment, which is transcribed in M-H *Wierix*, III.2, p. 549, doc. 57, 2nd item, under September 9, 1580.

[111] See the discussion of van den Broeck's work on this publication in 1581–1582 for these records.

[112] For this payment see MPM Arch. 60, fol. 167r (under October 10, 1582). The same payment is also recorded in MPM Arch. 14, bundle 4, fol. 11 rht, which is transcribed in M-H *Wierix*, III.2, p. 549, doc. 57, 3rd item, under October 10, 1582.

[113] For these payments, see MPM Arch. 60, fol. 135v (under August 25, 1582), and fol. 150v (under September 8, 1582) – this is transcribed in M-H *Wierix*, III.2, p. 541, doc. 35; and MPM Arch. 61, fols. 9v and 10v (both under January 15, 1583) – both of these are transcribed in M-H *Wierix*, III.2, p. 541, doc. 36, first two items, but with the dates incorrectly given as January 14 and 18. See also the discussion of this work in ch. 5 for Houwaert's own possible involvement in the employment of Wierix for the engraving of this last series of text illustrations for Plantin.

Table A1.1: Designers and etchers who worked on intaglio book illustrations for Plantin

Name of artist	1559	1560	1561	1562	1563	1564	1565	1566	1567	1568	1569	1570	1571	1572	1573	1574	1575	1576	1577	1578	1579	1580	1581	1582	1583	1584	1585	1586	1587	1588	1589
Designers:																															
L. van Noort								x																							
P. vander Borcht											x	x	x		x	x	x				x	x									x
C. van den Broeck												x	x			x	x	x					x	x							
M. van Heemskeck														x																	
G. van Groeningen																x	x														
H. Vredeman de Vries																								x							
O. van Veen																										x					
M. de Vos																													x	x	
Etchers:																															
Van Doetecums	x																										x	x			
P. vander Borcht																x							x	x	x		x	x		x	x

KEY: An "x" is placed by each year an artist is known to have worked for Plantin. If twenty or more images were completed by that artist in the given year, then that block is shaded black. If only one to four images were completed in that year, then the block is left white. If five to nineteen images are known to have been completed, then the block is shaded gray.

Table AI.2: Engravers and copper-plate printers who worked on intaglio book illustrations for Plantin

Name of artist ↓ / Date of activity →	1559	1560	1561	1562	1563	1564	1565	1566	1567	1568	1569	1570	1571	1572	1573	1574	1575	1576	1577	1578	1579	1580	1581	1582	1583	1584	1585	1586	1587	1588	1589
Engravers:																															
F. Huys				x																											
P. Huys						x	x	x			x	x	x		x																
P. van der Heyden											x		x	x		x				x											
Jan Wierix											x	x	x	x	x	x	x					x	x	x	x						
Hieronymus Wierix												x	x																		
J. Sadeler												x					x	x													
A. de B ruyn												x	x				x			x			x	x							
P. Galle														x						x											
P. Galle workshop																					x	x			x						
P. Dufour																x															
"Gil Hor"																	x														
P. Uten Waele																	x				x	x			x	x					
J. Goltzius																			x		x										
A. Huybrechts																						x									
B. Weerts																							x								
H. Goltzius																									x						
C. van de Passe																											x				
H. Collaert II																													x	x	
Intaglio Printers:																															
P. Huys								x	x	x																					
M. Liefrinck									x	x	x	x	x	x	x	x	x	x	x	x	x	x	x	x	x	x	x	x	x	x	x
J. vander Hoeven												x	x	x	x	x	x	x	x	x	x	x	x	x	x	x	x	x	x	x	x

NOTE: The shading system, indicating the relative quantity of work completed by individual engravers, is not applied to the intaglio printers.

PLANTIN'S PRICE CALCULATING SCHEMA FOR HIS LITURGICAL EDITIONS

When Plantin began to send large quantities of books with engraved illustrations to Philip II in Spain in the early 1570s, there was, apparently, a need to establish some general guidelines for determining both the cost of printing the text and the cost of including engraved illustrations. The following undated document provides a detailed summary of the primary prices for printing illustrated books.[1] It appears to have been compiled by early 1574. This dating is derived from two remarks in the text itself. One is that a set of illustrations for a book of hours in 24° had been made, but (the implication is) not yet used ("Secundum genus est earum quas paratas habemus ad imprimendum in horis in 24ᵗᵒ quarum specimina mittimus ex quibus dabimus," p. 72). Plantin's first reformed book of hours to be printed in 24° appeared in 1572 (PP 1767). However, there is no indication in the sales records of this edition that any copies were printed (or priced) with engraved illustrations. Rather, the primary option here was whether or not an accompanying hymnal was purchased for 1 extra stuiver.[2] The next book of hours that Plantin printed in 24° did not appear until 1575 (PP 1778). This edition, in contrast with the preceding, was illustrated with engravings, as there are clear references to copies with engravings ("fig. aeneis") in Plantin's records.[3] Thus, this is most likely the edition alluded to above. Consequently, this remark alone indicates that this document should be dated to sometime between 1572 and 1575.

The second significant statement for the dating of this document is that, at the time that the document was written, Plantin was having a missal printed in *octavo*.[4] Given that the dating of the document, on the basis of the preceding information, probably lies between 1572 and 1575, this reference to work on an *octavo* missal likely refers to a 1574 edition (PP 1688) – the first missal Plantin is known to have printed in *octavo*; Plantin's next known *octavo* missal was not published until 1577 (PP 1697).

In addition, when Plantin notes in a letter to Francisco de Villalva, from January 18, 1574, that he has determined the prices for his liturgical editions, he is probably

---

[1] See MPM Arch. 122, pp. 71–73.   [2] For examples of this, see the notes to PP 1767.
[3] See the notes to PP 1775.   [4] " . . . et quibus nunc imprimimus Missale in 8° cum lineis . . ." (p. 71).

referring to this schema, a copy of which is appended to the letter. This dating also coincides with the earliest known application of these guidelines for calculating the cost of editions with engravings.[5]

The only potentially problematic remark is the reference to missals and breviaries printed in folio and medium *quarto* ("Missalia et Breviaria in folio et in mediocri 4to," p. 72). For while Plantin had printed several editions of missals in both folio and *quarto* by 1574 (see PP 1675–1683) and one edition of a folio breviary in 1573 (PP 818), he did not complete a breviary in *quarto* until the late fall of 1574 (PP 823).[6] Nevertheless, it is possible that while the reference to folio editions did apply to both missals and breviaries, that to *quarto* editions pertained just to the missals.

Transcription

Eius generis papyri et typis quibus impressimus Breviarium Romanum in 16° in eadem 16^{a} vel in 24ta forma dabimus duo folia impressa pro uno stufero.

Eius generis papyri, typis, et formis quibus impressimus Missale in magno quarto Horas B. Mariæ in magno et maximo octavo (quas alias vocamus etiam in 4to) dabimus duo folia pro uno stufero. Quod namque uni accedit in pretio laboris alteri additur ad pretium papyri.

Eius generis papyri et typis quibus impressimus Breviaria in 8° uno et duobus tomis Diurnalia in 16° in 24° minima, et Horæ in 12°, 24°, et 32 atque Missalia et Breviaria in folio et in mediocri 4to communis papyri et dicta Missalia in parvo quarto dabimus septem folia pro duobus stuferis.

Eius generis boni et magni papyri et typis quibus impressimus Breviarium et Missale in f° et nunc rursus imprimimus dictum Missale etiam in folio et quibus parati sumus imprimere Breviarium maximum etiam in f° et quibus nunc imprimimus Missale in 8° cum lineis dabimus 3 folia bene et decenter impressa pro uno stufero.

Non autem eo inficias aut nego quin aliqua[7] ex supra scriptis et simul sub unico pretio coniectis formis typis et papyro unum sit altero parum sumptuosius sed ad evi<n>tandam prolixitatem et molestiam volui pauciora genera pretiorum indicare: existimo namque unum genus aliud compensaturum.

Hæ autem omnes impressiones intelliguntur debere fieri sine imaginibus aut saltem cum imaginibus illis quas iam habemus excusas aut successu temporis poterimus curare excindi in ligno.

Pretia vero figurarum in cupro vel aere incisarum hic postea sequentur iuxta earum magnitudines.

---

[5] For Plantin's letter to de Villalva, see Corr. IV, no. 508. For his use of this system to price some of his editions, see the cost accounting of missals in *quarto, octavo*, and folio, all completed in 1574, in MPM Arch. 5bis, fols. 29 rht and 30 rht. This is also discussed in ch. 4.

[6] Although this edition is dated 1575 on the title-page, copies with engravings were first sold in mid-December 1574 (see, e.g., MPM Arch. 52, fol. 194v, under December 11, 1574, and fol. 185v, under December 13, 1575).

[7] In the text (p. 71) this word was erroneously written as "alique."

Primum genus est earum quas impressimus in horis in 32 ex quibus dabimus quinque impressas in libris quibusvis pro uno stufero.

Secundum genus est earum quas paratas habemus ad imprimendum in horis in 24to quarum specimina mittimus ex quibus dabimus quatuor impressas in quibusvis libris pro uno stufero.

Tertium genus est quas impressimus in horis in 12° et quas etiam statuimus imprimere in 16° ex quibus dabimus tres impressas in quovis libro pro uno stufero.

Quartum genus est earum quas habemus paratas et iam incepimus curare imprimi in minoribus festis missalibus in magno quarto et in folio quarum aliquot specimina mittimus ex quibus dabimus duas impressas in quibusvis libris pro uno stufero.

Quintum genus est earum figurarum quas impressimus in horis in 8° in medio vignetarum quarum etiam specimina mittimus signata N° 5° ex quibus dabimus quatuor pro tribus stufferis.

Sextum genus est earum quas impressimus in horis maioribus typis ex quibus dabimus unam impressam in quolibet libro pro unico stuffero.

Septimum genus est vignetarum quas habemus paratas et eas imprimimus in missali in magno quarto ex quibus dabimus quatuor impressas pro quinque stufferis.

Octavum genus est earum quas quibus sunt impressæ imagines N° 6° in ipsis vignetis N° 7 ex quibus dabimus unam pro duobus stufferis.

Nonum genus est earum quas curavimus excudi imprimendas in max. fest. missalis in f° quarum mittimus specimen ex quibus dabimus unam quamque pro duobus stufferis cum dimidio, hoc est duas figuras impressas in quibusvis libris pro quinque stufferis.

Decimum genus est vignetarum quas curamus excindi pro magno missali quarum etiam mittimus specimen ex quibus dabimus unamquamque pro tribus stufferis impressam in quibusvis libris.

Addimus autem eas imprimendas esse in libris eo quod multo minori pretio darentur dictæ omnes figuræ impressæ in papyro candida separatim quam possint dari impressæ in dictis libris eo quod sit multo maior difficultas in imprimendis illis in ipsis libris et quod peius est sæpe accidat perperam imprimantur et tunc perditum sit illud folium et per consequens totus liber reddatur inutilis.

Est præterea considerandum typos talium figurarum non posse reddere ultra mille exemplaria figurarum quin sit detritus et proinde rursus est de novo alius typis excindendus id quod plurimos sumptus absumit et molestias ingentes nobis exhibet in quærendis et retinendis illis artificibus qui plerumque perditi sunt moribus, morosi seu difficiles et mendaces in suis promissis.

Translation

With the paper of that sort and with the letters with which we have printed the breviary in 16°, we reckon two sheets in the same 16° or 24° form at 1 stuiver.

With this sort of paper, letters, and forms with which we printed the missal in large *quarto* and the book of hours of the Virgin in large and very large *octavo* (which we have also called a *quarto* elsewhere), we reckon two sheets at 1 stuiver, as the cost of the work compensates the cost of the paper.

With this sort of paper and with the letters with which we have printed the breviary in 8° in one and two vols., the diurnal in 16° and most small 24°, the book of hours in 12°, 24°, and 32°, the missal and the breviary in folio and the medium *quarto* with common paper and the cited missal in small *quarto*, we reckon seven sheets for 2 stuivers.

With this sort of good and large paper and the letters with which we have printed the breviary and the missal in folio, with which we are now printing again the said missal in folio and with which we are going to print the extra large breviary also in folio and with which we are now printing the missal in *octavo* with borders, we reckon three well-printed sheets for 1 stuiver.

You may not suppose from this and I cannot deny that among the items noted above and brought together under the same price for the forms, letters, and paper, one is a little more expensive than the other. To avoid undue length and difficulty, I wanted to indicate fewer sorts of prices, for the one sort compensates the other.

One must understand that the prices for all this printing work are only valid if there are no illustrations, or with the illustrations that we already have available to us, or that we could have cut in wood in the course of time.

The prices of illustrations cut in copper are the following in order of their magnitude:

The first sort are the engravings that we have printed in the book of hours in 32° for which we reckon five printed engravings in books of any format for 1 stuiver.

The second sort are the engravings that we have prepared for the printing of the book of hours in 24° and from which we are sending examples: for these we reckon four printed engravings in books of any format for 1 stuiver.

The third sort are the engravings that we printed in the book of hours in 12° and which we also decided to print in the book of hours in 16°: for these we reckon three printed engravings in books of any format for 1 stuiver.

The fourth sort are the engravings that we have prepared and which we already have started to have printed in the lesser feast days in the missals in large *quarto* and in folio from which we are sending a few examples: for these we reckon two printed engravings in books of any format for 1 stuiver.

The fifth sort are the engravings that we have printed in the book of hours in *octavo* in the middle of the borders from which we are also sending examples signed N° 5: for these we reckon four printed engravings for 3 stuivers.

The sixth sort are the engravings that we printed in the book of hours with larger type: for these we reckon one printed engraving in books of any format for 1 stuiver.

The seventh sort are the borders that we prepared and already printed in the missal in large *quarto*: for these we reckon four printed engravings for 5 stuivers.

The eighth sort are the engravings with which the N° 6 illustrations were printed in the N° 7 borders: for these we reckon one printed engraving for 2 stuivers.

The ninth sort are the engravings that we arranged to have cut for the printing of the greatest feast days in the missal in folio from which we are sending an example: for these we reckon for every one engraving 2$^1/_2$ stuivers, in other words, two printed figures in whatever books for 5 stuivers.

The tenth sort are the borders that we had cut for the large missal from which we are also sending an example: for these we reckon for each one printed in whichever book, 3 stuivers.

We add to this that these figures must be printed in books in that all of the cited figures printed separately on white paper will be given at a much lower price than when they are printed in the named books. It is always more difficult to print the figures in the books themselves and, what makes more of a difference, it frequently happens that something is erroneously printed, and then the sheet is lost and the entire book is unusable as a result.

In addition, one must consider that the plates for such illustrations can give no more than one thousand copies of the illustration before the plate is worn, with the result that one must begin again to have another plate cut, which is very expensive for us and causes innumerable problems to find and keep engravers who are often depraved, pernickety, difficult, and do not keep their promises.

SALES OF PLANTIN'S EDITIONS WITH INTAGLIO ILLUSTRATIONS

In this appendix, we present the sales of a selection Plantin's editions with intaglio illustrations from three distinct periods in his career: in figure A3.1, sales of some of his first liturgical editions illustrated with engravings from the period 1573–1576; in figure A3.2, sales of his major illustrated editions from the early 1580s, when he had just started to use etchings in earnest; and in figure A3.3, sales of a sample of his last illustrated editions from the late 1580s, when he tended to favor etchings over engravings for his intaglio illustrations. For each book, we traced the first year of sales. In particular, under the title of each text considered, we present the following: the specific period for which the sales were noted; the usual selling price of the book; the total number of sales that we could localize; their subdivision into the primary groups of buyers Plantin sold works to in the course of his career; and the sources for these sales. Specific buyers who are discussed in the main text are also cited here in the notes, along with the source(s) for their purchase(s). The sales listed below represent the minimum number of copies sold to each category of buyers, as it was not always possible to identify the buyer or destination of each sale of the works considered. The order in which the groups of sales are presented was determined by the total number of books purchased by individuals in each group during the first period examined (1573–1576). These groups were then arranged from the largest total purchases (at the top of the lists given below, or on the left of the accompanying figure) to the smallest. This ordering of these groups is retained for the following two periods of sales considered in order to enhance comparisons of the varying markets for Plantin's books. The groups of buyers that appear in the three periods under consideration are:

> Philip II: his purchases of Plantin's editions were only significant during the first period under consideration (1573–1576; see fig. A3.1), when Philip II ordered thousands of the reformed liturgical editions from Plantin for local use in Spain and for further distribution in Spanish domains.

France: in the first period under consideration (1573–1576; see fig. A3.1), this consists primarily (but not always exclusively) of shipments to Plantin's own shop in Paris, then run by his son-in-law, Gillis (Egidius) Beys. By the 1580s (see figs. A3.2 and A3.3), Plantin had sold his shop to the Parisian bookseller Michel Sonnius I, who then came to dominate the subsequent purchases of Plantin's editions.

Iberian peninsula: this comprises the following two groups of buyers:

a) "special contacts": namely, Plantin's important contacts or middlemen for the Spanish government in the Low Countries or Spain. Prominent figures here are Benito Arias Montano, Cardinal Granvelle, and Gabriel de Çayas. Some of the books listed here were given by Plantin to the individuals concerned.

b) other buyers: namely booksellers, merchants, or private individuals based in Spain or Portugal.

Italy: this comprises sales (or gifts) to booksellers, merchants, or private individuals based in present-day Italy.

Low Countries: this comprises sales to booksellers and private individuals, clerics, etc., based in the Low Countries (roughly present-day Belgium and the Netherlands). This group is usually dominated by booksellers based in present-day Belgium. Sales of books made via Plantin's local Antwerp shop are not included in the first period under consideration (1573–1576; fig. A3.1) because these sales can rarely be linked, with certainty, to the editions examined. These sales are listed separately for some editions sold in the 1580s (see figs. A3.2 and A3.3), when they formed a more significant, identifiable part of the market for certain books. However, even in these cases, the often abbreviated and summary notation of these records occasionally made it impossible to determine which works, specifically, were sold and on what day.

Germany: this comprises sales to booksellers based in the former German Empire, including the international Birckman firm, which had its main office in Cologne in the periods considered and not, for example, Antwerp. Copies of Plantin's editions sold at the Frankfurt book fair are listed separately (see below), as those books were ultimately intended for unspecified international dealers who happened to be at Frankfurt in a given year.

England: this comprises sales to booksellers, merchants, or private individuals based in present-day England. In the periods considered here, these buyers were all based in London.

Frankfurt book fair: this consists of shipments of the selected books to Frankfurt for sale to unspecified dealers at the book fair there.

SALES OF LITURGICAL EDITIONS (1573–1576)

In figure A3.1, we have traced the sales of a sample of Plantin's early liturgical editions with engraved illustrations, printed between 1573 and 1576. We selected at least one of each of the three main types of books he published with engraved illustrations (missals, breviaries, and books of hours) and sought a format that was new for Plantin's editions with engraved illustrations which could be readily distinguished from his other

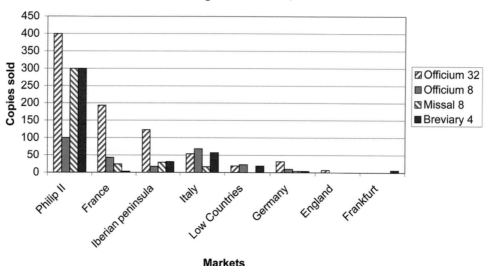

A3.1 Sales of Plantin's liturgical editions, 1573–1576.

editions of the same texts. The selected works are presented below in chronological order.

Officium beatae Mariae Virginis, printed twice in 32° between December 1572 and May 1573 (PP 1772–1773)[1]

We were able to localize the sale of 828 copies of this book with engraved illustrations, made between mid-January 1573 and mid-January 1574. While Philip II paid 6 st. per copy, other buyers usually paid 6 or 7 st. per copy.

> Philip II: 400 copies.[2]
> France: 193 (all but 1 to Plantin's shop in Paris).[3]
> Iberian peninsula: probably 123 copies in total, comprising:
>> a) "special contacts": 15 copies;[4]

---

[1] We have grouped the sales of these two editions together in order to obtain a comparable overview of the sales of one type of text in a given format for the duration of approximately one year. Plantin completed his first edition of the *Officium* in 32° in December 1572 and began to sell copies with engraved illustrations in January 1573 (see MPM Arch. 51, fol. 6r, under January 12, 1573, for a shipment of sixty such copies to his shop in Paris). Plantin had apparently underestimated the market for this book and began to print a new edition five months later in May 1573 (PP 1773). This second edition was completed in August 1573 (for the records of the printing of each edition, see Bowen 1997a, p. 241). As there are no clear records of exactly how many copies of each edition were illustrated with engravings, it is impossible (for sales post-dating August 1573) to know which edition, specifically, is represented. Consequently, we have not attempted to subdivide the sales noted here between these two editions. Hereafter, Plantin did not print another book of hours in 32° until 1580 (see PP 1785).

[2] See MPM Arch. 22, fols. 18r and 25v, and MPM Arch. 6, fols. 14r and 24r.

[3] MPM Arch. 51, fols. 6r, 12r (R. Clayson of St. Omer), 31r, 166v, and 192v.

[4] MPM Arch. 51, fols. 28v, 66v, 68v (G. de Çayas), 80r (Granvelle), and 81r (H. de Torres).

b) other buyers: at least 58 copies, and probably 108 copies.[5]

Italy: 54 copies.[6]

Low Countries: 19 copies.[7]

Germany: 32 copies, all but 8 to Georg Willer.[8]

England: 7 copies, all to Nicolas Jude in London.[9]

Frankfurt book fair: none.

Officium beatae Mariae Virginis, printed in 1573 in large octavo (PP 1769) (fig. 4.4)

We were able to localize the sales of 261 copies of this book with engraved illustrations, made between mid-April 1573 and mid-April 1574. While Philip II paid just 34 st. (= 1 fl. 14 st.) per copy, the base price for other buyers seems to have been 40 st. (= 2 fl.) per copy.

Philip II: 100 copies.[10]

France: 43 copies (all but 3 to Plantin's shop in Paris).[11]

Iberian peninsula: 17 copies in total, comprising:

    a) "special contacts": 14 copies;[12]

    b) other buyers: 3 copies.[13]

Italy: 68 copies.[14]

Low Countries: 23 copies.[15]

Germany: 10 copies, 8 to the Birckman firm and 2 to Georg Willer.[16]

England: none.

Frankfurt book fair: none.

---

[5] MPM Arch. 51, fols. 144v and 167r (F. de Canto); and MPM Arch. 52, fol. 1r (P. de Molina), for the obvious sales. Only the final destination of fifty copies sold to M. de Varron, a merchant in Antwerp of Spanish descent and son-in-law of Louis Perez, is uncertain (see MPM Arch. 51, fol. 193v). The Iberian peninsula seems likely given his family ties and the fact that, in 1581, de Varron signed a contract with Jan Poelman concerning the sale of books in Salamanca (Robben 1993, p. 39).

[6] MPM Arch. 51, fols. 26v (G. Antontio d'Antoni), 56r, 87r (G. Antontio d'Antoni), 142r, 195r, and 205r (P. and F. Tini); and MPM Arch. 52, fol. 2v (M. de Wesel).

[7] MPM Arch. 51, fols. 29v (2x) (widow van Salenson), 34r (2x) (H. Dungheus), 49r, 55r (widow van Salenson), 59v (J. Fowler), 72r (J. Fowler), 85v (J. Fowler), 182v (P. de Beaufeu), and 200v (J. Matheeus).

[8] MPM Arch. 51, fols. 16r (J. Gymnicus – although no format is given, the price of 7 st. per book matches that in other contemporaneous sales of this edition), 25r (G. Willer), 88v (G. Willer), 179r (G. Willer), and 193r (J. Aubri and C. de Marne).

[9] MPM Arch. 51, fols. 10v and 51r. As suggested by Dr. David McKitterick, Jude may have been related to the London-based merchant Sir Andrew Judde (see DNB 1993, pp. 367–368).

[10] MPM Arch. 22, fols. 23r and 25v, and MPM Arch. 6, fols. 21v and 24r.

[11] MPM Arch. 51, fols. 57v and 69v (M. Hernandez); and MPM Arch. 52, fols. 6r (R. Clayson of St. Omer), 8r, and 39r.

[12] MPM Arch. 51, fols. 66v (G. de Çayas), 68r (G. de Çayas), 81r, 131v (H. de Virbiesca), 140v, and 210r; and MPM Arch. 52, fols. 26v, 44r, and 47v.

[13] MPM Arch. 51, fols. 144v and 166r.

[14] MPM Arch. 51, fols. 61v, 80r, 81r, and 95v (J. C. Talignani); and MPM Arch. 52, fols. 2v (M. de Wesel), 3r (M. de Wesel), 3v (M. de Wesel), 16r (G. Piscatori), 19r (B. and B. Bonvisi), 31r, and 37r.

[15] MPM Arch. 51, fols. 62r, 69v, 72r (J. Fowler), 84v (J. Fowler), 103v, 126v (J. Fowler), 141v ("le gouverneur"), 154v, and 182v (P. de Beaufeu); and MPM Arch. 52, fols. 23r, 26r (P. de la Tombe), and 48r ("le gouverneur").

[16] MPM Arch. 51, fols. 88v (G. Willer), 142v and 185v (both to A. Birckman).

Missale Romanum, printed in 1574 in *octavo* (PP 1688) (fig. 4.11)

We were able to localize the sales of 373 copies of this book with engraved illustrations, made between May 1574 and April 1575. While Philip II paid just 30¹/₂ st. (=1 fl. 10¹/₂ st.) per copy, other buyers typically paid 42 st. (= 2 fl. 2 st.) per copy.

> Philip II: 300 copies.[17]
> France: 24 copies, all to Plantin's shop in Paris.[18]
> Iberian peninsula: 30 copies in total, comprising:
>> a) "special contacts": 15 copies;[19]
>> b) other buyers: 15 copies.[20]
>
> Italy: 16 copies.[21]
> Low Countries: no clear purchases of this issue with engravings in the first year.
> Germany: 4 copies, all to Georg Willer.[22]
> England: none.
> Frankfurt book fair: none.

Breviarium Romanum, printed in 1575 in *quarto* (PP 823) (fig. 4.13)

We were able to localize the sales of 420 copies of this book with engraved illustrations, made between mid-December 1574 and mid-December 1575. While Philip II paid just 54¹/₂ st. (=2 fl. 14¹/₂ st.) per copy, the base price for other buyers was 80 st. (= 4 fl.) per copy.

> Philip II: 300 copies.[23]
> France: 3 copies, all to Plantin's shop there.[24]
> Iberian peninsula: 31 copies in total, comprising:
>> a) "special contacts": 28 copies;[25]
>> b) other buyers: 3 copies.[26]
>
> Italy: 57 copies.[27]
> Low Countries: 19 copies.[28]
> Germany: 4 copies, all to Georg Willer.[29]
> England: none.
> Frankfurt book fair: 6 copies.[30]

---

[17] MPM Arch. 22, fol. 44v; and MPM Arch. 6, fol. 45r.

[18] MPM Arch. 52, fol. 158v; and MPM Arch. 53, fol. 2v.

[19] MPM Arch. 52, fols. 131v (Granvelle), 145v, 151v (B. Arias Montano), and 184r (B. Arias Montano); and MPM Arch. 53, fols. 63v (B. Arias Montano), 70v (Granvelle), and 79r (B. Arias Montano).

[20] MPM Arch. 52, fol. 66r (P. de Molina); and MPM Arch. 53, fols. 4r (H. Magnacavalli) and 71v.

[21] MPM Arch. 52, fols. 131v and 201v (A. Copus); and MPM Arch. 53, fols. 7v (B. and B. Bonvisi), 26v, 44r (M. de Wesel), and 113r.   [22] MPM Arch. 52, fol. 172r; and MPM Arch. 53, fol. 29v.

[23] MPM Arch. 22, fols. 55v–56v, and MPM Arch. 6, fols. 54v–55r.   [24] MPM Arch. 53, fol. 2v.

[25] MPM Arch. 52, fols. 185v (Granvelle) and 200r (H. de Torres); and MPM Arch. 53, fols. 13r (B. Arias Montano), 17r, 48v (B. Arias Montano), 51r (B. Arias Montano), 55r, 63v (B. Arias Montano), 87r (Granvelle), 99v, 176r, and 199r (B. Arias Montano).

[26] MPM Arch. 53, fols. 4r (H. Magnacavalli) and 177r.

[27] MPM Arch. 52, fols. 194v and 201v (A. Copus); and MPM Arch. 53, fols. 8r (J. Buysset), 26v, 27r (M. de Wesel), 113r, 120v (B. and B. Bonvisi), 151v (J. Buysset), 160r (M. de Wesel), 203v, and 215v (J. Harlemius).

[28] MPM Arch. 52, fol. 196v (J. de Zeelandre); MPM Arch. 53, fols. 30r (A, Sassenus), 36v, 53r (J. Fowler), 60r (J. Fowler), 63r, 66v (A. Sassenus), 86v, 96r (J. de Zeelandre), 148r, 151r, 198v, 217r (S. Pighius), 217v, and 220r.

[29] MPM Arch. 53, fol. 205v.   [30] MPM Arch. 53, fol. 20v.

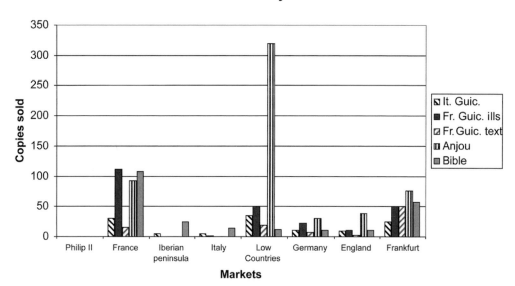

A3.2 Sales of Plantin's editions from the early 1580s.

SALES FROM THE EARLY 1580S

In figure A3.2, we have traced the sales of Plantin's major editions with intaglio illustrations from the early 1580s. These include Plantin's last, large-scale project with engraved illustrations (his 1583 folio bible), and two new types of publications (for Plantin) with etched illustrations, namely, Ludovico Guicciardini's description of the Low Countries and the 1582 state entry of the duke of Anjou. The books are listed below in chronological order.

L. Guicciardini, *Descrittione di tutti i Paesi Bassi*, in folio, 1581 (PP 1277)
(figs. 5.8 and 5.9)

We were able to localize the sales of 119 copies of this work with etched illustrations, made between February 1581 and January 1582. Illustrated copies were typically sold at 7 fl. (= 140 st.) per copy.

> Philip II: none.
> France: 30 copies, all to Michel Sonnius in Paris.[31]
> Iberian peninsula: 5 copies, none to "special contacts."[32]
> Italy: 5 copies.[33]

---

[31] MPM Arch. 59, fol. 52v.   [32] MPM Arch. 59, fols. 75r, 85v, 110v, 126r, and 143r.
[33] MPM Arch. 59, fols. 80v, 139r, 156r, 159r (G. Piscatori), and 191r.

Low Countries: 35 in total, comprising:
- a) local Antwerp buyers: 19 (at least);[34]
- b) other buyers: 16 copies.[35]

Germany: 10 copies.[36]

England: 9 copies, all but 1 to Ascanius de Renialme in London.[37]

Frankfurt book fair: 25 copies.[38]

L. Guicciardini, Description de touts les Pais-Bas, in folio, 1582 (PP 1278)

We were able to localize the sales of 244 copies with illustrations and 92 without, made between December 1581 and November 1582. Copies with illustrations were typically sold at 7 fl. (= 140 st.) per copy, while copies without illustrations generally cost 2 fl. 10 st. (= 50 st.).

Philip II: none.

France: 113 copies with illustrations, 15 without, comprising:
- a) Michel Sonnius in Paris: 87 copies with illustrations;[39]
- b) other buyers: 26 copies with illustrations, 15 without.[40]

Iberian peninsula: none.

Italy: 1 copy with illustrations;[41]

Low Countries: approximately 50 copies with illustrations and 19 without, comprising:
- a) local Antwerp buyers: 14 (at least), including at least 2 copies without illustrations;[42]
- b) artists: 6 copies with illustrations;[43]
- c) other buyers (primarily booksellers): 32 with illustrations, 17 without.[44]

Germany: 20 copies with illustrations, 6 without.[45]

---

[34] MPM Arch. 491, fols. 4r, 4v, 6r, 8r, 11r, 14v, 17r, 20r, 22v, 31v, 35r, and 37r. The sales of the Italian edition of this text via Plantin's shop in Antwerp may have been higher in the first year, but in these records the language of the copy of Guicciardini's text that was sold and the price per copy were not always noted, making it impossible to distinguish between the French and Italian editions.

[35] MPM Arch. 59, fols. 29r (2x, including one sale to Plantin's son-in-law, F. Raphelengius I), 37v, 41r, 52v, 54v (F. Raphelengius I) 77r, 90v, 132v, 144v, and 158v.

[36] MPM Arch. 59, fols. 21r and 56v (both to the Birckman firm), and fols. 157v and 190v; and MPM Arch. 60, fols. 3r and 13v (both to the Birckman firm).

[37] MPM Arch. 59, fols. 21v and 150v (both to A. de Renialme) and fol. 152r.

[38] MPM Arch. 59, fol. 95r.   [39] MPM Arch. 59, fol. 191r; and MPM Arch. 60, fols. 116v and 150r.

[40] MPM Arch. 60, fols. 4r (P. Porret and G. Beys), 10v, 18r, 58v, 82r, 86v, 93v, 107r (J. de Burdigale), and 117v (A. le Maire).

[41] MPM Arch. 60, fol. 122v, for this solitary sale to a certain Jaques van Brecht in Venice.

[42] Regrettably, sales of Guicciardini's text via Plantin's shop in Antwerp were usually not recorded specifically enough in 1582 to determine which edition (or variant thereof) was actually sold (see MPM Arch. 491, fols. 31v–65r).

[43] MPM Arch. 59, fol. 192r (C. van Roosendael); and MPM Arch. 60, fols. 13v and 113v (both to A. de Bruyn).

[44] MPM Arch. 60, fols. 6v, 12r (F. Raphelengius I), 21v (C. Claessens), 22v, 24v, 32r, 32v, 45v, 46r (C. Claessens), 64r, 66r, 88r, 97r, 98r (2x), 104v, 109v, 120r, 126v, 131r, 135v, 157v, 160r, 162r, 174r (F. Raphelengius I) 186r, 192v, and 197r.

[45] MPM Arch. 60, fols. 11v (H. Spierinck), 13v (Birckmans), 19v, 26v, 27r, 27v, 37r (G. Willer), 83r (H. Spierinck), 127v (A. Mylius), 156v, and 184v (A. Mylius).

England: 10 copies with illustrations, 2 without.[46]
Frankfurt book fair: 50 copies with illustrations, 50 without.[47]

[Pierre Loyseleur de Villiers?], *La ioyeuse et magnifique entrée de Monseigneur François . . . en sa tres-renommée ville d'Anvers*, in folio, 1582 (PP 1211) (figs. 5.10 and 5.11)

We were able to localize the sales of 556 copies, made between mid-April 1582 and mid-April 1583. These were typically sold at 1 fl. 10 st. (= 30 st.) per copy.

Philip II: none.
France: 92 copies in total, comprising:
    a) Michel Sonnius in Paris: 52 copies;[48]
    b) other buyers: 40 copies.[49]
Iberian peninsula: none.
Italy: none.
Low Countries: 319 copies in total, comprising:
    a) local Antwerp buyers: 158 copies;[50]
    b) members of the Antwerp city government: 80 copies, 74 of which were sold to the local government in a single, large order;[51]
    c) local artists and print dealers: 37 copies;[52]
    d) other buyers (primarily booksellers): 44 copies.[53]
Germany: 30 copies.[54]
England: 39 copies, including 13 to A. de Renialme, 18 to W. Herle, and 8 to H. François.[55]
Frankfurt book fair: 76 copies.[56]

---

[46] MPM Arch. 59, fol. 183r (A. de Renialme); and MPM Arch. 60, fols. 36r (W. Herle), 39r (W. Herle), 71r (H. François), and 74r (H. François).

[47] MPM Arch. 60, fols. 4r and 20r.   [48] MPM Arch. 60, fols. 75v, 116v, and 150r.

[49] MPM Arch. 60, fols. 68v, 76r (P. Porret), 77v, 80r (A. le Maire), 80v (A. le Maire), 82r, 86v, 107r, and 117v (A. le Maire).

[50] MPM Arch. 491, fols. 41v–73r.

[51] For the bulk purchase of this text by the city of Antwerp, see MPM Arch. 60, fols. 98r and 132v, as well as Antwerp City Archives, R 23, *Rekeningen 1582*, fols. 272r and 272v. For independent purchases by city employees, see MPM Arch. 60, fol. 85r, for a sale to "Mres. de la fortification" (Gentlemen of the fortification) and fol. 98r, for a sale to "De munitie camer par Jan Loef" (Munitions room via Jan Loef); and MPM Arch. 61, fol. 5v, for a sale to "Jan vander Langen, secretaire des Estats."

[52] MPM Arch. 60, fols. 72r, 78r, 86r, 114v, 175r, and 184r (all 6 records to P. Galle), fols. 78v, 81v, 109r, 150r, and MPM Arch. 61, fol. 21r (all 5 records to M. Liefrinck), MPM Arch. 60, fol. 81r (A. de Bruyn), fols. 73v, 77v, 133r, 151v, 168r, and MPM Arch. 61, fol. 1r (all 6 records to E. van Hoeswinckel), and MPM Arch. 60, fol. 72v (H. Scholliers, an Antwerp painter who traveled with Abraham Ortelius; see Imhof 1998a, p. 137).

[53] MPM Arch. 60, fols. 69v, 80v, and 107r (all to J. Matthias), 71v and 141r (both to L. Elsevier), 71v and 80r (both to C. Claessens), 71v, 77r, and 79v (all to F. Raphelengius I), fol. 72v (A. Ortelius), and, for additional isolated purchases by others, see fols. 70v, 72v (3x), 73r, 74v, 76r (2x), 78v, 94r, 172r, 186r, 192r, and 196r.

[54] MPM Arch. 60, fols. 72r, 83r (H. Spierinck), 93v (C. Clusius), 108v (G. Willer), 116r, 124r (H. Gundlach), and 132r (W. Coleman).

[55] MPM Arch. 60, fols. 68r (A. de Renialme), 70r (W. Herle), 71r (H. François), 76v (W. Herle), 77r (W. Herle), 99v (W. Herle), 103r (W. Herle), 104v (W. Herle), 120v (W. Herle), and 165v (A. de Renialme); and MPM Arch. 61, fol. 44v (H. François).

[56] MPM Arch. 60, fols. 92v and 120r; and MPM Arch. 61, fol. 18v.

Biblia sacra, in folio, 1583 (PP 690) (figs. 5.1, 5.2, 5.4, and 5.5)

We were able to localize the sales of 235 copies, made between November 1582 and November 1583. These were typically sold at approximately 15 fl. (= 300 st.) per copy.

> *Philip II*: none.
> *France*: 107 copies, all but 1 to Michel Sonnius in Paris.[57]
> *Iberian peninsula*: 24 copies in total, comprising:
>> a) "special contacts": 3 copies;[58]
>> b) other buyers (booksellers and merchants): 21 copies.[59]
> *Italy*: 14 copies.[60]
> *Low Countries*: 12 copies.[61]
> *Germany*: 11 copies, including 5 to Hans Gundlach.[62]
> *England*: 10 copies, including 7 to Ascanius de Renialme.[63]
> *Frankfurt book fair*: 57 copies.[64]

SALES FROM THE LATE 1580S

In figure A3.3 we have traced the sales of a sample of Plantin's last illustrated editions, each of which was embellished with etchings. The books are listed below in chronological order.

Petrus Canisius, Manuale catholicorum, in 16° from 1588 (PP 890–891) (fig. 5.16)

We were able to localize the sales of 213 copies with etchings and 498 copies with woodcuts, all made between September 1588 and August 1589. Copies with etchings were typically sold at 10 st. per copy, copies with woodcuts at 5 st.

> *Philip II*: none.
> *France*: 126 copies with etchings and 301 with woodcuts in total, comprising:
>> a) Michel Sonnius in Paris: 125 copies with etchings, 300 with woodcuts;[65]

---

57 For Sonnius's purchases, see MPM Arch. 60, fols. 195v and 207r, and MPM Arch. 61, fols. 37v, 53v, 60r, 64v, and 90v. For the purchase of one copy by an advisor to the king of France in Paris, see MPM Arch. 60, fol. 198r. It is possible that an additional sixteen copies of this bible reached France via either the Rouen-based merchant Balthasar de Spinosa or the Antwerp-based merchant Alonzo de Spinosa (see Corr., VIII–IX, no. 1478, pp. 543–544, for references to them), but the record of this large sale does not specify who made the purchase or its final destination clearly enough to be sure (see MPM Arch. 61, fol. 88v).

58 MPM Arch. 61, fols. 19v (B. Arias Montano) and 115r (B. Arias Montano and G. de Çayas).

59 MPM Arch. 61, fols.IV, 9r (F. Ximenes), 20r, 39r, 86v (F. Ximenes), 93v (B. de Roblas), and 101r (P. van Assche).

60 MPM Arch. 61, fols. 9r, 33v (G. Franzini), and 120v.

61 MPM Arch. 491, fols. 81v and 82v (for sales of 2 copies via Plantin's shop); MPM Arch. 60, fol. 197r; and MPM Arch. 61, fols. 11v, 67v, 73r, 77v, 92r, 115r, 130v, and 144r.

62 MPM Arch. 61, fols. 2r (H. Gundlach), 7r, 8r, 17v, 72v (H. Gundlach), 96r, and 124v.

63 MPM Arch. 61, fols. 26v, 42v, 70r (A. de Renialme), 140v, 142v (A. de Renialme), and 152v.

64 MPM Arch. 61, fols. 15v, 18v, 66r, 95r, and 105r.

65 MPM Arch. 65, fol. 128r, for his initial purchases of 200 copies with woodcuts and 100 copies with etched illustrations in September 1588, the first month that sales of this edition are recorded. See MPM Arch. 66, fol. 56r, for his supplementary purchase of 100 copies with woodcut illustrations (at just 4^{1}/2 st. per copy instead of the usual 5 st. per copy) and 25 copies with etched illustrations (at just 9 st. per copy, instead of the usual 10 st. per copy).

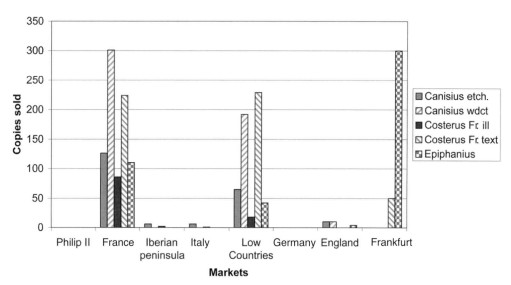

A3.3 Sales of Plantin's editions from the later 1580s.

b) other buyers: 1 copy with etchings, 1 with woodcuts.[66]

Iberian peninsula: 6 copies with etchings to an anonymous buyer in Spain.[67]

Italy: 6 copies with etchings for Alessandro Farnese's library.[68]

Low Countries: at least 65 copies with etchings and approximately 187 with woodcuts, comprising:

 a) local Antwerp buyers: at least 31 copies, 6 of which clearly had etched illustrations;[69]

 b) Douai booksellers: 12 with etchings, 100 with woodcuts, all to Jan Bogard II;[70]

 c) other buyers: approximately 47 with etchings and 62 with woodcuts.[71]

Germany: none.

England: 10 copies with etchings, 10 with woodcut illustrations.[72]

Frankfurt book fair: none.

---

[66] MPM Arch. 65, fol. 120r.   [67] MPM Arch. 65, fol. 125r, for the six copies sent to Spain.

[68] MPM Arch. 65, fol. 158v, for the purchase for Farnese's library.

[69] MPM Arch. 491, fols. 188v–196r (passim), and fols. 200r–201r; and MPM Arch. 495, fol. 14v, for the clearly identifiable sales of this book. Once again, the summary notation here of the books sold and the number of editions of this text Plantin had available at this time often made it impossible to determine precisely which edition was represented and whether the copy in question had intaglio illustrations.

[70] MPM Arch. 65, fol. 117r.

[71] MPM Arch. 65, fols. 116r, 116v (2x), 117r, 120v, 121r (2x), 122v, 124v, 124r, 126r (2x), 129v, 130v, 132v, 134v, 139v, 142v (2x), 146r, 155v, 160r, 168v, 169r, 170r, 171v, 173v, 180v, 183r, 184v, 186v; and MPM Arch. 66, fols. 5v, 24r, 25r, 47r, 57v, 60v, and 68v. These sales also include five copies with unspecified illustrations, hence the approximate values given above.

[72] MPM Arch. 65, fols. 170v–171r (A. de Renialme); and MPM Arch. 66, fol. 87r (H. Wouteneel).

Franciscus Costerus, *Cinquante meditations . . . de la Passion de Nostre Seigneur,*
in *octavo* from 1587 (PP 1049) (fig. 5.17)

We were able to localize the sales of 107 copies of the French edition with illustrations
and 508 without, made between September 1587 and August 1588. As the first year
of sales of the Dutch version, Costerus's *Vijftich meditatien . . . der passie ende des lijdens
Ons Heeren Jesu Christi* (PP 1048), were essentially limited to sales of the plain text (for a
total of 253 copies without the accompanying illustrations), made almost exclusively
to booksellers and a few clerics in the Low Countries (none, for example, was sent
to Sonnius or the Frankfurt book fair), these sales are not recorded in figure A3.3.[73]
Rather, only the sales of the French edition will be detailed below and represented in
the figure. Copies of the French edition without the illustrations typically cost 7 st.,
while copies with the fifty illustrations generally cost 2 fl. 5 st. (= 45 st.).

> *Philip II:* none.
> *France:* 86 copies with illustrations, 224 without, comprising:
>   a) Michel Sonnius in Paris: 50 copies with illustrations, 212 without;[74]
>   b) other buyers: 36 copies with illustrations, 12 without.[75]
> *Iberian peninsula:* 2 copies with illustrations to Gabriel de Çayas.[76]
> *Italy:* 1 copy with illustrations for Alessandro Farnese.[77]
> *Low Countries:* 18 copies with illustrations, 234 without, comprising:
>   a) local Antwerp buyers: 11 copies with illustrations, at least 5 of which appear to
>   have been the French edition; and 51 copies without illustrations, at least 1 of
>   which appears to have been the French edition. Only the clear sales of copies
>   in French are included in fig. A3.3;[78]
>   b) Douai booksellers: 3 copies with the illustrations, 146 without;[79]
>   c) other buyers (primarily booksellers): 10 copies with illustrations, 87 without.[80]
> *Germany:* none.
> *England:* none.
> *Frankfurt book fair:* 50 copies without the illustrations, none with.[81]

---

[73] Only Franciscus Raphelengius I's son Christopher purchased some copies (twelve) with the
accompanying illustrations (see MPM Arch. 65, fol. 93r). See ch. 5, n. 138, for examples of sales of the
Dutch text to others in the Low Countries.

[74] MPM Arch. 64, fol. 131r; and MPM Arch. 65, fols. 9v, 82v, and 109v.

[75] MPM Arch. 64, fols. 128r (A. L'Angelier) and 154r (N. Lescuyer); and MPM Arch. 65, fols. 43v–44r (G.
Bichon). The only other French buyer who purchased copies of Costerus's work (presumably in French,
but that was not specified) was Plantin's "brother" Pierre Porret in Paris, who bought four illustrated
copies (MPM Arch. 64, fol. 166r).

[76] MPM Arch. 65, fol. 101v.   [77] MPM Arch. 64, fol. 130r.

[78] For all of these purchases, see MPM Arch. 491, fols. 148v–167r (*passim*), and fols. 170r, 172v, 173v (two of
French edition with etchings), 179r, 179v, 184v (three of French edition with etchings), 187r, and 187v.

[79] MPM Arch. 64, fol. 144v, and MPM Arch. 65, fol. 21r (both to A. Fowler); MPM Arch. 64, fols. 131v, 150v,
164v, and MPM Arch. 65, fols. 36v and 41v (all to J. Bogard II); and MPM Arch. 64, fols. 138r and 164r,
and MPM Arch. 65, fol. 40r (all to J. Utens).

[80] MPM Arch. 64, fols. 116r, 126v, 127v, 133v, 134v, 138r, 139v, 140r, 141r, 146v, 150v, 152r, and 160r; and
MPM Arch. 65, fols. 5v, 6v, 12r, 15r, 15v, 22r, 23r, 24r, 28v, 35r, 36v, 37r, 46r, 47v, 60v, 79v, 101r, and 102r.

[81] MPM Arch. 64, fol. 140v.

Epiphanius of Constantia, *Ad physiologum*, in *octavo* from 1588 (PP 1126) (fig. 5.18)

We were able to localize the sales of 456 copies, made between August 1588 and July 1589. Illustrated copies were typically sold at 10 st. per copy.

> *Philip II*: none.
> *France*: 110 copies in total, comprising:
>> a) Michel Sonnius in Paris: 100 copies;[82]
>> b) other buyers: 10 copies.[83]
>
> *Iberian peninsula*: none.
> *Italy*: none.
> *Low Countries*: 42 copies in total, comprising:
>> a) local Antwerp buyers: 8 copies;[84]
>> b) Douai booksellers: 8 copies;[85]
>> c) other buyers (primarily booksellers): 26 copies.[86]
>
> *Germany*: none.
> *England*: 4 copies to Ascanius de Renialme.[87]
> *Frankfurt book fair*: 300 copies.[88]

---

[82] MPM Arch. 65, fol. 109v.   [83] MPM Arch. 65, fol. 152r–v; and MPM Arch. 66, fol. 22r.
[84] MPM Arch. 491, fols. 186v, 187r, 188v (2x), 189r, 189v, 190r, and 195r.
[85] MPM Arch. 65, fols. 117r (J. Bogard I), and 110v (A. Fowler).
[86] MPM Arch. 65, fols. 106r, 107r, 112r, 112v, 113r, 116v, 117r, 118r, 122v, 124r, 134v, 136r, 142v, 159v, and 186v; and MPM Arch. 66, fols. 7r and 24v.
[87] MPM Arch. 65, fols. 170v–171r.   [88] MPM Arch. 65, fol. 107v.

INVENTORIES OF PLANTIN'S STOCK OF COPPER PLATES

Between Plantin's death on July 1, 1589 and the final agreement between his heirs on March 16, 1590 regarding the settlement of his estate,[1] several lists of his property were compiled, including at least two distinct lists of the copper plates present at the *Officina Plantiniana* in Antwerp. One (referred to here as the 1589 A inventory) is part of a larger inventory dated to November 3, 1589.[2] It appears to be preserved in its original form and is the most detailed of all the known lists of Plantin's copper plates, comprising a total of 1,652 plates. This has, consequently, been used for the basic transcription of the list of Plantin's copper plates given below. A copy of this inventory also exists and is referred to here as the 1589 B inventory.[3] The items are listed in a different order here than in the 1589 A inventory (essentially backwards), and are interspersed with notations of some of Plantin's woodcuts (see p. 1, left-hand column) and his type (see p. 2). There are, nevertheless, only occasional significant divergences in the description of some of the plates – that is, more than simple variations in the spelling of individual words. Each important variation is recorded in a note at the end of the transcription of the item concerned. If no mention of the 1589 B inventory is made, then one must assume that the same item is listed in it in roughly the same manner as it is listed in the 1589 A inventory.

By February 1590, presumably as part of the preparation of the definitive settlement of his estate, final inventories of Plantin's possessions were compiled and valued. These include an updated list of Plantin's stock of copper plates (augmented with plates that were most likely completed in the intervening months[4]), referred to here as the 1590 A inventory.[5] This inventory begins with an abbreviated list of 1,536 "old plates,"

[1] See MPM Arch. 99, pp. 197–201, for a copy of this settlement.
[2] See MPM Arch. 98, pp. 513–514, for this list of copper plates. The inventory itself starts on p. 509 with a sort of title-page, which is dated November 3, 1589. This date is repeated on p. 511, when the actual inventory begins.
[3] See MPM Arch. 124, pp. 1, 3–4, for this copy.
[4] See, e.g., the references below to plates for an edition of Ovid's *Metamorphoses*, which Jan Moretus I published in 1591 with 178 illustrations (Imhof 1996a, cat. 20). While only twenty-five plates were noted in the 1589 inventories, eighty are listed in 1590.
[5] See MPM Arch. 99, pp. 13–14, for this document.

both engraved and etched ("veilles partie taillees partie faictes a eau forte"). As many of the plates in the 1590 A inventory are grouped together instead of listed individually, there are few clear repetitions of items cited in the 1589 A inventory. Consequently, when such a repetition does occur, it is mentioned in a note following the transcription of the pertinent listing from the 1589 A inventory.[6] The list of "old plates" is then followed by a list of 319 new etched plates ("Neufves faictes à eau fortes") and then 73 new engraved plates ("Neufves tailles"). Despite the reference to these plates being "new," they are all also included in the original 1589 A inventory. Rather, the essential distinction made here was not simply when a specific plate had been made, but whether or not it had been used. This distinction is underscored in the concluding valuation of the plates. A separate sheet of paper bound in at the end of the 1590 A list bears an attestation from Peeter vander Borcht, Abraham Ortelius, and Philips Galle that, on February 5, 1590, following careful consideration, they valued all the copper plates except that of the Seven Sorrows of the Virgin (see below) at 2,150 Brabant guilders (or fl.).[7] Comparing this value with those included at the end of the immediately preceding list indicates that vander Borcht, Galle, and Ortelius had, in fact, valued only the "Vielles figures" (old figures) (which were assigned the same 2,150 fl. value noted above), and not the 319 new etched plates or the 73 new engraved plates. The value of these plates is worked out (albeit anonymously) in exceptional detail, per plate, in a final document, referred to here as the 1590 B inventory.[8] The resulting sums were included summarily at the end of the 1590 A inventory. For the etched plates, the design and etching of each plate was valued individually per plate, while a lump sum for the copper plate itself was calculated at an average of 6 st. per plate. For the engraved plates, just a single sum per plate is noted. The individual values assigned to specific plates in the 1590 B inventory (but not the bulk value of the etched copper plates) are included in notes to the citations of the respective plates given in the transcription below.

In addition to these inventories of Plantin's stock of plates in Antwerp, a separate inventory dated to 1590 of, among other items, the copper plates Plantin had left in Leiden is preserved in two versions: one list that was part of the extensive inventory made of Plantin's possessions in Leiden in 1590, and a transcription of the same items in a slightly different order on a loose sheet.[9] Comprising just 461 plates valued at 637

---

[6] The following vague "group" references in the 1590 A inventory (MPM Arch. 99, p. 13) are not linked with more specific listings in the 1589 inventories: "71 Petites et quarees pour le Missel" (71 small and square [plates] for the missal); "10 Missel en petit f°" (10 [plates for the] missal in small f°); "12 Titres et cartes &c. in f°" (12 titles and maps, etc. in f°); "237 Diverses figures dont Mynken Liefrincks a faict les espreuves" (237 diverse figures from which Mynken Liefrinck has printed impressions); "30 Missale in f° longuet" (30 [plates for the] missal in f°, oblong); "64 Diverses figures, comme marques, armoires, &c." (64 diverse figures, such as printer's devices, coats of arms, etc.); "9 Figures servantes aux titres du Missel de diverses grandeures" (9 figures for the title-pages of missals, of various sizes); "29 Vignettes in f°" (29 borders in f°); and "8 grandes figures in f°" (8 large figures in f°).

[7] Their statement (MPM Arch. 99, p. 15) reads: "Op heden den vijfden feb. 1590. hebben wij onderschreven na rijpe deliberatie daer op gedaen ende gehadt, alle de copere plaeten geestimeert op de somme van twee duisent en hondert en vyftich gulden brabants. wt gesteken (?) de groote plaete vande seven weeen." Philips Galle performed a similar function when he helped estimate the value of Gerard de Jode's property following his death on February 5, 1591 (see Van der Stock 1998, p. 273).

[8] See MPM Arch. 124, p. 321, for this document.

[9] See MPM Arch. 99, pp. 31–94, for the entire inventory, pp. 33–34 for the detailed list of the copper plates, and p. 261 for the loose copy. The identification of the entire, original inventory as that of Plantin's

fl., the plates listed in the official inventory are included here following the list of plates left in Antwerp. Any significant divergences between this list and the loose copy of this list are recorded in a note by the group of plates concerned.

For both the Antwerp and Leiden inventories given below, the transcription of each item is followed by a brief translation of the reference given and, whenever possible, the identification of the book(s) in which the cited plates were used. If the plates are still preserved in the Plantin-Moretus Museum, the reference numbers for these plates are also given in the note at the end of the item concerned. However, it is not always possible to link these existing plates with occasionally vague, general references in these inventories. We have always tried to make a tentative link between the surviving liturgical images and one of these groups, primarily to underscore how few of these plates survive. Regrettably, it is usually too difficult to link the remaining "generic" and repeatedly reused images, such as title-page vignettes, with individual listings below. Similarly, it is impossible to determine which plates, specifically, were included in some of the groups of "diverse" plates cited below.[10] Consequently, not all of the plates commissioned by Plantin that are still in the collection of the Plantin-Moretus Museum will be cited in the transcription of the inventories given below.[11]

The inventories of Plantin's copper plates at Leiden and Antwerp also support the following general observations concerning these collections. The Leiden *Officina Plantiniana*, run by Plantin's son-in-law Franciscus Raphelengius I, had a total of 461 of Plantin's copper plates valued at 637 fl., which amounts to the notably small figure of around 1.38 fl. per plate, on average.[12] Used for the illustration of just seventeen distinct publications, a strikingly large quantity of these plates (346) were etchings made in the 1570s and 1580s (and not just, for example, when Plantin was in Leiden). The Antwerp *Officina Plantiniana* had nearly four times as many of Plantin's "Vielles figures" (old plates), namely, some 1,536 plates valued at 2,150 fl. (only approximately 1.40 fl.

---

possessions in Leiden is confirmed on MPM Arch. 99, p. 94. It is dated 1590 in an old hand on p. 23 of MPM Arch. 99. Extracts from the "livre de casse" noted on pp. 92 and 93 of MPM Arch. 99 (pp. 62 and 63 of the original inventory) include items dated from September 1589 through March 1590, which may reflect the specific time period in which this inventory was made up. These dates roughly coincide with those of the inventories taken of Plantin's stock of plates in Antwerp.

[10] Consider, e.g., MPM KP 952 B (= M-H 2149), an engraved medallion image of the Virgin, used on the title-page of Plantin's large 8° editions of his *Officium B. Mariae Virginis* from 1573 and 1575 (PP 1769 and PP 1776). Would this have been included in one of the groups of 8° plates for books of hours, breviaries, etc., noted below, or in the group of "48 diverses figures petites et grandes servants de tiltres" (48 diverse figures, small and large, used for titles)? For an example of a readily identifiable plate in the collection of the Plantin-Moretus Museum that is not cited below because there is no clear reference to it in the known inventories, see MPM KP 839 B, an engraved portrait of Ovid used in Hercules Ciofanus, *In P. Ovidii Nasonis Fastorum libros observationes* (Antwerp: Christopher Plantin, 1581) (PP 989). Both the technique (engraving) and the size of the plate (112 × 78 mm) would have kept it from being included among the smaller (in 16°) etched plates for a later edition of Ovid's *Metamorphoses*, which are cited below. MPM KP 68 E, an engraving of the boundaries of Antwerp by Philips Galle's workshop (see PP 569 and ch. 6), is another case in point.

[11] Other plates in the collection of the Plantin Museum that were likely ordered by Plantin, but cannot be associated with specific items listed below are: MPM PK 11/32 and MPM KP 65 B, 248 B, 825 B, and 947 B.h.

[12] In order to put this amount in some perspective, consider the evidence in Bowen and Imhof 2003 and pp. 235–236 above, that the charges for new engraved plates could range from c.2–4 fl. per plate for very small plates to c.30 fl. for extra large folio plates. Etchings appear to have cost roughly half as much to make as engravings.

per plate on average), which were used for the illustration of perhaps as many as a hundred distinct editions.[13] These surprisingly low monetary valuations of Plantin's fundamental stock of copper plates may be explained by a consideration of the extent to which the plates could actually be reused – the bottom line when determining their full, true value to Plantin's heirs. Specifically, while many of the plates left in Antwerp had a greater potential use for the illustration of a variety of religious texts, this very advantage also meant that they may have been significantly worn down already and consequently were of little actual value. As the Leiden plates consisted primarily of project-specific illustrations that Plantin himself had only printed once or twice – see the list below – they may have been in a better state generally. Nevertheless, their practical value may still have been relatively low because the subjects themselves were not in great demand.

The subdivision of Plantin's plates between his two *Officinae* was, in many ways, a logical one based upon the subject of the publications concerned. For example, those plates commissioned for the illustration of Justus Lipsius's publications (his *Saturnalium sermonum libri duo* and *De amphitheatro liber*) were left with the Leiden *Officina*, as Lipsius himself was still in Leiden at that time and preferred to continue publishing his works there.[14] Similarly, the Leiden *Officina* also appears to have retained all of the plates used to embellish the Polyglot Bible. This may have been done because Raphelengius was himself a linguist who had worked on the Polyglot Bible, and would in 1593, a few years after Plantin's death, republish many of these plates, together with a selection of Arias Montano's treatises from the Polyglot Bible, under the title *Antiquitatum Iudaicarum libri IX*.[15] In addition, those plates with a Protestant association were also left in the Leiden *Officina* – the etchings that would be used to illustrate Hendrik Jansen van Barrefelt's picture bibles, or those that had been used to illustrate both the state entry of the duke of Anjou (which the Calvinist leader, William of Orange, had helped arrange), and the Protestant humanist Dirck Volckertsz. Coornhert's recently published Dutch edition of *Recht ghebruyck ende misbruyck*.[16] Of the other plates left in Leiden, there were still three large sets: those used to illustrate (1) Joannes Sambucus's selection of portraits of physicians from 1574 (PP 2175), (2) Laurentius Gambara's 1577 collection of religious poems (PP 1235), and (3) Ludovicus Hillessemius's publication on figures from the Old Testament (PP 1335). While Raphelengius's son eventually republished Sambucus's work and later Dutch publishers reissued the illustrations to Hillessemius's, it is not

---

[13] When the definitive inventory was made of the stock of the Antwerp *Officina Plantiniana* on February 5, 1590, an additional 319 new etchings and 73 new engravings were also noted, which brought the total number of plates there up to 1,928, for a total value of 3,747 fl. and 14 st. The estimate of the number of projects the cited plates may have illustrated is based upon the number of distinct titles cited in the inventories, as well as the number of editions of certain frequently reprinted works (missals, breviaries, books of hours, and P. Canisius's *Manuale catholicorum*) that Plantin may have produced with intaglio illustrations. For Plantin's books of hours, see Bowen 1997a, pp. 228–229 (PP 1365–1368), and pp. 233–258. For all of the other editions, see the relevant entries in Voet, PP.

[14] See PP 1532–1533 and PP 1556–1558, respectively, for these editions. Ultimately, however, Franciscus Raphelengius I only reprinted the *Saturnalia* once (in 1590; see BB III, p. 1071, no. L 507) with the old etchings. All of the subsequent editions of the *Saturnalia* and the *De amphitheatro* printed by the *Officina Plantiniana* were printed in Antwerp with new illustrations (or else none at all).

[15] See TB 284 for this publication. The reuse of these plates is discussed in greater detail in ch. 3.

[16] See ch. 5 for more on the Barrefelt editions and the publication on Anjou's state entry (PP 1211), and ch. 6 for the last text, which is a Dutch version of B. Furmerius's *De rerum usu et abusu* (PP 1228).

clear whether Raphelengius had similar plans for Gambara's poems, which would clarify his possession of these plates.[17]

Of the 461 plates recorded in Leiden in 1590, the vast majority – 325 or more – appear to have still been in the hands of Franciscus Raphelengius II some twelve years later, in 1602, when Raphelengius wrote to his uncle, Jan Moretus I, asking if he would like them.[18] Raphelengius's remarks reveal which groups of plates were still in a reasonable condition and which were not, following limited reuse for the illustration of a solitary edition, or even none at all. He states: "Mais les figures de cuivre, je les veux vendre . . . Je ne pense pas aussi que vous les voudriez avoir. Toutesfois si les voulez, mandez-les moy. Ce sont les figures de vander Borcht, longuets, et quarrez, les prophetes de Hildesemius, et celles de Usus et Abusus. Le reste est usé, of uytgeslepen. Les Icones Medicorum je les ay accordé à Cornelis Claesz, à condition qu'il imprimera les 300 exemplaires pour moy." (But as for the figures on copper, I want to sell them . . . I do not think that you would like to have them. Nevertheless, if you want them, ask me. They are the figures by vander Borcht, "long" and "square," Hillessemius's prophets, and those for the "Usus et abusus." The rest are used up or worn out. I have an agreement with Cornelis Claesz concerning the *Icones medicorum*, on the condition that he print 300 copies for me.) If each of the sets of illustrations alluded to above was complete, they would represent all 180 biblical images (oblong and square) etched by vander Borcht for the Barrefelt editions, 26 plates for B. Furmerius's *De rerum usu et abusu*, 66 plates for J. Sambucus's *Icones . . . medicorum*, and as many as 53 plates associated with L. Hillessemius's *Sacrarum antiquitatum monumenta*. The main groups of plates not alluded to here that were originally left at the Leiden *Officina Plantiniana* are (as indicated in the inventory transcribed below): 22 plates used to embellish the Polyglot Bible, 56 plates to L. Gambara's *Rerum sacrarum liber*, 24 plates used to illustrate two Lipsius editions, and 20 plates used to illustrate the commemorative album for the 1582 state entry of the duke of Anjou into Antwerp. Perhaps these were part of the group of worn-out plates Raphelengius alluded to, for no subsequent editions bearing them are currently known. If that is the case, their worn-out state is all the more remarkable, for the Raphelengii had only used the plates for the *Saturnalia* and some of those made for the illustration of the Polyglot Bible once following the settlement of Plantin's estate.[19]

Franciscus Raphelengius II ultimately did not end his business in 1602, but seventeen years later in 1619. Once again, Raphelengius wrote to one of the managers of the Antwerp *Officina Plantiniana* (now Jan Moretus I's son Balthasar I) to ask if they would like to buy some of his remaining plates.[20] This time, however, only some non-specified printer's devices and a few title-plates were cited, namely, those for "Herbarii nostri"

[17] See the *Veterum aliquot ac recentium medicorum philosophorumque icones* (Leiden: Franciscus Raphelengius II, 1603), for the later edition of Sambucus's text; and *Holl. Dutch & Flemish*, XXI, p. 96, for references to later editions bearing the plates used to illustrate Hillessemius's work.
[18] See MPM Arch. 92, p. 141, for this letter from May 12, 1602, written at a time when Raphelengius was considering stopping his printing operations, supposedly owing to health concerns, and wanted to sell his stock of copper plates. The ambiguity as to precisely how many plates Raphelengius still had stems from his references to general groups or types of plates, without any specific references to exactly how many there were.
[19] See above regarding the reuse of these plates.
[20] See MPM Arch. 92, pp. 189–190, for this letter from January 25, 1619.

(= R. Dodoens's, *Cruydt-Boeck* [Leiden: Franciscus Raphelengius II, 1618]), M. Lobelius's *Kruydtboeck* (Antwerp: Christopher Plantin, 1581), and the Polyglot Bible. None of these plates appears to have made its way back to Antwerp. Many of the other Leiden plates – like those for Coornhert's variant of the *De rerum usu et abusu* and van-der Borcht's long and square biblical plates – had already appeared in other printers' publications by this time, suggesting that Raphelengius had sold at least some, if not most, of his copper plates by 1610 or so.[21] The evidence of these editions, combined with the occasional reuse of some of the other plates noted above – namely, those for Sambucus's work, the Polyglot Bible, and Lipsius's *Saturnalia* – suggests that the stock of plates left at the Leiden *Officina Plantiniana* did yield some returns despite their more project-specific content.

The copper plates at the Antwerp *Officina* were, by contrast, mostly plates used to illustrate Plantin's frequently reprinted Catholic liturgical or devotional editions. The primary exceptions here (at least in terms of the number of plates involved) were those used to illustrate Epiphanius's *Ad physiologum* (PP 1126), Ludovico Guicciardini's description of the Low Countries (PP 1277–1280), Jan-Baptist Houwaert's *Pegasides pleyn, ende den lust-hof der maeghden* (PP 1412), and Juan de Valverde's anatomical work (PP 2413–2416). It is not certain whether there were specific reasons why these plates were kept at the Antwerp *Officina*. While Plantin's successors did have impressions made of the Guicciardini and de Valverde plates on occasion (presumably to complement as yet unillustrated copies of these texts), they did not publish a full new edition with any of them.[22] Of the 1,928 or so plates listed in the inventories discussed here (see n. 13 above), at least 318 are still in the collection of the Plantin-Moretus Museum. Notably, except for the 18 plates associated with Houwaert's work, all of the "exceptional" groups of plates cited above – those used to illustrate Guicciardini's, de Valverde's, and Epiphanius's texts – are still preserved and amount to 149 plates, nearly half of the plates we were able to associate with items in the inventories. The bulk of Plantin's other plates that are still in the Plantin-Moretus Museum either were used to illustrate some of Plantin's last devotional works – vander Borcht's etchings for Franciscus Costerus's series of fifty meditations on the Passion of Christ (PP 1048 and 1049) and the fifteen etchings used to illustrate Michel d'Esne's brief verses for the devotion of the rosary (PP 1138) – or were newly made at the time of Plantin's death and ultimately never used.[23] Predictably, of the hundreds of plates made for Plantin's liturgical and related devotional texts, only a seemingly random sample of thirty-five or so remain, in addition to a few other isolated plates, like one of the views of forts made by Abraham de Bruyn for A. de Pasino's *Discours sur plusieurs poincts de l'architecture de guerre concernants les fortifications . . .* , from 1579 (PP 1955). Presumably, the bulk of the other religious images

[21] See the discussion of Raphelengius's 1602 letter above for his agreement with another printer concerning Sambucus's plates. See *New Holl.*, *Van der Borcht*, 1, pp. 4 and 133, for the reuse of the Barrefelt images by 1613 and 1610, respectively. See also *New Holl.*, *Van Groeningen*, 11, p. 24, for the reuse of the plates for the *De rerum usu et abusu* by 1609.

[22] For the later printing of the Guicciardini plates, see Imhof 1996a, pp. 59–60; for that of the de Valverde plates, see ch. 3, p. 82.

[23] See the listings below for the twelve new plates by Jan Wierix for a breviary or book of hours and the forty-six plates engraved by Crispijn van de Passe after designs by Maarten de Vos, with images of the Passion of Christ, as well as standard devotional and liturgical subjects.

that are cited in the inventories transcribed below were simply reused until they were worn out and then disposed of, worth only their weight in copper.[24] The other logical, but nevertheless striking aspect of the group of plates that have survived is the notable lack of engraved title-plates. While Plantin did not have many engraved title-plates made, it is notable that even when the related text illustrations remain – the city views for Guicciardini's description of the Low Countries, for example, or the images of St. Jerome and St. Augustine made for Plantin's publications of their collected works – the associated title-plates do not. Perhaps the title-plates were too text-specific to be reused, while the base copper was, like that of the worn-out plates, still worth something if simply remelted or beaten out for the creation of an entirely new plate. All told, the Moretuses were, like their relatives in Leiden, clearly able to profit from the plates they had inherited from Plantin. Many were reused, despite potential disadvantages of wear or highly subject-specific imagery, and the majority appear to have ultimately been sold, either for the illustration of another printer's books, or simply for their weight in metal, thereby yielding at least their rudimentary value, when the engraving itself was no longer serviceable.

1589 A INVENTORY OF PLANTIN'S COPPER PLATES IN ANTWERP (MPM ARCH. 98, PP. 513–14)

62 figures des villes de Guicc[ini] f° (62 figures of the cities of Guicciardini f°)

7 desdittes de $^1/_2$ fueille (7 of the same, $^1/_2$ page)

8 desdittes de $\frac{1}{4}$ fueille (8 of the same, $\frac{1}{4}$ page)

3 figuren vanden tytel met de wapen ende figure vanden Coninck (3 figures of the title with the coat of arms and the figure of the king)

= L. Guicciardini, *Descrittioni di paesi bassi*, 1581, and following editions (PP 1277–1279).[25]

16 figures du missale f° v (16 figures from the missal f°)[26]

12 vignettes f° p^r le missel v (12 borders f° for the missal)[27]

24 desdittes moyennes et petites (24 of the same medium and small)[28]

---

[24] For one example of the Moretuses selling their worn-out plates back to Cornelius Galle II, see Imhof 1996a, cat. 33a, p. 126 and n. 5.

[25] In the 1589 B inventory (MPM Arch. 124, p. 4), the number 4 was written over the 3 for the number of title-plates – four was the number of introductory plates typically included in Plantin's editions of this text – and the identification of the format as "in folio" was added. In the 1590 A inventory (MPM Arch. 99, p. 13) simply "82 Guicciardini" was noted. This figure is the same as the number of plates listed in the 1589 A inventory, if one counts the last group as three title-plates and two extra plates, one with the portrait of the king and one with his coat of arms. If that is what was tallied in 1589, then this group of plates may have comprised all of the plates Plantin used in his most recent (1588) edition of Guicciardini's text except one of the four title-plates and one of the seventy-eight city views. See MPM KP 1432 B, 1498 B, 10 C, 38 C, 92–94 C, 399–402 C, 404–405 C, 410 C, 208–220 D, 222 D, 224–227 D, KP 1–42 E, and 44–46 E, for all seventy-seven plates of city views and plans cited. None of the frontispieces or title-plates appears to be preserved.

[26] In the 1589 B inventory (MPM Arch. 124, p. 4), the relative scale of these figures is also given as "16 groote figueren vanden missael" (16 large figures from the missal).

[27] This and the preceding reference to sixteen figures for the folio missal may have been combined into one listing of "28 Missale in f°" (28 [plates for the] missal in f°) in the 1590 A inventory (MPM Arch. 99, p. 13).

[28] This and subsequent references to assorted plates for Plantin's missals may have been combined in some of the more imprecisely defined references to larger groups of plates for Plantin's missals

= Possibly for any of Plantin's editions of the *Missale Romanum* (PP 1675–1702).

4 Platen gebeten vignetten verborcht in 8° (4 plates etched borders [by] vander Borcht in 8°)[29]

1 figura novi testam. titulus f° (1 figure of the New Testament title f°)

5 figures p[r] le Canon f° cleyn en groot (5 figures for the Canon f° small and large)[30]
> = Possibly for some of Plantin's folio editions of the *Missale Romanum* (e.g., PP 1675–1678, 1680, 1685, 1689, 1694, 1700, and 1702), or for an independent publication of the "Canon Missae" (see PP 904).

45 figures de <u>Anatomie</u> (45 figures of Anatomy)[31]
> = J. de Valverde, *Vivae imagines partium corporis humani*, 1566, and subsequent editions (PP 2413–2416).[32]

1 ovile Christi pro pastorali 4° (1 Christ as shepherd for the Pastorale 4°)
> = *Pastorale*, 1589 (PP 1957).[33]

9 figures de fortification de Passino cleyn en groote (9 figures of the "Fortification" by Pasino, small and large)[34]
> = A. de Pasino, *Discours sur plusieurs poincts de l'architecture de guerre concernants les fortifications . . .*, 1579 (PP 1955).

1 tabula Calend. Antiqui B.A.M. (1 tablet of an ancient calendar, [text by] B.[enedictus] A.[rias] M.[ontanus])
> = *Calendarium Romanum*, 1574 (PP 863).

7 figures vielles de Guicciardini de Sylvius (7 old figures of [Willem] Silvius's Guicciardini [editions])
> = Possibly some of the plates included in copies of Willem Silvius's 1567 Italian edition and 1567–1568 French edition of Guicciardini's description of the Low Countries.[35]

---

found in the 1590 A inventory that are noted above (see n. 6) and not linked with specific citations below.

[29] This listing may refer to a group of four folio-size plates (c.280 × 182 mm), each of which bears four etched borders, each with a central opening of c.103 × 60 mm (see MPM KP 5–8 D). No impression or use of these plates is known. Comprising images of everyday occupations, they may have been used to decorate such everyday works as the almanacs Plantin had printed with intaglio illustrations (see e.g., MPM Arch. 20, fol. 194 rht, under September 17, 1584, for payments to Mynken Liefrinck for illustrating almanacs with intaglios).

[30] In the 1590 A inventory (MPM Arch. 99, p. 13), this group of plates is identified simply as "5 Canon missae" (5 Canons of the mass).

[31] This group of plates is similarly cited in the 1590 A inventory (MPM Arch. 99, p. 13).

[32] Although all editions of this text comprise forty-two text illustrations and an engraved title-frame, the fact that forty-five plates are listed must mean that two erroneously engraved plates, along with their two replacements, were kept together in one group (see the discussion of this work in ch. 3). This hypothesis is supported by the fact that all of these plates – the title-frame, forty-two correctly engraved images, and two in mirror image – are still preserved in the Plantin-Moretus Museum (see MPM KP 241–258 C, 284–291 C, 296–311 C, 315 C, and 320–321 C).

[33] This most likely refers to a full-page frontispiece of the resurrected Christ surrounded by sheep with seven medallions with images of the seven sacraments (see Voet, PP, IV, fig. 48).

[34] In the 1590 A inventory (MPM Arch. 99, p. 13), this group of plates is identified simply as "9 Fortifications de Passina" (9 Fortifications of Pasino). At least one of these plates is still preserved (see MPM KP 327 C, two horizontal views of forts, engraved by Abraham de Bruyn and inserted between pp. 64 and 65 in the copy of this book in MPM [A 960]).

[35] See Guicciardini 2001, pp. 28–31, for descriptions of these editions and maps "Nederlanden-1" and "Antwerpen-Stadhuis-1 [and]-2" for the three intaglio plates Silvius is known to have included in these

21 figures p^r le missel petit f° et 4° (21 figures for the missal [in] small f° and 4°)[36]

= Possibly for some of the following editions of Plantin's *Missale Romanum* (e.g., PP 1675–1678, 1680, 1681, 1683, 1685, 1686, 1689–91, 1694, 1695, 1699, 1700, and 1702).

2 Titres d Aug^{nus} et Hieronymus (2 titles of St. Augustine and St. Jerome)

2 figures d Aug^{nus} et Hieronymus (2 figures of St. Augustine and St. Jerome)[37]

= St. Augustine, *Opera D. Aurelii Augustini Hipponensis . . .*, 1576–1577 (PP 604), and St. Jerome, *Opera divi Hieronymi Stridoniensis . . .*, ed. by M. Victorius, 1579 (PP 1333), both of which have an engraved title-page and an engraved author's portrait.

16 vignetten tot missael cleyn f° et 4° (16 borders for the missal [in] small f° and 4°)

= Possibly for some of the following editions of Plantin's *Missale Romanum* (e.g., PP 1675–1678, 1680, 1681, 1683, 1685, 1686, 1689–91, 1694, 1695, 1699, 1700, and 1702).

1 tytel tot de groote misse boecken[38]

= This plate was used to illustrate several of Plantin's and Jan Moretus I's large folio music editions; the first (for which the plate was made) is G. de la Hèle, *Octo missae quinque, sex et septem vocum*, 1578 (PP 1306).

1 figure de nre. dame des douleurs Mofl. (1 figure of the [Seven] sorrows of the Virgin [for Jean] Moflin)[39]

1 Ville de Salamanca en 2 pièces (1 city of Salamanca in 2 pieces)[40]

1 Moscovia petite p^r le livre de Possevinus [1 Moscow, small, for the book of Possevinus]

---

editions. It is not clear which additional four plates are alluded to in this listing. See MPM KP 75 E for the original plate for "Antwerpen-Stadhuis-2."

[36] The following copper plates (all smaller, mostly square images, *c*.59 × 59 mm for the first two and *c*.70/72 × 70/72 mm for the rest) may have been included in this group of plates, or other listings for missals in *quarto* and folio in this inventory. See MPM KP 554 A, 565 A, 107 B, 121 B, 182 B, 485–488 B, 550 B, 662 B, and 717 B. MPM KP 804 B and 841 B are both slightly larger plates (*c*.118 × 79), that may also have served to illustrate these books, or *octavo* books of hours, although no impressions of any of these plates in Plantin's editions are known.

[37] See MPM KP 154 D and 157 D, respectively, for these two plates, both of which are believed to have been engraved by Jan Sadeler I after Crispin van den Broeck. The corresponding engraved title-pages do not appear to have been preserved.

[38] In the 1589 B inventory (MPM Arch. 124, p. 4), this plate is further identified as "1 tytel tot de groote missen musicael" (1 title to the large musical masses). See MPM KP 70 E for this plate, which is signed "P 1578 H" (for Pieter Huys) on the back.

[39] In the 1589 B inventory (MPM Arch. 124, p. 4), the relative scale of this plate is also given as "1 grande figure de nre. Dame de Moufflin" (1 large figure of Our Lady from Moflin). This plate is also cited in both the 1590 A and 1590 B inventories. In the 1590 A inventory (MPM Arch. 99, p. 14), it is simply identified as "1 Nostre Dame aux douleurs" (1 Sorrows of Our Lady), among the "new" engraved plates. In the 1590 B inventory (MPM Arch. 124, p. 321), the artists responsible for this engraving are also identified, as the citation there reads "1 Une grande image de nre. Dame de l'invention Crispiaen vande Broeke, et taille de Hier. Wiricks" (One large image of Our Lady designed by Crispin van den Broeck and cut by Hieronymus Wierix). According to this last reference, this plate was valued at 60 fl. This work is discussed in greater detail in ch. 2.

[40] While this listing suggests that this one image was printed from two plates, in each of the other three inventories made up of the copper plates in Plantin's estate, simply two plates of Salamanca are cited (see MPM Arch. 124, p. 4 [1589 B inventory]; and MPM Arch. 99, p. 13 [1590 A inventory], among the "new" etched plates. In the 1590 B inventory (MPM Arch. 124, p. 321), these plates were similarly cited in a list of etched ("ghebeten") plates and were valued at 12 fl.

= A. Possevinus, *Moscovia*, 1587 (PP 2094).[41]

1 Ascensio B. Mariae f° (1 Assumption of the Virgin f°)

= Most likely (given the large format) an illustration to one of Plantin's folio editions of the *Missale Romanum* (e.g., PP 1675–1678, 1680, 1685, 1689, 1694, 1700, and 1702), or his folio *Breviarium Romanum* from 1575 (pp 882).

1 Effigies D. Thomae (1 portrait of Thomas Aquinas)[42]

1 figura apocalypseos f° (1 figure of the apocalypse [in] f°)

113 figure p^r la Bible in f° et monumenta 4° et horae 4° (113 figures for the bible in f° and the Monumenta [in] 4° and books of hours [in] 4°)

= *Biblia sacra*, 1583 (PP 690); and the editions cited under the following two entries.[43]

21 tot Horae in 4° (21 [figures] for books of hours in 4°)

= *Officium BMV*, 1573 and 1575 (PP 1769 and PP 1776).[44]

18 tot monumenta 4° etc. (18 [figures] for Monumenta [in] 4° etc.)

= B. Arias Montano, *Humanae salutis monumenta*, 1583 (PP 590).[45]

5 tot den missael in 4° cleyn (5 [plates] for the missal in small 4°)[46]

= Possibly for some of the following editions of Plantin's *Missale Romanum* (PP 1681, 1686, 1690, 1699).

69 figures de monumenta y comprins le titre et effigies xri 8° (69 figures of the Monumenta, including the title and the image of Christ [in] 8°)[47]

= B. Arias Montano, *Humanae salutis monumenta*, editions from 1571, 1575, and 1581 (PP 588–589).[48]

---

[41] The inserted map in this book is actually not small (230 × 275 mm) and represents a region of the former country of Russia identified as Moscow and not the specific city that one thinks of today.

[42] In the 1589 B inventory (MPM Arch. 124, p. 4), the format "in f°" is added to the basic information in this listing.

[43] For at least some of the plates that might have been included in this group, see MPM KP 1440 B (an engraving of the *Capture of Christ* by Abraham de Bruyn after Crispin van den Broeck), 1444 B and 1463 B (anonymous engravings of the *Flagellation*, the former designed by Peeter vander Borcht), 1499 B and 90 C (anonymous engravings of *Christ on the Mount of Olives*), 1504 B (an anonymous engraving of the *Mocking of Christ*), and 77 C (an anonymous engraving of the *Kiss of Judas*).

[44] As these books usually had just eighteen text illustrations, this group of plates most likely comprises multiple plates of some subjects and not simply a single complete series of plates used to illustrate this text.

[45] This work actually contained seventy text illustrations *c*.165 × 115 mm, as well as an introductory circular image of Christ, which was also used to illustrate copies of Plantin's octavo editions of this book (see below). Given the preceding reference to plates used in Plantin's 1583 bible, *quarto* books of hours, and this book, this group of eighteen plates most likely comprises eighteen subjects that only appeared in this work (e.g., an engraving by Jan Wierix after Peeter vander Borcht of *Christ Carrying the Cross* [M-H 2254] that is still preserved under MPM KP 1357 B).

[46] The preceding four entries comprise 157 plates in quarto for use in any number of the cited titles. Combined, these plates most likely represent essentially the same group of plates that is listed in the 1590 A inventory (MPM Arch. 99, p. 13) as "156 Monumenta ejusdem [= Montani], Horae &c. in 4°" (156 [plates for the] Monumenta [by] Montano, books of hours, etc. in 4°).

[47] In the 1590 A inventory (MPM Arch. 99, p. 13), this group of plates is simply identified as "68 [versus 69] Monumenta Montani in 8°" (68 [plates for the] Monumenta [by] Montano in 8°). For at least one text illustration and the two bust portrayals of Christ used for these editions, see MPM KP 493 B (an engraving of the *Entombment* by Hieronymus Wierix = M-H 2211) and MPM KP 826 B (*Head of Christ* by Jan Wierix = M-H 2147) and 1052 B (*Head of Christ* by Jan Wierix = M-H 2147 a), respectively.

[48] See Bowen 2003 for a detailed discussion of the printing and illustration of each of these editions. A few of the *octavo*-scaled text illustrations must be missing from this group, as each of these editions contained seventy such text illustrations, in addition to the noted title-plate and smaller image of Christ.

43 vignettes in 8° p^r monumenta etc. (43 borders in 8° for the Monumenta etc.)[49]

    = B. Arias Montano, *Humanae salutis monumenta*, editions from 1571, 1575, and 1581 (PP 588–589).[50]

51 figures de le passion de verborcht gebeten (51 figures of the Passion, etched by vander Borcht)[51]

    = F. Costerus, *Vijftich meditatien . . . der passie . . . Ons Heeren Jesu Christi* [and] *Cinquante meditations . . . de la passion de Nostre Seigneur*, both published in 1587, with the same accompanying set of illustrations (see PP 1048–1049).

50 figures meditat. B. Mariae borcht gebeten (50 figures [of] meditations [on] the Virgin [by Peeter vander] Borcht, etched)[52]

    = F. Costerus, *Cinquante meditations de la vie et louanges de la vierge Marie*, 1590 (BB, I, p. 879, C 539; and BT 5505).[53]

15 figures p^r les 15 mysteres gebeten (15 figures for the 15 Mysteries, etched)[54]

    = M. d'Esne, *Les XV mysteres du rosaire de la Sacrée Vierge Marie*, 1588 (PP 1138).

27 figures d'Epiphanius gebeten (27 figures of Epiphanius, etched)[55]

    = Epiphanius of Constantia, *Ad physiologum*, 1588 (PP 1126).[56]

25 diverses in 8° p[r] Horae, brev, et missale (25 diverse [plates] in 8° for books of hours, breviaries and missals)[57]

[49] These plates may have been included in the slightly expanded group of plates listed in the 1590 A inventory as "46 Vignettes in 8°" (46 borders in 8°) (see MPM Arch. 99, p. 13).

[50] See Bowen 2003, table 2 and pp. 32–34, for the identification of the seventeen different borders that are known to have been used to illustrate these editions. Given the discrepancy in the total number of borders listed (forty-three compared with seventeen), this group of borders most likely also includes some that were only used to illustrate copies of Plantin's *octavo* books of hours (the "etc." in the inventory listing) (see the notes on PP 1367–1368, 1770 A, and 1775 D, E, and G [editions from 1570, 1573, and 1575, respectively] in Bowen 1997a, pp. 228, 238, and 243).

[51] In the 1589 B inventory (MPM Arch. 124, p. 3), the subject of the plates is described more fully as "51 figures des Meditations de la Passion de N. S. ghebeten P. B." (51 figures of the meditations on the Passion of Our Lord etched [by] P.[eeter] [vander]B.[orcht]). In the 1590 A inventory (MPM Arch. 99, p. 13), these plates are simply described according to the book for which they were made, namely as "51 Meditationes Costeri de passione" (51 [plates for] Costerus's Meditations on the Passion). See MPM KP 254–255 B, 261–308 B, and 529 B, for this group of fifty-one plates.

[52] In the 1590 A inventory (MPM Arch. 99, p. 13) and 1590 B inventory (MPM Arch. 124, p. 321) these plates are listed more succinctly according to the book for which they were made, namely as "50 Meditationes Costeri de vita n[ost]rae D[omi]nae" (transcription from the 1590 A inventory, where these plates are included in the list of the "new" etched ["ghebeten"] plates). According to the 1590 B inventory, they were valued at 2 fl. per plate.

[53] Included among the "new etched plates" in the 1590 A and 1590 B inventories (see p. 377), the first known use of them post-dates Plantin's death.

[54] In the 1589 B inventory (MPM Arch. 124, p. 3), the subject of the plates is described more fully as "15 figures pour les 15 Mysteres du Rosaire, ghebeten" (15 figures for the fifteen mysteries of the Rosary, etched). In the 1590 A inventory (MPM Arch. 99, p. 13), only the brief title "15 Mystere du Rosaire" (15 mysteries of the rosary) is given. See MPM KP 1119–1121 B and 1136–1147 B for these fifteen plates.

[55] In the 1589 B inventory (MPM Arch. 124, p. 3), the general small ("petites") scale of the images is also noted, while in the 1590 A inventory (MPM Arch. 99, p. 13), this group of plates is tersely identified as "27 Physiologus Epiphanii."

[56] Actually, only twenty-six plates (and not twenty-seven) were used to illustrate this work. See MPM KP 109–120 B, 138–149 B, 183 B, and 494 B for the twenty-six plates used to illustrate this work, and 491 B, which is an extra etching of the image "Night," represented by an owl (see fol. F2r of Epiphanius's work).

[57] This and a subsequent listing of fifteen comparable plates in 8° (see below) may have been grouped together for the 1590 A inventory and listed simply there as "40 Breviarium &c. in 8°" (forty [plates to the] breviary, etc. in 8°) (see MPM Arch. 99, p. 13). For some of the plates that may have once been part of this (or the subsequent) listing of illustrations in 8°, see MPM KP 492 B (an engraving of the

= Possibly used in any of Plantin's editions of these texts in 8° or larger.

20 oude figures vande passie (20 old figures of the Passion)[58]

13 figures monumenta Hillesemij (13 figures [for] Hillessemius's Monumenta)

= L. Hillessemius, *Sacrarum antiquitatum monumenta*, 1577 (PP 1335).[59]

18 figuren van Houwaert (18 figures of Houwaert)[60]

= J.-B. Houwaert, *Pegasides pleyn ende den lusthof der maeghden*, 1583 (PP 1412).

60 figuren tot missael in 4° cleyn (60 figures for missals in small 4°)

= Possibly for some of the following editions of Plantin's *Missale Romanum* (PP 1681, 1686, 1690, 1699).

275 figuren Cal. Rom. p' (275 figures for the Roman calendar small [petite]) [61]

= *Sanctorum kalendarii Romani* . . . (PP 865 and PP 867), and *Evangeliorum dominicalium* . . . (PP 1152 and PP 1153), all published in either 1580 or 1584.[62]

8 figures diurnalis 16° (8 figures [for the] diurnal [in] 16°)

= *Officium diurnum*, 1589 (PP 1806).

23 Manuale Canisij 24° gebeten (23 [plates for] Canisius's Manuale [in] 24°, etched)

= Possibly for P. Canisius, *Manuale catholicorum*, 1589 (PP 892).

23 dudit manuel 16 (23 for the same manual [in] 16°)[63]

23 dudit 16° gebeten oudt (23 of the same [in] 16°, etched old)

Purification of the Virgin by Jan Wierix = M-H 2188 A), 495 B (an engraving of the *Circumcision* by Jan Wierix = M-H 2185 A), 661 B (an anonymous engraving of the *Purification of the Virgin* = M-H 2188 a), 677 B (an anonymous engraving of *St. Luke*, similar to M-H 2224), 678 B (an anonymous engraving of the *Assumption of the Virgin*, similar to M-H 2219), 719 B (an anonymous engraving after Peeter vander Borcht of the *Flight into Egypt* = M-H 2190 b), and 723 B (an engraving of *Pentecost* by Jan Wierix = M-H 2216 A); as well as MPM PK 11/30 (an engraving of the *Death of the Virgin* = M-H 2218 by Hieronymus Wierix after Peeter vander Borcht), and MPM PK 11/31 (another engraving of the *Circumcision* by Jan Wierix after Peeter vander Borcht).

[58] In the 1590 A inventory (MPM Arch. 99, p. 13), only fifteen such plates are noted.

[59] This reference to just thirteen plates for the illustration of this work is problematic, as there is also a reference in the Leiden inventory (see below) to a group of fifty-three plates that were also supposedly used to illustrate this work. Not only would it have been unusual to have divided this series of plates, but the original series used by Plantin in 1577 comprised just thirty-nine plates and not sixty-six. The plates were, most likely, at the Leiden *Officina*, as later editions containing these plates were printed in Amsterdam (see *Holl. Dutch & Flemish*, XXI, p. 96). It is not clear, then, which plates are referred to in the Antwerp inventory and which extra plates were associated with the originals in the Leiden inventory. Perhaps this group of plates should be associated with the following comparable, but otherwise unidentifiable group of plates listed in the 1590 A inventory (MPM Arch. 99, p. 13): "13 Christus cum 12 Aptrs." (13 [plates of] Christ with 12 apostles).

[60] In the 1590 A inventory (MPM Arch. 99, p. 13), these plates are simply listed as "17 [rather than 18] Houwaert." It is not clear whether one plate was lost between the compilations of these inventories, or perhaps the author's portrait or coat of arms was listed together with other like items in the 1590 A inventory (see n. 6 above), separate from the sixteen text illustrations made for this work. Remarkably, the only plate related to this group that is still preserved in the Plantin-Moretus Museum (MPM KP 12 C) is a different engraved portrait of Houwaert that does not appear to have ever been used (see *Holl. Dutch & Flemish*, LXVIII, no. 2103).

[61] This group of plates is most likely included in the enlarged reference in the 1590 A inventory (MPM Arch. 99, p. 13) to "292 Kalendarium Gregorianum &c. in 24°" (292 [plates to] the Gregorian Calendar etc. in 24°), where the "etc." probably alludes to the fact that some of these plates were also used to illustrate other publications, such as books of hours in 24° and some of Plantin's *quarto* missals (see pp. 251–255 and 150, respectively). See MPM KP 157 A for one engraving after Peeter vander Borcht of St. Melchiades (now referred to as St. Miltiades), which was definitely used to illustrate editions of the calendar and KP 154 A, for an anonymous engraving of a pope that is stylistically comparable, although no impression of it in one of these works is known.

[62] See pp. 252–254 for more on the varying number of plates associated with these works.

[63] In the 1589 B inventory (MPM Arch. 124, p. 3), the technique ("gebeten" [etched]) is also noted.

23 dudit 16° de Colardt (23 of the same [in] 16° by Collaert)[64]

    = Each of the three preceding entries may have been used in P. Canisius's *Manuale catholicorum* from 1588 (PP 890). It is also possible that the same plates were used in Dutch and French editions of Canisius's text that were printed in the slightly larger 12° format in 1589 (see PP 894 and 895).[65]

35 des horae 12° vieles ¹/₂ par som (?) (35 [plates for] books of hours [in] 12° old . . .)[66]

    = Possibly used in any of the following of Plantin's editions of the *Officium BMV*, printed between 1573 and 1587 (PP 1771, 1777, 1778bis, 1779–1781, 1786, 1786ter, and 1786octies).[67]

19 Horae in 32° Raphael[68]

    = Possibly used in any of the following of Plantin's editions of the *Officium BMV*, printed between 1584 and 1588 (PP 1786quinquies, PP 1786sexies, and PP 1788bis).[69]

1 figure pᵣ Martyrologium Rom. f° (1 figure for the Martyrologium Romanum [in] f°)[70]

    = Most likely C. Baronius, *Martyrologium Romanum*, 1589 (PP 626).[71]

5 figures de Itinerarium Ortelij (5 figures from Ortelius's Itinerarium)[72]

    = A. Ortelius, *Itinerarium per nonnullas Galliae Belgicae partes*, 1584 (PP 1837).

48 diverses figures petites et grandes servants de tiltres (48 diverse figures, small and large, used for titles)[73]

---

[64] In the 1589 B inventory (MPM Arch. 124, p. 3), the preceding ninety-two plates are all listed by the title of the book they illustrated (*Manuale catholicorum*) and not by the author's name. In the 1590 A inventory (MPM Arch. 99, p. 13), these plates are most likely included in the enlarged reference to "115 Manuale catholicorum de diverses sortes et tailles" (115 [plates to the] Manuale catholicorum of diverse sortes [i.e., formats] and cutting [i.e., engraved and etched]). The artist referred to is probably Hans II or Adriaen Collaert.

[65] See the discussion of the "Group 9" set of illustrations to Plantin's books of hours in Bowen 1997a, p. 134, for evidence of other plates that were used to illustrate books in both 16° and 12°.

[66] This group of plates is also cited in the 1590 A inventory (MPM Arch. 99, p. 13).

[67] For a brief description of each of these editions, see Bowen 1997a, pp. 239–241, 245–247, 249–251, 253, and 255.

[68] In the 1589 B inventory (MPM Arch. 124, p. 3), this group of plates is listed as "19 Heures in 32. neufves" (19 [plates for a] book of hours in 32°, new), without the quizzical reference to "Raphael" (Sadeler?).

[69] For a brief description of each of these editions, see Bowen 1997a, pp. 254 and 257. Plantin's earliest known books of hours in 32° to contain engraved illustrations (PP 1772–1773 – see ch. 4) are not included in this list, as the artist responsible for making those engravings was most likely Pieter Huys (see appendix 1, p. 344).

[70] This plate is listed without a reference to a book format in the 1589 B inventory (MPM Arch. 124, p. 3).

[71] Given the ambiguity in the format of the book concerned between the 1589 A and 1589 B inventories, it is also possible that a smaller title-page vignette for an earlier edition of this text in 8° was meant instead. See MPM KP 514 B for this vignette and PP 1643 (and Voet, PP, IV, fig. 2, for a reproduction of the title-page) for Plantin's 1586 *Martyrologium Romanum* in 8°.

[72] This group of plates is also cited in the 1590 A inventory (MPM Arch. 99, p. 13).

[73] This broadly described group of title-plates may include the two plates used to introduce C. Baronius's *Annales ecclesiastici* (published under Jan Moretus I in 1589, following Plantin's death) that are listed separately in the 1590 A inventory (MPM Arch. 99, p. 13, among the "old" plates) as "2 Tituli Annalium" (2 titles of the Annales). There is no other specific, corresponding reference to these plates in the 1589 inventories. On these and the other plates used to print the title-page of the Moretuses' editions of this text, see Bowen and Imhof 2005.

15 Tot de horae, breviaria, 8° (15 [plates] for books of hours and breviaries [in] 8°)[74]

    = Possibly used in any of the following editions of Plantin's breviaries (PP 824, 826, 829, 833, and 834) and books of hours (PP 1365–1368, 1700, 1775, and 1777bis).[75]

4 du missel in 4° (4 of the missal in 4°)

    = Possibly for some of the following editions of Plantin's *Missale Romanum* (PP 1681, 1683, 1686, 1687, 1690, 1691, 1699).

11 tot de missal 4° cleyn (11 for the missal in small 4°)

    = Possibly for some of the following editions of Plantin's *Missale Romanum* (PP 1681, 1686, 1690, 1699).

7 diverses vieles et parmi ceulx deux de H. prod Pighij (7 diverse old [plates], among which two for Hercules prodicius [by] Pighius)[76]

    = S. Pighius, *Hercules prodicius seu principis iuventutis vita et peregrinatio*, 1587 (PP 2054).

1 tiltre de la bib. Latine (1 title from the Latin bible)[77]

    = Possibly for Plantin's *Biblia sacra*, 1583 (PP 690).

4 figures neuves de Colard pʳ missel f° (4 new figures by Collaert for the missal [in] f°)[78]

12 figures neuves pʳ brcv. 16° et 8° wirickx (12 new figures for breviary [in] 16° and 8° [by] Wierix)[79]

7 figures de Salve Regina (7 figures of [the] "Salve Regina")

    = Possibly intended for the illustration of the second part of F. Costerus's *Cinquante meditations de la vie et louanges de la vierge Marie*, published by Jan Moretus I in 1590 (see BB, I, p. 879, c 539; and BT 5505), namely, the *Sept meditations sur le cantique Salve Regina*.

25 fig. metamorphosis 16° (25 figures [for Ovid's] Metamorphoses [in] 16°)[80]

    = This edition was not published until 1591 (by Jan Moretus I), at which point it bore 178 illustrations.[81]

---

[74] See n. 57 above.

[75] See Bowen 1997a, pp. 228–229, 238–239, 242–244, and 247–248, for brief descriptions of the books of hours concerned.

[76] In the 1589 B inventory (MPM Arch. 124, p. 1), the title is given as "Hercules Proditius."

[77] In the 1589 B inventory (MPM Arch. 124, p. 1), the language of the bible is not specified, while the format (f°) is.

[78] In both the 1590 A inventory (MPM Arch. 99, p. 14, among the "new" engraved plates) and the 1590 B inventory (MPM Arch. 124, p. 321) this same group of plates is listed, with the additional reference to the designer, Maarten de Vos. According to the 1590 B inventory, these plates were valued at an average of 26 fl. 10 st. per plate. See Bowen and Imhof 2001 for a detailed discussion of these engravings.

[79] This group of plates is cited in both the 1590 A inventory (MPM Arch. 99, p. 14, among the "new" engraved plates) and the 1590 B inventory (MPM Arch. 124, p. 321), with the additional note that the plates were designed and engraved ("de la taille et invention" [as noted in the 1590 A inventory]) by Hans [= Jan] Wierix and the simplification of the format to just breviaries in 8° (with no extra reference to works in 16°). According to the 1590 B inventory, these engravings were valued at 10 fl. per plate. See MPM KP 171–181 B and 184 B for such a group of twelve plates.

[80] In both the 1590 A inventory (MPM Arch. 99, p. 13, among the "new" etched plates) and the 1590 B inventory (MPM Arch. 124, p. 321) this group of twenty-five plates is most likely incorporated in the enlarged citation of "80 [etched plates for] Metamorphosis Ovidii." According to the 1590 B inventory, they were valued at 2 fl. per plate.

[81] See n. 4 above.

12 figure p^r missale f° long^{tis} verborcht gebeten (12 figures for [the] missal [in] f°, oblong, etched by vander Borcht)^{82}

= Possibly used to illustrate one of Plantin's later editions of the *Missale Romanum* from 1587 or 1589 (see PP 1700 and 1702). Or, as suggested by the related reference to such plates in the 1590 inventories, if these were new plates, not yet used by Plantin, the reference might pertain to some of the plates seen in Jan Moretus I's *Breviarium Romanum* in 4° from 1592 (see BT 5326, and the discussion of this edition in Imhof 1996a, cat. nos. 7 and 8).

10 Horae in 24° (10 [plates for] books of hours in 24°)^{83}

16 figures des heures en 32 (16 figures for books of hours in 32°)

= Possibly used in any of the following of Plantin's editions of the *Officium BMV* (PP 1772–1773, 1786quinquies, 1786sexies, and 1788bis).^{84}

21 figures p^r manuale S. angl. (21 figures for [the] "manuale S. Anglois")^{85}

1 vignette p^r le missel f° ([1 border for the missal [in] f°)

= Possibly used in any of the following editions of Plantin's *Missale Romanum* in folio (e.g., PP 1676, 1678, 1680, 1685, 1689, 1694, 1700, and 1702).

10 figures de cuivre p^r Horae ^ ^{brev} 16 neuves (10 figures on copper for books of hours and breviaries [in] 16°, new)^{86}

36 de la Passion 16° martin de Vos (36 [plates] of the Passion [in] 16° [by] Maarten de Vos)^{87}

175 du testament forme de 8° (175 [figures] of the Testament, format 8°)^{88}

---

82 In both the 1590 A inventory (MPM Arch. 99, p. 13) and the 1590 B inventory (MPM Arch. 124, p. 321) a group of twelve etched oblong plates are similarly noted, but then for use in breviaries, in addition to missals, and with a slightly smaller format (4° instead of f°) (namely "12 Breviarium et Missale in 4° longues") (as noted in the 1590 A inventory, among the "new" etched plates). According to the 1590 B inventory, these plates were valued at 4 fl. per plate.

83 In the 1590 A inventory (MPM Arch. 99, p. 14) these plates are listed among the "new" engraved plates, with the extra note that they were engraved and designed ("taille et l'invention") by Hans [= Jan] Wierix. In the 1590 B inventory (MPM Arch. 124, p. 321), in which Wierix was not specified, the plates were valued at 4 fl. each. They do not appear to have ever been used.

84 For a brief description of each of these editions, see Bowen 1997a, pp. 241, 254, and 257.

85 In the 1589 B inventory (MPM Arch. 124, p. 1), these plates are listed as follows: "21 Manuale Catholicorum de l'Anglois."

86 The extra reference to breviaries in the 1589 A inventory was not added to the 1589 B inventory (see MPM Arch. 124, p. 1). In both the 1590 A inventory (MPM Arch. 99, p. 14, among the "new" engraved plates) and the 1590 B inventory (MPM Arch. 124, p. 321) there is a potentially related reference to ten new plates for a breviary (but then no mention of books of hours), with a slightly different format (8° instead of 16°) – recall that a comparable shift in format was also made for the twelve new Wierix plates for a breviary listed above. In the 1590 inventories, there is also a significant addition to the citation of these plates, namely, the identification of the designer (Maarten de Vos) and the engraver (Crispijn van de Passe). Most likely, these, together with the next group of thirty-six engravings of the Passion represent the group of forty-six plates by these artists that never appear to have been used. For all forty-six plates, see MPM KP 66–67 B, 150–170 B, 256–257 B, and 402–422 B. See the discussion of these plates in appendix 1 for more on the delivery of the plates and their potential, originally intended use. According to the 1590 B inventory, all of these plates were valued at 11 fl. per plate.

87 In both the 1590 A inventory (MPM Arch. 99, p. 14, among the "new" engraved plates) and the 1590 B inventory (MPM Arch. 124, p. 321) the reference to these plates includes the identification of Crispijn van de Passe as the engraver. According to the 1590 B inventory, these plates were valued at 11 fl. per plate. See also the preceding note.

88 In the 1589 B inventory (MPM Arch. 124, p. 1), the reference to the format of the plates is omitted, while the identification of the technique (etching ["ghebeten"]) was added. In both the 1590 A inventory (MPM Arch. 99, p. 13, among the "new" etched plates) and the 1590 B inventory (MPM Arch. 124,

INVENTORY OF PLANTIN'S COPPER PLATES IN LEIDEN
(MPM ARCH. 99, PP. 33–34)

1 Cornelii Valerii effigies (1 portrait of Cornelius Valerius)

1 Stewechii effigies (1 portrait of Stewechius)

   = G. Stewechius, *Commentarius ad Flavi Vegeti Renati libros*, 1585 (PP 2261).[89]

100 Figures de la Bible in f° quarré (100 figures from the bible in f°, square)[90]

   = H. Jansen van Barrefelt, *Imagines et figurae bibliorum . . .*, 1592 (see PP 631).[91]

80 Figures de la Bible in 4° longuet (80 figures from the bible in 4°, oblong)[92]

   = H. Jansen van Barrefelt, *Bibelsche figuren*, 1592 or 1593 (see PP 631).[93]

22 Figures de la Bible Royale (22 figures from the "Royal Bible")

   = *Biblia sacra* (= Polyglot Bible), 1568–1573 (PP 644).[94]

26 Usus et abusus rerum

   = B. Furmerius, *De rerum usu et abusu*, 1575 (PP 1228) and the 1585 edition in Dutch
   (PP 1229).[95]

56 Poëmata Gambarae (56 [plates to] Gambara's poems)

   = L. Gambara, *Rerum sacrarum liber*, 1577 (PP 1235).

66 Icones medicorum

   = J. Sambucus, *Icones veterum aliquot ac recentium medicorum*, 1574 (PP 2175).

53 Monumenta Hillesemii (53 [plates to] Hillessemius's Monumenta)

= L. Hillessemius, *Sacrarum antiquitatum monumenta*, 1577 (PP 1335).[96]

5 Effigies et Hierogl. Becani (5 [plates:] portrait and [illustrations to] Becanius's
   Hieroglyphica)

   = J. Goropius Becanus, *Opera*, 1580 (PP 1255).[97]

---

   p. 321) the subject matter of a comparable group of 175 etched plates is described as the Life of Christ
   ("Vita Christi" in the 1590 A inventory and "t leven Christi" in the 1590 B inventory). According to the
   1590 D inventory, these plates were valued at 2 fl. per plate.

[89] This portrait is the only engraving made by Hendrick Goltzius for Plantin (see appendix 1, p. 335–336).

[90] In MPM Arch. 99, p. 261, these plates are further specified as: "100 Figures de la Bible faictes à eau forte,
   les petites" (which is odd, as these plates are larger [roughly 190 × 155 mm] than those from the
   following series [usually *c*.98 × 224 mm] identified as "les grandes").

[91] See *New Holl., Van der Borcht*, pp. 3–5 and nos. 235–334, for this series, which does not appear to have
   been published until 1592.

[92] In MPM Arch. 99, p. 261, these plates are further specified as: "80 Figures de la Bible faictes à eau forte,
   les grandes." See n. 90 on the relative size of these plates.

[93] See *New Holl. Van der Borcht*, pp. 133–135 and nos. 335–422, for this series, which does not appear to
   have been published until 1592 or 1593 (and then with eighty-three plates, not just eighty), even though
   many of the plates were clearly executed in the 1580s.

[94] This group most likely comprised all of the engraved plates used to embellish the Polyglot Bible (one
   title-plate, five frontispieces, and sixteen text illustrations), with the possible exception of Philips
   Galle's original engraving of the shekel. For, when the original plates from volume VIII of the Polyglot
   Bible were reused in Franciscus Raphelengius's 1593 publication, the *Antiquitatum Iudaicarum libri IX*
   (which comprised many of Arias Montano's commentaries from the *Apparatus* of the Polyglot Bible),
   only Galle's engraving of the shekel was then replaced with an anonymous copy of the original
   engraving (see p. 334). For the original engraving (but not the copy), see in *New Holl., Galle*, 11, no. 226,
   where it is erroneously dated 1582 instead of 1572.

[95] See *New Holl., Van Groeningen*, 11, p. 24, for references to the subsequent use of these plates by other
   publishers.

[96] See the discussion of these plates above (pp. 379–380 and n. 59).

[97] As is evident from the copy of this text in MPM (A 293), this group of plates most likely comprised the
   introductory portrait of Goropius Becanus and the four engravings used to illustrate the section
   Hieroglyphica.

1 Effigies Iessei (1 portrait of Jessée)

    = J. de la Jessée, *Les premières œuvres françoyses*, 1583 (PP 1466).

1 Titulus Herb. Lobel (1 title-plate [to] Lobelius's herbal)

    = M. Lobelius, *Kruydtboeck*, 1581 (PP 1579).

1 Orbis terrarum Pomp. Melae (1 "orbis terrarum" [by] Pomponius Mela)

    = Pomponius Mela, *De situ orbis libri tres*, 1582 (PP 2082).

16 Saturnalia Lipsii (16 [plates to] Lipsius's Saturnalia)

    = J. Lipsius, *Saturnalium sermonum libri duo*, 4°, 1585 (PP 1557) and 1588 (PP 1558).

8 Amphitheatrum Lipsii (8 [plates to] Lipsius's Amphitheatro)

    = J. Lipsius, *De amphitheatro*, 1584 (PP 1530–1531) and 1585 (PP 1532–1533).

20 Ioyeuse entrée (20 [plates to] Joyous entry)

    = [Pierre Loyseleur de Villiers], *La joyeuse et magnifique entrée de Monseigneur Françoys . . . d'Anjou . . .*, 1582 (PP 1211)[98]

4 Plagghen[99]

Effigies Lipsii appartient au mesme Lipsius (portrait of Lipsius that belongs to Lipsius)[100]

Titulus inscriptionum aveq les blocqs en bois sunt curatorum (title-page of the "Inscriptionum" with the woodblocks, belong to the "curatores" [of the University of Leiden])[101]

461 Figures en cuivre taxees ensemble à fl. 637 st. _ (461 figures on copper, valued together at 637 fl.)

---

[98] The original publication comprised an engraved title-page and twenty-one illustrations, implying that two plates are missing from this group.

[99] This is not included specifically in the copy of the list of copper plates Plantin had at Leiden in MPM Arch. 99, p. 261.

[100] In MPM Arch. 99, p. 261, this plate is included in the list of Plantin's plates, among the other portraits with no indication as to who really owned it.

[101] In MPM Arch. 99, p. 261, this plate (listed together with the other plates, as the last item) is further specified as: "1 Titulus Inscriptionum, mais appartenant aux Curateurs de l'Université, comme faict à leur despens." (1 title of the "Inscriptionum," but belonging to the "curatores" of the University [of Leiden] as it was made at their expense.) The "Inscriptionum" presumably refers to the following work: Martinus Smetius (ed.), *Inscriptionum antiquarum quae passim per Europam, liber: Accessit auctarium a Justo Lipsio* (Leiden: Franciscus Raphelengius I, 1588) (see Adams 1967, II, S 1310).

EDITIONS WITH INTAGLIO ILLUSTRATIONS THAT PLANTIN PRINTED FOR OTHERS

In this appendix, we provide a list of all known works with engraved or etched illustrations for which Plantin was asked to print the accompanying text for a third party, who was partly or fully responsible for the project. Within this group of illustrated works, the third party, commonly defined as the "publisher" of the edition, was either a "pictorial printer" or print publisher – Philips Galle, Adriaen Huberti, Gerard de Jode, or Mynken Liefrinck – or the author of the text – Albert Hayen, Abraham Ortelius, Etienne Perret, or Lucas Janszoon Waghenaer. Occasionally, one of these figures also served as the engraver of the plates used to illustrate a given work, as Galle did, for example, for his publication *Instruction et fondements de bien pourtraire* from 1589 (see below). Generally, however, individuals who worked primarily as printmakers – the van Doetecum brothers, for example – were simply one of the "hired hands," like Plantin, and not the person who was organizing the project. The critical difference between the projects listed here and those discussed elsewhere in this book as Plantin's own is the matter of who controlled (owned) the plates.[1]

First we will present the works Plantin printed for print publishers and then the works published by independent authors. In both categories, the individuals will be discussed in alphabetical order, with their respective publications listed in chronological order. In the accompanying commentary, essential information on the publication and its illustrations is given, along with references to supplementary literature. Throughout, however, the focus will be on justifying the association of the publication with Plantin. The attribution of the printing of the text to Plantin is based upon one or more of the following types of evidence: (1) explicit references within the publication itself to Plantin as the printer or co-publisher of the edition; (2) archival data documenting the printing of the text at Plantin's Press; and (3) the decorative elements – in particular, the

---

[1] The primary exception to this rule is Clemens Perret's *Exercitatio alphabetica nova et utilissima* (PP 1961). Although Plantin did not own the plates making up this publication, it is, nevertheless, not included here because Plantin appears only to have loaned his name (and ability to procure a privilege) to the publication and did not print any text for it (see p. 66).

initials – that embellish the publication. Although an examination of the type used to print a text can also provide useful information concerning who may have printed it, we will not be drawing upon such analysis here. By the sixteenth century, it was common for various printers to own sets of matrices made from a single set of punches. Consequently, it is difficult to claim, for any common set of type, that it was the sole property of a single printer and, thus, an exclusive, identifying aspect of their work.[2]

Of the three aspects highlighted above, the identification of the decorative initials present in a publication is the most novel, although it is a recognized (and advocated) means of distinguishing a printer's work.[3] At first glance, it appears that this analysis can be easily and fruitfully applied in Plantin's case, thanks to Stephen Harvard's 1974 catalogue of Plantin's decorative initials and two publications of the woodcut initials in the collection of the Plantin-Moretus Museum. One of these, published by Max Rooses in 1896 and reprinted in 1905, contains both instructive samples of the typefaces still in the collection of the Plantin-Moretus Museum, in addition to impressions of decorative initials. Unfortunately, however, this publication is not as complete as it could be and also lacks the inventory numbers of the items reproduced, thereby making the specification of some letters difficult. An "in-house" publication with impressions of all of the woodblocks still preserved in the collection of the Plantin-Moretus Museum is complete – including text illustrations and other decorative elements used alongside of the initials. It also has the inventory references for each of the woodblocks that is reproduced.[4] While the Plantin-Moretus Museum's "publication" provides the most secure record of what Plantin may actually have owned and used, the Harvard catalogue is more complete (at least in terms of decorative initials), as it includes reproductions of initials from Plantin's publications where the original woodblock used to print it no longer exists.[5]

Such analysis must be used with caution, however, for there are three essential obstacles to identifying the printer of a text on the basis of the decorative materials used: (1) the regular practice of making more or less precise copies of woodblocks found in other printers' publications – thus, what one notes in one publication may actually have been copied from another printer's work; (2) the fact that some texts, while bearing the name of one printer-publisher, were actually printed for that person by an anonymous printer, possibly with the anonymous printer's own, independent typographical materials; and (3) the common convention among printers of buying up the type and other decorative materials formerly used by one printer to supplement their own stocks.

---

[2] Vervliet 1968, pp. 6, 10–11, and n. 3 on p. 6. Vervliet does believe that one can associate a printer with a collection of typefaces and identify him through this group. However, this sort of indepth analysis is beyond the scope of this work.

[3] For such recommendations, see, e.g., Janssen 2000, p. 192.

[4] See Harvard 1974 and Rooses 1896 for these publications. Regrettably, the Plantin-Moretus Museum's reproductions of its woodblocks are not published and serve simply as a visual record and internal inventory of all of the woodblocks in the museum that may only be consulted in its reading room.

[5] See, e.g., the discussion of Adriaen Huberti's 1587 Latin edition of R. Verstegen's *Theatrum crudelitatum haereticorum nostri temporis* below for an example of this.

Each of these practices is a concern when examining Plantin's production. He did use popular, commonly reproduced and copied sets of letters.[6] Plantin also periodically had texts that appeared under his name as publisher printed for him by independent printers, particularly in the period 1570–1576 when he was busy printing liturgical editions for Spain.[7] Finally, Plantin not only purchased other typographers' materials, but also endured having all of his own property sold at public auction in his absence on April 28, 1562. While he was able to recover part of his former stocks when restarting his business in 1563–1564, it is impossible to determine fully to what extent he was able to do so.[8] Consequently, some decorative letters that Harvard was only able to document in Plantin's earliest publications from the 1550s and for which the woodblocks are now lost, may not provide secure evidence of Plantin's involvement in the production of a text dated after 1562. For, those letters may have been sold at the auction of Plantin's goods in 1562 and then subsequently used by another printer in the late sixteenth-century.

The best single example of these problems is an 18 mm "Q" initial bearing the face of an old man with a hood over his head (fig. A5.1). Distinguishing Gerard de Jode's 1584 edition of his *Parvus mundus* (BT 1374), Stephen Harvard catalogues this as one of Plantin's "solitary" initials, present only in Plantin's 1555 edition (and 1556 reissue) of Antoine Mizauld's *Les ephemerides perpetuelles* (fig. A5.2).[9] But then again, the same initial – or is one an exceptionally close copy of the other? – also appears in some publications printed by Gillis Coppens van Diest I, including a 1540 edition of Petrus Apianus's *Cosmographia*, edited by Gemma Frisius, which he printed for Arnold Birckman, and his 1550 edition of Sebastian Serlio's *Des antiquites, le troisiesme livre translaté d'italien en franchois*, printed for Pieter Coecke van Aalst (fig. A5.3).[10] We compared enlarged reproductions of three of these initials, namely, from de Jode's 1584 edition of the *Parvus mundus*, Plantin's 1555 edition of Mizauld's *Les ephemerides perpetuelles*, and Serlio's *Des antiquites . . .* (fig. A5.4). While these enlargements reinforce our view that these three initials are exceptionally close, they also reveal minute discrepancies between the three impressions. Those distinguishing the initial from Coppens van Diest's edition of

---

[6] See, for example, Harvard 1974, cat. 20, for a set of 20 mm initials that Plantin regularly used (and had copied in wood for himself), that was also common to the work of other Antwerp printers. For example, a very similar set of initials was used by the Antwerp printer Gerard Smits for the 1578 edition of Gerard de Jode's *Speculum orbis terrarum* (BT 5577; Denucé, 1912–1913, I, pp. 181–198; and MPM [A 2880], 2 vols.). "Exact" copies could also be cast in metal (see Harvard 1974, pp. 5–6, for the problem of cast or cut copies of letters).

[7] For a list of these publications, many of which do not bear the name of the printers who did the work, see Voet, PP, VI, pp. 2592–2595. Occasionally, Plantin did lend out some of his typographical materials for such work. See, for example, Esteban de Garibay y Zamalloa's 1571 publication *Los XL libros d'el compendio historial de las chronicas . . .de España* (PP 1238), which is discussed below in conjunction with Gerard de Jode's 1579 edition of his *Parvus mundus* (BT 5898; MPM [R 55.18]).

[8] For examples of Plantin purchasing stocks of woodblocks from other printers, see Voet, GC, II, p. 229. On the public auction of Plantin's goods and his subsequent repurchase of at least a portion of the lost items, see Voet, GC, I, pp. 40–44 (on the sale of his possessions), Voet, GC, II, p. 106 (for his repurchase of some of his type), and the discussion of his de Valverde edition in ch. 3 for an example of his repurchase of some of his engraved plates.

[9] See Harvard 1974, cat. 58, for the initial; and PP 1704 and 1705 for the 1555 and 1556 editions of this text. We examined a copy of the 1555 edition, MPM (R 6.10).

[10] For the former, see NK 126; MPM (A 3486), fol. LVII v (= leaf PIV). For the latter, see BT 4330, MPM (R 17.11), fols. 35v, 50r, and 56v (among others).

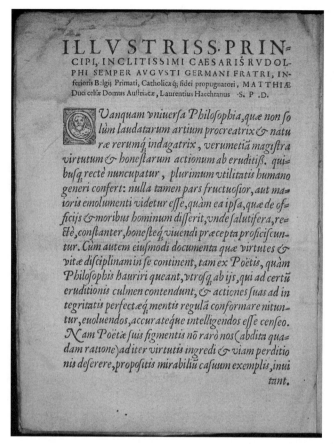

A5.1 Letter "Q" from Laurentius Haechtanus, Μικρόκοσμος. *Parvus mundus* (Antwerp: Gerard de Jode, 1584; 4°), fol. *2v, 18 × 16 (Brussels, The Royal Library, Rare Books Department, VH 22,364 A RP).

Des antiquites (fig. A5.4c) are the easiest to describe. Not only are the decorative diagonal lines in the lower right corner noticeably absent from the Coppens van Diest initial, but his initial alone also has slanting lines among the shortest background shading lines along the outer edges, in the middle of the right and left sides. These observations aside, the remaining two initials – that from de Jode's 1584 edition of his *Parvus mundus* (fig. A5.4a) and Plantin's 1555 edition of Mizauld's text (fig. A5.4b) – are themselves not identical. Compare, for example, the horizontal shading lines within the "Q" to the left and right of the man's head. Are these signs of wear or faults in a cut or cast copy of this initial? It is impossible to say on the basis of this limited sample.

A consideration of the type used to print the accompanying text is similarly inconclusive. On the one hand, it appears that Plantin did possess most, if not all, of the typefaces present in de Jode's publication.[11] The italic type featured in the body of the text was, for example, one of the types that Plantin had included in his 1567 *Index sive*

---

[11] We are indebted to Hendrik Vervliet for helping us identify these types.

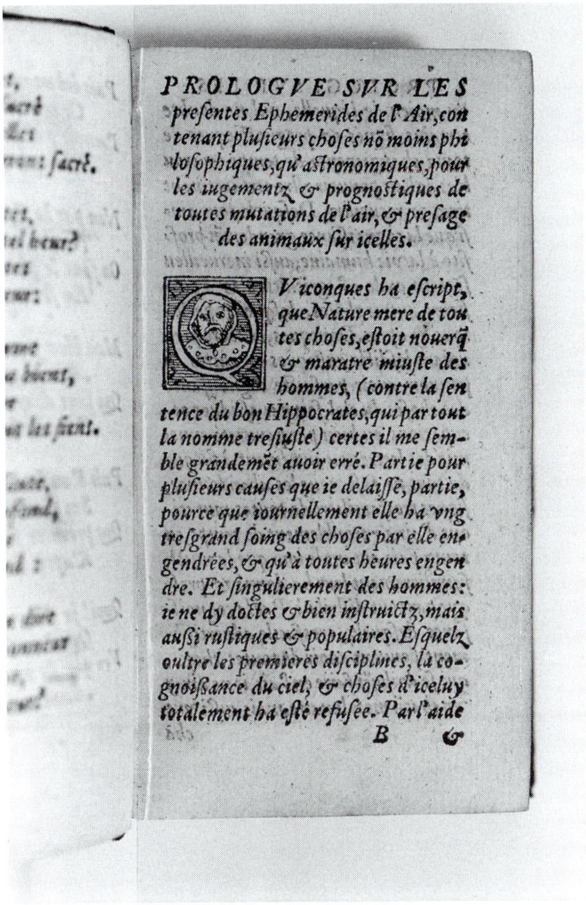
PROLOGVE SVR LES presentes Ephemerides de l'Air, contenant plusieurs choses nõ moins philosophiques, qu'astronomiques, pour les iugementz & prognostiques de toutes mutations de l'air, & presage des animaux sur icelles.

QViconques ha escript, que Nature mere de toutes choses, estoit nouerq̃ & maratre iniuste des hommes, (contre la sentence du bon Hippocrates, qui par tout la nomme tresiuste) certes il me semble grandemẽt auoir erré. Partie pour plusieurs causes que ie delaisse, partie, pource que iournellement elle ha vng tresgrand soing des choses par elle engendrées, & qu'à toutes heures engendre. Et singulierement des hommes: ie ne dy doctes & bien instruictz, mais aussi rustiques & populaires. Esquelz oultre les premieres disciplines, la cognoissance du ciel, & choses d'iceluy totalement ha esté refusée. Par l'aide

B &

A5.2 Letter "Q" from Antoine Mizauld, *Les ephemerides perpetuelles* (Antwerp: Christopher Plantin, 1566; 12°), fol. B1r, 18 × 18 (Antwerp, Museum Plantin-Moretus, R 6.10).

specimen characterum Christophori Plantini (see fol. B4 r, under "I. Offic.").[12] However, like the Roman typefaces used for the introductory lines of text at the top of the page, it was a popular typeface that was used simultaneously by other printers. In the case of the italic type, one of the other printers associated with it is, notably, Gillis Coppens van Diest I, whose "Q" initial of the hooded man so closely resembles that included in de Jode's 1584 text.[13]

It is tempting to associate Plantin's Press with the printing of the text for de Jode's 1584 edition of his *Parvus mundus*, simply because of the other printing jobs Plantin's sons-in-law executed for de Jode that same year (see below). Nevertheless, we believe that the evidence to date in support of this claim – a highly similar initial that Plantin

[12] We examined a copy of this work in MPM (A 2007). It is also reproduced in Vervliet and Carter 1972, as specimen no. 19 of Plantin's 1567 *Index sive specimen characterum Christophori Plantini* (PP 2075).

[13] See Vervliet 1968, It2, pp. 286–287.

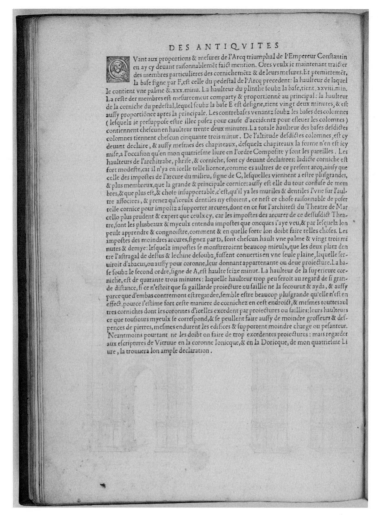

A5.3 Letter "Q" from Sebastian Serlio, *Des antiquites, le troisiesme liure translaté d'italien en franchois* (Antwerp: Gillis Coppens van Diest I for Pieter Coecke van Aalst, 1550; f°), fol. 56v, 18 × 16 (Antwerp, Museum Plantin-Moretus, R 17.11).

is only known to have used around 1555 and type that not only he but other Antwerp printers may have had in stock – cannot definitively support an attribution of this printing job to Plantin and does not preclude the possibility that the work was done by another printer, such as Gillis Coppens van Diest II.

The preceding example is far more ambiguous than any of the works discussed below. In all of these cases, we have endeavored to combine different types of evidence – archival data with typographical analysis, for example – or to draw our conclusions from typographical materials that appear to be unique to or pervasive among Plantin's publications in order to make attributions as firm as possible. The locations of copies of the work under consideration are given in the reference works listed with it. Specific copies are cited in the notes when these were important for the analysis.

| (a) De Jode | (b) Plantin | (c) Coppens van Diest |

A5.4 a, b, and c Enlarged details of the three preceding letters. Are these examples of the letter "Q" the same or different?

PRINT PUBLISHERS

PHILIPS GALLE

1574: *Fontium puteorumque iconicas delineationes* (Antwerp: [C. Plantin for] P. Galle, 1574) oblong 4°

Refs.: *Holl. Dutch & Flemish*, XLVIII, nos. 384–407; *New Holl., Van Doetecum*, III, nos. 703–726; Sellink 1997, I, p. 22.

The brothers Jan and Lucas van Doetecum executed this series of twenty-four etchings of "Precise Drawings of Springs and Wells" after designs by Hans Vredeman de Vries. Published without a title-page or title-plate, this series was occasionally sold with a typographically printed dedicatory text on the back of the first print.[14] Dated 1574, Galle's dedication to Melchior Lorch supplies not only the approximate date and title of the series, but also the evidence that Plantin was responsible for printing it. Specifically, the decorative letter "H," marking the start of the text, is part of a set of 30 mm Roman letters with stylized botanical decoration that Plantin regularly used throughout his career.[15] Although we did not find any archival references to the printing of this text, a manuscript version of it is preserved in the Plantin-Moretus Museum.[16] In this version, the dedication closes with: "Antverpiae, ex nostro chalcographia . . . MCCCCCLXIIII" (In Antwerp, from our printing house, 1564). The date (which was corrected to 1574 in the printed version) led Jan Denucé to conclude, incorrectly, that Galle had established a business in Antwerp by 1564.[17] Plantin does not appear to have purchased copies of this print series, nor did he include it in his own list of Galle's publications.[18]

[14] In each of the works cited above, a copy with the dedicatory text is said to be preserved in the Prentenkabinet of the Plantin-Moretus Museum. No call number is ever given for this copy, however, and we have yet to be able to trace it ourselves. For the following discussion, we examined the dedicatory text printed on the verso of the first plate of the series preserved in the Öffentliche Kunstsammlung in Basel (Bd. M 81, fols. 88–111).

[15] Harvard 1974, cat. 12.   [16] See MPM Arch. 82, fol. 381bis, for this text.

[17] Denucé, 1912–1913, I, pp. 221–223. Denucé apparently did not know of the printed version of this text.

[18] See ch. 6 for Plantin's purchases from Galle and his list of Galle's publications (MPM M 296, fol. 388r; see fig. 6.8).

1574: *Libellus varios regionum tractus continens* (Antwerp: [C. Plantin for] P. Galle, [1574]) oblong 4°

Refs.: *Holl. Dutch & Flemish*, III, nos. 164–193; *New Holl.*, *Galle*, IV, R 17; Sellink 1997, I, p. 22.

Hans Bol supplied the designs for this series of thirty landscapes, which were etched by an unknown artist. As with the prints of wells discussed above, while this series lacks a title-page, some copies do have a dedicatory text printed typographically on the back of the first plate.[19] Galle's dedication to Petrus Scoliers is concluded simply with the place of publication (Antwerp) and the date (1574). The 22 mm decorative initial "C" marking the start of the body of the text, however, clearly indicates that Plantin's materials were used to print it, for this same letter was also used for the printing of several other Plantin editions. Compare, for example, Caesar Baronius's *Martyrologium Romanum* (Antwerp: C. Plantin, 1589), p. 130 (among other pages), and Franciscus Aguilon's *Opticorum libri sex* (Antwerp: *Officina Plantiniana*, 1613), p. 328 (among others).[20] We have yet to find any archival references to the printing of this text, nor did Plantin ever appear to buy copies of it or include it in his list of Galle's publications.[21]

1575: *David, hoc est virtutis exercitatissimae probatum Deo spectaculum* (Antwerp: C. Plantin for P. Galle, 1575) oblong 4°

Refs.: BT 1205 and 5832; Hänsel 1991, pp. 118–127; Melion 2005, pp. 73–90; *New Holl.*, *Van Groeningen*, II, nos. 265–285; PP 580; Sellink 1997, I, pp. 25, 91–92.

Dedicated by Galle to Philip II, this series of forty-eight engravings from the life of the biblical King David was intended to serve as a model of behavior for contemporary rulers. With inscriptions composed by B. Arias Montano, the compositions are attributed in part to Gerard van Groeningen and in part to Crispin van den Broeck. Jan Sadeler I is credited with the engraving of the plates. Here, Plantin's involvement in the project is clearly stated in the imprint, which reads: "Antverpiae, Ex officina Christoph. Plantini, Architypog. Regij. M. D. LXXV." However, we have yet to find any archival data documenting either payments Plantin would have made to his staff for producing this edition, or a charge to Galle for the printing of this text. What is evident from archival documents is that Plantin periodically purchased copies of the finished book from Galle.[22] This suggests that Galle served as sole publisher of this edition and was not involved in a sort of joint venture with Plantin, as is suggested by both Sellink and

---

[19] See, e.g., the copy in Coburg, Kunstsammlungen der Veste (Inv. VII. 104. 724 [verso]).

[20] Although comparable in style to the set of 22 mm Roman initials with arabesque decoration that are described in Harvard 1974, cat. 19, this particular block is not included there or in the Plantin-Moretus Museum's inventory of its woodblocks. For Baronius's *Martyrologium Romanum*, see, e.g., PP 626; for Aguilon's *Opticorum libri sex*, see, e.g., Simoni 1990, A 36. We examined the following copies of these books: MPM (A 284), for the former, and MPM (A 946), for the latter.

[21] See n. 18.

[22] This work is included in Plantin's list of Galle's publications (MPM M 296, fol. 388r), under the title "Speculum Davidis," at a price of 20 st. (or 1 fl.) per copy. Plantin's earliest known purchase of this text dates to June 18, 1575, when he bought twenty copies at 20 st. per copy (see MPM Arch. 18, fol. 64 rht). Plantin continued to purchase copies of this text intermittently – for a total of approximately fifty copies – up until January 29, 1589. For these purchases, see MPM Arch. 18, fols. 64 rht, 187 rht, and 321 rht, and MPM Arch. 20, fols. 57 rht, 146 rht, and 307 rht.

Voet.[23] For, in other, better documented cases of Plantin's and Galle's joint projects (see chapter 6), not only were the costs, but also the resulting copies, divided equally between Galle and Plantin. Any subsequent purchases of copies by either Galle or Plantin were rare and limited to only a few copies.

1575: Furmerius, Bernardus, *De rerum usu et abusu* (Antwerp: C. Plantin [& P. Galle], 1575) 4° (figs. 6.9–6.11)

Refs.: BB, III, p. 57 (F 15); BT 1202; *Holl. Dutch & Flemish*, LXX, book no. 21; M-H 2289–2314; *New Holl.*, *Van Groeningen*, II, nos. 221–246; PP 1228; Sellink, I, pp. 26 and 33.[24]

Fashioned like an emblem book, this moralizing tract on justice and injustice comprises twenty-five engravings designed by Gerard van Groeningen and engraved, at least in part, by Jan Wierix.[25] Plantin's involvement in the publication is clear from the imprint, which reads: "Antverpiae, ex officina Christophori Plantini Architypographi Regij. M.D. LXXV." As is discussed in greater detail in chapter 6, this is the first clearly documented example of a "joint venture" between Plantin and Philips Galle, in which the production costs and the resulting copies were divided equally between the two men.[26]

1577: Heyns, Pieter, *Spieghel der werelt* (Antwerp: C. Plantin for P. Galle, 1577) oblong 4°

Refs.: BT 2293; Koeman 1967–1971, III, Ort. 47; PP 1828.

Galle's *Spieghel der werelt* ("Mirror of the World") was roughly based upon Abraham Ortelius's *Theatrum orbis terrarum*, which was first published in 1570. Representing the first edition of what would become an extremely popular pocket atlas, the 1577 *Spieghel der werelt* consists of seventy-two maps, which were accompanied by brief commentaries written in Dutch by Pieter Heyns. These plates, along with additional ones Galle commissioned for the enlargement of his pocket atlas in the 1580s, remained in Galle's possession throughout the period that he employed Plantin to print the accompanying texts for these editions. In 1612, Plantin's grandsons, Jan Moretus II and Balthasar Moretus I, purchased all of the plates for the pocket atlas at an auction of the possessions of Jan Baptist Vrints I's widow. Nevertheless, the Moretuses do not appear to have ever used these plates themselves and may well have sold them in turn, as they are no

---

[23] See Sellink 1997, I, p. 91, and PP 580, n. 2.

[24] In both Sellink 1997 and the Hollstein volumes, the authors follow one theory (see the respective literature lists) that this text was originally conceived of by Dirck Volkertsz. Coornhert and translated into Latin by Furmerius without mention of Coornhert's name due to Coornhert's sensitive position in the Low Countries at the time. However, in a recently up-dated overview of Coornhert's work (Bonger 2004, p. 287), the standard attribution of the original text to Furmerius is supported and Coornhert is credited with translating it.

[25] Plate 2 in this series (fig. 6.11) clearly bears the IHW monogram of Jan Wierix on the barrel in the lower left, while traces of his monogram are evident (according to Mauquoy-Hendrickx) on plates 3, 4, and 7. In both M-H *Wierix* and *Holl. Dutch & Flemish*, LXX (see above), Jan Wierix is credited with engraving the entire series.

[26] See ch. 6 for a detailed discussion of this text. Plantin's subsequent Dutch edition of it, *Recht ghebruyck ende misbruyck van tydlycke have*, published in Leiden in 1585 (PP 1229; BT 5826), is not listed here because, as argued above, it appears that by the time it was published, Plantin had compensated Galle for his share of the plates and thus had full control of (and financial responsibility for) the entire project.

longer in the collection of the Plantin-Moretus Museum.[27] Plantin's role as the printer of the texts for this first edition is clear from the imprint, which reads: "T'Antwerpen, ghedruckt by Christoffel Plantyn, hooft-drucker der Conincklycke M[teyt]. voor Philips Galle. M.D.LXXVII." This role is confirmed by Plantin's record books. Payments for the printing of the text were made to the pressman Hans Clas from August 9 through September 14, 1577, and by November 9, 1577, Galle was charged 21 fl. 3 st. for this work.[28] By August 16, 1578 (a little less than a year after the work's completion), Plantin had purchased a total of forty-four copies of this text from Galle.[29]

1578: *Text for a map* (precise title not known)

On November 22, 1578, the compositor Hans Han and the pressman Guillaume Rivière were paid 30 st. and 12 st., respectively, for setting and printing a "carte de Gal" (map of Galle).[30] This may refer to Galle's map of the Netherlands, which was first published in 1578 with an accompanying Latin text. In 1579, Plantin then printed both a Dutch and a French translation of the original Latin text in book form, under the titles, *Een cort verhael van de gedincweerdichste saken . . . in de XVII Provincien vande Nederlanden* and *Sommaire annotation des choses plus memorables advenues . . . és XVII provinces du Pais Bas.*[31]

1578: Vosmerus, Michael, *Principes Hollandiae et Zelandiae, domini Frisiae* (Antwerp: C. Plantin for P. Galle, 1578) f° (fig. 6.14)

Refs.: BT 4802; *New Holl., Galle*, IV, R 25; PP 2475; Sellink 1997, I, pp. 33–34 and p. 65.

Comprising thirty-six engraved, full-length portraits of the counts of Holland and Zeeland, Vosmerus's summary overview of the lives of these men was the first of several publications to feature this series of images.[32] Galle's role as the publisher of this work is indicated not only by the imprint, but by an inscription on the engraved vignette on the title-page, which reads: "Phillippus Galle. excud. Cum privilegio. Regis. 1578." (Philips

---

[27] See MPM Arch. 183, pp. 1–3, for a list of all the items the Moretuses purchased at the Vrints's auction, in April 1612 in Antwerp (and p. 3 for this particular case). For other examples of plates they bought at this auction, see the discussion below of Galle's editions of the *Deorum dearumque capita . . . ex musaeo Abrahami Ortelii* and Ortelius's atlas.

[28] For the payment to Clas, see MPM Arch. 32, fol. 234 rht. The general charge to Galle reads as follows: "Item pour compte faict avec C. Plantin de limpression du Miroir en flamen 23¹/₂ [rames] a 18 st. la rame font 21 fl. 3 st." (Item for the account with C. Plantin for the printing of the *Miroir* in Flemish, 23¹/₂ reams at 18 st. a ream, comes to 21 fl. 3 st.) (MPM Arch. 18, fol. 253 lft.)

[29] This publication is referred to generally (without the specification of the year of publication) in Plantin's list of Galle's publications (MPM M 296, fol. 388r), under the title "Spiegel der werelt," with a price of 22 st. per copy. For an overview of Plantin's part in the production of these pocket atlases and his subsequent purchase of them, see Imhof 1999b, pp. 89–90.

[30] See MPM Arch. 32, fol. 289 lft, for the payment to Han; and fol. 297 lft for the payment to Rivière.

[31] For Galle's map of the Netherlands, see, e.g., Schilder, II (1987), pp. 111–122, especially pp. 118–119. There is no known copy of Galle's 1578/1579 issue of this map. For more on the original map and the subsequent publications of it, see ch. 6 and Sellink 1997, I, p. 32. Neither the original map nor the Dutch or French editions of the subsequently printed book appear to be included in Plantin's list of Galle's publications in MPM M 296, fol. 388r.

[32] For the later use of these plates, see the discussions below of the French translation of Vosmerus's text that Galle published in 1583 and 1586.

Galle publisher. With royal privilege. 1578.)[33] Plantin's involvement in this project is similarly indicated by the imprint, which reads: "Antverpiae Excudebat Christophorus Plantinus Philippo Gallaeo. M.D.LXXVIII." Galle's employment of Plantin for the printing of the text is documented by a charge of 22 fl. for "het drucken vande graven van hollandt" (the printing of the counts of Holland), which was noted shortly after November 1577 in Galle's running accounts with Plantin.[34] Payments made to Plantin's staff make it clear that the actual work was done between early December 1577 and the first week of January 1578.[35] There is no evidence to support Sellink's or Van der Stock's supposition that this was another joint project between Plantin and Galle.[36] The charge to Galle for the printing of the text was not noted among the other accounts of their joint projects and there are no records of Plantin having to pay Galle for a portion of the total costs. Moreover, as was the case with other of Galle's own publications, Plantin regularly purchased completed copies of the book from Galle from February 1578 onwards.[37] Finally, as Plantin's production of his 1584 edition of Adrianus Barlandus's *Hollandiae comitum historia et icones* makes clear, Galle also maintained exclusive control over the plates used to illustrate this and related editions.[38] By 1673, the Moretuses had acquired all of the portraits, as well as the title-page vignette for the series, but there is no evidence that they ever used them for a new publication.[39]

1579: Freitagius, Arnoldus, *Mythologia ethica, hoc est moralis philosophiae per fabulas brutis attributas traditae amoenissimum viridarium* (Antwerp: C. Plantin for P. Galle, 1579) 8° (fig. 6.22)

Refs.: BT 5820; PP 1214.

This moralizing collection of 125 illustrated and annotated animal fables was clearly inspired by Edward de Dene's *De warachtighe fabulen der dieren* (Bruges: Pieter de Clerck for Marcus Gheeraerts I, 1567), in terms of both its content and the plates used to illustrate it. For all 107 of Gheeracrts I's etchings used to illustrate de Dene's text were reused here, along with 18 additional etched text illustrations and a new plate for the title-page. Precisely the same set of 125 illustrations (but a different title-plate) was

---

33 This same inscription was still on the plate when it was used for the printing of the 1583 French translation of this text (PP 2476), despite the then inaccurate dating. It was removed prior to the illustration of the 1586 edition (PP 2477). Both of these French translations are discussed below.

34 MPM Arch. 18, fol. 253 lft.

35 See MPM Arch. 32, fol. 270 rht, for payments to the compositor Hans Han, and fol. 272 rht and lft, for payments to the pressman Guillaume Rivière.

36 Sellink 1997, I, p. 65; and Van der Stock 1998, n. 86 (p. 243), where he also attributes the design of the portraits to Willem Thybaut of Haarlem.

37 This publication is listed among Philips Galle's publications in MPM M 296, fol. 388r, under the title "Comites Hollandiae Princip. Zeland," with two prices: 18 st. and 20 st. It is not clear what the difference between these two prices signified. Plantin usually – but not always, see MPM Arch. 20, fol. 57 rht – paid just 18 st. per copy. For Plantin's initial purchase of this text in 1578, see MPM Arch. 18, fol. 253 rht, under February 15. For examples of Plantin's later purchases of the French edition of this text, see, e.g., MPM Arch. 20, fol. 307 rht, between December 30, 1588 and August 17, 1589.

38 See ch. 6.

39 For the listing of these plates in the Moretuses' 1673 inventory of their stock of copper plates, see MPM Arch. 124, p. 45. Galle's original plates are still preserved in the Plantin-Moretus Museum, under the numbers: KP 43–76C, 91C, 98C, and KP 112C (for the title-page vignette).

also used to illustrate a French edition of this text, the *Esbatement moral des animaux*, that was similarly published by Galle, but with a text printed a year earlier (in 1578) by the Antwerp printer Gerard Smits. Thus, it appears that Galle had acquired the original Gheeraerts etchings – and not Plantin, as Delen once suggested – and was the one in control of them.[40] The additional 18 text illustrations are generally also attributed to Gheeraerts, who was back in Antwerp at this time (following a temporary flight to London) and was collaborating with Galle on the publication of his prints.[41] Consequently, if Galle had obtained the original set of illustrations, it would not have been difficult for him to commission Gheeraerts to make the additional images he desired. Plantin's involvement in the production of the text for Galle's *Mythologia ethica* is evident from the imprint on the title-page, which reads: "Antverpiae, Philippo Gallaeo Christophorus Plantinus excudebat, M.D.LXXIX." Plantin's exact contributions are revealed by records of the individual payments to Plantin's staff for the setting and printing of this text in July and August 1579, as well as the final charge of 60 fl. to Galle for the printing of the text and the paper used. If one totals the payments made to the compositor and to the pressmen who worked on this project, it appears that Plantin paid at least 28 fl. 18 st. for this work (20 fl. 8 st. for the setting and 8 fl. 10 st. for the printing). This would leave approximately half of the 60 fl. that Galle was charged to cover the costs of the paper used.[42] As is discussed in greater detail in chapter 6, Plantin purchased numerous copies of not only this edition of the text, but also Galle's 1578 French edition, the *Esbatement moral*, with texts printed by G. Smits instead of Plantin.[43]

---

[40] For Delen's postulation, see Delen 1924–1935, II.1, p. 141. Although E. Hodnett accepts this theory (see Hodnett 1971, pp. 13 and 33), we agree with Voet (see PP 1214, n. 3) that Delen's suggestion that Plantin had acquired the Gheeraerts plates seems improbable. Not only is Delen's evidence for this claim – a record of payment of 5 fl. to "la femme des fables" (the wife of the fables) in Bruges – far too vague, but it would also represent a remarkably inexpensive price of approximately 1 st. per plate for 107 etchings that were in a good enough state to be used to illustrate at least two more publications. Lucien Scheler mistakenly asserts that the illustrations in the *Mythologia ethica* are reversed copies of Gheeraerts's original illustrations (see Scheler 1968, p. 352). See ch. 6 for more on these editions.

[41] For examples of the collaboration between Galle and Gheeraerts in this period, see, e.g., Sellink 1997, I, p. 33. In *Holl. Dutch & Flemish*, VII, p. 100, all of these plates are attributed to Gheeraerts, although reproductions of them on p. 100 are regrettably printed in reverse, while the image of *Death Accosting a Man* was not included in the 1567 de Dene publication, but is, rather, one of the eighteen new plates included in Galle's fable editions from 1578 and 1579. For a broader overview of Gheeraerts's work for these publications and their subsequent influence see, e.g., Hodnett 1971, pp. 31–41. Finally, for an alternative view as to the authorship of these additional illustrations, see Harthan 1981, p. 75.

[42] See MPM Arch. 18, fol. 321 lft, for the following general charge of 60 fl. to Galle, noted between August 15 and September 2, 1579: "p[our] trois rames du papier etc. p[our] impression des fables en Latin p[ar] compte faict . . . fl. 60" (for three reams of paper and for the printing of the fables in Latin, for the entire account . . . 60 fl.). For the individual payments made to Plantin's staff between July 4 and August 14, 1579, see MPM Arch. 32, fol. 264 rht, for the pressman Hendrik Smesman, fol. 265 lft, for the compositor Adriaen vande Velde, fol. 297 rht, for the pressman Guillaume Rivière; and MPM Arch. 33, fol. 5 lft, for the pressman Nicolas van Linschoten.

[43] Both the French and Latin editions of this text are listed among Galle's publications in MPM M 296, fol. 388r, under the titles "Esbatiment moral" (at a price of 25 st. per copy) and "Mythologia ethica" (at a price of 27 st. per copy). Plantin's first purchase of the former is noted on October 21, 1578 (MPM Arch. 18, fol. 282 rht), while his first purchase of the latter is listed at an unspecified date at the end of 1579 (MPM Arch. 18, fol. 321 rht). Ultimately, by August 17, 1589, Plantin (or Jan Moretus) had purchased approximately fifty copies of each of these editions from Galle (see MPM Arch. 18, fols. 282 rht and 321 rht, as well as MPM Arch. 20, fols. 146 rht, 228 rht, and 307 rht).

1579: *Description of Maastricht* (precise title not known)

Refs.: Sellink 1997, I, p. 32.

In 1579 (possibly in the month of May), Galle was charged 7 fl. for "imprimé 2 rames d'escripture p. le pourtraict de Maestricht" (printed 2 reams of [the] text for the image of Maastricht).[44] This may refer to an accompanying text for a map of the Spanish siege of Maastricht that Galle published in 1579.[45]

1579: *Map of France* (precise title not known)

On January 10, 1579, the compositor Hans Han was paid 5 fl. for setting "lescriture de la carte de franc. de Galle in folio et recouru in 16° magno aut 8 parvo" (the text for Galle's map of France and rearranged in large 16 or small 8 [book formats]).[46] We have yet to identify precisely which map is meant.

1579: *Typographic work for unspecified projects*

In May 1579, Galle was charged 6 fl. and then an additional 3 fl. for unspecified printing work done for him by the Plantin Press.[47]

1579: Heyns, Pieter, *Le miroir du monde* (Antwerp: C. Plantin for P. Galle, 1579) oblong 4° (fig. 6.13)

Refs.: BT 2292; Koeman 1967–1971, III, Ort. 48; PP 1829.

This is the first French edition of Galle's popular pocket atlas, the "Mirror of the World," with seventy-two maps and new accompanying texts by Pieter Heyns, derived primarily from those included in Abraham Ortelius's 1572 French edition of his atlas, the *Theatre du monde*.[48] Plantin's involvement in the project is indicated by the imprint, which reads: "A Anvers, de l'imprimerie de Christophle Plantin, pour Philippe Galle. M.D.LXXIX." As with the Dutch edition, Plantin's precise role is clarified by archival records. For, in January 1579, Plantin made payments to his compositor, Andries Spors, and to the pressmen Nicolas van Cullen and Nicolas Spors, for the setting and printing of the text.[49] By May 1579, Galle was charged 33 fl. for the printing of 500 copies of the text.[50]

---

44 MPM Arch. 18, fol. 282 lft. This payment may refer to the work of the compositor, Andries Spors, who was paid (an unspecified amount) on February 28, 1579 for work on "la carte de Galles" (Galle's map) (MPM Arch. 32, fol. 296 lft).

45 Sellink 1997, I, p. 32. There is no clear reference to this map in Plantin's list of Galle's publications in MPM M 296, fol. 388r, nor any known copy of this specific edition.

46 MPM Arch. 32, fol. 289 lft.

47 See MPM Arch. 18, fol. 282 lft, for the following brief, unspecified entries: "pour limpression a 6 flor." (for printing at 6 fl.) and (several entries further down) "Item van drucken . . . fl. 3." (Idem for printing . . . 3 fl.).

48 Imhof 1999b, p. 90. Ortelius's atlases are discussed in greater detail below.

49 See MPM Arch. 32, fols. 296 lft (for the payments to A. Spors) and 231 rht (for the payments to van Cullen); and MPM Arch. 33, fol. 2 rht (for the payment to N. Spors).

50 For this general charge, see MPM Arch. 18, fol. 282 lft, which reads: "Item pour l'impression du Miroer en françois, de 22 bladeren tot eenen riem het blat tot 30 st. bedraecht fl. 33." (Idem for the printing of the French *Miroir*, of each of the 22 folios one ream, at 30 st. for each folio, comes to 33 fl.)

Galle thereby retained possession of the plates and appeared to serve as the publisher.[51] However, once Galle had added the illustrations to the printed text, Plantin then began to buy back all of the fully illustrated copies for further sale via his bookshop.[52] As will be documented below, similar arrangements were made for the following French editions of Galle's pocket atlas, which appeared in 1583 and 1588: Plantin first printed the text at Galle's expense and then repurchased all of the copies once Galle had seen to illustrating them. In all three cases, Plantin then sold the majority of the copies to Michel Sonnius I, the bookseller in Paris who had taken over Plantin's shop there.[53]

1580: *Divinarum nuptiarum conventa et acta* (Antwerp: C. Plantin for P. Galle, 1580) oblong 4°

Refs.: BT 1209; Hänsel 1991, pp. 100–118; *Holl. Dutch & Flemish*, LXX, book no. 13; M-H 1978–1982; Melion 2005, pp. 98–107; *New Holl., Van Groeningen*, II, nos. 286–313; PP 1215; Sellink 1997, I, pp. 88–91.

This series consists of twenty-eight allegorical images on the journey of the Christian soul towards Christ, portrayed as a sacred marriage.[54] The engravings were designed by Gerard van Groeningen and engraved, at least in part, by Jan Wierix. They were originally published in 1573 and 1574 – first with only Latin verses written by Arias Montano and then with an accompanying French version of the text by Pieter Heyns. Both of these editions bear colophons with the name of the printer Anthonis Coppens van Diest.[55] Arnoldus Freitagius wrote a new dedicatory text for the 1580 edition, while Arias Montano's verses were replaced with texts in prose. Plantin's involvement in the production of the 1580 edition is clearly indicated by the imprint, which reads: "Antverpiae, excudebat Christophorus Plantinus, Architypographus regius, Philippo Gallaeo. (I).I).LXXX [= M.D.LXXX]."[56] It is confirmed by Plantin's charge to Galle for 6 fl. for work "inde bruyloft" (in the wedding) in May 1579.[57] Plantin purchased numerous copies of this series of images between August 1573 and December 1581 at 35 st. per copy. While it is clear that the majority of these would have been copies of the

---

[51] For more on the plates, see the discussion above of the 1577 edition of Galle's *Spieghel der werelt*.

[52] For Plantin's repurchase of all 500 copies of this edition (for 450 fl.), see MPM Arch. 18, fol. 143 rht. Like the Dutch edition of this text, there is a general reference to it (without the specification of the year of publication) in the list of Galle's publications in MPM M 296, fol. 388r, under the title "Miroir du monde" (at a price of 26 st.).

[53] For examples of Sonnius's purchase of the 1579 edition, see, e.g., MPM Arch. 57, fols. 33v and 81r. These arrangements are discussed in greater detail in ch. 6 and in Imhof 1999b, pp. 90–91.

[54] Melion 2005, p. 98.

[55] For an example of the 1573 Latin edition with a colophon bearing the address of Anthonis Coppens van Diest, see SBA (H 152255) – although, this copy is clearly a patched-up version of the original, with some prints cut out and pasted on to other pages. For an example of the 1573–1574 French-Latin edition, see KBR (LP 129 A).

[56] In Sellink 1997, I, p. 34, he gives the date of the third publication of these engravings as 1583. This is presumably a typographical error for 1580. Rather, following the 1580 edition, these plates would not be published again until 1642 (see, e.g., *New Holl., Van Groeningen*, II, p. 69). For a copy of the 1580 edition, see, e.g., KBR (II 16,387).

[57] See MPM Arch. 18, fol. 282 lft, for this record, which reads: "Inde bruyloft blaederens gedruckt acht bladeren elck eenen boek tot 20 sts. fl. 6." (In the wedding sheets, printed: eight sheets, each one quire, at 20 st. [amounts to] 6 fl.)

original 1573 and 1574 editions, it remains unclear whether or not the last purchases (made in December 1581) were of the new, 1580 edition.[58]

1582: *Deorum dearumque capita . . . ex musaeo Abrahami Ortelii* (Antwerp: [C. Plantin for] P. Galle, 1582) 8°

Refs.: BT 2286; Hänsel 1991, p. 102; *Holl. Dutch & Flemish*, XLVIII, nos. 353–383; *New Holl., Van Doetecum*, III, nos. 657–702; *New Hollstein, Galle*, IV, R 22; *New Holl., Van Groeningen*, I, nos. 25–36, and II, nos. 406–417; Sellink 1997, I, p. 34.

Several artists – Gerard van Groeningen, Hans Vredeman de Vries, and Lucas or Johannes van Doetecum – contributed to the completion of this set of fifty-five plates, which illustrate a group of ancient coins in the possession of Abraham Ortelius.[59] On the basis of the decorative initials used in the printing of the text, it is clear that, while the first edition (from 1573) was printed for Galle with materials belonging to Gillis I or Anthonis Coppens van Diest, this second edition (from 1582) was printed for Galle by Plantin.[60] The latter attribution is confirmed by several of the decorative initials used. Specifically, the 15 mm "Q" initial on fol. Aij r, the 15 mm "P" initial on fol. Aij v, and the 20 mm "P" initial on fol. Aiij r, are all readily identifiable as Plantin initials.[61] The only known archival record that might reflect the printing of this edition is an unspecified charge of 3 fl. for "twee bladeren te drucken" (two sheets of printing), noted in Galle's accounts on or shortly after September 23, 1582.[62] Although Plantin purchased a few copies of the original edition of this text, we have yet to find records indicating that he purchased copies of this later edition as well.[63] The plates used to illustrate this work were eventually bought by Jan Baptist Vrints I and used for one of his own publications in 1602. Ultimately, however, in 1612, Plantin's grandsons, Jan Moretus II and Balthasar Moretus I, purchased all of these plates, together with unsold copies of books illustrated with them, at an auction of the possessions of Jan Baptist Vrints I's widow, and reissued the publication that same year. The Moretuses presumably sold the plates (and possibly their unsold copies) in turn at some point prior to François Foppens's publication of the work in Brussels in 1683.[64]

---

[58] In Plantin's list of Galle's publications in MPM M 296, fol. 388r, a work cited as "Nuptiae sacrae" (holy weddings) (at a price of 35 st.) may refer to any of the known editions of this text. For Plantin's first known purchase of this series, see MPM Arch. 16, fol. 172 rht. For his last, see MPM Arch. 18, fol. 394 rht.

[59] For these attributions see the Hollstein volumes cited under the references for this publication.

[60] For the attribution of the 1573 edition (BT 2286) to the Coppens van Diest family, see ch. 6, p. 257. Regrettably, owing to the overlapping dates of activity for Gilles I and Anthonis Coppens van Diest (see Rouzet 1975, pp. 45–46) it is impossible to determine which, precisely, was responsible for this work.

[61] The following discussion is based upon a copy in KBR (LP 595 A). See Harvard 1974, cat. nos. 29, 26, and 20, respectively, for these letters. The original woodblocks of each of the cited letters are also still preserved (see MPM HB nos. 12,834, 13,049, and 12,988, respectively).

[62] MPM Arch. 18, fol. 394 lft.

[63] The original (1573) edition is listed among Galle's publications in MPM M 296, fol. 388r, under the title "Capita deorum et dearum," with two prices: 16 st. and 18 st. For Plantin's earliest known purchase of this text, see MPM Arch. 18, fol. 64 rht, under February 22, 1574.

[64] For examples of copies of each of these editions, see the Hollstein editions cited above. Regrettably, we have not been able to compare the accompanying letterpress text in each of these subsequent editions to determine the degree to which the text was newly printed, or simply updated (following Vrints's 1602

1583: Heyns, Pieter, *Le miroir du monde* (Antwerp: C. Plantin for P. Galle, 1583) oblong 4°

Refs.: Koeman 1967–1971, III, Ort. 50; PP 1831.

Galle's second French edition of his pocket atlas contains eleven new maps, or eighty-three in total.[65] As with the other editions of this publication, Plantin is named in the imprint, which reads: "A Anvers, de l'imprimerie de Christophle Plantin, pour Philippe Galle. M.D.LXXIX." The role Plantin actually played is revealed by archival records. Specifically, between August 11 and October 13, 1582, Plantin paid his pressman Lorans Mesureur for the printing of the entire text.[66] Similarly in 1582 (sometime prior to November), Plantin charged Galle 34 fl. for printing 600 copies of this edition.[67] As already discussed (see above under the 1579 French edition of this text), although Galle retained possession of the plates and appeared to serve as the publisher of this edition, once he was charged for the printing of the text, Plantin then began to buy back all of the fully illustrated copies for further sale via his bookshop.[68] In December 1582, Michel Sonnius I (in Paris) was charged for the purchase of 250 copies.[69]

1583: Heyns, Pieter, *Spieghel der werelt* (Antwerp: C. Plantin for P. Galle, 1583) oblong 4°

Refs.: BT 8862; Koeman 1967–1971, III, Ort. 49; PP 1830.

Galle's second Dutch edition of his pocket atlas was actually a reissue of copies of the original 1577 edition, supplemented with eleven new maps and a new introduction, which replaced the original one.[70] Plantin was named, once again, in the imprint, which reads: "T'Antwerpen, by Christoffel Plantijn, voor Philips Galle. M.D.LXXXIII." The patched-up nature of this publication – implying that only the new introduction and the accompanying texts for the extra eleven maps had to be printed and not the entire book – is reflected in the archival records for the printing of these texts. For, only these gatherings are noted in payments Plantin made in September and October 1583 to his compositor, Philips Groenrys, and to his pressmen, Hans Stroosnijder and Hans Clas. Similarly, Galle was only charged 15 fl. in November 1583 for the printing of just seven and one half sheets for this publication.[71] As was the case with Galle's

---

edition), with, e.g., the address of the new publisher. See n. 26 for more on the Moretuses' purchases at this auction and MPM Arch. 183, p. 2, for these plates in particular.

[65] See n. 51 above.   [66] MPM Arch. 33, fol. 68 lft.

[67] See MPM Arch. 20, fol. 129 lft, for this charge which reads: "pour aultant qu'il doibt pour l'impression dudit miroir . . . fl. 34" (for what he owes for the printing of this Miroir . . . 34 fl.).

[68] For Plantin's repurchase of all 600 copies of this edition (for 630 fl.), see MPM Arch. 20, fol. 129 rht, for the following agreement: "Philippus Galleus pour compte apart du miroir du monde doibt avoir la somme florins 630 pour 600 p[ieces] dudit que C. Plantin a acheptes de luy . . ." (Philips Galle, for the separate account of the Miroir du monde, should have the sum of 630 florins for 600 [copies] of said book, which C[hristopher] Plantin purchased from him.) Like the Dutch edition of this text, there is a general reference to it (without the specification of the year of publication) in the list of Galle's publications in MPM M 296, fol. 388r, under the title "Miroir du monde" (at a price of 26 st.).

[69] See MPM Arch. 19, fol. 167 lft. These arrangements are discussed in greater detail in ch. 6 and Imhof 1999b, p. 90.

[70] See n. 51 above.

[71] See MPM Arch. 33, fols. 87 lft (for Groenrys), 75 rht (for Stroosnijder), and 71 lft (for Clas). See MPM Arch. 20, fol. 146 lft, for the general charge to Galle, which reads: "Voor 7¹/₂ bladeren gedrukt in den

first pocket atlas in Dutch (from 1577), Plantin did not systematically buy back copies of it.[72]

1583: Vosmerus, Michael, *Les vies et alliances des comtes de Hollande et Zelande, seigneurs de Frise* (trans. by Nicolas Clément de Trêles) (Antwerp: C. Plantin for P. Galle, 1583) f°

Refs.: BT 4803; *New Holl., Galle*, IV, R 25; PP 2476.

This French paraphrase (and simplification) of Vosmerus's text (see above) was the second publication to be illustrated with Galle's series of thirty-six engravings of the counts of Holland and Zeeland (along with an additional engraved portrait of Francis, duke of Anjou, numbered 37). As before, while Galle's role as the publisher is clear from the engraved vignette on the title-page, Plantin's role as the printer of the text for Galle is indicated by the imprint, which reads: "A Anvers, de l'Imprimerie de Christofle Plantin pour Philippe Galle. M.D.LXXXIII."[73] Galle's employment of Plantin for this work is confirmed by payments made to one of Plantin's pressmen, Cornelis Comper, for the printing of at least part of the text between December 31, 1582 and January 15, 1583.[74] Plantin then purchased twelve copies soon thereafter (by February 18, 1583).[75] We have yet to find a summary charge to Galle for this work. As is discussed in detail under the 1578 edition of this text, the plates used to illustrate this book would ultimately (by 1673) come into the possession of Plantin's successors, the Moretuses.

1585: Favolius, Hugo, *Theatri orbis terrarum enchiridion* (Antwerp: C. Plantin for P. Galle, 1585) 4°

Refs.: BT 2287; Koeman 1967–1971, III, Ort. 51; PP 1832.

In this first Latin edition of Galle's popular pocket atlas, the eighty-three maps featured in the previous French and Dutch editions from 1583 were now accompanied by new, original texts by the poet Hugo Favolius.[76] As with the other editions of this publication, the text was printed at Plantin's Press in Antwerp, as is indicated by the imprint, which reads: "Antwerpiae Excudebat Philippo Gallaeo Christophorus Plantinus. M.D.LXXXV." However, as payments for the setting and printing of this text were made between early June and early September 1584, the work must have been done under the direction of Plantin's sons-in-law, Jan Moretus I and Franciscus Raphelengius I, during Plantin's sojourn in Leiden.[77] By August 31, 1584, Galle was charged

Duyschen spiegel op elck bladt 7 boecken, 53 boecken tot 6 st. den riem 4 fl. 16 st. Voor het drucken ende setten ende ander oncosten gerekent voor de 7$\frac{1}{2}$ bladeren voors. tot 2 fl. het blad 15 fl." (For 7$\frac{1}{2}$ sheets printed for the *Spiegel* in Dutch, of each sheet 7 quires, 53 quires at 6 st. per ream, 4 fl. 16 st. For the printing and setting and other expenses for the above mentioned 7$\frac{1}{2}$ sheets at 2 fl. per sheet, comes to 15 fl.)

[72] This publication is referred to generally in Plantin's list of Philips Galle's publications (MPM M 296, fol. 388r), simply under the title "Spiegel der werelt," with a price of 22 st. per copy. For more on Plantin and these pocket atlases, see ch. 6 and Imhof 1999b, pp. 89–90.

[73] See n. 32 above for the inscription referring to Galle.   [74] See MPM Arch. 33, fol. 74 lft.

[75] For a possible reference to this edition in Plantin's list of Galle's publications in MPM M 296, see n. 36 above. For Plantin's cited purchase, see MPM Arch. 20, fol. 57 rht.

[76] See n. 51 above.

[77] For payments to Plantin's staff, see MPM Arch. 33, fol. 74 rht, for the pressman Cornelius Comper; fol. 77 rht, for the pressman Hans van Leuven; fol. 87 lft, for the compositor Philips Groenrys; fol. 96 rht,

48 fl. for the printing of 525 copies of this text.[78] Plantin purchased several copies of this book, including one group of fifty copies for resale at the Frankfurt book fair.[79]

c.1585–1590: *Prosopographia sive virtutum, animi, corporis, bonorum externorum, vitiorum, et affectuum variorum delineatio* (Antwerp: [C. Plantin for] P. Galle, s.a.) 8°

Refs.: *New Holl., Galle*, III, nos. 316–360; Sellink 1997, I, pp. 132–135.

Sellink identifies this series of forty-three engravings of personifications of virtues, vices, and other human qualities or general concepts, as possibly one of Galle's last signed works.[80] The dating of the series is, however, regrettably vague. Each image is accompanied by an engraved distich by Cornelius Kiliaan. While there is an extra plate with an engraved dedication by Galle to Marie de Meleun, countess of Ligne, Galle's foreword to the reader was printed typographically. The 15 mm decorative initial "E" used to mark the start of Galle's text indicates that it was printed with Plantin's materials.[81] We have yet to find any archival records pertaining to the printing of this text, or any clear evidence that he bought copies of it.

1586: *Virorum doctorum de disciplinis benemerentium effigies XLIIII* (Antwerp: [C. Plantin for] P. Galle, [1586]) 4° (fig. 6.7)

Refs.: Hänsel 1991, pp. 91–99; *New Holl., Galle*, IV, pp. 25–27; Sellink 1997, I, esp. pp. 48–53, and II, Appendix 2 B, 1572b ed.

The second of Galle's series of scholars, this publication consists of forty-four engraved portraits of learned men, with accompanying accounts of them written in verse by Arias Montano. As discussed in chapter 6, in Galle's original 1572 edition of this series, the title-page, introductory texts, and the accompanying verses were all printed for Galle by Gilles I or Anthonis Coppens van Diest. In this issue, all of Arias Montano's verses were engraved on to the plates and only the title-page and Galle's introduction to the work were reprinted. Although the name of the printer is not given, both the typographic material used and archival evidence indicate that Plantin printed the letterpress text for this issue in the summer of 1586. Typographically, the "Q" initial marking the start of

---

for the pressman Hans Stroosnijder; and fol. 105 lft, for the pressman Renier Artsens. On Plantin's Leiden period (from April 1583 through October 1585), see Voet, GC, I, pp. 106–113.

[78] See MPM Arch. 20, fol. 146 lft, for the following general charge to Galle: "pour limpression de 24 f° en son theatrum petit en Latin a raison de deux fl. la rame" (for the printing of 24 folios of his small *Theatrum* in Latin at 2 fl. per ream). In MPM Arch. 62, fol. 85r (under August 27, 1584), there is a more detailed reference to the printing of the text, which reads: "Philippus Galle doibt pour 24 rames imprimees pour son Theatre en Latin epitomiste in 4°, contenant 24 f° et chascun f° est de une rame et 1 main de papier a raison de deux florins la rame et la main par dessus." This indicates that one ream and one quire (i.e., twenty-five sheets) of paper were needed for the printing of each sheet, which amounts to 525 impressions of each sheet and implies that as many as 525 copies were printed.

[79] For this one large purchase, see MPM Arch. 20, fol. 146 rht. Periodic additional (and smaller) purchases are noted after this one and in MPM Arch. 20, fol. 228 rht, ff.

[80] Sellink 1997, I, pp. 132 and 134.

[81] We examined the copy in the Print Department of the Royal Library, Brussels (s.IV.2865–2090). The "E" initial used in the dedication is the same as the first "E" represented in Harvard 1974, cat. 28, Roman letters with pictorial historiation. It appears frequently, for example, in C. Baronius's *Martyrologium Romanum* (Antwerp: C. Plantin, 1589) (PP 626) (see e.g., pp. 79 and 161).

Galle's introductory text on fol. Aij r (fig. 6.7) is part of a set of 39 mm Roman initials with grotesque historiation that Plantin used throughout his career.[82] The printing of the title-page and introductory text for this issue of Galle's *Virorum doctorum* is most likely represented by the charge of 4 fl. 10 st. noted in Galle's accounts on July 3, 1586 for the printing of one ream "doctorum virorum."[83] This is clearly distinct from the subsequent charge (recorded between October 2, 1587 and April 13, 1588) for the printing of three reams of text "int boeck vande geleerde" (in the book of the learned men), which most likely reflects the printing of the text for Galle's third series of images of scholars, which he published in 1587.[84] As Sellink suggests, Galle may have reissued the 1572 edition in preparation for the appearance of his new, complementary edition of portraits of scholars in 1587.[85] Although Plantin periodically bought copies of "Effigies doctorum" (images of scholars) from Galle between 1572 and 1588, these purchases are rarely specific enough to determine precisely how many copies of each edition or issue Plantin purchased. Only the original 1572 edition appears to be cited in Plantin's list of Galle's publications.[86]

1586: *Verses (precise title not known)*

On April 24, 1586, Galle was charged 1 fl. 10 st. for "limpression dune rame des vers..." (printing of one ream of verses).[87] We have yet to identify which text this was.

1586: Vosmerus, Michael, *Les vies et alliances des comtes de Hollande et Zelande, seigneurs de Frise* (trans. by Nicolas Clément de Trêles) (Antwerp: C. Plantin for P. Galle, 1586) f°

Refs.: BT 4804; *New Holl.*, Galle, IV, R 25; PP 2477.

In 1586, Galle reissued his 1583 French edition of Vosmerus's account of the counts of Holland and Zeeland. Only the first and last gatherings (A and L) were reprinted, which accounts for the minimal cost (in relative terms) for Plantin's work on this edition: only 8 fl. 10 st. charged for the printing of just two reams of paper, versus, for example, Plantin's charge of 22 fl. for the printing of the original 1578 edition of this text.[88] In addition,

82 See Harvard 1974, cat. 10, and MPM HB 12,254 for this woodblock. For copies of Galle's *Virorum doctorum* with this setting of the typographical text, see, e.g., MPM PK (R 115) and RUG (Res. 1127).
83 MPM Arch. 20, fol. 228 lft. Part of this charge presumably included the payment recorded on July 5, 1586 to Plantin's pressman Nicolas Sterck for the printing of "2 fueilles in doctorum virorum Gallei 12 st." (2 sheets in Galle's *Doctorum virorum* [amounts to] 12 st.) (MPM Arch. 33, fol. 104 lft.)
84 See MPM Arch. 20, fol. 307 lft, for the subsequent charge. Galle's 1587 publication is discussed below.
85 *New Holl.*, Galle, IV, p. 25; and Sellink 1997, II, p. 223.
86 Plantin's purchases of this series is discussed in greater detail in ch. 6. The best example of some differentiation among these editions in Plantin's accounts is an entry noted under January 16, 1588, in which first the purchase of three copies of the "Effigies doctorum f°" at 16 st. is recorded and then a purchase of "3 Idem novi 20 st." (3 of the same, new [at] 20 st. [per piece]) (see MPM Arch. 20, fol. 288 rht). This indicates that the "new" edition – that from 1587, perhaps – cost 4 st. more than the original. See MPM M 296, fol. 388r, for the listing of the "Effigies Doctorum [in] f°; [for] st. 16; [from] [15]72."
87 MPM Arch. 20, fol. 228 lft.
88 For Plantin's charge of 8 fl. 10 st. for printing "2 Rames in Com. Holl." (2 reams in com[tes de] Holl[ande]) which was noted in Galle's accounts with Plantin on July 3, 1586 (see MPM Arch. 20, fol. 228 lft). See above for the charges for the printing of the 1578 edition. We compared copies of the 1583 and 1586 issues of this text in KBR (II 68.698 C LP), for the original 1583 edition, and KBR (VH 27.511 C/ 2), for the 1586 reissue.

the last leaf of gathering K was removed so that the portrait of the duke of Anjou that had been added in the 1583 edition was no longer present. Consequently, this issue was illustrated with just the original series of thirty-six engravings. Although this constituted Galle's third publication to feature this series of portraits, it was actually the fourth time that the majority of them were published. This was owing to Plantin's use – or, to be more precise, "borrowing" – of thirty-four of these plates for the illustration of his edition of Adrianus Barlandus's *Hollandiae comitum historia et icones*, which was published in Leiden in 1584.[89] As with Galle's preceding editions of the counts of Holland and Zeeland, Plantin's involvement in this project is indicated by the imprint on the title-page, which reads: "A Anvers, de l'imprimerie de Christofle Plantin pour Philippe Galle. M.D.LXXXVI." Galle's employment of Plantin to print texts for this work is confirmed by the general charge cited above. Plantin continued to purchase numerous copies of this book from Galle, particularly in the period December 30, 1588 to August 17, 1589.[90] As is discussed in detail under the 1578 edition of this text, the plates used to illustrate this book ultimately (by 1673) came into the possession of Plantin's successors, the Moretuses.

1587: *Imagines L. doctorum virorum, qui bene de studiis literarum meruere* (Antwerp: [C. Plantin for] P. Galle [1587]) 4°

Refs.: Hänsel 1991, pp. 97–98; *New Holl., Galle*, IV, pp. 27–29; Sellink 1997, I, esp. pp. 53–57, and II, Appendix 2 C.

The third of Galle's series of learned men, this publication consists of fifty new engravings with accompanying verses composed by Franciscus Raphelengius I. In his introductory text, Raphelengius identifies this as the supplement to Galle's second series of scholars, which was originally printed in 1572 and reprinted by Plantin in 1586.[91] Although the printer of the letterpress text is not identified in the publication, both the typographic material used and archival evidence indicate that Plantin was responsible for it. Specifically, the "P" initial marking the start of Raphelengius's introductory text on fol. A2r is part of the same set of 39 mm Roman initials with grotesque historiation from which the "Q" marking the start of Plantin's 1586 reprint of Galle's 1572 series of portraits was taken.[92] The printing of the *Imagines L. doctorum virorum* is most likely represented by the charge of 6 fl. noted in Galle's accounts between October 2, 1587 and April 13, 1588 for printing three reams "int boeck vande geleerde" (in the book of the scholars).[93] As noted in the discussion of Plantin's 1586 reprint of Galle's 1572 series, while Plantin was evidently interested in purchasing copies of these portrait

---

[89] See the discussion of this work in ch. 6. The following engravings were not included in Plantin's Barlandus edition: plate 28 of John of Bavaria, plate 36 of Philip II, and plate 37 of Francis of Anjou.

[90] For a possible reference to this edition in Plantin's list of Galle's publications in MPM M 296, see n. 75 above. For this last flurry of purchases, see MPM Arch. 20, fol. 307 rht.

[91] See Sellink 1997, II, Appendix 2 C, for a transcription of this text.

[92] See Harvard 1974, cat. 10, for this set of initials and MPM HB 12,252 for the "P" block in particular. We examined copies of Galle's *Imagines L. doctorum virorum* in KBR (VB 13.266.1 RP) and in MPM PK (R 115).

[93] See MPM Arch. 20, fol. 307 lft, for this record, which reads: "gedruckt int boeck vande geleerde de twee eerst bladeren 3 riemen tegen 2 gulden fl. 6 st." (printed in the book of the scholars the two first pages, 3 reams at 2 florins [amounts to] 6 fl.).

series from Galle, it is impossible to determine precisely how many copies he bought of each series.

1587/1588: *D. Seraphici Francisci totius evangelicae perfectionis exemplaris, admiranda historia* (Antwerp: [C. Plantin for] P. Galle, 1587/1588) oblong f°

Refs.: BT 1216; Gieben 1976; Sellink 1997, 1, esp. pp. 129–131.

This is the second, revised edition of a series of prints on the life of St. Francis that Galle published. It consists of a frontispiece and eighteen plates – mostly engravings, but also some etchings – fourteen of which had been used in an earlier edition that appears to have been published prior to 1580, potentially with an accompanying text printed by the widow of a certain Gerard Fabri.[94] The only page printed typographically in the revised edition is a dedicatory letter by Henricus Sedulius to Franciscus a Toloza, dated August 8, 1587, that was included immediately after the engraved title-page. Although we have yet to trace the 12 mm decorative "D" initial used to mark the start of the text, the woodcut with the three coats of arms bearing the insignia of the Franciscan order is still part of the collection of the Plantin-Moretus Museum and could, thus, have been part of Plantin's stock of typographical materials.[95] Consequently, it is possible that Plantin was responsible for printing the text for this edition. This supposition is confirmed by a charge of 3 fl. noted in Galle's accounts between October 2, 1587 and April 13, 1588 for the printing of "noch het eerst blat voor tleven van S^t franciscus" (also the first page for the life of St. Francis).[96] In 1593 and 1604, Jan Moretus I was also paid to print the text for new editions of this series, first for Philips Galle, and then for his son and successor, Theodoor Galle.[97] One of these printings may be represented by a deceptively similar copy of the dedicatory text (bound in with most of the prints from the second series) that is now in the collection of the Museo Francescano in Rome.[98] The content of the letter – down to the date of August 8, 1587 – as well as the decorative initial "D," the woodcut with the coat of arms, and the remaining decorative matter, all appear to be the same as those found in the other copies discussed above. Nevertheless, a close examination of the setting of the text reveals that this differs throughout.[99] We are dating the Roman copy after the Brussels and Antwerp copies

---

94 On the earlier version of this series, see Sellink 1997, 1, p. 130, and Gieben 1976, pp. 241–257. The eighteen plates of the second series are numbered 3–20, with the frontispiece numbered 1 and the page of letterpress apparently serving as (fol.) no. 2. Of these, plate numbers 6 and 20 are etchings.

95 The "D" initial is comparable in style to the set of 22 mm Roman initials with arabesque decoration that are described in Harvard 1974, cat. 19. This "D" initial is similarly absent from the Plantin-Moretus Museum's inventory of its woodblocks. A full transcription of the dedicatory text is given in Gieben 1976, pp. 263–265. For the block with the three coats of arms, see MPM HB 8095. For this discussion, we examined copies of this text in KBR PK (S.III.106,213–106,232), where no. 106,214 is the page of text, KBR PK (S.III.4090–4108), which does not have the dedicatory text, and a private collection in Antwerp.

96 MPM Arch. 20, fol. 307 lft.

97 On August 20, 1593 Philips Galle was charged 3 fl. for the following: "Item il y a une rame de lepistre de St. François fl. 3." (Idem. there is one ream of the letter of St. Francis, 3 fl.) (MPM Arch. 21, fol. 203 lft.) On September 6, 1604, Theodoor Galle was charged 3 fl. for the following: "Item pour limpression de un Rame de l'Epistre de vite S. Francisci fl. 3." (Idem for the printing of one ream of the letter of the life of St. Francis, 3 fl.) (MPM Arch. 127, fol. 211 lft.)

98 This copy (V-BA-2b) is discussed in detail in Gieben 1976; see pp. 257–280, in particular.

99 Consider, for example, the word "DIVI," with which the body of the text begins. In the copies from Antwerp and Brussels, which are associated here with Plantin's printing of the text, the top of the letters

because the woodblock with the three coats of arms in the Roman copy lacks the lower edge of the left-most shield, just like the woodblock, as it is preserved today. In both the Antwerp and Brussels copies, this shield is complete. The possibility still exists that the Roman copy represents the third known printing of this text (in 1604) and that the Antwerp and Brussels copies represent the second known printing (in 1594), with none representing Plantin's original work for Galle. Only the discovery of additional copies will resolve this final question.

1587/1588: *Indulgences* (precise title not known)

Between October 2, 1587 and April 13, 1588, Galle was charged 4 fl. for "gedruckt twee mael cleyn aflaet briefkens 2 riemen" (printed twice small indulgences [amounting to] 2 reams).[100] We have yet to identify which text this was.

1588: *Epitome du theatre du monde d'Abraham Ortelius* (Antwerp: C. Plantin for P. Galle, 1588) oblong 8°

Refs.: BT 2289; Koeman 1967–1971, III, Ort. 52; PP 1833.

Galle's third French edition of his pocket atlas comprises ninety-four maps – eleven more than his previous edition – and bears texts that are simply excerpts from Ortelius's *Theatre de l'univers*.[101] All references to the original author, Pieter Heyns, were removed, probably owing to the potential conflict between his now overt Calvinist persuasion and the current Catholic rule of Antwerp. As with the other editions of this publication, Plantin is named in the imprint, which reads: "A Anvers, de l'imprimerie de Christofle Plantin, pour Philippe Galle. M.D.LXXXVIII." Plantin's specific role as the printer of the texts is confirmed by archival records. Specifically, in July 1588 Plantin paid Jan Verwithagen II for his work on this text.[102] Similarly, in 1588 Plantin charged Galle 45 fl. 10 st. for the printing of 250 copies of the text and an additional 25 fl. 7 st. for the paper used for this edition.[103] Once Galle had added the illustrations to the printed texts, however, Plantin then proceeded to buy back all of the fully illustrated copies (for a total of 400 fl.) for further sale via his bookshop.[104] Thus, as was the case with Galle's other

---

"IVI" are aligned with the top of the woodcut "D." In the copy from Rome, the "I" that immediately follows the "D" is slightly larger than the remaining letters and sticks up slightly above them and the upper edge of the woodcut "D."

[100] MPM Arch. 20, fol. 307 lft.   [101] Imhof 1999b, p. 90. See also n. 51 above.

[102] See MPM Arch. 33, fol. 136 lft, under Verwithagen, whose occupation – compositor or pressman – is not indicated, although his work on the 1588 French edition of R. Verstegen's *Theatre des cruautez* . . . (see below) suggests that he was a pressman.

[103] See MPM Arch. 20, fol. 129 lft, for the following: "pour compte du miroir en françois imprimé anno 1588 doibt pour aultant que monte l'impression de 13 f° du petit miroir à 3 fl. 10 st. la somme de 45 fl. st. 10. Item pour 6^1/2 rames du papier à 3 fl. 18 st. rame fl. 25 st. 7." (for the account of the French *Miroir*, printed in 1588, owed for the printing of the 13 folios of the small *Miroir* at 3 fl. 10 st. [for each folio], the sum of 45 fl. 10 st. Idem for 6^1/2 reams of paper at 3 fl. 18 st. per ream [comes to] 25 fl. 7 st.) See PP 1833, n. 4, for the calculation that 250 copies were printed.

[104] See the following record: "Philippus Galle doibt avoir pour compte du miroir imprime a° 1588 ad 31 aug^{ti} p[our] 100 p[iece] a 32 st. receus fl. 160. Item pour 150 qu'il doibt encores livrer a 32 st. val. fl. 240." (Philips Galle should have for the account of the *Miroir* from 1588, on August 31, for 100 copies at 32 st., received 160 fl. Item for 150 copies which he still has to deliver, at 32 st., [comes to] 240 fl.) (MPM Arch. 20, fol. 129 rht.)

French editions of his pocket atlas, while Galle retained possession of the plates and appeared to serve as publisher, Plantin took on the full responsibility for distributing the completed copies. Once again, the Parisian bookseller Michel Sonnius I bought a significant number of the copies: 188 of the 250 completed copies were shipped to him in November 1588.[105]

1589: Canisius, Petrus, *Institutiones christianae, seu parvus catechismus catholicorum* (Antwerp: C. Plantin & P. Galle, 1589) 8° (fig. 6.12)

Refs.: BCNI 4053; BT 3981; PP 884 = PP 2149; Sellink, I, pp. 127–128.

Richly illustrated with 101 etchings by Peeter vander Borcht, this pictorial embodiment of Canisius's catechism is the second well-known example of a "joint venture" between Plantin and Galle.[106] In contrast with their 1575 co-production of *De rerum usu et abusu* (see above), Plantin and Galle's cooperative working relationship is indicated in the imprint on the title-page, which reads: "Antverpiae, Excudebat Christophorus Plantinus, Architypographus Regius, sibi & Philippo Gallaeo. M.D.LXXXIX." Completed in May 1589, only a few months prior to Plantin's death, the plates for this publication, officially the joint property of Galle and Plantin, were still in Galle's possession when Plantin's estate was being settled in 1590. Neither the Moretuses nor Galle or his successors appear to have used these plates again.

1589: Galle, Philips, *Instruction et fondements de bien pourtraire* (Antwerp: [C. Plantin for] P. Galle, 1589) f°

Refs.: BT 8360; *New Holl., Galle*, III, nos. 505–517; Sellink 1997, I, pp. 69–75 in particular, and II, Appendix 3 A.

Highlighted by Sellink as the first drawing book to be published in the Low Countries, this work consists of a brief introductory text by Galle, in which he dedicates the book to young artists, and a series of thirteen engraved anatomical studies. All signed by Galle himself, these may represent the last group of engravings he made.[107] According to Sellink, complete copies of this publication are extremely rare. It is clear, however, from those copies containing Galle's introductory text, that the decorative letter "A" used to mark the start of it came from Plantin's stock of initials.[108] The printing of at least the title-page, if not the introductory text, may be indicated by a payment made on March 4, 1589 to Nicolas van Linschoten for various tasks, including the printing of "1 titre de Philipe Galle" (1 title for Philips Galle).[109]

---

[105] For this sale, see MPM Arch. 65, fol. 151r, and MPM Arch. 19, fol. 205 lft. These arrangements are discussed in greater detail in ch. 6 and Imhof 1999b, pp. 90–91.

[106] See ch. 6 for a more detailed discussion of the production of this book.

[107] Sellink 1997, I, pp. 69 and 74.

[108] We examined a copy in SBA (H 16636), which lacks several of the prints – plates 4, 7, 8, and 13 – but not the letterpress text. The 39 mm initial "A," printed on the verso of the title-page, is included in Harvard 1974, cat. 10, Roman letters with grotesque historiation.

[109] MPM Arch. 33, fol. 131 rht.

1589: *Epitome theatri Orteliani* (Antwerp: C. Plantin for P. Galle, 1589) oblong 8°

Refs.: BT 6455; PP 1834; Koeman 1967–1971, III, Ort. 53.

Like his 1588 French edition, Galle's second Latin edition of his pocket atlas boasts ninety-four maps, which are accompanied here by new texts by an unknown author.[110] Reading "Antverpiae, Philippo Gallaeo excudebat Christophorus Plantinus. M.D.LXXXIX," this would be the last time that Plantin was named in the imprint and thereby associated with the production of this text. Indeed, as the payments for the setting and printing of the text were made between April and June 1589, shortly before Plantin's death, even the work on this edition was most likely done under the direction of Plantin's son-in-law, Jan Moretus I.[111] In August 1589, Galle was charged 45 fl. 10 st. for the printing of this text, after which Moretus bought back only a portion of the copies.[112]

ADRIAEN HUBERTI

1585 (or possibly 1586): *Seven Sacraments in Dutch and French* (precise title not known)

On September 20, 1585 (or possibly 1586) Plantin paid Nicolas Spors for his work printing the "7 sacrements de Adrian Huberti en flammeng et en françois 28 [or 18? st.]" (7 sacraments of Adriaen Huberti in Dutch and French 28 [or 18 st.]).[113] We have yet to identify the publication(s) concerned.

1587: Verstegen, Richard, *Theatrum crudelitatum haereticorum nostri temporis* (Antwerp: [C. Plantin for] Adriaen Huberti, 1587) 4°

Refs.: Allison and Rogers 1989, no. 1297; BT 4728; Petti 1963, p. 89, cat. A. i) 4a; Rombouts 1933, pp. 53–63.

Identified only by the initials R.V. on the first page of the preface (fol. A2r), Richard Verstegen, a Catholic refugee from England who eventually settled in Antwerp, is now generally recognized as the author of this graphically illustrated work on the persecution of Catholics. Verstegen has also been credited with executing the thirty engravings used to illustrate this edition of the text.[114] Only Adriaen Huberti is named on the title-page, where he is simply identified in the imprint as the publisher of this edition ("Apud Adrianum Huberti"). But, as is demonstrated below for a French translation of this work from 1588, Verstegen may have been the true financier of and organizing force

---

[110] See n. 51 above.

[111] See MPM Arch. 33, fol. 146 lft, for payments to the compositor Arnout Fabri, and fol. 150 lft, for payments to the pressman Cornelis Comper.

[112] This charge reads: "limpression du Theatrum Ortelianum in epitome redactum contenant 13 f° a rayson de 3 fl. 10 la feuille monte in NS fl. 45 st. 10" (the printing of the small atlas of Ortelius, containing 13 sheets, at 3 fl. 10 [st.] per sheet, amounts to 45 fl. 10 st.) (MPM Arch. 20, fol. 307 lft). For Jan Moretus's purchase of sixty copies of this edition on August 16, 1589, see MPM Arch. 20, fol. 307 rht.

[113] MPM Arch. 33, fol. 108 lft. The dating of this payment is uncertain because of jumps in the records from August 24, 1585 (just before this record) to June 20, 1587 (immediately after it).

[114] Petti 1959, p. 81.

behind this publication. Regrettably, no charges are known (to either Verstegen or Huberti) for the printing of this edition. The printer of this text is similarly not cited, but both payments to Plantin's staff and the typographical materials used reveal that Plantin undertook this work. Payments to Plantin's staff indicate that the printing of the text, begun by the end of August 1587, was completed in mid-October.[115] In addition, the 30 mm initial "S" that marks the start of dedicatory text (fol. A2r) was part of one of Plantin's frequently used sets of letters with animal and botanical decoration, while the initial "C" marking the start of the introductory text (fol. C2v) was part of another set of 13 mm letters with similar decorative elements.[116] By 1642, the plates used to illustrate this edition – or else a set of copies of these plates – were in the possession of Plantin's heirs, the Moretuses, although there is no evidence that they ever used them.[117]

1588: *Seven Sacraments [and?] St. Francis* (precise title not known)

On February 4, 1588, Huberti was charged 3 fl. for "1/2 rame descripture pour les sept sacramens" (1/2 ream of text for the seven sacraments) and an additional 3 fl. for "la figure de St Francois ende voor de sacramenten" (the figure of St. Francis and for the sacraments).[118] We have yet to identify the publication(s) concerned.

1588: Verstegen, Richard, *Theatre des cruautez des hereticques de nostre temps* (Antwerp: [C. Plantin for R. Verstegen] Adriaen Huberti, 1588) 4° (fig. 6.23)

Refs.: Allison and Rogers 1989, no. 1302; BT 4727; Petti 1963, p. 89, cat. A. i) 4F; Rombouts 1933, pp. 53–63.

This basic French translation of Verstegen's *Theatrum crudelitatum haereticorum* has much in common with the earlier Latin edition. Not only is it illustrated with the same set of engravings, but Huberti is the only figure named on the title-page, where he is, once again, simply identified as the publisher in the imprint, which reads: "Chez Adrien Hubert." In contrast with the 1587 Latin edition, however, there is now evidence that Verstegen himself bore the costs of having the text printed. For, while the typographical material used and the payments to Plantin's staff all indicate that Plantin was responsible for printing this text, Verstegen was charged for this work.[119] Although this charge is not dated, payments to Plantin's pressmen Jan Verwithagen II and Hans Stroosnijder

---

[115] See MPM Arch. 33, fol. 111 rht, under the compositor François vanden Bossche; fol. 123 rht, under the compositor Hans Stroosnijder; fol. 126 lft, under the pressman Guillaume Rivière; and fol. 131 lft, under the pressman Nicolas van Linschoten.

[116] See Harvard 1974, cat. 12, for the former set with the "S," and cat. 30, for the latter set with the "C." We examined copies of this edition in RG (3118 D 21) and SBA (K 265513).

[117] These observations are based upon an entry in a 1642 inventory of the Moretuses' stock of plates for: "30 Theatrum Crudelitatis" (MPM Arch. 124, p. 13). In an inventory from 1673, the thirty plates are cited again, but subdivided as one title-plate and twenty-nine text illustrations (MPM Arch. 124, p. 79). See the discussion below of the 1588 French edition of this text for references to another set of engravings of these subjects.

[118] MPM Arch. 20, fol. 259 lft.

[119] See MPM Arch. 20, fol. 298 lft, for the following charge to Verstegen: "pour limpression de 18 rames en (?) son livre en françois a 30 patt la rame, monte fl. 27" (for the printing of 18 reams in [?] his book in French at 30 st. per ream, amounts to 27 fl.).

indicate that the text was printed between mid-May and early June 1588.[120] This evidence of Plantin's involvement is supported by the decorative initials used. Specifically, the historiated "C" that marks the start of the dedicatory text on fol. A2r is part of a frequently used set of 30 mm letters with botanical decoration, while the "T" marking the start of the "prologue" (p. 16) is part of a set of 22 mm Roman letters with grotesque decoration that Plantin also used for an extended period of time.[121] A similar examination of the decorative elements included in the setting of a distinct French edition of Verstegen's text, published in 1587, and an expanded 1588 French edition suggests that neither of these was printed by Plantin.[122]

1588: Verstegen, Richard, *Theatrum crudelitatum haereticorum nostri temporis* (Antwerp: [C. Plantin for] Adriaen Huberti, 1588) 4°

Refs.: Allison and Rogers 1989, no. 1298; BT 7083; Petti 1963, p. 89, cat. A. i) 4B; Rombouts 1933, pp. 53–63.

Although commonly identified as "another edition" of the text Huberti originally published in 1587, this was actually a separate issue of the 1587 edition, with only an extra "I" printed on the title-page, so that it would read "M. D. LXXXVIII." instead of "M. D. LXXXVII."[123] Thus, the text that Plantin printed for Huberti and/or Verstegen in 1587 was simply reused and illustrated with the same set of thirty engravings for a new issue dated 1588.

1589: *Indulgences* (in Dutch and in Spanish) (precise title not known)

On March 29, 1589, Huberti was charged 9 fl. for "3 rames aflaetbrieven en flamen [and] ung desdits en espagnol" (3 reams of indulgences in Dutch [and] one of the same in Spanish).[124] We have yet to identify which texts these were.

1589: *Verses* (in Dutch) (precise title not known)

On April 26, 1589, Huberti was charged 1 fl. 16 st. for "vi c Refereyns flamen" (600 refrains [or verses] in Dutch).[125] We have yet to identity the publication(s) concerned.

---

[120] See MPM Arch. 33, fol. 136 lft (for Verwithagen), and fol. 139 lft (for Stroosnijder). We have not found corresponding payments for the setting of the text.

[121] See Harvard 1974, cat. 12, for the "C" initial, and cat. 17 for the "T" initial. Both sets were used by Plantin from around 1563 or 1564 through 1589. We examined a copy of this edition in MPM (R 16.4).

[122] For the 1587 French edition, see *Theatre de cruautez des hereticques de nostre temps par M. Richard Versteganus* (Antwerp: Adriaen Huberti, 1587) 4° (Allison and Rogers 1989, no. 1301; Petti 1963, p. 89, cat. A. i) 4E). Our information concerning this edition is drawn from a copy of the book at the Vrije Universiteit in Amsterdam (UBM: O 78–151). Our thanks to Dr. Tom Johnston for examining this and a copy of the 1588, expanded French edition in Amsterdam for us. For the expanded 1588 edition, see R. Verstegen, *Theatre des cruautez des hereticques* (Antwerp: Adriaen Huberti, 1588) 4° (Allison and Rogers 1989, no. 1304; BT 9316; Petti 1963, p. 89, cat. A. i) 4H). We examined the copy in RUG (Meul. 711). See ch. 6 for more on these editions.

[123] We are grateful to Dr. Thomas Jahn of the Rare Books and Manuscripts Department of the Bayerische Staatsbibliothek and Mrs. Ann Robinson of the Palace Green Division of the Durham University Library for examining their copies of the 1588 edition of this text for us (nos. ESlg 4° H.Eccl. 774 and Bamburgh L.4.71/2, respectively). See the discussion above of the 1587 Latin edition for the identification of Plantin as the printer of the text for the 1587 Latin edition and an account of the engravings.

[124] MPM Arch. 20, fol. 259 lft.   [125] MPM Arch. 20, fol. 259 lft.

GERARD DE JODE

1579: Haechtanus, Laurentius, Μικροκόσμος. *Parvus mundus* (Antwerp: [C. Plantin for] G. de Jode, 1579) 4° (fig. 6.24)

Refs.: BT 5898; Landwehr 1988, no. 263.

De Jode's *Parvus mundus* comprises seventy-four moralizing engravings, each of which is set in an emblematic format and complemented with accompanying commentary written by Laurentius Haechtanus. Although the printer of the text is not cited in the publication itself, an examination of the decorative letters used suggests that Plantin was responsible for this work. Specifically, the "M" that marks the start of the dedicatory text on fol. *4r is the same as the "M" listed by Stephen Harvard as part of a set of 20 mm Roman letters with botanical decoration.[126] The association of the typographical text in this publication with Plantin remains uncertain because the main sources for this particular letter are one of his early publications, a 1556 edition of Girolam Parabosque's *Lettres amoureuses*, and a 1571 publication of Esteban de Garibay y Zamalloa's *Los XL libros d'el compendio historial de las chronicas . . . de España*.[127] The difficulty with the former publication is that it clearly pre-dates the 1562 sale of Plantin's property, while the latter was printed for Plantin by two independent Antwerp printers, Jan Verwithagen I and Theodoor van der Linden. In the case of Garibay's text, however, it is also evident that other sets of initials used to embellish it were ones that Plantin regularly used in other publications. This includes one set of initials for which the woodblocks are still preserved in the Plantin-Moretus Museum.[128] Thus, it appears that Plantin loaned at least the initials to the hired printers. Consequently, even the typographical materials in Garibay's *Compendium* can support the attribution of the letterpress in this edition of de Jode's *Parvus mundus* to Plantin. De Jode's 1579 edition of the *Parvus mundus* would then represent the third such emblematic, moralizing print publication to be printed by Plantin for a third party in the period 1578–1579.[129] Plantin did buy some copies of this text from de Jode in the summer of 1579.[130] It also appears that in 1584 de Jode had

---

126 Harvard 1974, cat. 20. We examined a copy of this edition in MPM (R 55.18). The decorative initial Q on leaf *2v of the *Parvus mundus* is also included in the Harvard catalogue (no. 46, as part of a small set of 24 mm Roman letters with pictorial historiation and two-line borders). The impression of the Q included in Harvard's catalogue comes from this edition of the *Parvus mundus*, however, and we have yet to find another impression of it in a Plantin publication to confirm Harvard's association of the letter with Plantin's collection of decorative letters.

127 For the 1556 publication, see PP 1947 and fol. A3r, for the "M" initial. For the 1571 publication, see PP 1238 and vol. I, fol. V5r (= p. 237) for the "M" initial.

128 Harvard 1574, cat. nos. 5 and 20 are both present in the Garibay *Compendium*; the woodblocks for cat. 5 are inventoried under MPM HB 12,167–12,190.

129 The two other comparable, contemporary publications are Galle's *Mythologia ethica*, from 1579, and Etienne Perret's *XXV Fables des animaux*, from 1578.

130 This publication is included among Plantin's list of de Jode's publications in MPM M 296, fol. 389r, under its Greek title, Μικροκόσμος (at a cost of 28 st. per copy). The first clear record of Plantin's purchase of this text is listed in MPM Arch. 18, fol. 66 rht, under June 2, 1579, where it is noted that Plantin had bought six copies of the "Microcosmus" (= Parvus mundus) at 28 st. per copy. A contemporary record of Plantin's sale of five copies of this book to the Nuremberg merchant Jehan Gundlach (at 30 st. per copy) suggests that Plantin had bought these copies from de Jode for Gundlach. (For the sale to Gundlach, see MPM Arch. 57, fol. 79r, under June 1, 1579.) Plantin similarly purchased four additional copies of this book from de Jode between July 16 and 18, 1579, but no more immediately thereafter (for this second purchase, see MPM Arch. 18, fol. 66 rht and MPM Arch. 57, fol. 103r).

his first Dutch edition of this work, titled *De cleyn werelt*, printed at the Plantin Press (see below). But, as was discussed in detail in the introduction to this appendix, there is, as yet, no conclusive evidence that de Jode's 1584 Latin edition of this work was similarly printed at the Plantin Press. Following the publication of these editions in 1584, de Jode turned to another Antwerp printer, Joachim Trognaesius, for the printing of a French edition of this text, which de Jode published in 1589, the year Plantin died and within two years of de Jode's own death.[131]

1584: Moerman, Jan, *Apologi creaturarum* (Antwerp: C. Plantin for G. de Jode, 1584) 4° (fig. 6.25)

Refs.: BT 5092 and 7792; Hodnett 1971, pp. 51–52; Holl. *Dutch & Flemish*, VII, p. 100; Landwehr 1988, nos. 560–561; PP 1706–1706 bis.

In 1584, de Jode published his first edition of another moralizing emblem book, his *Apologia creaturarum*, with accompanying Latin verses written by Jan Moerman. This work comprises a title-plate and sixty-five illustrations – all of which are etched – and begins with several distinctive images featuring the heavens and nature (as in fig. 6.25), before continuing with more conventional fable subjects. Two variants of this publication are known, which differ only in the title-page image and the plates used to print figure numbers 17, 33, and 64. An examination of the images suggests that the copies catalogued under PP 1706 and Landwehr 1988, no. 560, bear the most uniform set of illustrations – all of which are commonly attributed to Marcus Gheeraerts I – while those copies listed under PP 1706 bis and Landwehr 1988, no. 561, bear a mix of plates.[132] For, while all of the plates used to illustrate PP 1706 are consistent both in size and style, the three distinct plates present in PP 1706 bis are not only smaller in scale than the other images, but also clearly differ stylistically, owing to, for example, the repeated occurrence of more elongated figures.[133] The distinction between the illustration of these two variants is significant because the setting of the text appears to be identical, down to the inclusion of the colophon "Excudebat Gerardo Iudae Christophorus Plantinus," in which Plantin's name is also given, even though, as with other publications from this period, the work was most likely done under the direction of Plantin's sons-in-law, Jan Moretus I and Franciscus Raphelengius I, while Plantin was in Leiden.[134] Thus, the variation in the illustration confirms what has already been deduced concerning Plantin's approach to producing publications with intaglio illustrations, namely, that the text was printed first and then the illustrations were added at potentially disparate moments in time (with the result that the set of

---

[131] Landwehr 1988, no. 557. The title of this publication is the same as the earlier Latin editions, because the old title-plate was used.

[132] For the attribution of these plates to Gheeraerts, see, e.g., Hodnett 1971, p. 51; Holl. *Dutch & Flemish*, VII, *Gheeraerts*, p. 100; PP 1706, n. 2; and Landwehr 1988, no. 560.

[133] For an example of PP 1706 see, e.g., MPM (R 55.18). For an example of PP 1706 bis, see, SBA (H. 78781). All of the illustrations in the MPM copy measure roughly 76 × 121 mm (including plate nos. 17, 33, and 64), while the alternative plates used to illustrate these figures in the SBA copy all measure roughly 67/68 × 119 mm.

[134] On Plantin's Leiden period, see ch. 5.

plates used to illustrate the text may vary from one copy to another).[135] The printing of this text at the Plantin Press is also confirmed by both various archival records and the decorative initials used. Specifically, between January 7 and 28, 1584, the compositor Christoffle Ghist was paid for setting a "livre de G. Jude" (book of G. Jude [= de Jode]), with a signature that agrees with that of the *Apologi creaturarum*. Immediately hereafter (between January 26 and February 10, 1584), charges were periodically noted under de Jode's name for the printing of this text.[136] Voet asserts that these charges, totaling 35 fl., were for both supplying the paper and printing the text. However, we have yet to find any indication that this was the case. Rather, in the charges made to de Jode, only the printing of the *Apologi creaturarum* is cited. Finally, the 39 mm decorative C initial on fol. *∗* 2r is part of a set of Roman letters with grotesque decoration that Plantin frequently used for his publications.[137] Plantin did occasionally purchase a copy of this book, but not until the fall of 1584, some seven or eight months after the text had been printed.[138] This break between Plantin's printing of the text and his purchase of completed copies may reflect the time de Jode needed to have the illustrations printed on to the sheets of text.

1584: Haechtanus, Laurentius, *De cleyn werelt* (trans. by Jan Moerman) (Antwerp: [C. Plantin for] G. de Jode, 1584) 4°

Refs.: BT 1373; Landwehr 1988, no. 563.

In addition to working on de Jode's *Apologi creaturarum* (see above), Jan Moerman also revised the texts for de Jode's Dutch edition of the *Parvus mundus*, similarly published for the first time in 1584. As was the case with the other editions of de Jode's *Parvus mundus*, although the identity of the printer is not given in the publication itself, it is possible to deduce this from the typographical material used. In this case, the 13 mm decorative initial "B" marking the start of the introductory text on fol. *∗* r is part of a group of Roman letters with figural and botanical decoration that Plantin regularly used.[139] As was the case with de Jode's 1584 edition of the *Apologi creaturarum* (see above), while the typographical materials may have belonged to Plantin, the actual printing of the text was most likely supervised by Plantin's sons-in-law, Jan Moretus I and Franciscus Raphelengius I, during Plantin's sojourn in Leiden.[140] For other editions of this text, see the original 1579 edition of the *Parvus mundus* discussed above. It does not appear as though Plantin (or his sons-in-law) purchased any copies of this text.

[135] For more on this topic, see Bowen 2003.
[136] For the payments made to Ghist, see MPM Arch. 33, fol. 69 lft and rht. For the summary charges to de Jode for the work on this text (the title is cited periodically in these records), see MPM Arch. 62, fols. 11r, 14v, and 17v. For transcriptions of these payments, see Denucé 1912–1913, I, p. 165, n. 2.
[137] See Harvard 1974, cat. 10.
[138] Purchases of first two and then six copies of the text (made sometime between September 14, 1584 and January 14, 1587) at 22 st. per copy are noted in de Jode's general accounts with Plantin (see MPM Arch. 20, fol. 266 rht). See MPM Arch. 62, fol. 104r, under December 17, 1584, for a duplicate record of Plantin's purchase of two copies of this text. This edition is not cited among the list of de Jode's publications in MPM M 296, fol. 389r.
[139] Harvard 1974, cat. 30. We examined the copy of this text in RG (3118 D 16). There is also an unusual 26 mm decorative initial "G" on fol. *∗* 2r that we have yet to trace.
[140] On Plantin's period in Leiden, see ch. 5.

Mynken Liefrinck?

1585: *Text for unspecified figures*

On September 7, 1585, the pressmen Guillaume Rivière and Cornelis Comper were both paid for work on "figures de Minken."[141] This is, presumably, a reference to the printing of text to accompany some prints published by Mynken Liefrinck, who saw to the printing of the vast majority of the intaglio book illustrations used by Plantin.[142] However, we have yet to identify the image(s) concerned.

AUTHORS

ALBERT HAYEN

1585: Hayen, Albert, *Amstelredamsche zee-caerten* (Leiden: C. Plantin for A. Hayen, 1585) f°

Refs.: Koeman 1967–1971, IV, Haey 1; PP 1303.

This maritime atlas contains four maps of the coasts of Holland, Zeeland, and northwest Germany, all dated 1585 and inscribed with the name of the designer – the author, Albert Hayen – and the engraver Henrik Rycken, both from Haarlem. In addition, one extra map of the islands of Zeeland dated 1586 and engraved by Harmen Jansz. Muller, was probably added later on. All of the maps were either inserted between or pasted on to sheets with typographically printed text and were not printed on to them directly. As was the case with the 1584 and 1585 editions of Lucas Janszoon Waghenaer's maritime atlas (see below), Plantin – then in Leiden – agreed to print the accompanying text for the author, presumably at his expense.[143] This working relationship is indicated by the imprint on the title-page, which reads: "Tot Leyden, by Christoffel Plantijn/voor Aelbert Haeyen van Amstelredam. M.D.LXXXV." (At Leyden by Christopher Plantin for Albert Hayen of Amsterdam, 1585.) Thus, Hayen appears to have served as the publisher of the edition – the one who organized the execution of the project – and would have retained possession of the plates.[144] Regrettably, no archival data are known pertaining to the production of this book, its sale, or the details of the arrangements between Plantin and the author. Subsequent editions of this text with the same plates were published by Cornelis Claesz in Amsterdam between 1591 and 1609 and then by Dirck Pietersz Pers in 1613, also in Amsterdam.[145]

---

[141] For these payments, see MPM Arch. 33, fol. 101 rht (for Rivière) and fol. 103 lft (for Comper). Although Rivière usually worked as a printer, he was occasionally paid for composing texts, which may account for the unusual overlapping records here of payments to two different pressmen. See n. 171 below (a discussion of Rivière's work as a compositor for Abraham Ortelius's 1587 French edition of his *Theatre de l'univers*).

[142] See ch. 2 for an overview of Liefrinck's work for Plantin.

[143] Strictly speaking (and as noted by Voet), because the privilege for the publication is dated October 12, 1585, when Plantin had just returned to Leiden, it seems likely that the actual work on this atlas was carried out under the direction of Plantin's wife, who was in charge of the Leiden Press at that time (see PP 1303, n. 4).

[144] This impression is substantiated by the lack of any further reference to the plates in the inventories of the stock of the Antwerp and Leiden branches of the Plantin Press at the time of Plantin's death.

[145] For these editions, see Koeman 1967–1971, IV, pp. 220–222.

ABRAHAM ORTELIUS

1579: Ortelius, Abraham, *Theatrum orbis terrarum* (Antwerp: C. Plantin for A. Ortelius, 1579) f° (figs. 6.16–6.17)

Refs.: BT 2301; Denucé 1912–1913, II, pp. 68–70 and 106–108; Koeman 1967–1971, III, Ort. 15 A en B; PP 1817.

As would be the case for each of the Latin and French editions of his atlas printed between 1579 and 1587, Ortelius acted as the publisher of the work and paid Plantin to print the text.[146] These roles are typically confirmed in the text itself, where Plantin's role as printer is usually stated in the colophon and on the title-page of the section *Nomenclator Ptolemaicus*. Plantin always bought back some number of copies of the atlas for further sale. In this case, the first of Ortelius's atlases for which Plantin printed the text, Plantin charged Ortelius 120 fl. in May 1579 for printing the texts. There are also corresponding payments to Plantin's compositors and pressmen for their work on the atlas.[147] Plantin systematically purchased significant quantities of this edition of Ortelius's atlas – a hundred in 1579 alone.[148] During his lifetime, Ortelius retained the ownership of the plates used to illustrate all of the editions of his atlas. Although his very first edition comprised just 50 maps, Ortelius had included 117 maps (printed on 93 sheets) in this 1579 edition, while his 1587 French edition – the last to be printed by Plantin – featured as many as 145 contemporary and historical maps (printed on 112 sheets). Plantin's grandsons, Jan Moretus II and Balthasar Moretus I, purchased all of these plates, along with many others, at an auction of the possessions of Jan Baptist Vrints I's widow. The Moretuses do not appear ever to have used them themselves, however, and presumably sold them in turn, as they are no longer in the collection of the Plantin-Moretus Museum.[149]

1579: Ortelius, Abraham, *Additamentum theatri orbis terrarum* (Antwerp: [C. Plantin for] A. Ortelius, 1579) f°

Refs.: BT 6451; Denucé 1912–1913, II, p. 106; Koeman 1967–1971, III, Ort. 14A; PP 1823.

The *Additamentum* was a separate publication of new maps (in this case, twenty-five) that Ortelius had added to the most recent edition of his atlas, following the publication of his previous editions.[150] This was done for the convenience of those who owned

---

[146] See pp. 290–291 for a discussion of the exceptional 1588 Spanish edition of Ortelius's atlas (PP 1822), whereby Plantin served as the publisher and paid Ortelius for the printing of the maps.

[147] See MPM Arch. 19, fol. 113 lft, for the general charge to Ortelius's accounts, which reads: "Pour aultant que monte l'impression de son theatrum pour 120 rames a rayson de xx patt. la rame monte in NS. la somme de fl. 120." (For the amount for the printing of his Theatrum for 120 reams at 20 st. per ream, comes to the sum of 120 guilders.) For payments to Plantin's staff, see MPM Arch. 32, fol. 295 lft (for the compositor Hans van Miloo), fol. 296 lft (for the compositor Andries Spors), fol. 288 lft and rht (for the pressman Hans Stroosnijder), and fol. 297 lft (for the printer Guillaume Rivière).

[148] Imhof 1999b, pp. 85.

[149] See MPM Arch. 183, pp. 1–3, for a list of all the items the Moretuses purchased at the Vrints's auction, in April 1612 in Antwerp (and p. 1 for these plates in particular). For other such purchases, see the discussion above of Galle's editions of his pocket atlas and the *Deorum dearumque capita . . . ex musaeo Abrahami Ortelii.*

[150] For more on the subsequent fate of the plates used here and for other editions of Ortelius's atlas, see the discussion of the 1579 *Theatrum* above.

copies of these earlier editions, so that they could update their atlases without having to purchase a complete new one. In the case of this edition of the *Additamentum*, Plantin's name is not mentioned in the text and there are no clear archival records documenting the independent printing of the text. The type used, however, indicates that Plantin was responsible for printing this edition.[151] This would be logical given that Plantin is known to have printed the associated *Theatrum* from 1579 and another edition of the *Additamentum* that appeared in 1580 (see below).

1580: Ortelius, Abraham, *Additamentum [II] theatri orbis terrarum* (Antwerp: [C. Plantin for] A. Ortelius, 1580) f°

Refs.: BT 6452; Denucé 1912–1913, II, pp. 108–110; Koeman 1967–1971, III, Ort. 14B; PP 1824.

In May 1580, a charge of 69 fl. for the printing of the *Additamentum* was noted in Ortelius's accounts with Plantin. This record reads: "Pour Additamentum imprimé pour luy 24 f° a 4 mains et f° pr fueille font 4 ram. et 18 mains item 2 mains a luy livrés font rames 5, a 9 fl. rame fl. 45. Pour l'impression desdits 24 f° fl. 24." (For the *Additamentum* printed for him, 24 sheets, 4 quires [of each], sheet per sheet comes to 4 reams and 18 quires; idem, delivered 2 [additional] quires to him, comes to 5 reams at 9 fl. per ream [amounts to] 45 fl. For the printing of these 24 sheets, 24 fl.)[152] If four quires were printed of every sheet, this record would indicate that a hundred copies of the *Additamenta* were produced. It is not clear, however, whether these accounts refer to a hundred new copies of the *Additamenta*, or to previously printed ones, such as those published in 1579 and discussed above.[153]

1580: Ortelius, Abraham, *Theatrum oder Schawbüch des Erdtkreijs* (Antwerp: C. Plantin for A. Ortelius, 1580) f°

Refs.: BT 2305; Denucé 1912–1913, II, p. 110; Koeman 1967–1971, III, Ort. 16 A–B; PP 1818.

Although Plantin is identified as the printer of this text in the colophon, remarkably few archival records pertaining to its printing are known. Indeed, thus far, only the minimal charge of 2 fl. "pour l'impression de ung privilege sur le Theatre en Allemand" (for the printing of a privilege for the *Theatrum* in German) has been found.[154] It does not appear that Plantin purchased copies of this edition for further sale.[155]

1581: Ortelius, Abraham, *Theatre de l'univers, contenant les cartes de tout le monde* (Antwerp: C. Plantin for A. Ortelius, 1581) f°

Refs.: BT 8863; Denucé 1912–1913, II, p. 110; Koeman 1967–1971, III, Ort. 17; PP 1819.

---

[151] PP 1823, n. 3. We examined a copy of this *Additamentum* in MPM (A 943, as part of a 1574 edition of Ortelius's *Theatrum*).

[152] MPM Arch. 19, fol. 118 lft.

[153] Two payments made to the pressman Renier Artsens on April 9 and 16, 1580 for nine and eleven "feules dorteli" (sheets of Ortelius) respectively, might refer to the newly printed texts on the maps of the *Additamentum* (MPM Arch. 33, fol. 23 lft). See also n. 150.

[154] MPM Arch. 19, fol. 118 lft.   [155] Imhof 1999b, p. 85.

Illustrated with the same collection of 117 maps (printed on 93 sheets) that were included in Ortelius's 1579 Latin edition of his atlas, this French edition is noteworthy because of Plantin's extra contributions to it. For, in addition to printing the text, Plantin also wrote a dedication to the Antwerp city government and the citizens of Antwerp, as well as a foreword for the reader. Here, at least, Plantin did not just serve as the "hired hand," but clearly had a greater interest in its publication. Plantin's role as the printer is confirmed by archival documents. Specifically, on February 13, 1582 Plantin charged Ortelius at least 200 fl. 19$^{1}/_{2}$ st. for his production of this text. There are also corresponding payments to one of Plantin's pressmen (Lorans Mesureur) for his work on the atlas.[156] As was the case with the 1579 Latin edition, Plantin systematically purchased large numbers of copies of this edition.[157]

1584: Ortelius, Abraham, *Theatrum orbis terrarum* (Antwerp: C. Plantin for A. Ortelius, 1584) f°

Refs.: Denucé 1912–1913, II, pp. 111–114; Koeman 1967–1971, III, Ort. 21; PP 1820.

This was the second Latin edition of Ortelius's atlases to be printed at the Plantin Press. The text was enlarged significantly to accommodate the inclusion of 28 new maps (resulting in 112 sheets with maps).[158] Although Plantin's name is cited in the colophon, the actual work of printing the atlas would have been overseen by Plantin's sons-in-law, Jan Moretus I and Franciscus Raphelengius I, as Plantin was then in Leiden.[159] Ortelius was charged 282 fl. 12 st. for the production of this text by May 23, 1584.[160] There are also corresponding payments to Plantin's compositors and pressmen for their work on the atlas.[161] According to an overview of payments made to printers and compositors between 1582 and 1585, 750 copies were printed.[162] In the five years following the printing of this edition, Ortelius sold Plantin at least 166 copies of the atlas.[163]

1584: Ortelius, Abraham, *Additamentum III theatri orbis terrarum* (Antwerp: [C. Plantin for] A. Ortelius, 1584) f°

Refs.: BT 2279; Denucé 1912–1913, II, p. 114; Koeman 1967–1971, III, Ort. 18; PP 1825.

---

[156] See MPM Arch. 19, fol. 157 lft, for the general charge to Ortelius, which reads: "pour la f^e du Theatre 1 fl. a^1/2 rame, papier, 10 ram. 13 m[ains] a 13 st. pap. pour les commencements a 15 st." The record here is difficult to interpret. It is possible that the charge for Plantin's printing of the text also included (some of?) the paper it was printed on. For payments to Plantin's pressman L. Mesureur, see MPM Arch. 33, fol. 54 lft.

[157] Imhof 1999b, pp. 85–86. See also n. 150.   [158] See n. 150.   [159] See ch. 5.

[160] See MPM Arch. 19, fol. 163 lft, for the following record: "Adi ditto 23e de Maii, conferant le compte trouvons que le Theatre Latin monte 235 rames et demi à 24 st. pour la rame." (On 23 May: having compared our accounts, we have found that the Latin *Theatrum* comes to 235 and ^{1}/2 reams at 24 st. per ream.)

[161] For payments to Plantin's staff, see MPM Arch. 33, fol. 67 rht (for the pressman Nicolas Spors), fol. 71 lft (for the pressman Hans Clas), fol. 73 rht (for the pressman Nicolas van Linschoten), fol. 75 rht (for the pressman Hans Stroosnijder), fol. 84 lft (for the pressman Josse Embrecht), fol. 90 lft (for the pressman Claeys Sterck II), fol. 91 lft (for the compositor Jan Lancelot), fol. 96 lft (for the pressman Hans Stroosnijder), and fol. 97 lft (for the pressman Nicolas van Linschoten). The work on this atlas is discussed in greater detail in Imhof 1999b, p. 86.

[162] MPM Arch. 788, fol. 4r, under Ortelius.   [163] Imhof 1999b, p. 86.

In 1584, Plantin simultaneously printed the texts for Ortelius's *Theatrum* and the third *Additamentum*, which comprised forty-seven maps (printed on twenty-four sheets). This is evident from the two records known pertaining to the production of these books. One payment covers the printing of 750 copies of the texts for the old maps of the atlas. Another payment was for printing the texts for "2 rames et demy" ($2\frac{1}{2}$ reams), or 1,250 extra copies of the new maps.[164] Thus, while 750 copies of the texts for the new maps were combined with the 750 copies of the existing maps to make up the new editions of the *Theatrum*, the remaining 500 sets of texts for the new maps could have been sold separately as the *Additamentum*. On April 28, 1584, one of Plantin's pressmen, Hans Stroosnijder, was paid for printing what was most likely the separate title-page of the *Additamentum*.[165]

1585: Ortelius, Abraham, *Augmentation III du theatre du monde universel* (Antwerp: C. Plantin for A. Ortelius, 1585) f°

Refs.: Denucé 1912–1913, II, p. 114–115; Koeman 1967–1971, III, Ort, 20; PP 1827.

Plantin's involvement in the production of this French version of Ortelius's third *Additamentum* (with forty-seven maps, printed on twenty-four sheets) was multifold.[166] The imprint on this edition's title-page, "A Anvers, de l'imprimerie de Christofle Plantin, pour l'aucteur," suggests the usual working relationship, namely, Plantin printed the texts for Ortelius. That Plantin saw to the printing of these texts is confirmed by payments made to one of his pressmen, Hans van Leuven (alias Elsevir), between February 23 and March 30, 1585.[167] In addition, however, Plantin also paid for the translation of the new texts from the original Latin into French.[168] Thus, as was the case with Ortelius's 1581 French *Theatre* – the edition for which this *Additamentum* was most likely intended – Plantin's involvement in the production of the work went beyond his basic task as the letterpress printer.

1587: Ortelius, Abraham, *Theatre de l'univers, contenant les cartes de tout le monde* (Antwerp: C. Plantin for A. Ortelius, 1587) f°

Refs.: BT 6457; Denucé 1912–1913, II, p. 115; Koeman 1967–1971, III, Ort. 22; PP 1821.

Ortelius's 1587 French edition of the *Theatre* comprised the same selection of maps that were included in his 1584 Latin edition.[169] As before, Plantin's involvement in the production of this edition is evident from the colophon, which reads: "A Anvers, de l'imprimerie de Christofle Plantin, pour Abraham Ortel autheur mesme de ce livre," and is confirmed by archival records. Specifically, in July 1587 Plantin charged Ortelius 177 fl. for printing the texts for this edition.[170] There are also corresponding payments to

---

[164] See MPM Arch. 33, fol. 96 lft, for this reference. See also n. 150.

[165] See MPM Arch. 33, fol. 96 lft, for the following payment to Stroosnijder: "B12 [Theatri] et Additamentum III etc."

[166] See n. 150.　　[167] MPM Arch. 33, fol. 106 rht.

[168] MPM Arch. 20, fol. 82 rht. See also Imhof 1999b, p. 87.　　[169] See n. 150.

[170] See MPM Arch. 20, fol. 263 lft, for the following record: "Pour l'impression de son Theatrum en françois contenant folia 118, montant a rayson de 30 patt. la fueille fl. 177." (For the printing of his *Theatrum* in French, which comprises 118 folios, at 30 st. per folio, comes to 177 fl.)

Plantin's compositors and pressmen for their work on the atlas.[171] In striking contrast with the previous French edition and the two preceding Latin editions, Plantin bought only an occasional copy of this edition – as few as thirty-nine copies between 1587 and 1589.[172]

1588: Ortelius, Abraham, *Theatro de la tierra universal* (Antwerp: C. Plantin, 1588) f°

Refs.: Denucé 1912–1913, II, p. 119–120; Koeman 1967–1971, III, Ort. 23; PP 1822.

Because this Spanish edition of Ortelius's atlas is the only edition for which Plantin, and not Ortelius, served as publisher, it does not truly belong among the other examples here of Plantin printing for others. For a more detailed discussion of this edition, see chapter 6.

ETIENNE PERRET

1578: Perret, Etienne, *XXV fables des animaux* (Antwerp: C. Plantin for E. Perret, 1578) f° (fig. 6.19)

Refs.: Landwehr 1988, no. 612; PP 1962.

Featuring twenty-five folio engravings, this work constitutes a visually stunning, but limited selection of moralizing animal fables. For while both the images and the accompanying commentary were clearly derived from E. de Dene's *De warachtighe fabulen der dieren* (Bruges: P. de Clercq for Marcus Gheeraerts I, 1567), the emphasis now is on the full-page images that counterbalance a noticeably reduced text.[173] Plantin's role as the printer of the text is evident from the imprint, which reads: "A Anvers, Imprimé par Christophle Plantin, pour l'Aucteur. M.D.LXXVIII." (At Antwerp, printed by Christopher Plantin for the author . . .) Plantin was to receive 104 illustrated copies of the text in exchange for his work. Given that Plantin subsequently sold copies of this book for 18 st. per copy, the 104 copies would have rendered 93 fl. 12 st. However, while Perret did deliver 70 copies of his book to Plantin by May 6, 1578, he does not appear to have ever delivered the remaining 34 copies.[174]

LUCAS JANSZOON WAGHENAER

1584 and 1585: Waghenaer, Lucas Janszoon, *Teerste deel vande spieghel der zeevaerdt* (Leiden: C. Plantin for L. J. Waghenaer, 1584 and 1585) f°; and *Het tweede deel vanden spieghel der zeevaert* (Leiden: C. Plantin for L. J. Waghenaer, 1585), f° (fig. 6.18)

Refs.: Koeman 1967–1971, IV, pp. 465–483; *New Holl.*, *Van Doetecum*, III, nos. 791–840; PP 2480–2489.

[171] For payments to Plantin's staff, see MPM Arch. 33, fol. 113 rht (for the setting of much of the text by Guillaume Rivière, who usually worked as a pressman, but also occasionally worked as a compositor); fol. 115 rht (for the pressman Nicolas van Linschoten); fol. 124 lft (for the pressman Hans Elsevir, alias Hans van Leuven); fol. 126 lft (for the conclusion of the setting of the text by Rivière).

[172] Imhof 1999b, p. 87.

[173] See Landwehr 1988, nos. 613–617, for references to later editions of this work (dated to 1617–1633).

[174] See ch. 6 for a full discussion of this matter.

In Leon Voet's own words, Plantin's editions of Waghenaer's maritime atlas represent "a nightmare – or a delight" for bibliographers, owing to the numerous variants known, particularly in terms of the selection and state of the maps illustrating them.[175] Because Plantin's role as the printer, hired by the author to print his text, does not vary, we will not repeat Voet's description of the numerous variants here. In addition to an engraved title-page, the first volume of this text (with variants dated to 1584 and 1585) bears several woodcuts, an engraved compass with a moving part, a graduated arc, and twenty-three charts of the coasts of western Europe, where almost all of these plates bear the name of the designer – the author, L. J. Waghenaer – and the engraver-etcher Joannes van Doetecum. The second volume contains an additional twenty-three charts of the coasts of England, Scotland, and the Baltic Sea, similarly designed by Waghenaer and executed by Joannes van Doetecum.[176] According to Voet, both the first and the second volume were reset and reprinted in part or in their entirety at least two or three times. In all cases, however, the imprint on the title-page indicates that Plantin produced the text for Waghenaer when in Leiden. There are, regrettably, no known archival data to clarify the production of these editions and the working relationship between Plantin and Waghenaer. Although this work is listed in Plantin's catalogues of his own publications,[177] it appears, nevertheless, that Waghenaer served as the publisher of the edition – the one who organized the execution of the project – and would have retained possession of the plates. This supposition is supported not only by the imprint, but by the lack of any further reference to the plates in the inventories of Plantin's copper plates compiled following his death (see appendix 4). Rather, the ownership of the plates – and, hence, the control over the publication – appears to have passed from Waghenaer to the Amsterdam print publisher, Cornelis Claesz, who engaged a variety of printers, including Plantin's successor at the Leiden branch of the Plantin Press, Franciscus Raphelengius I, to print new editions of these texts.[178]

[175] Voet, PP, V, pp. 2,417–2,418.
[176] For accounts of the plates and how they are signed, see Voet's notes on the illustrations to PP 2487 and *New Holl., Van Doetecum*, III, nos. 791–840. Copies of Waghenaer's atlas also vary in the number of plates included.
[177] See MPM M 296, fol. 18r.
[178] For an overview of the later editions, see Koeman 1967–1971, IV, pp. 469–470, and *New Holl., Van Doetecum*, III, pp. 230–232.

REFERENCES

ARCHIVAL SOURCES

The titles of the archival documents from the Plantin-Moretus Museum given below are taken from Jan Denucé's *Inventaris op het Plantijnsch Archief. Inventaire des Archives Plantiniennes* (Antwerp: De Sikkel, 1926). For a brief overview of the various systems of notation used in these documents, see the preliminary remarks.

Arch. 3: *Journal des affaires 1563–1567*
Arch. 4: *Grand livre des affaires 1563–67*
Arch. 5 and Arch. 5bis: *Biblia Regia. Missel. Compte du Roi d'Espagne 1568–1578*
Arch. 6: *Comptes espagnols 1571–1575*
Arch. 8: *Copie de lettres de Plantin 1572–78*
Arch. 9: *Copie de lettres de Plantin 1572–1581*
Arch. 10: *Copie de lettres de Plantin 1579–1589*
Arch. 14: *Livre de caisse 1576–1589*
Arch. 16: *Grand livre 1568–1573*
Arch. 17: *Grand livre des libraires 1568–1578*
Arch. 18: *Grand livre + ++ 1571–1582*
Arch. 19: *Grand livre signé C 1572–1589*
Arch. 20: *Grand livre 1582–1589*
Arch. 21: *Grand livre 1590–1599*
Arch. 22: *Envois de livres à Philippe II, 1571–1576*
Arch. 24: *Comptes avec Philippe II 1571–1574*
Arch. 27: *Verkoop van Plantijns goed 1562*
Arch. 28: *Livre de caisse 1570*
Arch. 29: *Livre de caisse 1571*
Arch. 30: *Livre de caisse 1589–1590*
Arch. 31: *Livre des ouvriers 1563–1574*
Arch. 32: *Livre des ouvriers 1571–1579*

Arch. 33: *Livre des ouvriers 1580–1590*

Arch. 35: *Journal 1558–1561*

Arch. 37: *Débiteurs 1565–1569*

Arch. 43^III: *Vente à la boutique 1569–1576*

Arch. 47: *Journal 1569*

Arch. 48: *Journal 1570*

Arch. 49: *Journal 1571*

Arch. 50: *Journal 1572*

Arch. 51: *Journal 1573*

Arch. 52: *Journal 1574*

Arch. 53: *Journal 1575*

Arch. 54: *Journal 1576*

Arch. 56: *Journal 1578*

Arch. 57: *Journal 1579*

Arch. 58: *Journal 1580*

Arch. 59: *Journal 1581*

Arch. 60: *Journal 1582*

Arch. 61: *Journal 1583*

Arch. 62: *Journal 1584–1585*

Arch. 63: *Journal 1586*

Arch. 64: *Journal 1587*

Arch. 65: *Journal 1588*

Arch. 66: *Journal 1589*

Arch. 67: *Journal 1590*

Arch. 82: *Lettres de F. Fabianus–A. Gassen*

Arch. 86: *Lettres de Fr. v. Immerseel-Loyens*

Arch. 92: *Lettres de Jac. van Quaille-Ryckius*

Arch. 93: *Lettres de Aug. Sabbetius–Ger. Symont*

Arch. 98: *Pièces de famille 1549–1589*

Arch. 99: *Papiers de famille des Moretus 1590–1596*

Arch. 101: *Livre des affaires de famille 1605–1657*

Arch. 109bis: *Index librorum Officinae Plant. 1630, 12 Julij*

Arch. 112: *Libraires d'Anvers DD 1590–1602*

Arch. 113: *Libraires d'Anvers EE. 1602–1616*

Arch. 117: *Imprimerie 1585–1599*

Arch. 122: *Missale et Breviarium 1572–1576*

Arch. 123: *Graveurs I. Galle. 1600–1692*

Arch. 124: *Graveurs, II, 1555–1825*

Arch. 126: *Grand livre signé D. 1590–1614*

Arch. 127: *Grand livre du soleil 1600–1608*

Arch. 179: *Journal 1607*

Arch. 183: *Société de J. & B. Moretus pour les planches de J. B. Vrients 1612–1614*

Arch. 204: *Dépenses diverses 1569–1603*

Arch. 490: *Inventaire livres Anvers-Francfort, 1602*

Arch. 491: *Journal 1581–1588 (librairie)*

Arch. 495: *Journal librairie 1589–1592*

Arch. 756: *Relieurs et graveurs 1565–1569*

Arch. 757: *Relieurs 1570–1575*

Arch. 788: *Ouvriers 1582–1589*

Arch. 1075: *Livre de caisse 1605–1617*

Arch. 1079: *Carnet de dépenses*

Arch. 1228: *Theatrum typographicum Plantinianae officinae 1576*

M 39: *Catalogue des éditions plantiniennes 1590–1651* (Denucé 1926, no. 1232)

M 121: *Catalogue de la bibliothèque en 1592* (Denucé 1926, no. 1233)

M 164: *Catalogue des éditions plantiniennes 1555–1586* (Denucé 1926, no. 1226)

M 296: *Catalogue d'éditions de Plantin et de ses contemporains 1555–1593* (Denucé 1926, no. 1227)

SECONDARY LITERATURE

Adams 1967: Adams, H. M., *Catalogue of Books Printed on the Continent of Europe, 1501–1600, in Cambridge Libraries*, 2 vols. (Cambridge: Cambridge University Press, 1967).

Adams 2000: Adams, Alison, "Les emblemes ou devises chrestiennes de Georgette de Montenay: Edition de 1567," *Bibliothèque d'Humanisme et Renaissance*, 62/3 (2000), pp. 637–639.

Adams et al. 2002: Adams, Alison, Stephen Rawles, and Alison Saunders, *A Bibliography of French Emblem Books*, 2 vols. (Geneva: Librarie Droz, 1999–2002).

Aerts et al. 1995: Aerts, E., M. Baelde, H. Coppens, et al., eds., *De centrale overheidsinstellingen van de Habsburgse Nederlanden (1482–1795)*, 2 vols. (Brussels: Algemeen Rijksarchief, 1995).

Allison and Rogers 1989: Allison, A. F., and D. M. Rogers, *The Contemporary Printed Literature of the English Counter-Reformation between 1558 and 1640: An Annotated Catalogue. I. Works in Languages other than English* (Aldershot: Scolar Press; Brookfield, VT: Gower, 1989).

Amsterdam 1975: *Leidse universiteit 400: stichting en eerste bloei 1575–c.1650*, catalogue of the exhibition held at Rijksmuseum, Amsterdam, March 27–June 8, 1975 (Amsterdam: Rijksmuseum, 1975).

Amsterdam 2003: Leeflang, H., G. Luijten, et al., *Hendrick Goltzius (1558–1617). Drawings, Prints and Paintings*, catalogue of the exhibition held at the Rijksmuseum, Amsterdam (March 7–May 25, 2003), the Metropolitan Museum of Art, New York (June 23–September 7, 2003), and the Toledo Museum of Art, Toledo (October 18, 2003–January 4, 2004) (Zwolle: Waanders Publishers, 2003).

Antwerp 16th Century: *Antwerpen in de XVIde eeuw*, ed. by Genootschap voor Antwerpse Geschiedenis (Antwerp: Mercurius, 1975).

Arblaster 2004: Arblaster, Paul, *Antwerp and the World: Richard Verstegan and the International Culture of Catholic Reformation* (Leuven: University Press, 2004).

Arias Montano 2005: Arias Montano, Benito, *Virorum doctorum de disciplinis benemerentium effigies XLIIII*, ed. by Fernando Navarro Antolín and Luis Gómez Canseco (Huelva: Universidad de Huelva, 2005) (reprint of the original edition, published by Philips Galle in 1572).

Armstrong 1954: Armstrong, E., *Robert Estienne Royal Printer* (Cambridge: Cambridge University Press, 1954).

Von Arnim 1984: Von Arnim, Manfred, ed., *Katalog der Bibliothek Otto Schäfer Schweinfurt. Teil I: Drucke, Manuskripte und Einbände des 15. Jahrhunderts* (Stuttgart: Dr. Ernst Hauswedell, 1984).

Balsamo and Simonin 2002: Balsamo, Jean, and Michel Simonin, *Abel L'Angelier and Françoise de Louvain (1574–1620)*, Travaux d'Humanisme et Renaissance 358 (Geneva: Librarie Droz, 2002).

Barberi 1985: Barberi, Francesco, *Paolo Manuzio e la stamperia del Popolo Romano (1561–1570)* (Rome: Gela Reprints, 1985).

Barker 2002: Barker, Nicolas, "The Polyglot Bible," in: Barnard and McKenzie 2002, pp. 648–651.

Barnard and McKenzie 2002: Barnard, John, and D. F. McKenzie, eds., *The Cambridge History of the Book in Britain*, vol. VI: *1557–1695* (Cambridge: Cambridge University Press, 2002).

BB: *Bibliotheca Belgica. Bibliographie générale des Pays-Bas. Fondée par Ferdinand Van der Haeghen. Rééditée sous la direction de Marie-Thérèse Lenger*, 7 vols. (Brussels: Culture et civilisation, 1964–1975).

BCNI: *Bibliotheca catholica Neerlandica impressa, 1500–1727* (The Hague: Martinus Nijhoff, 1954).

Bécares Botas 1999: Bécares Botas, Vicente, *Arias Montano y Plantino. El libro flamenco en la España de Felipe II* (León: Universidad de León, Secretariado de Publicaciones, 1999).

Beer 1905: Beer, R., "Niederländische Büchererwerbungen des Benito Arias Montano für den Eskorial in Auftrage König Philipp II. von Spanien, nach unveröffentlichen, aus den Musée Plantin-Moretus zu Antwerpen von Max Rooses Zur Verfügung gestellten Urkunden," *Jahrbuch der Kunsthistorischen Sammhungen des allerhöchsten Kaisershauses*, 25/6 (1905), pp. i–xi.

Benzing 1963: Benzing, Josef, *Die Buchdrucker des 16. und 17. Jahrhunderts im Deutschen Sprachgebiet* (Wiesbaden: Otto Harrassowitz, 1963).

Bialler 1993: Bialler, Nancy, *Chiaroscuro Woodcuts: Hendrick Goltzius (1558–1617) and his Time* (Amsterdam: Rijksmuseum, 1993).

Bland 1969: Bland, David, *A History of Book Illustration: The Illuminated Manuscript and the Printed Book*, 2nd edn. (London: Faber & Faber, 1969).

BMC: *Catalogue of Books Printed in the XVth Century now in the British Museum*, 13 vols. (London: British Museum, 1908–2004).

BN: *Biographie nationale*, 44 vols. (Brussels: L'Académie Royale de Belgique, 1866–1985).

Boer 1952: Boer, C., *Hofpredikers van Prins Willem van Oranje: Jean Taffin en Pierre Loyseleur de Villiers* ('s-Gravenhage: Martinus Nijhoff, 1952).

Bowen 1994: Bowen, Karen L., "Newly Discovered Wierix Prints for Plantin's Books of Hours," *Quaerendo*, 24 (1994), pp. 275–295.

— 1997a: Bowen, Karen L., *Christopher Plantin's Books of Hours: Illustration and Production* (Nieuwkoop: De Graaf Publishers, 1997).

— 1997b: Bowen, Karen L., "Wierix and Plantin: A Question of Originals and Copies," *Print Quarterly*, 14 (1997), pp. 131–150.

— 2003: Bowen, Karen L., "Illustrating Books with Engravings: Plantin's Working Practices Revealed," *Print Quarterly*, 20 (2003), pp. 3–34.

Bowen and Imhof 2001: Bowen, Karen L. and Dirk Imhof, "Book Illustrations by Maarten de Vos for Jan Moretus I," *Print Quarterly*, 18 (2001), pp. 259–289.

— 2003: Bowen, Karen L. and Dirk Imhof, "Reputation and Wage: The Case of Engravers who Worked for the Plantin-Moretus Press," *Simiolus: Netherlands Quarterly for the History of Art*, 30/3–4 (2003), pp. 161–195.

— 2005: Bowen, Karen L. and Dirk Imhof, "18,257 Impressions from a Plate," *Print Quarterly*, 22 (September 2005), pp. 265–279.

Van den Branden 1985: Van den Branden, Lode, "Archiefstukken betreffende het Antwerpse boekwezen in de 15de en 16de eeuw," ed. by E. Cockx-Indestege, in: De Nave 1985, pp. 169–187.

Brulez 1959: Brulez, Wilfrid, *De firma Della Faille en de internationale handel van Vlaamse firma's in de 16de eeuw* (Brussels: Koninklijke Vlaamse Academie voor Wetenschappen/Paleis der Academiën, 1959).

BT: Cockx-Indestege, E., G. Glorieux, and B. Op De Beeck, *Belgica typographica 1541–1600. Catalogus librorum impressorum ab anno MDXLI ad annum MDC in regionibus quae nunc Regni Belgarum partes sunt*, 4 vols. (Nieuwkoop: De Graaf Publishers, 1968–1994).

Burke 1993: Burke, Peter, "Antwerp, a Metropolis in Europe," in: Van der Stock 1993, pp. 49–57 (in both the English and Dutch versions of this text).

Bury 2001: Bury, Michael, *The Print in Italy, 1550–1620* (London: British Museum Press, 2001).

Caron 1998: Caron, Antoine, ed., *Des livres rares depuis l'invention de l'imprimerie* (Paris: Bibliothèque nationale de France, 1998).

Chambers 1983: Chambers, B. T., *Bibliography of French Bibles*, 2 vols. (Geneva: Librarie Droz, 1983).

Chartier and Martin 1982: Chartier, R., and H. J. Martin, eds., *Histoire de l'édition française, vol. 1: Le livre conquérant* (Paris: Promodis, 1982).

Chatelain 1992: Chatelain, Jean-Marc, "Lire pour coire: mises en texte de l'emblème et art de méditer au XVIIe siècle," *Bibliothèque de l'Ecole des Chartes*, 150/2 (1992), pp. 321–351.

Clair 1959: Clair, Colin, "Christopher Plantin's Trade-connections with England and Scotland," *The Library*, 5th series, 14 (1959), pp. 28–45.

 1960: Clair, Colin, *Christopher Plantin* (London: Cassel, 1960).

De Clercq 1956: De Clercq, Carlo, "Les éditions bibliques, liturgiques et canoniques de Plantin," *Gedenkboek der Plantin-dagen, 1555–1955*, ed. by Vereeniging der Antwerpsche Bibliophielen (*De Gulden Passer*, 34 [1956]), pp. 157–192.

Cockx-Indestege 1994: Cockx-Indestege, Elly, *Andreas Vesalius, a Belgian Census: Contribution towards a New Edition of H. W. Cushing's Bibliography*, Monografieën van de Koninklijke Bibliotheek Albert I, 81 (Brussels: The Royal Library, 1994).

Coppens 1989: Coppens, Chris, "Een kijk op het Woord. De titelbladen van Plantins bijbels. Een iconografische verkenning," in Marcus de Schepper and Francine de Nave, eds., *Ex Officina Plantiniana: Studia in memoriam Christophori Plantini (c.1520–1589)* (*De Gulden Passer*, 66–67 [1988–1989]), pp. 171–211.

 1993: Coppens, Chris, *Reading in Exile: The Libraries of John Ramridge (d. 1568), Thomas Harding (d. 1572) and Henry Joliffe (d. 1573), Recusants in Louvain* (Cambridge: LP Publications, 1993).

Corr.: Rooses, M. and J. Denucé, eds., *Correspondance de Christophe Plantin*, 9 vols. (Antwerp: De Groote Boekhandel-'s Gravenhage, Martinus Nijhoff, 1883–1918) (reprint: Nendeln, Liechenstein: Kraus, 1968).

Corr. supplément: Van Durme, M., ed., *Supplément à la correspondance de Christophe Plantin* (Antwerp: De Nederlandsche Boekhandel, 1955).

Cushing 1962: Cushing, Harvey, *A Bio-Bibliography of Andreas Vesalius*, 2nd edn. (Hamden, CT: Archon Books, 1962).

Dael 2004: Dael, Peter van, "Two Illustrated Catechisms from Antwerp by Petrus Canisius," in Koen Goudriaan, Jaap van Moolenbroek, and Ad Tervoort, eds., *Education and Learning in the Netherlands, 1400–1600: Essays in Honour of Hilde de Ridder-Symoens* (Leiden and Boston: Brill, 2004), pp. 277–296.

Darby 2001: Darby, Graham, ed., *The Origins and Developments of the Dutch Revolt* (London and New York: Routledge, 2001).

Darlow and Moule 1963: Darlow, T. H., and H. F. Moule, *Historical Catalogue of the Printed Editions of Holy Scripture in the Library of the British and Foreign Bible Society*, 2 vols. (New York: Kraus Reprint Corporation, 1963).

Dávila Pérez 2002: Dávila Pérez, Antonio, ed., *Benito Arias Montano Correspondencia conservada en el Museo Plantin-Moretus de Amberes*, 2 vols. (Madrid: Alcañiz, 2002).

De Dene 1978: De Dene, Eduard, *De warachtighe fabulen der dieren*, reprint, with concluding commentary by W. Le Loup (Roeselare: Den Wijngaert, 1978).

Dekoninck 2004: Dekoninck, Ralph, "*Imagines peregrinantes*: The International Genesis and Fate of Two Biblical Picture Books (Barrefelt and Nadal) Conceived in Antwerp at the end of the

Sixteenth Century," in Arie-Jan Gelderblom, Jan L. de Jong, and Marc van Vaeck, eds., *The Low Countries as a Crossroads of Religious Beliefs* (Leiden and Boston: Brill, 2004).

Delano-Smith and Ingram 1991: Delano-Smith, Catherine, and Elizabeth Morley Ingram, *Maps in Bibles, 1500–1600. An Illustrated Catalogue* Travaux d'Humanisme et Renaissance 256 (Geneva: Librarie Droz, 1991).

Delen 1920: Delen, A. J. J., "Les artistes collaborateurs de Christophe Plantin," in: Musée du livre, Brussels, ed., *Sept études publiées à l'occasion du quatrieme centenaire du célèbre imprimeur anversois Christophe Plantin* (Antwerp: J.-F. Buschmann; Brussels: J.-E. Goossens, 1920), pp. 85–123.

1924–1935: Delen, A. J. J., *Histoire de la gravure dans les Anciens Pays-Bas & dans les provinces Belges des origines jusqu'à la fin du XVIIIe siècle* (Paris: Editions d'art et d'histoire, 1924–1935), vol. I: *Des origines a 1500* (1924); vol. II.1: *Le XVIe siècle. Les graveurs-illustrateurs* (1934); vol. II.2: *Le XVIe siècle. Les graveurs d'estampes* (1935) (reprint: Paris: F. de Nobele, 1969, 3 vols. in 1).

1930: Delen, A. J. J., *Iconographie van Antwerpen* (Brussels: L. J. Kryn, 1930).

1932: Delen, A. J. J., "Christoffel Plantin als prentenhandelaar," *De Gulden Passer*, 10 (1932), pp. 1–24.

Denucé 1912–1913: Denucé, Jan, *Oud-Nederlandsche kaartmakers in betrekking met Plantijn*, 2 vols., Publications van de Maatschappij der Antwerpsche bibliophielen, nos. 27 and 28 (Antwerp: De Nederlandsche Boekhandel; The Hague: Martinus Nijhoff, 1912–1913).

1926: Denucé, Jan, *Inventaris op het Plantijnsch Archief. Inventaire des Archives Plantiniennes* (Antwerp: De Sikkel, 1926).

1927: Denucé, Jan, "Prentenhandel Theodoor Galle en Catharina Moerentorf. Inventaris van 1636," *Antwerpsch archievenblad* (April 1927), pp. 1–16.

Depauw 1993: Depauw, Carl, "Peeter vander Borcht (1535/40–1608): The Artist as *Inventor* or Creator of Botanical Illustrations?" in: Imhof and De Nave 1993, pp. 47–55 (the same article appears in Dutch in the Dutch version of this catalogue).

Dequeker and Gistelinck 1989: Dequeker, Luc, and Frans Gistelinck, *Biblia Vulgata Lovaniensis 1547–1574* (Leuven: Bibliotheek van de Faculteit der Godgeleerdheid, 1989).

Diels 2005: Diels, Ann, *"Wat d'yser can bemaelen": prenten van de Antwerpse graveursfamilie Collaert (1550–1630)*, catalogue of the exhibition held at the Royal Library, February 25–April 9, 2005 (Ouderkerk aan den Ijssel: Sound & Vision; Brussels: The Royal Library, 2005).

Di Filippo Bareggi 1994: Di Filippo Bareggi, C., "L'editoria veneziana fra '500 e '600," in Gaetano Cozzi and Paolo Prodi, eds., *Storia di Venezia VI, Dal Rinascimento al Barocco* (Rome: Istituto della enciclopedia italiana, 1994), pp. 615–648.

Dizionario dei tipografi: Menato, Marco, et al., eds., *Dizionario dei tipografi e degli editori italiani: Il Cinquecento*, 2 vols. (Milan: Editrice bibliografica, 1997).

DNB 1993: Nicholls, C. S., ed., *The Dictionary of National Biography: Missing Persons* (Oxford and New York: Oxford University Press, 1993).

Van Durme 1962: Van Durme, Maurice, "Lettres inédites de cardinal de Granvelle à Christophe Plantin (1567–1569)," *Gutenberg-Jahrbuch* (1962), pp. 280–286.

Duval 1998: Duval-Arnould, Louis, "Les premières éditions italiennes du Missel tridentin," in: *Miscellanea Bibliothecae Apostolicae Vaticanae VI, Collectanea in honorem Rev.mi Patris Leonardi E. Boyle, O. P. Septuagesimum quintum annum feliciter complentis* (Vatican City: Biblioteca Apostolica Vaticana, 1998), pp. 121–172.

Duverger: Duverger, Erik, *Antwerpse kunstinventarissen uit de zeventiende eeuw*, 13 vols. to date (Brussels: Paleis der Academie, 1984–).

Ehrle 1908: Ehrle, F., *Roma prima di Sisto V: la pianta Du Pérac-Lafréry del 1577* (Vatican City: Biblioteca Apostolica Vaticana, 1908).

Elliot 1987: Elliot, James, *The City in Maps: Urban Mapping to 1900* (London: The British Library, 1987).

Febvre-Martin 1990: Febvre, Lucien, and Henri-Jean Martin, *The Coming of the Book: The Impact of Printing, 1450–1800* (London: Verso, 1990) (originally published in French as *L'apparition du livre*, Paris: Michel, 1958).

Ferrary 1996: Ferrary, Jean-Louis, *Onofrio Panvinio et les antiquités romaines* (Rome: Ecole Française de Rome, Palais Farnèse, 1996).

Filser and Leimgruber 2003: Filser, Hubert, and Stephan Leimgruber, *Petrus Canisius der große Katechismus* Summa doctrinae christianae (1555) (Regensburg: Verlag Schnell und Steiner, 2003).

Gaskell 1972: Gaskell, P., *A New Introduction to Bibliography* (New York and Oxford: Oxford University Press, 1972) (reprint New Castle, DE: Oak Knoll Press, 1995).

Gaskell 2004: Gaskell, Roger, "Printing House and Engraving Shop: A Mysterious Collaboration," *The Book Collector* (Summer 2004), pp. 213–251.

Génard 1859: Génard, P., "Les grandes familles artistiques d'Anvers," *Revue d'histoire et d'archéologie*, 1 (1859), pp. 102–117 and 194–210.

Gheyn 1911: Gheyn, Joseph van den, ed., *"Album amicorum" de Otto Venius* (Brussels: Vromant, 1911).

Gieben 1976: Gieben, S., "Philip Galle's Original Engravings of the Life of St. Francis and the Corrected Edition of 1587," *Collectanea Franciscana*, 46/3–4 (1976), pp. 241–307.

Gielens 1940: Gielens, A., "De Kosten van de Blijde Intrede van den Hertog van Anjou (1582)," *Jaarboek Koninklijke Oudheidkundige Kring van Antwerpen*, 16 (1940), pp. 93–105.

Greenslade 1963: Greenslade, S. L., ed., *The Cambridge History of the Bible*, vol. III: *The West from the Reformation to the Present Day* (Cambridge: Cambridge University Press, 1963; reprinted in 1975 and 1976).

Grendler 1977: Grendler, Paul F., *The Roman Inquisition and the Venetian Press, 1540–1605* (Princeton: Princeton University Press, 1977).

Griffiths 1996: Griffiths, Antony, *Prints and Printmaking: An Introduction to the History and Techniques* (Berkeley and Los Angeles: University of California Press; London: British Museum Press, 1996).

Grivel 1986: Grivel, Marianne, *Le Commerce de l'estampe à Paris au XVIIe siècle*, Histoire et civilisation du livre 16 (Geneva: Droz, 1986).

Grove Dictionary of Art: Turner, Jane, ed., *The Dictionary of Art*, 34 vols. (New York: Grove Dictionaries and Macmillan Publishers, 1996).

Gruys and de Wolf 1989: Gruys, J. A., and C. de Wolf, *Thesaurus 1473–1800 Nederlandse boekdrukkers en boekverkopers met plaatsen en jaren van werkzaamheid/Dutch Printers and Booksellers with places and years of activity* (Nieuwkoop: De Graaf Publishers, 1989).

Guicciardini 1920: Guicciardini, Ludovico, *Description de la cité d'Anvers* (reprint, Antwerp: Zazzarini, 1920).

Guicciardini 2001: Deys, Henk, Mathieu Franssen, Vincent van Hezik, et al., *Guicciardini illustratus: de kaarten en prenten in Ludovico Guicciardini's beschrijving van de Nederlanden* ('t Goy-Houten: Hes & De Graaf, 2001).

Guilday 1914: Guilday, Peter, *The English Catholic Refugees on the Continent, 1558–1795* (London and New York: Longmans, Green, 1914).

GW: *Gesamtkatalog der Wiegendrucke*, multiple vols. (Leipzig: Verlag von Karl W. Hiersemann, 1925–).

Hamilton 1981a: Hamilton, Alastair, "From Familism to Pietism: The Fortunes of Pieter vander Borcht's Biblical Illustrations and Hiël's Commentaries from 1584 to 1717," *Quaerendo*, II (1981), pp. 271–301.

1981b: Hamilton, Alastair, *The Family of Love* (Cambridge: Clarke, 1981).

Hänsel 1991: Hänsel, Sylvaine, *Der Spanische Humanist Benito Arias Montano (1572–1598) und die Kunst* (Münster: Aschendorffsche Verlagsbuchhandlung, 1991).

Harthan 1981: Harthan, John, *The History of the Illustrated Book: The Western Tradition* (London: Thames & Hudson, 1981).

Harvard 1974: Stephen Harvard, *Ornamental Initials: The Woodcut Initials of Christopher Plantin* (New York: The American Friends of the Plantin-Moretus Museum, 1974).

Hessels 1887: J. H. Hessels, *Abrahami Ortelii (geographi Antverpiensis) et virorum eruditorum ad eundem et ad Jacobum Colium Ortelianum . . . epistulae* (Cambridge: Typis Academiae sumptibus ecclesiae Londino-Batavae, 1887).

Hind 1952: Hind, A. M. *Engraving in England in the Sixteenth and Seventeenth Centuries*, pt. 1, *The Tudor Period* (Cambridge: Cambridge University Press, 1952).

Hodnett 1971: Hodnett, Edward, *Marcus Gheeraerts the Elder of Bruges, London, and Antwerp* (Utrecht: Haentjens Dekker & Gumbert, 1971).

Hofer 1934: Hofer, Philip, "Early Book Illustration in the Intaglio Medium," *The Print Collector's Quarterly*, 21 (1934), pp. 203–227 (part I) and 295–316 (part II).

Holl. *Dutch & Flemish* (see also under *New Holl.*): F. W. Hollstein, *Dutch and Flemish Etchings, Engravings and Woodcuts, c.1450–1700* (Amsterdam: Menno Hertzberger, 1949–1964; Amsterdam: Van Gendt, 1974–1987; Roosendaal: Koninklijke van Poll, 1988–1994; Rotterdam, Sound & Vision, 1995–2004; Ouderkerk aan den Ijssel: Sound & Vision, 2005–):

vol. III (1950) (including Hans Bol and Crispin van den Broeck).

vol. IV (1951) (including Abraham de Bruyn).

vol. VII (1952) (including Marcus Gheeraerts I).

vol. VIII (1953) (including Jules Goltzius).

vol. IX (1953) (including Pieter van der Heyden, Frans Hogenberg, Frans and Pieter Huys).

vol. XV (1964) (including Crispijn van de Passe I), by K. G. Boon and J. Verbeek.

vol. XVI (1974) (including C. van de Passe I), compiled by J. Verbeek and Ilja M. Veldman.

vols. XXI–XXII (1980): Sadelers, compiled by Dieuwke de Hoop Scheffer, ed. by K. G. Boon.

vol. XXXII (1988) (including Otto van Veen), compiled by Ger Luijten, ed. by D. de Hoop Scheffer.

vols. XLIV–XLVI (1995–1996): Maarten de Vos (one text vol., then plates in two "parts"), compiled by Christiaan Schuckman, ed. by D. De Hoop Scheffer.

vols. XLVII–XLVIII (1997): Vredeman de Vries, compiled by Peter Fuhring, ed. by Ger Luijten.

vol. LV (2000) (including Paulus Wtewael), compiled by Jeroen de Scheemaker, ed. by D. de Hoop Scheffer.

vols. LIX–LXIX (2003–2004): Wierix family independent prints compiled by Zsuzsanna van Ruyven-Zemen, in collaboration with Marjolein Leesberg; ed. by Jan Van der Stock and Marjolein Leesberg.

vol. LXX (2006): Wierix family book illustrations, part I, compiled by Harriet Stroomberg, ed. by Jan Van der Stock.

Holt 1986: Holt, Mack P., *The Duke of Anjou and the Politique Struggle during the Wars of Religion* (Cambridge: Cambridge University Press, 1986).

Homann and Melion 2003: Homann, F. A., and W. Melion, *Annotations and Meditations on the Gospels*, multiple vols. (Philadelphia: Saint Joseph's University Press, 2003–).

ILE: Justus Lipsius, *Epistolae*, vol. II, ed. by M. A. Nauwelaerts (Brussels: Paleis der Academiën, 1983).

Imhof 1992: Imhof, Dirk, ed., *Christoffel Plantijn en de Iberische wereld/Christophe Plantin et le monde Iberique*, catalogue of the exhibition held at the Plantin-Moretus Museum, Antwerp, October 3–December 31, 1992 (Antwerp: City of Antwerp, 1992).

1994a: Imhof, Dirk, ed., *Gerard Mercator en de geografie in de Zuidelijke Nederlanden/Gerard Mercator et la geographie dans les Pays-Bas meridionaux*, catalogue of the exhibition held at the Plantin-Moretus Museum, Antwerp, April 30–July 24, 1994 (Antwerp: City of Antwerp, 1994).

1994b: Imhof, Dirk, "L' 'Officina Plantiniana', centre de distribution des globes, cartes et atlas de Gerard Mercator" ("De 'Officina Plantinia' als verdeelcentrum van de globes, kaarten en atlassen van Gerard Mercator"), in: Imhof 1994a, pp. 32–41.

1996a: Imhof, Dirk, ed., *The Illustration of Books Published by the Moretuses*, catalogue of the exhibition held at the Plantin-Moretus Museum, Antwerp, October 19, 1996–January 17, 1997 (Antwerp: Plantin-Moretus Museum, 1996; also in Dutch under the title: *De Boekillustratie ten tijde van de Moretussen*).

1996b: Imhof, Dirk, "The Illustration of Scientific Works Published by the Moretuses," in: Imhof 1996a, pp. 53–63.

1998a: Imhof, Dirk, ed., *Abraham Ortelius (1527–1598) cartographe et humaniste* (Turnhout: Brepols, 1998).

1998b: Imhof, Dirk, "Abraham Ortelius et Jean I Moretus: la production et la vente des œuvres d'Ortelius par l'Officine Plantinienne de 1589 à 1610," in: Imhof 1998a, pp. 193–206.

1998c: Imhof, Dirk, *De wereld in kaart. Abraham Ortelius (1527–1598) en de eerste atlas*, catalogue of the exhibition held at the Plantin-Moretus Museum, November 21, 1998–January 24, 1999 (Antwerp: Museum-Plantin Moretus, 1998).

1999a: Imhof, Dirk, "The Illustration of Works by Justus Lipsius Published by the Plantin Press," in G. Tournoy, J. De Landtsheer, and J. Papy, eds., *Iustus Lipsius Europae lumen et columen*, Proceedings of the International Colloquium, Leuven, September 17–19, 1997 (*Supplementa humanistica Lovaniensia [Journal of Neo-Latin Studies]*, 15) (Leuven: Leuven University Press, 1999), pp. 67–81.

1999b: Imhof, Dirk, "The Production of Ortelius's Atlases by Christopher Plantin," in Marcel van den Broecke, Peter van der Krogt, and Peter Meurer, eds., *Abraham Ortelius and the First Atlas: Essays Commemorating the Quadricentennial of his Death, 1598–1998* ('t Goy-Houten: Hes Publishers, 1999), pp. 79–92.

2001: Imhof, Dirk, "Return my Woodblocks at Once: Dealings between the Antwerp Publisher Balthasar Moretus and the London Bookseller Richard Whitacker in the Seventeenth Century," in Lotte Hellinge, Alastair Duke, Jacob Harskamp, and Theo Hermans, eds., *The Bookshop of the World: The Role of the Low Countries in the Book-Trade, 1473–1941* ('t Goy-Houten: Hes & De Graaf Publishers, 2001), pp. 179–190.

2004: Imhof, Dirk, "Aankopen van Peter Paul Rubens bij Balthasar I Moretus," in *Een hart voor boeken: Rubens en zijn bibliotheek/La passion des livres: Rubens et sa bibliothèque*, catalogue of the exhibition held at the Plantin-Moretus Museum, Antwerp, March 6–June 13, 2004 (Antwerp: City of Antwerp, 2004), pp. 22–26.

2007–2008: Imhof, Dirk, "De uitgave politiek van Jan I Moretus (1589–1610)," University of Antwerp, 2007–2008.

Imhof and De Nave 1993: Imhof, Dirk, and Francine de Nave, eds., *Botany in the Low Countries (End of the 15th Century–c.1650)*, catalogue of the exhibition held at the Plantin-Moretus Museum, Antwerp, March 13–June 13, 1993 (Antwerp: City of Antwerp, 1993) (simultaneously published in Dutch, under the title *De botanica in de Zuidelijke Nederlanden [einde 15 de eeuw–c.1650]*).

Imhof et al. 1994: Imhof, Dirk, Francine de Nave, and Gilbert Tournoy, eds., *Antwerp, Dissident Typographical Centre: The Role of Antwerp Printers in the Religious Conflicts in England (16th Century)*, catalogue of the exhibition held at the Plantin-Moretus Museum, Antwerp, October 1–December 31, 1994 (Antwerp: Plantin-Moretus Museum, 1994).

Ivins 1987: Ivins, William M., Jr., *How Prints Look*, revised by Marjorie B. Cohn (Boston: Beacon Press, 1987).

Iwai 1986: Iwai, Mizué, "L'Œuvre de Pierre Woeiriot (1532–1599)," dissertation for the Université de Paris-Sorbonne, Paris, submitted in May 1985 and defended in 1986.

Janssen 2000: Janssen, Frans A., "Stevig voedsel: Valkema Blouws Nederlandse bibliografie 1541–1600," *Jaarboek voor Nederlandse boekgeschiedenis*, 7 (2000), pp. 187–197.

Johnson 1936: Johnson, Alfred Forbes, *A Catalogue of Italian Engraved Title-pages in the Sixteenth Century* (Oxford: Oxford Univerisy Press for the Bibliographical Society, 1936).

Judson and Van de Velde 1977: Judson, J. R. and Carl Van de Velde, *Book Illustrations and Title-Pages, Corpus Rubenianum Ludwig Burchard* 21, 2 vols. (Brussels: Arcade Press, 1977).

Kingdon 1963: Kingdon, Robert M., "Christopher Plantin and his Backers, 1575–1590: A Study in the Problems of Financing Business during War," in Anne-Morie Piuz and Jean-François Bergier, eds., *Mélanges d'histoire économique et sociale en hommage au professeur Antony Babel*, vol. I (Geneva: Imprimerie de la tribune, 1963), pp. 303–316.

Koeman 1967–1971: Koeman, C., *Atlantes Neerlandici: Bibliography of Terrestrial, Maritime, and Celestial Atlases and Pilot Books, Published in the Netherlands up to 1880*, 5 vols. (Amsterdam: Theatrum orbis terrarum, 1967–1971).

Künast and Schürmann 1997: Künast, Hans–Jörg, and Brigitte Schürmann, "Joannes Rynman, Wolfgang Präulein und Georg Willer, Drei Augsburger Buchführer des 15. und 16. Jahrhunderts," in: H. Gier and J. Janota, *Augsburger Buchdruck und Verlagswesen von den Anfängen bis zur Gegenwart* (Wiesbaden: Harrassowitz, 1997).

Kunze 1993: Kunze, Horst, *Geschichte der Buchillustration in Deutschland das 16. und 17. jahrhundert*, 2 vols. (Frankfurt am Main and Leipzig: Inzel, 1993).

Labarre 1985: Labarre, A., "Les imprimeurs et libraires de Douai aux XVIᵉ et XVIIᵉ siècles," in: De Nave 1985, pp. 241–260.

Landau and Parshall 1994: Landau, David, and Peter Parshall, *The Renaissance Print, 1470–1550* (New Haven and London: Yale Univeristy Press, 1994).

Landwehr 1971: Landwehr, John, *Splendid Ceremonies: State Entries and Royal Funerals in the Low Countries, 1515–1791. A Bibliography* (Nieuwkoop: B. De Graaf; and Leiden: A. W. Sijthoff, 1971).

   1976: Landwehr, John, *French, Italian, Spanish, and Portuguese Books of Devices and Emblems, 1534–1827: A Bibliography* (Utrecht: Haentjens Dekker & Gumbert, 1976).

   1988: Landwehr, John, *Emblem and Fable Books Printed in the Low Countries, 1542–1813: A Bibliography*, third revised and augmented edition (Utrecht: Hes Publishers, 1988).

Laor 1986: Laor, Eran, with Shoshana Klein, *Maps of the Holy Land: Cartobibliography of Printed Maps, 1475–1900* (New York: Liss, 1986).

Lauwaert 1972: Lauwaert, R., "De handelsbedrijvigheid van de Officina Plantiniana op de Büchermessen te Frankfurt am Main in de XVIe eeuw," *De Gulden Passer*, 50 (1972), pp. 124–180.

Leeflang 1993: Leeflang, H., G. Luijten, N. Orenstein, and C. Schuckman, "Print Publishers in the Netherlands, 1580–1620," in G. Luijten, Ariane van Suchtelen, et al., eds., *Dawn of the Golden Age: Northern Netherlandish Art 1580–1620*, catalogue of the exhibition held at the Rijksmuseum, Amsterdam, December 11, 1993–March 6, 1994 (Zwolle: Waanders Uitgevers, 1993), pp. 167–200.

Lefèvre 1953: Lefèvre, Joseph, *Correspondance de Philippe II sur les affaires des Pays-Bas. Deuxième partie*, II (1580–1584) (Brussels: Palais des Académies/Paleis der Academiën, 1953).

Levarie 1995: Levarie, Norma, *The Art and History of Books*, 3rd edn. (New Castle, DE: Oak Knoll Press; London: The British Library, 1995).

Le Loup 1983: Le Loup, W., ed., *Hubertus Goltzius en Brugge, 1583–1983*, catalogue of the exhibition held at the Gruuthusemuseum, Bruges, November 11, 1983–January 30, 1984 (Bruges: Designdruk, 1983).

Levine 1966: Saint Augustine, *The City of God against the Pagans*, IV (books XII–XV), trans. by Philip Levine, Loeb Classical Library (Cambridge, MA: Harvard University Press, and London: William Heinemann, 1966).

Lipsius Antwerp 1997: Dusoir, Ronnie, Dirk Imhof, and Jeanine, De Landtsheer, eds., *Justus Lipsius (1547–1606) en het Plantijnse Huis*, catalogue of the exhibition held at the Plantin-Moretus Museum, Antwerp, October 18, 1997–January 18, 1998 (Antwerp: City of Antwerp, 1997).

Lipsius Leuven 1997: Tournoy, G., J. Papy, and J. De Landtsheer, eds., *Lipsius en Leuven*, Supplementa Humanistica Lovaniensia, no. XIII, catalogue of the exhibition held at the Central Library of the University of Leuven, September 18–October 17, 1997 (Leuven: Leuven University Press, 1997).

Van Mander 1994–1999: Van Mander, Karel, *The Lives of the Illustrious Netherlandish and German Painters*, ed. by Hessel Miedema and trans. by Derry Cook-Radmore, 6 vols. (Doornspijk: DAVACO, 1994–1999).

Marnef 2001: Marnef, Guido, "The Towns and the Revolt," in: Darby 2001, pp. 84–106.

Martin 1954: Martin, Henri-Jean, "L'influence de la gravure anversoise sur l'illustration du livre français," in *Anvers ville de Plantin et de Rubens*, catalogue of the exhibition held at the Galerie Mazarine, March–April 1954 (Paris: Bibliothèque Nationale, 1954), pp. 257–264.

1984: Martin, Henri-Jean, *Livre, pouvoirs et société a Paris au XVIIe siècle (1598–1701)*, 2 vols. (Geneva: Librairie Droz, 1984).

Martin Abad 1999: Martin Abad, Julián, "The Printing Press at Alcalá de Henares: The Complutensian Polyglot Bible," in John L. Sharpe III and Orlaith O'Sullivan, eds., *The Bible as Book: The First Printed Editions* (London: The British Library, 1999), pp. 101–115.

Mathiesen 1985: Mathiesen, Robert, *The Great Polyglot Bibles: The Impact of Printing on Religion in the Sixteenth and Seventeenth Centuries* (Providence, RI: The John Carter Brown Library, 1985).

Mauquoy-Hendrickx 1971: Mauquoy-Hendrickx, Marie, "Observations sur les illustrations de quelques ouvrages édités par Plantin," *Le Livre et l'Estampe*, nos. 65–66 (1971), pp. 63–79, plus eight plates.

May 1985: May, Peter, "Die Kunstfertigkeit der Perspektive zu Nürnberg," in Gerhard Bott, ed., *Wenzel Jamnitzer und die Nürnberger Goldschmiedekunst, 1500–1700* (Nuremberg: Klinhardt Biermann for the Germanisches Nationalmuseum, 1985), pp. 161–165.

Meeus 2000: Meeus, Hubert, "Antwerp as a Centre for the Production of Emblem Books," *Quaerendo*, 30/3 (2000), pp. 228–239.

Meier 1941: Meier, Henry, "The Origin of the Printing and Roller Press, parts I–IV," *Print Collector's Quarterly*, 28 (1941), pp. 8–55, 164–205, 338–374, and 496–527.

Melion 2005: Melion, Walter S., "Benedictus Arias Montanus and the Virtual Studio as a Meditative Place," in M. Cole and M. Pardo, eds., *Inventions of the Studio, Renaissance to Romanticism* (Chapel Hill and London: University of North Carolina Press, 2005), pp. 73–107.

Meyer and Wirt 1943: Meyer, A. W., and Sheldon K. Wirt, "The Amuscan Illustrations," *Bulletin of the History of Medicine*, 14 (1943), pp. 667–687.

M-H Wierix: Mauquoy-Hendrickx, Marie, *Les estampes des Wierix*, 3 vols. in 4 parts (Brussels: The Royal Library, 1978–1982).

McKitterick 2003: McKitterick, David, *Print, Manuscript and the Search for Order, 1450–1830* (Cambridge: Cambridge University Press, 2003).

2005: McKitterick, David, "Histories of the Book and Histories of Antwerp," *Quaerendo*, 35 (2005), pp. 3–19.

Miller 2001: Miller, Peter N., "Making the Paris Polyglot Bible: Humanism and Orientalism in the Early Seventeenth Century," in Herbert Jaumann, ed., *Die europäische Gelehrtenrepublik im Zeitalter des Konfessionalismus: The European Republic of Letters in the Age of Confessionalism* (Wiesbaden: Harrassowitz, 2001), pp. 59–85.

Moll 1987: Moll, Jaime, "Sobre el 'privilegio' a Cristóbal Plantin," in Francisco Javier Aguirre González, ed., *Homenaje a Justo Garcia Morales* (Madrid: ANABAD, 1987), pp. 809–819.

1990: Moll, Jaime, "Plantino, los Junta y el 'privilegio' del nuevo rezado," in: Hans Tromp and Pedro Peira, eds., *Simposio internacional sobre Cristóbal Plantino* (Madrid: Universidad Complutense de Madrid, 1990), pp. 9–23.

Morocho Gayo 1998: Morocho Gayo, Gaspar, "Avance de datos para un inventario de las obras y escritos de Arias Montano," *La ciudad de Dios*, 211/1 (1998), pp. 179–275.

Mortimer 1964: Mortimer, Ruth (under the supervision of Philip Hofer and William A. Jackson), *Harvard College Library Department of Printing and Graphic Arts, Catalogue of Books and Manuscripts: Part I: French 16th Century Books*, 2 vols. (Cambridge, MA: Harvard University Press, 1964).

Mortimer 1974: Mortimer, Ruth, *Harvard College Library Department of Printing and Graphic Arts, Catalogue of Books and Manuscripts: Part II: Italian 16th Century Books*, 2 vols. (Cambridge, MA: Harvard University Press, 1974).

Moxon 1958: Moxon, J., *Mechanick Exercises on the whole art of printing*, ed. by H. Davis and H. Carter (London: Oxford University Press, 1958; 2nd edn., 1962).

Mulryne et al. 2004: Mulryne, J. R., Helen Watanabe-O'Kelly, and Morgovet Shewring, eds., *Europa triumphans: Court and Civic Festivals in Early Modern Europe*, 2 vols. (London: MHRA, 2004).

Nash 1964: Nash, Ray, ed. and trans., *Calligraphy and Printing in the Sixteenth Century: Dialogue attributed to Christopher Plantin in French and Flemish Facsimile*, foreword by Stanley Morison (Antwerp: Plantin-Moretus Museum, 1964).

De Nave 1985: De Nave, F., ed., *Liber amicorum Leon Voet* (*De Gulden Passer*, 61–63 [1983–1985]) (Antwerp: Nederlandsche Boekhandel, 1985).

1993: De Nave, Francine, "A Printing Capital in its Ascendancy, Flowering and Decline," in: Van der Stock 1993, pp. 87–95.

De Nave and De Schepper 1990: De Nave, Francine, and Marcus de Schepper, eds., *De geneeskunde in de Zuidelijke Nederlanden (1475–1660)*, catalogue of the exhibition held at the Plantin-Moretus Museum, Antwerp, September 1–November 25, 1990 (Antwerp: Plantin–Moretus Museum, 1990).

NBW: *Nationaal biografisch woordenboek*, multiple vols. (Brussels: Paleis der Academiën, 1964–).

NCE: *The New Catholic Encyclopedia*, 15 vols. (New York: McGraw-Hill, 1967).

New Holl. (see also under Holl. Dutch & Flemish): *The New Hollstein Dutch and Flemish Etchings, Engravings, and Woodcuts, 1450–1700* (Roosendaal: Koninklijke van Poll, 1993–1994; Rotterdam: Sound & Vision, 1995–2004; Ouderkerk aan den Ijssel: Sound & Vision, 2005–):

New Holl., Van der Borcht, 4 vols. (2004–2007), compiled by Hans and Ursula Mielke, ed. by Ger Luijten.

New Holl., The Collaert Dynasty, 7 vols. (2005–2006), compiled by Ann Diels and Marjolein Leesberg: I–VI ed. by M. Leesberg and Arnout Balis; VII ed. by M. Leesberg and Karen L. Bowen.

New Holl., Van Doetecum, 4 vols. (1998), compiled by Henk Nalis, ed. by Ger Luijten and Christian Schuckman.

New Holl., Galle, 4 vols. (2001), compiled by Manfred Sellink and Marjolein Leesberg, ed. by Manfred Sellink.

New Holl., Van Heemskerck, 2 vols. (1994), compiled by Ilja M. Veldman, ed. by Ger Luijten.

New Holl., Van Groeningen, 2 vols. (1997), compiled by Christiaan Schuckman, ed. by Ger Luijten.

NK: Nijhoff, W. and E. Kronenberg, *Nederlandsche bibliografie van 1500 tot 1540*, 3 parts in multiple vols. (The Hague: Martinus Nijhoff, 1923–1971).

NNBW: *Nieuw Nederlandsch biografisch woordenboek*, vols. I–X (Leiden: A. W. Sijthoff's uitgevers-maatschappij, 1911–1937).

Norton 1999: Norton, F. J., *A Descriptive Catalogue of Printing in Spain and Portugal, 1501–1520* (Mansfield, CT: Martino, 1999: facsimile of the 1978 Cambridge University Press edition).

Orenstein 1996: Orenstein, Nadine, *Hendrick Hondius and the Business of Prints in Seventeenth-Century Holland* (Rotterdam: Sound and Vision Interactive, 1996).

2001: Orenstein, Nadine M., ed., *Pieter Bruegel the Elder: Drawings and Prints*, catalogue of the exhibition held at the Museum Boijmans Van Beuningen, Rotterdam, May 24–August 5, 2001, and the Metropolitan Museum of Art, New York City, September 25–December 2, 2001 (New Haven and London: Yale University Press, 2001).

Pallier 1981: Pallier, Denis, "Les impressions de la Contre-Réforme en France et l'apparition des grandes compagnies de libraires parisiens," *Revue Française d'histoire du livre*, new series, 31 (1981), pp. 215–273.

1982: Pallier, Denis, "Les réponses catholiques," in: Chartier and Martin 1982, pp. 327–347.

Parent 1974: Parent, Annie, *Les métiers du livre à Paris au XVIe siècle (1535–1560)* (Geneva: Librarie Droz, 1974).

Pastoureau 1982: Michel Pastoureau, "L'illustration du livre: comprendre ou rêver?" in: Chartier and Martin 1982, pp. 501–529.

Perini 1980: Perini, Leandro, "Giunti," in *Firenze e la Toscana dei Medici nell'Europa del Cinquecento*, vol. IV (Florence: Centro di Edizioni Alinari Scala, 1980), pp. 270–305.

Persoons 1989: Persoons, G., "Joannes I Bogardus, Jean II Bogard en Pierre Bogard als muziekdrukkers te Douai van 1574 tot 1633 en hun betrekkingen met de Officina Plantiniana," *De Gulden Passer*, 66–67 (1988–1989), pp. 613–666.

Pettas 2005: Pettas, William, *A History and Bibliography of the Giunti (Junta) Printing Family of Spain, 1526–1628* (New Castle, DE: Oak Knoll Press, 2005).

Petti 1959: Petti, Anthony G., "Richard Verstegan and Catholic Martyrologies of the later Elizabethan Period," *Recusant History*, 5 (1959), pp. 64–90.

1963: Petti, Anthony G., "A Bibliography of the Writings of Richard Verstegan (c.1550–1641)," *Recusant History*, 7 (1963), pp. 82–103.

Pohl 1977: Pohl, Hans, *Die Portugiesen in Antwerpen, 1567–1648: Zur Geschichte einer Minderheit* (Wiesbaden: Steiner, 1977).

Puraye 1968: *Abraham Ortelius Album amicorum*, ed. by J. Puraye, *De Gulden Passer*, 45–46 (1967–1968), pp. 1–99.

Purkis 1973: *Entrée de François d'Anjou Anvers 1582*, facsimile ed. with introduction by Helen M. C. Purkis, *Renaissance Triumphs and Magnificences* (Amsterdam and New York: Theatrum orbis terrarum, Johnson Reprint Corporation, s.a., [c.1973]).

Van Puyvelde 1942: Van Puyvelde, L., *The Flemish Drawings in the Collection of his Majesty the King at Windsor Castle* (London: Phaidon Press, 1942).

De Ramaix 1968: De Ramaix, I., "Frans Huys. Catalogue de l' œuvre gravé," *Le Livre et l'Estampe*, 55–56 (1968), pp. 258–293; and 57–58 (1969), pp. 23–54.

1992: De Ramaix, I., *Graveurs en uitgevers Sadeler/Les Sadeler graveurs et imprimeurs*, catalogue of the exhibition held at the Royal Library of Brussels, February 14–March 28, 1992 (Brussels: The Royal Library, 1992).

Von Rath 1927: Von Rath, Erich, "Die Kupferstichillustration im Wiegendruckzeitalter," in Johannes Hofmann, ed., *Die Bibliothek und ihre Kleinodien. Festschrift zum 250jährigen Jubiläum der Leipziger Stadtbibliothek* (Leipzig: Hiersemann, 1927), pp. 58–68.

Reed and Wallace 1989: Reed, Sue Welsh, and Richard Wallace, *Italian Etchers of the Renaissance and Baroque*, catalogue of the exhibition held at the Museum of Fine Arts, Boston, January 24–April 2, 1989 (Boston: Museum of Fine Arts, 1989).

Rekers 1972: Rekers, B., *Benito Arias Montano (1527–1598)* (London: The Warburg Institute, 1972).

Remmert 2005: Remmert, Volker, *Widmung, Welterklärung und Wissenschaftslegitimierung: Titelbilder und ihre Funktionen in der Wissenschaftlichen Revolution* (Wiesbaden: Harrasowitz, 2005).

Renouard 1965: Renouard, Philippe, *Répertoire des imprimeurs Parisiens, libraires, fondeurs de caractères et correcteurs d'imprimerie depuis l'introduction de l'Imprimerie à Paris (1470) jusqu'à la fin du seizième siècle* (Paris: M. J. Minard, 1965).

1979: Renouard, Philippe, *Imprimeurs et libraires parisiens du XVIe siècle. Ouvrage publié d'après les manuscrits de Philippe Renouard par le Service des Travaux historiques de la Ville de Paris avec le concours de la Bibliothèque nationale*, vol. III: *Baquelier-Billon* (Paris: Musées de la Ville de Paris, 1979).

Riggs 1977: Riggs, Timothy A., *Hieronymus Cock: Printmaker and Publisher in Antwerp* (New York and London: Garland, 1977).

Robben 1989: Robben, Frans, "De relaties van Christoffel Plantijn met de boekhandel in Spanje. Een voorlopige inventaris," *De Gulden Passer*, 66–67 (1988–1989), pp. 399–418.

1993: Robben, Frans, *Jan Poelman, boekverkoper en vertegenwoordiger van de firma Plantin-Moretus in Salamanca, 1579–1607* (*De Gulden Passer*, 71–72 [1993–1994]) (Antwerp: Vereeniging der Antwerpsche Bibliophielen, 1994).

Roberts 2002: Roberts, Julian, "The Latin Trade," in: Barnard and McKenzie 2002, pp. 141–173.

Van Roey 1989: Van Roey, J., "Het boekbedrijf te Antwerpen in 1584–1585," in Marcus de Schepper and Francine de Nave, eds., *Ex Officina Plantiniana: Studia in memoriam Christophori Plantini (c.1520–1589)* (*De Gulden Passer*, 66–67 [1988–1989]), pp. 419–433.

Rombouts 1933: Rombouts, E., *Richard Verstegen, Een polemist der Contra-Reformatie* (Brussels: Algemeene Drukkerij, 1933).

1934: Rombauts, E., "Een clandestien drukker te Antwerpen? Richard Verstegen," *De Gulden Passer*, 12 (1934), pp. 20–32.

Rombouts and Van Lerius 1961: Rombouts, P. and T. Van Lerius, *De liggeren en andere historische archieven der Antwerpsche Sint Lucasgilde*, 2 vols. (Antwerp: Baggerman, 1864–1872; reprint: Amsterdam: Israel, 1961).

Rooses 1880: Rooses, Max, "Plantijns koninklijke bijbel," from the series "de Gids," 8 (1880), pp. 1–36.

1882: Rooses, Max, "Les frères Wiericx à l'imprimerie Plantinienne," *Bulletijn van de Maatschappij der Antwerpsche Bibliophilen*, 1 (1882), pp. 225–248.

1888: Rooses, Max, "De plaatsnijders der *Evangelicae historiae imagines*," *Oud Holland* (1888), pp. 277–282.

1896: Rooses, Max, *Index characterum architypographiae Plantinianae* (*Proeven der lettersoorten gebruikt in de Plantijnsche drukkerij. Spécimens des caractères employés dans l'imprimerie plantinienne*) (Antwerp: De Nederlandsche Boekhandel, 1896; 2nd edn., with the translated titles, Antwerp: De Nederlandsche Boekhandel, 1905).

c.1900: Rooses, Max, *De platen van het getijdenboek gegraveerd door Crispijn van de Passe* (Antwerp: De Nederlandsche Boekhandel, c.1900).

1901: Rooses, Max, introduction to the facsimile edition of Joannes Sambucus, *Icones veterum aliquot ac recentium medicorum* (Antwerp: De Nederlandsche Boekhandel, 1901).

1914: Rooses, Max, *Le Musée Plantin-Moretus. Contenant la vie et l'œuvre de Christophe Plantin et ses successeurs, les Moretus, ainsi que la description du musée et des collections qu'il renferme* (Antwerp: G. Zazzarini, 1914).

Rosenau 1979: Rosenau, Helen, *Vision of the Temple: The Image of the Temple of Jerusalem in Judaism and Christianity* (London: Oresko Books, 1979).

Rosier 1997: Rosier, Bart A., *The Bible in Print: Netherlandish Bible Illustration in the Sixteenth Century*, trans. by Chris F. Weterings, 2 vols. (Leiden: Foleor Publishers, 1997).

Rouzet 1975: Rouzet, Anne, *Dictionnaire des imprimeurs, libraires et éditeurs des XVe et XVIe siècles dans les limites géographiques de la Belgique actuelle* (Nieuwkoop: De Graaf Publishers, 1975).

Ruiz Fidalgo 1994: Ruiz Fidalgo, Lorenzo, *La imprenta en Salamanca (1501–1600)*, 3 vols. (Madrid: Arco/Libros, 1994).

Van Ruyven-Zeman 1995: Van Ruyven-Zeman, Z., *Lambert van Noort: Inventor* (Brussels: Paleis der Academiën, 1995).

Saunders and O'Malley 1950: Saunders, John B. de C. M., and Charles D. O'Malley, *The Illustrations from the Works of Andreas Vesalius of Brussels* (Cleveland: World Publishing Company, 1950; reprinted New York: Dover Publications, 1973).

Saur: *Allgemeines Künstler-lexikon*, multiple vols. (Munich and Leipzig: K. G. Saur, 1992–).

Scheler 1968: Scheler, Lucien, "La persistance du motif dans l'illustration flamande des fables d'Esope du seizième au dix-huitième siècle," in S. van der Woude, ed., *Studia bibliographica in honorem Herman de la Fontaine Verwey* (Amsterdam: Hertzberger, 1968), pp. 350–355.

Schilder: Schilder, Günter, *Monumenta cartographica Neerlandica*, 2nd edn. (Alphen aan den Rijn: Canaletto, 1991–).

Schmidt 1962: Schmidt, Ph., *Die Illustration der Lutherbibel, 1522–1700* (Basel: Reinhardt, 1962).

Schmidt 2003: Schmidt, Peter, *Gedruckte Bilder in handgeschriebenen Büchern: zum Gebrauch von Druckgraphik im 15. Jahrhundert* (Cologne: Böhlau, 2003).

Scholliers 1976: Scholliers, Etienne, "De lagere klassen: Een kwantitatieve benadering van levensstandaard en levenswijze," in: *Antwerp 16th Century*, pp. 161–180.

Schrader 1998: Schrader, Stephanie, "'Greater than Ever He Was': Ritual and Power in Charles V's 1558 Funeral Procession," in Reindert Falkenburg, Jan de Jong, Morle Meadow, Bort Ram, and Herman Roodenburg, eds., *Hof-, staats- en stadsceremonies/Court, State and City Ceremonies*, *Nederlands Kunsthistorisch Jaarboek/Netherlands Yearbook for History of Art*, 49 (1998), pp. 68–93.

Schreiber 1982: Schreiber, Fred, *The Estiennes: An Annotated Catalogue of 300 Highlights of their Various Presses* (New York: Schreiber, 1982).

Schwetschke 1850: Schwetschke, Gustav, *Codex nundinarius Germaniae literatae biseicularis* (Halle: G. Schwetschke, 1850).

Seelig et al. 2001–2003: Bartrum, Giulia, Marjolein Leesberg, and Gero Seelig, *New Hollstein German Engravings, Etchings and Woodcuts, 1400–1700: Joost Amman*, 9 vols. (Rotterdam: Sound and Vision Interactive, 2001–2003).

Sellink 1997: Sellink, Manfred, "Philips Galle (1537–1612): Engraver and Print Publisher in Haarlem and Antwerp," 3 vols., doctoral dissertation, Vrije Universiteit of Amsterdam, 1997.

Seville 2000: Villaverde, Fernando, ed., *La fiesta en la Europa de Carlos V*, catalogue of the exhibition held at the Real Alcázar, Seville, September 19–November 26, 2000 (Seville: Sociedad Estatal para la Commemoración de los Centenarios de Felipe II y Carlos V, 2000).

Shalev 2003: Shalev, Zur, "Sacred Geography, Antiquarianism and Visual Erudition: Benito Arias Montano and the Maps in the Antwerp Polyglot Bible," *Imago Mundi*, 55 (2003), pp. 56–80.

Shirley 1984: Shirley, Rodney W., *The Mapping of the World: Early Printed World Maps, 1472–1700* (London: Holland Press, 1984).

Simon and Watanabe-O'Kelly 2000: Simon, Anne, and Helen Watanabe-O'Kelly, *Festivals and Ceremonies: A Bibliography of Works Relating to Court, Civic and Religious Festivals in Europe, 1500–1800* (London: Mansell, 2000).

Simoni 1990: Simoni, Anna E. C., ed., *Catalogue of Books from the Low Countries 1601–1621 in the British Library* (London: The British Library, 1990).

Sorgeloos 1990: Sorgeloos, Claude, *1589–1989 Labore et constantia: A Collection of 510 Editions Issued by Christopher Plantin from 1555 till 1589* (Brussels: Eric Speeckaert, 1990).

Southern 1977: Southern, A. C., *Elizabethan Recusant Prose, 1559–1582* (London and Glasgow: Sands, 1977).

STC: Pollard, Alfred William, G. R. Redgrave, et al., *A Short-Title Catalogue of Books printed in England, Scotland, and Ireland and of English Books printed Abroad, 1475–1640*, 2nd edn., 3 vols. (London: Bibliographical Society, 1976–1991).

STC Dutch and Flemish (1470–1600): *Short-Title Catalogue of Books Printed in the Netherlands and Belgium and of Dutch and Flemish Books Printed in Other Counties from 1470 to 1600 now in the British Museum* (London: British Museum, 1965).

STC Europe (pre-1601): Thomas, Henry, *Short-Title Catalogue of Books Printed in Spain and of Spanish Books Printed Elsewhere in Europe before 1601 now in the British Museum* (London: British Museum, 1921).

STC French (1470–1600): *Short-Title Catalogue of Books Printed in France and of French Books Printed in Other Counties from 1470 to 1600, in the British Museum*, 2nd edn. (London: British Museum, 1966).

STC Italian (1465–1600): *Short-Title Catalogue of Books Printed in Italy and of Italian Books Printed in Other Counties from 1465 to 1600 now in the British Museum* (London: British Museum, 1958).

STC Spanish: *Catalogue of Books Printed in Spain and of Spanish Books Printed Elsewhere in Europe before 1601 now in the British Library*, 2nd edn. (London: The British Library, 1989).

Strauss 1977: Strauss, Walter L., ed., *Hendrik Goltzius, 1558–1617: The Complete Engravings and Woodcuts*, 2 vols. (New York: Abaris Books, 1977).

Van der Stock 1990: Van der Stock, Jan, "De koperplaten gebruikt ter illustratie van de Plantijn-uitgaven van de Vivae imagines . . . Anatomie oft levende beelden van Joannes Valverda de Hamusco . . . Het project van Plantijn," in: de Nave and de Schepper 1990, pp. 328–331.

1993: Van der Stock, Jan, ed., *Antwerp, Story of a Metropolis, 16th–17th Century/Antwerpen, verhaal van een metropool, 16de–17de eeuw*, catalogue of the exhibition at the Hessenhuis, Antwerp, June 25–October 10, 1993 (Ghent: Snoeck-Ducaju & Zoon, 1993).

1998: Van der Stock, Jan, *Printing Images in Antwerp: The Introduction of Printmaking in a City: Fifteenth Century to 1585*, trans. by Beverley Jackson (Rotterdam: Sound & Vision Interactive, 1998).

Tanner 1990: Tanner, Norman P., ed., *Decrees of the Ecumenical Councils*, 2 vols. (Washington, D.C.: Sheed & Ward and Georgetown University Press, 1990).

TB: Blouw, Paul Valkema, *Typographia Batava, 1541–1600 . . . A Repertorium of Books Printed in the Northern Netherlands between 1541 and 1600*, 2 vols. (Nieuwkoop: De Graaf Publishers, 1998).

Timmers 1991: Timmers, J. J. M., *Christelijke symboliek en iconografie*, 7th edn. (Houten: De Haan, 1991).

Toubert 1982: Toubert, Hélène, "Formes et fonctions de l'enluminure," in Chartier and Martin 1982, pp. 87–129.

Vandewalle 1984: Vandewalle, Paul, *Oude maten, gewichten en muntstelsels in Vlaanderen, Brabant en Limburg* (Ghent: Belgisch Centrum voor Landelijke Geschiedenis, 1984).

Veldman 2001: Veldman, Ilja M., *Crispijn de Passe and his Progeny (1564–1670): A Century of Print Production* (Rotterdam: Sound & Vision Interactive, 2001).

Verheggen 2006: Verheggen, Evelyne M. F., *Beelden voor passie en hartstocht: bid- en devotieprenten in de Noordelijke Nederlanden, 17de en 18de eeuw* (Zutphen: Walburg Pers, 2006).

Vermeylen 2003: Vermeylen, Filip, *Painting for the Market: Commercialization of Art in Antwerp's Golden Age* (Turnhout: Brepols, 2003).

Vervliet 1968: Vervliet, Hendrik D. L., *Sixteenth-Century Printing Types of the Low Countries*, foreword by Harry Carter (Amsterdam: Hertzberger, 1968).

Vervliet and Carter 1972: Vervliet, Hendrik D. L., and H. Carter (commentary), *Type Specimen Facsimiles II: Reproductions of Christopher Plantin's "Index sive specimen characterum" 1567 and Folio Specimen of c.1585 together with the Le Bé-Moretus Specimen c.1599* (London: The Bodley Head, 1972).

Veyrin-Forrer 1982: Veyrin-Forrer, Jeanne, "Fabriquer un livre au XVIe siècle," in: Chartier and Martin 1982, pp. 279–301.

VH: Van Havre, G., *Marques typographiques des imprimeurs et libraires anversois*, 2 vols. Uitgaven der Maatschappij der Antwerpsche Bibliophilen, 13 and 14 (Antwerp: J. E. Buschmann, 1883 and 1884).

(For the devices for Plantin and the Moretuses, see vol. 11 [1884], pp. 87–116 [Plantin] and pp. 117–193 [for Plantin's successors].)

Visser 1988: Visser, Piet, "Jan Philipsz Schabaelje and Pieter vander Borcht's Etchings in the First and Final State: A Contribution to the Reconstruction of the Printing History of H. J. Barrefelt's *Imagines et Figurae Bibliorum*," *Quaerendo*, 18 (1988), pp. 35–70.

Visser 1999. *Emblem Books in Leiden*, compiled and ed. by A. S. Q. Visser and co-edited by P. G. Hoftijzer and B. Westerweel (Leiden: Primavera, 1999).

Visser 2004: Visser, Arnoud, "From the Republic of Letters to the Olympus: The Rise and Fall of Medical Humanism in 67 Portraits," in J. F. van Dijkhuizen, ed., *Living in Posterity: Essays in Honour of Bart Westerweel* (Hilversum: Verloren, 2004), pp. 299–313.

Voet 1975: Voet, Leon, "De typografische bedrijvigheid te Antwerpen in de 16de eeuw," in: *Antwerp 16th Century*, pp. 233–255.

1984: Voet, Leon, "Some Considerations on the Production of the Plantin Press," in Frans Vanwijngaerden, ed., *Liber amicorum Herman Liebaers* (Brussels: Gemeentekrediet van België, 1984), pp. 355–369.

1985: Voet, Leon, "Het geïllustreerde boek in de *Officina Plantiniana* (1555–1589)," in Arnout Balis, Frans Baudouin, and Nora de Poorter, eds., *Rubens and his World* (Antwerp: Het Gulden Cabinet, 1985), pp. 37–47.

Voet, GC: Voet, Leon, *The Golden Compasses: The History of the House of Plantin-Moretus*, 2 vols. (Amsterdam: Vangendt; London: Routledge & Kegan Paul; New York: Abner Schram, 1969 and 1972).

Voet, PP: Voet, Leon, *The Plantin Press (1555–1589): A Bibliography of the Works Printed and Published by Christopher Plantin at Antwerp and Leiden*, 6 vols. (Amsterdam: Van Hoeve, 1980–1983).

Vredeman de Vries 2002: Borggrefe, Heiner, Thomas Fusenig, and Barbara Uppenkamp, eds., *Tussen stadspaleizen en luchtkastelen: Hans Vredeman de Vries en de Renaissance*, catalogue of the exhibition held at the Koninklijk Museum voor Schone Kunsten, Antwerp, September 14– December 8, 2002 (Ghent and Amsterdam: Ludion, 2002).

Wadell 1985: Wadell, Maj-Brit, *Evangelicae historiae imagines: Entstehungsgeschichte und Vorlagen*, Gothenburg Studies in Art and Architecture 3 (Göteborg: Eric Lindgrens Boktryckeri, 1985).

Van der Wee and Materné 1993: Van der Wee, Herman, and Jan Materné, "Antwerp as a World Market in the Sixteenth and Seventeenth Centuries," in: Van der Stock 1993, pp. 19–31.

Wieck 1988: Wieck, Roger, Lawrence R. Poos, Virginia Reinburg, and John Plummer, *Time Sanctified: The Book of Hours in Medieval Art and Life* (Baltimore and New York: George Braziller, in association with the Walters Art Gallery, Baltimore, 1988).

Witcombe 1991: Witcombe, Christopher I. C. E., "Christopher Plantin's Papal Privileges: Documents in the Vatican Archives," *De Gulden Passer*, 69 (1991), pp. 133–145.

Zweite 1980: Zweite, A., *Marten de Vos als Maler. Ein Beitrag zur Geschichte der Antwerpener Malerei in der zweiten Hälfte des 16. Jahrhunderts* (Berlin: Mann, 1980).

INDEX